Elderly People and the Law

Second Edition

Gordon Ashton OBE

Caroline Bielanska

JORDANS

Published by
Jordan Publishing Limited
21 St Thomas Street
Bristol BS1 6JS

Whilst the publishers and the author have taken every care in preparing the material included in this work, any statements made as to the legal or other implications of particular transactions are made in good faith purely for general guidance and cannot be regarded as a substitute for professional advice. Consequently, no liability can be accepted for loss or expense incurred as a result of relying in particular circumstances on statements made in this work.

Crown Copyright material is reproduced with kind permission of the Controller of Her Majesty's Stationery Office.

British Library Cataloguing-in-Publication Data

A catalogue record for this book is available from the British Library.

ISBN 978 1 84661 722 5

Typeset by Letterpart Ltd, Caterham on the Hill, Surrey CR3 5XL

Printed in Great Britain by CPI Antony Rowe, Chippenham and Eastbourne

FOREWORD TO THE FIRST EDITION

There used to be three ages of man and womankind – childhood, adulthood and old age – but now there are four. Most of us can expect to enjoy several years in the third age – what used to be called ripe old age. Comparatively few will spend much if any time in the fourth age – when ripeness turns to decay in physical or mental faculties or even both. And all of us must die, with or without our faculties and property intact.

So most of the law which elderly people and those advising them need to know is about how to make the best of the third age – to obtain the right pension and other benefits, to make the most of their savings, investments and other property, to maximise the opportunities for useful if not necessarily gainful occupation, to gain access to the full range of educational, recreational, health and social services available, to secure ready redress if those who should be providing these things let them down, and generally to combat the pervasive ageism in our society.

But people in or approaching the fourth age also need to know how to secure the more specialist services they may need, to complain effectively if these are not provided, to obtain protection against neglect or abuse or exploitation, and to provide so far as possible for what they would like to happen to them should they become unable to decide for themselves. Although the proportion of people who may need to know these things is comparatively small, the numbers are large and expected to grow.

The legal provisions are also comparatively complex but still inadequate to meet the needs of this growing group. The proposals of the Law Commission to improve the protection given to mentally incapacitated and other vulnerable adults are due to be published in March 1995 but any legislation is bound to take some time.

And we all need to know how best to provide for our eventual death.

Any one of these subjects qualifies for a book in its own right, although some are better catered for than others in the more conventional legal literature. Gordon Ashton has produced a comprehensive, practical and readable guide which seeks to cover most if not all of the many areas of law which fall within his broad title. It is encouraging that now, six years after the International Society on Family Law held its world conference on the problems of ageing, practitioners are beginning to recognise its importance.

Not surprisingly, there is more material in this book which is directly relevant to the fourth age than to the third. But those of us who are – with what feels like increasing rapidity – approaching the third should not be dismayed. There is still a great deal for us to look forward to.

Mrs Justice Hale
Royal Courts of Justice
January 1995

PREFACE TO THE SECOND EDITION

It is just two decades since I started to write the first edition of this book. It was so much simpler then and having been a solicitor in general practice I was able to tackle the entire topic on my own. Community care was in its infancy, the courts had less involvement in healthcare, and mental incapacity was only addressed in respect of financial affairs. The social and legal climate has changed almost unrecognisably in the intervening years and the fields of law that need to be covered have expanded exponentially. Now we must address human rights, European Union law, equality legislation (including disability discrimination), civil partnerships, data protection and elder abuse, quite apart from the overarching mental capacity jurisdiction and the further development of the inherent jurisdiction. For this reason I invited Caroline Bielanska to join me as an equal partner in producing this second edition. She has an impeccable background as recently retired chief executive of *Solicitors for the Elderly*, and is thoroughly versed in those areas of law that I tended not to encounter as a district judge. I express my thanks to her for rising to the challenge.

I wrote the first edition in MS Word on an Apple Macintosh using two displays and a laser printer and now, after many years staring at Windows in my judicial work, I have returned to Apple. The computer may work faster and the displays are larger, but little else has changed in my writing environment. Yet technology seeks to challenge the traditional world of publishing. The internet has revolutionised the way the law is accessed and threatens us with information overload. We no longer need to rely upon a traditional law library, but with a suitable subscription can access all the books we need on a laptop. Statutory material and government guidance can be found through a Google search, organisations maintain their own websites providing valuable information and even law reports are freely available on Bailii. The problem for the individual, whether or not a professional, lies in bringing the relevant material together and achieving an overview in a world of legal specialisms. That is what this book seeks to do.

I hope that there will be further editions but they will not be written by me. As I prepare to enter my 70th year I have become a consumer of my own work. I was struck by the way that Brenda Hale (then Mrs Justice Hale but now Baroness Hale, a Justice of the Supreme Court) referred in her Foreword for the first edition to the 'four ages of mankind and womankind'. I hope now to enjoy the third age and that the fourth age will not, for me, be artificially prolonged, but it is all a matter of personal perspective. When I studied law at Manchester University half a century ago I would have commented that I did not wish to live beyond 80 years because there would be no quality of life. I am beginning to change my mind! I did not overlap with Baroness Hale during my time at Manchester but first had the opportunity to work with her as a member of a couple of working parties for the Law Commission mental incapacity project. Since then she has played a key role in developing the law for children and disabled adults whilst I have merely been able to work in and write about these fields. But it has been a pleasure to witness the law and our legal system developing a more human approach to the way it treats vulnerable people.

For many years I have intended to update this book but the desire to promote the new mental capacity jurisdiction in my writings has always taken priority. I wish to thank Sally Drever, who was editor of my first book *Mental Handicap and the Law* in 1990, for her persistent encouragement without which I may never have embarked upon the task. It has been a pleasure to work with her again on this my final publication.

Gordon R. Ashton OBE
Grange-over-Sands, Cumbria
November 2013

PREFACE TO THE FIRST EDITION

This book was initially written primarily for lawyers who become involved in the problems and challenges presented by old age, but with the intention of benefiting the elderly as a client group. My hope is that it will also be of value to other professionals, because the law is not the sole preserve of lawyers and may become less so with cuts in legal aid. Having adopted a policy of care in the community to cope with an increasingly ageing population, our society must become more aware of the needs of the elderly and develop its laws and procedures to cope with them. In these respects the caring professions, which include lawyers, should take the lead. They need to have ready access to the law that concerns them.

Law books have tended to concentrate on traditional legal subjects rather than the needs of particular groups, and legal education is structured in the same way. Thus there are books on contract, tort, matrimonial and criminal law, employment, trusts, taxation, and court procedure but none providing an overview of the law that relates to older people, written from their point of view and adopting a practical approach. Practitioners who specialise tend to do so on the basis of fields of work rather than types of client, and this can result in failure to understand the overall needs of a client who seeks advice as to what to do rather than what the law is. This is especially so in the case of older people. Knowledge of law and procedure can be dangerous without a feeling for how and when to apply it. Practising lawyers gain this by experience, sometimes at the expense of clients, yet such experience is seldom shared in the context of client groups as distinct from legal specialities. Personal experience is selective, and this leads to different approaches in areas such as dealing with people who lack mental capacity.

Having spent 28 years in general legal practice in a community with an exceptionally high proportion of retired people, I have come to see the law as a series of enabling and protective provisions to be drawn on as necessary in serving the needs of the client. These needs must be properly identified and, although the lawyer must act for the client, this is not simply a question of doing what is asked but entails giving comprehensive advice. The lawyer cannot work in a vacuum and may need to look beyond the instructions of the client (if these can be ascertained), but the solicitor/client relationship inhibits contact with others and the relationship between lawyers and doctors, social workers and other care professionals is seldom sufficiently developed to encourage a joint approach. Now that I have retired from private practice I am able to take a more objective view of my past performance and whether the legal profession is really satisfying the needs of the elderly. I believe that better communication between different professionals is needed, and this can only be achieved if there is wider knowledge and understanding of the relevant law and its procedures.

This book represents my attempt to provide in a single volume the information and guidance that I wish could have been available to me during my years in practice. I hope that it will lead to a more comprehensive knowledge and understanding of the law not only by lawyers but within the caring professions generally. I have endeavoured to state the law at 1 January 1995 and in a manner intelligible to those who do not practise law whilst still of value to those who do. Some topics, such as welfare benefits, will soon become out of date and should only be treated as a general guide, but others may not have been written about elsewhere.

I should like to thank the members of the Law Society's Mental Health and Disability Committee who have provided me with so much support and in particular the secretary Penny Letts; also the team at Age Concern England for commenting on my work and Evelyn McEwen for co- ordinating this. Of the many individuals who have assisted me in various ways I wish to mention Mrs A B Macfarlane, Master of the Court of Protection who has always proved willing to make time for me, Lydia Sinclair for providing material on the criminal law, Denzil Lush for discussions about mental capacity and Luke Clements for material on care. I am also indebted to all at Gedye & Sons, solicitors of Grange-over-Sands for my years with them and my former clients, many no longer with us, who taught me so much. Above all, I wish to recognise my family who tolerated a husband and father who spent more time with his books and word-processor than with them. I hope that it has all been worthwhile.

Gordon R. Ashton
Grange-over-Sands, Cumbria
January 1995

CONTENTS

Contents

TABLE OF CASES

References are to paragraph numbers.

TABLE OF STATUTES

References are to paragraph numbers.

TABLE OF STATUTORY INSTRUMENTS

References are to paragraph numbers.

TABLE OF ABBREVIATIONS

Legislation

CSA 2000	Care Standards Act 2000
CDCA 2000	Carers and Disabled Children Act 2000
C(RS)A 1995	Carers (Recognition and Services) Act 1995
CSDPA 1970	Chronically Sick and Disabled Persons Act 1970
CC (DD) Act 2003	Community Care (Delayed Discharges etc.) Act 2003
DP(SCR)A 1986	Disabled Persons (Services, Consultation and Representation) Act 1986
EA 2010	Equality Act 2010
FOIA 2000	Freedom of Information Act 2000
HASSASSAA 1983	Health and Social Services and Social Security Adjudications Act 1983
HSCA 2001	Health and Social Care Act 2001
HSCA 2008	Health and Social Care Act 2008
HSCA 2012	Health and Social Care Act 2012
HRA 1998	Human Rights Act 1998
HSPHA 1968	Health Services and Public Health Act 1968
HTA 2004	Human Tissue Act 2004
LGA 2000	Local Government Act 2000
LASSA1970	Local Authority Social Services Act 1970
MCA 2005	Mental Capacity Act 2005
MHA 1983	Mental Health Act 1983
MHA 2007	Mental Health Act 2007
NAA 1948	National Assistance Act 1948
NHSA 2006	National Health Service Act 2006
NHS(W)A 2006	National Health Service (Wales) Act 2006
NHSCCA 1990	National Health Service and Community Care Act 1990
NA (AR) Regs 1992	National Assistance (Assessment of Resources) Regulations 1992

General

AMHP	Approved Mental Health Professional
CA	Carer's Allowance
CGT	Capital Gains Tax
CCG	Clinical Commissioning Group
CPA	Care Programme Approach

CRAG	Charges for Residential Accommodation Guide
CTO	Community Treatment Orders
CTR	Council Tax Reduction
CSSIW	Care and Social Services Inspectorate for Wales
CQC	Care Quality Commission
DLA	Disability Living Allowance
DHP	Discretionary Housing Payments
DoLs	Deprivation of Liberty Safeguards
DST	Decision Support Tool
DWP	Department for Work and Pensions
EAP	Emergency Assistance Payments
ECHR	European Convention of Human Rights
ECtHR	European Court of Human Rights
ECJ	European Court of Justice
ECT	Electric Convulsive Therapy
EEA	European Economic Area
ESA	Employment and Support Allowance
FACS	Fair Access to Care Services
GMC	General Medical Council
HMCTS	HM Courts and Tribunals Service
HMRC	HM Revenue and Customs
IAP	Individual Assistance Payments
ICO	Information Commissioner's Office
IHT	Inheritance Tax
IIDB	Industrial Injuries Disablement Benefit
IMCA	Independent Mental Capacity Advocate
JSA	Jobseeker's Allowance
JSNA	Joint Strategic Needs Assessment
LAC	local authority circular
LATs	Local Area Teams
LCW	Limited Capability for Work
NF	National Framework
NSF	National Service Framework
LGO	Local Government Ombudsman
LHB	Local Health Board
LHA	Local Housing Allowance
LPA (H&W)	health and welfare lasting power of attorney
NHS CB	NHS Commissioning Board
NHSCHC	NHS Continuing Healthcare
NHS	National Health Service
NIC	National Insurance Contributions
OPG	Office of the Public Guardian
PALS	Patient Advice and Liaison Service
PEA	Personal Expense Allowance

PC	Pension Credit
PIP	Personal Independence Payments
PSED	Public Sector Equality Duty
Prioritising Need Guidance	Prioritising need in the context of Putting People First: a whole system approach to eligibility for social care – eligibility criteria for adult social care
RAS	Resource Allocation System
RC	Responsible Clinician
SAP	Single Assessment Process
SERPS	State Earnings Related Pension Scheme
SOAD	second opinion appointed doctor
SSAC	Social Security Advisory Committee
STBAs	Short-term Benefit Advances
SCT	Supervised Community Treatment
UC	Universal Credit
UFSAMC	The Unified and Fair System for Assessing and Managing Care
WOC	Welsh Office Circular

INTRODUCTION

DISTINGUISHING OLDER PEOPLE

Gordon Ashton

'Forty is the old age of youth; fifty the youth of old age.'
Victor Hugo

Old age should not be seen as a problem – it is a fortunate reality of life for an increasing number of people. A changing social climate has provoked a new legal environment. It is the attributes of older people rather than their age that may justify special treatment by the law.

0.1   People are living longer and the number of elderly people in the UK is increasing. Most are able-bodied and of sound mind, but many will at some stage become dependent upon others and perhaps also unable to make their own decisions. Policies in regard to their care and treatment have changed, the emphasis now being upon care in the community which points to an enhanced role for the law in respect of those who might previously have been cared for within a non-complaining family or 'institutions' imposing their own rules. In a consumer oriented society the individual or a carer is more likely to challenge decisions made by the authorities in regard to the provision of financial or other support or medical treatment. Human rights are at the forefront of legal thinking and discrimination is outlawed. Wider home ownership, greater personal savings, private pension provision and social security payments result in an increase in the number of elderly people who have property and income that need managing and, in many cases, passing on to the next generation. There are more opportunities for the abuse of older people, but this is coupled with greater awareness of the existence of abuse and willingness to tackle it.

0.2   Dealing with the legal rights, duties and needs of older people raises special challenges. An understanding of the problems they face and their special needs is essential, so we start by outlining some of these. We ascertain what it is about them that justifies their treatment as an identifiable group. Then in later chapters we consider how the law and the legal system may play its part in fulfilling society's expectations as to the preservation of the rights of older people and of other members of the community in their interaction with one another.

STATISTICS

0.3   The population of the UK is growing in size and becoming increasingly older as people are living longer. According to the Office of National Statistics[1] over the period

---

[1]   Available at: www.statistics.gov.uk/hub/population/ageing/older-people.

1985–2010 the number of people aged 65 and over in the UK increased by 20% to 10.3 million; in 2010, 17% of the population were aged 65 and over compared with 7.5% over 60 at the turn of the 20th century. Population ageing will continue for the next few decades. By 2035 the number of people aged 85 and over is projected to be almost 2.5 times larger than in 2010, reaching 3.5 million and accounting for 5% of the total population. The population aged 65 and over will account for 23% of the total population in 2035, while the proportion of the population aged between 16 and 64 is due to fall from 65% to 59%. Population ageing brings potential benefits but also challenges to society. Key policy areas are health and social care, the ageing of the workforce and pensions, housing and transport.

0.4   Age UK (a merger in 2010 of Age Concern and Help the Aged) produces a valuable collection of statistics about the ageing population.[2] There are 10.8 million people aged 65 or over in the UK, 1.4 million people aged 85 or over, and more than 22 million (over a third of the population) aged at least 50 years. More people are aged over 60 than under 18 and the percentage of the total population who are over 60 is predicted to rise from 22% at present to nearly 29% in 2033 and 31% in 2058. The numbers of centenarians in the UK has nearly quadrupled since 1981, from 2,600 to over 12,000 in 2010 and nearly one in five people currently in the UK will live to see their 100th birthday. When asked what stage of life they were currently in (given choices), 55% of 60–64 year olds said 'later life or old age', but 43% of them said 'middle adulthood'.

ATTRIBUTES

0.5   There is no specific age at which an individual may be legally classified as 'elderly', though the state pension age[3] may conveniently be used and this book is concerned with those who are about to reach or have passed that age. This is presently 65 years for men and 60 years for women,[4] so in general we are considering people over the age of 60 years. We thus contemplate an age span of 20 or more years, potentially one-quarter of the life of an individual, while the ageing process develops more slowly for some than for others.

0.6   The attributes of elderly people are generally as follows and become more pronounced as they get older:

- tend to live off pensions, income from savings and even the savings themselves rather than earn an income to support themselves. Some have surplus assets which they wish to transfer to the next generation but many become financially dependent upon state benefits or their families. They may become concerned at the cost of long-term care yet not realise that they can still plan for this;
- have more leisure time, but live at a slower pace;
- are more inclined to rely upon acquired attitudes and beliefs than develop new ones, so appear less flexible;

---

[2]   Available on www.ageuk.org.uk and the information is extracted from December 2013.
[3]   This is a different concept from 'normal retiring age' which may be younger or older than this depending upon the particular employment in question.
[4]   Since 2010 there is a gradual phasing in of an increase to the pension age for women so by 2018 it will also be 65 years.

- wish to be independent as long as possible and may live alone or in some degree of isolation;
- are more likely to become dependent upon younger members of the family or other persons than to remain responsible for the younger generation, though it is not unusual to find a retired person caring for a parent;
- may encounter failing health resulting in physical limitations and disabilities on an increasing, permanent basis;
- may ultimately become mentally incapacitated.

This last attribute has a profound effect upon the legal status of the individual and is considered in Chapter 2.

Disabilities

0.7   One of the problems of ageing is a potential for sensory impairment, a decline in physical abilities and in some cases a lack of mental capacity each of which create a greater dependence upon others and vulnerability to abuse. This may also result in a handicap in society which should be compensated for rather than reinforced by the law or legal system.

0.8   We now adopt a social model of disability which sees the problem in the barriers constructed in society rather than a medical model which concentrates on the physical or mental impairment of the individual. Thus to the wheelchair user, the problem is that the building has steps but no ramp, not that the person has problems walking. Similarly to the hearing impaired person, the problem may be that the room does not have the loop system not that he has problems hearing. Many other examples could be cited of the marginalisation of disabled and infirm people by the way that society conducts itself.

Terminology

0.9   The terms that we use in these circumstances cause much confusion and words with a distinct meaning are often used in a wrong context or as if they are interchangeable. This is particularly so of 'disability' and 'handicap'.[5] It is suggested that it would be correct to state that an individual suffers from an illness or disorder and that this may result in a disability. This disability comprises two elements: first, the limitation imposed upon the individual by reason of his or her physical, mental or sensory impairment; and second, the handicap which this imposes on the individual in his or her environment. If the disability is of a sufficient degree the individual may be treated as being legally incapacitated (or incompetent) and this may be due to mental incapacity or physical inability or both.

0.10   We should not make comparisons with 'normal', or refer to 'the disabled', 'the handicapped', 'the deaf' or 'the blind' as if they were a distinct class.[6] The expression 'people with disabilities' has been preferred to 'disabled people' and this is not simply political correctness but also represents an attitude of mind: we should recognise the person rather than the disability. If we attach labels to people there is a danger that we then use these, however inadvertently, to take away their rights.[7] But there is now a

---

[5]   The term 'disability' had a technical meaning in some fields of law, eg under the Limitation Act 1980 and court rules, but a different approach is now adopted.

[6]   The use of these adjectives as nouns is also grammatically incorrect.

[7]   A type of 'stereotyping' particularly prominent with people from ethnic minorities.

move back to referring to a 'disabled person'[8] because this is a correct use of terminology and emphasises that the individual is being disabled rather than having a disability.[9]

0.11 One of the difficulties is that proper terms have over the years tended to become used in a derogatory manner[10] and then new terms have to be created. Thus 'mental handicap' has been replaced by 'learning disability' and efforts are being made to find a new term for 'mentally ill'.[11] Sensitivity is necessary at all times in the choice of term used to describe a genuine condition and a judgmental approach should be avoided. The following use of terms is suggested:

Appropriate	Inappropriate
'Person with ...'	'Victim of ...'
'Hearing impaired'	'Deaf'
'Wheelchair user'	'Wheelchair bound'
'Non disabled' or 'Able bodied'	'Normal'
'Person who has ...'	'Afflicted by ...' or 'Suffering from ...'

Use of inappropriate terms can cause offence to the individual and also demonstrates prejudicial attitudes towards disabled people.

Physical disability

0.12 Physical impairment, sometimes severe, is often associated with the ageing process and may comprise impaired mobility and dexterity. There may also be sensory impairment such as defective vision or hearing loss. The ability to communicate may be affected (eg the consequence of a stroke) with implications that appear similar to but should not be confused with mental disability. Pain and discomfort, the need to take regular medication or go to the toilet and limited concentration spans all affect social functioning.

Mental disability

0.13 Mental health problems can take many forms and are more prevalent than is generally acknowledged. Anxiety affects more than one person in four at some stage in their lives, and depression as many as one person in four. 'Mental illness' may be distinguished from 'learning disability'[12] in that treatment is appropriate and a cure may be possible (although it seldom will be in the cases of mental illness arising due to the ageing process). The term covers both neurosis[13] and psychosis[14] although only the latter is meant when using old terms such as 'lunatic'. There is no statutory definition

---

8   The former Disability Rights Commission adopted this approach.
9   See the reference above to the 'social' as distinct from the 'medical' model of disability.
10 Eg *idiot, imbecile, lunatic, cretin, moron,* all of which appeared in earlier legislation or medical textbooks but now are confined to the school playground.
11 MIND, the national organisation, suggest 'mentally challenged'.
12 A condition of the developmental years in that the individual has a brain that will not develop normally and medical treatment is not possible.
13 A functional derangement due to disorders of the nervous system, eg hypochondria, hysteria, phobias, obsessive behaviour, depression.
14 A severe mental derangement involving the whole personality, eg paranoia, schizophrenia, manic depression (bi-polar).

but there are medical criteria, namely it is an acquired condition insofar as the person has not previously been affected and the condition must satisfy the diagnostic criteria of one or more particular groups.

0.14 A person who has attained a normal ability and subsequently loses it is classified medically as having acquired organic brain syndrome which constitutes a mental illness as recognised by the Mental Health Act 1983 even though treatment may not be possible. This is a neurotic disorder which is usually due to vascular changes. It includes dementia (often referred to as senile dementia when it arises in old age) of which Alzheimer's disease is the most common form. Dementia affects ever increasing numbers of older people[15] who in terms of needs and capability (at least legally) have much in common with people with severe learning disabilities though such term would not be applied to them.

Discrimination

0.15 Although for the purposes of this book it is necessary to distinguish older people and identify their attributes, discrimination in any form is now disapproved of and should be avoided even if not intended. Discrimination takes many forms: it may be actual or perceived and it may be direct or indirect.

- **Direct discrimination** occurs where a person is treated less favourably on grounds of race, colour, religion, gender, ethnic or national origin, age or disability, than others would be in similar circumstance.
- **Indirect discrimination** occurs where a requirement is applied equally to all groups, but has a disproportionate effect on the members of one group because a considerably smaller number of members of that group can comply with it.

Indirect discrimination should not be tolerated unless it can be objectively justified by a legitimate aim and the means of achieving that aim are appropriate and necessary. Even if there is no discrimination every effort should be made to avoid the perception that there has been.[16]

Components of discrimination

0.16 Discrimination may be deliberate but it may also be the result of prejudice, ignorance, thoughtlessness or stereotyping by individuals.

- **Prejudice:** we all have prejudices and it is best that these are identified and acknowledged. These prejudices should not then be allowed to influence our thinking and decisions.
- **Ignorance:** discriminatory behaviour may be the result of mere ignorance or lack of awareness.
- **Thoughtlessness:** the thoughtless comment, throw away remark, unwise joke or use of inappropriate terminology may confirm or create an impression (whether justified or not) of prejudice.
- **Stereotyping:** we should not assume that because people meet particular criteria (for example, being Asian or wheelchair users) they behave in a particular way or

---

[15] 6% of those over 65 years and 20% of those over 80. Half these cases are caused by Alzheimer's disease which is not curable at present.

[16] Legislation to tackle discrimination is considered in Chapter 1.

have specific limitations. We must also beware of attaching labels to people and then using these to take away their rights. Thus it should not be assumed that people over 90 years of age are incapable of handling their affairs or that an individual who has had a stroke is incapable of giving evidence in court.

Unwitting or unconscious prejudice is difficult to tackle. Ignorance of the cultures, beliefs and disadvantages of others encourages prejudices and these are best dispelled by greater awareness. Thoughtlessness may also create or reinforce stereotypes or encourage discrimination by influencing the way people act or respond to others.

0.17 Discrimination can be found in an entire organisation through its processes, attitudes and behaviour.[17] A culture of prejudice may have grown up within an organisation which is seen as acceptable by those involved and results in unquestioning behaviour that disadvantages a section of the community. If this arises in the legal system or in any environment (for example, failure to provide assistance to wheelchair users or to communicate in a friendly manner with people from ethnic minorities) it should be addressed in an appropriate way.

The new climate

0.18 There is now a new social climate that emphasises personal autonomy, favours care in the community and disapproves of discrimination in any form. Infirm elderly people and others with disabilities are more visible in society and have increased expectations fuelled by the availability of information on the internet. Their rights are increasingly being recognised and enforced by others if not by themselves.

0.19 In 2009 the United Kingdom ratified the UN Convention on the Rights of Disabled People and the optional Protocol. The Convention includes detailed provision on independent living, habilitation and rehabilitation, personal mobility, health, access to justice and participation in public life. It is not directly enforceable, but is relevant to the exercise of powers by public bodies and as an aid to interpreting domestic legislation. The protocol enables individuals and groups to petition the UN directly where a breach of the convention is alleged and where domestic and EC law proceedings have failed to secure an effective remedy.

0.20 In Wales a Commissioner for Older People has been appointed to have regard to the UN Principles and act as a watchdog charged with promotion, consultation, review, advocacy, education and investigative functions. The Commissioner is empowered to examine the case of a particular older person or persons if it involves an issue that has general application to the lives of older people in Wales. The review functions cover those organisations charged with the delivery of services to older people in Wales and extend to the mechanisms available for advocacy, the making of complaints and whistle-blowing.[18]

0.21 Driven by these social forces the legal climate has changed too over the past decade. Lawyers and the courts are having to cope with the needs of infirm elderly and disabled people. Four significant legislative initiatives provide the basis for the growth of legal activity and a wide range of new outcomes from the courts:

---

[17] A conclusion of *The Stephen Lawrence inquiry – Report by Sir William Macpherson* (Cmnd 4264-1 HMSO). 'Institutional racism' was identified in the police force.

[18] Commissioner for Older People (Wales) Act 2006. A 'Commissioner for Older People (Scotland) Bill' was introduced in the Scottish Parliament in September 2006 but not enacted.

(1) under community care policies introduced in 1993, the needs of the individual are assessed and should be provided for (rather than expecting the individual to cope with whatever services are available);[19]

(2) Law Commission proposals in regard to decision-making for those who lack capacity to make their own decisions have influenced the approach of the courts and finally borne fruit in the Mental Capacity Act 2005;[20]

(3) increased awareness of the effects of discrimination has resulted in the disability and age discrimination legislation and subsequently the Equality Act 2010;[21]

(4) the Human Rights Act 1998 has enhanced the rights of people with disabilities.[22]

0.22 The legal profession has also woken up to the benefits of providing services targeting the needs of older clients that go beyond the traditional wills and enduring powers of attorney (now lasting powers of attorney). The following chapters illustrate the areas of law that should be within the experience of elderly client practitioners, and at the forefront are now capacity issues[23] and discrimination and employment laws.[24]

0.23 The concept of the *elderly client practice* first advocated by the author at the Annual Conference of the Law Society in 1992 and encouraged in the first edition of this book, has become a reality with a professional group being formed.[25] However, the Law Society of England and Wales and law schools have so far refrained from including elderly or disabled people within their areas of specialism and there is no panel of solicitors who practice in this area.[26]

---

[19] See Ch 6.

[20] See Ch 2.

[21] See Ch 1.

[22] See Ch 1.

[23] Ch 2 deals with the new jurisdiction under the Mental Capacity Act 2005.

[24] See the government website at www.agepositive.gov.uk.

[25] *Solicitors for the Elderly* (SfE) has a membership of over 1,200 practitioners and a website at www.solicitorsfortheelderly.com. In the USA 'elder law' is considered a distinct practice area and the National Academy of Elder Law Attorneys has a website at www.naela.com.

[26] The nearest that the College of Law comes to this is a 'private client' elective, but the University of Northumbria runs a postgraduate course in law for the elderly. The Judicial College provides training to judges on addressing the special needs of elderly and disabled parties and witnesses.

CHAPTER 1

ROLE OF THE LAW

Gordon Ashton

'It is in justice that the ordering of society is centered.'
Aristotle (384 BC–322 BC)

The general law should apply to older people without distinction but some aspects may be of more relevance to them than to the community at large and other aspects need to be modified to accommodate their special needs. In this chapter we consider first how older people may achieve equal access to justice, followed by the impact of anti-discrimination and human rights legislation and finally the implications of a lack of mental capacity.

INTRODUCTION

1.1 There is no separate body of law dealing with the needs of older people, so the law that concerns them and their families and carers must be extracted from the general law. As an identifiable group they do not present any special problems or challenges and it would be discriminatory to have a separate body of law dealing with them, but some fields of law need to be modified or enhanced to provide for their specific needs and changed role in society. This could also be said of other categories such as married or cohabiting couples and younger people with disabilities. We identify the piecemeal modifications or enhancements relating to older people throughout this book under different topics, but very little of its content relates exclusively to them. The relevant legal provisions relating to this group have merely been identified and brought together for convenience.

1.2 Some of these provisions relate only to older people[1] or to those with special needs.[2] Those relating to decision-making and the management of financial affairs during periods of mental incapacity predominantly relate to older people.[3] Others provide for physical disabilities to which the older person is particularly susceptible yet some specifically exclude people over a specified age.[4] All this provision has grown up in a piecemeal fashion and many gaps can be identified where provision is needed but has not yet been made. In some areas the law is not fully understood or has not been developed to cope with special needs.[5] Increasing demands are now being made of the law by, or in respect of, infirm, older people.

---

[1] Examples are the rules relating to certain tax benefits or the payment of pensions.
[2] See the community care provisions in Ch 7.
[3] See Chs 2 and 11.
[4] Such as employment schemes and social security allowances for mobility.
[5] Eg the law as to undue influence and court rules relating to unrepresented parties.

1.3   Legislation deals with some issues and the common law has had to cope with others whilst policies and procedures are also important. The objectives of the law are fourfold, being to:

(a)   enhance the quality of the individual's life by ensuring appropriate support when this is needed;

(b)   increase personal autonomy by enabling decisions to be made by the individual or (for those who can no longer make their own decisions) on their behalf;

(c)   protect the individual from exploitation, abuse or neglect whether physical, mental or financial; and

(d)   enforce duties owed by society to the individual (and vice versa).

There is a constant tension between these roles. You cannot protect individuals from exploitation or abuse without in some way restricting or taking away their independence or autonomy. Nor can you always preserve the freedoms of the individual whilst respecting the legitimate interests of the rest of society. The support that may be available from the state is limited by lack of resources. When and to what extent it is necessary for the law to intervene may be a matter of opinion, but the situation is made worse by the fact that those involved are not always clear about their role and may only concentrate upon one aspect.

1.4   Older people enjoy the same rights and are subject to the same duties as other members of society, but whether an individual is able to exercise those rights or perform those duties depends upon the ability to make and communicate decisions and the willingness of others to recognise decisions properly made. Mental or physical disability may result in an older person being treated as incompetent. It is essential that every effort is made, using aids when these would assist, to communicate effectively with the individual. There are three guiding principles for the application and development of the law when considering personal autonomy:

(a)   all people are presumed to be competent and to have the same rights and status, except as specifically provided or determined;

(b)   any modification or intervention should be the minimum necessary in that case; and

(c)   people should be enabled to exercise and develop their own capacity and to participate in decisions to the maximum extent possible.

1.5   If the law is to enhance the quality of life for those who lack competence it may do so in two different ways: first, it may compensate for their inadequacies by giving them privileges not enjoyed by the rest of society; second, it may ensure that decisions can be made for them so that rights we all take for granted can be enforced on their behalf and they are protected from abuse or neglect. In general, a wider view of mental disability should be taken when the objective is to enhance the quality of life by providing some targeted entitlement than when it is to delegate decision-making which involves taking away a personal freedom.

EQUAL ACCESS TO JUSTICE

Preliminary

1.6 Whatever the personal impairment it is important that this does not prevent access to justice. Lawyers and the courts must conduct themselves and their affairs so that the individual does not encounter a handicap in accessing legal rights. Some matters of general application must first be considered before we concentrate on the role of lawyers and the courts.

Coping with older people

1.7 Communication and understanding are the keys to access to justice. Not only is the individual entitled to be heard and understood before any advice is given, but it is also a pre-requisite that the individual understands the choices to be made and their implications before any decision is made so that they are then able to make an informed choice. The first question is therefore whether the individual is indeed able and being permitted to make their own decisions and provided with enough genuine information for that purpose. Those who are frail and depend upon the support of others are vulnerable to undue influence and steps must be taken to ensure that any wishes they express are the product of their own free will.[6] Subject to this it may be necessary to assess whether there is the necessary capacity to make decisions and give instructions to a lawyer. Capacity will normally be assumed but when for some reason it is called into question there must be a proper assessment according to the appropriate legal test.[7]

Communication

1.8 Communication is a two-way process: it is as important for advisers to ensure that they understand what is being said to them as that their explanations are given in a manner that the older person can comprehend. A different technique is required when interviewing or taking evidence from those who are mentally frail or otherwise vulnerable. In general the person asking the questions should:

- speak slowly, using simple words and sentences;
- ensure that there are no distractions in the background;
- avoid questions requiring 'yes/no' answers;[8]
- refrain from questions suggesting the answer or containing a choice of answers which may not include the desired one;
- not keep repeating questions as this may suggest that the answers are not believed and encourage a change (although the same questions may be asked at a later stage to check for consistent replies);
- not move to new topics without an explanation (eg 'can we now talk about');
- not ask abstract questions (eg ask 'was it after breakfast' instead of 'was it after 9.00 am');
- allow the person to tell his or her story and not simply ignore information which does not fit in with assumptions; and

---

[6] The law relating to undue influence is dealt with in Ch 4 at **4.117**.
[7] This topic is covered in Ch 1 at **1.93** and Ch 2 at **2.19**.
[8] An assent may not be the real answer. Memory impairment or a misunderstanding is more likely to be revealed if the individual expresses a response in his own words.

- not go on too long without a break.

Aids to communication

1.9   Every effort should be made to overcome communication difficulties using available aids or an interpreter where this will assist. If verbal dialogue is not possible written notes or sign language may facilitate communication. A simple response to questions, such as movement of a finger, may be found reliable but in that event questions must be phrased so as to facilitate a range of responses. Impairment of communication does not necessarily indicate lack of mental capacity and where there is doubt a medical report may establish the capacity of the individual.[9]

Understanding

1.10   The responses received should not always be taken at face value. There may be differences in the use of language and it is easy to talk at cross-purposes. Old-fashioned politeness may result in a desire to please or not to contradict and there may be an attempt to conceal memory impairments. A learnt behaviour pattern may result in a plausible performance devoid of reality. Where there is a significant doubt as to whether an individual is capable of understanding what is required of him it will be necessary to carry out an assessment of mental capacity.

Support, protection and empowerment

1.11   Older people are potentially vulnerable to neglect, abuse and exploitation. The law must do three things for their benefit: regulate support, provide protection and ensure empowerment.

Support

1.12   There have traditionally been three sources of support that are regulated by the law although the respective roles of these providers are changing and overlapping:

(a)   the Department of Work and Pensions which provides state or welfare benefits generally on a weekly basis. These may be contributory, non-contributory or a means-tested top-up to ensure that everybody has a minimum income to meet their requirements;

(b)   social services departments of local authorities which are responsible for providing or arranging community care services and services for disabled persons for which means-tested financial contributions must be made;[10] and

(c)   the National Health Service (NHS) which, through NHS Trusts, provides free hospital and nursing care but is increasingly restricted to acute health care.[11]

Social services apply means-tests which take away state benefit yet now provide cash to pay for services, whilst state benefits are withdrawn from those in hospital. The NHS has withdrawn from many areas of care for elderly people such as long-term care and social services authorities are assuming that role, although joint funding is increasingly available.

---

[9]   Mental capacity as a whole is considered further in Ch 2.
[10]   See generally Ch 7.
[11]   This is considered in Ch 8 at **8.15** et seq.

Protection

1.13   The law must also ensure protection and may do so by providing a representative in the form of an *appropriate adult* for police interviews,[12] or a *statutory guardian* or *nearest relative* for Mental Health Act functions.[13] The authorities should investigate and intervene where there is a suspicion of abuse but unlike their role in regard to children, their powers are limited at present and there is no duty to intervene.[14] The view may be taken that if there was better empowerment there would be less need for protection; leaving a vulnerable incapacitated individual without anyone legally in control (or with inadequate means of assuming control) is a recipe for abuse.

Empowerment

1.14   Empowerment means enabling individuals to take decisions for which they are competent. There must be a proper assessment of capacity and any communication difficulties should be overcome. A suitable person should be empowered to take decisions for individuals who are not competent. At present we have a number of potential representatives:

(a)   *appointee* for state benefits;

(b)   *deputy* appointed by the Court of Protection for financial affairs (or personal welfare decisions);[15]

(c)   *attorney* under a lasting (or an enduring) power of attorney;[16]

(d)   *litigation friend* for civil or family proceedings;[17]

(e)   *personal advocate* – a useful role yet not recognised in law.

The court may need to facilitate decisions when necessary and in the absence of a procedure, the High Court found that it might make *declarations* supported by injunctions in regard to medical treatment. Subsequently this remedy extended to personal welfare decisions, but this procedure was inordinately expensive and scarcely available for everyday situations. In regard to those who lack capacity to make the decision it has been replaced by the Mental Capacity Act 2005.

Problems

1.15   Four significant problems have in the past been identified:

(a)   a lack of adequate public funding to cover the needs of vulnerable elderly people and of ring-fencing for the funds that could be available;

(b)   buck passing between the former DSS, local authorities and health authorities with the disabled individual becoming a pawn in the funding game and money that could have been expended on unquestionable needs being wasted on the argument over which funder must provide. In recent years many appeal decisions have sought to define responsibilities but there is now a move towards joint funding;

---

[12]   Criminal responsibility is considered in Ch 3 at **3.159** et seq.
[13]   Mental health issues are considered in Ch 8 at **8.94** et seq.
[14]   See generally Ch 7 in the context of community care and Ch 4 at **4.100** and **4.161** under the heading Elder Abuse.
[15]   Mental Capacity Act 2005. Before October 2007 this was a *receiver* under the Mental Health Act 1983.
[16]   This topic and the two above are dealt with in Ch 2 and for financial affairs Ch 11.
[17]   Appointed under the Civil Procedure Rules 1998 or Family Procedure Rules 2010 (see Ch 3 at para. 3.135).

(c)   the balance between protection and empowerment, because protection involves taking away the personal autonomy that we seek to preserve. This dilemma is frequently encountered by those seeking to support or make decisions on behalf of vulnerable persons; and

(d)   gaps in the powers of the legally available representatives resulting from a lack of procedures for personal and medical decision-making. This has been largely resolved by the Mental Capacity Act 2005.

Role of the lawyer

1.16   Lawyers have developed considerable skills in negotiating on behalf of, and promoting the rights of, individuals who for one reason or another are at a disadvantage in looking after their own interests. The lawyer can also act as a whistle blower to draw attention to situations where the rights of a vulnerable person are being overlooked or abuse is taking place. These skills can be put to good use in relation to infirm elderly persons.

Who is the client

1.17   The first task for the adviser is to identify the client, which does not change just because of communication difficulties or even lack of capacity. A solicitor receiving instructions from a third party on behalf of an individual who is, or may become, mentally incapacitated should at all times remember that the individual is the client, not the third party. This is so even if the third party has legal authority to represent the individual, whether as deputy appointed by the Court of Protection, attorney acting under a registered lasting or enduring power of attorney or litigation friend in court proceedings. The third party is merely an agent with a duty to act in the best interests of the incapacitated principal. Any solicitor who accepts instructions shares this duty even if it brings him into conflict with the agent through whom he receives instructions.

Duty to the client

1.18   It is important that the legal profession retains this role of safeguarding the best interests of vulnerable and incapacitated people because there may be no-one else to do so. Undue reliance should not be placed by lawyers on relatives or carers in identifying the wishes of the client especially where these persons may be affected by the outcome of any decision. Potential conflicts of interest should be identified at an early stage and if appropriate, independent legal advice recommended either for the would-be elderly client or for the relatives or carers. A solicitor who is asked to take on a new elderly client should enquire as to the existence of any former solicitor and the reason for any change. It may be wise to contact that solicitor in case the change has been initiated by the agent in an attempt to circumvent legal advice based upon full knowledge of the client's circumstances.

1.19   It is easiest to explain this concept through a situation that might arise in everyday practice:

> A woman consults a solicitor and indicates that her elderly father wishes to execute a lasting power of attorney in her favour so that she may continue to look after his affairs in the event of incapacity. The solicitor should consider who he is acting for in this transaction. If it be the father, the solicitor should arrange to see him alone in order to offer advice, confirm instructions and be satisfied that the client is capable of giving instructions and not under the influence of another person before preparing the document. If it be the daughter, the solicitor

should arrange for her father to consult an independent solicitor of his choice and decline to prepare the document. The father may indeed wish to sign a lasting power of attorney but not necessarily in favour of that daughter!

The reason for this approach becomes more apparent if the document was to be a gift of the home in favour of the daughter, because however compelling the reasons put forward by her, she has a conflict of interest which the legal adviser cannot share.

The retainer

1.20 Technically the solicitor/client relationship is terminated by the subsequent mental incapacity of a client notwithstanding that this is the stage at which the client most needs the protective services of a lawyer. However, rules of professional practice may impose continuing obligations upon the solicitor as to the welfare of the former client. In the absence of anyone else with clear legal authority, the solicitor previously chosen by, and acting for, the individual is likely to be recognised as having at least the semblance of authority until formal steps can be taken.

1.21 When asked by relatives or carers to act for an individual who lacks capacity, the solicitor will seek to act for that individual on the instructions of the third party unless, and until, a dispute arises. If someone else challenges this role, especially if another solicitor is instructed, then the respective solicitors will represent the persons giving instructions until some formal legal authority is acquired.[18] At that stage the solicitor instructed by the person with such authority will represent the individual who lacks capacity.

Taking instructions

1.22 The process of taking instructions includes both obtaining information and giving advice. The guidance set out above as to effective communication and mutual understanding is of vital importance to any solicitor seeking to take instructions from a frail or infirm elderly client. In all situations the solicitor should ensure that he is acting on the instructions of the client or, if these cannot be obtained because the client lacks capacity to give instructions, that he is acting in the best interests of the client.

1.23 Any instructions, however received, should be confirmed with the client direct and if there is any doubt, this should be at a personal interview when the demeanour of the client may be assessed. The client should be seen alone at some point to ensure that the instructions are given freely and without undue influence, and that they really do represent the client's wishes. The interview note should be comprehensive and record not only the matters discussed and conclusions reached but also who was present at each stage. It is surprising how often when disputes later reach the courts, solicitors are unable to produce adequate notes and must rely upon their memory as to past events. There can be no presumption in such circumstances that the solicitor has acted properly.

Role of the courts

1.24 It should not be thought that courts exist solely to punish people for offences. That is the role of the criminal courts and older people are more likely to become involved in these courts as victims and witnesses than as defendants.[19] The civil courts

---

[18] Eg appointment of a deputy by the Court of Protection.
[19] Criminal responsibility is considered in Ch 3 at **3.159**, and victims of crime in Ch 4 at **4.151**.

enforce the rights of the citizen, businesses and corporations and resolve disputes. An older person is as likely to become involved in these matters as the general population whether as a party or a witness.[20] The family courts have a valuable role to play when problems arise with a spouse or partner, or with children or grandchildren.[21] A proliferation of tribunals has also been developed to resolve other disputes.

1.25   Courts have traditionally appeared 'unfriendly and inaccessible' to those who use their services and 'engender fear and anxiety'.[22] A survey of the reactions of litigants stated:[23]

> 'With or without a lawyer, few lay people say that they feel at ease in this setting. Many litigants described in interviews how they were taken aback by their first sight of the courtroom and its formality ... The interviews were peppered with words like "intimidating", "daunting", "frightening", "terrifying", "forbidding", and "formidable" ... Less than half of the unrepresented litigants ... said that they coped well in this setting and even those who were represented by counsel frequently said that they found the court appearance a daunting experience ... a few described how they had gone to pieces when they realised what was expected of them.'

In the new social climate outlined in the Introduction our courts and tribunals are developing a different approach and recognising the diversity of society.

Unrepresented parties

1.26   Some litigants (traditionally known as 'litigants in person' or more recently 'self-represented parties') represent themselves rather than instruct a lawyer and everybody of full age and capacity is entitled to do so. This may be because they cannot afford a solicitor,[24] distrust lawyers or believe that they will be better at putting their case across. They find that they are operating in an alien environment because the courts and tribunals have not traditionally been receptive to their needs:[25]

> 'All too often the litigant in person is regarded as a problem for judges and for the court system rather than a person for whom the system of civil justice exists.'

The disadvantages faced by unrepresented parties whatever their age stem from a lack of knowledge of the law and court procedure. They tend to be unfamiliar with the terminology, unskilled in advocacy, confused about the presentation of evidence and lacking in objectivity. The aim of the judge or tribunal is to ensure that they understand what is going on and what is expected of them at all stages, and have the time and facilities to enable them to fully participate.

McKenzie friend and lay advocates

1.27   The traditional role of the so-called '*McKenzie* friend'[26] is to quietly assist and not act as an advocate. Such assistance is generally accepted, especially during trials in

---

[20]   Involvement with the civil and family courts by older people is dealt with in Ch 3 at **3.121**.
[21]   This topic is considered in Ch 4.
[22]   Money Advice Trust, Adjudicator's Office and Institute of Consumer Affairs respectively.
[23]   *Monitoring the Rise of the Small Claims Limit*, 1995, Professor Baldwin.
[24]   Many do not qualify for Legal Services Commission funding (commonly known as Legal Aid), either financially or because of the nature of their case.
[25]   Lord Woolf, *Access to Justice*, Interim Report June 1995.
[26]   The role was first explained in *McKenzie v McKenzie* [1970] 3 All ER 1034.

court, but the court can exclude the 'friend' if unsuitable.[27] It is more likely to do so during proceedings in private (ie not an open court trial) because a more informal approach is adopted and the judge is better able to provide the support that is needed, but an unjustified exclusion could be 'unfair' and a breach of human rights.[28]

1.28 Only a qualified lawyer has rights of audience in the civil and family courts,[29] but a judge has a discretion to hear anyone if this will assist in the attainment of justice. A litigant in person who wishes to have someone without rights of audience acting as an advocate on his behalf (for example, a wife who is too timid to argue her own case seeking to rely on her husband) should personally explain to the court why such assistance is wanted. A court would be slow to grant this but there is no general principle that it may only be allowed in exceptional circumstances.[30]

1.29 If the right is granted, the litigant should still be present in court when personal interests are involved so that the judge can involve him or her if doubts arise as to the conduct of the case and may dismiss the representative if acting in an inappropriate manner.[31] In the 'small claims track' in the county court[32] a *lay representative* has a right of audience but only in the presence of the party.[33] An attorney does not acquire the right to conduct proceedings or a right of audience. However, a *litigation friend* for an incapacitated party may have full rights of audience. It is illogical that a person who lacks the physical ability to cope with a hearing may not be represented by someone other than a lawyer, yet a person who lacks mental capacity may be represented by an unqualified person without supervision.

1.30 Continuing in the absence of the litigant might be appropriate when this person was unable to attend and could not afford a lawyer (for example, a son representing his mother who is too infirm to attend)[34] but the judge would have to be satisfied that the representative was competent and did not have a conflict of interest. Representation by an unqualified person seeking to provide general advocacy services, or where the advocate is pursuing a separate agenda, will not be permitted. The test is 'what is in the best interests of the litigant' and this is a prime example of the protective role of the courts with suitable empowerment being the objective.

Support for disabled litigants

1.31 Special facilities or procedures may be needed when people with physical or mental impairments appear before the courts either as litigants or witnesses. Whilst the court staff may be helpful, a litigant is only treated in a different manner by the rules in

---

[27] Eg pursuing his own agenda or otherwise obstructing the proceedings – see *R v Bow County Court ex p Pelling* [1999] 2 FLR 149; *Re G (Chambers proceedings: next friend)* [1999] 2 FLR 59, CA.

[28] *Re O (Children)* [2005] EWCA Civ 759.

[29] Courts and Legal Services Act 1990, s 27(2)(c). This will generally be a solicitor with a practising certificate, a practising barrister or Fellow of the Institute of Legal Executives.

[30] *Nouieri v Paragon Finance Plc (No)* [2001] EWCA Civ 1402.

[31] *Clarkson v Gilbert & ors* (2000) *The Times*, 4 July, CA; *Izzo v Phillip Ross & Co* (2001) *The Times*, 9 August.

[32] Restricted to suitable claims under £5,000 – Civil Procedure Rules 1998 Parts 26 and 27.

[33] Civil Procedure Rules 1998, PD 27 para 3.2 and Lay Representatives (Right of Audience) Order 1999, SI 1999/1225.

[34] For a high value claim the court would be concerned to enquire why the litigant could not obtain legal assistance.

the case of mental incapacity. These then ensure that a representative is appointed, compromises and settlements are approved by the court and there is supervision of money recovered.[35]

1.32 The courts are not exempted from the provisions of the Equality Act 2010[36] which apply to services[37] and they may be in breach of this legislation if they do not take into account the needs of disabled people. Reasonable adjustments include not only disabled access to the building, the courtroom and the ancillary facilities, but also, for example, the provision of hearing loops for those with impaired hearing. It would be unlawful not to provide an interpreter for a deaf witness or braille for a person with impaired sight.[38]

1.33 In the early 1990s the courts developed an equal treatment policy, but this only tackled racial and gender discrimination. It was soon realised that 'equal opportunity' would be more appropriate – the best case should succeed, not the strongest litigant – and that special needs should also be addressed for people with disabilities. An *Equal Treatment Bench Book* is now issued to all judges and the guidance not only ensures a more just outcome but also results in more efficient use of court time.[39] Judges are trained to be 'disability aware' and encouraged to adopt the wider range of options that is available.[40] The forms used by the court and completed by the parties enquire as to any special needs so that the administration and judiciary know in advance when disabled facilities or special directions are needed. Simple measures such as devising user friendly forms and producing documents and letters in large print may be all that is required.

Interpreters

1.34 There is nothing in the court rules about interpreters but they are routinely arranged when a person giving evidence does not speak the language of the court or has seriously impaired hearing. Where lawyers are involved they will make the arrangements and the fees of the interpreter will become part of the costs of the case.[41] Where funding is not otherwise available, it is now the policy of the court in compliance with discrimination legislation to arrange and pay for the interpreter.[42] This becomes imperative where the liberty of the individual is at stake or in children or domestic violence cases. When it is a party, as distinct from a witness, who needs an interpreter this facility should be provided for the duration of the case.

---

[35] See Ch 3 for civil proceedings and Ch 4 for family proceedings. There will be a *litigation friend* but this representative will have no authority outside the specific court proceedings.

[36] Previously the Disability Discrimination Act 1995.

[37] The courts provide legal services – see 3.131.

[38] A claims has been settled where the court failed to provide suitable facilities to a hearing impaired person.

[39] This is available from the JSB Website: www.jsboard.co.uk. It has almost been afforded the status of the law – see *R (on the application of King) v Isleworth Crown Court* [2001] All ER (D) 48 (Jan), Brooke LJ.

[40] The author has been a member of the *Equal Treatment Advisory Committee* of the Judicial Studies Board (JSB – now the Judicial College) and regularly gave lectures on disability issues to judges at seminars.

[41] An advocate should not, other than briefly in an emergency, seek to act as interpreter – the roles must not be confused. The costs of a sign language interpreter should not be passed on to the client and for this reason will be paid by the Legal Services Commission for a publicly funded party and not included in the statutory charge – see www.rnid.org.uk.

[42] The Court Service will generally pay for an interpreter for a party (not a witness) who cannot otherwise provide one. Applications are made to the Civil Projects Branch by fax on 0207 210 1685. The Legal Services Commission will meet the costs of a sign language interpreter for deaf people using legal aid lawyers.

1.35 The interpreter must be competent and independent and it is unwise for the same interpreter to act for more than one party. Communication aids and intermediaries or communicators rather than just interpreters may be permitted for parties or witnesses with other difficulties[43] (even if this may be the only person who could understand the witness[44]), but evidence from a psychologist or psychiatrist as to the reliability of the evidence to be given may not be accepted.[45]

Venue

1.36 Anyone involved in a hearing who has an impairment that prevents them attending should notify the court in advance so that appropriate steps can be taken.[46] The hearing may be transferred to a courtroom with better facilities or a court in a more suitable location. In civil proceedings the evidence of a witness who is unable to attend the hearing for genuine reasons such as being abroad at the time or too infirm to attend the courtroom may be taken in advance before a court appointed examiner in the presence of representatives of the parties.[47] When a party is unable to attend and it is inappropriate to proceed in his absence albeit with legal representation, it may be possible to arrange for some or all the trial to take place at a venue suitable to that party instead of in a courtroom.[48] Another option where the technology can be made available is to set up a video conference.

Conclusion

1.37 It will generally be possible to accommodate the needs of an infirm or disabled litigant or witness whilst still ensuring a fair trial for all involved. When this litigant is mentally incapable of conducting the proceedings or giving instructions to a solicitor, a representative will be appointed to undertake these tasks. When the disability falls short of this, the use of available aids or assistance from a suitable person may be sufficient.

EQUALITY

Preliminary

1.38 The nature of discrimination was identified in the Introduction. Elderly people are particularly susceptible to discrimination on account of their age or disabilities. During recent years certain forms of discrimination have been made unlawful and statutory remedies provided for a breach, more recently fuelled by European Directives. Standards have been set in these areas and enforced through the courts and tribunals.

---

[43] They are expressly mentioned in the special measures directions introduced by the *Youth Justice and Criminal Evidence Act 1999 Part II* to assist vulnerable and intimidated witnesses to give evidence in criminal proceedings.

[44] See *R v Duffy* (1993) *The Times*, 2 May – a criminal case.

[45] See *R v Robinson (Raymond)* (1993) *The Times*, 25 November which related to criminal proceedings. Evidence by experts as to the competence of a witness to give evidence should be heard by the judge alone and not in the presence of a jury – *R v Deakin* (1994) *The Times*, 3 May. In civil proceedings it would be for the judge to decide whether he accepted the evidence but it would appear that he can hear expert evidence in support.

[46] In civil proceedings the Pre Trial Checklist which is submitted about 8 weeks before the final hearing enquires about this, but this is not used for 'small claims'.

[47] See the Civil Procedure Rules 1998 Part 34. The evidence is known as a 'deposition'.

[48] Rule 2.7 of the Civil Procedure Rules 1998 provides that the court may sit anywhere (eg the lounge of a residential care or nursing home). This procedure was adopted by Butler-Sloss P in *Re B (Consent to treatment: Capacity)* [2002] EWHC 429 FD when she adjourned the court to the claimant's hospital bedside.

Failure to comply could lead to an expensive lesson but, whilst a few test cases achieved a high profile, discrimination remained rife in society without effective sanction.

1.39   Article 14 of the European Convention on Human Rights, now part of UK law,[49] is particularly relevant because it provides:

> 'Prohibition of discrimination: the enjoyment of the rights and freedoms set forth in this Convention shall be secured without discrimination on any ground such as sex, race, colour, language, religion, political or other opinion, national or social origin, association with a national minority, property, birth or other status.'

This provision is not, however, freestanding and has to be joined to other Articles.

History of anti-discrimination legislation

Sex discrimination

1.40   The Sex Discrimination Act 1975 made it unlawful to discriminate against men or women on the grounds of gender or marital status and established the *Equal Opportunities Commission*. A person discriminated against a woman under the Act if:[50]

(a)   on the ground of her sex he treated her less favourably than he treated or would treat a man; or

(b)   he applied to her a requirement or condition which applied or would apply equally to a man but it was such that a considerably smaller proportion of women would be able to comply with it, it could not be justified irrespective of the sex of the person and it was detrimental because she could not comply with it.

The first of these dealt with direct discrimination and the second tackled indirect discrimination, whereas justification applied only to the latter. The Act applied also to the treatment of men with such modifications as were requisite and discrimination against married persons in the employment field was defined in a similar way. Areas of discrimination dealt with included employment, education and the provision of goods, facilities and services.

Race discrimination

1.41   This was closely followed by the Race Relations Act 1976 which made it unlawful to discriminate on grounds of colour, race, nationality, ethnic or national origin and established the *Commission for Racial Equality*. The Act was modelled on the 1975 Act but areas of discrimination extended to the disposal and management of premises. Once again separate clauses dealt with direct and indirect discrimination and justification applied only to the latter. In response to the *Stephen Lawrence Inquiry Report* the Race Relations (Amendment) Act 2000 promoted race equality by imposing specific duties on public authorities. It was hoped that this would encourage good practice in the private sector.

---

[49]   Under the Human Rights Act 1998.
[50]   Sex Discrimination Act 1975, s 1.

Disability discrimination

1.42   It took a further two decades to achieve legislation to end the discrimination encountered by many disabled people, but the approach in the Disability Discrimination Act 1995 differed from that for race and sex in so far as the concept of indirect discrimination was not included and direct discrimination could be legally justified. Regrettably the *medical* model of disability was adopted which defines disability by reference to the individual's inability to perform certain physical or mental functions, rather than the *social* model which focuses on the barriers constructed in society. 'Disability' was defined in the following manner:

> '... a person has a disability for the purposes of this Act if he has a physical or mental impairment which has a substantial and long-term adverse effect on his ability to carry out normal day-to-day activities.'[51]

Physical impairment was not defined but it included sensory impairment. An impairment was further defined as something affecting:

> 'the ability of the person concerned to carry out normal day-to-day activities if it affects one of the following:
>
> mobility;
>
> manual dexterity;
>
> physical co-ordination;
>
> continence;
>
> ability to lift, carry or otherwise move everyday objects;
>
> speech, hearing or eyesight;
>
> memory or ability to concentrate, learn or understand; or
>
> perception of the risk of physical danger.'

The impairment had to have an adverse effect on at least one normal day-to-day activity, the emphasis being on what the person could not do, or could only do with difficulty rather than on what the person could do. The adverse effect might be direct, for example, where the impairment resulted in an inability to walk; or indirect, for example where walking was difficult because of fatigue or pain or where medical advice discouraged walking. A purposive approach was suggested with a series of questions:

- does the person have an impairment which is either mental or physical?
- does that impairment affect the person's ability to carry out normal day-to-day activities in one of the respects set out in Schedule 1 of the DDA, and does it have an adverse effect?
- is the adverse effect substantial?
- is the adverse condition long term?

---

[51]   Disability Discrimination Act 1995, s 1.

This definition was not dependent upon being 'registered disabled' with the local authority or in receipt of disability benefits under the social security system. Although in the majority of cases it was clear who fell within this definition, the Employment Appeal Tribunal observed that:

> '... a relatively small proportion of the disabled community are what one might describe as visually disabled, that is people in wheelchairs or carrying white sticks or other aids. It is important, therefore, that when ... approaching the question as to whether someone suffers from a disability, [you] should not have in [your] minds a stereotypical image of a person in a wheelchair or moving around with considerable difficulty.'

1.43 The Act was supplemented by Regulations and *Codes of Practice* providing detailed information that had to be taken into account when interpreting the statutory material. This legislation made it unlawful to discriminate against people with disabilities[52] and provided new rights in the areas of employment, the provision of goods, services and facilities, and the buying or renting of land or property. It also placed a duty on service providers and employers to take reasonable steps to change any practice, policy or procedure which made it impossible or unreasonably difficult for disabled persons to make use of a service which they provided to other members of the public. From December 2006 further provisions relating to public transport were brought into force and public bodies assumed a duty to promote equality of opportunity.[53]

1.44 Discrimination included 'less favourable treatment' and the proper *comparator* was for many years thought to be a person who was not disabled (or did not have the particular disability) and thus to whom that reason for the treatment did not apply.[54] So for exclusion of a blind person with a guide dog, the comparators would be 'others' without dogs rather than persons who were not blind. The House of Lords then decided that on a proper construction of the statute the comparator was a person without a disability and this significantly weakened the protection given to disabled people.[55]

1.45 The 1995 Act set up the *National Disability Council* to advise the Government on discrimination against disabled people and in April 2000 this was superseded by the *Disability Rights Commission* (DRC). Although the Commission supported cases, it had no right of audience before a court or tribunal in a case to which it was not a party and only in exceptional circumstances were representations allowed from the Commission direct.

1.46 This was a complex piece of legislation. Most cases related to employment under Part II of the 1995 Act and these came before Employment Tribunals with the law being interpreted through appeals.[56] Claims brought in the civil courts under the 'goods, facilities and services' provisions of Part III of the Act were generally dealt with as small claims because of the level of damages, typically under £2,000 although the court could make a declaration that there had been discrimination. The DRC supported some of these cases so, even though costs may not be recovered, there was specialist legal

---

52 There was also a criminal offence of 'knowingly or recklessly making a statement which is false or misleading in a material respect' as to the lawfulness of some action – s 57.
53 Disability Discrimination Act 2005.
54 *Clark v TDG Ltd (t/a Novacold)* [1999] 2 All ER 977.
55 *London Borough of Lewisham v Malcolm* [2008] UKHL 43. The Equality Act 2010 (see below) has overcome this obstacle.
56 Employment rights are considered in Ch 3 at **3.67** et seq.

representation. Considerable publicity might be sought (and obtained) and this gradually had the desired effect on businesses which realised the implications of persisting in discrimination against disabled persons.

Age discrimination

1.47 Until October 2010 there was no general law that prohibited discrimination on the grounds of age.[57] Most attempts to introduce legislation related to employment but the Government ultimately became obliged to tackle this (although with an exemption for the normal retirement age) in compliance with a European Directive.[58]

1.48 Adopting different qualifying ages for males and females may amount to sex discrimination. Thus where travel permits were issued to men at 65 but to women at 60 this was found to be in breach of the European Convention on Human Rights.[59] But selecting an individual for compulsory retirement because he was over the minimum retirement age was held not to be in breach of his contract of employment, even though this included an equal opportunities policy prohibiting discrimination on grounds of age.[60]

Other legislation

1.49 Further Regulations brought in as a result of European Directives addressed discrimination in employment on grounds of religion or belief and also sexual orientation.[61]

1.50 The Equality Act 2006 established a new *Equality and Human Rights Commission* (EHRC) from October 2007 which merged the three existing commissions.[62] The new Commission tackles prejudice based on race, gender and sexual orientation and disability as well as human rights, and has wide powers to enforce legislation. The Act also made provision about discrimination on grounds of religion or belief.

Equality Act 2010

Preliminary

1.51 In February 2005, the Government set up the *Discrimination Law Review* to address long-term concerns about inconsistencies in the current discrimination law framework, and this was followed by consultation resulting in legislation. The purpose of the Equality Act 2010 is to harmonise discrimination law and strengthen the law to support progress on equality. It brings together and re-states all the existing anti-discrimination legislation and a number of other related provisions and most provisions were brought into effect from October 2010. It also extends the categories by identifying the following 'protected characteristics':

---

[57] Employment Equality (Age) Regulations 2006 made discrimination in employment on grounds of age unlawful.

[58] Framework (Equal Treatment) Directive 2000/78/EC came into force in December 2006. Employment issues are dealt with in Ch 3.

[59] *Matthews v UK* ECHR (Application No 40302/98) 15 July 2002.

[60] *Taylor v Secretary of State for Scotland* [2000] IRLR 502.

[61] Employment Equality (Religion or Belief) Regulations 2003; Employment Equality (Sexual Orientation) Regulations 2003.

[62] The website is: www.equalityhumanrights.com.

- age (section 5)
- disability (sections 6 and 15, and Schedule 1)
- gender reassignment (sections 7 and 16)
- marriage and civil partnership (section 8)
- race (section 9)
- religion or belief (section 10)
- sex (ie gender) (section 11)
- sexual orientation (section 12)

1.52   The definitions are similar to those that applied before, but the application of disability discrimination is brought into line with the other categories. The Act also strengthens the law in a number of areas by:

- placing a new duty on certain public bodies to consider socio-economic disadvantage when making strategic decisions about how to exercise their functions;
- extending the circumstances in which a person is protected against discrimination, harassment or victimisation because of a protected characteristic;
- making it unlawful to discriminate against, harass or victimise a person when (a) providing a service (which includes the provision of goods or facilities), (b) exercising a public function or (c) disposing of (for example, by selling or letting) or managing premises;
- making it unlawful for associations (for example, private clubs) to discriminate against, harass or victimise members, associates or guests;
- requiring taxis, other private hire vehicles, public service vehicles (such as buses) and rail vehicles to be accessible to disabled people and to allow them to travel in reasonable comfort;
- establishing a general duty on public authorities to have due regard, when carrying out their functions, to the need: to eliminate unlawful discrimination, harassment or victimisation; to advance equality of opportunity; and to foster good relations.

1.53   The Act creates a duty on listed public bodies when carrying out their functions and on other persons when carrying out public functions to have due regard to the need to:

- eliminate conduct which the Act prohibits;
- advance equality of opportunity between persons who share a relevant protected characteristic and those who do not; and
- foster good relations between people who share a relevant protected characteristic and people who do not.

Enforcement continues to be through the county courts (in relation to services and public functions) and employment tribunals (in relation to work and related areas, and equal pay).

Prohibited conduct

1.54   Several forms of conduct are now defined for the purpose of prohibition.

Direct discrimination

1.55 This occurs where the reason for a person being treated less favourably than another is a protected characteristic.[63] This definition is broad enough to cover cases where the treatment is because of the victim's association with someone who has that characteristic (for example, is disabled). For age, different treatment that is justified as a proportionate means of meeting a legitimate aim is not direct discrimination. In relation to disability it is not discrimination to treat a disabled person more favourably than a person who is not disabled.

Discrimination arising from disability

1.56 It is discrimination to treat a disabled person unfavourably not because of the person's disability itself but because of something arising from, or in consequence of, his or her disability.[64] The perpetrator must know, or reasonably be expected to know, of the disability, and it is possible to justify such treatment if it can be shown to be a proportionate means of achieving a legitimate aim.[65]

Indirect discrimination

1.57 This would occur when a policy which applies in the same way for everybody has an effect which particularly disadvantages people with a protected characteristic.[66] Where a particular group is disadvantaged in this way, a person in that group is indirectly discriminated against if he or she is put at that disadvantage, unless the person applying the policy can justify it. Indirect discrimination can also occur when a policy would put a person at a disadvantage if it were applied and thus acts as a deterrent.[67] The treatment of the claimant must be compared with that of an actual or a hypothetical person – the comparator – who does not share the same protected characteristic as the claimant but who is (or is assumed to be) in not materially different circumstances from the claimant.

Duty to make adjustments

1.58 Section 20 defines what is meant by the duty to make reasonable adjustments to the 'provision, criterion or practice' whereby things are done. The duty comprises three requirements which apply where a disabled person is placed at a substantial disadvantage in comparison to non-disabled people:

- the first covers changing the way things are done (such as changing a practice);
- the second covers making changes to the built environment (such as providing access to a building); and
- the third covers providing auxiliary aids and services (such as providing special computer software or providing a different service).

---

[63] Equality Act 2010, s 13. Thus excluding old people would be discrimination.
[64] Equality Act 2010, s 15. This would cover the need to have a guide dog.
[65] This is a new provision designed to overcome the problem caused by *London Borough of Lewisham v Malcolm* [2008] UKHL 43 explained above.
[66] Equality Act 2010, s 19. This would cover the need to have a guide dog.
[67] The extension of indirect discrimination to disability is new, coming after consultation following *London Borough of Lewisham v Malcolm* [2008] UKHL 43.

For the second requirement, taking steps to avoid the disadvantage would include removing or altering the physical feature where it would be reasonable to do so. For the first and third a reasonable step might include providing information in an accessible format. Except where the Act states otherwise, it would never be reasonable for a person bound by the duty to pass on the costs of complying with it to an individual disabled person.

Failure to comply with a duty

1.59   A failure to comply with any one of the reasonable adjustment requirements amounts to discrimination against a disabled person to whom the duty is owed.[68]

Harassment

1.60   There are three types of harassment, but the one which applies to disability and age involves unwanted conduct which is related to the characteristic and has the purpose or effect of creating an intimidating, hostile, degrading humiliating or offensive environment for the complainant or violating the complainant's dignity.[69] There may be a need to balance the right of freedom of expression (as set out in Article 10 of the European Convention on Human Rights) against the right not to be offended in deciding whether a person has been harassed.

Victimisation

1.61   Victimisation takes place where one person treats another badly because he or she in good faith has done a 'protected act' or is suspected of having done so or intending to do so.[70] This might include taking or supporting any action taken in relation to any alleged breach of the Act. Only an individual can bring a claim for victimisation and a person is not protected from victimisation where he or she maliciously makes or supports an untrue complaint.

Premises

1.62   There is protection from discrimination in the disposal and management of premises across all the protected characteristics with the exception of age and marriage and civil partnership, although other provisions should be relied on where they apply.[71] It is unlawful for a person who has the authority to dispose of premises (for example, by selling, letting or subletting a property) to discriminate against or victimise someone else in a number of ways including by offering the premises to them on less favourable terms, not letting or selling the premises to them or treating them less favourably. It is unlawful for a person who manages premises to discriminate against or victimise someone who occupies the property in the way he or she allows the person to use a benefit or facility associated with the property, by evicting the person or by otherwise treating the person unfavourably.

---

[68]   Equality Act 2010, s 21.
[69]   Equality Act 2010, s 26.
[70]   Equality Act 2010, s 27. This is not really a form of discrimination.
[71]   Equality Act 2010, ss 32–35.

Associations

1.63 It is unlawful for an association to discriminate against, harass or victimise an existing or potential member, or an associate. This means that an association cannot refuse membership to a potential member or grant it on less favourable terms because of a protected characteristic. It does not, however, prevent associations restricting their membership to people who share a protected characteristic.[72] It is also unlawful to discriminate against, harass or victimise existing or potential guests. In particular, an association cannot refuse to invite a person as a guest because of a particular characteristic or invite that person on certain conditions which the association would not apply to other would-be guests. There is also a duty to make reasonable adjustments for disabled members and guests.

Implications of conduct

1.64 The protection in previous legislation from discrimination, harassment and victimisation in the provision of services and the exercise of public functions was not uniform for the different protected characteristics. For example, there was no protection for discrimination because of age either in the provision of services or in the exercise of public functions. Section 29 extends protection so that it is generally uniform across all the protected characteristics. It is unlawful to discriminate against or harass a person because of a protected characteristic, or victimise someone when providing services (which includes goods and facilities). The person is protected both when requesting a service and during the course of being provided with a service.

1.65 It is also unlawful to discriminate against, harass or victimise a person when exercising a public function which does not involve the provision of a service. Examples of such public functions include law enforcement and revenue raising and collection. Public functions which involve the provision of a service, for example, medical treatment on the NHS, are covered by the provisions dealing with services. This section also imposes the section 20 duty to make reasonable adjustments in relation to providing services and exercising public functions. A person is considered to have discriminated against a disabled person if he or she fails to comply with this duty.

HUMAN RIGHTS

Introduction

1.66 The British citizen has been free to do as he likes unless forbidden by the common law or statute. But Parliament is supreme and, unlike the United States of America and many Commonwealth countries which have a written constitution, there was no concept of 'fundamental rights' of the individual. Although our public authorities can encroach upon the rights and freedoms of the individual they may only do what they are authorised to do by the law. The role of judges is restricted to interpreting the law, which is to be found in legislation and the common law.[73]

1.67 The absence of a constitution or Bill of Rights does not mean that fundamental human rights have been denied to our citizens and it has often been argued that

---

[72] Equality Act 2010, ss 100–103.
[73] Although this is often referred to as 'judge made law' the courts merely deduce the law from previous decisions although new principles do emerge.

providing effective remedies is more important than declaring inalienable rights. The democratic nature and accountability of our government coupled with a free press has created a culture of liberty which, it was argued, was more significant than formal legal rights. But this did not always enable individual human rights to be recognised and there was no straightforward procedure for arguing that such rights had been breached. In 1948 the United Nations adopted the *Universal Declaration of Human Rights* and by 1950 three other countries with legal systems based upon the common law[74] gave constitutional protection to human rights.

The European Convention

1.68   The *European Convention on Human Rights*[75] is a treaty of the Council of Europe,[76] an international organisation established after World War II to promote democracy, the protection of human rights and the rule of law throughout Europe. It was largely drafted by British lawyers, signed in 1950 and ratified by the UK in 1951 which means that under international law the UK became obliged to abide by its terms. The right of individual petition was only afforded in 1966 but this did not mean that Convention rights could be relied upon in proceedings in our courts. The treaty has subsequently been amended by *Protocols* which are either mandatory or optional, the latter only binding states that choose to ratify them.

1.69   The Convention commences with the requirement for contracting states to 'secure to everyone within their jurisdiction the rights and freedoms' defined within it, and is then divided into three Sections:

(1)   Articles 2 to 18 define the rights and freedoms;

(2)   Articles 19 to 51 establish the *European Court of Human Rights* and provide for its operation; and

(3)   Articles 52 to 59 contain provisions such as territorial application, reservations and ratification.

It was initially supervised by the *European Commission on Human Rights* with a *Committee of Ministers* and a part-time *European Court of Human Rights* but since 1998, pursuant to the Eleventh Protocol, there has been a full-time, permanent court located at Strasbourg, France which fulfils the judicial role. Reports are available of the decisions of that Court[77] and information is available on the Internet.

1.70   In 1966 only two cases had been decided by the European Court but by 1988 there had been some 50 judgments in UK cases finding breaches of Convention rights. This was largely due to the publicity afforded to such decisions and the willingness of our lawyers to pursue Convention rights. The principles influenced decisions of British courts although they were not binding on them, but due to the supremacy of Parliament and the system of precedent our judges were denied the power to safeguard Convention rights. Repeated assurances that our law was generally in accord with Convention rights and that adequate remedies existed to protect the individual against the state were not supported by the number of individual petitions to the European Commission, many

---

74   United States, India and Ireland.

75   Full title: *Convention for the Protection of Human Rights and Fundamental Freedoms*.

76   This is a separate organisation from the *European Union* and now comprises more than 47 member states. For further information see http://hub.coe.int.

77   *European Human Rights Reports* (EHRR); *European Human Rights Law Review* (EHRLR).

concerning fundamental breaches and some challenging legislation. The result was a concerted campaign to introduce these rights into our law resulting in the Human Rights Act 1998 which came into force on 2 October 2000.

Equality and Human Rights Commission (EHRC)

1.71 The Equality Act 2006 established this new commission from October 2007 which tackles human rights as well as discrimination based on race, gender and sexual orientation and disability, and has wide powers to enforce legislation.[78]

Human Rights Act 1998

1.72 The long title to this Act states that it is 'to give further effect to' the Convention rights and it was said to be 'bringing rights home' on the basis that individuals within the UK would be enabled to rely on their rights in their home courts,[79] although the right to bring a case in Strasbourg was not prevented. The Act is a compromise, representing an attempt to incorporate the Convention into our law whilst still recognising the traditions of the common law and the sovereignty of Parliament. Every new Bill presented to Parliament must, when introduced, be supported by a *statement of compatibility* by the Minister responsible.[80]

Statutory interpretation

1.73 The courts must interpret our primary and secondary legislation 'so far as it is possible to do so' in a way which is not incompatible with the Convention whilst not having power to overrule any such legislation.[81] Where this cannot be done a *declaration of incompatibility* may be made[82] and it then becomes a matter for Parliament (which has a fast-track procedure for remedying the incompatibility[83]), although in the meanwhile the legislation must still be applied.[84] This is a significant change which will affect the doctrine of precedent because where human rights are involved courts may no longer be bound by decisions of higher courts reached before the commencement of the 1998 Act.

1.74 It has been stated that an Act must receive a 'generous and purposive' interpretation to ensure that Convention rights are effective rather than illusory. Techniques may include 'reading down' (choosing between two possible interpretations and opting for the narrower) and 'reading in' (inserting words to make the statute compatible). Strasbourg jurisprudence must be 'taken into account' by our courts and tribunals,[85] which means that decisions of the European Court now become part of our case-law. The Convention itself must be interpreted in the same way as any other treaty which means:

---

[78]   The website is: www.equalityhumanrights.com.
[79]   See the White Paper *Bringing Rights Home* (Cm 3782, 1997).
[80]   Human Rights Act 1998, s 19.
[81]   Human Rights Act 1998, s 3.
[82]   Human Rights Act 1998, s 4. This power is restricted to the High Court, Court of Appeal and House of Lords and the Crown is entitled to make representations – s 5.
[83]   Human Rights Act 1998, s 10. This procedure will also be appropriate when a finding of the European Court in proceedings against the UK renders a provision incompatible.
[84]   If subordinate legislation (eg a statutory instrument) is incompatible with Convention rights, and the incompatibility is not required by primary legislation, either the courts will find ways of interpreting it so as to be compatible or will set it aside.
[85]   Human Rights Act 1998, s 2(1).

'... in good faith and in accordance with the ordinary meaning to be given to the terms of the treaty in their context and in the light of its objects and purpose.'

The Convention rights

1.75 Only certain of the rights contained in the Convention have been designated as 'Convention rights' for the purpose of the 1998 Act,[86] but those omitted must be taken into account. The Convention rights of particular relevance to older people are:

Article 2:	the right to life
Article 5:	the right to liberty and security
Article 6:	the right to a fair trial
Article 7:	no punishment without law
Article 8:	the right to respect for private and family life
Article 9:	freedom of thought, conscience and religion
Article 10:	freedom of expression
Article 11:	freedom of assembly and association
Article 12:	the right to marry
Article 14:	prohibition of discrimination
1st Protocol, Article 2:	protection of property

On reading these rights it will be seen that some of them are 'absolute' in the sense that they do not include any qualification or allow for any derogation by a ratifying country[87] and others are qualified by some limitation or restriction.[88] Any such limitation must be in accordance with the law, directed to a 'particular purpose' and 'necessary in a democratic society'.[89]

'Derogations' and 'reservations'

1.76 Convention rights have effect subject to any 'derogations' or 'reservations'.[90] A derogation is an exceptional limitation imposed by the ratifying country on a particular right in specified circumstances. A reservation relates to some existing law of the country concerned which is not to be affected.[91] Both will generally be limited in time.[92]

The new duties on public authorities

1.77 The Act works by imposing a new statutory duty on 'public authorities' rather than giving individuals personal rights. It is now 'unlawful for a public authority to act in a way which is incompatible with a Convention right' and even a failure to act would be construed as non-compliance.[93] The term 'public authorities' is not defined in the Act but a function-based test is to be applied. Courts and tribunals are expressly included, as

---

[86]   Human Rights Act 1998, s 1. The text of these Articles is set out in Schedule 1 to the Act.
[87]   Eg Article 3: the right to protection from torture.
[88]   Eg Article 5: the right to liberty.
[89]   For further consideration see under 'proportionality' at **1.74**.
[90]   Human Rights Act 1998, s 1(2). See ss 14 and 15.
[91]   For those now existing see Sch 3.
[92]   Human Rights Act 1998, ss 16 and 17.
[93]   Human Rights Act 1998, s 6.

is 'any person certain of whose functions are functions of a public nature'. The scope for interpretation is thus wide. There are three potential categories and only the first two may be affected by the new duty:

(1)   bodies which are clearly public authorities as they carry out public functions (eg the police, local authorities);

(2)   'hybrid' bodies which carry out both public and private functions; and

(3)   bodies with no public functions.

The use of Convention rights

1.78   The fact that courts and tribunals must not act in a way which is incompatible with a Convention right means that these rights must be applied whenever they arise during the course of proceedings. So the human rights of individuals will be enforced by the courts but this does not impair more generous legal rights already enjoyed under our law.[94] In addition, an individual[95] who claims that a public authority has acted in an incompatible way may bring proceedings against that authority either directly or within the context of other proceedings.[96] This person must be a 'victim', which in this context means 'directly affected', so public interest groups will seldom have status to bring proceedings but they may assist victims or be allowed to intervene in existing proceedings.[97] The court will be restricted to considering the particular case before it and cannot consider human rights in the abstract.

1.79   Where the public body determining the civil rights or obligations is not a court or tribunal[98] a two-limbed test is applied: either that body must comply with the right to a fair hearing under Article 6 or there must be a right of appeal or review from that body to a court or tribunal which fully complies. The previous right to apply for judicial review is not sufficient because the Administrative Court cannot make findings of fact.[99]

1.80   The limitation period for bringing a claim against a public authority is one year but there can be an extension when it would be 'equitable having regard to all the circumstances'.[100] This period will be of no relevance when human rights arise in other proceedings and all existing rights under the common law are preserved.[101]

Positive obligations

1.81   The European Court has recognised that the obligations of states under the Convention are not limited to refraining from interfering with individual human rights. There is a positive obligation to ensure that one person's rights are protected from violation by another person and this has led to five duties being imposed on states in relation to Convention rights:[102]

---

[94]   Human Rights Act 1998, s 11.

[95]   This includes a non-government organisation, group of individuals or corporate body.

[96]   Human Rights Act 1998, s 7.

[97]   Representative actions can be brought where a victim lacks legal capacity and if the victim dies during the proceedings a relative with a legitimate interest in the outcome can continue the claim.

[98]   Eg a local housing authority, a health authority, social services and probably the Office of the Public Guardian.

[99]   *W v United Kingdom* (1987) 10 EHRR 29 at para 82.

[100]   Human Rights Act 1998, s 7(5).

[101]   Human Rights Act 1998, s 11.

[102]   Thus a failure by the police to prevent a campaign of harassment was a breach of the individuals' Convention rights – *Osman v UK* [1999] EHRLR 228.

(1)   to have a legal framework providing effective protection;

(2)   to prevent breaches;

(3)   to provide information and advice;

(4)   to respond to breaches; and

(5)   to provide resources to individuals to prevent breaches.

Remedies

1.82   When a Convention right is found to have been breached (or is about to be breached), the court or tribunal may grant such relief or remedy, or make such order, within its powers as it considers 'just and appropriate'.[103] The emphasis here is upon the court acting within such powers as it already has, because the Act does not give additional powers or create any criminal offences.[104] Damages may be awarded by a court or tribunal having that jurisdiction where this is necessary to 'afford just satisfaction' under Article 41 and in that event the court must take into account the principles applied by the European Court (to the extent that any such principles have emerged[105]). Costs are dealt with under the domestic court's jurisdiction.

1.83   The Act does not create new ways in which a judicial act may be challenged and decisions of the courts and tribunals may only be challenged through the normal routes of an appeal or judicial review.[106] There can be no claim for damages in respect of a judicial act done in good faith except in the case of a breach of liberty.

Discrimination

1.84   Although there is an obligation under Article 14 to ensure that the substantive rights in the Convention are secured without discrimination, there is no free-standing prohibition on discrimination. A breach of another Convention right does not need to be established, but the circumstances must fall within the ambit of a convention provision. Unlike our equal treatment legislation,[107] the grounds on which discrimination is prohibited are not limited to race, sex and disability and age discrimination in the application of a Convention right would be unlawful unless justified and otherwise compliant with the concepts that apply. Those stated in the article are merely examples and the phrase 'or other status' has been broadly interpreted so as to include marital status and sexual orientation.

New concepts

1.85   It follows from the above that each branch of government (legislature, executive and judicial) is responsible for giving effect to Convention rights when exercising public powers. These rights become 'the law's compass' where human rights are involved.[108] However, various concepts apply in the interpretation and application of Convention rights which will not be familiar to lawyers brought up on the common law and statute law. They are summarised under the following headings.

---

[103]   Human Rights Act 1998, s 8(1).
[104]   Human Rights Act 1998, s 7(8).
[105]   That Court has been conservative in awards of damages and has not awarded aggravated or exemplary damages although a domestic court will be entitled to do so.
[106]   Human Rights Act 1998, s 8.
[107]   For anti-discrimination law see **1.39** et seq.
[108]   Lester and Pannick, *Human Rights Law and Practice* (Butterworths, 2009).

'Horizontal' and 'vertical' effect

1.86 Not only can proceedings be brought against a public authority in relation to Convention rights (this is the 'vertical' effect), but as the courts are public authorities they must apply Convention rights when adjudicating on proceedings between private individuals (the 'horizontal' effect). So litigants can argue their human rights in the courts and these must be respected.

Margin of appreciation

1.87 To some extent the European Court adopts a hands-off approach to the way that individual countries apply Convention rights, although this 'margin of appreciation' has no application to national courts. This reflects the fact that those courts are in a better position to assess the needs and standards of their own society and the national authorities should be deferred to (especially in moral matters and social policy) as long as the whole process is fair and the outcome is true to the Convention.

Autonomous approach

1.88 The Convention is concerned with the substantive rights of the individual rather than their formal classification, so it is the realities rather than the appearance that matters. Thus the division in our legal system between criminal and civil matters will be ignored and sanctions under the civil law which involve loss of liberty will be tested according to criminal standards.[109]

Proportionality

1.89 Where a state interferes with a Convention right, the means (the limitation) must be balanced against the end (the permitted purpose) and shown to be necessary. There must be a reasonable relationship between the goal pursued and the means employed. This follows from the fact that any limitation on a Convention right must be in accordance with law and 'necessary in a democratic society'[110] and has become the principle of 'proportionality'. The European Court applies this test not in the abstract but in relation to the facts of each case. The question asked is: was there a pressing social need to limit this person's human rights in this situation and was a less restrictive alternative available? Other considerations will be whether there has been procedural fairness in the decision-making process and safeguards exist against abuse. Any restriction should not destroy the essence of the Convention right and it is for the state to justify the restriction.

The principle of 'legality'

1.90 This principle is derived from the use by the Convention of the phrases 'in accordance with the law' and 'prescribed by law' and the use of the word 'lawful'. It has been stated to mean:[111]

(1) the legal basis for any restriction on Convention rights must be identified and established by the domestic law;

---

[109] *Benham v UK* (1996) 22 EHRR 293 – imprisonment for failure to pay poll tax was characterised as criminal proceedings.

[110] A 'democratic society' means a society which is pluralistic and tolerant. The interests of minorities and individuals must be carefully considered.

[111] *European Human Rights Law*, Keir Starmer, Legal Action Group (1999) at para 4.29.

(2)   that law must be accessible;[112] and

(3)   the law must be clear to those affected by it so that they can understand it and avoid breaking it.[113]

A *living instrument*

1.91   The Convention is a living instrument so, unlike the common law where previous decisions of higher courts create precedents, it must be interpreted in accordance with present day conditions. This means that what was decided yesterday may be decided differently tomorrow, although this may be a whole generation later. The difficulty lies in determining what the contemporary standards are which merit protection. However, the Convention is intended to guarantee rights that are practical and effective rather than theoretical and illusory.[114]

Impact *of human rights*

1.92   In many ways the Human Rights Act 1998 has been a 'damp squib' and the 'flood' of human rights cases feared by some has not materialised. But it has already had, and will continue to have, a significant influence in areas where vulnerable elderly people have suffered prejudice and is of assistance in recognising and enforcing the rights of people with disabilities. These situations are mentioned as appropriate throughout this book. The real success of the Act will be measured not in individual cases but in the change of culture that it provokes.

COMPETENCE AND DECISION-MAKING

Preliminary

1.93   Everything we do is based upon a decision to take that specific step. The law assumes that an individual has the capacity to make, and the ability to communicate, decisions. In some cases there is concern that an elderly person is purporting to make decisions without being aware of the implications. In other cases although the individual can make decisions, others are unwilling to recognise them, either because of communication difficulties or behavioural characteristics which create an impression of lack of competence. It may therefore be necessary to decide whether an elderly person is still legally competent to make a particular decision and, if not, whether special procedures (if they exist) should be invoked for such decision to be taken by others.

1.94   This has been considered by the Law Commission[115] which identified the following guiding principles for the application and development of the law:

(1)   all people are presumed to be competent and to have the same rights and status, except as specifically provided or determined;

(2)   any modification or intervention should be the minimum necessary in that case; and

---

[112] It is not sufficient for the law to be published if it is interpreted according to unpublished criteria – this has affected the way that social security benefits are interpreted.

[113] Any discretion allowed by the law does not offend the rule as long as the limits of that discretion are clear.

[114] *Artico v Italy (A/37)* (1980) 3 EHRR 1.

[115] *Mental Incapacity* – No 231 – dated March 1995.

(3)   people should be enabled and encouraged to exercise and develop their own
        capacity and to participate in decisions to the maximum extent possible.

The recommendations of the Law Commission in regard to decision-making and mental
incapacity were not law, but they influenced the general approach and tended to be
followed by the courts in the interpretation of the existing law when there was no
binding authority on a particular point.[116] They cannot change any established legal
tests of capacity[117] although they may assist those tests to be applied in practice. This is
an area where there was previously a general lack of understanding amongst lawyers.

1.95   When talking about legal competence we are considering the ability of an
individual to decide or choose to do something and then make this clear to others, even
though assistance may be needed to carry the decision or choice into effect. It follows
that physical disability by itself should not affect competence. Lack of competence may
arise through mental incapacity, an inability to communicate or a combination of the
two. It is inevitable that the practitioner will encounter this from time to time when
dealing with older people. There may be doubts over the capacity of a client to execute
a will, purchase or sell a property or handle financial affairs generally. The family may
question the capacity of a parent to re-marry or even drive a car, or a doctor may be
concerned about the capacity of a patient to decide about medical treatment. We
therefore consider when the law treats an individual as incompetent and what can be
done to avoid or cope with the consequences.

Mental incapacity

Preliminary[118]

1.96   The term 'mental incapacity' is used loosely in society and although it conveys a
fairly consistent impression to most people, it does not have a precise meaning. It would
be convenient if there were a simple definition, so that we could readily identify those
members of society to whom different rules should apply or who are eligible for special
treatment, but this is not and could never be the case. No-one is incapable in all things
and it is wrong to attach discriminatory labels to people although some people may have
certain of their legal powers taken away from them.

1.97   Doubts about capacity may arise for several reasons but these should not be
confused with tests of capacity. Thus the status of the individual such as being elderly
and living in a nursing home, or the outcome of a decision such as a widow declaring
that she is going to live with her husband (long since deceased) or an elderly spinster
proposing to sell her house to a stranger for one-tenth of its value, may cause capacity to
be questioned. It may simply be the appearance, behaviour or conversation of the
individual that causes doubts. It is not unusual for outward appearances to create a false
impression of incapacity. Conversely, the absence of any of these indications does not
mean that the individual is capable. In all these situations a proper assessment should be
made according to appropriate criteria.

---

[116]   This process was encouraged by the rapid progress of the Law Commissioner responsible for the Report
        (Professor Brenda Hoggett) through the High Court and the Court of Appeal to her present status as Lady
        Hale of Richmond sitting on the Judicial Committee of the House of Lords and thence the Supreme Court.
[117]   Eg in regard to making a will or signing an enduring power of attorney.
[118]   Refer to Ch 2 for the jurisdiction now established under the Mental Capacity Act 2005.

Approach of professionals

1.98 One of the difficulties is that the various professionals who may be involved with the elderly individual all approach the question of capacity from a different standpoint. Their respective opinions may be perfectly valid according to their own criteria but should not be treated as interchangeable. In some instances these opinions may conflict simply because of the difference of approach. The lawyer who is considering legal capacity needs to be quite specific. Valuable evidence may be obtained from other professionals but they should not be relied upon to make the decision as to whether the individual lacks capacity.

Medical

1.99 The medical profession tends to be concerned with diagnosis and prognosis rather than the severity and implications of mental disability. Notwithstanding this restricted approach, lawyers continue to rely upon medical practitioners for opinions about mental capacity. The doctor may well be able to identify the cause of the disability and indicate its likely future consequences, but what is in issue for the lawyer is the effect on the individual at this moment in time. When expert evidence is needed the report of a consultant psychiatrist is to be preferred.

Social

1.100 Care workers classify people according to their degree of independence which involves consideration of levels of competence in performing skills such as eating, dressing, communication and social skills. These skills may be affected by mental or physical causes. An assessment based upon a medical diagnosis is of little use to the care worker other than to explain the reason for the present impairment and indicate whether improvement or deterioration is to be expected. Practicalities tend to dominate arrangements rather than considerations of legality, though a carer may become concerned as to the legal capacity of the individual cared for, the vulnerability of that person and the entitlement of others to take decisions on the person's behalf.

Legal

1.101 The lawyer wishes to establish whether the individual is capable of making a reasoned and informed decision (the test of *capacity*), although there may be the need to assess the degree of dependence, for example when considering what financial provision should be made. The medical diagnosis will be largely irrelevant except in so far as it points to a cause and the degree of capacity that may be anticipated and the carer's view may be helpful but will not be based on any particular legal test. Thus the lawyer may need to consult the doctor and carer (or social worker) but their views merely form part of the evidence when considering the question of legal capacity. Having gathered this evidence the lawyer is in the best position to form a considered view as to legal capacity or to refer the issue to the court for determination.

The legal approach

1.102 The Law Commission[119] identified three approaches to the question of legal capacity which have been adopted in different circumstances:

---

[119] Consultation Paper No 119: *Mentally Incapacitated Adults and Decision-Making: An Overview* (May 1991).

(1)   the *outcome* approach whereby capacity is determined by the content of the individual's decision. Thus if a decision is judged as foolish it may be deemed to be incompetently made;

(2)   a *status* test such as age, place of residence or diagnosis without any further consideration of the actual competence of the individual; and

(3)   a test based on *understanding* or *function* whereby the personal ability of the individual to make the particular decision is assessed.

Whilst the status test may still apply in certain situations[120] it is no longer favoured in regard to mental capacity and a test of understanding is generally appropriate.[121] Understanding is not the same as wisdom so the quality of the decision is irrelevant as long as the person understands what he is deciding. In addition it is inevitable that the individual must be able to communicate the decision.

1.103 Incapacity may be total or partial and it is important that this is recognised. Having identified a mental disability the individual may be treated, almost by definition, as being unable to make any decision or assert any legal rights. That would be the application of a status test and it is wrong to categorise or label the individual in this way. It is equally wrong to conclude that because an individual is incapable of making one decision he is also incapable of making another. No-one should be regarded as legally incapable in the total sense.

Legal tests

1.104 Although the general approach to capacity has been identified, there is no overall test for all decisions. The appropriate test of capacity (or rather incapacity) should be applied in each instance[122] and it is the personal ability of the individual to make the particular decision that is assessed. Thus a person who is incapable of handling his general financial affairs may nevertheless be capable of signing an enduring power of attorney or a will. Similarly, a person who is incapable of entering into one contract (eg a hire-purchase agreement) may be capable of entering into a different contract that is easier to comprehend (eg to purchase a particular item of clothing).

Specific definitions

1.105 Legal tests of capacity vary according to the circumstances but these usually relate to the matters which the individual is required to understand. In some situations specific tests have been developed by case-law or provided by statute, but otherwise general principles must be relied upon and these are based upon the individual's understanding rather than judgment.[123] Some statutes rely upon undefined phrases such as 'unsoundness of mind' which appear to beg the question, though this phrase is defined in the Trustee Act 1925 as 'incapable from infirmity of mind of managing his own affairs'. The terminology tends to reflect the period when the statute was enacted rather than the interpretation that should now be placed on the words chosen. The following tests of capacity are explained elsewhere:

---

[120] For example, in respect of a child whose legal capacity is limited.

[121] Thus a detained mental patient is not automatically deprived of the right to make decisions about general medical treatment or financial matters – see generally Ch 2.

[122] The Law Society/BMA publication *Assessment of Mental Capacity* (3rd ed. 2010) provides guidance as to the various legal tests of capacity and these are also identified in the following pages.

[123] Only the general principles are explained here and specific legal tests are described in later chapters as and when topics arise.

- to sign an enduring power of attorney – Chapter 11;
- to conduct civil proceedings in the courts – Chapter 3;
- to be convicted of a crime – Chapter 3;
- to enter into a marriage – Chapter 4;
- to consent to medical treatment – Chapter 8;
- to make a gift – Chapter 12; and
- testamentary capacity – Chapter 12.

Components

1.106 In a medical treatment context, the decision-making process has been analysed into three stages: first, *comprehending* and *retaining* treatment information; second, *believing* it; and third, *weighing* it in the balance to arrive at a choice.[124] This was subsequently reduced to the first and third stages in one of the clearest judicial definitions of lack of mental capacity:[125]

> 'A person lacks capacity if some impairment or disturbance of mental functioning renders the person unable to make a decision whether to consent to or refuse treatment. That inability to make a decision will occur when:
>
> (a)   the patient is unable to comprehend and retain the information which is material to the decision, especially as to the likely consequences of having or not having the treatment in question.
> (b)   the patient is unable to use the information and weigh it in the balance as part of the process of arriving at the decision. If ... a compulsive disorder or phobia from which the patient suffers stifles belief in the information presented to her, then the decision may not be a true one.'

In the context of conducting litigation it has been held by the Court of Appeal that the court should only take over the individual's function of decision making:[126]

> 'when it is shown on the balance of probabilities that such person does not have the capacity sufficiently to understand, absorb and retain information (including advice) relevant to the matters in question sufficiently to enable him or her to make decisions based upon such information.'

In the same case Lord Justice Chadwick emphasised that the understanding may be achieved with the assistance of such explanation as may be given and he identified three features:

(1)   the need for the person to have 'insight and understanding of the fact that he has a problem in respect of which he needs advice';
(2)   the need to be able to instruct an appropriate adviser 'with sufficient clarity to enable him to understand the problem and advise him appropriately'; and
(3)   the need 'to understand and make decisions based upon, or otherwise give effect to, such advice as she may receive'.

---

[124]   *Re C (Adult: Refusal of Medical Treatment)* [1994] 1 All ER 819, Thorpe J.
[125]   *Re MB (Caesarian Section)* [1997] 2 FLR 426, Butler-Sloss LJ.
[126]   *Masterman-Lister v Brutton & Co and Jewell & Home Counties Dairies* [2002] EWCA Civ 1889, [2002] All ER (D) 297 (Dec), CA, Kennedy LJ.

1.107 Whilst understanding information supplied might be the criteria for conducting litigation and medical treatment decisions, in other situations such as capacity to make a will this becomes retention of adequate knowledge of family and personal circumstances. Although some prompting may be acceptable, if the decision-maker were too dependent upon others for the supply of such information there would be potential for influence by the supply of selective or slanted information. Information, knowledge and comprehension must all be sufficient for the particular decision to be made.

1.108 The law is still developing and there are indications that, in the context of managing property and financial affairs, understanding is not the only criteria that should be included in the assessment of capacity. Qualities such as impulsiveness, recklessness and being easily manipulated may also need to be taken into account where these are the consequence of a mental disorder such as a brain injury. Being unstable and volatile may impair the decision-making process.

Requirement for mental disorder

1.109 Some qualifying reason for the incapacity is usually required when the decision-making powers of the individual are to be taken away to prevent a person who is merely eccentric from being deprived of autonomy simply because other people consider that irrational decisions are being made.[127] In the past the person needed to be incapable 'by reason of *mental disorder*' as defined in the Mental Health Act 1983:[128]

> 'mental illness, arrested or incomplete development of mind, psychopathic disorder and any other disorder or disability of mind.'

This definition makes no reference to the degree of impairment so merely provided a useful screening process.[129] However, the phrase was sometimes used inappropriately in situations where it was the extent of the mental impairment rather than the existence of mental disorder that was relevant. For example, it might be stated that 'a person who is mentally disordered may not ...'. That is an inappropriate application of a status test of capacity.

Assessment of capacity

General

1.110 Capacity should be assessed for each individual at the relevant time in respect of the particular transaction to be entered into or step to be taken. Assessment is not a medical or psychiatric diagnostic art and rests on a judgment of the type that an informed lay person may make using a relatively simple checklist. Various medical and psychometric tests have been devised[130] but whilst these may provide some evidence and assist in supporting conclusions they should not be confused for the actual tests of capacity that are prescribed by the law.

---

[127] As in the statutory jurisdiction of the old Court of Protection until October 2007 or the definition of a 'patient' under civil court rules – see Chs 2 and 3 respectively.

[128] Mental Health Act 1983, s 1(2). It is expressly provided that this shall not be 'by reason only of promiscuity or other immoral conduct, sexual deviancy or dependence on alcohol or drugs'.

[129] The Law Commission was concerned that the term 'mental disorder' has long been used and interpreted in other contexts, and proposed that a newly defined term should be adopted.

[130] Examples are the *Abbreviated Mental Test Score* (AMTS), the *Mini-Mental State Examination* (MMSE) and the *Wechsler Adult Intelligence Scale – Revised* (WAIS-R).

1.111 A judgment on decision-making capacity can deprive an individual of rights and liberties enjoyed by most adults and safeguarded by the Human Rights Act 1998. Alternatively, it could permit a person lacking capacity to do something whereby serious prejudice results, either putting that person at risk or causing harm to others. It is therefore important that anyone required to assess another person's capacity does so properly and is prepared to justify their assessment.

When is an assessment required

1.112 Where doubts are raised about a person's ability to make a decision the following questions should first be considered:

(1) Does the person have all the relevant information needed to make the decision? If there is a choice, has information been given on any alternatives?

(2) Could the information be explained or presented in a way that is easier for the person to understand?

(3) Can the decision be put off to a time when the person's understanding is better, or a location where they may feel more at ease?

(4) Can anyone else help or support the person to make choices or express a view, such as an advocate or someone to assist communication?

If all these steps have been taken without success in helping the person make a decision, an assessment of their capacity to make the decision in question should be made.

Who makes the assessment

1.113 In daily life assessments of capacity are made and relied upon by a variety of people, frequently by carers on an intuitive basis and these may be soundly based and perfectly valid. Such assessments may be influenced by their own perceptions or according to the personal interests of the persons applying them, yet may not have legal implications or may not be challenged. The more serious the decision, the more formal the assessment may need to be, but whoever assesses capacity must be prepared to justify their findings. Where consent to medical treatment is required, the doctor proposing the treatment must decide whether the patient has capacity to consent and should record the assessment process and findings in the person's medical notes. Where a legal transaction is involved, such as making a will or a power of attorney, the solicitor handling the transaction will need to assess, perhaps assisted by a doctor's opinion, whether the client has the required capacity to satisfy the relevant legal test. In case of dispute, or where there is reluctance to act on a decision made by the individual and an outcome is needed, capacity must be determined by the courts.

Timing

1.114 The assessment of capacity must not only be made on the basis of the appropriate test but also at the correct time. Thus if a will is to be signed, there must be capacity to take that step at the time of signing. It is not conclusive that the testator may have been capable the previous day or on the following day. Hence the attraction of having a doctor witness the document rather than merely providing a report the week beforehand. Even a person who is generally incapable may have a lucid interval, so an adverse medical report at another date is not always the end of the matter. Evidence of conduct at other times is admissible and the general pattern of life of the individual may be of great weight, although it is the state of mind at the time of the act that is material.

Fluctuating capacity

1.115 It is recognised that capacity, or rather lack of it, is not a static concept and a person's level of capacity may fluctuate over a period of time and from time to time. Hence the *lucid interval* of a person who previously and subsequently would be treated as lacking capacity. Acts done during such a period are generally treated as valid. The general public would talk of 'good days and bad days' and indeed for an elderly person there may be times of the day when the individual is at his or her best. An experienced legal practitioner will enquire about this and choose the best time to call on the client so as to achieve effective instructions, but a further visit may then be made on a later date to verify those instructions. It is important not to rush such visits because this may cause anxiety on the part of the client which diminishes capacity.

Implications of different conditions

1.116 Different mental conditions affect the individual in different ways. Dementia affects recent memories but may leave distant memories intact, so that the individual talks of previous homes and relationships but cannot recall more recent ones. This may have significant implications as to capacity, because the person presently providing care and support may be overlooked completely in favour of a relative with whom there has been little contact for many years. A depressed person is likely to have a negative outlook, ignoring personal needs and making inappropriate decisions, but there could be episodes of manic depression where the mood becomes one of elation and delusions of wealth can lead to the dissipation of money.

Vulnerability

1.117 Infirm older people are often extremely vulnerable to the influence of others, especially the influence of someone whom they are with at the time they make a decision. If based upon a desire to please this may give rise to concerns. It frequently gives rise to disputes between children, each of whom thinks they have achieved a favourable decision from the parent. Undue influence is recognised by the law and may be addressed.[131] Vulnerability should not be confused with lack of capacity:[132]

> 'The courts have ample powers to protect those who are vulnerable to exploitation from being exploited; it is unnecessary to deny them the opportunity to take their own decisions if they are not being exploited. It is not the task of the courts to prevent those who have the mental capacity to make rational decisions from making decisions which others may regard as rash or irresponsible.'

Whilst it is not clear what these 'ample powers' are, it is suggested that when extreme vulnerability is perceived, the correct approach is to analyse the reason for this and such analysis may lead to an assessment of lack of capacity.

Communication

1.118 Physical disabilities may obstruct the power of speech or movement even where mental capacity is not affected. A reasoning mind may be locked inside a body that lacks the ability to communicate in a normal manner. When considering competence the law is concerned with the *capacity* of the individual, but in practice the test applied may be

---

[131] The law relating to undue influence is dealt with in Ch 4 under the heading *Elder abuse*; see **4.136** et seq.
[132] *Masterman-Lister v Brutton & Co and Jewell & Home Counties Dairies* [2002] EWCA Civ 1889, [2002] All ER (D) 297 (Dec), CA, Chadwick LJ.

based upon physical *ability*, or at least the outward appearances of this, with inappropriate consequences. Thus a person who is unable to communicate due to physical disabilities may not be thought competent to open a bank account even though his thought processes are unaffected. Conversely, a person who can both talk coherently and sign his name may be allowed to open an account even though he has a serious mental illness which, if realised, would establish that he did not have the capacity to do so.

1.119 Whilst the law is concerned with what is going on in the mind, society tends to be concerned with the outward manifestations. It is not unusual for communication difficulties (which may have a physical cause) to disguise mental capacity. Other methods of communication must then be established, or at least attempted. Yet just as physical disabilities can create an impression of mental inadequacy which is not justified, so may the absence of physical features disguise an underlying mental disability. The difference between apparent *ability* and underlying *capacity* must be recognised, and the method of assessment, whether formal or informal, may thus become as significant as the legal test to be applied.

Methods

1.120 It should not be assumed that communication must be either verbal or in writing and that the process must be initiated by the individual concerned. Modern technology assists in this respect, but the ability to control any movement (lifting a finger, blinking an eye) could form the basis for communication. The movement in question can be treated as 'yes' and the absence of movement as 'no', but a series of test questions is needed to establish the reliability of this process and if significant questions are reached, care must be taken to ensure that these are not framed in such a way as to achieve responses that are expected or desired.

1.121 Questions must be put in a way that enables the individual to exercise a free and unrestricted choice and a structured series of questions is usually needed. For example, in the case of a will a solicitor would not ask 'Do you wish A, B and C to receive legacies of £1,000 each', but instead start by asking 'Are there any other people you wish to receive a legacy?' and subsequently repeat this question until a negative response is received. Having then, perhaps by a process of elimination, identified the legatees, in each case you would ask 'Is this more than £X' and 'Less than £Y' until a figure is reached. More than one session is usually necessary and a later session can be used to verify any instructions previously expressed in this way. A report from the individual's doctor as to capacity is desirable if significant legal steps are to be taken on the basis of instructions obtained in this way.[133]

Presumptions

1.122 Because of the importance of personal freedom and autonomy there is a long established legal presumption, at least as regards mental illness, that adults are competent unless, and until, the contrary is proved.[134] It follows that when there is

---

[133] Eg the execution on behalf of the individual of an enduring power of attorney or will.

[134] 'In all cases every man is presumed to be sane unless the contrary is proved, and it must be clearly proved, that, at the time of committing or executing the act, the party was labouring under such a defect of reason from disease of the mind as not to know the nature and quality of the act he was doing; or if he did know it, that he did not know that he was doing what was wrong' – Tyndal LCJ (1843). See now *Re MB (Caesarian Section)* [1997] 2 FLR 426.

doubt the question should be '*Is he incapable?*' rather than '*Is he capable?*' though this seldom applies in practice. All too often when the issue arises, perhaps because an elderly person is in a nursing home or seems confused, there is a pre-judgment and the latter question is asked. However, this presumption does yield to practical considerations. There may come a stage when, from a medical point of view, a patient with a serious condition must be presumed to be incapable unless the contrary is shown.[135]

1.123 There are also other presumptions. In civil proceedings there is a strong presumption that if an act and the manner in which it was carried out is rational, the individual was mentally capable at the time. Conversely, if a person is proved incapable in contract generally, the law presumes such condition to continue until it is proved to have ceased, although a lucid interval may still be established.[136] Also, the longer the time that has elapsed since an act which it is being sought to set aside on grounds of mental incapacity, the stronger will be the evidence required to do so.

1.124 These presumptions are relevant to the burden of proof. In general the person who alleges that an individual lacks capacity must prove this, but the standard of proof is the civil standard, namely upon the balance of probabilities rather than beyond reasonable doubt. It is often helpful to point this out to doctors when asking for their opinion.

The need for formal assessment

1.125 A formal assessment may be required for more complex or serious decisions, sometimes involving different professionals.

Legal requirements

1.126 In some cases it is a requirement of the law that a formal assessment of capacity be carried out. These include the following situations:

(a) where a doctor or other expert witness certifies a legal document (such as a will) signed by someone whose capacity could be challenged;[137]

(b) to establish that a person requires the assistance of the Official Solicitor;[138]

(c) where a civil court is required to determine a person's capacity to make a particular decision.[139]

Under the Mental Capacity Act 2005, an assessment is required to provide a certificate of capacity to make a lasting power of attorney or to establish that a person comes within the jurisdiction of the (new) Court of Protection.[140]

---

[135] *Simpson v Simpson* [1989] Fam Law 20.

[136] This has recently been questioned though it was conceded that if there is clear evidence of incapacity for a considerable period then the burden of proof may be more easily discharged – *Masterman-Lister v Brutton & Co and Jewell & Home Counties Dairies* [2002] EWCA Civ 1889, [2002] All ER (D) 297 (Dec), CA.

[137] The so-called 'golden rule' established in *Kenward v Adams* (1975) *The Times*, November 29. See Ch 12 in regard to wills.

[138] Civil Procedure Rules 1998, r 21.1; Practice Note *(Official Solicitor: Declaratory Proceedings: Medical and welfare decisions for adults who lack capacity)* [2001] 2 FLR 158, para 7.1.

[139] *Masterman-Lister v Brutton & Co and Jewell & Home Counties Dairies* [2002] EWCA Civ 1889, CA at 54.

[140] Mental Capacity Act 2005, Sch 1, para 2(1)(e) and ss 15(1), 16(1) respectively. See generally Ch 2.

Evidence

1.127 Mental capacity is a question of fact, though a legal test based upon understanding must be applied and the matters to be understood will vary according to the circumstances.[141] Any issue as to capacity can only be determined by a judge in civil proceedings acting not as a medical expert, but as a lay person influenced by personal observation and on the basis of evidence of doctors and those who know the individual. Capacity must be judged for each individual in respect of each transaction at that particular moment.

1.128 General reputation is not admissible in evidence, but the treatment by friends and family of a person alleged to be suffering from mental disorder may be admissible as between them respectively. An order of the (old) Court of Protection based upon a finding of lack of capacity to manage affairs by reason of mental disorder was admissible as prima facie evidence of this fact. The registration of an enduring power of attorney may also be relied upon as evidence of lack of capacity unless there is a dispute in which case other evidence will be required.[142]

Medical opinions

1.129 In many cases, all that may be needed is an opinion from the person's GP who is likely to have knowledge of the patient's medical condition and the effect that it has had over a period of time. Any opinion offered will follow a perusal of the case notes and will not be based merely upon a superficial assessment (although it should take into account information provided by those caring for the patient). The doctor may even have indicated that there was doubt about the patient's mental capacity in the first place and thereby prompted the further enquiry.

1.130 In more serious cases or where a challenge may be anticipated, care should be taken to ensure that the medical professional who gives an opinion is suitably qualified. A neurologist deals with physical ailments of the brain whereas a psychiatrist concentrates upon mental illness. The psycho-geriatrician is trained as a psychiatrist but also deals with physical problems and is experienced in the needs of elderly people. It is best to avoid relying on a treating doctor where there is a dispute because of the confusion over roles. The doctor acting purely as an expert witness will have access to the treating doctor's notes so any views will emerge and be assessed. In some cases, a multi-disciplinary approach is best, using the skills and expertise of different professionals.

1.131 If a case comes to court, medical evidence is admissible and usually important, so it is not surprising that when applying the tests in practice, lawyers rely heavily upon the medical profession. Unlike other witnesses, the medical practitioner is regarded by the courts as an expert (even though he may not be) and is therefore entitled to express an opinion about capacity. A doctor's opinion should not be treated as the definitive judgment; it is merely an opinion, part of the evidence, no more and no less. An explanation should be given as to how and why the opinion has been formed. It may not necessarily be given greater weight than other relevant evidence, such as the views of a solicitor where capacity to undertake a legal transaction is involved.[143]

---

[141] See generally *Masterman-Lister v Brutton & Co and Jewell & Home Counties Dairies.*
[142] The position is different in regard to the new lasting powers of attorney – see generally Ch 2.
[143] *Richmond v Richmond* (1914) LT 273; *Birkin v Wing* (1890) 63 LT 80.

Instructing a doctor

1.132 Solicitors requesting a professional assessment should take care to ensure that:[144]

- *the relevant legal test is spelt out.* It should be explained that different tests apply to different types of decision. It may be helpful for the doctor in his report or certificate to state that it relates to the particular situation involved and that no opinion is expressed about capacity in other respects;

- *all relevant information is provided.* For example, if the test is whether the individual is incapable of managing his affairs the doctor must be given some idea what those affairs are; and

- *it is made clear why an opinion about capacity is required.* Thus the doctor should be told if a finding of incapacity would take away the freedom of the individual or prevent other people from abusing the individual. Will it assist the patient (eg provide an additional financial benefit) or empower someone to deal with the patient's financial affairs (eg an application to the Court of Protection), or protect the patient (eg prevent misappropriation of his money)? Will it empower the patient (eg signing a will), change the patient's life (eg getting married) or restrict the patient (eg admission to hospital)? The doctor may be influenced by his perception of the implications and if this is wrongly based the outcome may not be what was intended.

The doctor's approach

1.133 For the purpose of any assessment, a doctor will wish to obtain a history of the patient and then confirm the factual information from medical notes or by talking to family, friends or carers. There will then be a *mental state examination* which extends to appearance, speech, mood, thinking processes, orientation, memory and insight. Previous personality will also be considered along with any perceptual disorders, delusional ideas and cognitive functions. A diagnosis will be made based upon the overall picture including whether the patient suffers from a mental disorder within the Mental Health Act 1983 or within the meaning of ICD10 (*International Classification of Disease*, 10th edn).

1.134 A distinction should be made between physical and psychological illnesses, both of which can result in impaired capacity. If there is an impairment it may be necessary to look at the cause because pain and discomfort can affect concentration and the ability to make decisions. Investigations may include a blood test, ECG or brain scan if a stroke or heart attack is suspected, or a chest examination or urine analysis if there may be an infection. Treatment in these circumstances could result in capacity being restored.

Other evidence

1.135 The views of a carer, social worker or nurse who has worked with the patient for extended periods of time and in different circumstances may be as pertinent as those of a medical practitioner who may only see the individual for short consultations often in the presence of a carer. Their evidence is less likely to be relied upon in practice, but there is no reason why they should not also give evidence as to the facts and circumstances even though they may not express opinions as experts. Such evidence may be very persuasive as to the state of mind of the individual.

---

[144] Sample letters have been provided in Denzil Lush *Elderly Clients: A Precedent Manual* (Jordans, 2nd edn).

Problems with the assessment

Confidentiality

1.136 Carrying out an assessment of capacity requires the sharing of information about the personal circumstances of the person being assessed, yet doctors, lawyers and professional persons generally (including social workers) owe a duty of confidentiality to their patients or clients. This means that personal information should only be revealed to others with the consent of the patient or client.[145] This duty is not absolute and may be overridden where there is a stronger public interest in disclosure.[146] Where the individual lacks the mental capacity to consent to (or refuse) disclosure, it may be desirable to permit disclosure in certain circumstances. This has been expressed as follows:[147]

> 'C's interest in protecting the confidentiality of personal information about himself must not be underestimated. It is all too easy for professionals and parents to regard ... incapacitated adults as having no independent interests of their own: as objects rather than subjects. But we are not concerned here with the publication of information to the whole wide world. There is a clear distinction between disclosure to the media with a view to publication to all and sundry and disclosure in confidence to those with a proper interest in having the information in question.'

During an assessment as to mental capacity, it is essential that information is shared by the professionals involved. The patient's consent to this should be obtained wherever possible, but in the absence of this, relevant disclosure may be permitted. However, this does not extend to confidential information about the patient unrelated to the assessment. Disclosure will be based upon a need to know and the overall test will be in the best interests of the patient.

Refusal to be assessed

1.137 The person whose capacity is in doubt may be reluctant to undergo an assessment. It will usually be possible to persuade someone to agree if the consequences of refusal are carefully explained. For example, it should be explained to a person wishing to make a will that evidence of their capacity could prevent the will being challenged and held to be invalid after their death. If there is a lack of capacity to consent to, or refuse, assessment it will normally be possible for an assessment to proceed so long as the person is compliant and this is considered to be in the person's best interests. In some cases, a 'reasonable belief' of lack of capacity will be sufficient. However, where a formal assessment is needed, no one can be forced to undergo an assessment in the face of an outright refusal unless required to do so by a court. Even then, entry to a person's home cannot be forced and a refusal to open the door to the doctor may prevent a personal meeting. Other evidence may then be pursued and the conduct of the individual may be taken into account.

---

[145] This may be imposed by codes of professional conduct or by the law, e g Data Protection Act 1998 or European Convention on Human Rights, Art 8.

[146] *W v Egdell* [1990] Ch 359 at 419; 1 All ER 835 at 848.

[147] *R (on the application of Ann Stevens) v Plymouth City Council and C* [2002] EWCA Civ 388, per Hale LJ.

Decision-making

Preliminary

1.138 Where decisions need to be taken which a person is incapable of making or communicating, these can only be made by others. Legal powers and procedures are needed to authorise or appoint decision-makers and resolve disputes. The absence of such procedures causes problems and uncertainty throughout the whole range of personal decision-making. In practice, routine decisions are taken and carried out on the basis of practicalities without reference to legal procedures, but the person taking responsibility for the decision may feel vulnerable. Those concerned with the welfare of the individual often feel uncertainty as to their rights and duties and the procedures to be followed. Problems arise especially when:

- a decision is taken which someone concerned will not accept;
- there is disagreement as to what decision should be taken; or
- a decision is needed that no-one can or will take.

Types of decision

1.139 In a legal context one can divide decisions into three basic categories. In each category there are decisions which can be regarded as routine, daily matters and those which have more serious implications. This distinction may be relevant as to the level of formality required for the decision to be made. The categories are:

(a) financial (or management) decisions;

(b) medical treatment (or health care) decisions; and

(c) personal (or welfare) decisions.

We consider each of these separately. Historically our courts have been more concerned with property than the person and there has been a choice of delegation procedures available for financial decisions,[148] though they may not have been adequate. Until October 2007, our law did not enable other types of decision to be made on behalf of an incapable individual although the courts became imaginative in devising procedures to enable these decisions to be made.

Financial decisions

1.140 When an individual is unable to handle his own financial affairs it is necessary for someone else to be able to do so on his behalf, with safeguards to prevent the misuse of funds. Financial affairs may comprise claiming benefits, managing money, buying and selling property and making a will. Where there are only limited resources, relatives or carers find informal ways of dealing with financial matters as they arise. The methods adopted may be of doubtful legal validity but are unlikely to be questioned and those involved are only concerned with whether or not they work. Where more than a small amount of money is involved or there is a dispute, it is necessary to use one of the legally recognised procedures that is available.

---

[148] See generally Chs 2 and 11.

Background

1.141 The Lunacy Act 1890 gave various powers to the Office of the Master in Lunacy (which was not renamed the Court of Protection until 1947) and these were the basis of the provisions contained in Part VII of the Mental Health Act 1983. Until October 2007 that court had powers over the property and affairs of an individual who was 'incapable, by reason of mental disorder, of managing and administering his property and affairs'. However, this was restricted to financial affairs, thereby denying a procedure for dealing with other decisions. Usually an individual was appointed as a *receiver* to handle those affairs under the supervision of the court, but a *short order* was available for small or straightforward cases.

1.142 Demand for a less expensive and simpler procedure of choice coupled with the inability of the Court of Protection to cope with the financial affairs of all mentally incapacitated persons, resulted in the passing of the Enduring Powers of Attorney Act 1985. This overcame the problem with ordinary powers of attorney that they were revoked by the subsequent mental incapacity of the donor under normal agency principles. Some formality was introduced into the documentation and the power had to be registered with the Public Guardianship Office upon the donor becoming mentally incapable, but there was no supervision. Again, only financial decisions could be dealt with in this way.

Statutory powers of delegation

1.143 The law thus provided for delegation to an agent of the power to handle the financial affairs of the individual. In respect of civil proceedings, court rules provided for litigation to be conducted on behalf of those who were deemed to be 'patients'.[149] There was also an *appointee* procedure[150] which enabled weekly state benefits to be paid to someone on behalf of the claimant and this was widely relied upon but there were few safeguards against abuse. If other sources of income were involved or capital funds or assets had to be dealt with, then application usually had to be made to the (former) Court of Protection for specific authority unless the individual had completed an enduring power of attorney before losing capacity.

Medical treatment decisions

1.144 This category is often referred to as 'heath care decisions' and three types of decision have been identified:[151]

(1) minor routine medical treatment (eg dentistry, cervical smear tests, vaccinations);

(2) medical treatment with advantages and disadvantages (eg replacement of teeth by dentures); and

(3) controversial medical treatment (eg sterilisation, participation in medical research).

The ultimate medical decision is whether treatment should be withdrawn and the patient allowed to die.

---

[149] See Ch 3 at **3.129** et seq.
[150] Social Security (Claims and Payments) Regulations 1987, SI 1987/1968, reg 33. See Ch 11 at **11.5**.
[151] Law Commission Consultation Paper No 119 *Mentally Incapacitated Adults and Decision-Making: An Overview*.

The reality

1.145 Medical treatment requires the patient's consent. A mentally competent adult has an absolute right to give or refuse consent to medical treatment, however damaging the consequences may be to him.[152] If consent cannot be given but the treatment is non-controversial and the close relatives or those concerned with the patient's care approve, treatment may in practice be given. In an emergency, the doctor responsible for a patient who is unable to give or refuse consent to treatment may act in accordance with good medical practice and give treatment which is designed to preserve the life of the patient, assist recovery or ease suffering but limited to treatment that is both necessary and reasonable.[153]

1.146 Patients who do not have, or will not regain, competence to make their own decisions are entitled to more than such restricted treatment and the doctor may give treatment which he considers to be in the patient's best interest.[154] This raises problems over withholding or withdrawing treatment from a mentally incompetent patient which would merely prolong the process of dying. A previously expressed objection to treatment, such as an advance directive, could rebut the doctor's view of best interests if it contemplated the actual situation that had arisen.[155]

Powers of the courts

1.147 Most of the references to the courts prior to the Mental Capacity Act 2005 related to medical treatment decisions which have serious ethical implications and are normally only taken by the individual.[156] The courts concluded that no-one, not even the court, had legal authority to give consent to medical treatment in these circumstances. However, they got round this in essential cases by making *declarations* that the proposed operation or action would be in the best interest of the patient so would not be unlawful. Whilst these cases achieved publicity they merely represented the tip of the iceberg so far as the underlying problem was concerned. The needs for a mental capacity jurisdiction were becoming overwhelming.

Personal decisions

1.148 Three types of personal decision were identified:[157]

(1) day-to-day living (what to eat or wear, whether to have a bath or haircut);

(2) activities involving more risk (going out alone, sports, holidays, making new friends); and

(3) major life decisions (where to live, whether to enter residential care, getting married or having children).

---

[152] *T (Adult: Refusal of Medical Treatment)* [1993] Fam 95, per Lord Donaldson MR.
[153] See *Bolam v Friern Hospital Management Committee* [1957] 2 All ER 118.
[154] *F v West Berkshire Health Authority* [1989] 2 All ER 545, HL; also reported as *Re F (Sterilisation: Mental Patient)* [1989] 2 FLR 376.
[155] These matters are considered in greater detail in Ch 8.
[156] Eg to have a sterilisation or refrain from treatment where death may result.
[157] Law Commission Consultation Paper No 119 *Mentally Incapacitated Adults and Decision-Making: An Overview.*

The reality

1.149 A mentally competent adult has an absolute right to determine where and with whom he should live and with whom he should associate.[158] Although there may be an urgent need to make some personal decisions, apart from a few exceptions in the Mental Health Act 1983, English law made no provision for delegation in respect of an incapacitated adult. Such decisions might simply not be made at all, or might have been made by the wrong person or for the wrong reasons. Routine personal decisions were usually made by carers, and sometimes by others, without legal authority but on grounds of necessity or expediency.

1.150 The financial procedures enabled some personal decisions to be carried into effect even though no-one had authority in law to make them.[159] In some cases the financial agent would be a relative willing to make both personal and financial decisions, but if he was a professional person he would consult the carers who might make the personal decision leaving him to deal with the money. In other cases this agent made personal decisions by default simply because there was no-one else to do so, or those decisions were not taken at all. In either event the individual was vulnerable to abuse or neglect due to the absence of a proper system for delegated personal decision-making and the person taking responsibility for the decision could feel vulnerable. The biggest problem was often the uncertainty of those concerned with the welfare of the incapacitated individual as to their rights and duties and the procedures to be followed. The more personal decisions (such as getting married) are not capable of delegation so could not legally be made at all if the individual did not have the personal capacity to make them.

Jurisdiction of the Court to grant a declaration

1.151 If a decision made in respect of a mentally incapable person was challenged, or the lack of a decision became an issue, the courts had to decide what was to be done. Initially the *declaration* procedure was only used for medical treatment, but in 1995 Mrs Justice Hale[160] not only applied the procedure to a personal welfare decision[161] but also backed it up with an injunction and was upheld by the Court of Appeal.[162] In that same year the High Court also held that the court had jurisdiction to grant a declaration that an adult with cerebral palsy and learning difficulties was entitled to choose where to live and with whom to associate, and to restrain the parents by injunction from interfering.[163] However, the making of a declaration or an injunction was a discretionary remedy. From October 2007 the jurisdiction of the High Court to grant declarations in these circumstances is largely replaced by the jurisdiction of the new Court of Protection under the Mental Capacity Act 2005.

Basis for decisions

1.152 Where courts made declarations or delegation took place, it was necessary to know the basis upon which the decision should be made. It could be on the basis of:

---

[158] *Re S (Hospital patient) (Court's jurisdiction)* [1996] Fam 1, [1995] 1 FLR 1075.
[159] He who controls the money generally controls the person. Thus the person who finances the care and accommodation may by default decide where the incapacitated person is to live and who the carer will be.
[160] As Professor Brenda Hoggett she was architect of the Law Commission Report on *Mental Incapacity*.
[161] *Re S (Adult Patient: Jurisdiction)* [1995] 1 FLR 302. An injunction was granted to stop the wife of an elderly, infirm man taking him abroad out of the care of his mistress.
[162] *Re S (Hospital Patient: Court's Jurisdiction)* [1996] Fam 1, [1995] 1 FLR 1075.
[163] *Re V (Declaration against Parents)* [1995] 2 FLR 1003, Johnson J.

(a)   the *best interests* of the incapacitated person. There is a danger that this is interpreted as 'what the decision maker (usually the carer) thinks is best'; or

(b)   *substituted judgment,* namely that which the individual would have decided if capable of making the decision. There might be evidence of this from the manner in which an elderly person lived before becoming incapacitated.[164]

The Law Commission proposed[165] a new statutory definition in this context that took into account all relevant factors and the Mental Capacity Act 2005 has adopted a similar approach although it is referred to as 'best interests'.

Decision makers

1.153 There is a long list of persons who have in the past represented the interests of a mentally disabled individual to a greater or lesser extent. This includes:[166]

(1)   receivers, attorneys, appointees or trustees for financial affairs;

(2)   litigation friends, next friends or guardians ad litem for litigation;

(3)   statutory guardians and nearest relatives under Mental Health Acts;

(4)   appropriate adults when investigated for a crime; and

(5)   personal advocates in a community care context.

Despite the length of this list the authority of such representatives in England and Wales extended to very few ordinary decisions for the individual and there were large gaps where no-one had any power to make such decisions. This has been resolved by the Mental Capacity Act 2005, dealt with in Chapter 2.

---

[164] There may be no evidence in the case of someone with serious learning disabilities who has never had capacity.

[165] Report No 231 *Mental Incapacity.*

[166] In Scotland there are curators bonis and ad litem, tutors-dative and tutors-at-law, managers, judicial factors and the negotiorum gestio.

CHAPTER 2

THE MENTAL CAPACITY JURISDICTION

Gordon Ashton

'It is our choices ... that show what we truly are, far more than our abilities.'
J. K. Rowling, 'Harry Potter and The Chamber of Secrets', 1999

Under the Mental Capacity Act 2005 a statutory jurisdiction now enables decisions to be made on behalf of mentally incapacitated adults and regulates the way this is done. Only time will tell whether this is effective and produces an appropriate balance between empowerment and protection. This chapter first explains the fundamental principles of capacity and best interest, and then outlines the powers and duties of decision makers and the procedures of choice. This is followed by an overview of the new Court of Protection which oversees the jurisdiction and resolve disputes, the Public Guardian and the supporting services.

BACKGROUND

The reform process

2.1   During the 1980s it became apparent that our law and procedures failed to address in a comprehensive manner the difficulties raised by those who were incompetent in the sense that they could not take their own decisions.[1] The courts did not have power to fill the vacuum and such legislation that there had been was piecemeal and not based upon an underlying philosophy. Comprehensive reform in this area was essential. The Law Society first highlighted these issues at a conference[2] in 1989.

Law Commission Report

2.2   In consequence the Law Commission considered the whole question of decision making and mental incapacity over the following 5 years and produced four successive consultation papers resulting in a healthy debate involving practitioners, professionals and service organisations. The final Report was published in March 1995[3] and recommended that there should be a single comprehensive piece of legislation to make new provision for people who lack mental capacity.[4] This would provide a coherent

---

[1]   See Ch 1 at **1.78** et seq for a further explanation.
[2]   *Decision-making and Mental Incapacity*, May 1989.
[3]   *Mental Incapacity* – No 231. A similar review was undertaken by the Law Commission of Scotland and a Report produced for that country.
[4]   A draft Mental Incapacity Bill was annexed to the Report.

statutory scheme to which recourse could be had when any decision (whether personal, medical or financial) needed to be made for a person aged 16 or over who lacked capacity.

2.3   Two concepts were identified as being fundamental to any new decision-making jurisdiction, namely capacity and best interests, so new statutory definitions were proposed. Key points in the recommendations were:

(1)   A 'general authority to act reasonably', which would remove the uncertainties of the present law as to what action may lawfully be taken by someone caring for a person without capacity or what medical treatment a doctor can give to such a person.

(2)   The principle that people be encouraged and enabled to take their own decisions be extended to future health care, with living wills (including advance refusals of medical treatment and the appointment of someone to take treatment decisions) being given statutory authority subject to safeguards.

(3)   Independent supervision of certain medical and research procedures (the withdrawal of artificial feeding from patients in a persistent vegetative state was given special consideration).

(4)   Enduring powers of attorney be replaced by 'continuing powers of attorney' which would extend to the full range of decision making (ie personal welfare and health care as well as property and affairs) and be subject to a new registration procedure.

2.4   The proposals extended to a new statutory jurisdiction for the making of all types of decision on behalf of persons without capacity, with a new regional Court of Protection able to make declarations and one-off orders or, where appropriate, appoint a manager with substitute decision-making powers. A Code of Practice would provide guidance and there would be further public law protection with social services departments being under a duty to investigate where they had reason to believe that a vulnerable person was suffering or likely to suffer significant harm or serious exploitation.[5]

The Government's response

2.5   Following an emotional but ill-considered attack on the Law Commission by the Daily Mail in support of 'family values'[6] the Government announced that it did not intend to proceed with legislation 'in its present form' but would undertake further consultation on the Report. That consultation did not materialise until December 1997 following a change of government.[7] In October 1999 the Lord Chancellor published the Government's proposals in the Report *Making Decisions*. It was announced that there would be legislation 'when Parliamentary time allows' but much of the detail had still to be worked out.

Adults with Incapacity (Scotland) Act 2000

2.6   This Act was passed by the Scottish Parliament on 29 March 2000 and received the Royal Assent on 16 May 2000. It followed the Scottish Law Commission *Report on*

---

5   The public law protection recommendations have not been implemented.
6   Living wills were singled out for condemnation but little was said of the many other recommendations.
7   *Who Decides? Making Decisions on Behalf of Mentally Incapacitated Adults*, Cm 3803 issued by the Lord Chancellor's Department.

Incapable Adults[8] and was widely welcomed as a significant and much-needed reform of the law, protecting the rights and interests of adults who are incapable of managing their own affairs, acknowledged to be one of the most vulnerable groups in society.[9] The Act dealt with the management of their property, financial affairs and personal welfare, including medical treatment and was implemented over 2 years.

Legislation for England & Wales

Mental Incapacity Bill

2.7   On 27 June 2003 the Government published a draft Mental Incapacity Bill with the following explanation:[10]

> 'The overriding aim of the Bill is to improve the lives of vulnerable adults, their carers, families and professionals. It provides a statutory framework for decision making for people who lack capacity, making clear who can take decisions, in which situations and how they should go about this.
>
> The Bill is based on clearly defined principles. Its starting point is that everyone has the right to make his or her own decisions, and must be assumed to have capacity to do so unless it is proved otherwise. No-one should be labelled as incapable – each decision should be considered individually and everyone should be helped to make or contribute to making decisions about their lives. The Bill sets out clear guidelines for, and limits on, other people's role in decision making.'

Following scrutiny of the Bill and a draft Code of Practice by a Joint Committee of both Houses of Parliament during which the title was changed, the Mental Capacity Act 2005 ('the Act') received the Royal Assent on 7 April 2005.

Mental Capacity Act 2005

2.8   The preamble states that it is:

> 'An Act to make new provision relating to persons who lack capacity; to establish a superior court of record called the Court of Protection in place of the office of the Supreme Court called by that name; to make provision in connection with the Convention on the International Protection of Adults signed at the Hague on 13th January 2000; and for connected purposes.'

Part 1 deals with 'persons who lack capacity', Part 2 establishes the new Court of Protection and the Public Guardian, whilst Part 3 deals with miscellaneous matters. There are 69 sections followed by seven Schedules. Implementation took place on 1 October 2007.

---

[8]   No 151 dated July 1995.
[9]   Up to 100,000 adults in Scotland and their relatives and carers were affected by incapacity at any time.
[10]   David Lammy, Parliamentary Under Secretary of State for Constitutional Affairs, *Hansard*, HC Deb, col 67WS (18 June 2004).

Codes of Practice

2.9   The Act merely creates a broad framework and heavy reliance is placed on Codes of Practice which will be reviewed at intervals in the light of experience and decisions of the new Court of Protection. A Code or Codes must be issued and revised by the Lord Chancellor with respect to:[11]

- persons assessing whether a person has capacity;
- persons acting in connection with care or treatment;
- donees of lasting powers of attorney ('LPAs');
- deputies appointed by the court;
- research involving people lacking capacity;
- Independent Mental Capacity Advocates ('IMCAs');
- advance decisions to refuse treatment.

2.10   Any Codes are intended to give practical guidance and examples to illustrate the provisions of the Act, rather than imposing any new legal or formal requirements.[12] Those acting in relation to a person who lacks capacity as the donee of a lasting power of attorney, a deputy appointed by the court, in a professional capacity or for remuneration 'must have regard to' any relevant Code. This includes lawyers, health and social care professionals and others such as paid carers. Whilst a strict requirement to comply with the Codes is not imposed on informal carers, the Codes comprise appropriate guidance and assistance in promoting good practice. A court or tribunal must take into account the provisions of the Codes in deciding any question affected thereby in any criminal or civil proceedings.

THE PRINCIPLES OF THE MENTAL CAPACITY ACT 2005

Preliminary

2.11   The Act establishes a new integrated jurisdiction for the making of personal welfare decisions (which include healthcare) and financial decisions on behalf of people without the capacity to make such decisions for themselves. It enshrines in statute current best practice and former common law principles concerning such people and those who take decisions on their behalf. The statutory framework is based on two fundamental concepts: lack of capacity and best interests. For those who lack capacity to make particular decisions, the Act provides a range of processes, extending from informal arrangements to court-based powers, to govern the circumstances in which necessary decisions can be taken on their behalf and in their best interests.

Overriding principles

2.12   Section 1 sets out the overriding principles which permeate the new jurisdiction and must never be overlooked:[13]

---

[11]   Codes may be issued for other matters but initially a single Code of Practice dealt with all the stipulated matters. Subsequently a further Code of Practice deals with Deprivation of Liberty Safeguards.

[12]   Mental Capacity Act 2005, ss 42–43. There are extensive requirements for consultation and approval by Parliament and accessible versions of any Code will be published in various formats.

[13]   See generally Code of Practice, para 2.

(a) a person must be assumed to have capacity unless it is established that he lacks capacity;

(b) a person is not to be treated as unable to make a decision unless all practicable steps to help him to do so have been taken without success;

(c) a person is not to be treated as unable to make a decision merely because he makes an unwise decision;

(d) an act done, or decision made, under this Act for or on behalf of a person who lacks capacity must be done, or made, in his best interests; and

(e) before the act is done, or the decision is made, regard must be had to whether the purpose for which it is needed can be as effectively achieved in a way that is less restrictive of the person's rights and freedom of action.

Presumption of capacity

2.13   At common law if a question of capacity comes before a court the burden of proof is generally on the person who is seeking to establish a lack of capacity and the matter is decided according to the usual civil standard, the balance of probabilities. The Law Commission recommended that the new statutory provisions should expressly include and re-state both the common-law principle of presumption of capacity and the relevant standard of proof. This becomes the first key principle. The Code of Practice stresses that the starting point for assessing someone's capacity to make a particular decision is always the assumption that the individual does have capacity:[14]

'Some people may need help to be able to make a decision or to communicate their decision ... this does not necessarily mean that they cannot make that decision.'

Support for decision making

2.14   The second key principle clarifies that people should not be treated as unable to make a decision until everything practicable has been done to enable them to make their own decision without success. There are a number of ways in which people can be supported to make their decisions and these will vary according to the decision to be made, the time available and the circumstances of the individual. The steps to be taken might include using specific communication strategies, providing information in an accessible form, or treating an underlying medical condition to enable the person to regain capacity.

2.15   The Code of Practice points to a range of practicable steps which may assist decision making. The relevance will depend on the particular circumstances but the following should always be considered:[15]

(1) Try to minimise anxiety or stress by making the person feel at ease. Choose the best location where the client feels most comfortable and the time of day when the client is most alert.

(2) If the person's capacity is likely to improve, wait until it has improved (unless the decision is urgent). If the cause of the incapacity can be treated, it may be possible to delay the decision until treatment has taken place.

---

[14]   Code of Practice, para 3.3.
[15]   Code of Practice, paras 3.1–3.16.

(3)   If there are communication or language problems, consider using a speech therapist or interpreter, or consult family members on the best methods of communication.

(4)   Be aware of any cultural, ethnic or religious factors which may have a bearing on the person's way of thinking, behaviour or communication.

(5)   Consider whether or not a friend or family member should be present to help reduce anxiety. But in some cases the presence of others may be intrusive.

The right to make unwise decisions

2.16   The Law Commission was influenced by the strongly held views they received to include this recommendation in its proposals. It reflects the nature of human decision making. People make different decisions because they place greater weight on some factors than others, taking account of their own values and preferences. Some are keen to express their own individuality or more willing to take risks, and people with mental disabilities which could affect their decision-making capacity should not be expected to make 'better' or 'wiser' decisions than anyone else. Although an unwise decision should not, by itself, be sufficient to indicate lack of capacity there may be circumstances where a person has an on-going condition which affects the capacity to make a range of inter-related or sequential decisions. One decision on its own may make sense but the combination of decisions may raise doubts as to the person's capacity or at least prompt the need for a proper assessment.

Best interests

2.17   The Law Commission proposed a single criterion of 'best interests' to govern all decision making, this being a compromise between the proposed approaches of what the decision maker considers best and 'substituted judgment' (ie what the person would have wished). 'Best interests' is a concept already recognised by the courts especially in the field of child care law (although using different terminology),[16] but it is amplified in the Act and explained further below.

Least restrictive alternative

2.18   The Law Commission originally proposed that the 'least restrictive alternative' principle should be one of the factors to be taken into account in determining best interests. However, in response to the Joint Committee's recommendation it has been adopted as the fifth key principle. Where there is more than one course of action or a choice of decisions, the least restrictive option should be adopted.

People who lack capacity'

Definition

2.19   Section 2(1) of the Act defines incapacity as follows:

> 'For the purposes of the Act, a person lacks capacity in relation to a matter if at the material time he is unable to make a decision for himself in relation to the matter because of an impairment of, or a disturbance in the functioning of, the mind or brain.'

---

[16]   Children Act 1989, s 1(1): '... the child's welfare shall be the court's paramount consideration'. The more paternalistic approach should be avoided when dealing with adults.

This is a two-stage test in that it must be established that (a) there is an impairment of, or disturbance in the functioning of, the person's mind or brain, and (b) this is sufficient to render the person incapable of making that particular decision.[17]

The diagnostic test

2.20   The first stage is a new 'diagnostic test', namely 'an impairment of, or a disturbance in the functioning of, the mind or brain'. This replaces mental disorder under the former Court of Protection jurisdiction but covers a wide range of conditions. It does not matter whether the impairment or disturbance is permanent or temporary. Lack of capacity cannot be established merely by reference to a person's age or appearance, or any condition or aspect of his/her behaviour which might lead others to make unjustified assumptions about the person's capacity. However, the Act does not in general apply to persons under 16 years of age.

The function test

2.21   The second stage is inability to make the decision because of the condition. The Act further provides that a person is unable to make a decision for himself if he is unable to:[18]

(a)   understand the information relevant to the decision;

(b)   retain that information;

(c)   use or weigh that information as part of the process of making the decision; or

(d)   communicate his decision (whether by talking, using sign language or any other means).

Applying the test

2.22   The first principle described above confirms that the onus is upon the person who alleges lack of capacity to establish this but any question must be decided on the balance of probabilities. The second principle that a person should not be treated as unable to make a decision until every practical step possible has been done to help him to do so is also triggered here. There is a link between the function test and the diagnostic test insofar as the inability to make the decision must be a consequence of the condition, namely impairment of, or disturbance in the functioning of, the person's mind or brain. So a person will not be treated as incapable and deprived of the right to make his own decisions just because he is eccentric, or has an approach that is radically different than that of the person who is making the assessment. This reinforces the third principle described above, namely the right to make unwise decisions.

Information

2.23   The information relevant to a decision includes information about the reasonably foreseeable consequences of deciding one way or another, or failing to make the decision. The fact that a person is able to retain the information relevant to a decision for a short period only does not prevent him from being regarded as able to make the decision, but he must be able to retain the information for long enough to make the decision based upon it. A person is not to be regarded as unable to understand the information relevant to a decision if he is able to understand an explanation of it given

---

[17]   See generally Code of Practice, para 4.
[18]   Mental Capacity Act 2005, s 3(1).

to him in a way that is appropriate to his circumstances (using simple language, visual aids or any other means) and every effort should be made to give such explanation.

'Use or weigh'

2.24 In the initial period following implementation of the Act there was a tendency, including amongst psychiatrists, to concentrate so much on understanding that the further requirement of using or weighing the understanding in the process of decision making was overlooked. As stated in Chapter 1, the effects of a mental disability (especially an acquired brain injury) may prevent the individual from using information in the decision-making process even if he or she can understand it.[19]

Communication

2.25 The functional test has been extended to cover those who cannot communicate in any way. This is inevitable because a person who is unable to communicate a decision must be treated as incapable of making it. But strenuous efforts must be made to facilitate communication before any finding of incapacity is made, and the Code of Practice recommends that in cases of this sort, professionals with specialist skills in verbal and non-verbal communication will be required to assist.

Implications

2.26 The majority of decisions made on behalf of people lacking capacity will be informal day-to-day decisions and it will not be necessary to carry out or record a formal assessment. It is sufficient for the decision maker to 'reasonably believe' that the person lacks capacity to make the decision or consent to the action in question.[20] However, if the assessment is challenged, the decision maker must be able to point to objective reasons to justify why they hold that belief. Where professionals are involved, for example a doctor providing medical treatment or a solicitor obtaining a signature to a document, good practice requires that a proper assessment of capacity is made and the findings recorded in the relevant records. In some instances a more detailed report or certificate will be required, for example in court proceedings or to invoke the jurisdiction of the Court of Protection.

Conclusion

2.27 The Act thus adopts a functional approach, requiring capacity to be assessed in relation to each particular decision at the time the decision needs to be made. So a person may lack capacity in regard to one matter but not another and capacity may fluctuate over time. However, decisions are not made in isolation. Although an unwise decision should not, by itself, be sufficient to indicate lack of capacity, a combination of decisions or a sequence of inconsistent decisions may raise doubts and prompt the need for a proper assessment.

2.28 The reference to 'For the purposes of the Act ...' is used by some critics to severely restrict the scope of the Act but it should not be overlooked that the underlying purpose of this legislation is regulating decision making for those who lack capacity (including the need to assess capacity) and that extends beyond the potential role of the Court of Protection.

---

[19]   See *Re MB* [1997] 2 FLR 426; *R v Collins and Ashworth Hospital Authority ex parte Brady* [2001] 58 BMLR 173. The Mental Capacity Act 2005, s 3(1)(c) recognises this.

[20]   Mental Capacity Act 2005, ss 4(8) and 5(1).

Best interests

The statutory checklist

2.29 The Act repeats the common law principle that any act done, or any decision made, for or on behalf of a person who lacks capacity must be done, or made, in that person's best interests. This only applies once it has been determined that the person lacks the capacity to make their own decisions, or where someone exercising powers under the Act 'reasonably believes' that the person lacks capacity. The concept of best interests is not defined as such but is to be addressed on the basis of a checklist that must be gone through.[21] This seeks to identify those issues most relevant to the individual who lacks capacity (as opposed to the decision maker or any other persons) in the context of the decision in question. Not all the factors in the checklist will be relevant to all types of decisions or actions, but they must still be considered if only to be disregarded as irrelevant to the particular situation. The decision maker must, so far as reasonably practicable, permit and encourage the person to participate, or to improve his ability to participate, as fully as possible in any act done for him and any decision affecting him. Those who lack capacity should not be excluded from the decision-making process.

2.30 All the relevant circumstances must be taken into account and the statutory checklist merely sets out matters that must never be overlooked. Relevant circumstances are defined as those of which the person making the determination is aware, and which it would be reasonable to regard as relevant, because he or she may not be in a position to make exhaustive enquiries as to every issue which may have some relevance.

Addressing best interests

Assumptions

2.31 Decisions should not be based on any preconceived ideas or negative assumptions, for example about the value or quality of life experienced by older people or those with mental or physical disabilities. The Act specifically provides that a determination of someone's best interests must not be based merely on the person's age or appearance, or any condition or aspect of behaviour which might lead others to make unjustified assumptions about the person's best interests.

Prospect of recovery

2.32 In determining what is in a person's best interests, the decision maker must consider in particular whether the person may at some time have capacity in relation to the matter and, if so, when that is likely to be. It may be possible to put off the decision until the person can make it personally. Any delay may allow time for additional steps to be taken to restore the person's capacity or to provide support and assistance which would enable the person to make the decision.

Input from incapacitated person

2.33 The decision maker must also consider, so far as is reasonably ascertainable:

(a) the person's past and present wishes and feelings;

---

[21] Mental Capacity Act 2005, s 4. See generally Code of Practice, para 5.

(b)   the beliefs and values that would be likely to influence his decision if he had capacity; and

(c)   the other factors that he would be likely to consider if able to do so.

The following guidance has been given by the court, making it clear that too much weight must not be given to the person's own wishes:[22]

> 'Having gone through these steps, the decision maker must then form a value judgment of his own giving effect to the paramount statutory instruction that any decision must be made in P's best interests. In my judgment this process is quite different to that which applied under the former Mental Health Acts. ... The only imperative is that the decision must be made in P's best interests ... although P's wishes must be given weight, if, as I think, Parliament has endorsed the "balance sheet" approach, they are only one part of the balance ... those wishes are to be given great weight, but I would prefer not to speak in terms of presumptions ... any attempt to test a decision by reference to what P would hypothetically have done or wanted runs the risk of amounting to a "substituted judgment" rather than a decision of what would be in P's best interests.'

Persons to consult

2.34   The decision maker must take into account in regard to all these matters, if it is practicable and appropriate to consult them, the views of:

(a)   anyone named by the person as someone to be consulted on the matter in question or on matters of that kind;

(b)   anyone engaged in caring for the person or interested in his welfare;

(c)   any donee of a lasting power of attorney granted by the person; and

(d)   any deputy appointed for the person by the court.

2.35   As a safeguard, it is provided that there is sufficient compliance if, having done all these things, the decision maker reasonably believes that what he does or decides is in the best interests of the person concerned. The Code of Practice suggests:[23]

> 'Decision-makers must show they have thought carefully about who to speak to. They must be able to explain why they did not speak to a particular person – it is good practice to keep a good record of their reasons. It is also good practice to give careful consideration to the views of family carers, if it is possible to do so.'

The requirement for consultation must be balanced against the right to confidentiality. Consultation should only take place where relevant and with people whom it is appropriate to consult.

Least restrictive alternative

2.36   Before any action is taken, or any decision is made in relation to a person lacking capacity, consideration should be given to whether it is possible to act or decide in a way that interferes less with the person's rights and freedom of action. Where there is more than one course of action or a choice of decisions to be made, all possible options should be explored (including whether there is a need for any action or decision at all) in order

---

[22]   *Re P (Statutory Will)* [2009] EWHC 163 (Ch), Lewison J.
[23]   Code of Practice, para 5.51.

to consider which option would be the least restrictive. However, other options need only be considered so long as the desired purpose of the action or decision can still be achieved.

Reasonable belief

2.37   In cases where the court is not involved, carers (both professionals and family members) and others who are acting informally can only be expected to have reasonable grounds for believing that what they are doing or deciding is in the best interests of the person concerned, but they must still, so far as possible, apply the best interests checklist and therefore be able to point to objective reasons to justify why they hold that belief. This also applies to donees and deputies appointed to make welfare or financial decisions and to those carrying out acts in connection with the care and treatment of a person lacking capacity. In deciding what is 'reasonable' in any particular case, higher expectations are likely to be placed on those appointed to act under formal powers and those acting in a professional capacity than on family members and friends who are caring for a person without any formal authority.

GENERAL POWERS AND DUTIES

Acts in connection with care or treatment

Protection from liability (section 5)

2.38   There has in the past been uncertainty about what actions could lawfully be taken by carers in looking after the day-to-day personal or health care needs of people unable to consent. This could include helping individuals to wash, dress and attend to their personal hygiene, feeding them, taking them out for walks and leisure activities or taking them to the doctor or dentist. In consequence, health care professionals have been hesitant about carrying out examinations, treatment or nursing care. Usually the common law 'principle of necessity' has been relied upon.

2.39   Section 5 applies where someone acts in connection with the care or treatment of another person and affords statutory protection against liability for acts which are in the person's best interests.[24] If they first take reasonable steps to establish and then reasonably believe that the person lacks capacity and that the act will be in the person's best interests, then they will not incur any liability which they would not have incurred if the person did have capacity and had consented. This is sometimes regarded as a general authority (as proposed by the Law Commission) but in reality it is a statutory defence. The intention is to allow carers and health care professionals to do whatever is necessary to safeguard and promote the welfare and health of individuals who lack capacity, so long as it is appropriate for the particular carer or professional to take the action and the act is in the best interests of the incapacitated person.

2.40   This does not exclude any civil liability for loss or damage, or any criminal liability, resulting from negligence in doing the act. Nor does it authorise a person to do an act which conflicts with a decision made, within the scope of his authority, by a donee of an LPA or a deputy appointed by the court.

---

[24]   See generally Code of Practice, para 6.

2.41 Guidance on the exercise of these powers is to be found in a judgment of Mr Justice Baker:[25]

> '(i)   The vast majority of decisions about incapacitated adults are taken by carers and others without any formal general authority. That was the position prior to the passing of the MCA under the principle of necessity ... In passing the MCA, Parliament ultimately rejected the Law Commission's proposal of a statutory general authority and opted for the same approach as under the previous law by creating in section 5 a statutory defence to protect all persons who carry out acts in connection with the care or treatment of an incapacitated adult, provided they reasonably believe that it will be in that person's best interests for the act to be done. Crucially, however, all persons who provide such care and treatment are expected to look to the Code ...
>
> (ii)   The Act and Code are therefore constructed on the basis that the vast majority of decisions concerning incapacitated adults are taken informally and collaboratively by individuals or groups of people consulting and working together. It is emphatically not part of the scheme underpinning the Act that there should be one individual who as a matter of course is given a special legal status to make decisions about incapacitated persons.
>
> (iii)   It will usually be the case that decisions about complex and serious issues are taken by a court rather than any individual. In certain cases, as explained in paragraphs 8.38 and 8.39 of the Code, it will be more appropriate to appoint a deputy or deputies to make these decisions. But because it is important that such decisions should wherever possible be taken collaboratively and informally, the appointments must be as limited in scope and duration as is reasonably practicable in the circumstances. ... the appointment of deputies is likely to be more common for property and affairs than for personal welfare.'

Restraint

2.42 This power is qualified by s 6 which provides that acts of restraint will not be covered unless there is a reasonable belief that it is necessary to do the act in order to prevent harm and the act is a proportionate response to the likelihood of suffering harm and the seriousness of that harm. Restraint means the use of, or threats to use, force to secure the doing of an act which is resisted, or restricting the person's liberty of movement, whether or not the person resists. Restraint may take many forms. It may be verbal or physical and may vary from shouting at someone to locking them in a room. It may also include the prescribing of a sedative which restricts liberty of movement.

2.43 This does not stop a person providing life-sustaining treatment, or doing any act which he reasonably believes to be necessary to prevent a serious deterioration in the person's condition, while a decision as respects any relevant issue is sought from the court. 'Life-sustaining treatment' means treatment which in the view of a person providing health care for the person is necessary to sustain life.

Conflict situations

2.44 Where formal decision-making powers already exist, for example under an LPA or through an order made by the Court of Protection, these will take precedence so anyone acting contrary to a decision of a donee or deputy will not have protection from liability so long as the donee or deputy are acting within the scope of their authority.

2.45 Where an advance decision to refuse treatment is known to exist, is clear and unambiguous and is valid and applicable in the circumstances which have arisen, any

---

[25]   *G v E* [2010] EWHC 2042 (Fam) (COP).

health professionals who knowingly provide treatment contrary to the terms of the decision may be liable for battery or assault, or for breach of the patient's human rights.[26] Section 5 does not provide protection from liability in these circumstances.

2.46 In cases of dispute (for example when carers or health professionals feel that a donee or deputy is acting outside the scope of any authority, or contrary to the incapacitated person's best interests) an application may be made for permission to apply to the Court of Protection to resolve the matter. Where the dispute (for example, as to the application of an advance decision to refuse treatment) involves serious health care decisions, life-sustaining treatment, or treatment necessary to prevent a serious deterioration in the person's condition, treatment can be given pending a ruling from the court.

Serious acts relating to medical treatment or welfare

2.47 Concerns were expressed that the scope of the statutory defence in s 5 'remains unclear and is too wide'. The previous requirement, confirmed in a Practice Direction, to seek a declaration from the court in cases where it is proposed to withdraw or withhold life-sustaining treatment from patients in a permanent vegetative state ('PVS') has continued.[27] An additional safeguard is provided where serious medical treatment or a change of residence involving a health or local authority is proposed, but *only* where the person concerned has no family or friends to speak up on his or her behalf. An 'independent mental capacity advocate' must be appointed to advise on the person's best interests.[28]

Life-sustaining treatment

2.48 Special consideration is given to the provision of 'life-sustaining treatment'.[29] In determining whether the treatment is in the best interests of the incapacitated patient, the decision maker must not be motivated by a desire to bring about the individual's death.[30] The starting point is an assumption that it is in the person's best interests for life to continue. There will be some cases (for example in the final stages of terminal illness), where there is no prospect of recovery and it may be in the best interests of the patient to withdraw treatment or give palliative care that might incidentally shorten life. All the factors in the best interests checklist must be considered, but the decision maker must not be motivated in any way by the desire to bring about the person's death.

Financial affairs

Payment for necessary goods and services

2.49 Section 7 provides that if necessary goods or services are supplied to a person who lacks capacity to contract for the supply, he must pay a reasonable price for them. 'Necessary' means suitable to a person's condition in life and to his actual requirements at the time when the goods or services are supplied. What is 'necessary' extends to

---

[26] Advance decisions are dealt with in ss 24–26 and considered below and in Ch 8.

[27] See *Practice Direction E: Applications relating to serious medical treatment (PD 9E)*.

[28] See Mental Capacity Act 2005, ss 35–41. This role is considered in Ch 8.

[29] This is defined as treatment which a person providing health care regards as necessary to sustain the life of a person lacking capacity to consent to that treatment.

[30] Mental Capacity Act 2005, ss 4(5) and (10). Section 62 confirms that the Act does not have the effect of authorising or permitting euthanasia or assisted suicide.

ordinary drink, food and clothing or the provision of domiciliary or residential care services. 'Condition in life' means place in society, rather than any mental or physical condition.

2.50   The responsibility to make payment lies with the person for whom they are supplied even though that person lacks the capacity to contract for them, but the carer who has arranged for the goods or services may have to arrange settlement. However, s 8 provides that if an act within s 5 (dealt with above) involves expenditure, it is lawful for the person doing the act to pledge the credit of the incapacitated person for the purpose of the expenditure, and to apply money in that person's possession for meeting the expenditure or in reimbursing any expenditure actually borne.

2.51   The mechanics of payment are described in the Code of Practice as follows:[31]

'If neither the carer nor the person who lacks capacity can produce the necessary funds, the carer may promise that the person who lacks capacity will pay. A supplier may not be happy with this, or the carer may be worried that they will be held responsible for any debt. In such cases the carer must follow the formal steps ...

If the person who lacks capacity has cash, the carer may use that money to pay for goods or services (for example, to pay the milkman or the hairdresser).

The carer may choose to pay for the goods or services with their own money. The person who lacks capacity must pay them back. This may involve using cash in the person's possession or running up an IOU. ... The carer must follow formal steps to get money held in a bank or building society account.'

The intention is to make it possible for ordinary but necessary goods and services to be provided for people who lack the capacity to organise and pay for them. However, this does not authorise a carer to gain access to the incapacitated person's income or assets or to sell the person's property.

General safeguards

Excluded decisions

2.52   There are certain acts which cannot be done and certain decisions which can never be taken on behalf of people who lack capacity either because they are so personal or are governed by other legislation.[32]

Family relationships etc

2.53   Consents in relation to marriage or a civil partnership (including divorce or dissolution on the basis of 2 years' separation), sexual relations and adoption are included in a list of decisions that cannot be made.

---

[31]   Code of Practice, para 6.61.
[32]   See Mental Capacity Act 2005, ss 27–29.

Mental Health Act matters

2.54   Consent may not be given in respect of treatment for mental disorder which would otherwise be regulated by Part 4 of the Mental Health Act 1983.[33] Thus the 2005 Act cannot be used as a means to avoid the protection afforded by the Mental Health Act.

Voting rights

2.55   The Act does not permit a decision on voting at an election for any public office, or at a referendum, to be made on behalf of a person.

The offence of ill-treatment or neglect

2.56   There were concerns that the ability to acquire powers over another person who lacks capacity may result in abuse. In consequence new offences have been created of ill-treating or wilfully neglecting such person.[34] These apply to 'anyone who has the care of' a person lacking, or reasonably believed to lack, capacity so will include not only family carers, donees of LPAs[35] and deputies, but also health and social care staff in hospital or care homes or providing domiciliary care.[36]

Ill-treatment

2.57   It is necessary to establish deliberate conduct which could properly be described as ill-treatment, whether or not it had caused or was likely to cause harm, but a single act may be sufficient.[37] The accused must either realise that he is inexcusably ill-treating the other person, or be reckless as to whether he is doing so.[38]

Wilful neglect

2.58   It has been held in the context of children that neglect cannot be described as *wilful* unless the person either had directed his mind to whether there was some risk that the child's health might suffer from the neglect and had made a conscious decision to refrain from acting, or had so refrained because he did not care whether the child might be at risk or not.[39] The Court of Appeal has expressed concern about the difficulty of adopting this offence in the context of mental incapacity.[40]

---

[33]   That Part clarifies the extent to which treatment for mental disorder can be imposed on detained patients in hospital and provides specific statutory safeguards concerning the provision of treatment without consent.

[34]   Mental Capacity Act 2005, s 44. There is a maximum penalty of 5 years' imprisonment so these are 'arrestable offences' under s 2 of Police and Criminal Evidence Act 1984.

[35]   Or an attorney under an enduring power of attorney that is still subsisting.

[36]   In the majority of cases, an appointee for state benefits will have care of the person and therefore be covered by the offence.

[37]   See *R v Holmes* [1979] Crim LR 52.

[38]   See *R v Newington* (1990) 91 Cr App R 247, CA.

[39]   *R v Sheppard* [1981] AC 394, [1980] 3 All ER 899, HL (re Children and Young Persons Act 1933, s 1).

[40]   *R v Dunn* [2010] EWCA Crim 2935; *R v Hopkins and R v Priest* [2011] EWCA Crim 1513; *Ligaya Nursing v R* [2012] EWCA Crim 2521.

PROCEDURES OF CHOICE

Overview

2.59 Although there are informal procedures for decisions to be made as described above, and the Court of Protection[41] has power to make decisions or appoint a deputy who may do so, there is a need for adults who have capacity to be able to nominate someone to make decisions for them in the event that they become incapacitated in the future. The law regarding decisions made in advance relating to medical treatment also needed to be clarified. The Act addresses these needs and seeks to provide safeguards.

2.60 The ability to create enduring powers of attorney has been replaced with effect from 1 October 2007 by lasting powers of attorney but the former will continue to operate under their own jurisdiction, although within the framework of the 2005 Act.[42] Thus different procedures as well as laws will operate side by side for many years to come, and the Public Guardian and the Court of Protection will be responsible for administering the two sets of procedures and laws.

Enduring powers of attorney

2.61 A power of attorney is a document whereby a person (the *donor*) gives another person (the *attorney*) power to act on his behalf in his name in regards to his financial affairs. Only a competent person can appoint an attorney, and an attorney under an ordinary power can only continue to act if the donor remains mentally capable. In response to demand for a procedure of choice, legislation in 1985 created the enduring power of attorney (EPA) which remains valid notwithstanding the donor's subsequent incapacity to manage his own affairs.[43] These EPAs provided a practical, inexpensive way in which elderly or infirm people might anticipate incapacity. However, they could only be used for financial affairs and there were few safeguards so it was feared that there was considerable abuse in the use of these powers. An improved procedure was considered necessary. The continued use of EPAs is considered in Chapter 11 as part of financial management.

Lasting powers of attorney

2.62 The Act creates a new statutory form of power of attorney, the lasting power of attorney ('LPA') which replaces the EPA.[44] There are two separate forms applying respectively to financial management and personal welfare decisions (which includes health care). An individual may complete either or both. Unlike the EPA, an LPA can only be used where, in relation to the matter for which capacity to make a decision is required, the donor lacks capacity. The procedures involved in their creation and registration also involve material differences.

---

[41] See **2.102** for more detail.
[42] Mental Capacity Act 2005, s 66(3) and Sch 4.
[43] Enduring Powers of Attorney Act 1985. Replaced by Mental Capacity Act 2005, Sch 4.
[44] Mental Capacity Act 2005, ss 9–14 and Sch 1.

Creation

2.63   Any person who has reached the age of 18 and has capacity to do so may create an LPA.[45] This is done in two stages. First, the donor completes the prescribed form, by signing (or 'executing') it[46] in the presence of a witness or if by someone else at the direction of the donor then in the presence of two witnesses. The second stage is registration with the Public Guardian. Until the LPA is registered, it is ineffective as a power of attorney.

Choice of attorney(s)

2.64   The donee or attorney must be an adult or (in the case of financial management) a trust corporation. Individuals may be appointed jointly or jointly and severally in respect of the entire power or specified matters.[47] The appointment of successive attorneys is permitted, but the attorneys cannot themselves appoint their own successors in the same way that trustees can. A person who is bankrupt can be an attorney under a welfare power but not in respect of property and affairs.

2.65   Where two or more attorneys are appointed *jointly*, they must act together. This provides some protection because they need to co-operate, but is cumbersome to operate and fails if either attorney cannot act. Where appointed *jointly and severally*, each may act independently of the other. Usually they will work separately either with a clear division of responsibility or with one taking a lead role and the other acting as a default attorney. Whilst a professional person might well be suitable to act as an attorney under an EPA for financial management, either alone or jointly with a relative, an attorney acting in respect of a donor's welfare will generally be a relative or friend.

Form

2.66   An LPA must be in the prescribed form and executed in a prescribed manner, comply with certain requirements as to the appointment of an attorney and be registered.[48] The separate LPAs relating to property and affairs and personal welfare (including health care) may need to be used at different times and by different people but the former (unless restricted) can be used at any time after it has been registered, whereas the latter can only be used where the donor lacks capacity. The form must contain statements that:

(a)   the donor has read or had read to him the information explaining the form and intends the attorney to make decisions when he no longer has capacity;

(b)   the attorney has read or has had read to him the information contained in the form and understands the duties imposed on him.

---

[45]   A 'creation and registration pack' which includes the form may be downloaded from the Internet at: www.justice.gov.uk/forms/opg/lasting-power-of-attorney.

[46]   The LPA is a deed so must be executed in accordance with s 1 of the Law of Property (Miscellaneous Provisions) Act 1989. See also Powers of Attorney Act 1971, s 1.

[47]   Where this is unclear there is a presumption in favour of their appointment jointly.

[48]   Lasting Powers of Attorney, Enduring Powers of Attorney and Public Guardian Regulations 2007, SI 2007/1253; Lasting Powers of Attorney, Enduring Powers of Attorney and Public Guardian (Amendment) Regulations 2009, SI 2009/1884. The original form has been revised.

Persons to be notified

2.67 The donor must nominate the person or persons (not being a donee) to be notified of an application to register the LPA, or state that there are no such persons (in which event the LPA must contain two certificates – see below).

Certificate of capacity

2.68 The LPA must contain a certificate by a person of a prescribed description[49] that in his opinion when the instrument was executed:

(a)   the donor understood its purpose and the scope of the authority given;

(b)   no fraud or undue pressure was used to induce the donor to create an LPA; and

(c)   there was nothing else which would prevent an LPA from being created.

This is an important safeguard aimed at protecting the donor from undue influence or abuse and avoiding subsequent doubts about the validity of the power. The LPA must contain two certificates if the donor does not require any person to be notified of registration.

Defective forms

2.69 Despite the requirement for an LPA to be in the prescribed form, the Act provides that the Public Guardian can ignore an immaterial difference, and the Court of Protection may:[50]

> 'declare that an instrument which is not in the prescribed form is to be treated as if it were, if it is satisfied that the persons executing the instrument intended it to create a lasting power of attorney.'

Scope

2.70 An attorney's authority is potentially very extensive because he can do whatever the donor could do for himself. This authority may be limited by the terms of the power, the common law, statute and the Court of Protection. At common law there are certain personal acts that cannot be delegated and an attorney cannot act to benefit himself or delegate his authority. The Act imposes some limitations, and the Court of Protection has powers to intervene in the operation of the power.

2.71 An LPA is described as 'a power of attorney under which the donor confers on the donee [*the attorney*] authority to make decisions about ... the donor's ... personal welfare ... and property and affairs ...'. It 'includes authority to make such decisions in circumstances where (*the donor*) no longer has capacity'.[51] The attorney does not require permission to make an application to the Court of Protection, and the court is given power to determine questions arising in respect of LPAs which reflect those under existing procedures relating to enduring powers.

---

[49]   Defined by regulations and set out in the prescribed form – Mental Capacity Act 2005, Sch 1, Part 1, para 1(3). Lasting Powers of Attorney, Enduring Powers of Attorney and Public Guardian Regulations 2007, SI 2007/1253.

[50]   Mental Capacity Act 2005, Sch 1, Part 1, para 3(2).

[51]   Mental Capacity Act 2005, s 9(1).

Finance limitations

2.72 The attorney will have access to and authority to administer all the donor's property and affairs, but must act in the best interests of the donor and in accordance with the principles of the Act. The donor must therefore take into account matters such as the donor's past and present wishes and feelings, beliefs and values and the other factors the donor would consider if able to do so. A balance may need to be achieved between these wishes and prudent management of the estate.

Power to maintain others

2.73 Unlike the Enduring Powers of Attorney Act 1985, the 2005 Act makes no reference to the maintenance of anyone other than the donor. There is no express power for the attorney to act upon any moral obligation the donor might have to maintain, for instance, a spouse or a minor child. Doing so may, of course, fall within the best interests criteria which are not confined to selfish interests, and in such cases no specific authority is required, however in all other cases, such as maintaining a disabled adult child or paying university fees for a teenage child the Court of Protection is required to confirm the need for such support.

Gifts

2.74 An attorney has no general power to make gifts but, subject to any restriction contained in the power, may make gifts:[52]

'(a) on customary occasions to persons (including himself) who are related to or connected with the donor, or

(b) to any charity to whom the donor made or might have been expected to make gifts,

if the value of each such gift is not unreasonable having regard to all the circumstances and, in particular, the size of the donor's estate.'

'Customary occasion' includes all types of family, seasonal or religious events which justify the making of a gift. This would appear to exclude gifts for tax planning purposes unrelated to such occasions, but an attorney could continue an established pattern of giving, for instance maintaining standing orders to charities.

2.75 Where there is any doubt about the attorney's authority to make the gift or a proposed gift exceeds the statutory authority, the Court of Protection can authorise the gift under its powers in relation to the operation of LPAs. The court cannot ignore an express limitation in the power itself and allow the attorney to exceed his authority under the power,[53] but the attorney or any other person may request the court to authorise a gift under its general powers.

The donor as trustee

2.76 An attorney acting under an LPA has no power to act as a trustee unless the power complies with s 25 of the Trustee Act 1925 or the provisions of s 36 of the Trustee Act 1925 (as amended) apply. This latter provision saves most domestic situations where a property is owned by husband and wife under a trust for land. Where

---

[52]   Mental Capacity Act 2005, s 12(2), (3).
[53]   See *Re R (Enduring Power of Attorney)* [1990] Ch 647, [1990] 2 All ER 893.

one of the owners, who is also a trustee for land, becomes incapable the attorney of the incapable trustee – acting under a registered power[54] – can appoint a new trustee to join in the sale and give a valid receipt for capital moneys.

The donor as a litigant

2.77 An attorney acting under an LPA has no standing as an attorney to bring or defend court proceedings on behalf of the donor. A person's right to conduct proceedings is governed by the rules of the court in which those proceedings take place.[55] Whether a person has capacity to conduct proceedings is specific to the matter for which capacity is required. A person may therefore have capacity to conduct proceedings even though he or she might otherwise be unable to administer his property and affairs.[56]

Welfare limitations

2.78 The donor of an LPA may authorise the attorney to make decisions on his or her behalf about personal welfare or specified matters concerning personal welfare. This includes where and with whom the donor shall live and whether to give or refuse consent to medical treatment. The attorney may not make decisions if the donor has capacity to do so, and must act in accordance with the donor's best interests. He may not make any of the excluded decisions mentioned above in regard to the general authority, and may not restrain the donor unless the criteria of s 6 are fulfilled.

2.79 The attorney may give formal consent to treatment and thus avoid the need for the doctor to rely on s 5, but in any event should be consulted and may veto the exercise of that authority.[57] The authority of an attorney under an LPA made after an advance decision in respect of treatment takes precedence over the refusal of consent contained in that advance decision, but is subject to a valid and applicable advance decision made after the LPA.[58]

2.80 The attorney only has authority to give or refuse consent to life-sustaining treatment if this is expressly allowed by the LPA and the authority is subject to any restrictions or conditions in the power. This power of 'life and death' is subject to two further safeguards:

(1) a person considering whether a life sustaining treatment is in a person's best interests must not be motivated by a desire to bring about his death; and

(2) the declaration in s 2 that the existing law relating to murder or manslaughter is not affected by anything contained in the Act.

These provisions are controversial. How can the authority's refusal of consent to 'life-sustaining treatment' be reconciled with the requirement that 'best interests' cannot include a desire to bring about the death of the donor? Presumably any decision to withhold treatment must be made on the basis that it is unduly burdensome or futile and not in the best interests of the donor, the motive being to relieve pain and suffering and

---

[54] 'Registered power' is defined as an 'Enduring Power of Attorney or Lasting Power of Attorney registered under the Mental Capacity Act 2005' (Trustee Act 1925, s 36(6C)).

[55] See Ch 3 for civil proceedings and Ch 4 as regards family proceedings.

[56] *Masterman-Lister v Jewell* [2002] EWCA Civ 1889.

[57] Mental Capacity Act 2005, ss 4(7) and 6(6)(a).

[58] Mental Capacity Act 2005, ss 25(2)(b), 11(7)(b) and 25(7).

not to bring about the death of the patient.[59] It should not be assumed that an attorney will merely refuse consent to treatment; the refusal might equally be of consent to the withdrawal of treatment which prolongs the donor's life. Donors will have different views as to the prolongation of life by medical treatment, and it is they who choose their attorneys.

Conditions and restrictions in the LPA

2.81 The authority of an attorney is subject to any conditions or restrictions in the LPA as well as limitations imposed by the Act. The donor may wish to 'tailor' the power to meet personal requirements, but imposing too many restrictions may make it inflexible in practice and lead to the expense and inconvenience of an application to the Court of Protection.

Finance restrictions

2.82 Restrictions in a property and affairs LPA could relate to:

- remuneration for a professional attorney;
- authorising disclosure or safe custody of the donor's will;
- requiring the attorney to render an account to a third party such as another member of the family, a solicitor or an accountant;[60]
- restricting its operation to specified circumstances;
- setting a maximum amount for gifts or prohibiting gifts without the consent of the court or a third party;
- restricting the amount of capital which can be applied or limiting the value of transactions that may be entered into;
- confirming the revocation of an earlier LPA or EPA;
- requiring the consent of a third party to the disposal of a particular asset, such as the family home or shares in a family company.

Welfare restrictions

2.83 The donor of a welfare LPA may have strong views as to whether or not it extends to the giving or refusing of consent to life-sustaining treatment. Special conditions might include:

- requiring decisions to be taken in consultation with or subject to the agreement of a named person or subject to medical advice;
- restricting the right to refuse consent to life-sustaining treatment so that it does not include the right to refuse artificial nutrition and hydration.

---

[59] This is the approach that has been developed at common law – see Ch 8.
[60] The Court of Protection has authority to require an attorney to deliver an account, but it is unlikely that this will be widely exercised – Mental Capacity Act 2005, s 23(3)(a). Any such direction will be for the account to be delivered to a specified relative, accountant or solicitor – not the Public Guardian.

Registration

2.84 The LPA is not properly created and so cannot be used until it is registered.[61] Early registration is encouraged and the fact of registration does not give rise to a presumption of incapacity. This avoids the misuse that arises with EPAs which are often used when they should be registered with the result that the donor's interests are not protected and the attorney (who may be acting in good faith) is acting without authority.

Implications of early registration

2.85 There are disadvantages in this approach to registration. A third party dealing with the donor cannot make any assumption as to the donor's lack of capacity, but must make his own assessment at the relevant time. It follows that, unlike the EPA, a bank cannot rely on the fact of registration to prevent the donor using his account so there will be less protection than at present. The expense and inconvenience of registration may also discourage this step being taken at the time the power is signed. Many LPAs may stipulate that they are only to be used (and thus are registered) on incapacity.

Status of attorney prior to registration

2.86 The attorney is not given transitional or temporary authority to act under the LPA whilst an application to register is pending.[62] In this respect the LPA differs from an EPA, and the apparent omission may cause difficulties for an attorney who needs to manage the donor's affairs while the power is being registered. If registration is seriously delayed by a dispute over the validity of the power or the conduct of the attorney, an application must be made to the Court of Protection for a specific order unless s 5 can be relied upon or a payment is for necessaries.

Procedure on registration

2.87 Registration is with the Public Guardian[63] and the application may be made by the donor as well as by an attorney. The procedure is relatively straightforward (in contrast to that for an EPA), involving the completion and submission of the prescribed form with the original LPA and payment of a fee. The form is prescribed by regulations and contains enough information about the donor, the donee or donees and service of notices to enable the Public Guardian to deal with the registration process. Where the donor has created separate LPAs in respect of financial affairs and welfare matters, they may be registered separately and not necessarily at the same time. Many donors whose property and affairs are dealt with by an attorney will carry on being cared for informally without the need for intervention by a welfare attorney but it is prudent to register a welfare power following signature because it can never be anticipated when the authority of an attorney is required to resolve a dispute or contentious treatment.

2.88 The person applying to register the LPA must give notice in the prescribed form of the intention to register the power to any person named in the LPA for that purpose.[64] The form of notice and method of service are prescribed by regulations. The Public Guardian is responsible for notifying the donor (where the application is made by a

---

[61] Mental Capacity Act 2005, s 9(2)(b), Lasting Powers of Attorney, Enduring Powers of Attorney and Public Guardian Regulations 2007, SI 2007/1253.

[62] Compare the provisions that relate to enduring powers of attorney – see Ch 11.

[63] In accordance with Sch 1 of the 2005 Act and Lasting Powers of Attorney, Enduring Powers of Attorney and Public Guardian Regulations 2007, SI 2007/1253.

[64] Mental Capacity Act 2005, Sch 1, para 6. There is no requirement to notify any close relatives or carers unless they are so named.

donee) or the donees where the application is made by the donor. The court can dispense with the service of notice on a named person (but not the donor) if satisfied that no useful purpose would be served by giving notice.

Completion of registration

2.89   The Public Guardian must register the LPA at the end of the prescribed period unless there is an objection or it appears not to be a valid power, in which event it cannot be registered unless directed by the court.[65] If a deputy has already been appointed and it appears to the Public Guardian that the powers conferred on the deputy would conflict with the powers conferred on the attorney the power cannot be registered unless directed by the court.

2.90   The Public Guardian notifies the donor and donees of registration in a prescribed form. The original LPA is sealed and endorsed with details of the registration and returned to the applicant or any solicitor involved, but office copies comprise conclusive evidence of registration and the contents of the power.[66]

Objections to registration

2.91   Schedule 1 of the Mental Capacity Act 2005 deals with objections to registration.

Role of the Public Guardian

2.92   An objection to registration from a donee or a named person may be made to the Office of the Public Guardian on one of the following technical grounds:

(1)   the bankruptcy of the donor or donee (for a financial LPA only);

(2)   disclaimer by the donee (attorney);

(3)   death of a donee;

(4)   dissolution or annulment of the marriage or civil partnership between the donor and the donee (unless the power excludes revocation in these circumstances); or

(5)   the donee lacks capacity.

2.93   If it appears that the ground for making the objection is satisfied, the Public Guardian can refuse to register the power without reference to the court.[67] In these cases the LPA is either revoked or the appointment of the attorney terminated by operation of law rather than the intervention of the Public Guardian. Any dispute will be referred to the court which may refuse to register the LPA or, if the donor lacked capacity, revoke the LPA.[68] If the donor objects to registration, the Public Guardian must refuse to register the LPA unless the court is satisfied that the donor lacks capacity to object.[69]

---

[65]   Mental Capacity Act 2005, Sch 1, para 11(1). For example, where the power was made using the incorrect form or there was a technical defect in the form which prevented it from operating as a valid LPA.

[66]   Mental Capacity Act 2005, s 16(1).

[67]   Mental Capacity Act 2005, Sch 1, para 13(1) and (2). These are the narrow grounds defined in s 13(3) and (6)(a)–(d).

[68]   Mental Capacity Act 2005, s 22(4). The power to refuse registration or revoke the power is without prejudice to the court's powers to give directions under s 22.

[69]   Mental Capacity Act 2005, Sch 1, para 14.

Intervention by the Court of Protection

2.94   There may also be an objection from the donee or a named person on one of the 'prescribed' grounds, and the Public Guardian must not then register the power unless directed by the court.[70] The 'prescribed grounds' are not defined by the 2005 Act but mirror the grounds on which the court can revoke a power, namely:

(1)   revocation or termination of the power;

(2)   fraud or undue pressure used to induce the donor to execute the power;

(3)   that the donee has behaved, is behaving or proposes to behave in a way that contravenes his or her authority or contrary to the donor's best interests.

2.95   The court can determine any question relating to whether or not any of the requirements for creating or revoking a lasting power have been met.[71] This question may relate to the formal requirements of completing and executing the power or the capacity of the donor to grant the power. The court will assume that an LPA which has been correctly executed and contains the required certificate has been validly executed, so the burden of proving otherwise lies with the objector. Unless there is clear and compelling evidence that the donor lacked capacity at the time of execution or that there was fraud or undue influence, the court must register the LPA. The court's powers are not limited to the period of registration, but can be exercised at any time after a person has executed a power or a power has been registered as an LPA. However, an objection to registration made after the power has been registered will require the leave of the court.

Advance decisions

2.96   The Act gives statutory force to the existing law relating to what became known as 'living wills' or 'advance directives'.[72] This topic is dealt with in Chapter 8.[73]

2.97   In response to public concerns there is a declaration that nothing in the Act is to be taken to affect the law relating to murder or manslaughter or the operation of s 2 of the Suicide Act 1961 which relates to assisting suicide.

POWERS OF THE COURT OF PROTECTION

Overview

2.98   The Act only sets out the basic powers of the new Court of Protection and how these are to be implemented depend on the new Court Rules and Practice Directions.[74] The court may make declarations as to whether a person lacks capacity in regard to a particular decision or class of decisions, and if there is a lack of capacity may make decisions concerning personal welfare or property and affairs or appoint a deputy to do so. The court may also control deputies and attorneys. This represents the core

---

[70]   Mental Capacity Act 2005, Sch 1, para 13(3) and (4).
[71]   Mental Capacity Act 2005, s 22(2).
[72]   This is often incorrectly quoted as 'advanced directives'.
[73]   See also Mental Capacity Act 2005, ss 24–26.
[74]   Court of Protection Rules 2007, SI 2007/1744.

jurisdiction of the court which will adopt a best interests approach but also choose the least restrictive intervention. These functions are summarised in the following paragraphs.

Declarations

2.99 In regard to serious medical treatment and, more recently, welfare decisions the High Court has found it necessary to make declarations as to both capacity and then best interests when there is uncertainty or dispute over these issues in relation to an individual. The High Court has had to do this under its inherent powers because there was no power to make decisions on behalf of those who lack capacity. This vacuum in the law has now been resolved by the Mental Capacity Act 2005 which not only puts declarations on a statutory basis but also enables decisions to be made. The new Court of Protection may make declarations as to:

(a) whether a person has or lacks capacity to make a specified decision;

(b) whether a person has or lacks capacity to make decisions on matters described in the declaration;

(c) the lawfulness of any act done, or to be done, in relation to that person.[75]

Declarations as to capacity

2.100 Under the new jurisdiction there is a constant need to reassess capacity in regard to different decisions and at different times. This power to make declarations as to capacity in regard to a particular decision or range of decisions is therefore of considerable importance.

Declarations as to medical treatment

2.101 Although the Court of Protection may make decisions concerning medical treatment, it is likely that in serious or developing situations a declaration as to the lawfulness of treatment will be preferred because this delegates to the medical profession on a continuing basis the decision as to whether treatment is still appropriate in the circumstances. For situations where the treatment will definitely be provided if it is authorised (eg non-therapeutic dental treatment or cosmetic surgery for a learning disabled adult) there is no reason why the court should not exercise its power to make the treatment decision.

Decisions and deputies

2.102 If a person lacks capacity in relation to a matter or matters concerning personal welfare, or property and affairs, the court is given certain powers. These are subject to the provisions of the Act and, in particular, to the principles set out in s 1 and the best interests criteria set out in s 4. In these situations the court may by an order:

(a) make any decisions on the person's behalf; or

(b) appoint a person (a 'deputy') to make decisions on the person's behalf in relation to those matters.[76]

---

[75] Mental Capacity Act 2005, s 15. An 'act' includes an omission and a course of conduct.
[76] Mental Capacity Act 2005, s 16.

An order of the court may be varied or discharged by a subsequent order.

Making decisions

Personal welfare

2.103 The power to make decisions as respects the person's personal welfare extends in particular to:[77]

(a)   deciding where to live;

(b)   deciding what contact, if any, to have with other persons (including family);

(c)   giving or refusing consent to the carrying out or continuation of a treatment by a person providing health care;

(d)   allowing a different person to take over responsibility for health care.

Property and affairs

2.104 The power as respects the person's property and affairs extends in particular to:[78]

(a)   the control and management of property;[79]

(b)   carrying on any profession, trade or business;

(c)   dissolving a business partnership;

(d)   carrying out a contract;

(e)   the discharge of debts or obligations, whether legally enforceable or not;

(f)   the settlement of any property;

(g)   the execution of a will;

(h)   the exercise of any power held beneficially or as trustee or otherwise;

(i)   the conduct of legal proceedings.

Wills and settlements

2.105 The court can thus, if the person is an adult who lacks testamentary capacity, authorise someone else to execute a will on his or her behalf[80] which has the same effect for all purposes as if the person had had the capacity to make a valid will, and the will had been duly executed by him or her. The will may make any provision which could be made by a will executed by the person if he or she had capacity to make it.[81] The court now approaches this on the basis of the statutory test of 'best interests' rather than the approach of the former Court of Protection which was to deem a lucid interval.[82]

2.106 Further provisions enable the court to preserve the interests of others (eg under a will or in intestacy) in property disposed of on behalf of the person lacking capacity.

---

[77]   Mental Capacity Act 2005, s 17.

[78]   Mental Capacity Act 2005, s 18.

[79]   Including the acquisition, sale, exchange, charging, gift or other disposition of property.

[80]   There are provisions as to execution of wills in Sch 2 of the 2005 Act. Special provisions in regard to settlements are also to be found in Sch 2.

[81]   See *Practice Direction F: Applications relating to statutory wills, codicils, settlements and other dealing with P's property (PD9F)*.

[82]   *Re P (Statutory Will)* [2009] EWHC 163 (Ch); *Re M (Statutory Will)* [2009] EWHC 2525 (Fam).

This might involve transferring the interest to another property or imposing a charge on property that has been improved at the person's expense.[83]

Appointment of deputies

2.107 Instead of making decisions itself, the court may appoint a person (a 'deputy') to make decisions on the incapacitated person's behalf in relation to matters concerning personal welfare, or property and affairs, or both.[84] A deputy becomes the person's agent in relation to anything done within the scope of the appointment. When deciding whether to appoint a deputy the court must have regard (in addition to best interests) to the principles that:

(a)   a decision by the court is to be preferred to appointment of a deputy; and

(b)   the powers conferred on a deputy should be as limited in scope and duration as is reasonably practicable in the circumstances.

Thus a one-off decision will be preferred to the appointment of a deputy where that will suffice.

Who to appoint

2.108 A deputy must consent to the appointment and be an adult or (in the case of financial management) a trust corporation but could be a specified office holder. Two or more deputies may be appointed to act jointly, jointly and severally, or jointly in respect of some matters and jointly and severally in respect of others. The court may also appoint successors in such circumstances as may be specified.

Control

2.109 The court may, on an application (which may be made by the Public Guardian in the event of abuse having been reported), revoke the appointment or vary the powers conferred on a deputy if satisfied that the deputy's behaviour breaches his authority or is not in the person's best interests. The court may require a deputy:

(a)   to give to the Public Guardian such security as the court thinks fit for the due discharge of his or her functions; and

(b)   to submit to the Public Guardian such reports at such times or at such intervals as the court may direct.

Powers

2.110 The court may confer on a deputy powers to take possession or control of all or any specified part of the person's property and to exercise all or any specified powers in respect of it, including such powers of investment as the court may determine. The deputy is entitled to be reimbursed for reasonable expenses and, if the court so directs, also to remuneration out of the person's property.

2.111 The authority conferred on a deputy is always subject to the provisions of the 2005 Act and, in particular, to the principles set out in s 1 and the best interests criteria set out in s 4. A deputy does not have power to make a decision if he knows or has

---

[83]   Mental Capacity Act 2005, Sch 2, paras 8 and 9.
[84]   Mental Capacity Act 2005, s 19.

reasonable grounds for believing that the person has capacity to do so, and may not impose restraint unless he reasonably believes that this is necessary to prevent harm and a proportionate response to the likelihood of the person suffering harm and the seriousness of that harm.

2.112 There are various restrictions on the powers that the court may give to deputies.[85] In particular a deputy may not be given power:

(a)   to prohibit a named individual from having contact;

(b)   to direct that a different person take over responsibility for health care;

(c)   with respect to the settlement of property;

(d)   with respect to the execution of a will;

(e)   with respect to the exercise of any power vested in the person; or

(f)   to make a decision which is inconsistent with a valid decision made by an attorney under an LPA.

A deputy may not refuse consent to the carrying out or continuation of life-sustaining treatment.

Control of attorneys

2.113 The court retains statutory powers which are exercisable at any time, to revoke or cancel the registration of an EPA or LPA or attach conditions to the attorney's conduct, and also to guide the attorney or provide authority where the attorney requires this to carry out his or her duties under the power.[86] This is in addition to the court's general powers which are exercisable in respect of any matter in which a person lacks capacity, whether or not the attorney has authority to act in respect of the same matter.

2.114 A donor or an attorney under an LPA does not require permission from the court to make an application for the exercise of any of its powers. Neither does the Act appear to prevent the court from exercising its powers of its own volition, for instance in response to a report made to it by the Public Guardian or a Visitor.

THE COURT AND SUPPORTING SERVICES

Overview

2.115 The Act establishes the new Court of Protection, creates the office of Public Guardian and makes provision for the Visitors and also Independent Mental Capacity Advocates.[87] The court is supported by the Official Solicitor and the Court Funds Office.

2.116 References in the Act to the Lord Chancellor have been overtaken by the Constitutional Reform Act 2005 and a subsequent Concordat established between the Lord Chancellor and the Lord Chief Justice. The aim of these reforms is to put the relationship between the executive, legislature and judiciary on a modern footing,

---

85   See Mental Capacity Act 2005, s 20.
86   These matters are considered under Lasting Powers of Attorney above.
87   Mental Capacity Act 2005, ss 44–61.

respecting the separation of powers. The Secretary of State at the Ministry of Justice now ensures that there is an efficient and effective system to support the courts, whilst judiciary-related functions have been transferred to the Lord Chief Justice. Appointment of judges is the responsibility of the Judicial Appointments Commission whilst their training remains with the Judicial College. The Mental Capacity Act 2005 must be interpreted subject to these changes.

Court of Protection

Structure

2.117 From 1 October 2007 a new superior court of record known as the Court of Protection came into existence and the former Court of Protection, which was merely an office of the Supreme Court, ceased to exist. The new court may sit at any place in England and Wales on any day and at any time. It has a President, a Vice-President and a Senior Judge having administrative functions[88] and a central office and registry in London with additional registries at any district registry of the High Court or county court office. The jurisdiction of the new court is exercised by nominated High Court, circuit and district judges.

Powers of the court

2.118 The court has in connection with its jurisdiction the same powers, rights, privileges and authority as the High Court. This gives it an extremely wide range of powers but these may only be exercised 'for the purposes of this Act'. Office copies of orders made, directions given or other instruments issued and sealed with its official seal are admissible in all legal proceedings as evidence of the originals without any further proof.

Interim orders and directions

2.119 The court may, pending the determination of an application to it in relation to a person, make an order or give directions in respect of any matter if there is reason to believe that this person lacks capacity in relation to the matter, the matter is one to which its powers under this Act extend, and it is in the person's best interests to make the order, or give the directions, without delay. This enables the court to make interim orders even before making a finding of incapacity.

Power to call for reports

2.120 The court may require a report to be made to it in writing or orally, by the Public Guardian or a Court of Protection Visitor.[89] It may also require a local authority or an NHS body to arrange for a report to be made by one of its officers or employees, or such other person as the authority or body considers appropriate.[90] The report must deal with such matters relating to the person to whom the proceedings relate as the court may direct or the Court of Protection Rules specify.[91]

---

[88] The President of the Family Division and the Chancellor of the High Court have hitherto been appointed President and Vice-President respectively and the former Master of the (old) Court of Protection is the first Senior Judge.

[89] See para 2.124 for more detail.

[90] Mental Capacity Act 2005, s 49.

[91] Court of Protection Rules 2007, r 117; Practice Direction E: *Section 49 reports* (PD14E).

2.121 When preparing a report the Public Guardian or a Court of Protection Visitor may, at all reasonable times, examine and take copies of any health record, any record of, or held by, a local authority and compiled in connection with a social services function, and any record held by a person registered under Part 2 of the Care Standards Act 2000 so far as the record relates to the person.

Practice and procedure

Rules and Practice Directions

2.122 New Rules[92] set out the practice and procedure of the court and make provision as to such matters as the way in which proceedings are to be commenced, the persons entitled to be involved, dealing with cases without a hearing or in private, the presentation of evidence and enforcement of orders.[93] In addition the President may make Practice Directions as to the general practice and procedure of the court.

Permission to apply

2.123 There is a screening process to prevent those who seek to interfere without justification from causing inconvenience and expense to others whilst hopefully not discouraging genuine applications. Certain categories of person have a right to apply but others must obtain permission from the court.[94]

2.124 No permission is required for most property and affairs applications or for an application by a person who lacks, or is alleged to lack, capacity. Similarly for the donee of an LPA or a deputy appointed by the court for a person to whom the application relates, or for a person named in an existing order of the court if the application relates to the order. Permission may be required for any other application and this is dealt with in the Rules.[95] In deciding whether to grant permission the court must have regard to the applicant's connection with the person to whom the application relates, the reasons for the application, the benefit to the person to whom the application relates of a proposed order or directions and whether the benefit can be achieved in any other way.

Rights of appeal

2.125 There is some flexibility as to how appeals may be dealt with, but appeal routes have been established to a higher level of nominated judge and thence to the Court of Appeal although appeals raising important issues may go direct to the Court of Appeal. Permission is required to appeal in specified cases.[96]

Fees and costs

Fees

2.126 It was Government policy that the former Court of Protection should be self-funding, raising its income from court fees, although some subsidy was necessary for those who could not afford the fees. This policy is continued but the subsidy must

---

92   Court of Protection Rules 2007, SI 2007/1744.
93   Mental Capacity Act 2005, s 51.
94   See Court of Protection Rules 2007, Part 8, rr 50–60.
95   See Part 8, rules 50–60. Most applications for permission to pursue a full application will be dealt with on paper (ie without an attended hearing) but there is a right to be heard in the event that permission is refused.
96   Mental Capacity Act 2005, s 53, Court of Protection Rules 2007, Part 20, rr 169–182.

inevitably be enhanced for the new enlarged jurisdiction because many applications will relate to situations where there is no money available or involved.[97]

Costs

2.127 The general rule is that in property and affairs cases the costs of and incidental to the proceedings of all parties are payable out of the funds of the incapacitated person. It is different for personal welfare applications where costs orders are not generally made. But the court has a discretion and can deny costs to a party who has behaved inappropriately or even order a party to pay the costs of other parties. The court may even order the legal or other representatives concerned to meet any 'wasted costs'. These are costs incurred by a party as a result of any improper, unreasonable or negligent act or omission on the part of the representative.[98]

Challenges for the new court

2.128 The former Court of Protection was little known and often misunderstood within the court system, but this has changed with generic judges becoming involved and a regional presence. The new court no longer operates in isolation and there is more involvement with the civil and family courts with the jurisdiction no longer restricted to financial affairs.

2.129 Hearings may now take place at a venue more local to the parties but having a centralised administration with satellite courts can create problems.[99] One of the advantages is that more provincial lawyers are appearing before the 'local' Court of Protection and thereby gaining experience with which they may better advise their clients. Telephone conferences and video links are increasingly being utilised.

The workload

2.130 There is a wider range of cases under the new jurisdiction because this relates to the entire range of personal decision making for adults who lack capacity. More people are involved because those entitled to be consulted as part of a best interests determination include 'anyone engaged in caring for the person or interested in his welfare'. The previous unmet need for a decision-making body is emerging but lack of public funding results in a high proportion of unrepresented parties. Resolution techniques are being developed (eg referring welfare and health care issues initially to multi-disciplinary case conferences) but the more intransigent cases inevitably reach the court.

2.131 The following are examples of situations concerning an elderly person that need to be dealt with under the new jurisdiction but were not encountered by the former Court of Protection or the High Court under its declaratory judgment jurisdiction:

> **Care dispute** – Dispute between a son and daughter who live some distance apart as to which residential care or nursing home their mother should move to. She has Alzheimer's disease and is incapable of participating in the decision but has adequate funds to meet the fees.

---

[97] Mental Capacity Act 2005, s 54 provides for scales or rates of fees, exemptions from and reductions in fees and remission of fees in whole or in part. See Court of Protection Fees Order 2007 (updated at intervals).

[98] Court of Protection Rules 2007, Part 19, rr 155–168 and various Practice Directions.

[99] These were largely resolved in a pilot under the former court whereby from September 2001 District Judge Ashton heard northern cases at Preston as a Deputy Master.

Welfare dispute – A local authority moves an elderly person who lacks capacity into a care home for protection from an abusing family carer and the carer challenges this action.

Procedural issues

2.132 There are many issues faced by the new Court of Protection. How formal should hearings be? Should the public be admitted and anonymised case reports published, or will it be a contempt to publish information about the hearing? Flexibility is desirable because the various categories of case that come before the court require different treatment. There is a world of difference between contested hearings involving a dysfunctional family and fund management meetings intended to reassure hesitant deputies.

2.133 Who is, or may be, party to the proceedings and must this include the incapacitated person to whom the proceedings relate, in which event should this party be represented by a litigation friend? An adversarial approach may not assist when all the parties are failing to address the best interests of this person and how is such representation to be funded especially where the issue does not concern financial affairs? Many hearings may be conducted informally in the judge's chambers with an inquisitorial approach. It may not then be necessary to identify parties to the proceedings as long as everyone with a legitimate interest is given the opportunity to attend. Only those cases where significant findings of fact are required (eg allegations of serious financial defalcations or ill-treatment) will necessitate a formal trial with an adversarial approach, the parties being identified in advance and evidence being given on oath.

Overlapping issues

2.134 Cases in the civil or family courts with a capacity element can be transferred to a nominated Court of Protection judge who has the necessary experience and may arrange to sit in a dual jurisdiction where appropriate. For example:

Ancillary relief – Following a divorce between an elderly couple financial claims are made which include the future of the former matrimonial home. The husband proposes that she remain in the home for life but she cannot grasp the implications and the judge questions whether she lacks mental capacity but she refuses to be medically examined. *A nominated judge to whom the case is transferred could resolve all the issues locally with minimum delay and expense.*

Possession – A landlord or mortgagee brings a possession claim for non-payment of sums due and the elderly tenant or mortgagor attends but appears confused and unable to cope. Doubts arise as to mental capacity and the judge is in great difficulty knowing how to proceed. *A nominated judge could deal with the capacity issue, the need for practical support and the merits of the possession claim, invoking the jurisdiction of the Court of Protection if necessary.*

Residence dispute – Following a divorce between elderly parents there is a dispute as to which parent is to continue to care for their 40-year-old mentally disabled child and the future of the matrimonial home may depend on this. *A nominated district judge could simultaneously deal with the care issue under the new jurisdiction and the ancillary relief claims in the county court, these being interdependent.*

Contact dispute – Older parents with a learning disabled adult son became involved in a bitter divorce which results in father being excluded from the matrimonial home where mother continues to care for this son. The father and a daughter who has sided with him are then denied contact with the son and seek to establish that it is in his best interests to see them on a regular basis. *A nominated judge could resolve the issue under the new jurisdiction in the context of the divorce proceedings thereby having an overview of the whole family situation.*

The Public Guardian

Background

2.135 The former Court of Protection depended upon the support that it received from the Public Guardianship Office ('PGO').[100] This administrative office also provided services to promote the financial and social well-being of those who were not able to manage their own financial affairs because of mental incapacity. The court might, following an application, treat such person as a 'patient' and appoint a receiver to manage the person's affairs. The PGO supported receivers in their duties (the Protection function) and maintained working relationships with patients, their families, carers and any other people or organisations involved in their welfare. As a last resort the Chief Executive of the PGO would act as receiver (the Receivership function) and officers would then be involved in the patient's financial and legal affairs. But the PGO was merely an agency with a chief executive and no independent powers.

2.136 One of the key reforms is the creation of an officer with a statutory function known as the 'Public Guardian' and appointed by the Lord Chancellor. The Public Guardian has an office and staff to whom he may delegate his functions, known as the Office of the Public Guardian ('OPG').[101] This in concept is a very different body from the PGO and it is hoped that the Public Guardian (through his senior staff) will act fearlessly and independently, becoming a facilitator of mediation and a problem solver as well as performing administrative functions.

Functions of the Public Guardian

2.137 The Public Guardian has the following basic functions:[102]

(a)   maintaining registers of LPAs and orders appointing deputies;

(b)   supervising deputies appointed by the court;

(c)   directing a Court of Protection Visitor to visit and to make a report;

(d)   receiving security which the court requires a person to give for the discharge of his functions;

(e)   receiving reports from donees of lasting powers of attorney and deputies appointed by the court;

(f)   reporting to the court on such matters as the court requires;

(g)   dealing with representations (including complaints) about the way in which a donee of a lasting power of attorney or a deputy appointed by the court is exercising his powers.

---

[100]   Previously the Public Trust Office (PTO).

[101]   Office of the Public Guardian, PO Box 16185, Birmingham B2 2WH. DX 744240 Birmingham 79. Tel: 0300 456 0300 (phone lines are open Monday–Friday 9am–5pm, except Wednesday 10am–5pm). Fax: 0870 739 5780. Textphone: 0115 934 2778. Website – www.justice.gov.uk/about/opg.

[102]   Mental Capacity Act 2005, s 58.

(h) publish information about the discharge of his functions and make an Annual Report.

Some of these functions may be discharged in co-operation with any other person who has functions in relation to the care or treatment of the incapacitated person. The Lord Chancellor may confer other functions in connection with the Act on the Public Guardian. There are regulations as to the giving of security, fees, and the making of reports by deputies and others.[103]

2.138 Although the 2005 Act did not expressly provide that the Public Guardian should provide the administration for the Court of Protection, this was the initial arrangement. It raised issues as to independence especially as the Public Guardian may become a party to proceedings with a right of appeal. The administration has since been transferred to Her Majesty's Courts Service (HMCS) which also provides the administration for other courts.

The new role

2.139 The Public Guardian thus has three distinct and sometimes conflicting roles: administrative, supervisory and policymaking. He must:

- be a supporter of incapacitated people and their families and carers;
- be an ally of good attorneys and deputies;
- be an enemy of abusers and a channel for whistle-blowers;
- develop the right public image and educate the public by promoting his services;
- monitor standards in decision making for vulnerable adults that everyone is expected to follow;
- establish procedures for investigating allegations of abuse;
- work with local authorities and other agencies.

The OPG may encourage dispute resolution and has established an Investigations Unit which seeks to safeguard vulnerable adults. It also maintains a panel of suitably experienced lawyers who are available to be appointed as deputies when the need arises. The office is expected to become a 'centre of excellence in service provision for the mentally incapacitated' developing partnerships with social services and health authorities and also those charitable organisations working in this area.

Powers

2.140 In carrying out his functions the Public Guardian may examine and take copies of health and social services records, and any record held by a person registered under Part 2 of the Care Standards Act 2000 so far as the record relates to the incapacitated person and may interview that person in private.[104] The Public Guardian is empowered to apply to the Court of Protection in connection with his functions under the Act in such circumstances as he considers it necessary or appropriate to do so.

---

[103] Lasting Powers of Attorney, Enduring Powers of Attorney and Public Guardian Regulations 2007, SI 2007/1253, Part 4.

[104] Mental Capacity Act 2005, s 58(5).

Fees

2.141 The OPG charges fees for its services independently of the Court of Protection and has a range of fees that apply in different situations.[105] Although the Public Guardian has inherited the objective of full cost recovery in regard to client orientated functions, this will be harder to achieve in a jurisdiction which extends beyond cases where there is money to be administered. The need for waiver of fees on hardship grounds in more cases will exacerbate the shortfall in fee income. It is hoped that lack of resources will not inhibit performance.

Court of Protection Visitors

Background

2.142 The office of Visitor dates from the Lunatics' Visitors Act 1833 which authorised the appointment of two physicians and a barrister to visit patients and report on their care and treatment. The majority of these visits required a combination of social work, public relations and plain common sense and did not warrant the expense of being made by a psychiatrist or counsel, so in 1981 a panel of lay General Visitors was created. Visits were carried out as appropriate on an ad hoc basis and in March 2000 there were six General Visitors each covering a particular region of England and Wales.

2.143 Medical Visitors were asked to address particular issues in their reports, such as:

- capacity to manage and administer property and financial affairs;
- capacity to create or revoke an EPA; and
- testamentary capacity.

These visits were only commissioned where other medical evidence was conflicting, unsatisfactory, or non-existent.

2.144 The General Visitors regarded themselves as 'the eyes and the ears of the Court, and the voice of the patient'. They were the human face of the system and in most cases the only face-to-face contact a patient or receiver had with the authorities. The purpose of their visits was to consider whether a patient's needs were being properly addressed and to draw attention to any action needed to bring about improvements.

2.145 A General Visitor would be asked to carry out a special visit when a particular problem arose. Otherwise routine reports commented on overall care, present and future problems for the court and possible action.

The present regime

2.146 This past experience has been drawn upon for the new mental capacity jurisdiction as regards the role of the Visitors. Although the court may seek reports from the OPG these are generally paper based and when contact with the incapacitated person is required a Visitor will be instructed.

---

[105] Public Guardian (Fees, etc) Regulations 2007, SI 2007/2051 (as amended at intervals). See www.legislation.gov.uk/uksi for the latest version.

Panels of Visitors

2.147 For the purpose of the new jurisdiction there are two panels of Court of Protection Visitors appointed by the Lord Chancellor: a panel of Special Visitors and a panel of General Visitors.[106] They are appointed to carry out visits and produce reports as directed by the court and the Public Guardian in much the same way as previously although the brief may be wider.

2.148 The Special Visitors are registered medical practitioners with knowledge and experience in cases of impairment of or disturbance in the functioning of the mind or brain, but the General Visitors need not have a medical qualification although they are likely to have experience of social work.

Powers

2.149 When exercising their functions Visitors may, at all reasonable times, examine and take copies of any health record and any record held by a local authority in connection with a social services function so far as the record relates to the incapacitated person, and may also interview that person in private.[107] A Special Visitor when making a visit may, if the court so directs, carry out in private a medical, psychiatric or psychological examination of the person's capacity and condition.

The Official Solicitor

Background

2.150 The Official Solicitor to the Senior Courts is an independent statutory office holder and an officer of the court[108] whose main function is to represent parties to proceedings who are without capacity, deceased or unascertained when no other suitable person or agency is able and willing to do so. The purpose is to prevent a possible denial of justice and safeguard the welfare, property or status of the party.

2.151 The office[109] is part of the Ministry of Justice and there are some 140 staff, of whom 22 are lawyers. Most of the staff are caseworkers with access to in-house legal advice.

The incapacity work of the Official Solicitor

Representing adults who lack capacity

2.152 The role in county court and High Court proceedings is recognised by the court Rules.[110] An order directing the Official Solicitor to represent a protected party will either be made with his prior consent or will only take effect if his consent is obtained so he should be consulted in advance about any proposed application which seeks his involvement. He requires evidence or judicial determination of incapacity and operates a 'last resort' acceptance policy, namely that he will only accept appointment when there is no other suitable and willing person.

---

[106] Mental Capacity Act 2005, s 61.
[107] Mental Capacity Act 2005, s 61(5)–(6).
[108] Appointed by the Lord Chancellor under Senior Courts Act 1981, s 90.
[109] The Official Solicitor, Victory House, 30–34 Kingsway, London WC2B 6EX. DX 141423 Bloomsbury 7. Tel/fax: 020 3681 2726. E-mail: *enquiries@offsol.gsi.gov.uk*. Website: www.offsol.demon.co.uk.
[110] See the Civil Procedure Rules 1998, Part 21; Family Procedure Rules 2010, Part 15.

2.153 He may act as his own solicitor, or instruct a private firm of solicitors to act for him, and in appropriate cases will require security for his charges and expenses before agreeing to act.

Assisting the civil and family courts

2.154 The Official Solicitor may also be asked to assist or to investigate and report to a court (eg to ascertain the mental capacity of a party to proceedings). It may be a contempt of court to interfere with an investigation by the Official Solicitor.

Assisting the Court of Protection

2.155 The Official Solicitor is frequently appointed as litigation friend for an incapacitated party who is the subject of contested Court of Protection proceedings relating to personal welfare, especially serious medical treatment cases. He may also be asked to represent the incapacitated person in property and affairs cases where the deputy or attorney has a personal interest in the outcome (eg applications for statutory wills or gifts). He does not need the consent of the court to bring an application.

Court Funds Office

2.156 The Court Funds Office (CFO)[111] provides investment and banking administration services for clients whose money is held under the control of the civil courts of England and Wales, including the Court of Protection.[112] The Mental Capacity Act 2005 now provides greater choice for the deputy and only some Court of Protection clients have to keep money at the CFO.

Independent Mental Capacity Advocates

2.157 There are detailed provisions whereby Independent Mental Capacity Advocates ('IMCAs') must be available to represent and support incapacitated persons where serious treatment is proposed or accommodation is to be provided by an NHS body or local authority.[113] The advocate will become involved where there is no other appropriate person to be consulted, but not where the incapacitated person has himself nominated a person to be consulted or there is a donee of a lasting power of attorney or a deputy appointed by the court. Much of the detail is provided by regulations[114] and these provisions do not apply where such action is to be taken under the Mental Health Act 1983.

2.158 Advocacy involves helping people to express their views and wishes, access information and services, explore choices and options, and secure their rights. The IMCA should be independent of any person who will be responsible for the act or decision and may interview in private the person in relation to whom he has been asked for advice, and may examine any prescribed record of a kind which the person holding the record considers may be relevant to the advocate's investigation. The IMCA may initially use informal methods to challenge decisions and ask for a meeting with the decision maker to explain any concerns and request a review of the decision. Where

---

[111] The Court Funds Office, Glasgow, G58 1AB. Tel/fax: 0845 223 8500/0141 636 4398. Email: enquiries@cfo.gsi.gov.uk.
[112] Court Funds Rules 2011, SI 2011/1734.
[113] Mental Capacity Act 2005, ss 35–41.
[114] Mental Capacity Act 2005 (Independent Mental Capacity Advocates) (General) Regulations 2006, SI 2006/1832.

there are serious concerns about the decision made, an IMCA may decide to use formal methods to challenge the decision. These include using the relevant complaints procedure, approaching the Official Solicitor and referring the case to the Court of Protection.

OTHER RESOURCES

Medical Research

2.159 Another controversial area was medical research. This is dealt with in Chapter 8.[115]

Deprivation of liberty safeguards

Background

2.160 Adults who reside in hospitals or care homes may have consented to be there or been sectioned under the Mental Health Act 1983. There are, however, many who lack the capacity to consent but are compliant insofar as they may not have objected to their admission nor to their continued stay in the hospital or care home. Concerns arose as to whether such residents are being detained and thereby deprived of their liberty contrary to Art 5(1) of the European Convention on Human Rights. The British courts did not think so[116] but the European Court of Human Rights took a different view being concerned that that detention was arbitrary and not in accordance with a procedure prescribed by law, and there were no safeguards against unjustified deprivations of liberty.[117] This became known as the 'Bournewood Gap' because the appeal case related to a person admitted to Bournewood Hospital. It was necessary to introduce new procedures into our law.

Legislation

2.161 The Government chose to set up procedures within the mental capacity jurisdiction with appeals being dealt with by the Court of Protection. With effect from 1 April 2009 it was rendered lawful[118] to deprive a person of their liberty either:

(a) if it is a consequence of giving effect to an order of the Court of Protection on a personal welfare matter; or

(b) where the deprivation of liberty is in a hospital or care home, if a standard or urgent authorisation is in force (referred to as the Deprivation of Liberty safeguards or 'DoLs').

Mental Health Act 1983 procedures if applied will take precedence over these processes, but the interaction of orders of the Court of Protection and DoLs is problematic and the

---

[115] See also Mental Capacity Act 2005, ss 30–34.

[116] _R v Bournewood Community and Mental Health NHS Trust ex parte L_ [1999] 1 AC 458, HL; [1998] 2 WLR 764, CA.

[117] _HL v United Kingdom_ (45508/99) (2005) 40 EHRR 32, judgment on the merits given on 5 October 2004.

[118] Mental Health Act 2007 amended Mental Capacity Act 2005 by inserting new provisions including Sch A1.

best view may be that the two operate in parallel. The operation of these provisions is monitored and reported on by the Care Quality Commission.[119]

Authorisations

2.162 The managing authority of a hospital or care home may lawfully deprive a patient or resident of their liberty if they are detained for the purpose of being given care or treatment and a standard or urgent authorisation is in force which relates to the relevant person and to the hospital or care home in which they are detained. The managing authority is put in the same position as if the resident had capacity to consent and had consented to their detention.

2.163 An authorisation should not be used to foreclose a genuine dispute about where it is in the incapacitated adult's best interests to reside, and significant welfare issues that cannot be resolved by discussion should be placed before the Court of Protection.[120]

2.164 The authorisation procedure usually begins with a request by the managing authority[121] to the supervisory body[122] which then arranges for assessments to be carried out to determine whether the following requirements are met in relation to the detained resident:[123]

(a) *the mental health requirement* – the person must be suffering from a mental disorder within the meaning of Mental Health Act 1983;

(b) *the mental capacity requirement* – the person must lack capacity in relation to the question whether or not they should be accommodated in the hospital or care home for the purpose of being given the care or treatment concerned;

(c) *the best interests requirement* – it must be in the person's best interests to be a detained resident and the deprivation of liberty must be necessary to prevent harm and be a proportionate response to the likelihood and seriousness of that harm;

(d) *the eligibility requirement* – a person is ineligible if already subject to certain Mental Health Act 1983 procedures; and

(e) *the no refusals requirement* – there must not be a valid and effective advance decision by the detained resident refusing the treatment in question, nor a valid refusal of the proposed care or treatment by a deputy or donee of an LPA within the scope of their authority.

Standard authorisations

2.165 A standard authorisation is an authorisation given by the supervisory body after it has been requested to do so and once the prescribed procedure has been followed. The request must be dealt with within 21 days but the authorisation cannot be given unless assessments have been commissioned by the supervisory body which conclude that all the qualifying requirements are met. Regulations[124] specify who can carry out assessments, covering the need for more than one assessor, the professional skills,

---

[119] See the Mental Capacity (Deprivation of Liberty: Monitoring and Reporting; and Assessments – Amendment) Regulations 2009, SI 2009/827.

[120] *LB Hillingdon v Neary* [2011] EWHC 1377 (Fam).

[121] Generally the managers of the hospital or care home involved.

[122] This is now the relevant local authority.

[123] Mental Capacity Act 2005, Sch A1, Part 3.

[124] Mental Capacity (Deprivation of Liberty: Standard Authorisations, Assessments and Ordinary Residence) Regulations 2008, SI 2008/1858, as amended by SI 2009/827.

training and competence required and independence from decisions about providing or commissioning care to the person concerned and the time frame within which the assessments must be completed. The mental health and best interests assessments must be carried out by different assessors. It is the responsibility of the supervisory body to appoint eligible and suitable assessors. Anyone carrying out assessments (other than the age assessment) must have undergone specific training.

2.166 The best interests assessor must first decide whether a deprivation of liberty is occurring or is likely to occur. He must consult the managing authority and take into account the views of anyone named by the person, anyone caring for or interested in the welfare of the person, any donee of an LPA or deputy appointed by the court. If the person does not have anyone to speak for them who is not paid to provide care an IMCA must be appointed to support and represent them during the assessment process.

2.167 If that assessor concludes that deprivation of liberty is not in the person's best interests but becomes aware that they are already being deprived of their liberty, the assessor must draw this to the attention of the supervisory body. If the assessment recommends authorisation the assessor must state the maximum authorisation period, which may not be for more than a year, and may recommend conditions to be attached to the authorisation. The best interests assessor must also identify someone to recommend for appointment as representative of the person being deprived of their liberty.

2.168 If any of the assessments conclude that the person does not meet the criteria the supervisory body must turn down the request for authorisation and inform all persons with an interest. If all the assessments recommend it, the supervisory body must give the authorisation and:

- set the period of the authorisation and attach any appropriate conditions;
- issue the authorisation in writing, stating the period for which it is valid, the purpose for which it is given and the reason why each qualifying requirement is met;
- appoint someone to act as the person's representative during the term of the authorisation;[125] and
- provide a copy of the authorisation to the managing authority, the person being deprived of their liberty and their representative, any IMCA who has been involved and any other interested person consulted by the best interests assessor (in due course notifying them when the authorisation ceases to be in force).

2.169 The managing authority in acting on the authorisation must:

- ensure that any conditions are complied with;
- take all practicable steps to ensure that the detained resident understands the effect of the authorisation, their right of appeal to the Court of Protection and their right to request a review;
- give the same information to the person's representative; and

---

[125] Someone who will maintain contact with the resident and support and represent them in relation to the authorisation, including requesting review or appealing to the Court of Protection on their behalf. See the Mental Capacity (Deprivation of Liberty: Appointment of Relevant Person's Representative) Regulations 2008, SI 2008/1315.

- keep the person's case under consideration and request a review if necessary.

The supervisory body may review a standard authorisation at any time and must do so if requested by the detained resident, their representative or the managing authority.

Urgent authorisations

2.170 Urgent authorisations[126] may be given by the managing authority of a care home or hospital to provide a lawful basis for a deprivation of liberty whilst a standard authorisation is being obtained when it is urgently required and the qualifying requirements appear to be met. The managing authority must record the reasons in writing and take all practicable steps (verbally and in writing) to ensure the person understands the effect of the authorisation and their right of appeal to the Court of Protection and to notify any IMCA who has been involved.

2.171 An urgent authorisation takes effect at once and can only last for 7 days. It can be extended once for a further 7 days by the supervisory body if there are exceptional reasons why it has not been possible to complete a standard authorisation and it is essential that the detention continues. Otherwise an urgent authorisation can only be extended by a standard authorisation or a court order.

'Deprivation of liberty'

2.172 One of the problems has been deciding what is, and what is not, a deprivation of liberty. The Court of Appeal attempted to give guidance in *Chester West and Chester Council v P*[127] but subsequent judgments of the European Court of Human Rights have cast significant doubt upon the correctness of that approach. The Supreme Court is to consider the position in October 2013 and until then the law remains in an unsatisfactory state of uncertainty.

Review by the Court of Protection

2.173 A person who has been deprived of their liberty or their representative may apply to the Court of Protection for a review of the lawfulness of their detention.[128] The court has wide powers to review the authorisation and, if satisfied that there is a lack of capacity, to make decisions on the person's behalf in relation to matters concerning his personal welfare or property or affairs.

International protection of adults

Background

2.174 The ageing of the world's population, combined with greater international mobility, has created the need for improved international protection for vulnerable adults through legal regulation and international co-operation. In particular, the tendency for retired persons to move to warmer countries, leaving some of their property behind and acquiring a home in the new country, and sometimes making

---

[126] Mental Capacity Act 2005, Sch A1, Part 5.
[127] [2011] EWCA Civ 1257, [2012] COPLR 37.
[128] Mental Capacity Act 2005, s 21A; Court of Protection Rules 2007, Part 10A. Practice Direction – *Deprivation of Liberty Applications*.

advance arrangements for their care or representation in the event of incapacity, made it essential to have clear rules specifying which national authorities should take any necessary protective measures.

International Conventions

2.175 The *Hague Convention on Private International Law* seeks to establish international agreements over jurisdiction and related matters. Under its auspices the *Convention on the International Protection of Adults* was concluded on 13 January 2000. It applies to the protection in international situations of 'adults who, by reason of an impairment or insufficiency of their personal faculties, are not in a position to protect their interests'.[129]

2.176 The objects as set out in Article 2 are:

'(a) to determine the State whose authorities have jurisdiction to take measures directed to the protection of the person or property of the adult;

(b) to determine which law is applied by such authorities in exercising their jurisdiction;

(c) to determine the law applicable to representation of the adult;

(d) to provide for the recognition and enforcement of such measures of protection in all Contracting States; and

(e) to establish such co-operation between the authorities of the Contracting States as may be necessary to achieve the purposes of the Convention.'

Commencement

2.177 The Convention is not yet in force in the UK, but because there is provision for it in Sch 3 of the Mental Capacity Act 2005 it is possible to give effect to and ratify the Convention in relation to England and Wales. The Schedule provides private international law rules to govern jurisdictional issues between Scotland and England and Wales irrespective of whether the Convention is in force.

Implications

2.178 Under the Convention the country of habitual residence has the primary right to exercise jurisdiction. As a secondary rule, presence will suffice for urgent and temporary measures, in relation to refugees and displaced persons, and where property is located. The State of nationality may take jurisdiction, but this is subordinate to any measure taken by the State of habitual residence. The State of habitual residence can, with the agreement of the receiving State, transfer jurisdiction to another State connected with the adult.

2.179 The State with jurisdiction will apply its own law but may instead choose to apply the law of another State with which the adult has a connection. Parties to the Convention are required to recognise measures taken under the Convention, subject to specific fairly narrow grounds of refusal.

---

[129] For the text of the Convention see www.hcch.net/upload/conventions/txt35en.pdf.

Non-Convention countries

2.180 Dealing with capacity issues in non-Convention countries can be a nightmare. The issues that arise in private international law are jurisdiction, applicable law, recognition and enforcement. The first question to ask is: do the courts of England and Wales have jurisdiction? Then, which law will the country apply: that of England and Wales or another state? There will be concern as to whether the other country recognises the authority of an attorney or deputy appointed in this country or even an order of our Court of Protection. If not, one must investigate the procedures available in that country.[130]

---

[130] A series of Questionnaires dealing with such issues in a range of countries is published in *Court of Protection Practice 2013* (Jordan Publishing).

CHAPTER 3

THE OLDER PERSON

Gordon Ashton

'Anyone can get old. All you have to do is to live long enough.'
Groucho Marx

Individuals enjoy legal rights in and owe duties to society but what is important in relation to older people is the extent to which they are afforded access to these rights and enabled to cope with their corresponding duties. In this chapter we consider first the rights and duties of the individual in the context of contracts, bank accounts, investments and trusteeship. Then we identify civil status and civil duties before addressing civil responsibility including debts and other liabilities. Finally we address work and leisure activity and involvement in civil court proceedings including criminal responsibility.

INTRODUCTION

3.1 The basic principle is that older people enjoy the same rights and are subject to the same duties as other members of society, although whether an individual is able to exercise those rights or perform those duties may depend upon personal competence. Some modification of these rights and duties may be needed for the support or protection of the individual or in the interests of other members of society. In this chapter we identify the extent to which normal legal rights and duties apply or may be modified or supplemented according to the status or needs of the older individual. The objective may be to protect those who are regarded as vulnerable, to enable their affairs to be dealt with or to afford them privileges of status.

3.2 In England and Wales there is neither a Bill of Rights nor a Constitution setting out fundamental and inalienable rights, but the Human Rights Act 1998 has incorporated the European Convention on Human Rights into our law. The Act is a compromise, representing an attempt to incorporate the Convention into our law whilst still recognising the traditions of the common law and the sovereignty of Parliament. The implications of human rights are mentioned throughout this book, and the general principles are briefly explained in Chapter 1. The United Nations Declaration of Human Rights in 1948 provided that everyone has the right to a standard of living adequate for the health and well-being of himself and his family, including food, clothing, housing, medical care and necessary social services, and the right to security in the event of disability. This provided the basis for the European Social Charter in 1965 but is not legally enforceable in this country.

RIGHTS AND DUTIES

Preliminary

3.3   In this part we consider the legal rights and duties of older people in relation to normal transactions with particular reference to the changed role that they have in society and a potential decline in physical or mental competence. The starting point is that they have the same rights and duties as other members of the community unless there is a rule of law or procedure to the contrary. The reasons for any variations have already been considered in previous chapters.

Contract

General

3.4   Anyone who has the necessary capacity may enter into a contract. It has been stated, although this may now be an oversimplification, that:[1]

> 'the mental capacity required by the law in respect of any instrument is relative to the particular transaction which is being effected by means of the instrument and may be described as the capacity to understand the nature of that transaction when it is explained.'

It follows that a person may have the capacity to enter into one contract but not another, depending upon the complexities or implications. If doubt arises in a particular instance it is necessary to consider whether at the time the contract is to be or was entered into the individual:

(a)   understood the transaction;

(b)   was capable of deciding whether to reach the agreement;

(c)   was aware of any choices and able to make them; and

(d)   was capable of committing himself to the transaction.[2]

The implications of the contract should be taken into account when considering whether the party understood what he was doing because some transactions are much simpler than others and no-one should be regarded as legally incapable in the total sense. It may also be necessary to consider whether the party intended to enter into legal relations (thus a bargain struck within a domestic context may not be legally enforceable).

3.5   A distinction has been drawn between a lack of understanding due to mental incapacity or drunkenness and illiteracy or language limitations:[3]

> 'All four conditions are disabilities which might prevent the sufferer from possessing a full understanding of a transaction, but the former might not only deprive the sufferer of understanding the transaction, but also deprive him of the awareness that he did not understand it. An illiterate knew that he could not read. A man who was unfamiliar with English was aware of that. If he signed a document which he did not understand he had only himself to blame. A man who signed a document in a language with which he was

---

[1]   *Gibbons v Wright* (1954) 91 CLR 423 approved in *Re Beaney* [1978] 1 WLR 770.

[2]   The question of capacity in general is considered in Ch 1 at **1.93** et seq. The statutory definition of capacity in the Mental Capacity Act 2005 (explained in Ch 2 at **2.19**) may not apply directly in this context but will influence case-law.

[3]   *Barclays Bank plc v Schwartz* (1995) *The Times*, 2 August, Millett LJ.

insufficiently familiar to understand could be in no better position than the man who signed a document which he did not read because he was too busy.

> ... mental incapacity and drunkenness provided defences to a claim in contract if the other party was aware of the defendant's condition. But illiteracy and unfamiliarity with the English language did not ... even if the other party was aware of their existence. ... They might found a claim in equity to set the transaction aside as a harsh and unconscionable bargain: it was not enough in order to invoke that equitable doctrine that the defendant should establish that he was the weaker of the parties. He had to establish that there was a substantial unfairness in the transaction itself, so that there had been an unfair advantage gained by the unconscientious use of power by the stronger party against the weaker.'

Setting aside

3.6   With one past exception,[4] a contract entered into by a party who lacks capacity is merely voidable, not void. If a contract is to be set aside at the option of a party on the ground of his incapacity it must be shown that the other party knew, or should have been aware, of the disability at the time the purported contract was entered into.[5] The fact that the contract is unfair is not by itself sufficient.[6]

3.7   It may not always be apparent on meeting an elderly person that there is limited capacity, because lack of understanding may be disguised by a convincing manner. Thus reversing a cash purchase made in a shop by an older person who lacks capacity may depend upon the goodwill of the shopkeeper. But if prolonged negotiations are involved suspicion may arise which is enough to put the other party on enquiry.[7] It is more difficult in mail order or internet-based contracts where there is no personal contact between the parties (but there may be a time limited right of cancellation which can be adopted by a carer).

3.8   The question of whether the contract was fair is irrelevant except as regards the purchase of necessaries, but in regard to some arrangements made by older people it may be appropriate to consider whether there was an intention to create legal relations. For social and domestic arrangements it is presumed that there is no such intention, and this may also be the case in regard to financial arrangements within the family but the presumption may be rebutted by evidence to the contrary.

Necessaries

3.9   It has for long been provided by statute that:[8]

> 'Where necessaries are sold and delivered to an infant ... or a person who by reason of mental incapacity or drunkenness is incompetent to contract, he must pay a reasonable price therefor.'

---

4   Contracts entered into by a patient subject to the jurisdiction of the (former) Court of Protection were invalid but might later be given retrospective approval – *Re Walker* [1905] 1 Ch 160; *Re Marshall* [1920] 1 Ch 284. It is unlikely that these cases have survived the Mental Capacity Act 2005 in view of the new approach to capacity.

5   *Imperial Loan Co v Stone* [1892] 1 QB 599, 601. This has long been the case in regard to contracts for the sale of land: *Broughton v Snook* [1938] Ch 505. The need to avoid prejudicing the other party thus takes priority over protection of the incapable party. It is different in Scotland.

6   *Hart v O'Connor* [1985] 2 All ER 880.

7   Eg on negotiations for a mobile telephone it may become apparent that the customer is never going to be able to cope and does not understand the implications.

8   Sale of Goods Act 1979, s 3 re-enacting Sale of Goods Act 1893, s 2 which put the common law obligation to pay a reasonable price on a statutory footing.

Quasi-contractual liability is founded on the request, and the fact that it was for the supply of necessaries merely results in the incapacity being overlooked. The obligation is only to pay a reasonable price and not any contract price that may have been stipulated, so in case of dispute the court would determine the amount on the basis of a *quantum meruit*. Of course the price stipulated will be taken into account and this may be found to be reasonable.

3.10 'Necessaries' mean goods suitable to the condition in life of the person[9] and to his actual requirements at the time,[10] which will generally cover the purchase of ordinary food, drink, clothing or other items that are considered necessary in everyday living. The burden of proof is on the person supplying the goods. It follows that a care home or nursing agency should be entitled to payment for essential services provided before a deputy is appointed.

3.11 Although the supply of goods is dealt with by statute the principle of 'necessaries' was derived from common law and it was considered that this principle applied to expenditure on professional services necessary to preserve the property of a person who lacked mental capacity. It was not clear whether it would also apply to steps taken to enhance the value thereof. The doubt has now been resolved and the liability re-stated by s 7 of the Mental Capacity Act 2005 which provides:

'(1) If necessary goods or services are supplied to a person who lacks capacity to contract for the supply, he must pay a reasonable price for them.

(2) "Necessary" means suitable to a person's condition in life and to his actual requirements at the time when the goods or services are supplied.'

Restitution

3.12 Situations also arise where necessaries are supplied to an incapacitated person in an emergency without a request. In these circumstances the court could order reimbursement of the value on the basis of an implied contract. The principles have been stated as follows:[11]

'Before a supplier can obtain payment for necessaries supplied to a mentally disordered person in a case of necessitous intervention, he must satisfy the following conditions. He must show that there was some necessity, which may be done by proving that he supplied necessaries; that he was a suitable person to intervene (such as, for example, a relation), and that he intervened *bona fide* in the interests of the mentally disordered person. Moreover, he must intend to charge, and it has been said that the onus is on him to prove such an intention.'

This principle might not be restricted to an emergency. Where a person spent money on behalf of a disabled person for 'necessaries' and expected to be repaid, the law would acknowledge a liability to repay out of the estate or financial resources of the disabled person.[12]

---

9   This means place in society rather than mental or physical condition.
10   Goods will not be necessaries if the person's existing supply is sufficient. It is irrelevant that the seller did not know that this was the case.
11   Goff and Jones *The Law of Unjust Enrichment* (8th edn, 2011).
12   *Re Rhodes* [1890] 44 Ch D 94. See also Mental Capacity Act 2005, ss 7 and 8 as explained in Ch 2 at **2.49**.

Agency

3.13   A traditional agent can only act for a person with contractual capacity, so whilst this facility may be available to those who are physically disabled it cannot be relied upon where there is a lack of mental capacity (except in regard to 'necessaries' as stated above). However, in that situation the agent may become personally liable. A general power of attorney may nevertheless be useful if the elderly individual is likely to be out of action for a while (for example, in hospital or even residing abroad).[13]

Court of Protection

3.14   The former Court of Protection authorised transactions on behalf of a person who was 'incapable, by reason of mental disorder, of managing and administering his property and affairs'. A contract involving the assets or money of a person who had become subject to the jurisdiction of that court (known as a 'patient') might only be made under its authority which may have been delegated to a receiver. The patient could not personally enter into a contract and any contract purportedly entered into would be void.[14] Similarly the patient could not make a gift, as illustrated by the following case:

> A receiver paid the fees for an elderly lady to reside in a residential care home and arranged for some of her antique furniture to be placed in her room. Without his knowledge she purported to give an oak chest to the manager of the home who sold it and spent the proceeds. The manager was convicted of theft. He knew of the receiver's appointment so should have known that the lady had no authority to make the gift notwithstanding that she appeared to know what she wanted.

3.15   Any money or assets remaining under the control of the patient would in practice be vulnerable to transactions with persons having no knowledge of the lack of capacity. Beneficial contracts were likely to be ratified. Any receiver appointed by the former court would seek to take control of all accounts, investments and other assets but the court or the receiver might in practice authorise a patient to have control of some money so as to have personal freedom in small financial transactions. It would be difficult for third parties to know of such authorisation or any limitations. That is effectively the position under the new mental capacity jurisdiction whereby individuals may exercise such capacity as they have and the appointment of a deputy (the modern equivalent of the former receiver) by the Court of Protection will not by itself render any personal transactions voidable.[15]

Banking accounts

3.16   Contractual capacity is required to conduct an account with a bank or building society. In the case of older people problems arise in opening an account or in continuing to use an account following a decline in mental capacity.

Opening an account

3.17   In the past a savings account could be opened with minimum formality and the customer might not even need to attend at the premises. All that was usually required

---

[13]   For the statutory provisions which enable the financial affairs of a mentally incapacitated person to be administered see Ch 11.

[14]   *Re Walker* [1905] 1 Ch 160.

[15]   For the position after October 2007 under the Mental Capacity Act 2005 reference should be made to Chs 2 and 11.

was the completion of a simple form with a specimen signature. More enquiry was made before a current account with a cheque-book could be opened and an interview might be necessary with references being taken up especially if an overdraft-limit was to be authorised. Recent money laundering regulations have made the opening of bank accounts much more difficult and proof of identity is required which provides safeguards but may also result in obstacles for infirm older customers.

3.18   The previous regulations in respect of National Savings Bank accounts covered deposits made on behalf of and in the name of persons of unsound mind, so ordinary or investment deposit accounts were suitable for an incapable elderly person with the account in the name of the individual but administered by someone else.[16] This facility appears no longer to be available.

3.19   When an account is opened by an attorney or a deputy for a person who is incapable of handling his affairs, it should be in the name of that person. The account is to be operated on an agency basis and is not a trust account. In practice some banks and building societies have insisted upon the account being opened in the name of the attorney or deputy. The difference may not appear significant but has had serious consequences in the past. When some building societies changed their status and issued shares to their members, this was on the basis of a fixed allocation to each individual member. Thus the attorney or receiver at the time was treated as the member and only received a restricted allocation to cover all accounts held (thereby losing any allocation on personal accounts).[17]

Conduct of the account

3.20   The production of a consistent signature has in the past been a pre-requisite to operating an account,[18] although this merely relates to physical ability and is not an indication of mental capacity.[19] If physical ability to sign becomes impaired arrangements should be made for some form of mark to be accepted or for someone else to sign.[20] If this causes capacity to be questioned because of a failure to distinguish between ability and capacity, medical evidence of capacity may be produced. A customer owes a duty of care not to draw a cheque in a manner that facilitates fraud or forgery and to notify any fraud or forgery, so a bank would be justified in refusing to continue an account for a customer who could not fulfil this duty.

3.21   The development of electronic and internet banking with the use of PIN numbers rather than signatures makes it easier for an account to be conducted by or on behalf of an infirm older person but also creates vulnerability over the use of the PIN and because there will be less occasions when personal capacity may be tested.

3.22   All transactions should be treated as confidential between the bank and its customer. The customer who has capacity can authorise the release of information, but

---

[16]   National Savings Bank Act 1971, s 8(1)(f); National Savings Bank Regulations 1972, SI 1972/764, regs 6 and 7. Similar rules initially applied to Trustee Savings Banks until they acquired the status of a full bank in 1985.

[17]   A similar problem arose with accounts held by care workers for adults with learning disabilities. The Building Societies (Distributions) Act 1997 was rushed through Parliament to remove the injustice.

[18]   In response to a questionnaire in 1997 the big six building societies all stated that they would insist upon a trust account for an individual who could not produce a consistent signature.

[19]   The issues of physical ability and mental capacity should be separately addressed. Banks are vulnerable to proceedings under the Equality Act 2010 if they do not make reasonable adjustments – see Ch 1 at **1.58**.

[20]   Any attempt to have the account put in the name of the signatory as trustee or nominee should be resisted.

problems arise where an existing elderly customer loses capacity. Until any lasting (or enduring) power of attorney has been registered or a deputy has been appointed there will be a vacuum with no-one having a legal right to information. However, the lack of capacity may be of a temporary nature,[21] and whilst it may be appropriate for a degree of discretion to be exercised where a carer or professional adviser is known to be assisting the elderly customer, this cannot be guaranteed.

3.23 Conversely, if the account of an elderly person is in the name of a relative or carer, the elderly person will be deprived of the normal facilities of a customer such as access to information, receipt of statements and the right to control the account directly. Maintaining an account in joint names may be the answer but note the potential problems outlined below.

Overdrafts and loans

3.24 A bank has a customary right to charge simple interest at a reasonable rate on an overdraft so if the customer is considered capable of conducting the account capacity to accept interest and charges will be assumed. A banker has been held not to be entitled to interest and bank charges in respect of an overdraft where the money had been applied to maintain a person of unsound mind, but the implications of this are not clear.[22] When authorising a loan a commercial lender (including a bank or building society) must be satisfied that the borrower understands the transaction, and interest charges on a loan will be a matter for agreement. Fixed charges for unauthorised borrowings may be challenged as an unlawful penalty if they do not reflect the expenses incurred by the bank.

Joint accounts

3.25 A joint account with either party to sign is often seen as a convenient way of handling the finances of an elderly person, but this can lead to problems in two respects:

(a) joint account holders are jointly and severally liable for any overdraft incurred on the account consequent on borrowing by either holder without reference to the other.[23] So a period of financial instability by the elderly person could have serious consequences for both parties;

(b) the effect of incapacity of an account-holder is not generally realised. Upon the incapacity becoming known the mandate is terminated so that the bank is entitled to decline any further transactions until it has new instructions from all account-holders, including the legally authorised representative of the incapacitated one.

Guarantors

3.26 At common law the overdraft of a minor was not enforceable if the fact of such minority was known to all parties, so a guarantor would not be liable unless treated as principal debtor. A similar approach may apply where an adult is known to lack mental capacity to take a loan. The position has been reversed by statute in respect of minors[24] but the law may be unchanged for other forms of incapacity. In practice when loans or

---

[21] Eg a period of illness or the result of a stroke where a degree of recovery is anticipated.

[22] *Re Beavan* [1912] 1 Ch 196. This decision may no longer be followed as the interest (but perhaps not the charges) may be treated as 'necessaries'.

[23] *Royal Bank of Scotland v Fielding* (2003) *The Times*, 16 May, Hart J.

[24] Minors' Contracts Act 1987, s 2.

overdrafts are arranged for persons of doubtful mental capacity a separate indemnity is required and this would not be caught by the rule.

Capacity

3.27 If it becomes apparent that an account holder does not understand the transactions involved the account will be frozen until appropriate legal procedures have been brought into effect.[25] This will usually involve an application to the Court of Protection unless there is an enduring or lasting power of attorney which can be registered. The size and nature of any cheque is relevant, so if it is for a small sum in keeping with the balance normally held or in payment for necessaries there may be no reason for enquiry, but if it is unusual and disproportionate in amount payment may be refused. If the only payments from an account are to a nursing or residential care home for normal weekly fees the bank may be willing to give the benefit of any doubt as to mental capacity to the customer, especially if supported by close family, but with the closure of smaller branches this type of understanding based on personal knowledge is less common.[26]

3.28 Problems have tended to arise not only in continuing to use an account following a decline in mental capacity but also in the take-over or opening of an account by an attorney or deputy. A bank is not obliged to accept any particular customer, but if it adopts a policy that discriminates against disabled persons a claim may arise under the Equality Act 2010.[27] It is not clear how banks will cope under the new mental capacity jurisdiction whereby capacity is to be determined in respect of each transaction, because in these days of computerised banking there is less personal contact with the customers.[28]

Investments

3.29 Elderly people often have money invested and no special provisions apply to them in this respect, but if they become mentally incapable no further transactions may take place except under appropriate procedures. Problems may also then arise in regard to the receipt or disposal of income from investments. An application to the Court of Protection may be necessary unless an enduring or lasting power of attorney has been completed in which event it must be registered.[29]

Stocks and shares

3.30 Where securities are offered for sale direct to the public all that is required is a signed application form accompanied by a cheque or other form of payment and the capacity of the investor is not questioned. If investments are dealt with through a financial intermediary he will be obliged to give best advice and accordingly to 'know the client' so mental incapacity may then be identified. The intermediary is potentially vulnerable if he proceeds with an investment for a mentally incapacitated client because he could be liable for any loss on the investment but the client would retain any profit. If members of the family make investments in their own names on behalf of a parent

---

[25]　The obligation to pay a customer's cheque is determined by notice of mental disorder where this is of a sufficient degree to prevent an understanding of the transaction – *Drew v Nunn* (1879) 4 QBD 661, CA.

[26]　There is statutory authority for payments for necessaries in s 7 of the Mental Capacity Act 2005 and these provisions may authorise the bank to make the payments – see Ch 2 at **2.49**.

[27]　See Ch 1 at **1.58** et seq.

[28]　See Ch 2 generally.

[29]　For the procedures see Chs 2 and 11.

without adequate documentation confirming the beneficial ownership, problems may arise over ownership, taxation and inheritance. A declaration of trust may be appropriate to confirm the beneficial ownership.

Property ownership

3.31 There is no simple test of capacity to buy or sell land and interests in land, but the general contractual principle outlined above applies.[30] Textbooks on real property tend to use non-specific phrases such as 'unsoundness of mind', but sometimes refer to 'mental disorder' as if this means incapacity when it is simply a condition which may affect capacity.

3.32 A contract for the sale or purchase of land entered into by a party who does not have the mental capacity to understand the nature of the transaction is voidable at the option of that party if it can be shown that the other party was aware of the disability at the time.[31] The need for documentation and involvement of lawyers usually results in the question of capacity being considered, and if an elderly person were encouraged by the other party to sign a document without advice this may indicate an attempt to take advantage of lack of capacity thereby enabling the transaction to be set aside.[32]

Execution of deeds

3.33 Inability to provide a coherent signature need not be an obstacle to executing a deed providing that this is not due to mental incapacity. A person's signature is what he chooses it to be and a mark is sufficient if acknowledged as the signature even if assistance has been proved to position the hand and pen in the correct position on the paper. An explanation of the mark in the attestation clause may be helpful to avoid future doubt or argument as to valid execution. The alternative is for someone to sign on the individual's behalf at his direction and in his presence, and this is authorised but must be done in the presence of two independent witnesses who will also sign in that capacity.[33] Whether this means four persons being present (the party executing the deed, the proxy signer and the two witnesses) is a matter for argument but the safer course is to arrange this rather than to rely upon the proxy signer as a witness. The alternative is for the individual to execute a lasting power of attorney (unless there is already an enduring power of attorney) and the attorney can then sign future documents on his behalf – other than a will.[34]

Insurance

3.34 Insurance is a contract *uberrime fides* (of the utmost good faith) so a policy could be void if any relevant disability is not disclosed on the proposal or on renewal if there has been any change of circumstances. There may be an express declaration for some types of policy, such as those relating to health or holidays, that there is no pre-existing medical condition or disability so the proposal form should be carefully examined. Any material disability must be disclosed when taking out motor insurance and medical

---

[30] See also Ch 1 at **1.93** et seq and Ch 2 at **2.19** et seq.
[31] *Broughton v Snook* [1938] Ch 505. A deed entered into by a patient of the (former) Court of Protection would be invalid to dispose of property – *Re Walker* [1905] 1 Ch 106.
[32] Undue influence and unconscionable bargains are dealt with in Ch 4 at **4.160** and **4.173** respectively. For the procedure to adopt if an owner of real property becomes incapable see Ch 11.
[33] Law of Property (Miscellaneous Provisions) Act 1989.
[34] A 'statutory will' may be authorised by the Court of Protection where testamentary capacity is lacking.

evidence may be required before a policy is issued to an older driver. The fact that the non-disclosure was a consequence of the lack of capacity of the policyholder would not preserve the policy although some discretion may be exercised by the insurer especially if there has been no prejudice.

3.35   If the insured is incapable when money is to be paid by the insurers, they may insist upon the appointment of a deputy before paying out unless there is a registered enduring or lasting power of attorney. To avoid this it may be appropriate, in some cases, to appoint trustees of a policy and give them power to expend the monies for the beneficiary.

Elderly people as trustees

Preliminary

3.36   The making of wills by elderly people is dealt with in Chapter 12 and under this heading we merely consider the situation of the individual who is appointed an executor or trustee and becomes unable to perform that role.

Grants of probate and administration

3.37   Neither age nor physical disability is a bar to appointment as an executor or entitlement to be administrator of an estate, though it is important that the individual be able to carry out the duties involved because there are limits to the extent to which these may be delegated. A person who is mentally incapable may not prove a will (despite being named as executor) nor be appointed as an administrator. The usual practice where a sole executor is mentally incapable is to make a grant for his use and benefit.[35]

3.38   Some textbooks state that a person who is suffering from mental disorder is regarded in law as incapable not only of carrying out the duties of executor but also of deciding whether to assume the office. This is an inadequate interpretation of the law because the statutory definition of mental disorder under Part VII of the Mental Health Act 1983 did not take into account the degree of impairment and that is of more relevance than the mere existence of the mental disorder. The Mental Capacity Act 2005 adopts a different diagnostic threshold for mental capacity.[36] It will not be known by the Probate Registry if there is a mental impairment unless the application for a grant is challenged and the issue would then have to be tackled, usually on the basis of medical evidence. Any solicitor instructed to act in an application for a grant of probate or administration who is concerned as to the mental capacity of the client must address the issue because he is an officer of the court and may have a professional duty to the beneficiaries.

Trustees

3.39   There is no upper age limit but problems arise if a trustee becomes 'incapable of acting', whether this be due to mental incapacity or any other cause.[37] In that event the

---

[35]   See the Non-Contentious Probate Rules 1987, SI 1987/2024, r 35.

[36]   This is dealt with in Ch 2 at **2.20**.

[37]   Textbooks suggest that the incapacity could be by reason of lunacy, age or infirmity and that a person suffering from mental disorder could be replaced. In all these cases the test to be applied is one of capacity to perform the task rather than of status and there is no age bar as such unless one is imposed by the trust instrument.

persons with power to appoint new trustees may exercise that power so as to appoint a replacement for the trustee who is incapable.[38] They may be the persons stated by the trust instrument to have the power of appointment or, if there are no such persons, the surviving or continuing trustees (not including the trustee being removed). A trustee for sale of land who is incapable, by reason of mental disorder, of exercising his functions of trustee, must be replaced or otherwise discharged before there can be any dealing with the land.[39]

3.40 The court has power to appoint a new trustee in substitution for a trustee who lacks capacity to exercise his functions as trustee but will only do so where this is necessary, such as where a sole trustee is incapable and there is no-one else with power to make the appointment.[40] Where the trustee is also entitled to a beneficial interest in possession in the trust property, no appointment of a new trustee in his place shall be made unless leave has been given by the Court of Protection.[41] The court has power to vest trust property in trustees on various occasions, including where a person entitled is under disability[42] and also has an inherent jurisdiction to remove a trustee where it is necessary for the safety of the trust property or the welfare of the beneficiaries.

Costs

3.41 Before engaging in court proceedings trustees (especially charity trustees who have no personal financial involvement in the outcome) should seek personal protection in the form of a 'Beddoe order' entitling them to payment of costs out of the trust fund. A trustee who defends proceedings brought against him in a representative capacity without obtaining such an order does so at his own risk on costs. Even if he has been advised by counsel that he has a good defence to the claim he would not receive his costs unless the court was satisfied that it would have authorised the defence at the expense of the trust fund had such an application been made.

Delegation

3.42 It is one of the basic principles of equity that trustees may not delegate their task unless authorised to do so by the trust instrument, but there are exceptions including the ability to employ people to do administrative acts and to transact business through an agent.[43] There has for some years been a limited statutory power to appoint an attorney which was initially limited to periods when the trustee was outside the jurisdiction.[44] This only permits delegation for a period not exceeding 12 months other than to a co-trustee (unless a trust corporation), and notice of the delegation and the reason for it must be given to the other trustees and any person with power to appoint a new trustee.

---

[38] Trustee Act 1925, s 36. The appointment of a trustee under this section is in the place of a retiring trustee, so the appointment of one new trustee is incapable of discharging two retiring trustees. In such circumstances a second retiring trustee could only obtain a discharge pursuant to the retirement provisions contained in s 39 – *Adam & Co International Trustees Ltd v Theodore Goddard (a firm)* [2000] 13 LS Gaz R 44, Ch D. Further provisions whereby beneficiaries may appoint trustees are contained in Trusts of Land and Appointment of Trustees Act 1996, s 20.

[39] Law of Property Act 1925, s 22(2). This causes problems when a joint owner of land becomes incapable. See also the Trust of Land and Appointment of Trustees Act 1996.

[40] Trustee Act 1925, s 41(1) as amended by the Mental Capacity Act 2005.

[41] Trustee Act 1925, s 36(9) as amended by the Mental Capacity Act 2005.

[42] Trustee Act 1925, s 44(ii)(a).

[43] This must be in the 'proper and ordinary course of business' and the trustee must take proper care in the appointment of the agent – *Speight v Gaunt* (1883) 9 App Cas 1, HL. The Trustee Act 2000 has enabled trustees to delegate investment decision making and appoint nominees and custodians.

[44] Law of Property Act 1925, s 25 later amended by Powers of Attorney Act 1971, s 9.

Such delegation would not survive the mental incapacity of the donor. It should be noted that the donor remains liable for the acts or defaults of the attorney.[45]

3.43   An attorney under both a general or an enduring power of attorney whenever made can exercise a trustee function of the donor if it relates to land, or the capital proceeds or income from land, in which the donor had a beneficial interest.[46] An 'appropriate statement' made by the attorney at the time of a sale or within 3 months thereafter confirming that the donor had a beneficial interest in the property shall be conclusive evidence of this fact.[47] But it will not be sufficient if the joint owner (for example, a spouse) is the sole attorney because a capital receipt by trustees needs two signatures. In all other cases the provision mentioned in the above paragraph must be complied with or (in case of incapacity) a replacement trustee appointed by the continuing trustee or trustees. It follows that, unless advantage can be taken of the 1999 Act, if a joint legal owner of freehold property becomes incapable by reason of mental disorder of exercising his functions as a trustee, a new trustee will have to be appointed in his place before the legal estate can be dealt with.

Civil status

Driving licences

3.44   It is an offence to drive a motor vehicle on a road unless the driver holds a licence authorising him to drive a vehicle of the class being driven. Applications for driving licences are dealt with by the Driver and Vehicle Licensing Agency (DVLA)[48] which may refuse to issue a licence to, or revoke the licence of, a person who suffers from a relevant disability.[49] Drivers must renew their licence on reaching 70 years of age and at 3-yearly intervals thereafter. Although drivers over the age of 70 years must indicate that they consider themselves fit to drive, this statement does not have to be supported by medical evidence and they will only be requested to undergo a medical examination if a report has been received questioning the ability to drive.

3.45   An applicant for a driving licence must state whether he is suffering from a relevant disability, which means either a disability prescribed by the Secretary of State or any other disability which is likely to cause the driving of a vehicle by the applicant to be a source of danger to the public.[50] The holder of a licence must also report 'forthwith' any subsequent disability that arises unless it is not expected to last for more than 3 months, or any notified disability that becomes worse. Failure to notify without reasonable excuse is an offence.

3.46   Although the obligation is placed upon the driver to notify any disability, a deputy or an attorney under a registered lasting (or enduring) power of attorney would be expected to notify the incapacity although it would not necessarily render the person incapable of driving. Doctors are requested to inform DVLA if they consider that there is

---

[45]   Trustee Act 1925, s 27(7).

[46]   Trustee Delegation Act 1999.

[47]   See Land Registry practice leaflet 32.

[48]   Swansea SA6 7JL (tel: 01792 772151). The website is: www.dft.gov.uk/dvla/.

[49]   See generally Road Traffic Act 1988.

[50]   This may include epilepsy, multiple sclerosis, cardiac conditions, failing vision, dementia and other mental illness. Being subject to a guardianship order under the Mental Health Act 1983 is a prescribed disability – Motor Vehicles (Driving Licences) Regulations 1987, SI 1987/1378.

any question about a patient's ability to drive. Doctors thus have a discretion,[51] but face a conflict between their duty of confidentiality and a wider duty to protect the patient and society.

3.47   Once a disability has been notified, DVLA medical officers tend to adhere to rigid guidelines so it is difficult to persuade DVLA to reverse a decision. A right of appeal against refusal to grant or revocation of a driving licence lies to the magistrates' court for the petty sessional area in which the person resides. DVLA usually instruct lawyers and call medical evidence[52] so substantial costs may be awarded against an unsuccessful appellant. Legal aid is not available, yet an appellant will usually need to rely upon a lawyer for advocacy and a doctor for medical evidence. Few appeals succeed.

Passports

3.48   The Identity and Passport Service was established as an Executive Agency of the Home Office on 1 April 2006. The Agency replaces the UK Passport Service (UKPS).[53] Any applicant who is physically unable to sign should make a mark and enclose a letter from the person completing the form on the person's behalf explaining the situation. The passport will bear an observation that the holder is not required to sign.

3.49   When someone is unable to sign a passport application form due to mental disability, a declaration signed by a person responsible for the applicant's welfare may be accepted. For an infirm elderly applicant this could be a son, daughter, doctor, social worker or manager of a residential care home but other categories may be considered. The signatory should explain in the 'Other Information' section of the form, or in a separate letter, that the applicant is mentally disabled and that the signatory has signed on the applicant's behalf in some relevant capacity.

Privileges

Concessionary payments

3.50   Reduced sums may be payable for various services by people over a specified age, but this may be for commercial reasons as well as due to national or local policy. The concession may be provided for in a statute or regulations. Examples are:

(a)   reduced fees for television licences for elderly or disabled people living in certain types of home.[54] A free television licence is also available to persons over 75 in respect of their own home.[55]

(b)   all local authorities must offer a minimum bus concession for all people of pensionable age, and Senior Railcards are available providing savings on most rail fares.[56]

---

[51]   Guidance is to be found in *Medical Aspects of Fitness to Drive: A Guide for Medical Practitioners* (4th edn, 1985) by the Medical Commission on Accident Prevention. See also *Fitness to drive: a guide for health professionals* available at: www.dft.gov.uk/pgr/roadsafety/drs/fitnesstodrive/fitnesstodrive.pdf.

[52]   *At a glance Guide to the current Medical Standards of Fitness to Drive* (September 2009) DVLA publication.

[53]   The Service may be accessed at: www.passport.gov.uk/index.asp or the Adviceline on 0870 521 0410.

[54]   Wireless Telegraphy (Television Licence Fees) Regulations 1997, SI 1997/290.

[55]   A *Factsheet* is available from *AgeUK* at: www.ageuk.org.uk/publications/age-uk-information-guides-and-factsheets.

[56]   There is an *AgeUK Factsheet* on travel and transport (see above).

Parking schemes

3.51 The Blue (formerly Orange) Badge Scheme provides a national arrangement of on-street parking concessions enabling people with severe walking difficulties who travel either as drivers or passengers to park close to their destinations. The Scheme also applies to registered blind people and people with severe upper limb disabilities who regularly drive a vehicle but cannot turn a steering wheel by hand. The Scheme is administered by local authorities who deal with applications and issue badges.[57]

Civic duties

Voting

General

3.52 Everyone is entitled to vote in local government, Parliamentary and European elections[58] if they satisfy certain conditions of residency,[59] citizenship and age[60] and are not barred from voting.[61] People can exercise their right to vote only if their name is on the Electoral Register. The name of every resident should be entered on the registration form completed by a householder in October each year in order that such resident may be included on the Electoral Register. However, people may be added or deleted at any time of the year, the register may be inspected during a specific period in November and December and if a name has been omitted application may then be made for its inclusion under a claims and objections procedure.

3.53 There are two versions: the full register and the edited register (which anyone can buy), and a box may be ticked to omit details from the latter. The householder who completes the form should ask each person included whether they wish their details to appear on the edited register. Although there is no age restriction the form requires an indication to be given of those over the age of 70 years on the relevant date in connection with eligibility for jury service.

Capacity to be on the register

3.54 The form does not raise the question of mental capacity.[62] There is no provision in the legislation dealing with persons who are mentally disabled but registration officers will not enter on the register people whom they have good reason to believe lack capacity to vote under common law because of mental impairment.[63] This will depend upon personal knowledge or being asked to advise. Too high a standard of capacity should not be required and each case should be considered on its own merits. It is sufficient if the individual understands in broad terms the nature and effect of voting and is able to make a choice between candidates. The Electoral Commission advice to electoral registration officers is to err, if at all, on the side of inclusion rather than

---

57   Further information is available at: www.gov.uk/government/organisations/department-for-transport.
58   See generally the Representation of the People Act 1983 (as amended). Further information is available at www.aboutmyvote.co.uk.
59   *Kevin Lippiatt v Electoral Registration Officer, Penwith District Council* (21 March 1996, unreported).
60   18 years and over with no upper age limit. A homeless man may claim residency at his local day centre: *Kevin Lippiatt v Electoral Registration Officer*, above.
61   *Convicted* prisoners are barred from voting.
62   Legal incapacity to vote has been defined as 'some quality inherent in the person, which either at common law, or by statute, deprives him of the status of Parliamentary elector' – *Stowe v Joliffe* [1874] LR9 CP 750.
63   At common law an 'idiot' could not vote but a 'lunatic' might during a lucid moment. This terminology acknowledges the difference between learning disability and mental illness but is not helpful in deciding whether an elderly person has capacity to vote.

omission and to consider how they would justify to the courts any decision to register or not to register a particular person.[64] In practice the decision on whether a frail elderly person will vote may be made by a carer who makes the arrangements.

Capacity to vote

3.55   Any subsequent assessment of competence will be based upon ability to comply with voting formalities rather than mental capacity.[65] The presiding officer may challenge an individual who requests a ballot paper at the polling booth if lack of mental capacity is suspected and must then decide as a question of fact whether the prospective voter at that moment is sufficiently *compos mentis* to discriminate between the candidates and to answer certain statutory questions in an intelligible manner. These include 'Are you the person whose name appears on the Register as ....?' and 'Have you already voted?'.

3.56   A candidate or the election/polling agent may require the questions to be put to the prospective voter. If the questions are not answered satisfactorily a ballot paper should not be issued, but they do not assist in determining mental capacity and no further questions may be put. Electors who are unable to read may ask the presiding officer to mark their vote on the ballot paper but they must be capable of giving directions as to how they wish to vote. A relative or carer may not assist in this way unless the elector is blind and so entitled to have the assistance of a companion.

Postal and proxy voting

3.57   The problem of an elector being unable to attend the polling station is now overcome by the extension of the postal voting facility which used to be available to disabled people and their carers although application must be made in advance.[66] Additional safeguards were introduced from 1 January 2007 in the form of 'personal identifiers' which include a specimen signature and the need to state the date of birth, although the requirement for the signature may be dispensed with in appropriate circumstances.[67] There appears to be no other procedure whereby the vote of an absent voter could be questioned, although the systematic orchestration of inappropriate postal votes from a care or nursing home could no doubt be identified.[68]

3.58   The Mental Capacity Act 2005 specifically provides that the power to vote may not be delegated under that legislation.[69] An elector who satisfies the postal voting qualifications may apply to the registration officer for the appointment of a proxy at a specific election or for an indefinite period and this must be granted if the registration officer is satisfied that the elector is or will be registered as an elector and the proxy is able and willing to be appointed.[70]

---

[64]   *Managing Electoral Services: a good practice guide for electoral administrators in England,* The Electoral Commission, 2002: Appendix XIV.

[65]   Local Elections (Parish and Community) Rules 1986, SI 1986/2215; Local Elections (Principal Areas) Rules 1986, SI 1986/2214.

[66]   Representation of the People Act 2000, s 12.

[67]   Electoral Administration Act 2006, s 14(8).

[68]   There are offences under the Representation of the People Act 1983 (as amended by the 2006 Act) which include undue influence and inappropriate use of postal votes.

[69]   Mental Capacity Act 2005, s 29.

[70]   Representation of the People Act 2000, ss 8 and 9.

Hospital patients

3.59   Ordinary hospital patients do not usually lose their residence at their home address for the purpose of electoral registration. Those residing permanently in residential care or nursing homes should be treated as ordinary members of the community and will register at that address. The officer-in-charge should not be asked to make a judgment as to which residents have the mental capacity to vote.

Mental hospitals

3.60   Voluntary patients in a mental hospital may register as electors by completing the 'patient's declaration' (Form RPF 35) if various conditions are fulfilled. In particular they must be able to make the declaration unaided, though assistance may be given because of blindness or physical incapacity, and it must be witnessed by an authorised member of the hospital staff. They cannot be registered in respect of the hospital where they are a patient but must nominate an address where they have resided in the past or would otherwise be living. The regulations were designed to ensure that no-one loses the right to vote for want of an address and effectively voluntary patients may choose any address within these criteria without the consent of those who live there and even if the address no longer exists, but long-term patients may still be unable to specify one.[71]

3.61   It is for the electoral registration officer to decide which hostels or registered homes for mentally ill or elderly people come within the definition of 'mental hospital', if necessary after obtaining advice from the health authority and Department of Health. For other hostels or registered homes that officer must decide which residents or patients are entitled to be registered, if necessary after considering medical advice. The Home Office guidance[72] states that the warden or person in charge should not be asked to make a judgment as to which residents have the capacity to vote, as such practice would be both objectionable and open to abuse.

Detained mental patients

3.62   The right to vote exists whether patients are detained or voluntarily resident in hospital, in a care home or a hostel. However detained offenders[73] are not entitled to vote. Under the previous Home Office guidance[74] detained patients could not be treated as being resident at the place where detained or be regarded as resident elsewhere because they were not at liberty to leave the hospital, so they were effectively disenfranchised by statute on grounds relating to mental disorder. In 1995 MIND challenged this policy and the government conceded that it was unlawful and that detained patients may have a residence outside the hospital. New guidance was issued[75] but this suggests that a patient detained in hospital for more than 6 months might have difficulty in claiming residency at an address outside the hospital.

---

[71]   There are now special provisions for 'sectioned' (ie compulsorily detained) patients.
[72]   Circular RPA 379, 23 August 1993.
[73]   For example, those detained under the Mental Health Act 1983, ss 37, 38 and 47.
[74]   Circular RPA 379, 23 August 1993.
[75]   Circular RPA 407, 7 May 1996.

Jury service

General

3.63 Jurors are chosen at random from the electoral roll to serve on a jury.[76] Unless ineligible or disqualified under a specific provision, an adult aged under 70 years who fulfils a residence qualification[77] and is registered as an elector is qualified to serve as a juror in the courts and liable to attend for jury service when summoned.[78] It is an offence to fail to comply with a summons, to give false information or to serve on a jury knowing that you are not qualified to do so. If a person called for jury service is not thought fit to sit the jury officer or court clerk should be informed and the summons may be withdrawn.

3.64 Applications for excusal will only be considered for exceptional circumstances but deferral may be considered though only once. Such applications are considered by summoning officers carefully, sympathetically and with regard to individual circumstances. A policy is adopted that is both fair to the individual and consistent with the need to provide a representative jury. Officers therefore can refuse a request if no good reason is given.

Ineligible persons

3.65 The categories of person who are ineligible include anyone who suffers or has suffered from a mental health problem and because of that is either resident in a hospital or similar institution or regularly attends for treatment by a medical practitioner. Also, anyone under guardianship or whose property and affairs are administered by the Court of Protection.[79]

3.66 The decision to discharge a juror, where on account of physical disability or insufficient understanding of English there is doubt as to capacity to act effectively as a juror, must be made by the judge and may not be made on an administrative basis.[80]

Disabled jurors

3.67 A juror with a disability or a special need will be asked by HMCTS to provide further information on the 'Reply to Your Summons for Jury Service'. This information is then used to decide what reasonable adjustments can be made. If it is not possible to make the necessary adjustments then their jury service may be transferred to a court nearby where adjustments can be made to suit their needs.

3.68 Some older people see jury service not as a duty but as a right, and they would not wish to be excluded because of physical infirmity. Many courts do not have wheelchair access but if only some of the courts sitting in the building are so restricted the disabled individual should remain on the panel and raise the issue of access with the judge if it arises upon selection; the judge may wish the juror to return to the panel to await further selection or move to another court to enable the juror to sit.

---

[76] Further information is available at: www.gov.uk/jury-service/overview.
[77] They must have been ordinarily resident in the United Kingdom (or the Isle of Man or the Channel Islands) for at least 5 years since the age of 13 years.
[78] Juries Act 1974, s 1. The government has announced that the upper age limit for jurors in England and Wales is to be raised from 70 to 75.
[79] Juries Act 1974, Sch 1, Part I as amended by Mental Health Act 1983 and Mental Capacity Act 2005.
[80] Juries Act 1974, s 9B. 'Each such application should be dealt with sensitively and sympathetically', Practice Direction by Lord Lane CJ on 19 September 1988.

3.69 Restrictions upon contact with jurors whilst they are considering their verdict may pose problems for those who need personal care at intervals, but a jury bailiff may be able to assist and is covered by his oath not to discuss matters overheard when entering the jury room. There have been many cases in which persons who are blind have served on juries. However, it has been held that a person who is profoundly deaf and unable to follow the proceedings in court, or deliberations in the jury room, without the assistance of an interpreter in sign language should be discharged from jury service because such a person could not act effectively as a juror and it would be an incurable irregularity in the proceedings for the interpreter to retire with the jury to the jury room.[81] The same reasoning would apply if a person called for jury service required the full-time attendance of a carer.[82]

Civil responsibility

Preliminary

3.70 Under this heading we consider the legal liability of elderly people for their actions and the extent to which they might be excused because of their age or state of health. Those who have not made adequate financial provision for retirement or encounter unexpected ill-health may get into financial difficulties so an overview of the tactics then available is included. The special procedures that apply to those who become involved with the courts in civil or criminal proceedings are dealt with later in this chapter.

Tort

3.71 There is little case-law on the extent to which mental incapacity affects liability in tort. The question appears to be whether the individual has the requisite state of mind for the particular tort for which he is to be held responsible, and he must behave as would be expected of a person of normal intelligence in the situation. It is no defence that he acted to the best of his own judgment if this is below that of the reasonable man. There is some indication that a lower standard of care is required from an infant, and it may be that this should also be applied to a frail elderly person.

3.72 In the case of negligence, which depends upon damage arising from breach of a duty of care, the personal characteristics of the defendant do not appear to be relevant save that a higher duty of care may be required from an expert (eg a professional person in the conduct of his business). Mental incapacity may not therefore be a defence to an action in negligence because the test is objective, but there is no direct authority on the point. Some torts involve strict liability and the mental capacity of the defendant will then be irrelevant, although if the acts complained of were involuntary there may be a defence. If a person who is mentally disordered but who knows the nature and quality of his act commits a tort, it is no defence that he does not know that what he is doing is wrong.[83] The circumstances of the individual (eg being in a care home) may be relevant to the existence of a duty of care.

---

[81] *Re Osman* [1996] 1 Cr App R 126, Sir Lawrence Verney, Recorder of London. The Disability Discrimination Act 1995 did not apply because jury service is not deemed to be a 'service to the public'.

[82] In a case in Liverpool, a disabled person's carer was allowed to sit near to this person in the court room but when it came to retiring the carer remained outside the jury room and the other members of the jury attended to their colleague's needs.

[83] *Morriss v Marsden* [1952] 1 All ER 925.

Debts and insolvency

3.73 Older people are particularly vulnerable when they get into debt because their opportunities to raise money are restricted and there is the prospect of carrying mounting debts to the grave. Easy access to loans and credit cards, and costs associated with medical treatment, are causing many older people to incur liabilities that ultimately have to be faced up to. The most important thing is not to ignore the problem in the hope that it will go away. Support is available from Citizens Advice Bureau[84] and many debt advice agencies, Money Advice Centres or Law Centres which provide their services without charge.[85] The much advertised commercial debt firms are best avoided. The following strategies and options are available.[86]

Consolidation loans

3.74 It is seldom possible to borrow one's way out of unmanageable debts, although a consolidation loan may reduce outgoings especially when a series of expensive credit and store card loans have accumulated. The consolidation loan may be appropriate in some cases, and if it is secured on the home the interest rate may be less but there is the prospect of losing the home if the agreed instalments are not regularly paid. The temptation to increase the loan to provide for a few 'luxuries' should be resisted as this is merely repeating the excessive expenditure which may have produced the debt problems in the first place.

Debt management plans

3.75 Where several debts are involved the first step is to make a list of these and of all sources of income and outgoings, and work out a weekly or monthly budget. The possibility of claiming additional welfare benefits should not be overlooked. Priority debts must then be identified, these being rent or mortgage payments, utility payments and council tax which will result in serious consequences if not paid. Civil court judgments or fines may also come within this category especially if a bailiff is threatened. Comprehensive proposals for payment by instalments can then be worked out and put to all creditors in the hope that they will accept these. Non-priority creditors will be offered pro rata payments from what is left after priority debts have been dealt with in the proposals. Debt management firms offer this service but charge a significant proportion of the monthly payments that are made thereby compounding the problem although their intervention may assist in securing agreement with all creditors. In some instances creditors may be prepared to write off debts for people with long-term serious health problems.

Credit agreements

3.76 If financial obligations have been taken on under hire purchase or credit sale agreements, surrendering the goods may still result in a residual liability. Payment by revised instalments may be agreed or stipulated by the county court which has

---

[84] Website: www.adviceguide.org.uk.

[85] The National Debtline can give free information to people living in England and Wales. It also provides an information pack on dealing with debt. The line is available on Monday to Friday 9.00 to 9.00 and on Saturday 9.30. to 1.00. The National Debt Helpline is 0808 808 4000 and the website is: www.nationaldebtline.co.uk.

[86] For possession proceedings relating to a tenanted or mortgaged home see Ch 5 at **5.105**.

additional powers to interfere with the terms when there is an 'extortionate credit bargain' or there are 'unfair contract terms'. A 'time order' can allow more time to pay a regulated credit agreement.[87]

County Court judgment

3.77 Civil court proceedings are only a threat to debtors who have assets that may be seized, property that may be charged or income that may be attached. There is the prospect of obtaining a judgment payable by instalments and sensible proposals should be put to the district judge who will take these into account. Where a judgment is to be enforced by a *warrant of execution* an application may be made for this to be suspended on terms that weekly or monthly instalments will be made.

3.78 It is important to attend any hearing, preferably with an adviser or friend for support, to explain the proposals and any health difficulties may be mentioned. The court will seek to achieve a balance between enforcement of the debt and protection of the debtor. An *attachment of earnings* order may be made when there is income from employment but this must leave the debtor with sufficient income with which to manage – both a normal deduction rate and a protected earnings rate are fixed. If a *charging order* is made against the debtors home this provides security for the judgment creditor and the court will be reluctant to force a sale if a reasonable monthly instalment is paid. A *third party debt order* may recover a debt from a balance in a bank account or an investment.

Administration order

3.79 Where there are a number of debts which do not amount to more than £5,000 in total and a county court judgment is obtained for one of these, the debtor may apply for an *Administration Order*.[88] Under this the county court consolidates all the debts and stipulates a monthly payment that will be distributed by the court between the creditors. The court has a discretion to write off the balance of the debts after a period (usually 3 years) under a composition order. An application form is available from the local county court and there is no fee on the application because the court deducts this from each payment This procedure is a very useful way of getting small debts under control and is often referred to as 'the poor person's bankruptcy'.

Individual voluntary arrangement (IVA)

3.80 An IVA is a legal agreement with creditors (usually non-priority creditors) to repay debts, either in part or in full.[89] The arrangement is negotiated and set out in writing by a licensed Insolvency Practitioner acting as a 'nominee' who generally then becomes a 'supervisor' of the arrangement if it is accepted by the creditors. If 75% in value of the creditors approve the proposals when put to the vote it becomes binding on them all. There is scope for flexibility and creditors usually accept proposals because they offer a better return than the alternative of bankruptcy.

---

[87] See Consumer Credit Acts 1988 and 2006.
[88] Civil Procedure Rules 1998, Sch 2; CCR Ord 39.
[89] Insolvency Rules 1986, SI 1986/1925, Part 5.

Bankruptcy

3.81   There is now much less stigma associated with bankruptcy which is the ultimate means of making a new start financially.[90] Most bankruptcies now relate to people who get out of their depth with consumer loans and spending and relatively few are the result of failed business ventures. The bankrupt is allowed to keep certain items such as household goods, 'tools of trade' and a reasonable amount to live on, but will lose any assets such as a dwelling house. Provided the rent is being paid a tenanted home will not usually be at risk. There are restrictions on taking credit during bankruptcy but discharge usually follows within 12 months although liability to pay a monthly instalment order may continue for 3 years.[91]

3.82   Disadvantages include the cost of the Petition,[92] the consequent publicity,[93] closure of any business and a damaged credit record (although this is likely to be damaged anyway). A 'bankruptcy restriction order' may be made in the case of culpability and this severely restricts financial affairs for up to 15 years.

Debt relief orders

3.83   A simpler procedure known as 'Debt Relief Orders' was introduced on 6 April 2009 for those who do not own their home, have debts below £10,000, assets less than £300 and a low income.[94] Applications must be through an authorised debt adviser who will help with the paperwork.

Taxation

3.84   The topics of personal taxation and payment of National Insurance contributions and council tax are dealt with in Chapter 10. Liability is generally unaffected by mental or physical disability although reliefs and allowances are available in certain specific instances. Procedures whereby tax affairs may be dealt with where the individual is mentally incapable are considered in Chapter 11.

WORK AND LEISURE ACTIVITY

Preliminary

3.85   Some employees choose to remain at work after reaching their normal retirement age and many remain as partners in businesses or company directors. Others seek new fields of full or part-time employment, self-employment or voluntary work. We now consider some legal implications of continuing activity of this nature. Employment law may also be relevant from the other perspective for those who employ cleaners, home helps or personal carers. The pursuit of further education is also considered here in the context of discrimination against people with disabilities, and finally we consider some implications of holidays and travel. The topics of National Insurance and pension contributions and of pensions as a source of income are dealt with in Chapter 10.

---

[90]   Some debts such as fines and student loans are not written off.
[91]   Insolvency Act 1986; Insolvency Rules 1986, Part 6.
[92]   A deposit of £300 for the Official Receiver and a court fee, although the latter may be waived.
[93]   Local newspapers may publish the fact and a list of bankrupt people appears on the internet.
[94]   Tribunals, Courts and Enforcement Act 2007 amended the Insolvency Act 1986. See www.gov.uk/options-for-paying-off-your-debts/debt-relief-orders.

Employment

General

3.86 The climate has changed since today's older people first went out to work. Employment was then largely a matter of contract with disputes being resolved in the civil courts. The distinction between a contract of employment and a contract for the provision of services (self-employment) was clear and the taxation of wages or salary was straightforward. Since then, and especially during the past couple of decades, employment law has become a complex legal subject inhabited by specialist lawyers and with its own tribunals to resolve the majority of disputes. Most of the issues raised in the following paragraphs will be addressed by employment tribunals. Indeed the civil courts have been largely excluded from this rapidly developing field of law and practice.

3.87 Only an overview of provisions relevant to older employees is provided in the following pages. Even the terminology has changed and references are now made to 'workers' and 'non-workers' in some contexts. There are no legal restrictions in relation to older people working but their employment rights are reduced in some areas and protected in others.

Legislation

3.88 The principal legislation that relates to employment is:

- Trade Union and Labour Relations (Consolidation) Act 1992
- Employment Rights Act 1996
- National Minimum Wage Act 1998
- Working Time Regulations 1998[95]
- Employment Relations Act 1999
- Employment Act 2002

but in addition there are numerous further regulations such as the Part-time Workers (Prevention of Less Favourable Treatment) Regulations 2000.[96] The Equality Act 2010 replaces former anti-discrimination legislation (as explained in Chapter 1) and covers employment, equal pay and services, public functions, associations/clubs and education.

Employment or self-employment?

3.89 The common law and most early legislation relating to employment only applied to those working under a *'contract of employment'*. Section 230(1) of the Employment Rights Act 1996 defines an employee as:

> '... an individual who has entered into or works under (or where the contract has ceased, worked under) a contract of employment ...'

and a contract of employment is:

> '... a contract of service or apprenticeship, whether express or implied, and (if it is express) whether oral or in writing.'

---

[95] SI 1998/1833.
[96] SI 2000/1551.

The Act also defines a worker as follows:

> 'In this Act "worker" (except in the phrases "shop worker" and "betting worker") means an individual who has entered into or works under (or, where the employ-ment has ceased, worked under):
>
> (i) a contract of employment, or
> (ii) any other contract, whether express or implied and (if it is express) whether oral or in writing, whereby the individual undertakes to do or perform personally any work or services for another party to the contract whose status is not by virtue of the contract that of a client or customer of any profession or business undertaking carried on by the individual.'

The crucial points are that the contract need not be in writing, and the terms can be express (therefore more likely to be written down) or implied (when evidence of conversations and custom and practice will be relevant). The worker must perform the work personally for another party to the contract.

3.90 The status of worker should be distinguished from self-employment or a contract to provide services, but courts and employment tribunals look at the reality of the situation rather than the terminology applied.[97] They have devised a number of tests of employment and no single one is determinative. These include:

(a) the degree of control and of integration;

(b) the basis of remuneration and taxation;

(c) whether someone is an entrepreneur in their own right; and

(d) whether there is an obligation to provide work and be provided with work.

The definition is more extensive for some employment protection legislation. In particular anti-discrimination legislation extends to those who work under a contract to do personal work. A person may thus be a 'worker' for some purposes but not for others and it becomes necessary to look at the definitions in particular statutes and regulations rather than categorise the individual. Issues also arise in regard to the status of agency and casual workers including 'bank' or 'pool' workers who may be called on 'as and when required'. Even though not employees in the conventional sense, they may be able to contend that they are 'workers' having agreed to perform, personally, any work available for a business which is not a customer.[98]

Voluntary workers

3.91 The nature of the relationship may have to be considered where the worker does not get paid or merely receives 'expenses'. Any expenses will have to be analysed to see if they represent genuine recompense or are a disguised form of remuneration. But pay is not the only factor and even the existence of a contract is not by itself conclusive.[99] Thus the answer to the question: 'is the individual an employee, worker or independent contractor?' may depend on the reason for the enquiry. The existence and contents of a

---

[97] Thus a person may be treated as a worker *even* if taxed on a self-employed basis – *Airfix Footwear Ltd v Cope* [1978] ICR 1210, [1978] IRLR 396, EAT.

[98] Thus the National Minimum Wage Act 1998, Working Time Regulations 1998 and Equality Act 2010.

[99] See *Murray v Newham Citizens Advice Bureau* [2001] ICR 708, EAT where an applicant for the post of 'trainee voluntary adviser' claimed disability discrimination when rejected.

document called a contract will be important evidentially and the type and method of tax deduction will be another factor as will the mutuality of obligation which exists between the parties.

Equal treatment

3.92   For many years all employees have had a right not to be discriminated against on the grounds of sex, race, disability or trade union membership or activity during their employment. The Equality Act 2010 now makes provision to eliminate discrimination including harassment in the workplace (for all employees, not just older workers) as well as for those in vocational training, contract workers, officeholders of public sector appointments and those in partnership. An overview of this legislation and the 'protected characteristics' is provided in Chapter 1[100] and its impact in the field of employment is mentioned below but it should be borne in mind that it applies to all aspects including recruitment, remuneration and other terms of employment, and termination.

Age discrimination

3.93   In consequence of the European Union Directive, from 1 October 2006 regulations prohibiting direct and indirect age discrimination as well as age-related victimisation and harassment were introduced.[101] All ages were affected, not just old age. This required a culture change with employers adopting 'age positive' practices and no longer recruiting, training, promoting or retiring employees on the basis of age. Skills, experience and ability to do the job became important rather than age. Inevitably there are some exceptions such as 'objective justification', which arises where the treatment or practice is a 'proportionate means of achieving a legitimate aim'.[102]

3.94   This has been overtaken by the Equality Act 2010. Job applicants, employees, self-employed people, contract workers, company directors and partners are all eligible to bring claims. There is no restriction on the amount of damages that may be awarded but a claim must be made within 3months of the act complained of.

Victimisation and harassment

3.95   Victimisation is adverse treatment of someone in response to action taken by them under the equality provisions. For example, treating an employee less favourably because of a complaint about age discrimination, but not if the complaint was made in bad faith.

3.96   Harassment occurs when someone's dignity has been violated or they are subjected to an intimidating, hostile, degrading, humiliating or offensive environment. This must be on the grounds of one of the protected characteristics such as age or disability, but not necessarily that of the claimant. Unwanted comments about age or the age of a partner might be sufficient and this may extend to office banter. A tribunal will look at this in both an objective and a subjective way, taking into account the employee's perception and whether it was reasonable to consider the offending conduct as having

---

[100]   Refer to **1.51**.

[101]   Employment Equality (Age) Regulations 2006, SI 2006/1031.

[102]   There is also a narrow 'occupational requirement' which may be met by, for example, the need for a young actor to play a young part in a play.

that effect. Employers are responsible for the conduct of their employees unless they can show that they took reasonable steps to prevent this.

Commencement of employment

3.97 The terms of employment may be express, implied or statutory and may be deduced from custom or implication insofar as not expressly agreed. In addition to any letter offering employment, job descriptions and document setting out the terms, these may be deduced from collective agreements between unions and employer, works rules or handbooks, signs or notices in the workplace and even conversations between the employer and the worker or other workers.

Recruitment

3.98 An employer cannot discriminate when recruiting on the grounds of a protected characteristic[103] under the Equality Act 2010 or trade union membership and the exception for refusal to recruit over the age of 65 no longer applies now that the default retirement age of 65 years has been phased out. Questions about health may not be appropriate because relying on the information for recruitment may amount to disability discrimination, although this could be relevant as to whether reasonable adjustments would be required. Questions such as 'why would you want such a challenge at this stage of your career?' and comments such as 'you are over qualified' demonstrate age bias and are unlikely to be justified. Advertising for staff to join a 'young, dynamic team', asking an applicant's age at interview and advertising only in journals with a readership in a particular age group could all lead to discrimination claims.

3.99 Employees who work with children or vulnerable groups must have particular checks before commencing employment.[104] From June 2013 the Disclosure and Barring Service (DBS)[105] helps employers make safer recruitment decisions and prevent unsuitable people from working with vulnerable groups, including children. It replaces the Criminal Records Bureau (CRB) and Independent Safeguarding Authority (ISA).

Statement of terms of employment

3.100 It is a legal requirement that a written statement of particulars be given to most employees within 2 months of commencement of the employment or within one month of certain changes.[106] The main terms and conditions must be specified including the rate of remuneration and intervals at which it is paid, hours, holidays, sickness and sick pay. Certain other basic terms must also be specified and these include the period of notice, disciplinary and grievance procedures, and any terms relating to pensions.

3.101 The stated terms are not conclusive if there is evidence that other terms have been agreed or are generally applied in practice. If the parties have behaved in a manner inconsistent with them that behaviour is likely to be the best evidence relating to the relevant term. Insofar as not specified the terms of the contract may be deduced from long established custom or practice or simply because it is reasonable to do so. There may be a financial sanction on an employer for failure to provide this document.[107]

---

[103] For the protected characteristics see Ch 1 at **1.51**.
[104] Safeguarding Vulnerable Groups Act 2006; Protection of Children Act 1999.
[105] This is an executive non-departmental public body of the Home Office. See: www.gov.uk/government/organisations/disclosure-and-barring-service.
[106] Employment Rights Act 1996, ss 1 and 4(3).
[107] Employment Act 2002, s 38.

The employment relationship

3.102 Duties of the employer that may be implied by common law include payment of wages, provision of a minimum amount of work and proper information and provision of a safe environment and system of work. Implied duties on the part of the employee include: to act in good faith and pass on relevant information; to follow lawful orders and provide personal service; and to exercise reasonable care and skill in the performance of duties. There will be mutual duties of trust and confidence although this may be expanded upon or restricted by the express terms.

3.103 There has been legislative intervention over the years which is now consolidated in the Employment Rights Act 1996 and the agreed terms cannot override certain terms implied by statute. These include statutory minimum provisions in regard to the notice period, equal pay and rights relating to time off and union membership or activities.

Remuneration

3.104 All relevant workers (including agency workers and home workers) became entitled to the National Minimum Wage (NMW) with effect from 1 April 1999.[108] The rates are increased every year in October.[109] There is no maximum age and the worker has the right not to be victimised for claiming the minimum wage.

3.105 All employees should receive an itemised pay statement giving the breakdown of the amount actually paid.[110] No employee can have a deduction made from his wages other than for overpayment of wages or expenses unless this has been agreed in writing (eg in the contract of employment) or under some statutory provision. The Attachment of Earnings Act 1971 allows debts to be collected in this way but only under a court order.

3.106 Employees are entitled to equal pay with the opposite sex which includes all benefits and pensions.[111] Pay and non-pay benefits which depend on length of service requirements of 5 years or less or which recognise and reward loyalty and experience and motivate staff may continue. Offering staff benefits contingent upon length of service beyond this will amount to indirect age discrimination because some age groups are more likely to have completed the required length of service than others.

Sick pay

3.107 The contract of employment should set out the basis on which payment of wages is made during periods of sickness, and this may be on a sliding scale with an overall maximum for any stated period. In the absence of a discernible agreement the obligation will be to pay for a reasonable period which may depend upon the treatment of other employees in the past and custom and practice in the industry. Statutory sick pay may be available for up to 26 weeks and it is common for employers to deduct this from the contractual pay so that the employee receives only the net amount.

---

[108] National Minimum Wage Act 1998, s 54.
[109] They are available at www.gov.uk/national-minimum-wage-rates.
[110] Employment Rights Act 1996, s 8.
[111] Equality Act 2010, Part 5, Chapter 3 (formerly Equal Pay Act 1970).

Working hours

3.108 The hours during which the employee may be required to work are a matter for agreement between employer and employee. But limits are imposed on the hours that an employee can be required to work,[112] with rest breaks at work and minimum daily and weekly rest periods.[113] There must also be paid annual leave. This extends to the majority of agency workers and freelancers, but most employees in the transport sector are excluded. 'Workforce agreements' may be reached which to some extent override these provisions.

3.109 Workers may not be discriminated against for asserting an entitlement. Night workers should have health assessments with the right to be moved to day jobs if they become ill, and they should be treated no less favourably than day workers. Since April 2007 carers of a spouse, partner, near relative or someone else living at the same address have been able to apply for flexible working hours and employers are obliged to consider these requests.[114]

Part-timers and time off work

3.110 Many older people will wish to work part-time and their employment situation is now more secure. Part-time employees are entitled to the same rights (pro rata) as their full-time colleagues doing the same work.[115] Similar provisions now apply to fixed term employees.[116]

3.111 Holidays are normally a matter for agreement. Recently the courts have confirmed that the right to paid holiday can be accrued during periods of ill-health absence and may be rolled over to the following year in some circumstances. Workers are entitled to reasonable time off for certain purposes, including looking for another job or undergoing training, performing duties as a union official or employee representative, and undertaking public duties (eg as a JP).[117] The question of payment is for negotiation between the parties, there being no general right to paid time off. There is a right to take up to 13 weeks off to care for dependants in a family emergency, the time allowed being that which is reasonable in order to take action that is necessary.

Conduct of the employee

3.112 New rules for disciplinary procedures came into force in October 2004.[118] Employees may be disciplined by oral, written or final written warnings for misconduct such as poor timekeeping or repeated absences. Provided that a fair hearing is given at which the employee may be accompanied by a work colleague or union representative, the employer may impose sanctions. There should be a right of appeal. In the event of long-term absence the employer may wish to arrange a medical examination rather than rely upon the employee's GP. In the case of gross misconduct it is preferable to suspend the employee pending an investigation and hearing rather than impose instant dismissal.

---

[112] Presently 48 hours a week over a 17-week period, or for night work normal hours not exceeding an average of 8 hours in 24.

[113] Working Time Regulations 1998, SI 1998/1833.

[114] This includes in-laws, uncles, aunts and step-relatives. Employment Rights Act 1996, s 80F.

[115] Part-time Workers (Prevention of Less Favourable Treatment) Regulations 2000, SI 2000/1551.

[116] Fixed-term Employees (Prevention of Less Favourable Treatment) Regulations 2002, SI 2002/2034.

[117] Trade Union and Labour Relations (Consolidation) Act 1992.

[118] Employment Act 2002, Sch 2. See also the ACAS Code of Practice on Disciplinary and Grievance Procedures.

Whistleblowing

3.113 There are provisions to protect employees who express concerns about a breach of an obligation, such as a health and safety duty within the workplace or some wrongdoing.[119] In the event of reprisals the employee may take the employer to a tribunal who can award compensation to the employee and may effect disclosure to the relevant authority.

Transfer of employment

3.114 The employee's job may be protected when the business is sold as a going concern to a different employer. Such protection may extend to a situation where a service is transferred from one service provider to another and substantially the same services are provided by the new contractor. In these circumstances all the employee's rights under the contract of employment are transferred to the new owner or contractor.[120] Membership of an occupational pension scheme will not transfer but the new employer must offer a comparable scheme.[121] Continuity of employment is also preserved for redundancy pay and statutory notice pay.

Termination of employment

3.115 The contract of employment may be terminated by agreement, resignation of the employee, operation of law, notice from the employer, 'constructive dismissal' or expiration of a fixed term. It may also be frustrated, for example by sickness or injury.

Notice

3.116 There are statutory minimum notice periods of one week after a month, 2 weeks after 2 years and thereafter one week per year up to a maximum of 12 weeks.[122] The contract may stipulate for longer periods and reasonable notice must be given where it does not, which may be more than the statutory minimum. There may be instant dismissal without notice for gross misconduct, but where this is not justified employment may in most cases be terminated immediately with wages paid in lieu of notice.

Entitlement

3.117 Upon dismissal an employee is entitled to net salary and benefits for the entire notice period if termination is with immediate effect. This is subject to the duty to mitigate the loss by finding other work which is usually more difficult for older workers. There may be a right to work during the full notice period in some circumstances. After 2 years' service the employee is entitled to a written statement of reasons for the dismissal.[123]

Wrongful dismissal

3.118 Damages may be claimed for any dismissal in breach of contract regardless of age. Either the courts or employment tribunal have jurisdiction but the tribunal cannot award more than £25,000.

---

[119]　Public Interest Disclosure Act 1998.
[120]　Transfer of Undertakings (Pension Protection) Regulations 2006, SI 2006/246 (TUPE).
[121]　Transfer of Employment (Protection of Employment) Regulations 2005, SI 2005/649.
[122]　Employment Rights Act 1996, s 86.
[123]　Employment Rights Act 1996, s 92.

Unfair dismissal

3.119 After 2 years' continuous employment[124] an employee has a right not to be unfairly dismissed, and since October 2006 this applies to those over normal retirement age, giving older workers the same rights to claim unfair dismissal as younger workers, unless there is a genuine retirement. Claims must be made within 3 months of the 'effective date of termination', which means the date on which the notice expires. In the case of dismissal without notice this would be 'the date on which the termination takes effect', and for fixed term contracts it is the date on which the contract expires without being renewed.

3.120 The employer must have a valid statutory reason for dismissal and have acted reasonably in treating that reason as justifying dismissal taking into account all the circumstances, including size and administrative resources.[125] Valid reasons for dismissal generally relate to the employee's conduct, capability, redundancy or breach of an enactment although there may be 'some other substantial reason'. There are some automatically unfair reasons, including dismissal for asserting statutory rights (including taking leave to care for dependents) or taking part in trade union activities.

3.121 Dismissal may be fair where it relates to the capability of the employee for performing work of the kind he is employed to do assessed by reference to skill, aptitude, health or any other physical or mental quality. Also on grounds of incapacity including due to prolonged sickness (provided this does not amount to disability discrimination) but full medical information should be obtained. Dismissal may only be justified on grounds of incompetence or ill-health if proper procedures have been followed.[126]

3.122 Unfair dismissal claims are distinct from claims for wrongful dismissal. Remedies are provided by the employment tribunal and an unfairly dismissed employee can request re-employment or compensation, which is normally based upon a compensatory award plus a basic award. The former is to cover financial loss resulting from the dismissal insofar as the employer is responsible, thus allowing a reduction to be made for contributory conduct on the part of the employee or failure to mitigate the loss. The latter is calculated according to a formula which takes into account weekly pay, age and length of employment. Re-employment is seldom sought, but if ordered and not complied with a further sum could be awarded which can be doubled if the dismissal was for discriminatory reasons. Compensation for an employee dismissed before normal retiring age may take into account that employment should have continued beyond that age, but the Equality Act 2010 provides that a person who has reached 65 cannot normally bring an unfair dismissal claim if they have been retired in accordance with the statutory retirement procedures.[127]

Redundancy

3.123 A redundancy occurs where there is a closure of the business or in the place where the employee works, or a cessation or diminution in the need for employees to carry out work of a particular kind. Employees who are made redundant after 2 years' continuous employment are entitled to a redundancy payment based on the number of

---

[124] Increased from one year since 6 April 2012.

[125] Employment Rights Act 1996, s 94.

[126] It should be ascertained if there are reasons for this, both at work or outside work and monitoring is essential.

[127] Part 2 of Sch 9.

years' service with a maximum payment.[128] Older workers have the same rights to claim and receive a redundancy payment as younger workers, unless there is a genuine retirement. Claims must be made within 6 months of the 'relevant date' which is normally the date on which the employment ended. An employer can avoid a redundancy payment by offering suitable alternative employment to the redundant employee (ie employment on the same or very similar terms and conditions without any significant loss of status).

3.124 Unfair selection for redundancy may amount to unfair dismissal and selection of older workers has been held to be an improper criterion and unfair. In addition, under the new regulations selection criteria should not be discriminatory on grounds of age. A redundancy notice served on a chief executive with the aim of dismissing him before his 49th birthday in order to save the expense of early retirement at an enhanced pension was held to be fair, being in pursuance of a legitimate aim.[129] An employee should take care when volunteering for redundancy (eg for early retirement) because this could be interpreted as termination by agreement rather than dismissal for state benefits purposes.

Retirement

3.125 The default retirement age (formerly 65) has now been phased out and most people can work for as long as they wish to. Few businesses set a compulsory retirement age for their employees, but some can set a compulsory retirement age if they can clearly justify it. So the retirement age normally becomes when an employee chooses to retire, and if an employee chooses to work longer they cannot be discriminated against. It is an employee's responsibility to discuss when and how to retire with their employer and this could include phasing retirement by working flexibly.

Self-employment

3.126 Self-employment may continue to any age[130] and there may be tax incentives to retain a business or a share in a business. Tax-efficient schemes should be considered where it is desired to hand on the business to the next generation, but tax planning generally is beyond the scope of this book.[131]

Sole traders

3.127 Those who wish to trade or engage in business on their own are known as sole traders or proprietors and their activities are governed by the general principles of contract and commercial law. Some businesses may only be carried on by duly qualified persons[132] or if licences are obtained.[133] A sole trader who works exclusively for one customer may appear to be an independent contractor but on closer examination may prove to be an employee.

---

[128]   Employment Rights Act 1996, s 135.
[129]   *Woodcock v Cumbria Primary Care Trust* [2012] EWCA Civ 330.
[130]   A checklist is available via: www.adviceguide.org.uk/index/life/employment.htm.
[131]   For capital gains tax advantages on retirement and inheritance tax advantages in respect of business assets see Ch 10 and for gifts and testamentary provision Ch 12.
[132]   Eg solicitors, pharmacists, investment businesses.
[133]   Eg the sale of intoxicating liquor, consumer credit or consumer hire businesses and businesses which involve the taking of deposits.

3.128 There is no system of registration and a sole trader may choose a name for the business provided that this is not misleading, but if this is a name other than his or her own it is a 'business name' and requirements regarding disclosure of information about the proprietor apply.[134]

Partnership

3.129 The law of partnership is governed by the Partnership Act 1890. Section 1 defines partnership as the relationship which subsists between persons carrying on business in common with a view of profit. This is based on a contract between two or more parties which affects their liability to one another and also to persons dealing with them as a partnership. The requirement of a profit motive excludes most clubs and voluntary associations and is to be tested according to laid down criteria. Individuals and companies can form partnerships, and a business carried on in partnership is generally known as a 'firm'.

3.130 A partnership does not have legal personality which means that the partners themselves are the joint owners of partnership property and are personally liable for the debts and liabilities of the firm. Although partners may agree between themselves as to their shares in the partnership and the division of duties, their liability to others is unlimited and each may take part in the management of the partnership business. It has been stated that '... each partner is the unlimited agent of every other in every matter connected with the partnership business'. But if the partners agree to restrict the usual authority of partners, no act done in contravention of this agreement will bind the firm with respect to third parties who were aware of the restriction.

Partnership agreements

3.131 Although a formal agreement in writing is not essential the partners should decide their intentions as to the business of the partnership, what money or assets they are putting in, the manner in which they will share any profits or losses (and whether they will take any prior salaries) and what will happen to the business if a partner leaves or dies. The partnership agreement will normally contain clauses covering issues such as the identity of the partners, the nature of the business, partnership property, decision making and provisions dealing with the death, retirement or expulsion of a partner. The advantage of a partnership deed or written agreement is that this can set out the terms from the outset, although these can be changed by a course of conduct or subsequent agreement.

Limited liability partnerships

3.132 Since July 2000 there has been a new form of legal entity known as a 'limited liability partnership'.[135] Relations between the partners follow partnership law. There must be one or more partners who have unlimited liability but subject to this the partners are free to reach agreement as to their liabilities and duties as partners between themselves. The partners who have limited liability contribute to the partnership a specified amount of assets in money or money's worth and enjoy immunity from liability beyond the amount so contributed. An important condition of this immunity is that the limited partner has no part in the management of the business and no power to bind the

---

[134] Companies Act 2006, ss 1200–1206. These provisions apply also to partnerships.
[135] Limited Liability Partnerships Act 2000; Limited Liability Partnerships Regulations 2001, SI 2001/1090.

firm. A limited partner who goes beyond this limitation becomes liable. There are substantial regulatory provisions such as filing an annual return and audited accounts with Companies House.

Termination

3.133 A partnership will be dissolved on the expiry of a fixed term or termination of a project or undertaking which was its sole purpose. Also by any partner giving notice of intention to dissolve the partnership and on the death or bankruptcy of a partner (subject to what the partners may have agreed should happen in these circumstances). A partner may seek a court order of dissolution of the partnership in certain circumstances, including where a partner becomes permanently incapable of performing his part of the partnership contract.

3.134 Where the partnership is dissolved, the assets must be collected in and used firstly to discharge any debts and liabilities and then any remainder shared between the partners in accordance with their original agreement as to share of the capital. If the partnership agreement does not provide for notice of retirement, the only way in which a partner can retire from the partnership will be bring about a general dissolution of the partnership (although a new partnership may then be established by the continuing partners). Many partnership agreements provide for purchase of an outgoing partner's share by the continuing partners.

Age and capacity

3.135 In the absence of specific provision in the partnership agreement neither age nor infirmity is a bar to entry into partnership unless the party lacks sufficient capacity to enter into the contract, and even then that party may still be bound by the arrangement if the other partner or partners did not know of the incapacity. Subsequent mental incapacity does not automatically dissolve a partnership (unless this triggers a specific termination provision in the partnership agreement) but it is a ground for asking the court to decree a dissolution. In dealings with third parties a purported partner could be liable under the principle of holding out if he represents himself, or knowingly allows himself to be represented, as partner of the incapacitated party even if there is in fact no valid partnership.[136]

3.136 The Equality Act 2010 prohibiting age discrimination in employment applies to partnerships. So a partnership will have to establish objective justification of any retirement age and a policy of retiring partners early may be difficult to sustain. Ageist harassment within a partnership could also give rise to a compensation claim. Obliging a partner to retire who is no longer seen as an effective contributor might also amount to age discrimination unless there are clearly documented performance-related reasons which do not also apply to younger partners.[137] The Supreme Court has held that a provision in a partnership deed for a firm of solicitors that partners must retire at 65 years may be 'objectively justified' on the basis that it was 'a proportionate means of achieving a legitimate aim'.[138]

---

[136] Partnership Act 1890, ss 35 and 14(1).
[137] The Employment Appeal Tribunal has criticised 'unfounded stereotypical assumptions' that a partner's performance starts to drop away at a certain age.
[138] *Seldon v Clarkson Wright and Jakes* [2012] UKSC 16.

Voluntary work

General

3.137 Those wishing to engage in voluntary work should check the effect on any state benefits and take care not to become personally liable under any contracts that are entered into. The normal law of negligence will apply as regards any injury caused to any person or damage caused to property during the course of such work so some form of insurance may be appropriate. Those wishing to establish or participate in a members club[139] or an association[140] should take advice on the appropriateness of the form or structure and the implications of personal involvement. If the purpose is to promote some objective beneficial to the wider community it may be possible to register as a charity but a constitution of some form will still be required whether this be a trust deed, a constitution or the formation of a company limited by guarantee.

Committee member

3.138 Before becoming a committee member of an unincorporated society, club or association it is important to consider the rules or other constitution of the organisation and its financial state. The annual accounts should be examined. Committee members are jointly and severally liable for any liabilities incurred although they may usually seek indemnity from the assets of the organisation.

3.139 It is becoming increasingly desirable to form a limited liability company, usually incorporated by guarantee without a share capital, especially where there are employees or substantial contracts or risks may be involved. Committee members are then technically directors of the company. The directors can still be personally responsible if the company has traded whilst insolvent or they have acted imprudently or beyond the powers of the company and insurance against directors' liability should be arranged by the company.

Club trustees

3.140 A members club may loosely be defined as an association for the purposes of social, educational or recreational pursuit. As such, there will be no object of acquiring gain and this type of association is not for business purposes. The club will be based on a contract between its members. If the members pay money to the club, this property becomes the property of all members and ceases to be their individual property. If the club is then wound up by order of the court as an unregistered company the surplus assets are distributed to the members for the time being, unless the members have agreed some other distribution in their contract. Clubs may operate through a management committee or by forming a private company limited by guarantee.

3.141 The club may appoint trustees to hold assets and enter into contracts. They should seek to limit their liability under any contracts to the amount of the club assets from time to time under their control, or exclude the right of any creditor to claim against them personally for any shortfall. Merely describing themselves as trustees does not limit liability and trustees may also wish to obtain an indemnity from the individual club members or at least the members of the club management committee.

---

[139] As distinct from a 'proprietory club' which is actually owned by someone and in which members acquire only limited (if any) rights.

[140] The organisation may be described as a club, society, association or by some other description and may, or may not, have a body of members apart from those in control. What is important is how it has been set up.

Charity trustees

3.142 Those who are charity trustees, whether in the capacity of ordinary trustees, committee members or directors, assume further responsibilities. Full particulars are available from the Charity Commissioners.

Education
Preliminary

3.143 It may seem strange to mention education in the context of older people, but many seek to widen their knowledge during retirement and even to gain academic qualifications. In the past there existed effective barriers to those with physical or mental impairments participating in such pursuits but the extension of disability discrimination legislation to further and higher education creates valuable new opportunities.

Disability discrimination

3.144 The Equality Act 2010 applies to further and higher education institutions and to local authorities that provide adult or continuing education, and relates to both full- and part-time courses, including short courses, evening classes and distance learning. All stages (admissions, enrolment, education, training, examinations and assessments) are covered, and also provision of student services such as residential accommodation and leisure facilities, catering, library facilities and welfare services.[141]

Implications

3.145 The legislation does not aim to lower academic standards but rather to ensure that disabled people have equal opportunity to benefit from, and contribute to, education of the nature covered. It is 'anticipatory' in the sense that providers must consider what sort of adjustments may be needed for disabled people in the future. Once they have made appropriate adjustments their market for recruitment will be wider and the needs of some disabled students will be met automatically, but for others adjustments will still be required in response to particular needs.

3.146 The education provider should make reasonable attempts to find out about a person's disability-related needs, in particular by asking the right questions on application forms, at enrolment, prior to any outings and on the introduction of a tutor. An understanding environment should be created with an explanation being given as to why this information is being sought and how the individual will be supported. Assurances of confidentiality may be appropriate. If despite all this a student chooses not to disclose any such needs then the provider will not be liable for any failure to make adjustments.

3.147 The steps that it is reasonable for an education provider to take will depend upon the type of services being offered, the size and resources of the institution and the effect of the disability on the student. When considering what is reasonable there will be taken into account the need to maintain academic and other standards, the financial resources available to the responsible body and the grants or loans likely to be available to disabled students for the purpose of enabling them to receive student services.

---

[141]　For a general explanation see Ch 1 at **1.51**.

Remedies

3.148 Any claims relating to disability discrimination in further or higher education are to be brought as civil proceedings in the county court and may result in an award of damages.

Holidays and travel

Preliminary

3.149 Many retired people who have savings or a sufficient pension choose to spend their additional leisure time travelling or taking holidays abroad. Some of the legal implications are considered under this heading.

Contractual relationships

3.150 One or more contracts will be involved, whether for travel or accommodation, and some of these may involve other jurisdictions. Bookings may be made personally, by post or by telephone and the more adventurous will organise their own travel arrangements through the internet, but most people prefer to book a 'package'. However, when something goes wrong with one of the components of a holiday the legal position can be complex, and additional protection has been provided for the package holiday. The travel industry is quite sophisticated but dominated by a small number of companies which have become household names due to extensive promotion and advertising. There are also small operators which provide tailor-made holidays often to more exotic locations.

3.151 Bookings may be made direct with the tour operator or through a travel agent, although some travel agents are subsidiaries of the leading operators. There are also consortia of independent travel agents and truly independent agents. In addition many airlines, whether providing a full traditional service or of the 'no frills' type, enable hotel booking and even car hire which may be treated as part of a package. If follows that there may be one or more contracts with the tour operator, the travel agent and/or those who actually provide the services. Where there is no contractual liability a separate liability in tort may arise, or there may be a liability in both tort and contract.[142] When something goes wrong the route for a remedy will be uncertain and it may be best initially to approach this through complaints procedures or by referring to a trade association such as the Association of British Travel Agents (ABTA) or the Federation of Tour Operators (FTO).[143]

Package travel

3.152 In 1990 the Council of the European Communities adopted the Package Travel, Package Holidays and Package Tours Directive and this has now been given effect in UK law.[144] It supplements the common law and creates a new statutory framework within which tour operators must work when supplying packaged products. In summary these are pre-arranged combinations of transport, accommodation or other tourist services at

---

[142] The significance of this is that rules as to damages may be different so it may be appropriate to bring a claim in both contract and tort (eg negligence).
[143] The websites are: abta.com and www.fto.co.uk.
[144] Package Travel, Package Holidays and Package Tours Regulations 1992, SI 1992/3288. Available at: www.legislation.gov.uk/uksi/1992/3288/contents/made.

an inclusive price. The operator becomes liable for all aspects of the package (even if delivered in other countries by different services providers) not only to the contracting party but also to other persons included in the holiday and any persons to whom the benefit of the holiday is transferred.[145]

3.153 The operator is obliged to give the consumer essential information about the holiday package so that an informed choice may be made and rights of cancellation arise if changes have to be made before commencement of the holiday. Compensation may be payable in certain circumstances and there is protection against insolvency by compulsory bonding (or equivalent).

Air travel

3.154 The rights of disabled air passengers leaving or arriving at European airports were increased from July 2008.[146] The onus of helping a passenger from the airport entrance to the plane is now placed with the airport authorities, as opposed to the airline which takes over during the flight. An extra charge must not be made and staff should receive disability awareness and disability equality training. The ambit of disability is far wider than that in disability legislation and includes temporary reduced mobility.

3.155 If a passenger needs assistance this must be communicated at the time of booking (or at least 48 hours before departure). It is unlawful for an airline, travel agent or tour operator to refuse a booking on the ground of disability or to refuse to allow a disabled person to board an aircraft when they have a valid ticket or reservation. Where for exceptional circumstances legitimate safety or technical reasons prevail the individual must be provided with an explanation and offered a reasonable alternative such as reimbursement or re-routing.

3.156 There are rules on enforcement and a range of penalties.[147] Passengers whose rights have been infringed may seek compensation in the county court which may include injury to feelings, but it will be a defence to show that reasonable steps were taken to comply with the regulations. Conciliation is available through the Equality and Human Rights Commission.

COURT PROCEEDINGS

Preliminary

3.157 Old age by itself is not a barrier to conducting proceedings. An older person may become involved with the civil courts as a claimant or defendant, or with the family courts as an applicant or respondent. The topic of access to justice in general has been considered in Chapter 1 and involvement with the criminal justice system is dealt with separately under the next main heading Criminal Responsibility.

---

[145] Contracts (Rights of Third Parties) Act 1999 would give named third parties the right to enforce the terms in any event.

[146] Rights of Disabled Persons and Persons with Reduced Mobility when Travelling by Air, EC Regulation 1107/2006.

[147] Civil Aviation (Access to Travel for Disabled Persons and Persons with Reduced Mobility) Regulations 2007, SI 2007/1895.

Tribunals

3.158 In addition to the traditional courts such as the High Court of Justice and the county court there is an extensive range of tribunals[148] most of which have recently been reformed and more closely aligned to the courts.[149] These deal with appeals on a wide range of decisions by government departments and public authorities on matters such as social security benefits, immigration and mental health treatment and (with the exception of the employment tribunals which stand alone) have all been brought within a unified system.

3.159 There are First-tier Tribunals divided into Chambers including the Social Entitlement Chamber and the Health Education and Social Care Chamber, with further appeals progressing to an Upper Tribunal and ultimately the Court of Appeal. The legally qualified chairs of these tribunals are now known as Tribunal Judges and the Administrative Justice and Tribunals Council has replaced the Council on Tribunals as the supervisory body. An older person may well become involved in an appeal which is taken before one of these tribunals and they are mentioned as appropriate throughout this book. Their procedures are generally more informal than those of the courts.

Procedures

Court Rules

3.160 Courts are governed by their own rulebooks and there are at present the following sets of rules:

- Civil Procedure Rules 1998 (CPR) for civil proceedings;[150]
- Family Procedure Rules 2010 (FPR) for family proceedings;[151]
- Insolvency Rules 1986 for insolvency proceedings;[152] and
- Court of Protection Rules 2007.[153]

These Rules are supplemented by Practice Directions that apply throughout the country and provide a guide as to how the rules should be applied.[154] In the tribunal system each Chamber has its own rules.

Civil Justice Reforms

3.161 The introduction in April 1999 of a new procedural code for civil proceedings in the High Court and county courts represented a change of culture in the civil justice system.[155] The problems of the old system were identified as delay, cost and inequality of the parties, and the aim of the reforms was to achieve access to justice for all with

---

[148] A list is available at: www.justice.gov.uk/tribunals.

[149] Tribunals, Courts and Enforcement Act 2007. HM Courts and Tribunals Service (HMCTS) now administers both the courts and the tribunals.

[150] Replacing Rules of the Supreme Court 1965 (RSC) and County Court Rules 1981 (CCR). See *Civil Court Service 2013* (Jordan Publishing) – published annually.

[151] SI 2010/2955, replacing Family Proceedings Rules 1991, SI 1991/1247. See *The Family Court Practice* (Family Law) – published annually.

[152] SI 1986/1925.

[153] See *Court of Protection Practice 2013* (Jordan Publishing) – published annually.

[154] These are made by the senior judiciary and can be amended more readily than the Rules which must be put before Parliament. Local practice directions should no longer be made.

[155] Referred to as the 'Woolf Reforms' after Lord Woolf's *Access to Justice* Report (July 1996).

procedures that are easier to understand.[156] Proceedings are henceforth governed by the *overriding objective* of enabling the court to deal with cases justly, which means:

(a)   ensuring that the parties are on an equal footing;

(b)   saving expense;

(c)   dealing with cases in ways which are proportionate to the money involved, importance of the case, complexity of the issues and financial position of each party;

(d)   ensuring that cases are dealt with expeditiously and fairly; and

(e)   allotting to cases an appropriate share of the court's resources.

3.162 The court must seek to give effect to the overriding objective and the parties are required to help. Instead of leaving them to progress litigation, the judge acts as 'case manager' and adopts an interventionist role. This includes encouraging the parties to co-operate, identifying the real issues at an early stage, deciding how these can best be resolved, and fixing a timetable. Cases are allocated to one of three 'tracks' according to the amount in issue, complexity and other factors.[157] Alternative forms of dispute resolution are encouraged and attempts should be made to settle proceedings at an early stage.

Family Justice Reforms

3.163 Similar reforms to the rather outdated rules for family proceedings were introduced in 2010 and these also adopt the overriding objective. Hitherto the family justice system has been part of the civil courts but separate family courts are now being created which better integrate the work of the former Family Proceedings Court (part of the Magistrates Court) and the county court together with the Family Division of the High Court.

Implications for older people

3.164 There is much in these reforms of potential benefit to the elderly individual, but more could have been achieved. As the intention was to ensure that the parties are on an equal footing (or that there is a level playing field) this represented an opportunity to address the needs of people with disabilities or other disadvantages who encounter the civil courts. The writer submitted during the consultations that unless this was spelled out it would be overlooked and that an express duty should be imposed upon the court to:

> 'ascertain if any of the parties has a physical or mental impairment which substantially affects that party's ability to conduct or participate in the proceedings.'

This was not included in the new rules and the emphasis remains upon financial inequality. There is no specific mention of a duty to address the personal needs of litigants, but the overriding objective is wide enough to encompass other personal handicaps and the judge in managing cases should take these into account.[158]

---

[156]   Simpler language is adopted and Latin expressions are no longer used. The party bringing the claim is described as *claimant* rather than plaintiff, but the party defending is still described as *defendant*.

[157]   These are the 'multi-track', the 'fast track' and a small claims track.

[158]   The writer has been involved in training judges in disability issues and training has recently included the Equality Act 2010 which has implications for all courts and tribunals.

3.165 An older person may have difficulty coping as a party to proceedings or as a witness at a hearing because of some physical disability or sensory impairment. For example:

(1)   impaired mobility may render it impossible to gain access to the court or cope in a particular courtroom;

(2)   impaired hearing or vision may make it difficult to identify what is going on;

(3)   communication limitations may prevent others from understanding the individual;

(4)   limited concentration spans or the need for regular medication may make it impossible to remain in court for more than a limited period; and

(5)   some ailments may make it impossible to attend court at all.

The steps that may be taken to overcome such problems, including having personal assistance from a *McKenzie* friend or lay representative, are considered in Chapter 1 under the heading 'Role of the Courts' because they apply to proceedings before any court or tribunal.

Mental capacity

3.166 When a party to proceedings lacks capacity to conduct those proceedings, a procedure is needed to enable the proceedings to continue with a representative acting on behalf of that party.[159] These procedures are to be found in Part 21 of the Civil Procedure Rules 1998 (CPR) in respect of civil proceedings and in Part 15 of the Family Procedure Rules 2010 (FPR) in respect of family proceedings.[160] Such party is known as a 'protected party'[161] and the representative is referred to as a 'litigation friend'.[162] The civil procedures also ensure that compromises and settlements are approved by the court, and there is supervision of money recovered. Courts control their own procedures and principles of agency do not apply, so a power of attorney cannot confer a right to conduct litigation or of audience.[163]

Protected parties

3.167 A protected party is a party, or an intended party, who lacks capacity (within the meaning of the Mental Capacity Act 2005) to conduct the proceedings. There is thus introduced into the CPR the principles of the 2005 Act which provides:

> 'A person lacks capacity in relation to a matter if at the material time he is unable to make a decision for himself in relation to the matter because of an impairment of, or a disturbance in the functioning of, the mind or brain.'

3.168 A party is unable to make a decision for himself if he is unable to understand the information relevant to the decision, to retain that information, to use or weigh that information as part of the process of making the decision, or to communicate his

---

[159]   Capacity in general is dealt with in Ch 1 at **1.93** et seq.

[160]   For insolvency proceedings refer to the Insolvency Rules 1986 which rely upon the CPR to fill any gaps.

[161]   The former rules described such parties along with infants as being 'under disability' and those who lacked capacity were termed 'patients' or 'mental patients'.

[162]   Previously a 'next friend' for the party bringing the proceedings and a 'guardian ad item' for the party responding.

[163]   *Gregory v Turner, R (on application of Morris) v North Somerset Council* [2003] EWCA Civ 183, [2003] 1 WLR 1149, CA.

decision (whether by talking, using sign language or any other means).[164] This is a two-stage test, because it must be established first, that there is an impairment of, or disturbance in the functioning of, the person's mind or brain (the diagnostic threshold); and secondly, that the impairment or disturbance renders the person unable to make the decisions needed to conduct the proceedings. Merely being eccentric is not a basis for being deprived of one's right to conduct litigation, but qualities such as impulsiveness and volatility may render an individual incapable of conducting litigation if they are a consequence of an acquired brain-injury.[165]

Is a party a 'protected party'?

3.169 Courts should investigate the question of capacity whenever there is any reason to suspect that it may be absent.[166] If doubt arises during proceedings the court may need to determine not only whether the party is a protected party but also when this condition first arose. The proceedings should be stayed whilst the court deals with this as a preliminary issue. The court hearing the proceedings decides as a question of fact whether a party is a protected party and if it is unclear will receive evidence to determine the matter. If that decision has already been made by the Court of Protection it should be followed and that court will then normally decide who shall conduct any proceedings.

3.170 It is the capacity of the party to conduct the particular proceedings that is relevant so a person might be a protected party for complex personal injury proceedings yet not for a simultaneous small claim. In view of the issue-specific nature of tests of capacity the Court of Appeal has held that the test relates to the individual and his immediate problems:[167]

> '[T]he test to be applied ... is whether the party to legal proceedings is capable of understanding, with the assistance of such proper explanation from legal advisers and experts in other disciplines as the case may require, the issues on which his consent or decision is likely to be necessary in the course of those proceedings. If he has capacity to understand that which he needs to understand in order to pursue or defend a claim, I can see no reason why the law — whether substantive or procedural – should require the interposition of a next friend or guardian ad litem (or, as such a person is now described in the CPR, a litigation friend).'

The mental abilities required to conduct litigation were identified by the Court of Appeal as comprising the ability to recognise a problem, obtain and receive, understand and retain relevant information, including advice; the ability to weigh the information (including that derived from advice) in the balance in reaching a decision; and the ability to communicate that decision.

Relying on advice

3.171 The extent to which an individual with impaired capacity may rely upon the advice of others has been considered:[168]

---

[164] Mental Capacity Act 2005, s 3(1). Assessment of capacity under the Act is considered in Ch 2 at **2.19**.

[165] *Mitchell v Alasia* [2005] EWHC 11 (QB), [2005] All ER (D) 07 (Jan), Cox J. For an early decision on the new test of capacity in regard to a brain injured claimant see *Saulle v Nouvet* [2007] EWHC 2902 (QB).

[166] *Masterman-Lister v Brutton & Co and Jewell & Home Counties Dairies* [2002] EWCA Civ 1889, [2002] All ER (D) 297 (Dec).

[167] *Masterman-Lister v Brutton & Co and Jewell* [2002] EWCA Civ 1889 at [75], [2002] All ER (D) 297 (Dec).

[168] Boreham J in *White v Fell* (1987) unreported but quoted by Wright J in *Masterman-Lister v Brutton & Co and Jewell & Home Counties Dairies* [2002] EWHC 417 (QB), [2002] All ER (D) 247 (Mar).

'Few people have the capacity to manage all their affairs unaided. In matters of law, particularly litigation, medicine, and given sufficient resources, finance professional advice is almost universally needed and sought. For instance, if the plaintiff succeeds in her claim for compensation ... then she will need to take, consider and act upon appropriate advice. ... It may be that she would have chosen, and would choose now, not to take advice, but that is not the question. The question is: is she capable of doing so? To have that capacity she requires first the insight and understanding of the fact that she has a problem in respect of which she needs advice. ...

Secondly, having identified the problem, it will be necessary for her to seek an appropriate adviser and to instruct him with sufficient clarity to enable him to understand the problem and to advise her appropriately.

Finally, she needs sufficient mental capacity to understand and to make decisions based upon, or otherwise give effect to such advice as she may receive. ... she may not understand all the intricacies of litigation, or of a settlement, or of a wise investment policy. ... But if that were the appropriate test then quite a substantial proportion of the adult population might be regarded as under disability.'

Litigation friends

Appointment

3.172 A protected party must have a litigation friend to conduct proceedings on his behalf and any step taken before such appointment has no effect, but the court may permit proceedings involving a protected party to continue to a limited extent even though a litigation friend has not been appointed and may validate proceedings that have continued in breach of the requirements.[169] Any step which might normally have been taken in the proceedings may be taken by the litigation friend and he need not act by a solicitor though failure to do so in a significant claim may render him unsuitable for the role.

3.173 A person seeking to become a litigation friend on commencing proceedings or filing an acknowledgement to a claim files and serves an office copy of any authorisation from the Court of Protection or a 'certificate of suitability' and a 'certificate of service'.[170] A court order is only required when no acknowledgement is filed by a litigation friend, the litigation friend is to be changed or a party becomes a protected party after proceedings have been begun. If recovery of a substantial sum of money is likely it may be best to involve the Court of Protection which has more experience and will have responsibility at a later stage for any money recovered.

Appointment by the court

3.174 There are procedures whereby the court may, on application or of its own initiative, appoint, replace or debar a litigation friend. The court will be concerned to see that the person to be appointed satisfies the requirements of the certificate of suitability (see below). Any application will be dealt with by a Master or district judge in chambers. Most of these applications are straightforward but where there is a dispute as to whether an appointment is necessary or who is to be appointed, directions will usually be given

---

[169] CPR 1998, r 21.3 and FPR 2010, r 15.3. Note the phrases 'without the permission of the court' and 'unless the court orders otherwise'.

[170] CPR 1998, r 21.5. Service in this context is upon everybody on whom the claim form would have to be served but strangely this does not include the (alleged) protected party although it would be good practice to include this person.

as to the determination of this issue which may include the filing of statements and medical reports. The proceedings will be stayed in the interim although the court may authorise some steps to be taken. There are general powers to compel the attendance of witnesses (including medical attendants and the party concerned) and the production of documents.

Suitability of litigation friend

3.175 A deputy appointed by the Court of Protection with power to conduct legal proceedings on behalf of a protected party is entitled to be the litigation friend in any proceedings to which his authority extends.[171] Apart from this, a person may act as a litigation friend who meets the criteria of suitability for appointment, namely that he:

(1) can fairly and competently conduct proceedings on behalf of the protected party;

(2) has no interest adverse to that of the protected party; and

(3) (where the protected party is a claimant) undertakes to pay any costs which the protected party may be ordered to pay in relation to the proceedings, subject to any right he may have to be repaid from the assets of the protected party.

3.176 It is desirable that the litigation friend be a person of standing and related to or connected with the protected party. Apart from this, there is no restriction on the person appointed save that he or she must not be a child or mentally incapable and (in practice) should normally be within the jurisdiction. The court may remove a person who proves to be unsuitable and substitute another person, but there is no express duty to monitor the situation.

3.177 An attorney under a registered enduring power of attorney (EPA) or a lasting power of attorney for property and affairs (LPA) is not specifically mentioned in the CPR but would be an obvious person to act as litigation friend because he will control the financial affairs of the protected party and there will, in consequence, be no need for a financial deputy.

Certificate of suitability

3.178 A 'Certificate of suitability of litigation friend' must be filed and served before a litigation friend is appointed.[172] It is verified by a statement of truth signed by the person to be appointed and states that he:

(1) consents to act;

(2) believes that the party is a protected party, stating the grounds of his belief and if his belief is based upon medical opinion attaching any relevant document to the certificate;

(3) meets the criteria whereby a person may be regarded as suitable for appointment as litigation friend (including giving an undertaking as to costs where the protected party is a claimant).[173]

---

[171] CPR, r 21.4(2). An office copy of the order or other authorisation sealed with the official seal of the Court of Protection should be filed. The appointment of a deputy (whether for financial affairs or personal welfare) does not by itself give authority to conduct proceedings.

[172] Form N235 for civil proceedings and FP9 for family proceedings.

[173] The undertaking is not required for a defendant in civil proceedings (CPR, r 21.4(3)(c)) but strangely is required for family proceedings (FPR 2010, r 15.4(3)). It is not required where the intended litigation friend is authorised by the Court of Protection to conduct the proceedings.

Although this certificate is not specifically required before the court appoints a litigation friend by an order, the court must first be satisfied that the person to be appointed meets the criteria of suitability for appointment and it is generally more convenient for the certificate to be completed and filed than to set out the criteria in the statement in support of the application.

Official solicitor

3.179 In the absence of any other suitable or willing person the Official Solicitor is available to be appointed as litigation friend of a protected party.[174] Any appointment by the court should be expressed as being subject to consent and this will usually be forthcoming, subject to appropriate medical evidence, provided that his costs will be met. Where there are practical difficulties in obtaining medical evidence the Official Solicitor may be consulted.

3.180 When the circumstances justify involving the Official Solicitor a questionnaire should be completed and submitted with a copy of the Order appointing him subject to his consent. Save in the most urgent cases (eg where immediate medical treatment is in issue) it is unlikely that the Official Solicitor will be able to complete his enquiries in less than 3 months so a lengthy adjournment might be necessary and a substantive hearing will not be fixed within such period without consulting him.

Service and admissions

3.181 Where a document commencing proceedings is to be served upon a protected party it must be served upon the person, if any, who is authorised by the Court of Protection to conduct the proceedings on behalf of that party (including a registered attorney). If there is no such person it must be served upon the person with whom the protected party resides or in whose care he is.[175] Service upon the protected party is technically invalid, but may bring the appropriate response. The court may make an order for deemed service or dispensing with service in appropriate circumstances.[176]

3.182 The aim is to reach a responsible adult who will ensure that the protected party is properly represented in the proceedings. In addition to formal service it may be prudent to communicate with any person concerned with the welfare of the protected party in the hope that a suitable representative will emerge. Occupants of a residential care or nursing home will be in the care of the registered proprietor who should bring the proceedings to the attention of any concerned person. If such care is funded by the local authority it would be appropriate to involve the social services department which will have carried out a community care assessment.

Evidence

3.183 In civil proceedings evidence may only be given by a witness who is considered by the judge to be competent to give evidence. Unlike criminal proceedings, the oath is not obligatory so there is no requirement of ability to understand the nature and consequences of taking the oath. Much depends upon the approach of the judge, and this in turn depends upon understanding of mental disability, tolerance and prejudice.

---

[174] The Official Solicitor may be contacted at 81 Chancery Lane, London WC2A 1DD; telephone 0171 911 7127, fax 0171 911 7105.

[175] CPR 1998, r 6.6(1); FPR 2010, rr 6.28 and 6.14(2).

[176] Service should not be dispensed with on the ground that the party is a detained patient in a mental hospital, because such party may still be capable of conducting proceedings.

Evidence may be admitted as to the capacity of the witness in general terms but not as to the likelihood of the witness being able to give a truthful account.

Enforcement

Limitation periods

3.184 A claim may become 'statute barred' and a person precluded from pursuing a claim in the courts because one of the 'limitation periods' has expired.[177] These are 12 years for a claim on a deed and 6 years for breach of contract or a claim based on tort (eg negligence) but 3 years for personal injury claims. For inheritance claims[178] the period is 6 months from the date of a grant of representation to the estate, and under the Human Rights Act 1998 there is a one year time limit from the act complained of. The period runs from accrual of the 'cause of action' or date of knowledge (if later) but there can be constructive knowledge. Time may not run where there has been fraud, concealment or a mistake. The court has a discretion in certain circumstances to waive these periods.

3.185 If on the date when the right to bring the claim accrued the potential claimant lacked capacity to do so, the claim may be brought within the prescribed period from the date when the incapacity ceases or the person dies even though the period of limitation has expired. The extension of time in these circumstances is mandatory, but in the case of supervening incapacity the court has a discretion.[179]

Default judgments

3.186 There may not be a default judgment against a protected party who does not have a litigation friend. There are also restrictions on obtaining a judgment by or against a protected party based on an admission.[180]

Stay of execution

3.187 If a money judgment is obtained against a protected party a court would be sympathetic towards an application for a stay of execution to enable appropriate steps to be taken on the that party's behalf, and should grant a stay to enable an application to be made to the Court of Protection for the appointment of a deputy who would endeavour to pay the judgment debt out of the party's estate. A stay may also be appropriate if it was necessary for an EPA to be registered before the party's affairs could be administered. Of course, if the judgment was entered before a litigation friend was appointed (see above), it will not be valid and should be set aside.

Injunctions

3.188 The fact of incapacity is not itself a bar to the granting of an injunction against a protected party but the court's powers are in practice restricted. The question is whether such person understood the proceedings and the nature and requirements of the injunction. If he was incapable of understanding what he was doing or that it was wrong, an injunction should not to be granted because he would not be capable of complying with it and the injunction would not have a deterrent effect and, furthermore,

---

[177] Limitation Act 1980 (as amended).
[178] Inheritance (Provision for Family and Dependants) Act 1975 – see Ch 12.
[179] Limitation Act 1980, s 33.
[180] CPR 1998, rr 12.10(a)(i) and 14.1(4).

any breach would not be subject to effective enforcement proceedings since he would have a defence to an application for committal for contempt.[181]

3.189 The appropriate way of restraining unacceptable behaviour by such a person may be the use of the powers under the Mental Health Act 1983 of admission and detention for assessment and treatment in hospital,[182] although a limited interlocutory injunction might be appropriate while the mental condition of the person concerned is investigated. However, the criteria for compulsory treatment are not the same as those that apply to the grant of an injunction, and the medical authorities may take a different view of their powers thereby leaving other people vulnerable to abuse where the courts are incapable of granting relief. Other than in criminal proceedings it appears that the courts do not have the power to require a person to submit to treatment or the authorities to provide treatment.[183] An effective remedy may in consequence be denied to another person. This could arise in a domestic abuse situation or in a simple trespass claim and is likely to be a more frequent problem under community care policies.

Insolvency proceedings

3.190 An older person is not exempt from the prospect of bankruptcy. The Insolvency Act 1986, Parts VIII–XI provide a comprehensive code for dealing with 'insolvency proceedings' and the Insolvency Rules 1986 regulate such proceedings.[184] Special provisions apply where it appears to the court that a person affected by the proceedings lacks capacity within the meaning of the Mental Capacity Act 2005 to manage and administer his property and affairs.[185]

3.191 The person concerned is referred to as 'the incapacitated person' and the court appoints such person as it thinks fit to appear for, represent or act for the incapacitated person. The appointment may be made either generally or for the purpose of any particular application or proceeding, or for the exercise of particular rights or powers which the incapacitated person might have exercised but for his incapacity. It is not expressly stated that in the absence of a representative the proceedings are ineffective but it remains open to the court to adopt that approach, which is consistent with that under the CPR.

3.192 The appointment of a representative is made either by the court of its own motion or on application by:[186]

(1) a person who has been appointed by a court in the UK or elsewhere to manage the affairs of, or to represent, the incapacitated person; or

(2) any relative or friend of the incapacitated person who appears to the court to be a proper person to make the application; or

(3) the official receiver; or

---

[181] *Wookey v Wookey* [1991] 3 All ER 365, CA.

[182] See Ch 8 at **8.129** et seq.

[183] *Wookey v Wookey* held that Contempt of Court Act 1981, s 14(4) empowered the court to make a hospital order where the party was suffering from serious mental incapacity at the time of the contempt proceedings but if that incapacity had existed earlier it would have precluded any contempt.

[184] CPR 1998 apply except insofar as inconsistent with the Insolvency Rules 1986 and *CPR PD Insolvency Proceedings* provides guidance.

[185] Insolvency Rules 1986, Pt 7, Ch 7, rr 7.43–7.46.

[186] Insolvency Rules 1986, r 7.44(3). Unlike other types of proceedings, concerned persons are expressly authorised to intervene.

(4)   the person who, in relation to the proceedings, is the responsible insolvency practitioner.

An application may be made ex parte (ie without notice) but the court may require notice to be given to the person alleged to be incapacitated or any other person and may adjourn to enable notice to be given. The application is supported by an affidavit of a registered medical practitioner as to the mental or physical condition of the incapacitated person unless it is made by the Official Receiver in which case his report is sufficient. Any notice served on, or sent to, a person appointed by the court under these rules has the same effect as if it had been served on, or given to, the incapacitated person.

Costs

3.193 Unless the court otherwise directs, the costs payable in any proceedings by a protected party to his own solicitor must be assessed by the court, usually on the standard basis, and no costs are payable to that solicitor except the amount so allowed.[187]

Liability of litigation friend

3.194 The requirement for a litigation friend to give an undertaking to pay any costs which the protected party may be ordered to pay[188] imposes a severe limitation upon the ability of a protected party to bring a claim. The undertaking is not required from a deputy or the Official Solicitor or the litigation friend of a defendant. One way of circumventing the undertaking is to obtain the authority of the Court of Protection to bring the proceedings.

Liability of solicitor

3.195 A solicitor may be ordered to pay all the costs incurred where he acts for a protected party without a litigation friend.[189] The basis of this personal liability is a breach of warranty of authority to the opposite party. When during the course of proceedings it is determined that a party is a protected party the proceedings are stayed until a litigation friend is appointed. If the litigation friend once appointed adopts the proceedings to date this liability will be avoided.

Approval of settlements

3.196 Where money is claimed for a protected party, no settlement, compromise or payment and no acceptance of money paid into court is valid without the court's approval.[190] Without this approval the settlement, compromise or payment is unenforceable and made entirely at the risk of the parties and their solicitors.[191] It would

---

[187]   CPR 1998, r 48.5. This applies also to family proceedings.
[188]   CPR 1998, r 21.4(3) and PD 21 at para 2.3(2)(e). It is contained in Form N235 *Certificate of Suitability of Litigation Friend.*
[189]   *Yonge v Toynbee* [1910] 1 KB 215, CA.
[190]   CPR 1998, r 21.10(1). This extends to any costs of the proceedings.
[191]   In view of the cost of obtaining the court's approval, small claims are often settled on indemnities being given by the person to whom the money is paid.

be an abuse of process for the parties and their solicitors in any subsisting proceedings to make or act on any such settlement, compromise or payment without the court's approval.[192]

3.197 There is a procedure whereby the court can approve a settlement reached before the commencement of proceedings, which is intended to protect parties from lack of skill or experience on the part of their legal advisers and provide a means whereby the defendant can obtain a valid discharge from the claim.[193] It also ensures that the solicitors involved are paid their proper costs and no more, and that the money recovered is properly looked after and wisely applied.

Approach of the court

3.198 In considering whether to give approval the overriding consideration is the interest of the protected party, having regard to all the circumstances of the case.[194] Matters taken into account include the risks in the litigation, the adequacy of the amount in question, the desirability of an early end to the litigation and the amount of the costs involved and on whom they fall.

3.199 The court will usually expect the protected party and litigation friend to be present (unless there is good reason for them not to attend) and will consider whether all necessary medical and other evidence has been obtained and considered by those who have advised on the settlement. This evidence should be available to the court and counsel's opinion on the settlement will be produced in all but small claims. In the event that the court does not approve the settlement it may adjourn the hearing for further negotiations to take place or give directions as to what is to be done next. These may be directions to bring the action to trial if the proceedings have already been begun or, if not, for the issue of a claim.

Protected beneficiary

3.200 The court must decide whether the protected party is also a 'protected beneficiary' who is incapable of managing any moneys recovered. In that event the money may only be dealt with pursuant to the directions of the court; the litigation friend has no authority as such to receive or expend. The former practice of setting up a trust on behalf of the protected party and paying the money to the trustees should not now be adopted.

Administration by the court

3.201 Small amounts may be administered by the court in which they were recovered or transferred to the protected beneficiary's local county court.[195] This may be relevant where the amount is less than £50,000 and the protected beneficiary does not have other savings that would bring the total above this figure or need a procedure for administration. If the local district judge can be persuaded to supervise the fund in court and to reserve applications to himself for that purpose, a carer may apply to that judge at intervals with proposals for spending the income or capital. If these proposals are

---

[192] *Barker v S Green & Sons Ltd* [1950] WN 416.

[193] CPR 1998, r 21.10(2). See *Black v Yates* [1992] QB 526, [1991] 4 All ER 722.

[194] The court relies heavily on those advising on, or conducting, litigation on behalf of a protected party: *Re Barbour's Settlement* [1974] 1 All ER 1188, at 1191.

[195] See CPR, PD 21 at para 11.2. This is the procedure adopted for infants who, on attaining majority, will be able to handle their own financial affairs.

thought to be in the best interests of the protected beneficiary (having in mind that the intention is to spend the money on that person[196] rather than preserve it for those who would inherit on death) the judge may direct that a lump sum is released or regular payments (eg the income from the fund) are made.

3.202 This money will generally be credited direct to an account in the name of the carer or relative who made the application. On a subsequent application the judge is likely to ask for production of receipts or other proof of payment for the authorised items before releasing further money to the same applicant.

Involvement of Court of Protection

3.203 If more money is involved (as in brain injury cases) the damages will be paid over to the Court of Protection,[197] and it is then appropriate when formulating a claim for damages for personal injuries to include an element for the fees and costs that will be involved in administering those damages, whether through the Court of Protection or under a registered EPA.

3.204 It is wise to consult this court at the outset and certainly before any offer is accepted. A procedure for receiving and investing the damages should be set up before these are recovered otherwise there could be long delays.[198]

Conclusion

3.205 Although providing, of necessity, a procedure for the appointment of a representative to conduct the litigation, court rules do not address fundamental aspects of decision making for people who lack mental capacity, despite the fact that courts control their own procedures and decisions relating to litigation are likely to be among the more important made on their behalf. There is minimal scrutiny as to who is appointed, little guidance as to the basis on which that person should act and no supervision except in regard to compromise or settlement of claims. No mention is made of a duty to consult with or involve the protected party, even as to the choice of representative. That party may not even need to be notified of the proceedings in which he is involved, notwithstanding that he might wish to dispute the lack of capacity. Reliance is placed on the certificate of suitability (see above) and upon service on the person with whom the alleged protected party resides or in whose care he or she is. It cannot be assumed that this person will inform the protected party in every situation where this would be prudent, and there is a risk that older people may be marginalised in proceedings involving their affairs when they could make some contribution.

CRIMINAL RESPONSIBILITY

Preliminary

3.206 Special consideration should be given to elderly people who are suspected or accused of crimes for several reasons. They may not understand the process of

---

[196] This might be for equipment such as a wheelchair, appliances such as a washing machine, items such as a television, services such as a regular visit from a hairdresser, or even for day outings or holidays (which may include the cost of a carer).

[197] For the jurisdiction and procedures of the Court of Protection see Chs 2 and 11.

[198] Interim awards are common and a deputy should be in place to deal with this.

investigation and prosecution, and safeguards are needed to prevent false self-incriminating statements being made if they are mentally vulnerable. If prosecuted they may be found to be *unfit to plead* in relation to the trial so that the trial cannot proceed, or they may wish to plead that they were insane at the time of the offence and pursue a verdict of not guilty by reason of insanity *(special verdict)*. There may be concern about detention in prison while awaiting trial or when sentenced, and if convicted they may need medical treatment or care in the community rather than punishment.

3.207 Most of the special provisions turn upon the individual being 'mentally disordered' but the definition of this term is not limited to mental illness and is wider than generally believed.[199] It may include confused elderly people more often than is generally realised. The policy is that people who are mentally disordered should not be prosecuted unless it is in the public interest, and if they are prosecuted various additional sentencing options are available. It is therefore important to identify any mental disorder at an early stage if appropriate treatment is to be afforded, prosecution is to be avoided or any relevant reports are to be obtained prior to sentence.[200] It may also be appropriate to seek a community care assessment of the person's needs because provision to meet those needs may help to justify diversion from the criminal justice system.

Safeguards

3.208 Protection is afforded to those being investigated and there is a discretion whether to prosecute for non-serious offences.

Code of Practice (PACE)

3.209 When any person is detained by the police the procedures under the Police and Criminal Evidence Act 1984 (PACE) must be followed. These seek to strike the right balance between the powers of the police and the rights and freedoms of the public, *Codes of Practice* supplemented by *Notes for Guidance* provide rules as to:

(1)   exercising powers of stop and search (Code A);

(2)   search of premises and seizure of property (Code B);

(3)   the treatment and questioning of detainees and interviewees (Code C);

(4)   identification of persons (Code D);

(5)   audio recording (Code E) and video recording (Code F) of interviews with suspects;

(6)   powers of arrest (Code G).

The latest versions of Codes A, B and D came into effect on 6 March 2011, Code C on 10 July 2012, Codes E and F on 30 April 2010 and Code G on 12 November 2012.[201] A breach in circumstances which are regarded as unreasonable would raise questions

---

[199]   Mental disorder is defined as 'mental illness, arrested or incomplete development of mind, psychopathic disorder and any other disorder or disability of mind'— Mental Health Act 1983, s 1(2).

[200]   A Law Society publication for duty solicitors, *Advising Mentally Disordered Offenders; A Practical Guide* deals with these matters.

[201]   These may be downloaded through the website: www.gov.uk/government/organisations/home-office/series/police-and-criminal-evidence-act-1984-pace-current-versions.

about the validity of police evidence, particularly statements made by vulnerable people in the absence of an appropriate adult (see below) or confessions given in circumstances of discomfort and duress. The trial judge may decide not to admit such evidence.

Persons in custody (Code C)

3.210 Elderly people have the same general rights when in police custody and when being questioned as other detained persons including the rights mentioned below and the right to consult the Code. Anyone in custody must be dealt with expeditiously and released as soon as the need for detention no longer applies. The general provisions provide for appropriate and considerate treatment by the police and these relate also to those voluntarily attending police stations to assist with investigations.[202] The Equality Act 2010 makes it unlawful for police officers to discriminate against, harass or victimise any person on the grounds of the 'protected characteristics' of age, disability, gender reassignment, race, religion or belief, sex and sexual orientation, marriage and civil partnership, pregnancy and maternity when using their powers.

3.211 If a detained person needs medical attention or appears to be suffering from physical illness or mental disorder then the custody officer must call the police surgeon (who is in fact a medical practitioner) or send the person to hospital.[203] The person does not need to request this. The police surgeon can assess fitness for detention and interview, and advise on any safeguards that are necessary.

3.212 The custody officer must inform a person under arrest at a police station of his right to have someone informed at public expense as soon as practicable of the arrest and the detained person's whereabouts. The person informed can be someone known to the detained person or someone likely to have an interest in his welfare. If that person cannot be contacted the detained person can choose two alternative people to be informed and if they cannot be contacted the custody officer has discretion to allow further attempts to inform another person. This right may be exercised at any stage and also each time there is a move to another police station, and can only be delayed in exceptional circumstances.

3.213 A detained person also has the right to consult a solicitor in private, either in person or by telephone, and to be told that free independent legal advice is available. The custody officer must act promptly to secure advice without delay except when the interests of the police investigation would be hindered. No attempt must be made to dissuade the detained person from seeking legal advice and when he has requested this he may not be interviewed or continue to be interviewed until his solicitor arrives.[204] Where a solicitor is not available or the detained person does not wish to instruct the duty solicitor the enquiry can continue without representation.

3.214 Interviews with detained persons must be conducted fairly and in regard to confessions PACE states:[205]

---

[202] The definition of detention includes those who are mentally disordered and detained at a police station as a place of safety under the provisions of Mental Health Act 1983, ss 135 and 136.

[203] Code C, para 9.5.

[204] There are exceptions to this which generally cover delays which would cause risk or harm to persons or unreasonable delay to the investigation.

[205] Police and Criminal Evidence Act 1984, s 76(2).

'... where ... it is represented to the court that the confession was or may have been obtained ... (b) in consequence of anything said or done which was likely, in the circumstances existing at the time, to render unreliable any confession which might be made by him in consequence thereof, the court shall not allow the confession to be given in evidence against him except in so far as the prosecution proves to the court beyond all reasonable doubt that the confession in court (notwithstanding that it may be true) was not obtained as aforesaid.'

Where the detained person is interviewed and fails to answer certain questions satisfactorily or at all, a 'special warning' must be given after which the court can draw inferences if the detained person fails or refuses to account for objects/marks or substances found in his possession or in the place he was arrested or fails to account for his presence at the place or time the offence was committed.[206]

3.215 If there are grounds to suspect that the detained person committed an offence, he must be cautioned before being questioned. The Code provides that an accurate record of the interview including place, time of beginning and end, breaks and names of those present must be made. Such record must be read and signed by the detained person, and any solicitor present at the interview should also read and sign the record.[207]

The appropriate adult

3.216 Additional safeguards for vulnerable elderly people may be found in para 1.4 of Code C which states:

'If an officer has any suspicion, or is told in good faith, that a person of any age may be mentally disordered or otherwise mentally vulnerable, in the absence of clear evidence to dispel that suspicion, the person shall be treated as such for the purposes of this Code.'

The approach of a police officer is unlikely to be comparable to that of those working in the field of mental disorder. A police surgeon may be called in the event of uncertainty and his view relied upon without further consideration, but he may apply the wrong test, namely: is the individual fit to be detained. The Notes for Guidance at para 1G expressly provide that when the custody officer has any doubt about the mental state or capacity of a detainee, that detainee should be treated as mentally vulnerable and an appropriate adult called.[208]

3.217 When a detained person has been so identified, an *appropriate adult* must be brought in to safeguard his rights by being present at interviews and having certain other functions.[209] This should be a relative, guardian or other person responsible for his care or custody, or else someone who has experience of dealing with mentally disordered persons[210] but is not a police officer or employed by the police. In the absence of such a person, some other responsible adult aged 18 or over who is not a police officer or

---

[206] Criminal Justice and Public Order Act 1994, ss 36 and 37.
[207] Code C, paras 11.7 and 11.12.
[208] A helpful summary of provisions relating to mentally disordered or otherwise mentally vulnerable people is to be found at Annexe E to Code C.
[209] This only applies to questioning in the police station yet the individual could be required to answer questions elsewhere.
[210] Such as an approved social worker (ASW) as defined by the Mental Health Act 1983 or a specialist social worker. It seems that the mentally disordered person can nominate the appropriate adult (even if that person seems to others to be inappropriate) but cannot instruct a solicitor due to incapacity (the appropriate adult does this).

employed by the police may adopt the role. A solicitor in the police station in a professional capacity may not act as an appropriate adult because his is a different role.[211]

3.218 A custody officer who authorises the detention of a person who is mentally disordered must as soon as practicable inform the appropriate adult of the grounds of the detention and ask the adult to come to the police station to see the person. The detained person's rights must be stated to him in the presence of the appropriate adult, or later repeated to him in that presence if the appropriate adult was not present in the police station when they were first stated. Where the appropriate adult has been informed of the detained person's right to legal advice and considers that such advice should be taken, the Code applies as if legal advice has been requested and prompt action to secure such advice must be taken.[212]

3.219 A mentally disordered person (whether or not a suspect) must not be interviewed or asked to provide a written statement in the absence of an appropriate adult who should also sign the record of the interview.[213] This adult is not present at the interview simply as an observer and must be asked to participate as an adviser to the individual being questioned and as an observer that the interview is conducted properly and fairly. If necessary the appropriate adult will be asked to assist communication with the person being interviewed. Any caution delivered without an appropriate adult present must be repeated in the presence of an appropriate adult. If there is concern that the caution has not been understood it should be explained by the officer in his own words and if necessary further explanation of the significance of the caution must be given.[214]

3.220 An appropriate adult available at the time of review of the detention must be given an opportunity to make representations to an officer or superintendent about the need for continuing detention. If a custody officer charges a mentally disordered person with an offence this must be done in the presence of the appropriate adult to whom a written notice is given.[215] A search of the individual can only be conducted in the presence of an appropriate adult of the same sex unless there is a specific request for a particular adult of the opposite sex.

3.221 Despite these provisions there remains uncertainty as to the role of the appropriate adult and there is little training for the task. In general the functions of the appropriate adult are to:

(1) facilitate communication between all parties;

(2) facilitate the suspect's comprehension of the ideas expressed in any way necessary and to explain what is happening and the consequences of this;

(3) ensure that the police act properly.

---

[211] See *Notes for Guidance* 1E and 1F. The appropriate adult is not governed by a duty of confidentiality, so the solicitor should not take instructions in his presence but should instead tell him what the instructions are so that if they are then related to anyone else the hearsay rules would apply.

[212] See generally para 6 of Code C.

[213] Paras 11.15 and 11.12. There is provision for interview of detained persons or suspects to be carried out in the absence of an appropriate adult when an officer of the rank of superintendent or above considers that further delay will cause risk to personal property, but this should only be exercised in exceptional cases.

[214] See generally para 10 and *Note for Guidance* thereto.

[215] See generally paras 15 and 16.

The suspect's right to legal advice is separate and the appropriate adult should assist with this when necessary.

Alternatives to prosecution

Diversion

3.222 A Home Office Circular[216] draws the attention of the courts and those services responsible for dealing with mentally disordered persons who commit, or are suspected of committing, criminal offences to the legal powers which exist and the desirability of ensuring effective co-operation between agencies to ensure that the best use is made of resources. The overall aim is to divert mentally disordered people from the criminal justice system and keep them out of prisons where this is appropriate. Wherever possible they should receive care and treatment from the health and social services, and the use of Mental Health Act powers is encouraged. This policy can be effective only if the courts and criminal justice agencies have access to these services and this requires consultation and co-operation.[217] The police should establish close working relationships with local health, probation and social services to assist them in exercising the range of powers available to them.[218]

Caution

3.223 Cautioning is recognised as an increasingly important way of keeping offenders out of the courts and in many circumstances reducing the risk that they will re-offend. Whilst simple cautions are available for any offence they 'are generally intended for low level, mainly first time offending. An assessment of the seriousness of the offence is the starting point for considering whether a simple caution may be appropriate.' There should be uniform principles that apply across all age groups, but special considerations that apply additionally to the elderly and infirm and other vulnerable groups result in cautioning rates being higher for those groups than for others.[219]

3.224 A Code of Practice governs the use by police of Conditional Cautions, under Part 3 of the Criminal Justice Act 2003[220] and the CPS may recommend a caution. This procedure enables offenders to be dealt with appropriately without the involvement of the usual court processes. The key to determining whether a Conditional Caution should be given – instead of prosecution or a simple caution – is that the conditions attached to the caution will be an appropriate and effective means of addressing the offender's behaviour or making reparation for the effects of the offence on the victim or the community.

The decision to prosecute

3.225 The initial decision to charge may be taken by the police. After any charge the Crown Prosecution Service (CPS) will review the case and decide whether to continue on

---

[216] *Provisions for Mentally Disordered Offenders*, Circular 66/90.

[217] The Department of Health sent copies to all health and social services authorities and drew attention to their responsibilities for ensuring that sufficient facilities are available for the care of mentally disordered offenders.

[218] See Home Office Circular 12/95 *Mentally Disordered Offenders: Inter-Agency Working*: www.homeoffice. gov.uk/documents/ho-circular-inter-agency-working.

[219] Home Office Circular 16/2008 for Simple Cautioning was replaced on 8 April 2013 by the Ministry of Justice – Simple Caution for Adult Offender guidance: www.justice.gov.uk/out-of-court-disposals.

[220] Available at: www.justice.gov.uk/downloads/oocd/code-practice-adult-conditional-cautions-oocd.pdf.

this or another basis, although they may be consulted prior to any charges being brought.[221] Review is on a continuing basis. Prosecutors will need information and evidence about any mental health problems at the earliest opportunity in order to review the case and the police have responsibilities to provide this although it may come from many other sources including relatives and friends.[222] Where the court has a scheme to facilitate the process of assessment and the provision of reports the offender should be referred to it for investigation and a report.

3.226 Each case must be considered on its merits, taking into account all available information about any mental health problem, and its relevance to the offence, in addition to the principles set out in the Code for Crown Prosecutors. If the person is elderly, frail or mentally disordered and has no recent involvement with the criminal justice system and the allegation is not serious, representations may be made that there should be no charge or that proceedings should not continue. The CPS will also decide whether to accept a plea of guilty to the charge or a lesser charge.

Code for Crown Prosecutors

3.227 The functions of investigating and prosecuting crime are distinct and have been separated. The primary roles of the CPS are to provide an objective assessment of the results of the police investigation and to prosecute only those cases which pass the tests laid down in the Code for Crown Prosecutors.[223] The Code provides general guidance in three specific areas, namely the decision to prosecute, selection of appropriate charges and representations to magistrates as to where the trial should be (where there is a choice).[224]

3.228 There is a threshold *evidential* test for any prosecution based upon the 'realistic prospect of conviction', namely: 'On the basis of the evidence is it more likely than not that a conviction will result'. If this is passed the *public interest* must then be considered. The Code sets out factors in favour of and against a prosecution, and it is here that the age and mental state of the defendant (and the victim) may be relevant. Prosecution should not follow unless wider public interest and the gravity of the offence requires it. The impact of the offence upon a particular community may be taken into account, as well as the consequences for the victim and any views expressed by the victim.

3.229 Thus where there is evidence to show that a mentally disordered person has committed an offence, consideration should be given to whether prosecution is appropriate taking into account alternatives such as cautioning, admission to guardianship or to hospital (if the person's mental condition requires hospital treatment), or informal support in the community by the social services department. Regard will be had to the welfare of the accused as well as the need to ensure that the offence will not be repeated. A defence solicitor may be able to persuade the CPS to discontinue a prosecution, but will wish to have in mind that mentally disordered people should be given the same opportunity as others to clear their names or accept responsibility for their actions. Any information provided by the police with the papers regarding the person's mental condition, or discussions held with other agencies, will be

---

221   The Director of Public Prosecutions (DPP) is the head of the CPS which was established under the Prosecution of Offences Act 1985.

222   Home Office Circular 12/95 (see above).

223   The latest edition issued January 2013 may be found on the CPS website at: www.cps.gov.uk/publications/ code_for_crown_prosecutors/index.html.

224   The Attorney General has commended the Code to other prosecutors such as HM Revenue & Customs, but in practice they may be more influenced by other factors.

taken into account by the CPS, and where it is satisfied that the probable effect upon his mental health outweighs the interests of justice in the particular case it will consider discontinuing the proceedings.

Mens rea

3.230 Unless there is statutory authority to the contrary, the onus is on the prosecution to establish *mens rea* (the necessary intention for the offence) beyond all reasonable doubt.[225] When deciding whether to prosecute it is necessary to consider the impact of a mental disorder on the offender's ability to form the necessary *mens rea*. An independent medical report may be helpful.

Confessions

3.231 People who are mentally disordered or otherwise mentally vulnerable may be particularly prone to provide information that may be unreliable, misleading or self-incriminating. Care should always be taken when questioning such a person, and the appropriate adult should be involved if there is any doubt about a person's mental state or capacity. Corroboration of any facts admitted should be obtained wherever possible. It should be borne in mind that a confession by a mentally disordered offender may be excluded[226] or the jury must be warned of the special need for caution before convicting in reliance on that confession.[227]

Remand in custody

3.232 A defendant charged with a serious offence may be remanded in custody or on bail, and age and physical or mental health will be taken into account when considering this. Conditions of bail can be imposed and if the defendant requires medical treatment a condition of residence in hospital or a bail hostel with a condition for medical treatment may be imposed.

3.233 If the defendant appears to be mentally disordered but bail is not appropriate the court has powers to remand to hospital rather than prison. This may be for psychiatric reports for periods of 28 days at a time to a maximum of 12 weeks, or for treatment.[228] Evidence from one (or more) registered medical practitioner of mental disorder of an appropriate nature and extent is required and also confirmation that arrangements have been made for the defendant's admission to hospital within 7 days. In addition the Home Secretary has the power to transfer a mentally disordered remand prisoner from prison to hospital when there is an urgent need for treatment.[229]

Prosecution

Mode of trial

3.234 Offences are divided into three types, namely summary only offences (such as driving offences) tried in the magistrates' court, either way offences which are more serious but can be tried in that court or the Crown Court, and indictable only offences (such as murder and rape) which must be tried in the Crown Court with a jury. Usually

---

[225] *Woolmington v DPP* [1935] AC 462.
[226] Under Police and Criminal Evidence Act 1984, s 76 or 78.
[227] Police and Criminal Evidence Act 1984, s 77.
[228] Mental Health Act 1983, ss 35 and 36.
[229] Mental Health Act 1983, s 48.

the magistrates decide whether either way offences may be tried by them but the defendant and the CPS will have an input into these decisions.

Fitness to plead

3.235 In Crown Court proceedings a person who is judged unable to understand the trial, conduct a proper defence, challenge a juror to whom he may wish to object or understand the substance of the evidence is considered to be 'under a disability in relation to the trial' and special provisions apply.[230] There will be a 'trial of the facts' to determine whether the jury is satisfied beyond reasonable doubt that he did the act or made the omission charged, and the court is given a wider range of disposal options. A circular provides guidance to the courts, police, probation service and health and social services departments.[231]

3.236 What constitutes disability is not set out in the statute but is described as 'any disability such that apart from the act it would constitute a bar to his being tried ...' so depends on common law.[232] There is authority that an accused person who is unable to communicate with his legal adviser should be found unfit to plead.[233] The finding of a disability is based upon the capacity to understand and communicate, so the presence of a mental disorder will not automatically mean that the defendant will be found unfit to plead. Equally, it is not essential to establish a mental disorder, though the definition of this is so wide that it is likely to be satisfied in most cases.

Procedure

3.237 The procedure has two stages:

(1)   whether the offender is under a disability (ie 'unfit to plead'); and if so

(2)   whether he did the act or made the omission charged against him.

The question of fitness to plead can be raised by the defence, the prosecution or the court and should normally be determined as soon as it arises, although the court may postpone this until the defence opens its case which enables the prosecution case to be tested. Thus the accused may be acquitted without the issue of fitness to be tried being considered and without a finding of disability being recorded. The judge determines the question of disability on the evidence of two or more medical practitioners of whom one must be duly approved by the Secretary of State under s 12 of the Mental Health Act 1983.[234] If raised by the defence the question must be proved on balance of probabilities and if raised by the prosecution it must be proved beyond all reasonable doubt. There is a right of appeal for the accused against a finding of unfitness, but there is no appeal against a finding of fitness to plead though the accused retains the right to

---

[230]   Criminal Procedure (Insanity) Act 1964 as amended by Criminal Procedure (Insanity and Unfitness to Plead) Act 1991 and Domestic Violence, Crime and Victims Act 2004.

[231]   Home Office Circular No 93/1991, 20 November 1991.

[232]   See *R v Pritchard* (1836) 7 C & P 303. The Law Commission has proposed that a test in line with that in the Mental Capacity Act 2005 may be more appropriate because the common law test can lead to injustice by excluding participation – *Unfitness to plead* (2010 Law Com CP No 197).

[233]   *R v Burles* [1970] 1 All ER 642, CA.

[234]   Prior to the 2004 Act there was a separate jury.

appeal against any subsequent conviction and sentence. Where the accused recovers between a finding that he had done the act complained of and the disposal, a further hearing may be arranged.[235]

Trial of the facts

3.238 If the judge finds that the accused unfit, a trial of the facts follows in which a jury examines the evidence and determines whether the accused did the act or made the omission charged. The prosecution must prove this beyond reasonable doubt, but such a finding is not a conviction and if the jury is not so satisfied the accused is acquitted. The court will not look at the intentions of the accused as this is meaningless for someone who is unfit to plead.

3.239 An accused found unfit to be tried should be legally represented during the subsequent trial of the facts and if, because of mental disorder, he repudiates his legal representative the court appoints a person whom it considers may properly be entrusted to pursue the accused's interests to put the case for the accused. This may be the previous advocate or any other solicitor known to the court to have experience in such matters.[236] The Official Solicitor is appointed when no-one else is available and usually instructs a solicitor in private practice experienced in both criminal law and the law relating to mental health.

Disposal options

3.240 When a person is found unfit to plead the court is in most cases no longer obliged to order detention in hospital subject to a restriction order without limitation of time.[237] Other disposal options are an order that the accused should be admitted to such hospital as may be specified by the Secretary of State, a guardianship order or an absolute discharge. There may also be a supervision and treatment order which requires the accused to co-operate with supervision by a social worker or a probation officer for a period of not more than 2 years and with treatment (for all or part of that period) by a registered medical practitioner.

3.241 If on a trial of the facts the accused is found to have done the act or made the omission charged, and admission to hospital is directed, the Secretary of State may remit the accused to stand trial if while still detained in hospital he subsequently becomes fit to plead.

Sentencing

3.242 If there is reason to believe that a defendant is mentally disordered the court must obtain a medical report before sentencing. There is a wide range of sentencing options open to the court when dealing with a defendant with a mental disorder, including a community rehabilitation order (probation) with or without a condition of psychiatric treatment. The court has various powers under the Mental Health Act 1983 to impose a sentence not involving custody in prison. It may, in strictly defined circumstances, authorise admission to and detention in such hospital as may be specified in the order or

---

[235] *Hasani v Blackfriars Crown Court* [2005] EWHC 3016 (Admin).
[236] Legal aid is not available but costs are payable from central funds – Prosecution of Offences Act 1985, s 19(3) inserted by 1991 Act.
[237] Domestic Violence, Crime and Victims Act 2004 amended Criminal Procedure (Insanity) Act 1964, s 5 to provide three disposal options when a defendant is found unfit to plead or not guilty by reason of insanity.

place the person under guardianship of the local social services authority, but only if satisfied, taking into account the circumstances of the offence and the character and antecedents of the offender, that this is the most suitable method of disposing of the case.[238]

3.243 The court can also, in certain circumstances, make an interim hospital order[239] if there is reason to suppose that the mental disorder from which the offender is suffering renders this appropriate and the court is satisfied that a bed will be made available within the required time period. The court cannot compel a hospital to admit a particular person, but can put some pressure on a Regional Health Authority to explain its bed provision. If the court thinks the offender is suffering from a mental disorder a psychiatric report must be obtained before sentencing, and when contemplating a custodial sentence the court must consider the effect this will have on the mental condition of the offender and his need for treatment.[240]

3.244 When mentally disordered persons are detained in prison, whether on remand or following sentence, carers or other representatives should monitor their progress and press for transfer to hospital if mental health is deteriorating, because they are unlikely to receive appropriate medical care in prison.[241]

---

[238] Mental Health Act 1983, s 37.
[239] For a period not exceeding 28 weeks renewable for further periods of not more than 28 days up to a maximum of 6 months – Mental Health Act 1983, ss 38 and 39.
[240] Criminal Justice Act 1991, s 4.
[241] Transfer powers are found in Mental Health Act 1983, ss 47 and 48.

CHAPTER 4

FAMILY AND CARERS

Gordon Ashton

'Family isn't about whose blood you have. It's about who you care about.'
Trey Parker and Matt Stone, South Park, Ike's Wee Wee, 1998

As people become older relationships with their partners and families assume a different emphasis and the role of carer may develop. There is a potential for neglect and abuse which must be addressed. The law may be expected to resolve some of the problems that arise. In this chapter we consider personal relationships and the implications of breakdown, including marriage, civil partnership and cohabitation. We also consider relationships with any children in the wider family. Finally we outline the role and status of carers and the remedies available for elder abuse.

INTRODUCTION

4.1   Older people enjoy personal relationships like everyone else, but the death of contemporaries may leave a void and they may become unable to develop or cope with new relationships. It is undesirable for an older person to live in isolation although those who do not have a partner often choose to live alone or are obliged to do so. Most continue to rely upon established relationships with family, friends and neighbours but these do not always provide the daily care or support that is required with the onset of mental or physical impairments, so informal or professional carers may be needed.

4.2   The needs of the informal or family carer can be just as great as those of the older person being cared for yet are generally neglected. Carers need to know their rights and responsibilities and it becomes necessary to consider the legal implications of arrangements made with companions or carers.[1] In all these situations there is scope for neglect and abuse, so under the heading Elder Abuse (at **4.136**) we identify the types of abuse that arise and the remedies that are available when older people are victims of abuse.

4.3   An added difficulty which may be superimposed upon these situations is a decline in mental capacity causing doubt as to the ability of the older person to make decisions which should be respected by others. Facilitated or supported decision making may then become important but this generally involves significant role changes within the family and can result in conflict between those wishing to adopt a dominant role. We address in

---

[1]   The regulation of professional carers is dealt with in Ch 7.

this chapter the legal aspects of some of these situations, but the more specific implications of mental incapacity are dealt with in other chapters.[2]

PERSONAL RELATIONSHIPS

Preliminary

4.4   Everyone has the right to form their own personal relationships. The United Nations Declaration on Human Rights in 1948 includes the right of adults to freedom and equal treatment.[3] The European Convention on Human Rights of 1950[4] provides in Article 8 that 'Everyone has the right to respect for his private and family life ...' and in Article 12 that 'Men and women of marriageable age have the right to marry and found a family ...'. Any interference with these rights can only be justified by the need to protect the individual from potentially abusive relationships. It is a difficult balance to maintain. In general there is only a right to interfere in personal relationships when an individual lacks mental capacity or there is undue influence.[5]

4.5   Following the loss of a partner or the breakdown of a relationship an elderly person may wish to live with someone else or even remarry, and some marry for the first time at an advanced age. The breakdown of a son or daughter's marriage may result in the need to look after a grandchild or contact with grandchildren ceasing. Older people often have families with whom they live or are in contact but despite age and maturity, and sometimes because of the effects of ageing, relationships break down. All these situations have legal implications.

Marriage

Overview

4.6   Under this heading we consider first the long-standing law relating to marriage and then the recent legislation in respect of civil partnerships between persons of the same sex. In many respects a civil partnership mirrors a civil marriage in that the legal consequences are the same.

Implications of marriage

4.7   When an elderly couple are considering whether it is in their best interests to marry rather than merely live together they will wish to take into account the implications. Sharing a home or full cohabitation may be an alternative from the point of view of legal relationships, and this is considered later in this chapter. On occasion an elderly person seeks to marry someone very much younger and there are no legal barriers to this but different considerations may then apply.

---

[2]   In particular refer to Ch 2.
[3]   Further information is available at: www.ohchr.org/en/udhr/pages/introduction.aspx.
[4]   The implications of the Human Rights Act 1998 which incorporated the Convention into our law with effect from October 2000 are considered in Ch 1. For the Convention see: www.hri.org/docs/ECHR50.html.
[5]   For assessment of capacity see Ch 1. Undue influence is considered in the context of elder abuse later in this chapter.

4.8   Despite the relative ease with which a person can enter into matrimony, marriage creates a change of status with long-term financial implications. No warning is given to the parties of this and they may not realise the full implications especially if elderly. In particular:

- one spouse may become liable to maintain the other;[6]

- pension entitlements may be affected;

- entitlement to state benefit could be affected (eg a widow's pension may be lost);[7]

- the spouse may become entitled to succeed to any tenancy or acquire the right to buy the freehold;[8]

- the spouse becomes entitled to be the nearest relative;[9]

- there are changes in capital taxation[10] but no longer any tangible income tax benefits for married couples;

- succession rights change, any existing will is revoked unless made in contemplation of the marriage and future claims may arise under the Inheritance (Provision for Family and Dependants) Act 1975.[11]

If there is a possible conflict of interest, and this will inevitably be the case where one or both of the parties has been married before and has a family, each party should be separately advised. Each of them should make a new will following or in contemplation of the marriage especially if they have their own families, but even then inheritance rights may arise.

4.9   The anxiety of a parent over the marriage of a son or daughter may be trivial compared with the anxiety of a son or daughter over the proposed marriage of an elderly parent. In both situations any attempt to influence or advise may be misunderstood and even be counter-productive, but serious conflicts of interest arise when a parent contemplates re-marriage which seldom arise on the marriage of a son or daughter. The younger members of the family may not only be concerned about the welfare of a parent or grandparent and their continuing caring obligations, but also a long awaited financial inheritance. The act of marriage will put this in jeopardy unless some new testamentary provision is made, yet an attempt to discuss this at the relevant time may create a breakdown in the relationship which in itself influences testamentary intentions. Problems may arise due to the low capacity threshold for marriage and the high threshold of testamentary capacity, but a statutory will may be made in appropriate circumstances.[12]

Capacity to marry

4.10   Marriage is 'a simple contract which it does not require a high degree of intelligence to understand'.[13] More recently it has been stated that:[14]

---

[6]   This could arise on a claim by the spouse or by a local authority obliged to provide support for the spouse. The former is dealt with later in this chapter and the latter in Ch 10.

[7]   See Ch 10.

[8]   Housing is covered in Ch 5.

[9]   Mental health law is dealt with in Ch 8.

[10]   The status of marriage may be useful in tax and estate planning. See Ch 10.

[11]   These topics are addressed in Ch 12.

[12]   This is dealt with in Ch 12.

[13]   *Durham v Durham* (1885) 10 PD 80, at 82, per Sir J Hannan P.

[14]   *Sheffield City Council v E* [2004] EWHC 2808 (Fam), Munby J.

'There are many people in our society who may be of limited or borderline capacity but whose lives are immensely enriched by marriage. We must be careful not to set the test of capacity to marry too high, lest it operate as an unfair, unnecessary and indeed discriminatory bar against the mentally disabled.'

4.11 The parties must understand the nature of marriage and the duties and responsibilities it creates and also truly consent to the particular marriage, but lack of consent only makes a marriage voidable and not void.[15] Consent will not be validly given if it was given under duress or there was mistake as to the person being married or the nature of the ceremony, but the fact that a party is totally unfit for marriage appears to be irrelevant, though it may result in resistance by others to the marriage and could render the marriage voidable.[16] It is only capacity in a general sense that is required, and the particular marriage proposal does not have to be taken into account. The court will not adjudicate upon the wisdom of the choice of partner and has no jurisdiction to consider whether a particular marriage is in the best interests of a party.[17]

Relevance of sexual intercourse

4.12 Although, generally speaking, a sexual relationship is implicit in any marriage, it is not a vital ingredient and its absence does not invalidate a marriage. The marriage contract must be understood as providing the parties to the marriage with the right to choose whether to engage in sexual activity within that union. It may be that a marriage 'at a time of life when the passions are subdued' is 'contracted only for comfortable society', the spouses being 'fairly left to just reflection and more placid gratifications'.[18] The law has been clearly stated as follows:[19]

'For although it has been said that the procreation of children is one main object of marriage, yet it cannot be doubted that marriages between persons so advanced in years as effectually and certainly to defeat that object, are perfectly legal and binding. The truth is, *consensus non concubitus facit matrimonium*.'

Protection

4.13 The High Court has demonstrated a willingness to use its inherent protective jurisdiction to protect otherwise competent adults from marriage where there may be a lack of understanding or coercion depriving them of capacity to make their own decisions. Where a deaf woman was unable to communicate with her family in her own language (British Sign Language) or to lip read their first language, an order was made to ensure that she was properly informed in a manner that she could understand about any specific marriage before entering into it.[20] In another case an injunction was granted to prevent a British citizen who was a competent adult from entering into a marriage against her will whilst she was abroad and being kept out of the country.[21] In other cases parents have been restrained by an injunction from taking their incapacitated child to

---

[15]   *Re Park's Estate* [1953] 2 All ER 1411, CA.
[16]   It is now possible for a marriage ceremony to take place in a mental hospital for a detained patient – Marriage Act 1983, s 1.
[17]   *Sheffield City Council v E* [2004] EWHC 2808 (Fam).
[18]   *Briggs v Morgan* (1820) 3 Phill Ecc 325, at 331–332, Sir William Scott.
[19]   *A v B* (1868) LR 1 P&D 559, at 562, Sir J P Wilde.
[20]   *Re SA (Vulnerable Adult with Capacity: Marriage)* [2005] EWHC 2942 (Fam).
[21]   *Re SK (An Adult) (Forced Marriage: Appropriate Relief)* [2005] 3 All ER 421, [2005] 2 FLR 230.

Pakistan for the purpose of marriage there.[22] The principles established by these cases are equally applicable to elderly people where questionable marriages are contemplated.

Objections

4.14   There are procedures whereby objection may be raised to a proposed marriage before it takes place.

Caveat

4.15   A *caveat* can be entered at the relevant registration office or church by a person who believes that a party to a proposed marriage does not have the necessary capacity, and this puts the registrar or clergyman on notice and creates a requirement to investigate the matter.[23] The burden of proof of lack of capacity is on the person seeking to oppose the marriage and medical evidence may be required. The Superintendent Registrar gives the person who gave notice of marriage an opportunity to answer the objection and to produce evidence in rebuttal, and there is a right of appeal to the Registrar General against a refusal to issue a certificate of marriage because a caveat has been entered.

Banns

4.16   Most Anglican weddings take place after the reading of three banns in church and this gives an opportunity to concerned persons to record an objection to the proposed marriage. An enquiry is then made as to capacity of the parties to enter into the ceremony.

Pre-nuptial agreements

4.17   Before getting married the parties will usually discuss, to a greater or lesser extent, the nature and implications of their relationship following marriage because of the effect that marriage will have on the existing and perhaps long established pattern of their lives. Raising a family will not usually be on the agenda, but coping with an existing family or families may be and other matters to be considered include where to live, how to handle their financial arrangements, longer-term financial provision and even how intimate the relationship is to be. The marriage is unlikely to be successful if one party merely seeks companionship whereas the other desires a full relationship.

4.18   Ideally agreement will be reached on the key financial aspects of the proposed relationship and it is possible to record this in a written document. Such agreements are particularly appropriate for second, or subsequent, marriages usually between an older couple, when either or both have children and wish to keep their own property separate in order to protect the children's inheritance.

4.19   For those domiciled in England and Wales there is no legislation specifically governing marriage contracts and they are not enforceable as such but may be relevant either on marriage breakdown or in the event of an inheritance claim. When resolving financial matters following a divorce the court must take into account 'all the

---

[22]   *M v B, A and S (by the Official Solicitor)* [2005] EWHC 1681 (Fam), [2006] 1 FLR 117; *Re MAB, X City Council v MB, NB and MAB (by the Official Solicitor)* [2006] EWHC 168 (Fam).

[23]   Marriage Act 1949, s 29. A doctor or anyone else may take this step, but there must be good grounds for doing so or liability could arise for the costs of the registrar and damages to the couple.

circumstances of the case' including 'the conduct of each of the parties if ... it would ... be inequitable to disregard it'.[24] In a case dealing with a separation agreement Mr Justice Eastham stated:

> '... the existence of an agreement is a very relevant circumstance ... and in the case of an arm's length agreement based on legal advice between parties of equal bargaining power, is a most important piece of conduct to be considered.'

The Court of Appeal, having approved this proposition, considered that the court would not enforce an agreement where there had been, for example, undue pressure by one side, exploitation of a dominant position to secure an unreasonable advantage, inadequate knowledge, possibly bad legal advice, or an important change of circumstances unforeseen or overlooked at the time of making the agreement. However, 'formal agreements, properly and fairly arrived at with competent legal advice, should not be displaced unless there are good and substantial grounds for concluding that an injustice will be done by holding the parties to the terms of their agreement'.[25]

4.20   It has more recently been held that marriage contracts may comprise valuable evidence[26] and their existence and evidential weight are factors to be taken into account by the court when deciding how to exercise its discretion under the Matrimonial Causes Act 1973.[27] In this respect they would not need to be in any particular form so an exchange of letters might be sufficient. The onus is upon the party seeking to rely upon the contract to prove that the party to be bound had fully understood its nature and effect, and had entered into it of his own free will.[28] A contract might also be invalid if it purports to restrict the right of one party to apply to the court for relief, so if this is desired it should contain a severability clause to prevent the entire agreement being declared void.[29]

4.21   A marriage contract may thus comprise valuable evidence especially in the case of a companionship marriage between an elderly couple which proved to be of short duration. It would be of less significance in the case of a long marriage where the parties had brought up children. But other factors such as the needs and resources of the parties may outweigh the intentions expressed in any such contract.

Post nuptial settlements

4.22   Similar principles apply to contracts entered into between the parties during the marriage. They are not binding but can be persuasive although issues of undue influence may arise.[30]

---

24   Matrimonial Causes Act 1973, s 25.
25   *Edgar v Edgar* [1980] 3 All ER 887, CA.
26   For the interpretation of a pre-nuptial agreement made in New York see: *S v S (Divorce: Staying proceedings)* [1997] 2 FLR 100.
27   *N v N (Jurisdiction: Pre-Nuptial Agreement)* [1999] 2 FLR 745.
28   *Zamet v Hyman* [1961] 1 WLR 1442, CA. For a checklist see: *K v K (Ancillary relief: Prenuptial Agreement)* [2003] 1 FLR 120.
29   *Hyman v Hyman* [1929] AC 601, HL. A precedent will be found in Denzil Lush, *Cohabitation and Co-Ownership Precedents* (Family Law, 1993).
30   For a case where the law was analysed see *NA v MA* [2006] EWHC 2900 (Fam).

Marriage breakdown

4.23 The law that governs the breakdown of marriage is to be found in the Matrimonial Causes Act 1973 as amended by the Matrimonial and Family Proceedings Act 1984 and the rules governing court procedure are the Family Procedure Rules 2010. To the older person whose marriage has failed, especially if it was a second marriage, the important question is likely to be the financial consequences rather than the granting of a divorce or the arrangements for children. Most proceedings are now brought in the local county court and the full powers of the court only become exercisable once there is a decree of nullity or dissolution (divorce). The petitioner commences the proceedings by filing and serving a petition and the respondent responds by completing an acknowledgement and then serving an answer if the proceedings are to be defended, though they seldom are.

Nullity

4.24 Marriages may be void or voidable.[31] A marriage entered into after 31 July 1971 will be void only if certain of the necessary formalities have not been complied with, the parties are within the prohibited degrees of relationship or not respectively male and female, or one of them is under 16 years of age or already married. In all other circumstances the marriage will be voidable only. For marriages entered into prior to that date certain of the grounds on which a marriage may now be voidable would have rendered the marriage void, though on a more restricted basis.

4.25 There are several grounds upon which a marriage may be voidable at the instance of one of the parties[32] and these include incapacity by either party to consummate the marriage, wilful refusal by the other party to consummate the marriage, that the other party was suffering from VD or pregnant by another at the time of the marriage and that either party did not validly consent to the marriage. A marriage is also voidable if at the time of the marriage either party, though capable of consenting, was suffering from mental disorder within the meaning of the Mental Health Act 1983, of such a kind or to such an extent as to be unfitted for marriage.

4.26 There must be apparent consent for the ceremony to take place, so the question is whether this is accompanied by the necessary intention. Consent may not be valid due to duress, mistake, unsoundness of mind or otherwise. Mental disorder only vitiates consent if the party was, at the time of the ceremony, incapable of understanding the nature of the marriage and the duties and responsibilities it creates.[33] The fact that the party is totally unfit for marriage is irrelevant in the context of consent, but the mental disorder ground was introduced to cover the case where the afflicted party is capable of giving a valid consent but has a mental disorder which makes him or her incapable of carrying on a normal married life. Such person may even petition on the basis of his or her own mental disorder.

4.27 There are now no bars to the granting of a decree if it is established that the marriage is void. Nullity proceedings on the basis of lack of consent must be commenced within 3 years of the marriage, though the court may give permission for the proceedings to be instituted at a later date if the petitioner has at some time during the 3-year period

---

[31] It is necessary to check whether the marriage was before or after 31 July 1971 because the Nullity of Marriage Act 1971 changed the common law from that date.

[32] The Matrimonial Causes Act 1973 as amended by Marriage Act 1983, s 2(4) consolidated earlier legislation.

[33] *Re Park's Estate* [1953] 2 All ER 1411, CA.

suffered from mental disorder and it is in all the circumstances just to do so. In addition the court may not grant a decree in the case of a voidable marriage if the respondent satisfies the court that the petitioner, with knowledge that it was open to him or her to have the marriage avoided, so conducted himself or herself in relation to the respondent as to lead the respondent reasonably to believe that he or she would not seek to do so and it would be unjust to the respondent to grant a decree.[34] This may be relevant in respect of a marriage entered into for companionship only.

Divorce

4.28   Historically the dissolution of marriage has been based upon the matrimonial offences of adultery, cruelty and desertion, but an exception to this was introduced in 1937 when unsoundness of mind became a ground for divorce available to the other party subject to certain limitations. The Divorce Reform Act 1969 made radical changes by providing that 'the sole ground on which a petition for divorce may be presented to the court by either party to a marriage shall be that the marriage has broken down irretrievably'. However, the court may only be satisfied of this if the petitioner establishes one of five 'facts', namely:[35]

(1)   the respondent has committed adultery and the petitioner finds it intolerable to live with the respondent;

(2)   the respondent has behaved in such a way that the petitioner cannot reasonably be expected to live with the respondent;

(3)   the respondent has deserted the petitioner for a continuous period of at least 2 years immediately preceding the presentation of the petition;

(4)   the parties to the marriage have lived apart for a continuous period of at least 2 years immediately preceding the presentation of the petition and the respondent consents to a decree being granted;

(5)   the parties to the marriage have lived apart for a continuous period of at least 5 years immediately preceding the petition.

A respondent may oppose dissolution on the grounds of hardship when the petition is based upon 'living apart' (ie the final fact above), and this will usually mean financial hardship so loss of pension rights would be relevant.[36] No petition may in any event be presented before the expiration of one year from the marriage.

4.29   Before 1969 when cruelty was one of the grounds for a divorce, it was necessary to show wilful conduct, or that the cruel conduct was aimed at the other party. This made it difficult to obtain a divorce on this ground where the intended respondent was incapable of appreciating the effect of his or her behaviour. It is now the effect of behaviour on the petitioner that is relevant.

4.30   The validity of a spouse's consent to a decree of divorce following 2 years' separation depends on whether he or she has the capacity to understand the nature of the consent and to appreciate the effect and result of expressing it.[37] If the respondent is incapable of managing his or her property and affairs so that a litigation friend must be appointed, a divorce may not be obtained on the basis of consent.

---

[34]   Matrimonial Causes Act 1973, s 13(1).
[35]   Matrimonial Causes Act 1973, s 1(2).
[36]   See Matrimonial Causes Act 1973, ss 5 and 10.
[37]   *Mason v Mason* [1972] 3 All ER 315.

Judicial separation

4.31   A decree of judicial separation is obtained on the same basis as a divorce and a petition may be presented in the first year of the marriage. Orders relating to financial matters and children may still be made, but when a decree has been granted the parties are not free to remarry and pension and inheritance rights will not generally be affected. These petitions are rare and generally arise from religious convictions, but the respondent can in most instances obtain a divorce after 5 years of separation regardless of conduct.

Financial provision

4.32   In the context of the breakdown of the relationship there is an important difference between marriage or civil partnership (see below) on the one hand and cohabitation on the other. The courts have power to redistribute assets and require financial support following the failure of a marriage or civil partnership. Upon termination of cohabitation the courts may only give effect to the ownership of assets and any agreements reached, or deemed to have been reached, between the parties.

Orders that can be made

4.33   The court dealing with a nullity, divorce or judicial separation petition has power to provide a range of *financial remedies* for the benefit of either spouse.[38] On or after the filing of the petition it can make an interim maintenance order (known as *maintenance pending suit*), and on or after granting a decree, but with effect in the case of divorce or nullity from decree absolute, it may make orders for periodical payments (which may be secured), a lump sum, property adjustment,[39] pension sharing and the avoidance of a disposition. The court may also order the release of future inheritance claims against the estate of the other spouse. Periodical payments orders can be made on an interim basis or varied following a change of circumstances, but the other orders once made are usually final and a party cannot later come back to the court for a further order. Most cases are resolved by *consent orders* negotiated between the solicitors to the spouses, but these must be approved by the district judge after full disclosure of the financial position of the parties if they are to be legally binding.

Matters taken into account

4.34   When making financial orders the court must 'have regard to all the circumstances of the case'. First consideration is given to the welfare of any minor child of the family, but the court will refer to a statutory list of matters[40] which include:

(1)   the income, earning capacity, property and other financial resources which each of the parties to the marriage has or is likely to have in the foreseeable future, including in the case of earning capacity any increase in that capacity which it would in the opinion of the court be reasonable to expect a party to the marriage to take steps to acquire;

(2)   the financial needs, obligations and responsibilities which each of the parties to the marriage has or is likely to have in the foreseeable future;

---

[38]   Matrimonial Causes Act 1973, ss 21 to 24. These financial orders were previously known as *ancillary relief orders*.

[39]   This may be for the transfer or settlement of property, or variation of a settlement.

[40]   See Matrimonial Causes Act 1973, s 25 (as amended by Matrimonial and Family Proceedings Act 1984 and Pensions Act 1995).

(3)   the standard of living enjoyed by the family before the breakdown of the marriage;

(4)   the age of each party to the marriage and the duration of the marriage;

(5)   any physical or mental disability of a party to the marriage;

(6)   the contributions made by each of the parties to the welfare of the family, including any contribution made by looking after the home or caring for the family;

(7)   the conduct of each of the parties, if that conduct is such that it would in the opinion of the court be inequitable to disregard it.

Maintenance and the home

4.35   The court seeks to achieve a *clean break* with no continuing maintenance provision, but this may not be possible following a long marriage where there is little further employment potential, unless adequate capital (including pension entitlement) is available to provide for the security of both parties or both are likely to be dependent on state benefits. Ownership and continued occupation of the former matrimonial home is usually of paramount importance, but the home may be ordered to be sold and the net proceeds divided in specified proportions with a view to each party making their own provision. Alternatively, the home may be transferred to one party with a deferred charge to the other, though this is more likely when there are young children.

Implications of incapacity

4.36   Where financial provision is to be made for a party to the marriage who is a protected party[41] then, unless the Court of Protection is already involved, the court dealing with the marriage may order the payments to be made or property to be transferred to a person 'having charge of' that party.[42] This might be a carer or some relative dealing with the financial affairs, but if substantial capital was involved it is likely that a deputy would have to be appointed by the Court of Protection.[43] In cases where this party was in a nursing or residential care home, or otherwise receiving substantial means-tested support, it might be appropriate for any capital provision to be made through a discretionary trust[44] in favour of that party and the children, and the court has power to order this.[45]

4.37   Orders for financial provision may also be made against a spouse who is a protected party even if a deputy has been appointed by the Court of Protection, although such representative would usually be authorised to conduct the proceedings as litigation friend for the spouse. In appropriate cases the Court of Protection may already have ordered provision for the other spouse because it seeks to honour the obligations of persons within its jurisdiction.[46]

---

[41]   Ie incapable within the meaning of the Mental Capacity Act 2005 of managing and administering his or her property and affairs.

[42]   Matrimonial Causes Act 1973, s 40.

[43]   See generally Ch 11.

[44]   See generally Ch 12.

[45]   Matrimonial Causes Act 1973, s 24(1)(b).

[46]   See generally Ch 2.

Civil partnership

Background

4.38   The Civil Partnership Act 2004 reflects more liberal social attitudes. It had become widely accepted that it is both logically and morally indefensible to prevent gay and lesbian couples having access to formal recognition of their relationships and to the 'next of kin' rights and the tax, pension and other advantages that flow from marriage. Encouraging stability in relationships, whether heterosexual or homosexual, should involve the same sorts of protections as come with marriage, and the Civil Partnership Act 2004 ('the 2004 Act') addresses these issues in considerable detail.

4.39   The Act took effect on 5 December 2005 and introduced greater recognition for same sex relationships in England and Wales, Scotland and Northern Ireland by an option of registration as 'civil partners'. It does not address the problems in the legal treatment of those cohabiting without registration by marriage or by civil partnership. Heterosexual couples are specifically excluded because they have the option of marriage.

Creation and termination

4.40   A 'civil partnership' is defined as:[47]

> '... a relationship between two people of the same sex ... which is formed when they register as civil partners of each other ...'

It ends only on death, dissolution or annulment. The general approach is to make detailed provision for the formation and ending of civil partnerships, and for the consequences that flow from them. It deals with these matters by treating civil partners in very much the same way as married couples. There is provision for recognition of overseas relationships.

4.41   To create a civil partnership a specific document is required, signed in the presence of each other and of a civil partnership registrar and two witnesses. No religious service is to be used during the registration formalities, and it cannot take place in religious premises. A couple cannot register if one is already married or a civil partner of someone else, nor if either is under 16 or within prohibited degrees of relationship.

Termination

4.42   The provisions for court proceedings to end partnerships[48] in most cases mirror existing provisions for married couples. The partnership may be dissolved when it is established that the relationship has irretrievably broken down due to unreasonable behaviour, desertion or 2 years' separation with consent or 5 years' separation (adultery is omitted).

---

[47]   Civil Partnership Act 2004, s 1.
[48]   Including nullity, presumption of death and separation orders as well as dissolution.

Finances and children

4.43 In this area too most of the provisions mirror those for married couples. The court can make orders for financial provision including pension sharing,[49] and in the case of disputes about property either civil partner may apply to the county court, and the court may make such order with respect to the property as it thinks fit, including an order for sale. Contributions to property improvement if substantial and in money or money's worth are recognised. Pre-registration agreements may be considered in the same way as pre-nuptial agreements.

Status

4.44 Other amendments align civil partners with married persons, for example in certain parts of the law relating to housing and tenancies, in domestic violence proceedings under the Family Law Act 1996, Part IV and in claims under the Fatal Accidents Act 1976. Interpretation of statutory references to step relationships (eg stepson, stepmother, etc), and the terms '... in-law' (eg brother-in-law and daughter-in-law) are amended to apply in civil partnerships. There are amendments to the Sex Discrimination Act 1975, social security, child support and tax credits legislation. Civil partners have inheritance rights similar to marriage and an insurable interest in each other, and the partnership will revoke any previous will made by a partner unless made in contemplation thereof. Their inheritance and capital gains tax treatment is the same as that for spouses but they will be treated as 'connected persons' for tax purposes.

Incapacity issues

4.45 Civil partnership is not merely a matter of contract but affects status and creates a completely new legal relationship. Clearly this has implications for our mental capacity jurisdiction. The civil partner must be recognised to the same extent as a spouse when decisions are to be made, whether relating to financial matters, personal welfare or healthcare. Comparable duties and responsibilities may also arise on the part of the civil partner.

4.46 The civil partner is afforded the same status as a spouse as regards participation in any of the procedures. This is not as radical as it may seem, because the new social attitudes have already resulted in domestic partners being involved in many situations, and this has included same sex partners even in the absence of a civil partnership. To this extent there has been a move away from relationships of blood and marriage to de facto relationships. The Scottish mental incapacity legislation provided 'next of kin' rights to same sex partners by including them within the definition of nearest relative whose views must be taken into account,[50] and the equivalent provision under the Mental Capacity Act 2005 includes 'anyone engaged in caring for the person or interested in his welfare' as well as 'anyone named by the person as someone to be consulted on the matter in question or matters of that kind'.[51]

---

[49] It is not yet clear whether the courts will adopt the same approach to financial provision as for married couples. There cannot be any discrimination between the sexes, but can long periods of cohabitation before the Act be taken into account?

[50] Adults with Incapacity (Scotland) Act 2000, ss 1(4)(b) and 87(2).

[51] Mental Capacity Act 2005, s 4(7).

Cohabitation

Overview

4.47 An elderly couple may contemplate living together and it could be convenient, economical and mutually supportive for them to do so. There are moral implications which are more likely to be of concern to the older generation, but the attitude of the respective families may be an influential factor. The younger generation may display dual standards, not being comfortable with this type of relationship for their parents yet content to cohabit themselves. However, it is important to realise that a change of status may arise when parties live together and they may not both have the same expectations, so it is important to consider the practical and legal implications in advance.

Status

4.48 The change of status will be far more limited than that which arises on marriage or civil partnership. There is no such thing as a 'common law marriage' and whilst the court has wide discretionary powers to distribute property and income fairly following the breakdown of a marriage or civil partnership, this is not so following a period of cohabitation, however lengthy that may have been. But cohabiting partners are recognised in some statutes. For example, they may be able to claim compensation for the death of the partner under the Fatal Accidents Act 1976, or make a claim against the estate of the deceased partner under the Inheritance (Provision for Family and Dependants) Act 1975 without having to prove dependency. They may also obtain an occupation order under the Family Law Act 1996, Part IV or be able to apply for a transfer of a tenancy under Sch 7 to that Act.

Practical implications

4.49 The matters to be discussed and agreed are similar to those when the parties contemplate marriage, but may be more extensive because certain aspects of a relationship are assumed by the act of marriage. They include:

(1) where they are to live. Who is to own the home or hold the tenancy, and if the other party is to make a capital contribution, on what basis is that to be done? If the home is to be owned jointly, on what basis will it be held beneficially?

(2) the sharing of and manner in which they are to meet household and other expenses. Will there be a joint bank account and a pooling of expenses, or if one party is to be merely a lodger, on what terms will that be?

(3) the basis on which they are to live together. Is an intimate relationship intended or merely companionship? Will there be a change of name? Will they take holidays together and share leisure activities?

(4) the effect on any pensions, state benefit claims or services provided by the local authority. Will they be treated as 'living together as man and wife' for benefits purposes, and will any services be withdrawn or restricted? Will increased charges be made for services?

(5) whether the relationship is intended to be mutually supportive for life. Does this mean financially or on a caring basis, or both? If financial, is this until the first death or the second death, and if until the death of the survivor, what steps are to be taken to secure that intention? Should lasting powers of attorney and new wills be signed?

4.50   Just as an ante-nuptial agreement may be useful for older couples, so may a cohabitation contract be desirable for those who choose to live together if only because it will oblige them to consider the implications of their proposed course of conduct before giving up their separate homes. Precedents are available.[52] If the relationship does not work it is seldom possible for the parties to restore their previous way of life and the experience can be extremely disruptive, especially for an older person.

Legal implications

4.51   Despite the benefits of reaching an agreement over significant aspects of the relationship, a cohabitation contract is of doubtful legal effect. Attitudes of previous generations have resulted in the general freedom of contract being overridden by public policy considerations and there are several hurdles to overcome. The contract may be illegal on grounds of public policy (where sexual services are involved) or void for uncertainty, there may be no intention to create legal relations or an absence of consideration, or it may be voidable where there is undue influence.

4.52   A deed which concentrates upon the division of property and financial support in the event of a breakdown in the relationship[53] would probably overcome these hurdles. In any event care should be taken over the investment of money and any documentation such as house deeds, tenancy agreements, bank accounts and household bills so that there is not an unfair outcome if the parties separate. A decision will be needed over whether to pool financial resources and the parties should also reconsider their wills. In order to avoid the suggestion of undue influence, especially in the case of older people who may be mentally frail or dependent on others, independent legal advice should be obtained by the parties when they are negotiating an agreement or dealing with significant matters such as buying a house for joint occupation.

4.53   The living together relationship will have greater legal significance when it is seen as being a substitute for the married relationship. A finding that the parties are cohabiting as distinct from merely sharing a house on another basis can have serious adverse consequences in regard to means-tested benefits, pensions or maintenance payments. It follows that where this is not intended steps should be taken to record the intentions of the parties and a written agreement may assist. However, a relationship that starts off on one basis may become something quite different: the housekeeper may become a 'common law spouse' or the cohabitee a mere lodger. The change of status may be gradual and is not always easy to recognise, despite the possible legal significance.

4.54   Definitions are not precise and the actual nature of the relationship is a question of fact which can be difficult to determine. The parties may be married in all but name, or the reality of the relationship may be closer to that of householder and housekeeper or lodger. The difference may seem less significant in the case of older people as it tends to be assumed that a sexual relationship is non-existent, yet that might also be the case in a marriage between younger people and is not the deciding factor.

4.55   For means-tested benefits the question is whether the parties are 'living together as husband and wife or civil partners', the test now being the same for same-sex couples

---

52   Denzil Lush, *Cohabitation and Co-ownership Precedents* (Family Law); Jill Bowler and others, *Living Together Precedents* (Sweet & Maxwell).
53   This could be a trust deed or settlement where substantial wealth is involved.

as for heterosexual couples.[54] The existence of a sexual relationship will only be one of the criteria to take into account, others being whether the parties live in the same household, have a stable relationship and have children, the nature of the financial arrangements and how the parties appear in public.[55] The outcome depends upon the reality of the relationship and a court or tribunal having to decide the issue will look behind any agreement between the parties, but how they have chosen to deal with their financial affairs will be very material.

Breakdown of the relationship

4.56   The courts are now facing many claims, usually but not necessarily by unmarried mothers, relating to the future of the home where a living together relationship has broken down. Where there is a dispute as to the ownership of property the general law is merely declaratory of existing rights. Any dispute will be resolved pursuant to the Trusts of Land and Appointment of Trustees Act 1996 and orders for sale can be made.[56]

4.57   Where a transfer or deed of trust states the proportions in which the property is held this is usually determinative unless there is a finding of mistake, fraud or duress which may allow rectification. The House of Lords held that where a property was conveyed into the joint names of a cohabiting couple without any explicit declaration of their respective beneficial interests, the starting point where the property had to be divided upon the breakdown of the relationship was that where there was joint legal ownership, there was also joint beneficial ownership. The onus is upon the person seeking to show that the parties intended their beneficial interests to be different from their legal interests and in what way, but context is everything and each case turns on its own facts.[57]

4.58   In the case of dispute the question becomes what the parties agreed, yet usually they will not have addressed the future ownership at all or there are conflicting interpretations. Where there is no agreement the starting point is who owns and who paid for or contributed to the purchase and improvement of the property, but complex equitable doctrines such as proprietary estoppel and resulting or constructive trusts are then called in aid. The needs of the parties are not relevant, although they would be if the parties had been married or in a civil partnership. Litigation of this nature is expensive and the outcome uncertain so negotiated settlements are generally reached which may be disadvantageous to the party whose name is not on the legal title. Those concerned about this area of law should look out for recent appeal cases.

Resulting trust

4.59   The presumption of an implied or resulting trust arises where one party contributes to the purchase of a property which is taken in the name of another with the common intention that it be held in trust for them both in shares proportionate to the

---

[54]   An *unmarried couple* was previously defined as 'a man and woman who are not married to each other but are living together as husband and wife' – Social Security Contributions and Benefits Act 1992, s 137(1).

[55]   This analysis is based on the rule for claiming certain means-tested benefits as a couple – see Commissioners' decision R(SB) 17/81.

[56]   The criteria laid down in this Act should be applied in preference to cases pre-dating it.

[57]   *Stack v Dowden* [2007] UKHL 17.

contributions to the purchase price. This can be rebutted by a presumption of advancement (where a gift has been made) but only between married couples or parent and child.

Constructive trust

4.60   It is more usual for a cohabitant to rely upon a constructive trust which usually arises where property has been conveyed to one party but the other claims a beneficial interest despite the absence of a written agreement as to how the property is to be held. This has been explained as follows:[58]

> 'The first and fundamental question which must always be resolved is whether, independently of any inference to be drawn from the conduct of the parties in the course of sharing the house as their home and managing their joint affairs, there has at any time prior to acquisition, or exceptionally at some later date, been any agreement, arrangement or understanding reached between them that the property is to be shared beneficially. The finding of an agreement or arrangement to share in this sense can only, I think, be based on evidence of express discussions between the partners, however imperfectly remembered and however imprecise their terms may have been. Once a finding to this effect is made it will only be necessary for the partner asserting a claim to a beneficial interest against the partner entitled to the legal estate to show that he or she has acted to his or her detriment or significantly altered his or her position in reliance on the agreement in order to give rise to a constructive trust or proprietary estoppel.
>
> In sharp contrast with this situation is the very different one where there is no evidence to support a finding of an agreement or arrangement to share, however reasonable it might have been for the parties to reach such an arrangement if they had applied their minds to the question, and where the court must rely entirely on the conduct of the parties both as the basis from which to infer a common intention to share the property beneficially and as the conduct relied on to give rise to a constructive trust. In this situation direct contributions to the purchase price by the partner who is not the legal owner, whether initially or by payment of mortgage instalments, will readily justify the inference necessary to the creation of a constructive trust. But, as I read the authorities, it is at least extremely doubtful whether anything less will do.'

4.61   The claimant has to establish both a common intention and that she (it is usually the woman) has acted to her detriment in reliance upon this. The test of a common intention is strict but this may be established either through an agreement, arrangement or understanding relating to the beneficial ownership of the property or, in the absence of express discussions, through conduct. It seems that such conduct is confined to making financial contributions to the acquisition or enhancement of the property (payment of the mortgage may be sufficient) and general contributions to household expenses or the cost of bringing up children will not be sufficient. The further hurdle of proving detriment brings in the proprietary estoppel principle whereby it would be inequitable to overlook the changed position of the party who has been prejudiced.

Quantifying the interest

4.62   Once a beneficial interest has been established it must be quantified, and the law in this respect has developed in recent years. With a resulting trust it will usually be based upon the actual financial contribution as a proportion of the purchase price. Where a person has expended money on the property of another subsequent to

---

[58]   *Lloyds Bank Plc v Rosset* [1990] 1 All ER 1111; See also *Pettitt v Pettitt* [1969] 2 All ER 385; *Gissing v Gissing* [1970] 2 All ER 780.

acquisition with no intention that this be a loan or a gift, that person can seek the return of the money and arguably a share of the increased value resulting from the expenditure on the basis of a resulting trust.[59] For a constructive trust the interest may be quantified by the agreement but in the absence of this all the circumstances are taken into account. These may include the whole course of dealing between the parties relevant to their ownership and occupation of the home up to the date of the dispute.[60] But although wider contributions in terms of home-making can be taken into account in quantifying the interest they may not be relied upon when determining whether a beneficial interest arises in the first place.[61]

4.63   The Court of Appeal attempted to clarify the developing and sometimes conflicting case law in *Oxley v Hiscock* where a broad brush approach was adopted and Chadwick LJ stated:[62]

> '... [T]he second question to be answered in cases of this nature is "what is the extent of the parties' respective beneficial interests in the property?" Again, in many such cases, the answer will be provided by evidence of what they said and did at the time of the acquisition. But, in a case where there is no evidence of any discussion between them as to the amount of the share which each was to have – and even in a case where the evidence is that there was no discussion on that point— the question still requires an answer. It must now be accepted that (at least in this Court and below) the answer is that each is entitled to that share which the court considers fair having regard to the whole course of dealing between them in relation to the property. And, in that context, 'the whole course of dealing between them in relation to the property' includes the arrangements which they make from time to time in order to meet the outgoings (for example, mortgage contributions, council tax and utilities, repairs, insurance and housekeeping) which have to be met if they are to live in the property as their home.'

This introduces an element of discretion in regard to quantifying the share once a beneficial interest has been established under traditional principles. Uncertainties include whether this only applies to unmarried couples living as man and wife or also to same sex relationships or even friends who buy a house together for economic reasons, and the significance of financial contributions to the household but not the property as such.

Proprietary estoppel

4.64   Under this doctrine, first expounded by Scarman LJ, there is no need to establish an agreement or common intention. Instead this will be presumed from the conduct of the other party where:[63]

- the claimant has a mistaken belief as to his legal rights;

- the claimant has acted to his detriment in reliance on that mistaken belief;

- the defendant knows of his own rights and that they are inconsistent with the claimant's belief;

- the defendant knows of the claimant's mistaken belief;

- the defendant has encouraged the claimant to act to his detriment either actively or passively by refraining from asserting his own legal rights.

---

[59]   *Hussey v Palmer* [1972] 3 All ER 744. This may require a complicated valuation exercise.
[60]   *Drake v Whipp* [1996] 1 FLR 826, CA.
[61]   *Midland Bank Plc v Cooke* [1995] 4 All ER 562.
[62]   [2004] EWCA Civ 546, [2004] 3 All ER 703.
[63]   *Crabb v Arun District Council* [1975] 3 All ER 865 affirmed in *Matharu v Matharu* [1994] 2 FLR 597. A recent reiteration of the law is to be found in *Lissimore v Downing* [2003] 2 FLR 308.

The detriment does not have to include financial expenditure and may comprise looking after the other party for many years in reliance on assurances of a home for life.[64] Once encouragement and detriment is proved reliance may be inferred. The court must look at the matter in the round and the fundamental principle is that equity is concerned to prevent unconscionable conduct, and this consideration permeates all elements of the doctrine.[65]

4.65   A broader range of remedies is available under proprietary estoppel than constructive trust. In addition to declaring ownership rights the court can grant the right to occupy the property or award compensation. Any other benefits received by the claimant will be taken into account. The position was summarised by the Court of Appeal in *Jennings v Rice*[66] when it was indicated that the ultimate result must be just and proportionate in the circumstances. However, in *Oxley v Hiscock* (mentioned above) Chadwick LJ concluded that the outcome should be the same whether the case proceeds on constructive trust or in proprietary estoppel.

Law Commission proposals

4.66   The law has yet to catch up with the trend in society for informal relationships and there have been many proposals for reform. In 2007 the Law Commission for England and Wales recommended the introduction of a new scheme of financial remedies which would not apply to all cohabitants and where it did apply would only give rise to remedies relating to contributions made to the relationship.[67] Remedies would respond to the economic impact of the parties' contributions to the relationship and first consideration would be given to any dependent children of the couple. Cohabitants would not be expected to meet each other's future needs by means of maintenance payments and there would be no principle that the parties should share their assets equally. The scheme would apply to those couples who have had a child together or who have lived together for a minimum period within a range of 2 to 5 years. Couples who wished to do so could opt out of the scheme by a written agreement to that effect. They would then be free to make their own arrangements for what would happen to their assets in the event of separation. There seems to be little prospect of these proposals being enacted at present.

Children

Preliminary

4.67   The legislation relating to children has little application once the child attains 17 years of age. In most instances any children will have grown up and the elderly person will be concerned about maintaining a relationship with grandchildren so this is considered below after an explanation of the general law and procedure that applies under the Children Act 1989 and associated legislation.

---

64   *Greasley v Cooke* [1980] 3 All ER 710.
65   *Gillett v Holt* [2001] Ch 210.
66   [2002] EWCA Civ 159.
67   *Cohabitation: The Financial Consequences of Relationship Breakdown* (31 July 2007). Available at: www.lawcom.gov.uk/cohabitation.htm.

Financial support

4.68 Maintenance orders for children following a divorce usually cease when the child is beyond compulsory school age but may continue even into adulthood if there are special circumstances or the child is at an educational establishment or undergoing training for a trade or profession.[68] Special circumstances may include physical or other handicap, and the expenses attributed to the child's disability should be taken into account in the broadest sense.[69] It is generally better for any financial support for a disabled child to be provided on a voluntary basis because a court order for the benefit of the adult child may be vulnerable to means-testing for local authority services or state benefits.

4.69 A child who has reached 18 and is continuing in education may obtain an order for periodical payments or a lump sum against parents in the situations specified above where they are not living with each other in the same household and there was no periodical payments order in force in respect of the child before he reached the age of 16.[70] If there was such an order, the child's remedy is to apply in the proceedings in which that order was made to extend that order and for payments to be made to him. If, however, there was no such order and the parents are living with each other in the same household, then the adult child has no remedy against his parents. An application may only be made against a parent for the support of an adult disabled child if the parents are not living together. Thus, for instance, the adult child whose parents are living together and for no valid reason are refusing to support him or her through university is in a markedly worse situation than an adult child whose parents have separated.

Parental responsibility

4.70 Parental responsibility comprises the authority, along with others similarly entitled, to make normal decisions relating to education, medical treatment, etc. A person with parental responsibility for a child does not require permission to apply to the court in relation to that child. Only the mother, or both parents if married or (after 1 December 2003) the father's name appears on the birth certificate, have parental responsibility but others may acquire it by court order or by a registered agreement. A residence order confers parental responsibility during its subsistence, but a parental responsibility order may be made by itself.[71] Parental responsibility has no significance after the child attains 17 years save that it may have some influence if an application is made to the Court of Protection in respect of a mentally disabled adult child.

Guardianship

4.71 There are several types of guardianship[72] but in the present context it is the legal status under which a person has parental responsibility for a child who has not attained majority following the death of one or both of the parents. A parent with parental responsibility or guardian can in writing appoint one or more individuals to be guardian of any infant children following death.[73] In practice this is often done in a will. A later

---

68 Matrimonial Causes Act 1973, s 29. In the case of unmarried parents an order may be made under Children Act 1989, Sch 1.
69 *C v F (Disabled Child: Maintenance Orders)* [1998] 2 FLR 1.
70 Children Act 1989, Sch 1.
71 Children Act 1989, ss 2–4 as amended by the Adoption and Children Act 2002.
72 For the use of guardianship under the Mental Health Act 1983 see Ch 8.
73 Children Act 1989, ss 5 and 6. There is no longer any concept of parental guardianship whereby the father of a legitimate child became the guardian on the death of the mother.

appointment will revoke an earlier one unless it is clear that an additional appointment is being made and the destruction of the document with that intent will also amount to revocation. The appointment may also be disclaimed.

4.72 A guardian may also be appointed for a child by the court. This would be done where the child has no parent with parental responsibility or a residence order has been made for the child in favour of a parent or guardian who has died while the order was in force. In other words the appointment of a guardian fills a vacuum in responsibility for the child. Anyone may apply or the court may make an order of its own initiative.

4.73 The guardian must be an 'individual' so cannot be a local authority but more than one guardian may be appointed. For many purposes a guardian will be in the same position as a parent with parental responsibility, but no liability can arise for financial provision or child support and no rights of succession are acquired on the child's death. The guardian's duties cease when the child dies or attains 18 years, and of course also in the event of the prior death of the guardian. The court also now has power to remove a guardian. The status of guardian may be of great significance for grandparents in respect of grandchildren where their own son or daughter has died and there is a dysfunctional family.

Private law applications

Orders

4.74 A wide range of orders can be made by the county court and these are often referred to as *section 8 orders* because they are made under that section of the Children Act 1989.

- A *residence order* settles the arrangements as to the person with whom a child is to live.
- A *contact order* requires the person with whom a child lives, or is to live, to allow the child to visit or stay with the person named in the order, or for that person and the child otherwise to have contact with each other.
- A *prohibited steps order* provides that no step which could be taken by a parent in meeting his parental responsibility for a child, and which is of a kind specified in the order, shall be taken by any person without the consent of the court.
- A *specific issue order* gives directions for the purpose of determining a specific question which has arisen, or which may arise, in connection with any aspect of parental responsibility for a child.

Interim orders can be made, for example to deal with an emergency or until such time as a final order can be made, although there is in reality no final order in relation to a child.

Principles

4.75 The emphasis is upon agreement being reached between the parents as to the future upbringing of their children. The welfare of the child is the paramount consideration and the court will not make any order unless it considers that doing so is better for the child than making no order at all. When considering whether to make most orders, the court must have particular regard to the ascertainable wishes and feelings of the child, the physical, emotional and educational needs of the child and the likely effect on the child of a change of circumstances.

4.76 Other factors will be the age, sex, background and any characteristics of the child which the court considers relevant, any harm which the child has suffered or is at risk of suffering and how capable each of the child's parents (and any other person) is of meeting the child's needs. The court will take into account the range of powers available to it and, although the wishes and feelings of the child are important if of sufficient age and maturity, a child should not be expected to choose.[74]

Conciliation

4.77 The courts encourage the parents or other parties 'competing' for the child to behave as responsible parents and to make their own arrangements for the upbringing of any children. Wherever appropriate conciliation will be attempted and each court has its own arrangements for involving a court welfare officer or an independent local family mediation service. The court has power to make a family assistance order requiring a Cafcass[75] officer or officer of the local authority to advise, assist and (if appropriate) befriend any person named in the order.

4.78 Disputes about children are dealt with separately from other disputes relating to the breakdown of the marriage and the financial consequences. It may, however, not be possible to resolve a dispute about residence independently of the financial arrangements because of the need to ensure that there is a suitable home for the parent with whom the child resides.

The adult child

4.79 Where an adult child lacks mental capacity any issues as to residence and contact may be dealt with by the Court of Protection pursuant to the Mental Capacity Act 2005.[76] It has been held that there is no presumption of a right to contact between a parent and an adult child, albeit one with mental health problems or a learning disability.[77]

Public law applications

4.80 The Children Act 1989 also exclusively governs cases brought by the local authority which may be for *care orders*.[78] Grandparents may apply for leave to be made parties and to be heard when such applications are brought, and an order for reasonable contact may be made in their favour. If a care order is made in favour of the local authority, the child may be accommodated with grandparents. The court cannot order this but could revoke the care order later if its expressed wishes were not thereafter carried out by the authority. If this procedure is adopted the grandparents may be paid an allowance whereas they may not receive financial support under a residence order unless the parents are able to provide this.

Adoption

4.81 If a grandchild is placed for adoption all legal ties with the grandparents are severed, and although there can be post-adoption contact this is likely to be restricted in

---

[74] These factors are known as the 'welfare checklist'. See generally Children Act 1989, s 1.
[75] Children and Family Court Advisory and Support Service.
[76] See generally Ch 2.
[77] *D-R v D-R and another* (1999) *The Times*, 8 February, CA.
[78] See Children Act 1989, Part IV, ss 31–42.

its nature.[79] An adoption order is treated as a last resort and will only be made if it is in the best interests of the child, so if support for the parents (or one of them) is not sufficient the grandparents may apply for leave to intervene and seek to oppose the adoption. The court will then be concerned as to the future upbringing of the child especially if the parents are not offering any viable alternative, so faced with this the grandparents may consider applying for a residence order themselves. They are unlikely to be permitted to adopt the grandchild because of their age and the confusion of roles that would result.

Grandchildren

4.82   Grandparents play an important part in the care and upbringing of their grandchildren, and generally become emotionally attached to them. This role is not always welcomed by both parents and there may be an attempt to restrict it, especially after the death or departure of one parent. Yet in the event of the death, incapacity or inadequacy of both parents, or simply because of their need to earn a living, grandparents may need to take over or contribute to the parental role and there may be a dispute as to which grandparents should do so.[80] Where the parents are not suitable there is a tendency for social services to encourage grandparents to seek a residence order following which any financial support may cease.[81]

4.83   Grandparents may also become involved in disputes following the breakdown of the marriage of the parents. They often, though not always, tend to take the side of their own son or daughter, but if able to avoid doing so they may retain an important stabilising influence especially where grandchildren are concerned. They may find themselves looking after the grandchildren on a regular basis or wish to seek regular contact when this is being denied to them. The Children Act 1989 governs both *private law* disputes (involving the family) about the upbringing of children and *public law* applications (involving local authorities) relating to the welfare of children. Grandparents may become involved in either of these types of application and may initiate the former or provoke the latter. The emphasis is now on conciliation and mediation, and grandparents can often support and assist in this process.

4.84   A study[82] has shown that the nature and style of grandparenting in a given family seemed to be established before the parents divorced. While the divorce accentuated the role the grandparents played in the immediate or medium-term aftermath, it did not alter their fundamental approach to grandparenting. Grandparents who had been closely involved in the family before the break-up – typically the maternal grandparents – were likely to become even more so afterwards, while those who were more distant – often the paternal grandparents – might expect to become even more cut off. Regrettably the impression was gained that grandchildren are usually more important to grandparents than vice versa.

Campaigns

4.85   The legal status of grandparents in relation to their grandchildren has in recent years become a topical issue among lawyers and policy makers. Pressure groups have

---

[79]   Adoption Act 1976; Adoption and Children Act 2002.
[80]   It is estimated that about 1% of all grandparents have children living with them.
[81]   A report in September 2003 by the *Family Rights Group* funded by the Joseph Rowntree Foundation highlights the financial costs experienced by family and friends who have taken over the care of a child.
[82]   A team at Cardiff University funded by the Nuffield Foundation between 2000–2002.

been set up to lobby for greater recognition of the importance of grandparents and the extended family as potential carers of children who would otherwise be placed with unrelated foster carers.[83] There are campaigns for improved rights in relation to contact with grandchildren. Grandparents feature in the new parenting plans devised for use in England, Wales and Scotland, and these plans make it clear that parents are expected to give serious consideration to grandparent contact. Whilst children may benefit from contact with their grandparents, there is no conclusive evidence of this and the promotion of grandparent/grandchild contact may have a detrimental effect on the resident parent, often the mother.

4.86   There is no legal presumption that it is in the best interests of a child to have contact with a grandparent. Nevertheless, there is judicial support in so far as it has been stated in the Court of Appeal that trial judges:[84]

> '... should recognise the greater appreciation that has developed of the value of what grandparents have to offer, particularly to children of disabled parents.'

This was in the context of care proceedings where the local authority was advocating adoption, but the general approach may be equally relevant in some private law proceedings. To date the European Court of Human Rights has not ruled that grandparents have the same right to respect for family life as a parent in respect of their grandchild.[85] Much depends upon what the grandparents actually do with their grandchildren and the part that they have played in their lives. This may present difficulties to those grandparents who are infirm.

Applications by grandparents

4.87   Grandparents must justify any approach to the court on the basis of the actual relationship they have with their grandchild and cannot merely rely on their status as grandparents. It will not be appropriate for them to seek to make their own application for an order regulating contact with their grandchildren when the same result can be achieved through a parent. On the whole grandparents are reluctant to apply because this step may be seen as hostile by the resident parent and they will generally have to bear their own costs of the proceedings without legal aid whereas the parent may be publicly funded.[86]

4.88   A grandparent who has a satisfactory relationship with one of the parents may arrange contact without a court order if the child lives with that parent, or during a period when that parent has contact. When appropriate in the best interests of the child grandparents may be joined as a party in proceedings between the parents, but normally only when they are at odds with both parents and seek an order of their own. The alternative is to support the case of one of the parents and this may be appropriate when they seek contact through that parent.

---

[83]   The Grandparents' Association celebrated its 20th Anniversary in 2007. A website is maintained at: www.grandparents-association.org.uk/.
[84]   *Re J (Leave to issue application for residence order)* [2003] 1 FLR 114, Thorpe LJ.
[85]   In *Boyle v UK* (1994) 19 EHRR 179 it was stated that 'Access by relatives to a child is normally at the discretion of the child's parents ... a restriction of access which does not deny a recoverable opportunity to maintain the relationship will not of itself show a lack of respect for family life'.
[86]   In 1998 researchers at Bristol University found that only 4% of contact applications were made by grandparents, although this was based on a relatively small sample.

4.89   A grandparent requires permission of the court to apply for an order in respect of a grandchild.[87] When considering such an application the court must have particular regard to the nature of the proposed application, the connection with the child and any risk that the proposed application might disrupt the child's life to such an extent that he would be harmed by it. In addition, where the child is being looked after by a local authority, the court must have regard to the authority's plans for the child's future and the wishes and feelings of the child's parents.[88] At this stage the child's welfare is not the paramount consideration but the applicants 'must satisfy the court that there is a serious issue to try and must present a good arguable case'.[89]

4.90   An order may be made requiring the person with whom a child lives, or is to live, to allow the child to visit or stay with a grandparent, or for that grandparent and the child otherwise to have contact with each other. Alternatively, although it is generally in the best interests of a child to remain with the parents or one of them, grandparents may be able to make out a stronger case especially if the parents are not stable.[90] Residence with a close relative will generally be preferable to a care order in favour of the local authority. Where a child is living with grandparents with the agreement of parents, it may become necessary to apply for a residence order to achieve stability and this would also have the advantage of giving the grandparent(s) parental responsibility. Where the mother of a young child has died the courts will generally seek to encourage contact with the maternal grandparents so that the child will grow up with knowledge of that side of the family even if the father remarries.[91]

CARERS

Preliminary

4.91   Older people may increasingly become dependent upon support and services provided by others, either by reason of physical disability or mental impairment. Those who make such provision are generally described as 'carers'. They may be members of the family, friends and neighbours or they may be employed persons with or without professional training. A person may be a carer on a full-time or merely casual basis, but the word is generally used to describe someone who takes on a commitment to care either for a particular individual or for a class of persons in the community. In this context the categories identified below may be found helpful when considering carers generally.

4.92   The following material relates to informal carers. Having considered who these carers are, we identify their needs and then examine their status having in mind that responsibilities may be placed upon them by the mere fact of caring.

---

[87]   In the USA only one state requires this when grandparents wish to apply for 'visitation rights'. The court has power to make such order even if no application has been made.
[88]   Children Act 1989, s 10(9).
[89]   *Re A and W (Minors) (Residence Order: Leave to Apply)* [1992] 2 FLR 154; *Re M (Care: Contact: Grandmother's Application for Leave)* [1995] 2 FLR 86.
[90]   Eg a single parent who is an alcoholic or drug abuser.
[91]   A similar approach may be adopted in respect of a father with parental responsibility.

The role of carers

Categories

Informal carers

4.93 Most caring relationships could be described as informal because there is no legally binding agreement to provide care – it just happens.[92] There will be no express payment for the caring role although there may be reimbursement of expenses or even a pooling of resources. The stereotypical carer is a daughter looking after an infirm elderly parent, but this could be one spouse looking after another or even an elderly parent looking after a disabled adult child. Usually such a carer will only assume responsibility for a particular individual, although a daughter may care for both parents simultaneously, or a helpful resident may provide support for several neighbours.

4.94 The duties assumed by informal carers may comprise services such as shopping, washing clothes, household cleaning, meals and transport or may involve more extensive support such as supervision, respite care or the provision of accommodation and nursing. This provision may be made on an infrequent basis as required or on a regular basis, and it may take up merely short periods of time or become a full-time occupation. Informal carers have been referred to in the following terms:[93]

> '... we are dealing with a formidable number of people. According to the general household survey data, which are now somewhat out of date and therefore probably understate the numbers, there are some 6.8 million carers throughout Great Britain. At one end of the continuum, they may care for a few hours a week. At the other extreme, I have met people who care literally around the clock for a loved one – for someone with dementia or someone with a major physical handicap. I am particularly struck by the fact that an estimated 1.5 million carers provide care for 20 hours a week or more. It is often considerably more ... That caring army of 1.5 million people is a larger labour force than the national health service and social services combined.'

Professional carers

4.95 The second general category of carer comprises those who have adopted the role as part of their employment or vocation. They usually provide services or support for a class of persons in the community but may be restricted to one individual. This is an extensive class, including home helps, social workers, care workers, community nurses and others. Various duties and responsibilities are imposed by statute upon professional or paid carers, sometimes involving registration with and supervision by the local authority or another body.[94]

Statutory definitions

4.96 There is no specific meaning of carer in this context. One statutory definition of carer is 'a person who provides a substantial amount of care on a regular basis for a disabled person living at home'.[95] This does not include a person employed to provide care by a local authority or similar body in the exercise of its functions under any enactment. In practice the expression does not have so restricted a meaning. Specific recognition of the role of carers is to be found in legislation whereby carers who feel that

---

[92] One in eight people in Britain is now a carer in the wider sense (almost 6 m people).
[93] Malcolm Wicks MP, *Hansard*, 258 HC Official Report (6th series), col 426.
[94] See generally Chs 6, 7 and 8.
[95] Disabled Persons (Services, Consultation and Representation) Act 1986, s 8.

they need community care services in their own right can ask for a separate assessment. In this context a carer is 'an individual [who] provides or intends to provide a substantial amount of care on a regular basis for [a person in need of community care services]'.[96]

Caring for carers

Understanding

4.97   Anyone may become an informal carer, and seldom is this by choice. Caring takes place within a relationship, but it is wrong to assume that informal carers have chosen this role and sometimes it is resented. Often they are *involuntary* carers in that the caring role becomes thrust upon them or merely develops over a period of time. As a result they may have a severely restricted lifestyle and face substantial costs of caring and loss of personal income. They may feel a mixture of emotions including inadequacy, frustration, resentment, embarrassment, anxiety and guilt that they are not doing enough. The conflict between these emotions can be quite intense and result in confusion, indecision and even abuse.

Recognition

4.98   It is easy for informal carers, especially when involuntary, to feel that no-one cares about them. In consequence they need recognition, reassurance and information but above all practical help in the form of services, financial support and respite care.[97] There is a danger that professional carers along with the rest of society concentrate so much upon the needs of the infirm older person that they overlook the needs of the informal carer. This carer may simply be seeking to improve the quality of life of the older person, but if it were not for this informal input some more formal, and certainly more expensive, form of care provision might be needed. There are many older people who would need to be provided with residential or even nursing home care if adequate support was not available within the family. A duty is imposed on the local authority to take into account the ability of any carer to continue to provide care when deciding what services should be provided.

4.99   The Government has recognised that most care is provided by family, friends and neighbours who need help to manage what can become a heavy burden.[98] Their lives can be made easier if the right support is there at the right time, and statutory services providers should do all they can to assist and support carers. Help may take the form of providing advice and support as well as practical services such as day, domiciliary and respite care.

Information

4.100   The next priority for carers as well as older people is information as to what is, or could be, available either now or in the future by way of financial support or services. The former may be available from the Department for Work and Pensions (DWP)[99] or from the local authority. A helpful range of leaflets is available and these can be obtained

---

[96]   Carers (Recognition and Services) Act 1995.
[97]   See Ch 7. For further consideration of the role of carers see Jill Pitkeathley, *It's My Duty, Isn't It? The Plight of Carers in Our Society* (Souvenir Press, 1989).
[98]   Hence the enactment of the Carers (Recognition and Services) Act 1995.
[99]   Previously Department of Social Security (DSS) operating through the Benefits Agency.

from Post Offices and offices of the DWP.[100] Social services departments are responsible for community care and welfare services and are expected to disseminate information about statutory and voluntary services in their areas which would be of assistance to carers and their dependants.[101] General medical practitioners (GPs) are given a gatekeeping role in regard to the provision of services and they and other professionals also need this information. GPs are well placed to ensure that factors which affect the quality of life other than medical ones are taken into consideration, and their present contract imposes an obligation to refer on patients where there are problems needing specialist services and provide advice to enable patients to take advantage of local authority social services.[102]

4.101 The Government promotes a website aimed at health and social care professionals who work with carers and this contains guidance and regulations affecting carers.[103]

Cost of caring

4.102 Even though informal carers may not charge for their time it should not be assumed that they are able or willing to be out of pocket. The true cost of being a carer is seldom recognised especially if this becomes a full-time occupation. It may not be covered by weekly state benefits, although it is worth checking that all available state benefits are being claimed by both the individual and the carer.[104] Regular extra expenditure may arise,[105] and heavy wear and tear may result in regular replacement of items such as washing machines and dryers. Not only do carers often have to bear these extra costs but they may also suffer major loss of earnings and reduced employment prospects. This should be borne in mind when administering a discretionary trust for the benefit of an infirm elderly person living with the family. It is easy to conclude that there are few financial needs when in reality this is because family carers are providing an entire environment at great financial and emotional cost to themselves. The funding of extra facilities in the home, respite care and holidays not only for the elderly person but also for the carers should all be considered as being within the objects of the trust.

Community care for carers

Services

4.103 The stage may be reached where practical help is needed in the form of services and these would normally be provided or arranged by the social services department of the local authority under community care policies.[106] The emphasis has moved away from providing institutionalised care in hospital and elsewhere (for those who do not need medical treatment) to the provision of services and support to enable disabled and infirm people to live as independently as possible in their own homes, or in homely

---

[100] This topic is covered in Ch 10.
[101] Where appropriate, this should be available in Welsh or Gaelic and in the languages of the main ethnic minority groups in the area, as well as in English.
[102] This topic is covered in Ch 7.
[103] www.gov.uk/carers-uk. See also www.carersuk.org and www.direct.gov.uk/carers.
[104] State benefits are covered in Ch 10.
[105] Eg from unprescribed medicines and creams, incontinence aids, special diets, extra heating and washing, mobility and transport problems.
[106] Community care is dealt with in Ch 7.

settings in the community. A consequent danger is that more will be expected of family members and neighbours without the services and support that is the very essence of the policies.

Assessment

4.104 The first step is to assess the needs of the person cared for and to see how these needs may be best fulfilled, and assessments should be reviewed on a regular basis. A local authority is required to assess a disabled person when requested by a carer and to have regard to the ability of a home carer to continue to provide care on a regular basis.[107] Although the community care legislation makes no direct reference to carers, it permits them to request an assessment of need for those for whom the authority cares.[108] *The Policy Guidance* states:

> 'The assessment will need to take account of the support that is available from ... carers. They should feel that the overall provision of care is a shared responsibility between them and the statutory authorities ... The preferences of carers should be taken into account and their willingness to continue caring should not be assumed.' (para 3.28).

4.105 Carers now have an entitlement to have their own needs assessed. The Carers (Recognition and Services) Act 1995 provides that when a local authority assesses someone's needs for community care services, a person who provides or intends to provide substantial regular care for that person has the right to request an assessment of his ability to provide and to continue to provide care. The authority must take that assessment into account when making any decision about services for the cared-for person.

4.106 The carer's right to request an assessment is no longer dependent on the local authority carrying out an assessment of the needs of the person cared for. Under the Carers and Disabled Children Act 2000 if a carer '... asks a local authority to carry out an assessment of his ability to provide and to continue to provide care for the person cared for ... the local authority must carry out such an assessment if it is satisfied that the person cared for is someone for whom it may provide or arrange for the provision of community care services'. The local authority must consider the terms of the 1995 Act when carrying out such an assessment and is empowered to provide certain services to meet the carer's needs and help the carer provide care.

Provision of services

4.107 A carer's needs and wishes will not always be the same as those of the person cared for, but should be taken into account and services should be designed to meet the needs of carers as well as those cared for. Local authorities are made responsible for assuring these needs, nominating a case manager to review them and ensuring that resources are managed efficiently and that each service user has a single point of contact. The needs of each individual will be different, so assessments should lead to a personal care plan or individual programme plan which is a package of care intended to meet the needs of the individual.[109]

4.108 The legislation does not create an absolute right to obtain services but there is a complaints procedure which enables carers to make a complaint on behalf of the person

---

[107] Disabled Persons (Services, Consultation and Representation) Act 1986, ss 4 and 8.
[108] National Health Service and Community Care Act 1990, s 47.
[109] This topic is more fully considered in Ch 7.

cared for. The threshold at which services are provided tends to be constrained by the funding that is available to the particular authority and there is power to charge for services provided.[110]

Respite care

4.109 Respite care is more than just crisis intervention. It can be of considerable benefit to carers, whether on a regular basis or just for holidays, and may be provided in different ways and at different times. Thus it may comprise in-patient accommodation for the most severely infirm or residential care and nursing home places near to home, with hospice care for the terminally ill. Day care facilities of many sorts may be provided, and these should have flexible hours. Carers and their organisations should be involved in designing different types of respite facilities, and information about these should be made available to carers.

Implementation

4.110 The Government expects local authorities and health services to agree and publish local standards in six main areas:

- helping users and carers to find out about services;
- understanding and responding to the needs of users and carers;
- finding a suitable place to live;
- helping people to stay independent;
- getting the right health care; and
- helping carers to care.

The Carers (Equal Opportunities) Act 2004 came into effect on 1 April 2005 and seeks to give carers more choice and better opportunities to lead a more fulfilling life by ensuring that they receive information about their rights to an assessment of their needs. Those assessments must now consider the carer's wishes in relation to leisure, training and work activities. There is to be co-operation between local authorities and other public authorities, including housing, education, transport and health, in relation to the planning and provision of services that may help support the carer in the caring role.

4.111 On 19 September 2007 the government announced the establishment of a *Standing Commission on Carers* which is an independent advisory body providing expert advice to ministers and the Carers Strategy Cross Government Board on progress in delivering the national carers strategy.[111]

Status of carers

Background

4.112 Responsibilities may be placed on carers by the mere fact of caring. It may be left to the carer to ensure that the rights of the person cared for are not overlooked, and carers are often concerned about their right to make decisions on behalf of that person,

---

[110] The Government introduced from 1 April 2003 a uniform policy of means-testing where charges are levied by local authorities.

[111] Information is available on: www.gov.uk/government/policy-advisory-groups/standing-commission-on-carers.

especially as they will be taking, or at least communicating, such decisions on a daily basis.[112] Conversely, carers will be liable for damages in respect of any assault upon the person cared for, and in serious cases could be prosecuted if a criminal offence has been committed which can include neglect or ill-treatment.

4.113 In practice carers find informal ways of dealing with situations as they arise and the practical solution is usually of more significance than the legal solution (if there is one), but when a dispute arises it becomes necessary to identify the legal position. Neither family relationship nor the status of carer by itself confers any legal rights in respect of another individual. It follows that there may be no legal remedy or procedure available to deal with problems that arise. In certain situations there may be a duty to consult the next of kin and this will be in preference to a cohabitee who has (or has had prior to incapacity) a far closer relationship with the individual than any member of the family. In so far as the carer has any legal status this can only be based upon agreement with the individual cared for, either express or implied, and a de facto relationship may be the only evidence of this. The important point is usually whether the relationship is recognised by others, even though it may not at present be recognised by the law.

Relationships

4.114 Informal carers may encounter difficulties in their relationships with others, including professional carers. Despite their contribution, they have no right to be consulted (although it would be sensible to do so) and their role is often taken for granted. Many of the services which people who are infirm or disabled need are provided by or through the social services department, and a satisfactory relationship with a social worker can be supportive and the gateway for contact with other service providers. Carers feel threatened if the social worker takes a different view of a situation and difficulties can arise where the relationship with the social worker breaks down so care must be taken to avoid this.

4.115 Problems of communication can also arise, sometimes unknowingly, between professionals and carers. Professionals use language which is misunderstood, or simply not understood, by the people they are talking to. Community care is creating its own jargon and this should be discouraged; advisers who come across phrases and concepts that they do not understand should seek an explanation and encourage their clients to do likewise.

Data protection

4.116 Carers may encounter obstacles in gaining access to the personal records held in respect of an elderly person who lacks capacity because the consent of such person is required under the Data Protection Act 1998. There is no specific provision for applications for access to be made by others and common law principles of agency do not apply where there is a lack of capacity. The official view has been that access may be gained by an attorney under a registered enduring or lasting power or, if there is none, by a person authorised by the Court of Protection. This has not been a satisfactory solution because those powers generally only relate to financial affairs and the data access may be unrelated to these. Involvement of the Court of Protection may not be justified merely for data access. In practice voluntary disclosure may be made when there is clearly a justification for this on a 'need to know' basis.

---

[112] The Mental Capacity Act 2005 now fills the vacuum that previously existed in regard to personal welfare and health care decisions for mentally incapacitated adults. This legislation is covered in Ch 2.

Control of an adult

4.117 Disputes can arise between members of the family, or between the family and carers or between competing carers, about the arrangements to be made for an elderly person who is vulnerable to persuasion or no longer able to make decisions. Where capacity exists the law assumes that the elderly individual will determine the matter. The Mental Capacity Act 2005 now enables such disputes to be resolved where there is a lack of capacity and it may no longer be a question of 'he who controls the purse controls the person', but an application to that court is a last resort.

Financial

4.118 The financial management of another person's affairs is dealt with in Chapter 11. However, a problem as perceived by family or carers may be that in law an individual is either treated as incapable in which event financial powers may be delegated, or as not incapable, in which event no restrictions are imposed on that individual's financial management. There may be a period when great concern is felt as to the quality of financial decisions and the individual is not susceptible to persuasion, but nothing else can be done. The topic of undue influence is considered later in this chapter.

Medical treatment

4.119 With the exception of the procedures under the Mental Capacity Act 2005[113] no-one has the power to make medical treatment decisions on behalf of another adult, least of all family or carers, but any doctor who is considering giving treatment without express consent should consult such persons. Traditionally the next of kin has been consulted[114] especially in the hospital environment notwithstanding that such person may not have been a dominant carer and may not even have maintained a close relationship with the patient. An older person on admission to hospital should ensure that there is recorded in the medical records the name and details of the persons whom it is desired should be consulted, and even the identity of any family members who should not be consulted.

4.120 The purpose of such consultation should be to ascertain the patient's best interests including what he or she would have wished, if capable of making a decision. In this respect a current or recent personal carer may be best qualified to provide information and guidance.

Statutory guardianship

4.121 The Mental Health Act 1983[115] offers a limited form of adult guardianship and a member of the family or the local authority may be appointed. The guardian only has the right to require the patient to live in a specified place and to attend at specified times and places for the purpose of medical treatment,[116] occupation, education or training and also to provide access to the patient by the social worker, doctor or other specified person. There is no power over the property of the patient. A private guardian has

---

[113] In case of dispute or uncertainty the High Court could previously make a declaration as the best interests of the patient.

[114] The order of priority for intestate succession is usually followed, namely spouse, adult children, parents, etc.

[115] Section 8. The procedures are dealt with in Ch 8.

[116] There is no power to compel the patient to have such treatment, nor can the guardian consent to treatment on the patient's behalf.

various duties which relate to notification of the local authority and the appointment of a medical practitioner. It is an offence to ill-treat or wilfully neglect a person subject to a guardianship order.

Contact

4.122 Where an infirm elderly person resides in the home of a carer, relatives may complain that they are being denied access. In the past the High Court has progressively developed jurisdiction over such matters by making and enforcing declarations of best interest in the event that the elderly person lacked capacity to make the decision.[117] The Mental Capacity Act 2005 now enables such disputes to be resolved in the future.

Disposal of the body

4.123 The court is reluctant to interfere with any decision of the executors as to funeral arrangements at the suit of a near relative, and in the case of a person who dies intestate this approach will apply to the persons entitled to be administrators who will in any event be the next of kin.[118] This overlooks the interests of a cohabitee, regardless of the length of the relationship and whether or not of the opposite sex. However, where the deceased leaves no money to pay for a funeral, arrangements will be made by those prepared to pay, or the environmental health department of the local authority.[119]

Risk or restraint?

4.124 Carers may need to impose some restraint to prevent the elderly person from causing self-harm or harm to someone else. There are many types of restraint including physical force, locked doors, intimidation and using equipment or furniture which restricts movement. The degree of restraint used is important, as any act of touching another person's body is technically an assault if there is no consent. Providing it was not a hostile act it will not generally be treated as an assault, and if reasonable force is used an act will not be hostile. Each case will depend upon the particular circumstances, and in practice one may be forced to make snap decisions where there is little time to judge the reasonableness of the action required. Circumstances will be taken into account.[120] The Mental Capacity Act 2005 may have an input into such situations.

4.125 Carers will be liable for damages in respect of any assault upon the person cared for, and in serious cases could be prosecuted if a criminal offence has been committed which can include neglect or ill-treatment.

Right to intervene

4.126 We are all entitled to put ourselves at risk and no one can restrain us unless we are likely to cause harm to others or their property. This is underlined by the fact that we may engage in hazardous activities such as motor sports and mountaineering, and can refuse medical treatment even if death may result. These are personal freedoms and no one can legally interfere in our lives simply because they consider that we are not acting in our own best interests. We have autonomy in that sense even if we voluntarily

---

[117] *Re S (Adult Patient: Jurisdiction)* [1995] 1 FLR 302. An injunction was granted to stop the wife of an elderly, infirm man taking him abroad out of the care of his mistress and this power was upheld by the Court of Appeal in *Re S (Hospital Patient: Court's Jurisdiction)* [1996] Fam 1, [1995] 1 FLR 1075.

[118] See *Re Grandison* (1989) *The Times*, 10 July.

[119] This is considered in Ch 12.

[120] Emergency action to stop someone walking in front of a car may have to be very firm.

surrender it to those that we love or respect. But a carer will routinely protect a person cared for who is incapable of recognising and guarding against risks, and even restrain such person from a course of conduct that may cause harm. This may be part of the accepted role of caring and a duty to care may even arise in some situations, but it must not become domination. If the intervention is not authorised or welcomed it can only be justified on the basis of necessity or when the individual is mentally incapable of taking the particular decision involved.[121]

Professional carers

4.127 Special rules do not apply simply because a professional carer is involved or the individual is in a residential care home. Many such residents are quite capable of taking their own decisions and they should not be vulnerable to the dictates of those in charge. Care staff should consider whether the individual understands the nature and severity of the decision and its implications, and is able to take this into account when making a choice. So if an elderly resident in a care home wishes to go out for a walk alone the test becomes whether he can understand the consequences of doing so, taking into account his own particular limitations, and act on the basis of such understanding. If so, the activity may not be restrained (though it may be discouraged). Relatives may complain of a lack of care but they are not entitled to impose a more restrictive care regime.

4.128 On the other hand, if capacity is lacking the resident will not be making a decision, or choice, that should be respected by others and will merely be embarking upon a course of action without any properly formed intention behind it. There is then no reason why care staff should not gently deflect the resident from this course of action and encourage some other activity that does not create risk for the resident or others. If there is a serious risk positive restraint may be justified and this intervention will be lawful if it is in the best interests of the incapacitated person. In any professional care setting where physical restraint is likely to be needed from time to time, guidelines and training should be provided to protect everybody's interests.[122]

Policies and procedures

4.129 The law merely defines the following framework:

(1)   individuals may be restrained in cases of necessity, to prevent damage to property or injury to themselves or others;

(2)   apart from this, only those who lack capacity may be restrained;

(3)   any restraint must be proportional to the risk and the minimum necessary;

(4)   the person who intervenes must act in the best interests of the person being restrained.

Policies and procedures on risk and restraint should be developed in a residential or care setting that fit within this framework. This may include avoiding situations that pose a danger but not merely suiting the convenience of those 'in charge'. Of course, individuals may be prevented from doing things that they are not entitled to do[123] regardless of capacity, because that is a question of enforcing someone else's rights rather

---

[121]   Mental Capacity Act 2005, s 5.

[122]   Mental Health Act 1983, s 139 gives protection from civil or criminal proceedings for anything done in pursuance of the Act, unless done in bad faith or without reasonable care.

[123]   Eg residents in a care home may be prevented from entering the rooms of others or private rooms.

than restricting the rights of the individual. Capacity, or rather lack of it, becomes relevant when someone wishes to do something that he would be entitled to do.

4.130 We should not become so obsessed with empowering mentally incapacitated individuals that we seek to exempt them from the rules of society or of their own environment. If they accepted arrangements when they had capacity it is reasonable to assume that these may continue following a loss of capacity. The autonomy of the individual may need to yield to the rights of others, for example not to be offended or denied privacy. Those who have chosen to enter a care home will have accepted its regime so they do not become excused just because they cease to be capable of behaving rationally. They may then need to be encouraged, or even persuaded, to conform and some form of restraint may even be necessary.[124] It may be in the best interests of a care home resident to impose some restraint, especially if the alternative would be eviction from the home.

Types of restraint

4.131 Any restraint should relate to the particular situation and not be out of proportion or wrongly motivated.[125] There is no scope for punishment or anger – it is a matter of care management not retribution.[126] The needs of each individual should be considered and standard procedures for all residents cannot be justified. Recognised behaviour modification techniques may be appropriate and diversion or distraction may prove effective. Of more concern are standard procedures such as locking doors, removing clothing or appliances, the use of drugs and electronic tagging. It is not possible to provide a list of procedures that are acceptable and those that are not; each situation must be tested according to the principles set out here. Consider some examples:

(1) If a resident's behaviour is a problem, is it appropriate to modify such behaviour with drugs? The general rule is that consent is required for any medical treatment but in cases of incapacity treatment can be given that is in the best interests of the individual. So hard questions have to be addressed. Are the drugs in the best interests of the resident or merely for the convenience of others? Do the drugs have any non-beneficial effects? It may be difficult to separate the interests of the resident from those of carers and other residents, but drug restraint should not be used as an easy way out or to compensate for insufficient trained staff.

(2) Monitoring by cameras in private rooms is recognised as being intrusive but a more recent development is electronic tagging. In some situations the use of tagging may meet the criteria outlined above as a practical response to a real problem. It may enable doors to remain unlocked without putting at risk those who may inappropriately pass through them. It may also enable care staff to spend more time with other residents but should not be used as a way of reducing the number of staff.

---

[124] If they persist in undressing in public areas they must be removed and discouraged from doing so.
[125] Residents should not simply be locked in their room as a general form of prevention.
[126] Discipline such as slapping or deprivation of food or facilities will not be justified; we are considering people who are mentally incapable so unable to respond to discipline.

Financial support

Family

4.132 Voluntary carers, including members of the family, may provide necessary support for an elderly person at not inconsiderable cost to themselves, and the true cost may not be met by that person notwithstanding that ample resources are available. To this extent the relationship may become one-sided, simply because the financial realities are not faced up to and resolved at the time. Conversely, the making of payments in these circumstances can give rise to suspicion within families, so it is desirable that arrangements are openly discussed if disputes at a later stage are to be avoided. Undue reliance should not be placed upon inheritance rights or expectations because these may not be fulfilled.

4.133 Children may wish to provide support for elderly parents who have little money themselves, but need to be careful how they do so. If the parents are eligible for means-tested state benefit and local authority support, any money paid by the children, especially if on a regular basis, may be means-tested and thereby counter-productive unless so substantial that it lifts the parents above the state benefits threshold. It will usually be more beneficial for children and others to provide the use of facilities (including perhaps the right to occupy a home), and clothing and personal effects by way of gift.

State benefits

4.134 There are few financial benefits for the carer despite the financial burden that may be undertaken. A carer's allowance may be claimed by those who provide more than a certain amount of care and earn less than a specified weekly amount.[127]

Income tax

4.135 The policy now seems to be to provide financial assistance in respect of disabled people through the social security system rather than by way of tax allowances. There are no longer tax reliefs or allowances specifically targetted at carers, save that certain social security benefits are not taxable

ELDER ABUSE

Overview

4.136 Abuse of elderly people is more prevalent than has previously been recognised and a charity has been formed to address the perceived problem.[128] In 2004 it was estimated that about 5% of the elderly population in the community suffered verbal abuse and up to 2% were the victims of physical or financial abuse.[129] The abuser may be an informal carer, a relative, a friend or neighbour, or even a professional. Abuse may take place in a family or domestic environment, in the community or in a residential care or nursing home. Sometimes it may be the result of desperation due to lack of support

---

[127] The topic of social security benefits is dealt with in Ch 10.
[128] *Action on Elder Abuse*, Astral House, 1268 London Road, London SW16 4ER. A website is maintained at: www.elderabuse.org.uk/.
[129] Evidence submitted to the Parliamentary Health Select Committee on Elder Abuse.

from other relatives, the NHS and/or Social Services, for example, where the caring role places undue pressure upon the carer who takes out their frustration on the cared for person.

Vulnerability

4.137 The individual may not be in a position to complain or to seek a remedy so other people (including doctors, care workers, solicitors, family, friends and neighbours) must be vigilant. Whistle blowing procedures are needed with someone in authority available to hear the whistle and empowered to take appropriate action, and with no victimisation of the whistle blower.[130] Even when there is an available legal remedy, an older person may be reluctant to use a legal process because it is perceived as unpleasant and confrontational. Abuse tends to happen to people who are vulnerable and who, in consequence, may not make a good witness, so proof of the abuse may not be possible. Such people may also fear the implications to them of any action that is taken. The reality is that the outsider will be seeking to intervene but attempts to do so may not be welcomed by any of those involved including the vulnerable, abused individual.

No Secrets guidance

4.138 Guidance has been given to local agencies who have a responsibility to investigate and take action when a vulnerable adult is believed to be suffering abuse.[131] It offers a structure and content for the development of local inter-agency policies, procedures and joint protocols which draw on good practice nationally and locally. It defines abuse in terms of vulnerability as:

> 'A vulnerable person is one who is or may be in need of community care services by reason of mental or other disability, age or illness; and who is or may be unable to take care of him or herself or unable to protect him or herself against significant harm.'

Separate guidance is available in Wales.[132]

4.139 All local authorities should have vulnerable adults' procedures in place including an Adult Protection Officer and multi-agency teams to tackle cases as they come to their attention. Nevertheless it has been stated that: 'The voice of older people is rarely heard by those who have a responsibility for commissioning, regulating and inspecting services.'[133] Abuse can be reduced by changing the culture and in particular raising awareness of the way in which vulnerable adults should be treated in the community and the standards of care to which they should be entitled. Abuse is difficult to identify and tackle because the person abused is often dependent on the abuser, does not recognise the action as abuse, is embarrassed and fears that they will not be believed. There may be communication problems and lack of training of professionals who should be alert to the existence of abuse and know where to report its occurrence.

---

[130]   This is particularly important where the abuse is by professional carers (eg in a residential care home) and the 'whistle blower' is another employee.

[131]   *No secrets: guidance on developing and implementing multi-agency policies and procedures to protect vulnerable adults from abuse* published by the Department of Health and Home Office in March 2000 (Local Authority Circular LAC (2000) 7). Available on the Internet at: www.gov.uk/government/publications/no-secrets-guidance-on-protecting-vulnerable-adults-in-care.

[132]   'In Safe Hands: Implementing adult protection procedures in Wales' (Welsh Government 2000). Available at: wales.gov.uk/topics/health/publications/socialcare/reports/ishnov09/?lang=en.

[133]   Gary Fitzgerald, Chief Executive of *Action on Elder Abuse*, in evidence to the Parliamentary Committee on Elder Abuse.

Disclosure and confidentiality

4.140 There have been concerns that where abuse arises in professional care situations an employee will be reluctant to report this for fear of adverse consequences. Employment protection rights are now extended to staff who reveal confidential information during their employment.[134] If an employee makes a *protected disclosure* and suffers a *detriment* as a direct consequence this may justify a complaint to an employment tribunal. A dismissal or redundancy may be treated as unfair dismissal, but other forms of detriment may comprise a demotion, lack of promotion or withholding a pay rise or bonus.

4.141 A protected (or qualifying) disclosure must relate to, inter alia, a criminal offence or lack of compliance with a legal obligation. Clearly many forms of abuse of an older person would qualify. If the person making the disclosure reasonably believes in the accuracy of the information and makes the disclosure in good faith and not for personal gain the situation will be covered by these provisions. Disclosure must generally be to the employer or certain official bodies and disclosure to the press (or councillors) may only be justified if the matter has first been raised with the employer or relevant regulatory body.

What is elder abuse?

4.142 The term 'elder abuse' originated from the USA but has no legal meaning. It may take the form of physical assault (including sexual abuse) or threatening behaviour, verbal or emotional pressure, neglect, abandonment or isolation, or misuse of money, property or medication. Any or all of these forms of abuse may be perpetrated as the result of deliberate intent, negligence or ignorance, and may be the consequence of discrimination. Failure to recognise the personal and civil rights of an elderly person is a form of abuse, including undue influence and denial of access to independent legal advice. So also is medical paternalism whereby the doctor administers treatment on the basis that he knows best without troubling to obtain the informed consent of the patient or ascertain what the patient would have wished. Professional attitudes have had to change.

4.143 The *Commission on Equality and Human Rights* defines abuse in these terms:

> '... Abuse may consist of a single or repeated act. It may be physical, verbal or psychological. It may be an act or omission of an act or may occur when a vulnerable person is persuaded to enter into a financial or sexual transaction to which he or she has not consented or cannot consent. Abuse can occur in any relationship and result in significant harm and exploitation of the person subjected to it.'

According to *Action on Elder Abuse* (AoEA) it is:

> 'A single or repeated act or lack of appropriate action, occurring within any relationship where there is an expectation of trust, which causes harm or distress to an older person.'

Calls to their helpline during 2006 related to over £2m reported as stolen, defrauded, or coerced from elderly victims. Some 18 houses were allegedly sold or taken without consent and an additional 13 houses given away under pressure, including blackmail, or

---

[134] Public Interest Disclosure Act 1998.

without full awareness (a total value of £5.7m). The majority of victims were women aged over 81 years and the majority of perpetrators were sons and/or daughters aged 41–60 years.[135]

Types of abuse

4.144 Physical abuse would include hitting or slapping, burning, pushing, restraining or giving too much medication or the wrong medication. The older person may complain of being hit, slapped, kicked or mistreated, or there may be physical signs of the abuse. Psychological abuse comprises behaviour such as frightening, blaming, ignoring or humiliating a person. Financial abuse is defined by AoEA as 'stealing from, defrauding someone of, or coercing someone to part with, goods and/or property'. It may comprise improper use of a power of attorney or misuse of the pension book. Neglect is generally depriving a person of food, clothes, warmth and hygiene needs but could be denial of health care treatment or medication.[136]

Abuse of carers

4.145 There is a danger that we concentrate so much on the rights of the vulnerable older person that we overlook the normal responsibilities of this person. Many carers are abused because they carry the direct and indirect costs of caring without a contribution from the person cared for. Does apparent financial abuse sometimes result from the desire of the elderly individual to have it all ways, for example giving the home to the children to avoid means-testing whilst still expecting to live in it or be provided for until they die? This can create open ended obligations that it might be impossible to fulfil. Older people are not always fair or consistent in their interpretation of financial situations.

Civil remedies for abuse

Overview

4.146 Abuse may amount to the torts of negligence or trespass to the person (assault, battery or false imprisonment), a criminal assault or a theft but in some situations non-legal remedies may be appropriate. Thus if the abuser is a carer who cannot cope without additional help, steps should be taken to secure that help or, where the circumstances warrant this, to remove the abuser or move the elderly person to a more suitable environment.

4.147 We consider here those situations where an application is made to a court or elsewhere for compensation or other relief. The victim may obtain compensation for damage to his property or person by bringing a claim for damages in the civil courts. The objective may be to prevent further abuse rather than seek compensation for what has happened in the past, and the courts have powers in a range of circumstances to grant and enforce injunctions. Sometimes the authorities may apply for an injunction rather than the abused individual. In a serious case a prosecution may be brought against the abuser and a criminal compensation order may be made or there may be a claim to the Criminal Injuries Compensation Authority.

---

[135] *The Cost of living: 'growing up is free, growing old is expensive'*. See AoEA website.
[136] *Counsel + Care* has produced a factsheet *'Abuse: older people at risk'* available on their website: www.counselandcare.org.uk.

4.148 Where there is neglect a request should be made to the local authority social services department for a community care assessment of needs with a view to appropriate provision being made to meet those needs as explained in Chapter 7. If the abuse is taking place in a situation involving care professionals the use of available complaints procedures may be appropriate and sufficient. The regulation of residential care and nursing homes and of domiciliary carers, including Care Standards and the *Protection of Vulnerable Adults* scheme, is covered in Chapters 6 and 7. In the case of financial abuse the individual's affairs should be put on a proper footing or a reference made to the Court of Protection in accordance with the procedures outlined in Chapter 11.

Objectives

4.149 Recourse to the law, whether civil or criminal, may not be the only way of achieving a remedy. Unless the abuse is particularly serious the victim (or victim's family) will not be seeking compensation or retribution, but will merely wish to ensure that the abuse does not continue or is not repeated. There will of course be cases that are so serious that action must be taken on behalf of society, but in other cases it is important to ascertain what the victim wishes to happen. Taking up the case and seeking remedies without consulting the victim may in itself amount to further abuse especially if the alleged abuser is a relative or carer or someone with whom the victim has an emotional attachment. It may also result in the individual being removed from an environment in which he would prefer to remain even if some degree of abuse is inevitable. A reasonable balance between personal autonomy and protection from per-ceived abuse is very difficult to maintain. Failure to intervene may allow abuse to continue, yet too much intervention may be a greater abuse to the individual than that which it is intended to prevent.

Limitations of remedies

4.150 Claims in the civil courts are expensive to pursue and there is no certainty that costs will be recovered. Public funding (often referred to as Legal Aid) is now only available in a very limited range of cases for those on low incomes, and it is necessary to establish that there is a cause of action with a reasonable prospect of success. Nevertheless an application for Legal Aid can be made on behalf of someone who lacks capacity with subsequent proceedings being brought by a representative.[137] Some firms of solicitors will act on a conditional fee basis for personal injury claims which may amount to a 'no win no fee' arrangement with an insurance policy covering the risk of an adverse costs award. But the whole process can take a long time which may be a problem for an elderly claimant.

4.151 The claimant, in this situation the abused person, must establish the facts on 'the balance of probabilities' by producing evidence. In criminal proceedings the police will do this but the proof must be 'beyond reasonable doubt'. It is therefore important that sufficient evidence is obtained as soon as possible after the event of abuse. This may take the form of medical reports, photographic evidence, written records and statements from parties involved.

4.152 Establishing the facts may be more difficult for a victim without capacity who cannot give evidence of the abuse, but there are special measures that now enable a vulnerable person to give evidence. However, the victim may not wish there to be

---

[137] See Ch 3.

intervention especially when family members are involved. Also the perpetrator may not have any financial means so may not be worth pursuing. All these factors mean that appropriate action is not always taken in cases of abuse.

Civil claims

4.153 A victim will have a civil claim in assault in cases of personal violence and in trespass for loss of or damage to property. If the conduct was not intentional a claim may lie in negligence where there has been a breach of a duty of care causing injury or loss. Damages may be awarded but other relief is available including an injunction to prevent a repetition. A claim will usually be commenced in the county court, and this may be a court in any location although transfer may take place at a later stage to a more suitable court depending upon the convenience of the parties and their witnesses. Where a claimant has a physical or mental disability this should be made clear so that it can be taken into account in any decision as to transfer.[138]

4.154 The victim must be able to fund the action or qualify for legal aid. The standard of proof in civil courts is 'on the balance of probabilities' but in criminal courts is 'beyond all reasonable doubt', so a civil claim may be pursued in a case where a criminal trial did not take place or the defendant was acquitted. The decision about whether to pursue financial compensation will depend on whether the abuser has the means to pay or is insured although conditional fees are increasingly available.[139]

4.155 Although it can be justified in some circumstances, physical restraint of an elderly person may amount to the tort of negligence or trespass to the person and/or the criminal offence of assault and false imprisonment. It may comprise locking people in their rooms and ignoring their needs, the placement of furniture, physical confinement or electronic tagging. Medication may also be used as an artificial form of restraint. Some unsafe or outmoded restraint practices risk physical injury. The common law doctrine of 'necessity' provides a defence to conduct which would otherwise be tortious, especially when making decisions in the best interests of an incapacitated person. The Mental Capacity Act 2005 makes provision for personal welfare decisions but only allows restraint in limited circumstances.[140]

Criminal Injuries Compensation Scheme

Claims

4.156 Anyone who has been injured as a result of a crime of violence can apply to the Criminal Injuries Compensation Authority for payment of compensation even if the injuries were caused by someone who is unknown, has not been prosecuted or could not be held responsible under the criminal law (eg because of insanity). The incident must have been reported to the police without delay and the claimant must have helped the police in bringing the offender to justice and not have been responsible for the incident, or the award may be reduced or refused. The claimant's character and way of life are taken into account.

---

[138] For the special provisions to allow claims to be brought on behalf of mentally disabled persons see Ch 3.

[139] An arrangement where the solicitor funds the action but charges an enhanced fee if it suc-ceeds. This is often described as a 'no win, no fee' arrangement. An insurance policy may cover the risk or an adverse costs order.

[140] This is dealt with in Ch 2.

4.157 Claims may be pursued on-line.[141] There is a time limit of 2 years from the date of the injury, but late claims may be accepted if there is good reason for the delay (eg the mental condition of the victim and possibly also ignorance of the scheme). A claim can be made on behalf of a person who is mentally disabled with the application form being completed by a responsible person. It may then be necessary to involve the Court of Protection, though payment could be made to trustees or ex gratia to anyone considered suitable.

Awards

4.158 Awards were originally on the basis of what a court would have awarded for the injury with a minimum level below which an award would not be made. Thus the award might have included compensation for pain and suffering, loss of earnings, and a sum to reflect difficulty in obtaining future employment. Since 1996 there has been a tariff according to the nature of the injury, thus disregarding the effect on the particular victim. Awards are usually paid as a lump sum, but will be reduced to take into account any other compensation received for the injury and social security payments must be deducted in full.

Appeals

4.159 There is no right of appeal but if not satisfied with the decision initially made the claimant may ask for a review and thereafter appeal to the independent *Criminal Injuries Compensation Appeals Panel.*

Undue influence

General

4.160 One of the problems when dealing with individuals who are frail or of limited mental capacity is undue influence. Some adults prefer to have many of their decisions made by others and tests of capacity encourage the acceptance of support even though this may amount to influence. But there may be cause for concern if an older individual is too readily influenced or becomes too much under the influence of another person. Understanding of relevant factors may be corrupted by the manner and selectivity in which information is provided. A person who is constantly given incomplete or even incorrect information is likely to make choices that they would not otherwise have made, and in extreme cases this may amount to fraud. The ability to make a choice may also be affected by threats, perceived or actual. Thus a decision which appears to have been competently made could be the outcome of at best a limited perception of the choices available or at worst fear of the consequences of making a different decision.

4.161 The problem is magnified by the fact that those encouraging a challenge to a decision may themselves be seeking to exert an influence over the individual. All too often these situations of conflict develop from a power struggle between otherwise concerned relatives with the frail older person becoming a pawn in the game. A tendency by this person to agree with the party who presently has their audience either because of a short term desire for peace or the strength of that party's personality merely provides evidence which fuels the problem. By the time such a conflict reaches the court the situation has become intractable and removing the older person from the influence of the parties in conflict may appear to be the only solution.

---

[141] www.justice.gov.uk/victims-and-witnesses/cica.

4.162 Of more concern is the situation where financial or emotional abuse is taking place. An individual who needs assistance from others before making significant personal decisions is vulnerable. There is a tendency to delegate decisions to others who demonstrate a willingness to take them, and when those others are influenced by personal gain or improper motives there is likely to be abuse. The courts are prepared to set aside transactions adverse to an individual when these are the result of undue influence but these matters are expensive to litigate and the interaction between improper influence and mental capacity has yet to be developed.

4.163 Elderly people who are dependent on the care or support of others are exceptionally vulnerable to threats not merely of physical abuse but also of withdrawal of support. Such threats may not be express but could be implied by conduct and perceived even if not intended. A full time carer is in a powerful position especially when the person cared for feels vulnerable and these situations often arise of necessity rather than choice.

Approach of the courts

4.164 People may not be saved from their own foolishness but will be protected from being victimised by other people. The common law developed a principle of duress but equity supplemented this by enabling gifts and other transactions[142] to be set aside if procured by undue influence or they are otherwise unconscionable. The manner in which the intention to enter into the transaction was secured may be investigated and if produced by an unacceptable means, the law will not permit the transaction to stand – it will be 'set aside'.

4.165 Whether a transaction was brought about by the exercise of undue influence is a question of fact and the person who claims to have been wronged must prove this. All the circumstances of the relationship will be considered, but the principle is not confined to cases of abuse of trust and confidence, and includes cases where a vulnerable person has been exploited. However, there are circumstances in which undue influence may be presumed and the burden of proof then passes to the other party.

4.166 There are thus three situations relevant to the older person where transactions may be set aside:

(1)   where duress or undue influence has been actually used for the purpose of achieving a gift or benefit – the burden of proof is on the party alleging this;

(2)   where undue influence is presumed – the burden is then on the other party to justify the transaction;

(3)   where a contract of an improvident nature has been made by a poor and ignorant person acting without independent advice, and the other party cannot show that it was fair and reasonable – this is a fall-back remedy for unconscionable conduct.

The law is analysed in *Bank of Scotland plc v Etridge (No 2)* which related to security provided by a wife for her husband's business loans.[143]

---

[142]   This could be a purchase at an undervalue or a sale at an excessive price.
[143]   [2001] UKHL 44, [2001] 4 All ER 430.

Actual undue influence

4.167 Whilst actual undue influence usually involves 'specific overt acts of persuasion', this is not necessarily so and it may comprise some action which 'twisted the mind' of the individual. The exploitation of a vulnerable person is a relevant factor. The crucial question is:[144]

> 'Whether or not the persuasion or advice has invaded the free volition of the donor to accept or reject the persuasions or advice or withstand the influence. The [individual] may be led, but she must not be driven and her will must be the offspring of her own volition, not a record of someone else's.'

In this case an 85-year-old lady who intensely disliked any form of confrontation and was frightened by the prospect of litigation was persuaded to retire as trustee of a family trust of a farm by threats from her nephew to take her to court.

Presumptions of undue influence

4.168 The law has appeared to approach the issue of undue influence according to the specific relationship between the parties but the question is whether one party has placed sufficient trust and confidence in the other, rather than whether the relationship between the parties is of a particular type.[145] However, a presumption may arise in two ways:

(1) *the type of relationship*: where there is a recognised relationship in which one party acquires influence over another who is vulnerable (for example, client and solicitor, patient and doctor, beneficiary and trustee). There is then an irrebuttable presumption of influence and it is not necessary to establish that the relationship was based upon trust and confidence. If it appears that this influence has been inappropriately exercised then the party with influence must prove that this was not the case. Thus the making of a large gift to a solicitor or doctor gives rise to a presumption that would only be rebutted by a finding that the gift was made after full, free and informed thought and the absence of any pressure from the donee would not by itself be sufficient.

(2) *the evidential presumption*: where there is evidence that the relationship was based on trust and confidence in relation to the management of the complainant's financial affairs, coupled with a transaction giving rise to suspicions which must be addressed. Examples of relationships which may (on the facts) raise the evidential presumption include husband and wife, cohabitants, son and parents, employer and employee. There may then be a rebuttable presumption of undue influence and it is for the other party to produce evidence to counter the inference which otherwise should be drawn. The evidence required depends on the nature of the alleged undue influence, the personality of the parties, their relationship, the extent to which the transaction cannot readily be accounted for by the ordinary motives of ordinary persons in that relationship, and all circumstances of the case.

The need for disadvantage

4.169 There are thus two prerequisites to the burden of proof shifting to the other party. First, that trust and confidence was placed in the other party, or that party was in a position of dominance or control. Second, that the transaction is not readily explicable by the relationship of the parties. The mere existence of influence is not enough, but it is

---

[144] *Daniel v Drew* [2005] EWCA Civ 507.
[145] Treitel, *The Law of Contract* (10th edn, 1999), pp 380–381.

not essential that the transaction should be disadvantageous to the pressurised or influenced person, either in financial terms or in any other way.[146] However, questions of undue influence will not usually arise where the transaction is innocuous.[147] It would be absurd for the law to presume that every gift by a patient to his doctor, or every transaction between a client and his solicitor, was brought about by undue influence unless the contrary is proved. Some proof of the exercise of the influence of the donee must be given; thus it has been stated:[148]

> '... if the gift is so large as not to be reasonably accounted for on the ground of friendship, relationship, charity, or other ordinary motives on which ordinary men act, the burden is upon the donee to support the gift.'

When that proof is present, the greater the disadvantage to the vulnerable person, the more convincing must be the explanation to rebut the presumption of inappropriate influence. In a case where a widow allowed her half-sister to look after her finances following the death of the husband, a presumption of undue influence arose because of the number and size of alleged gifts which amounted to almost half of the widow's estate. A relationship of dependence existed, so the two pre-requisites for presumed influence were made out and required rebutting if the transfers were to remain valid.[149]

Family and caring relationships

4.170 Evidence of undue influence may exist in many family relationships such as that between a husband and wife, or elderly parent and mature child. It may also arise in a caring relationship, such as this example:[150]

> The donor an elderly bachelor who lived alone, was befriended and became dependent for his daily needs on the donee. Following a stay in hospital the donor without being put under pressure by the donee but without taking advice, realised assets and transferred £297,000 to her. He was left with his home, an annual pension and substantial tax liabilities. The donor died intestate. Letters of administration were granted to the claimant, the donor's cousin, who sought to have the gift set aside.

> On appeal it was held that there was a relationship of trust and confidence between the donor and donee and a gift so large as to give rise to the presumption of undue influence. The law applicable was well settled, most by the House of Lords decision in *Royal Bank of Scotland plc v Etridge*. However there continued to be misconceptions by the courts as to the circumstances in which transactions should be set aside. What was required to rebut the presumption was proof that the gift had been made by the donor only after full, free and informed thought. He had taken no advice and had incurred detrimental liabilities from realising his assets. The presumption was not rebutted and the gift to the donee should be set aside.

It should not be overlooked that many carers are 'abused' by the expectations imposed upon them without prospect of recompense, so proportionate gifts should not give rise to a presumption of undue influence. A transaction may be set aside as having been

---

[146] The label 'manifest disadvantage' adopted by Lord Scarman in *National Westminster Bank plc v Morgan* [1985] 1 All ER 821 can give rise to misunderstanding and should no longer be adopted – see the judgment of Lord Nicholls in *Bank of Scotland plc v Etridge* (No 2) referred to above.

[147] *CIBC Mortgages plc v Pitt* [1993] 4 All ER 433, [1994] 1 AC 200, HL.

[148] *Allcard v Skinner* (1887) 36 Ch D 145, [1886–90] All ER Rep 90, Lindley LJ.

[149] *Watson v Huber* [2005] All ER (D) 156. For a transaction between father and daughter/son-in-law that was readily explained see *Turkey v Awadh & another* [2005] EWCA Civ 382.

[150] *Hammond v Osborne and another* [2002] EWCA Civ 885.

procured by undue influence even though the actions and conduct of the person who has benefited from it cannot be criticised as wrongful and the claimant had been advised at the time by a solicitor.[151]

Independent advice

4.171 The absence of independent advice may be a significant factor, as illustrated by the above example. In another recent case the court found that an agricultural tenancy entered into by the deceased 7 weeks before his death was void for undue influence. There was a relationship of trust and confidence between the deceased and the 'tenant'. The deceased had received no independent advice as to the detrimental effect the grant of the tenancy would have on the value of the rest of the estate.[152]

4.172 Proof of outside advice does not, of itself, show that the subsequent completion of the transaction was free from the exercise of undue influence. The importance to be attached to such advice depends on all the circumstances. In the normal course, advice from a solicitor can be expected to result in a proper understanding of, for instance, the implications of a substantial gift, yet the individual may still be acting under the undue influence of another.

Unconscionable bargains

4.173 This is an equitable remedy based upon the principle in *Fry v Lane*[153] that: 'where a purchase is made from *a poor and ignorant* man at *a considerable undervalue*, the vendor having *no independent advice*, a Court of Equity will set aside the transaction'. If these three constituent elements are proved relief may be available. The claimant generally seeks a declaration that the defendant holds the claimant's share on trust, a declaration as to the value of that trust, and an order for sale. This principle overlaps that relating to undue influence. It may be applied where the transaction is with or the gift made in favour of a stranger and it is not possible to establish undue influence. In those circumstances the donor's mental capacity may also need to be closely examined and a gift would be likely to be set aside if there was lack of capacity to make it. In the event of a contract it would be necessary to show that the other party knew, or should have been aware, of this.[154]

Injunctions

General

4.174 An injunction is one of the remedies available in the civil and family courts to restrain conduct that is threatened or has taken place and is likely to be repeated. It may follow a declaration that the conduct in question is unlawful. Breach of an injunction is punishable as a contempt of court and could result in a fine or a period of imprisonment. It is therefore a powerful remedy, but its weakness is that the person being abused must generally initiate and actively pursue the proceedings. Other people can only counsel and advise, although if there is a lack of capacity the proceedings can be brought on behalf of the individual by a representative (see Chapter 3).

---

[151] *Pesticcio v Huet* [2004] EWCA Civ 372.
[152] *Re Rochelle deceased* [2002] WTLR 1483.
[153] (1888) 40 Ch D 312. See also *Cresswell v Potter* [1978] 1 WLR 255.
[154] See Ch 3 at **3.4**.

4.175 An injunction may be obtained to restrain the commission of a tort, such as trespass to the person or to property. A claim for damages is made based upon the tort and an injunction is sought to restrain further acts; once an interim injunction is granted the damages claim is seldom pursued. This would be the case where a person kept entering an elderly person's home without permission. However, it is usually necessary to resolve ownership and occupation rights first because the legal remedy is available to support these rather than protect the individual.

Mental disability of the defendant

4.176 There remain problems where the abuser is mentally disordered and this may arise in family situations. An injunction ought not to be granted against a person who is incapable of understanding what he is doing and that it is wrong, because a breach could not then be the subject of effective enforcement proceedings.[155] The fact that an abuser is incapable of conducting proceedings and requires a representative to pursue a defence is not by itself a bar to an injunction although someone must first be appointed by the court to represent the individual.[156] It has been held that it is not necessary to show a wilful intention to disobey a court order but merely a wilful and deliberate intention to do a prohibited act knowing the consequences:[157]

> The husband suffered from Usher's syndrome, was deaf and virtually blind, whilst the wife and two of the three children were also deaf. The parties separated following violence by the husband and an injunction was granted to the wife. The husband was re-housed by the local authority but kept returning to the former home where the wife and children were still living. This was in breach of the injunction and the power of arrest was often activated. The judge, having heard evidence from a psychiatrist, found that the husband had an average IQ but his ability to understand was limited by his disability and experience. He knew right from wrong and that if he went to the former home he may end up in prison. He did so on a voluntary basis and there was nothing (or no-one) forcing him to go. On appeal it was held that the judge had not erred in refusing to discharge the earlier injunction, because there was no need for a full understanding of the law. It was sufficient that he understood what he must not do and what the consequences of breach were.

4.177 Injunctions are usually applied for in an emergency and the court may be in some difficulty deciding what the individual is capable of understanding. Some judges will be cautious at that stage where the individual apparently has mental health problems, but others will grant the injunction regardless and rely upon any issue as to enforceability being dealt with in the event of committal proceedings when Legal Aid is likely to be available and the court can obtain a medical report.[158]

4.178 Where contempt of court has been established (ie on breach of an injunction) the court has power to remand in custody for a medical report to be obtained[159] and to make a hospital order.[160] The problem is that the degree of mental disorder that would justify these powers being relied on may have prevented the conduct being a contempt in

---

[155] *Wookey v Wookey* [1991] 3 All ER 365, CA. In *Re de Court* (1997) *The Times*, 27 November the Vice-Chancellor looked for an intention to do what he did and doing it consciously.

[156] The procedure is set out in Ch 3 at **3.172**.

[157] *P v P (contempt of court: mental capacity)* [1999] 3 FCR 547, [1999] 2 FLR 897, CA.

[158] The court has this power at an earlier stage in proceedings under Family Law Act 1996, Pt IV – see s 48.

[159] Contempt of Court Act 1981, s 14(4A) – there appear to be two similarly numbered paragraphs! The report is obtained under Mental Health Act 1983, s 35.

[160] Contempt of Court Act 1981, s 14(4). The order is made under Mental Health Act 1983, s 37, and there may be an interim order under s 38.

the first place. These powers will thus only really be effective when the mental disorder has arisen (or become substantially worse) since the breach of injunction.

4.179 It may be that judges who would be minded to exercise their power to make a hospital order will initially take a generous view of the individual's ability to understand the implications of the injunction, but the issue as to whether an injunction can be granted should be dealt with at that stage rather than later on committal. Where threatening behaviour is due to mental disorder and in consequence of a lack of understanding an injunction cannot be granted or enforced, it may be appropriate to invoke Mental Health Act powers.[161] However, there may be a 'gap' between the different approaches of the courts and the authorities, with a mentally disordered individual causing considerable disruption to the lives of others which is not restrained by the health or social services authorities yet cannot be tackled by the courts.

Family homes and domestic violence

4.180 Domestic violence within marriages and personal relationships is a social problem[162] and results in a significant proportion of crimes.[163] Legislation has progressively been introduced to enable the victim to obtain urgent relief in the local county court or magistrates' court in a wide range of circumstances.[164] This relief is generally in the form of a non-molestation injunction or an 'occupation' order. Applications may be free-standing or made in other family proceedings, and the court must have regard to all the circumstances of the case including the need to secure the health, safety and well-being of the applicant or other person for whose benefit the order is to be made.

4.181 The parties must be 'associated persons' but the definition now includes not only persons who are or have been married to each other or cohabitants (being a man and a woman not married to each other but living together as husband and wife), but also immediate relatives, parents of a child and those who have agreed to marry, had an intimate personal relationship with one another or lived in the same household (other than one of them being the other's tenant, lodger, boarder or employee).[165] It follows that a local court can now provide immediate and effective remedies in a wide range of situations that would be regarded as elder abuse within a household or a relationship. Courts that have been accustomed to dealing with 'wife-beating' must now tackle 'granny-bashing' and the extent that they may do so has yet to be fully explored.

Non-molestation orders

4.182 These injunction[166] may cover behaviour ranging from serious violence to silent telephone calls and are made to protect the health, safety and wellbeing of the applicant and any relevant child. There are two types: a prohibition against using or threatening violence against the applicant, and a prohibition against intimidating, harassing or pestering the applicant. When appropriate the order will spell out the particular behaviour which is to cease, for example the making of unwanted telephone calls or

---

[161] These powers are dealt with in Ch 8 at **8.132**.
[162] The term 'domestic violence' is a misnomer as it includes all kinds of 'domestic' abuse.
[163] It is now recognised that violence within such relationships should not simply be dismissed by the police as 'a domestic' and that prosecution should result.
[164] Initially Domestic Violence and Matrimonial Proceedings Act 1976 but now Family Law Act 1996, Part IV as amended by Domestic Violence, Crime and Victims Act 2004.
[165] Family Law Act 1996, s 62 (as amended).
[166] Family Law Act 1996, s 42.

sending text messages. A time limit is imposed, typically 12 months but if there is further misconduct the order will be extended or renewed. A breach of these orders is now a criminal offence so a vulnerable or incapacitated elderly person may now rely upon enforcement by the police rather than having to pursue this personally.

Occupation orders

4.183 These orders[167] may give or confirm a person's right to live in a property and oust the perpetrator from or prevent him from returning to that property. Alternatively occupation may be regulated, for example by excluding a party from certain rooms (typically a 'bedroom exclusion' order). The property will be the home of the victim (not necessarily the matrimonial home) but the order may extend to a defined area around that home. The order does not alter property rights and is only a temporary remedy, but does enable a property owning spouse or cohabitee to be excluded for a lengthy period whilst the future of the home is resolved.

4.184 Mortgagees or landlords must be given notice or an opportunity to make representations. Where the parties are not existing or former spouses or cohabitants but are within some other category of 'associated person' the applicant must have some pre-existing right to occupy before an occupation order can be made. Which provisions may be included in a particular order and how long the order may last depends to some extent upon whether or not the applicant has an estate or interest in the home or matrimonial home rights.[168]

4.185 The court is to have regard to all relevant circumstances including:

- the housing needs and resources of the parties;
- the financial resources of the parties;
- the nature and length of their relationship (and otherwise);
- their conduct in relation to each other; and
- the effect of any order upon the health, safety or well-being of the parties or any child.

4.186 It is necessary to study the particular section of the Act under which the order is to be made in order to determine the terms of a particular order and the dominant circumstances. Where a party is to be excluded from the home a 'balance of harm' test must be applied.[169] Although these orders relate to 'dwelling-houses' this will include a part of a building occupied as a such, a caravan, houseboat or structure occupied as a dwelling-house, together with any yard, garden, garage or outhouse belonging to or occupied with it.[170] In addition when an occupation order is made the court can require a party to maintain and repair the home or furnishings and contents, and to pay rent or mortgage payments.[171] Either party may be given possession or use of furnishings or other contents of the home. The court has power to transfer tenancies on divorce or between cohabitants in certain circumstances.[172]

---

[167] Family Law Act 1996, ss 33–38.
[168] The detailed provisions are to be found in Family Law Act 1996, ss 33, 35, 36, 37 and 38. A spouse has a right to occupy the matrimonial home.
[169] 'Harm' means ill-treatment or impairment of health and 'ill-treatment' includes non-physical forms.
[170] Family Law Act 1996, s 63.
[171] Family Law Act 1996, s 40.
[172] Family Law Act 1996, s 53 and Sch 7.

Without notice orders

4.187 Such orders may be applied for without notice, which means that the applicant initially appears before the court as a matter of urgency without giving notice to the other party. The court may make an order when this is justified at that stage[173] but will give notice to the respondent of a later hearing when the need for continuing orders will be further considered and both parties will have the opportunity to make representations and may be expected to give evidence.[174]

Undertakings

4.188 Before 1996 it was common for the courts to accept undertakings as to future behaviour without the need for a full hearing, and the proceedings were then adjourned. The alleged behaviour would not be admitted and the court would not be making findings, but breach of the undertaking would amount to contempt of court so committal proceedings could be brought in the same way as for breach of an injunction. This avoided lengthy, contested hearings so costs orders were seldom made but a power of arrest could not be attached to the undertaking. This may still be appropriate in less serious cases and the undertaking may be enforced on an application for committal should there be a breach, but the court is now constrained not to accept an undertaking in any case where it would attach the power of arrest to an injunction if granted.

Power of arrest

4.189 A power to arrest the abuser in the event of future breaches may be attached to an occupation order where there has been violence or threats of violence, unless the court is satisfied that there will be adequate protection without this.[175] The arrested person must be brought before a court within specified time-limits.[176] The court can remand the arrested person in custody or on bail pending a hearing and may remand for the purpose of enabling a medical report to be obtained.[177] If a power of arrest was not attached to the order or the police have not arrested a party alleged to be in breach, the other party may apply to the court for the issue of an arrest warrant if a breach of an injunction is alleged or merely apply to the court on notice for a committal order under the 'show cause' procedure.

Third party applications

4.190 The Act provides that the Lord Chancellor may make rules providing for any person in a prescribed category ('a representative') to act on behalf of another person in applying for an occupation order or a non-molestation order, subject to conditions.[178]

---

[173] Eg if the service of an application is likely to provoke further violence, or there is reason to believe that the respondent is aware of the application but is deliberately evading service and the delay will seriously prejudice the applicant.

[174] Family Law Act 1996, s 45. Some courts do not fix a date for a further hearing but give the defendant an opportunity to request one.

[175] Family Law Act 1996, s 47. This enables a constable to arrest without warrant a person whom he has reasonable cause for suspecting to be in breach of any such provision.

[176] 24 hours excluding Christmas Day, Good Friday and a Sunday. This may comprise a judge attending at the police station at a weekend.

[177] This would usually follow a medical examination unless a relevant report is already available. The power will be useful in cases of mental disorder and may be used to provoke an intervention by the social services or health authority.

[178] Family Law Act 1996, s 60. This provision has not yet been implemented and its wording demonstrates that it is experimental, in particular the reference to rules being made for a specified period and being replaced by further rules.

This might, for example, enable a local authority to apply for an injunction on behalf of a vulnerable older person and to exclude an abuser from the home. The provision of relief would not then depend upon the abused person taking action but it is not clear whether that person's consent to the proceedings would be required.

Protection from harassment

4.191 Although the purpose of the Protection from Harassment Act 1997 was to deal with the problem of 'stalking' which became a high profile issue in 1996, the wording of the Act is broad enough to encompass a far wider range of activities which may include aspects of 'elder abuse'. Harassment is made a criminal offence as well as a tort, and breach of a civil injunction granted under this Act is also made a criminal offence in addition to the usual civil enforcement procedures. Civil proceedings will be brought in the High Court or (more usually) the county court, whilst criminal proceedings are dealt with in the magistrates' court or (for the more serious offences) the Crown Court.

Course of conduct

4.192 A person must not pursue a course of conduct which amounts to harassment of another and which he knows or ought to know amounts to harassment of the other.[179] If a reasonable person would know that the course of conduct would amount to harassment then the person whose conduct is in question ought to know that. It is expressly provided that references to harassing a person include 'alarming the person or causing the person distress', but this is not intended to be an exhaustive definition. 'Conduct' includes nuisance phone calls, stalking, threats, excessive noise etc but there must be a course of conduct involving conduct on at least two occasions. There are some exclusion such as preventing or detecting crime and where the pursuit of the course of conduct was reasonable.

Civil remedies

4.193 An actual or apprehended breach may be the subject of a claim in civil proceedings by the victim of the course of conduct, and damages may be awarded for (amongst other things) any anxiety caused by and any financial loss resulting from the harassment. The court may also grant an injunction to restrain such conduct,[180] and if the claimant thereafter considers that the defendant has done anything which is prohibited by the injunction he may apply without notice to the court for a warrant of arrest against the defendant. This will be granted if the judge after hearing evidence on oath has reasonable grounds for believing that the defendant is in breach. When brought before the court there will be a hearing and if after considering all the evidence the defendant is found to have been in breach of the injunction he may be fined or committed to prison for up to 2 years for contempt.

4.194 Instead of hearing the evidence and granting an injunction the court may accept an undertaking from the defendant, but this is likely to be objected to by the claimant victim because it provides inferior remedies. A breach can be dealt with as a contempt in the same way as breach of an injunction but will not by itself be a criminal offence.[181]

---

[179] Protection from Harassment Act 1997, s 1.
[180] An injunction could be granted against a corporate body that bombarded the claimant with computerised demands for a disputed debt – *Ferguson v British Gas* [2009] EWCA Civ 46.
[181] *Carpenter v Carpenter* [1988] 1 FLR 121.

4.195 The civil court is not empowered to attach a power of arrest to such an injunction, but because the offence of breach of that injunction is punishable with up to 5 years' imprisonment police officers have the power to arrest without warrant anyone they reasonably suspect of having committed the offence, relying on their normal arrest powers.[182] They must then bring the arrested person before the criminal court.

Anti-social behaviour

4.196 Although this chapter primarily deals with family and carers, abuse may arise from neighbours and it is convenient to address this here. Legislation to control anti-social behaviour may be used to prevent the abuse of elderly people.

ASBOs

4.197 Magistrates' courts and in certain circumstances county courts may grant anti-social behaviour orders where a person '... has acted in an anti-social manner, that is to say, in a manner that caused or was likely to cause harassment, alarm or distress to two or more persons not of the same household as himself'. Breach of such orders amounts to a criminal offence.[183]

Housing estates

4.198 It was recognised that when tenants suffered from anti-social behaviour in the form of violence and harassment on housing estates there was a lack of effective measures to alleviate this. Older people are particularly vulnerable to this type of behaviour and ill-equipped to cope with it. The problem is best tackled by evicting the abusers rather than moving the victims from their homes to other accommodation. Measures were included in the Housing Act 1996 to facilitate the making of possession orders and increase enforcement powers without having to rely upon other tenants to come to court and thereby risk being singled out for further ill-treatment. However, there is no obligation upon the landlord to act when repeated complaints are made.[184]

Possession orders

4.199 A new discretionary ground for possession against secure tenants is now available[185] where the tenant or a person residing in or visiting the dwelling-house has been guilty of conduct causing or likely to cause a nuisance or annoyance to a person residing, visiting or otherwise engaging in lawful activity in the locality, or has been convicted of certain offences. The court procedures for obtaining possession under this ground are simplified and expedited.

Injunctions

4.200 Injunctions against anti-social behaviour on housing estates can be granted in favour of a local authority and public sector landlords.[186] These usually prohibit a person from 'engaging in or threatening to engage in conduct causing or likely to cause a nuisance or annoyance to a person residing in, visiting or otherwise engaging in a

---

[182] Police and Criminal Evidence Act 1984, s 24(6).
[183] Crime and Disorder Act 1998, Part I as amended by Police Reform Act 2002 and Anti-Social Behaviour Act 2003.
[184] *Hussain v Lancaster City Council* (1998) 96 LGR 663, 77 P&CR 89, CA.
[185] Housing Act 1996, s 144 introduces a new Ground 2 to Housing Act 1985, Sch 2.
[186] Housing Act 1996, Part V, ss 152–158 as amended by Anti-Social Behaviour Act 2003.

lawful activity in residential premises ... or in the locality of such premise' but may prohibit the person from 'entering residential premises ... or being found in the locality of any such premises'. The protected party can be a person residing in the residential premises (not necessarily the tenant), a lawful visitor or even a person in the locality of the premises (ie outside the estate) who is the victim of nuisance caused by a tenant.

4.201 If the court considers it 'just and convenient to do so', an injunction may be granted without notice, but the respondent should have the opportunity to make representations as soon as just and convenient. The court may attach a power of arrest to any of the provisions in these injunctions. If there is no power of arrest the landlord may apply to the court for a warrant of arrest if a breach is alleged. These enforcement provisions are similar to those under the Family Law Act 1996 (see **4.182**) and the procedure to be followed is set out in the court rules.[187]

Criminal remedies

Specific offences

4.202 Serious elder abuse may amount to a criminal offence especially where there is physical violence or fraud. A wide range of criminal charges can be brought against the perpetrator including common assault, sexual assault, rape, actual and grievous bodily harm, manslaughter and murder. Evidence should be obtained as soon as the abuse has been identified, and although it may be difficult to obtain a report from the victim's own medical practitioner (especially if he cares for both the perpetrator and the victim) the local police surgeon is likely to be involved. There are some specific statutory offences designed to protect vulnerable adults.

Domestic Violence, Crime and Victims Act 2004

4.203 This Act creates an offence of 'causing or allowing the death of a child or vulnerable adult'. Members of the household are required to take reasonable steps to prevent foreseeable harm, and if they do not they could be prosecuted and face a maximum sentence of 14 years if someone else in the household has killed the victim. A household can include people who live outside the home but are frequent visitors. An adverse inference can be drawn from silence at the trial when an explanation could be expected. This legislation followed a case where an elderly lady died of many injuries that could not have been self-inflicted but it could not be shown which member of the household caused the injuries.

Mental Capacity Act 2005

4.204 The second recent legislative initiative is to be found in the Mental Capacity Act 2005. Under s 44 anyone who has the care of a person who lacks, or whom he reasonably believes to lack, capacity is guilty of an offence if he ill-treats or wilfully neglects that person. This applies also to the donee of a lasting or enduring power of attorney or a deputy appointed by the Court of Protection. Ill-treatment and neglect are separate offences. On summary conviction the penalty may be imprisonment for a term not exceeding 12 months or a fine not exceeding the statutory maximum or both. On indictment the term of imprisonment may be up to 5 years thus making it an arrestable offence.[188]

---

[187] Civil Procedure Rules 1998, Part 65.
[188] Police and Criminal Evidence Act 1984, s 2.

Protection from Harassment Act 1997

4.205 A person who knowingly pursues a course of conduct which amounts to harassment is guilty of a criminal offence, and on summary conviction may be fined and imprisoned for up to 6 months.[189] There is a more serious offence of knowingly by a course of conduct putting a person in fear of violence on at least two occasions which is punishable on indictment by a fine or imprisonment for up to 5 years, and on summary conviction a fine and imprisonment for up to 6 months. A restraining order may also be made against a person convicted of either of these offences, and future breach of that order will itself be an offence with the more severe range of penalties.

4.206 In addition, where a court grants an injunction to restrain harassment and without reasonable excuse the defendant does anything which he is prohibited from doing by the injunction, he is guilty of an offence. The penalties are: if convicted on indictment a fine or imprisonment for up to 5 years, and on summary conviction a fine and imprisonment for up to 6 months.

Mental Health Act 1983

4.207 Section 127 of this Act makes it a criminal offence for staff to ill-treat or willfully neglect a patient receiving treatment, subject to a guardianship order or subject to after-care under supervision for a mental disorder in hospital or in a mental nursing care home.

Prosecution

Procedure

4.208 When it is alleged that an offence has been committed, there must be an immediate decision about involving the police and any serious offence should be reported promptly.[190] The victim may go to the police direct or with help from a third party, but should be consulted and where possible should consent to a referral to the police. Once the matter is reported the victim is asked whether he wishes to press charges and if so, or if the police decide to proceed anyway, the police investigation takes over. A statement can be taken immediately the offence is reported or left until later if the victim is upset or confused,[191] but there is no legal requirement for a statement to be taken before the complaint is noted and investigated. The victim may be asked to take part in identification of suspects either informally or by means of a formal identification parade, and to identify photographs.

4.209 There is a discretion whether to prosecute but the victim will not be involved in this even though the effect of a prosecution on the victim's physical or mental health is a factor taken into consideration.[192] The guidance in the Code for Crown Prosecutors that there should only be a prosecution if there is a 'realistic prospect of conviction' favours

---

[189] Protection from Harassment Act 1997, s 2.
[190] In cases of physical or sexual abuse, immediate police involvement is important to enable them to conduct a physical examination of the victim and collect corroborative forensic evidence.
[191] There is a right to a copy, see Home Office Circular 82/1969.
[192] The discretion has been considered in Ch 2 in the context of offences committed by an older person.

those who are likely to be believed and penalises victims who would not make good witnesses.[193] In some cases there will be no prosecution because of lack of reliable evidence or corroboration.

4.210 Policy varies as to how much information is given to victims, but the general practice is to tell them of an arrest, of a decision to prosecute or not, and of the outcome of a trial. Many victims feel excluded from the process and require advice and support to clarify their role as a prosecution witness and not as a party to proceedings. Reports in the local press of offences, particularly assaults, can be distressing for the victim and in cases of vulnerable victims a request should be made to the police to withhold the name and address. There will be press coverage of any trial and the victim may be subjected to considerable media attention, though rape victims must not be identified.[194]

Compensation orders

4.211 On convicting an individual of an offence the court can make an order for compensation in addition to or instead of another sentence.[195] If the offender cannot pay both adequate compensation and fine, the former should be given priority but in practice there are few compensation orders and awards tend to be low. The amount should reflect the damage resulting to the victim from the offence for which the accused is convicted or any other offence taken into consideration by the court in deciding on sentence, but the maximum amount in the magistrates' court is £2,000. The courts have laid down guidelines for such an order. It is not an alternative to sentence and should not be oppressive. The amount should take into account the defendant's finances and be realistic, possibly being payable by instalments but not over a long period. An order should only be made when it is clear that the defendant is under a legal liability to compensate.

Vulnerable victims

Competence as a witness

4.212 Problems arise for elderly victims of crime if they appear confused or have poor memories. First, it may be difficult to obtain convictions for offences against them if evidence in corroboration is unavailable; second, they may suffer unacceptable levels of stress when giving evidence; and third, judges and juries tend to regard their evidence with suspicion. This may be through unfamiliarity with the nature and effects of particular kinds of mental disability. The victim's capacity to give clear evidence and cope with cross-examination and the trauma of a public appearance in the witness box may be crucial to the trial. In the case of an adult witness, screens to prevent eye-contact with a defendant have only in the past been used in exceptional circumstances, and age or infirmity by themselves were not sufficient.[196]

4.213 It is for the judge to examine potential witnesses to ascertain whether they have the necessary competence and the burden of proving this rests with the party calling the witness. A person is not competent to give evidence in criminal proceedings if it appears to the court that he is not a person who is able to (a) understand questions put to him as

---

[193] Should the test for prosecution be whether the court ought, on the evidence and on the balance of probabilities, to convict?

[194] Sexual Offences (Amendment) Act 1976.

[195] Powers of the Criminal Courts Act 1973 as amended by the Criminal Justice Act 1982.

[196] *R v Schaub* (1994) 138 Sol Jo LB 11, CA.

a witness and (b) give answers to them which could be understood.[197] Once the decision has been made to admit the evidence it is for the jury to decide what weight to attach to it. The prosecution cannot call medical evidence to support the reliability of one of its witnesses unless this is to rebut a challenge by the defence.[198]

Special measures in the Crown Court

4.214 A range of 'special measures' has since July 2002 become available under Part 11 of the Youth Justice and Criminal Evidence Act 1999 to assist 'eligible witnesses' (but not defendants) in criminal proceedings.[199] These are witnesses the quality of whose evidence is likely to be diminished. They fall into three categories: first children, second those with a mental disorder[200] or physical disability, and third those who are likely to suffer fear or distress in giving evidence. There is no automatic right to any of these measures, and where a witness is eligible the court must decide whether to make them available balancing improvement in the quality of their evidence against the likelihood that the evidence will not be tested effectively.

4.215 The 'special measures' which may be taken include:

- excluding the public;
- giving evidence behind screens;
- removing wigs and gowns;
- the giving of evidence by means of a live television link or a video recording;
- the examination of a witness through an interpreter or other person approved by the court as an 'intermediary';
- the use of communication aids or techniques;
- restrictions on cross-examination.

The Court of Appeal has held that evidence of a vulnerable but competent witness may comprise merely a video recording without any cross-examination, and if it is in the interests of justice to admit the evidence taking into account the risk to the defendant there is unlikely to be a breach of the defendant's human rights.[201]

Intervention by the authorities

Background

4.216 Where the abuse involves neglect the intervention is likely to be by the local authority or the NHS under statutory powers. There are several provisions that are relevant and although these comprise part of community care services dealt with in Chapter 7 or health care considered in Chapter 8 they may be summarised here. In addition social services departments of local authorities are required to carry out

---

[197] Youth Justice and Criminal Evidence Act 1999, s 53, replacing the former test of capacity to understand the oath and appreciate the seriousness of the situation.

[198] *R v Robinson* [1994] 3 All ER 346, CA. Any such evidence should be given in the absence of the jury – *R v Deakin* [1994] 4 All ER 769, CA.

[199] Such measures were previously available to children in abuse cases. Some of them may not be available in the magistrates' courts.

[200] Within the meaning of the Mental Health Act 1983. This includes a significant impairment of intelligence and social functioning.

[201] *R v D (Video Testimony)* [2002] EWCA Crim 990.

assessments for people who may be in need of community care services,[202] so vulnerable neglected adults should be entitled to an assessment which may be multi-agency. Service provision may be made where the individual qualifies under the local authority's eligibility criteria. It is unlikely that the neglected person will ask for an assessment so 'whistle blowers' must be relied upon to notify possible neglect.

National Assistance Act 1948

4.217 A 'removal order' under s 47 of this Act enables a person to be removed from their home to a hospital or other specified place in extreme cases, in order to provide necessary care and attention. The person would have to be (a) suffering from a grave chronic disease, elderly, infirm or physically incapacitated and living in unsanitary conditions and (b) unable to devote to himself and not receiving from anyone else, proper care and attention. The removal must be in the interest of the person or to prevent injury to the health of, or serious nuisance to other people.

4.218 Application is made by social services with medical support to the local magistrates' court. The order can last up to 3 months and is renewable with no right of appeal so this section is rarely used. In urgent situations an order for immediate removal, which lasts only 3 weeks, can be obtained without giving notice to any person involved.[203] However, conditions will need to be extreme and other means pursued as well so this order is difficult to get and rarely sought by local authorities.

Mental Health Act 1983

4.219 Under s 115 of the Mental Health Act 1983 an Approved Social Worker (ASW) can enter and inspect any premises occupied by a mentally disordered person, if there is cause to believe that the person is not receiving proper care, but this does not allow forced entry. Section 136 enables a police constable to remove a person to a place of safety, if he finds that person in a public place, who appears to be suffering from a mental disorder and removal is in the interest of that person or for the protection of others. Detention can be for up to 72 hours, during which time an assessment would take place.

4.220 Section 135 enables a mentally disordered person to be removed from specific premises or from a public place to a place of safety. This can be a hospital, care home or even a police cell. The ASW makes an application to a magistrate for a warrant to be issued, authorising a police constable to gain entry (which can be forced) and remove the person to a place of safety for up to 72 hours. The person must reasonably be believed by the ASW to be suffering from a mental disorder and be a person who has been or is being neglected or ill-treated. This section can also be used to protect a mentally incapacitated victim of violence. A guardianship order may also be made under s 7 requiring, amongst other things, that the person reside at a particular place and attends at a place or a time specified for the purpose of medical treatment.

---

[202] National Health Service and Community Care Act 1990, s 47.
[203] Under the National Assistance (Amendment) Act 1951.

CHAPTER 5

HOUSING

Gordon Ashton

'A good home must be made, not bought.'
Joyce Maynard, Domestic Affairs

The law must accommodate the changing housing needs and vulnerabilities of older people and facilitate special arrangements but is not as flexible as it might be. In this chapter we consider housing options for older people including owner occupation, leases and tenancies and the implications of possession proceedings. We then look at various forms of special provision, housing and arrangements and conclude with guidance on gifts of the home and equity release.

INTRODUCTION

5.1   People do not automatically contemplate moving home on reaching retirement age, but it is a good time to consider future plans and sooner or later health, finances or other personal circumstances may dictate a move. An individual or couple will wish to consider whether they are happy and comfortable in their present home and able to cope physically and financially, and how long this situation is likely to continue. The presence of other people in the home and their wishes and intentions should be taken into account, and these should be expressed frankly before any plans are finalised rather than afterwards.

5.2   Before actually making a move it is important to consider whether the proposed new home and environment are suitable. Questions to ask include: will it be possible to cope in the new home both physically (access, stairs, convenience of layout, garden, security) and financially (outgoings, heating, maintenance and repairs)? Is there room for all the personal possessions that are to be kept? Is the location suitable, with adequate facilities (shops, transport, library, post-office) and all necessary services (doctor, dentist, social services assistance)? Will there be enough to do in the area and is it a safe and congenial environment at all times of the day and night? Is it a wise move, or will there be a loss of friends and acquaintances who cannot be replaced? If moving nearer to relatives, is there a risk that they will need to move? Is it too hasty after a bereavement or, in the case of a couple, would the survivor wish to remain in the new home? Finally, what will be the implications as regards any state benefits or local authority provision, and can the costs of the move be coped with (removal, estate agent, solicitor)? Putting off a move may reduce the options at a later stage, but a move once made can seldom be reversed. It may be wise to anticipate future needs by applying to go on a council or housing association waiting list.

5.3   Older people usually continue independent lives in their own homes, though as they get older they may need increasing support from family, neighbours or outside agencies. Such an approach is encouraged under community care policies. If the stage is reached when they can no longer cope in their own home, and no member of the family is able to provide a home and personal care, residential care may be needed either on a long-term basis or for short periods as respite care.[1] This may be seen as housing plus care, but total dependence upon a care establishment should be avoided or postponed for as long as possible as it is this which leads to an institutionalised existence.

5.4   We consider first the different bases upon which individuals may occupy their own homes and a few aspects of particular relevance to the older occupier. The age of the occupier is seldom relevant by itself although it may influence the exercise of a discretion or the ability of the individual to create or vary the legal relationship involved. An older person may be either a tenant or a landlord, so we deal not only with the basis of their own accommodation but also the situation if they allow another person to occupy or share their home. Special types of home and provision that may be available to the older person are then identified, and various types of arrangement that might be entered into by such persons are dealt with, including shared occupation, gifts of the home and home income plans. Finally, special situations such as second homes, time share and foreign properties are mentioned in relation to the older owner.

Capacity

5.5   A person who seeks to acquire an interest in a freehold or leasehold property must have the capacity to do so, and this topic is considered in Chapter 3. However, in many cases the provision of a home for an elderly individual will merely depend upon the creation of a tenancy. The legal test of capacity to enter into a tenancy or a licence to occupy is the general contractual test of ability to understand the nature of the transaction and make a decision based thereon. Simple forms of tenancy agreement or licence written in plain English are therefore to be encouraged,[2] and it would seem that a lower level of capacity may be required to take on a weekly tenancy than to execute a long lease. Where the tenancy or licence is clearly in the best interests of the individual and the agreement does not contain unusual or onerous terms, it may come within the special principles that apply to the purchase of items that are deemed to be necessary for normal living.[3]

5.6   In the absence of capacity there are procedures to enable a property to be purchased and held for the incapacitated person and these are dealt with in Chapter 11. Whether it is necessary to invoke these procedures on the grant of an ordinary weekly or monthly tenancy or licence may depend upon the attitude of the landlord and the availability of other persons willing to make the arrangements and undertake payment of the rent. If the individual is physically capable of signing, the landlord may be persuaded to accept this signature especially if it is witnessed by a close member of the family or a solicitor. A letter from a solicitor confirming that he has advised the tenant and is satisfied with the terms and that the tenant understands them may satisfy a landlord who has doubts about capacity but is otherwise prepared to accept the tenant. In practice licences to occupy are regularly arranged on behalf of incapacitated people with weekly fees being paid by an appointee out of state benefits and the legality of such arrangements is not questioned.

---

1   Care homes and nursing are considered in Ch 6.
2   They would refer to 'we' and 'you' instead of 'the landlord' and 'the tenant'.
3   See Ch 2 at **2.49** et seq for the way the Mental Capacity Act 2005 deals with this.

5.7 If the owner of a property becomes mentally incapable and it is desired to dispose of that property or an interest therein, in the absence of an attorney acting under a registered enduring or lasting power of attorney an application must be made to the Court of Protection for the appointment of a deputy. If a joint legal owner of property becomes incapable by reason of mental disorder of exercising his functions as a trustee, a new trustee must be appointed in his place before the legal estate can be dealt with but reference to the Court of Protection will still be required in the absence of such an attorney.[4] Single orders (ie not involving the appointment of a deputy) may be available in the case of a tenancy where a large capital sum is not involved, although in practice such tenancies may be surrendered by a joint tenant or even informally.[5]

Owner occupation

Introductory

5.8 Many older people own their homes, either on a freehold or long leasehold basis, and a substantial proportion have paid off any mortgage during their lifetimes. The home is often the biggest capital asset of an older individual, and care may be needed if its value is to be preserved for the next generation. Whilst this outcome may be desired in many family situations, the view may also be taken that the home is a resource to be used in meeting the cost of whatever provision is needed by the owner prior to death. In particular this is the view taken by the state or a local authority when called upon to support the individual.[6]

5.9 One should always examine the implications as regards means-testing for state benefits and local authority provision when the sale, purchase or gift of a home is being considered. The home may not be taken into account as an asset of the owner if it is occupied by that person as a sole or principal dwelling or, in some circumstances, if it continues to be occupied by a partner or by a relative of that person who is incapacitated or has attained 60 years. In other circumstances its value will be taken into account, and if it is sold and a cheaper home is acquired, the cash sum realised will be means-tested as an available resource.

Joint ownership

Joint tenancy or tenancy in common

5.10 Where a property is purchased or otherwise placed in joint names, it is important for there to be a precise statement as to how the beneficial interest is held. This should stipulate whether the parties are joint tenants or tenants in common and, if tenants in common, the proportions or shares in which they own the property. If joint tenants the property passes to the survivor on the death of one owner.[7] This statement should be in the purchase or transfer deed or in a separate deed of trust, and the statement to the Land Registry as to whether the survivor can give a valid receipt for capital money is not sufficient.

---

[4] See Ch 3 at **3.42** and Trustee Act 1925, s 36(9). Also further provisions in Trusts of Land and Appointment of Trustees Act 1996, s 20.

[5] See generally Ch 11.

[6] See Ch 10 at **10.234**. This is also the approach to be adopted by attorneys or deputies for elderly persons who are incapable of handling their own affairs – see Ch 11.

[7] The *commorientes rule* provides that where two joint tenants die instantly (eg in a plane crash) the younger is deemed to have survived the elder.

5.11   This is especially important when the joint owners are not married to one another. Although the court can redistribute property following a divorce, there are no procedures for property adjustment in the case of unmarried joint owners. In that situation the court can only give effect to the intentions and contributions of the parties, and any statement in the purchase deed is the starting point and will normally be relied upon to the exclusion of other evidence. Where a property is conveyed into the joint names of a cohabiting couple without any declaration of their respective beneficial interests, the starting point if the property has to be divided upon the breakdown of the relationship is that there is also joint beneficial ownership. A party seeking to challenge this must show that there was an intention that the beneficial interests would be different and in what way.[8]

Occupation rights

5.12   The legal estate is held by co-owners as joint tenants and used to be held 'on trust for sale' with those beneficially entitled having an appropriate interest in the proceeds of sale, but this concept has now been abolished and they now have an interest in possession in the property which is held under a 'trust of land'.[9] Those not entitled to immediate possession (eg there is a prior life interest) do not have a right of occupation. Rights of occupation arise where that is the purpose of the trust (eg an unmarried couple buy a house as their home). The court may declare whether occupation rights exist in a particular case.

Severence of a joint tenancy

5.13   If the parties are beneficial joint tenants one of them can later serve a notice to sever the joint tenancy and thereafter they will hold the property as tenants in common in equal shares.[10] This may be appropriate on a divorce or the breakdown of a personal relationship, but of course this will prevent the giver of the notice from inheriting the other half as well as the other owner doing likewise. It can be a difficult decision to take. It may also be appropriate to equalise estates for tax and estate planning purposes, particularly to safeguard at least half the value from care fees, should a surviving joint owner subsequently need to fund care.

5.14   Severance may also be effected in other ways. This includes a court order, homicide[11] or a merger of interests. It may also be by mutual agreement or conduct[12] or a course of dealing that is inconsistent with a joint tenancy such as a transfer or mortgage of the share or bankruptcy.[13] However, purporting to leave the share by will is not usually sufficient because the will is revocable until death and thereafter it is too late to effect severance, but mutual wills may evidence an irrevocable common intention to effect severance.[14]

Financial contributions

5.15   Case law established that an interest in a house or flat belonging to another could arise where a person made a financial contribution towards the cost of buying the

---

8   See the House of Lords' decision in *Stack v Dowden* [2007] UKHL 17.
9   Trusts of Land and Appointment of Trustees Act 1996, s 5.
10   Law of Property Act 1925, s 36(2).
11   A joint tenant who unlawfully kills the other joint tenant cannot benefit from the wrong.
12   For there to be such severance all the joint tenants must be involved.
13   The severance will be deemed to have taken place on the first available act of bankruptcy – Bankruptcy Act 1914, s 372; *Re Pavlou (A Bankrupt)* [1993] 2 FLR 751.
14   *Re Goodchild (Deceased)* [1997] 2 FLR 644.

property, or paid for or contributed towards the cost of extending or improving the property. Merely contributing to the household budget or the mortgage subscriptions would not be enough. This is likely to be of particular significance where the incentive for the financial input was the prospect of living in or sharing the home and that expectation is not fulfilled. Ideally the expectations of the parties should be clarified and confirmed in a legal document before the arrangement is entered into, though this seldom happens within families.

5.16 In a much quoted early case the House of Lords held that in the absence of agreement or an estoppel, a husband who does work or expends money upon the property of the wife has no claim upon the property. On the facts of that case it was not possible to infer any common intention that he should acquire any beneficial interest in the property.[15] Subsequent cases indicated that contributions to the household and carrying out decorating work on the home were not sufficient to justify an inference of a common intention.[16] However, in a later case an elderly widow who was invited to live in the home of her daughter and son-in-law and paid £607 for an extension, left after 15 months when differences arose. It was held that the money was not intended to be a gift and the house was held on a resulting or constructive trust for the widow proportionate to her payment.[17] An estoppel arose where a widow became housekeeper for a wealthy man and they began to live together as man and wife. He bought a new house of her choice and assured her that it was to be hers whereupon she spent money on improving it with his knowledge.[18]

5.17 The social climate has changed since these cases were decided and the courts must now cope with many living together relationships which break up resulting in disputes over ownership of the shared home. It seems that a person can now claim a beneficial interest in a property without having made a direct financial contribution.[19]

Purchase of former council house

5.18 A common situation for older people is the purchase at a discount of a former council house of which they were tenant. Sometimes children will become involved, perhaps because they can provide the purchase price, and questions then arise as to the extent of their beneficial interest in view of the fact that the discount, which may be substantial, was only available to the former tenant. Where such a purchase was taken in joint names of the former tenant and her daughter because only the daughter could get the necessary mortgage, it was held that the daughter did not have a beneficial interest because she had not actually paid any part of the price, did not pay the mortgage and it was not intended that she should. She merely facilitated the purchase of the house by her mother.[20]

5.19 The outcome might have been otherwise had the common intention been different. In another case of a council house purchase at a 60% discount the son agreed to pay the mortgage and under a trust deed acquired the property subject to the right of his parents to live there rent free for life. The transaction was subsequently challenged

---

[15] *Petitt v Petitt* [1970] AC 777.
[16] *Burns v Burns* [1984] Ch 317; *Lloyds Bank v Rosset* [1990] 1 All ER 1111, HL.
[17] *Hussey v Palmer* [1972] 1 WLR 1286, CA, Denning MR.
[18] *Pascoe v Turner* [1979] 1 WLR 431.
[19] This topic is further considered under the heading *Sharing the home* at **5.149**.
[20] *Carlton v Goodman* [2002] EWCA Civ 545.

on the grounds of undue influence but upheld.[21] In such cases, it is usually appropriate for the parties to enter into a declaration of trust to set out their respective interests. Failure to do so may cause later difficulties, such as where the older person moves into a care home and has to fund their care. Local authorities must take into account the declaration of trust when valuing the older person's interest in the property.[22]

Orders for sale under Law of Property Act 1925

5.20 Any person with a financial interest in a property could apply to the court for an order that the property be sold and the proceeds of sale distributed between the persons beneficially entitled.[23] The court could make such order as it thought fit, but would usually order sale where there was an express or statutory trust for sale with power to postpone sale and the trustees could not agree about the future of the property.[24] However, when the purpose of the joint acquisition was to provide a home for the joint owners neither of them could demand a sale whilst this collateral purpose still subsisted and an application would need to be made to the court if there was a dispute.[25] Where a widow transferred her home into joint names with her daughter on terms that it would not be sold during her lifetime, and the daughter then forged her mother's signature on a mortgage and defaulted on the loan, the Court of Appeal was not willing to grant an immediate order for possession and sale on the application of the mortgagee on the ground that the trust for sale could not be implemented without the consent of the mother.[26] The collateral purpose was thus binding on the mortgagee who, as assignee of the donee, could not acquire a better title than the donee had.

5.21 Thus there was a distinction between investment property and property acquired with the further purpose that it be used as a home. Where the marriage or relationship broke up this collateral purpose might not survive, but where dependent children were involved an order for sale might be refused or postponed. Even if there was an order for sale, it might be postponed to give an occupier the chance to make other arrangements. The court might also order a co-owner remaining in possession to pay a rent to the other owner.

Trusts of Land and Appointment of Trustees Act 1996

5.22 There were difficulties of interpretation under the 1925 Act and the law was reformed by this legislation in 1996.[27] The effect of the former provisions was re-enacted with amendments to ensure that the powers of the court are sufficiently broad and flexible in order to reflect the nature and the purpose of the trust.[28] Anyone who is a trustee or who has an interest in trust property may make an application to the court which is then required in determining the application to have regard to the following matters:

---

[21] *Popowski v Popowski* [2004] EWHC 668 (Ch). Contrast *Humphreys v Humphreys* [2004] EWHC 2201 (Ch) where a constructive trust on a 60-40 basis was declared.

[22] *Nottingham City Council v Berresford and the Adjudicator to HM Land Registry*, 10 March 2011 (ref 2010/0577); *Cunningham v East Lothian Council* [2011] CSOH 185.

[23] Law of Property Act 1925, s 30.

[24] *Re Mayo* [1943] 2 All ER 440.

[25] *Jones v Challenger* [1961] 1 QB 176, CA; *Evers v Evers* [1980] 1 WLR 1327, CA.

[26] *Abbey National plc v Moss* [1994] 1 FLR 307, CA. Contrast *Re Citro (a bankrupt)* [1991] Ch 142, CA where on the bankruptcy of the husband the collateral purpose had come to an end. For further consideration of this topic see *Sharing the home* at **5.149**.

[27] Law Commission Working Paper No 181: *Transfer of Land, Trust of Land*.

[28] Trusts of Land and Appointment of Trustees Act 1996, ss 14 and 15.

(1)   the intention of the person or persons who created the trust;

(2)   the purpose for which the property is subject to the trust is held;

(3)   the welfare of any minor who occupies or might reasonably expected to occupy any land subject to the trust as his home; and

(4)   the interests of any secured creditor of any beneficiary.

5.23   Older case law may still be relevant in interpreting these statutory guidelines, and it has been held that three principles could be transferred from the former provisions:[29]

(1)   the court as a matter of discretion should order what was equitable, fair and just;

(2)   where there is conflict between the chargee's interest in a matrimonial home and the interests of an innocent spouse, the former will prevail unless there are special circumstances; and

(3)   where there is a collateral purpose of a trust still subsisting, the court should not defeat that purpose by ordering a sale.

However, in a later case it was pointed out that the interests of a secured creditor are now only one of four factors to be taken into account with no order of priority, so this may have tipped the balance away from banks and other chargees towards families.[30]

5.24   Where there is a dispute the court[31] may make such order as it thinks fit relating to the exercise of the trustees' functions or declare the nature or extent of a person's interest in a property subject to a trust. This may include rights of occupation, exclusion of a joint owner and orders about payment of outgoings or occupation rent. There is no longer any presumption in favour of an order for sale.

5.25   In cases decided under the 1925 Act, the courts generally held that no order for sale should be made where the underlying purposes for which the trust was originally created continue to exist.[32] Where, however, an application for a sale is made by a trustee in bankruptcy or a creditor with a charging order on the beneficial share of one of them, a sale will usually be ordered unless there are exceptional circumstances.[33] For example, it has been held that the fact that the family concerned would lose their home and that the children would have to change school were not sufficient to delay a sale.[34]

Shared ownership

5.26   Some housing associations operate shared ownership schemes under which homes are part purchased (perhaps with a mortgage) and part rented on a long lease, sometimes with an option to purchase a greater share at a later date.[35] The landlord usually remains responsible for repairs and maintenance and in some cases provides personal services such as a warden. Most schemes are marketed for first-time buyers but

---

[29]   *TSB Bank Plc v Marshall* [1998] 2 FLR 769.

[30]   *Mortgage Corporation v Shaire* [2001] 3 WLR 639.

[31]   This is usually the local county court but in complex or high value cases it may be the Chancery Division of the High Court.

[32]   *Re Buchanan-Wollaston's Conveyance* [1939] Ch 738, CA.

[33]   These applications are under Insolvency Act 1986, s 335A which imposes further criteria.

[34]   *Re Citro (a bankrupt)* [1991] Ch 142, CA.

[35]   Known as 'staircasing'. In some cases it is possible eventually to acquire full ownership although some shared ownership leases exclude this.

some are designed for retired or disabled people.[36] Sheltered housing schemes include buying (and selling) at a discount, loan stock schemes and a 'life share' in the whole or part of the property.[37]

5.27 The scheme enables those with limited capital to enjoy the benefits of home ownership without borrowing. Investing available capital in this way may have advantages in regard to means-tested benefits, but increasing rents could become a problem and in some cases there are restrictions which would inhibit resale.

Mortgages

5.28 There is no age bar to taking on a loan secured by mortgage or legal charge. Building societies no longer insist upon any mortgage loan being structured so as to be repaid prior to reaching state pensionable age, and those who are approaching or have reached that age may now take on a mortgage if they can establish capacity to pay the monthly subscriptions. There are even schemes that encourage taking on a mortgage to increase the net income of the individual, though this may be at the expense of capital.[38]

5.29 Mortgage interest tax relief is no longer available. A ceiling has been placed since August 1993 on the maximum mortgage that can be taken into account for income support or its replacement, universal credit, purposes.[39] Further restrictions apply to loans taken out or increased whilst the claimant was entitled to income support, but there are savings where a tenant has become an owner-occupier or where the loan is to meet the special needs of a disabled person.[40]

Vulnerable mortgagors

5.30 Cases have arisen where a wife has signed a charge over the jointly owned family home to secure a loan to the husband or to his business. The question then arises whether there has been undue influence and the charge should be enforced against the wife. This issue is less likely to arise where the loan was for the benefit of the wife as well as the husband. Of course it is not only between husband and wife that this situation may arise: elderly parents may be prevailed upon to charge their homes as security for their children's activities, and if the child's finances collapse the parent risks losing the home. Similar principles are likely to apply.[41]

5.31 In a landmark decision[42] the House of Lords tried to balance the interests of sureties and lenders when providing security to support third party borrowings in non-commercial situations. It was held that if a wife is induced by the undue influence or misrepresentation of her husband to stand surety for his debts, or those of his company, the lender will, in circumstances which should have put it on enquiry, be fixed with constructive notice of the wife's right to set aside the transaction, unless the lender had

---

[36] Further information at: www.gov.uk/affordable-home-ownership-schemes/shared-ownership-schemes.

[37] Guidance is available at: www.ageuk.org.uk/home-and-care/housing-choices/sheltered-housing/.

[38] More details of these home income plans are provided later in this chapter.

[39] In respect of claims from 10 April 1995 this was reduced to £100,000. Universal credit is being phased in and replacing income support. The mortgage allowance is being removed and replaced by a housing allowance, with the total benefit being subject to a cap.

[40] Income Support (General) Regulations 1987, SI 1987/1967 as amended.

[41] For a cautionary tale where a mother charged her home as security for her son's borrowing and the same solicitors acted for both parties see: *Clark Boyce v Mouat* [1993] 4 All ER 268, PC.

[42] *Barclays Bank Plc v O'Brien* [1994] 1 AC 180, HL.

advised the wife to take independent advice or explained the transaction to the wife at a private interview in the absence of the husband.

5.32 A subsequent appeal offered guidance as to the minimum requirements expected of lenders and solicitors involved in such transactions in order to avoid the allegation of undue influence.[43] However, this can apply equally to other relationships where there is trust and confidence or reliance placed by the surety in the borrower, in circumstances where the relationship between the surety and borrower is not a commercial one. The following principles were laid down in addition for the need for the wife to establish the undue influence of the husband:

(1) When the wife offers herself as surety for the husband's debts the lender is put on enquiry and should take steps to ensure that the wife is aware of the risks she is proposing to take.

(2) The lender should refer the wife to a solicitor for independent legal advice and not proceed without confirmation that such advice has been given.[44]

(3) The position would be the same for an unmarried couple where the lender was aware of the relationship.

(4) Where the couple contract the debt jointly the lender is only on enquiry if it knows that the loan is solely for the husband's purposes.

(5) Where the wife is a shareholder or officer of a company benefiting from the transaction, the lender should still be on enquiry as a shareholding in a company, or being an office holder, does not always reflect the true guide to the controller of a company's business.

5.33 Comment was also made about the nature of undue influence. It may be actual or presumed. The former does not depend on a pre-existing relationship and the person who seeks to assert actual undue influence must prove it. By contrast, presumed undue influence necessarily involves some legally-recognised relationship, that can be described as one where one party is legally presumed to place trust and confidence in the other person. The burden of proof is on the wife to show that in reality such a relationship existed with her husband. Having done so, and providing the nature of the transaction was such that the lender ought to have been put on enquiry, then the burden of proof will shift to the lender to show that reasonable steps were taken to ensure that no undue influence exerted.

Long leases

Preliminary

5.34 A lease is a deed whereby an interest is created in land. It is required where a tenancy is to be created for a term of more than 3 years and usually contains covenants which are binding on the landlord (or lessor) and tenant (or lessee) for the time being. Although freehold ownership is more common, a dwelling may be held on a lease either at a market rent or a lower rent but with a premium payable. The lease can then be sold and assigned in just the same way that a freehold title can be conveyed. There can even be a sub-lease granted out of a head-lease, with the term being shorter.

---

[43] *Royal Bank of Scotland v Etridge* [2002] 1 AC 773.
[44] Detailed guidance was given as to the role of the solicitor in these situations.

Security of tenure

5.35   This is given to residential tenants who hold under long leases at a rent.[45] Where a term exceeding 21 years ends the tenancy is automatically continued (if the tenant so desires) until the landlord serves a notice in prescribed form either to convert the tenancy or seeking possession. Until 15 January 1999 conversion would have been to a statutory tenancy under the Rent Act 1977 with the tenant no longer paying the former ground rent under the lease but instead paying a 'fair rent' registered by a rent officer. The procedures relating to such tenancies applied as to security of tenure and rent review. If the lease is determined after that date the tenant acquires an assured tenancy with more limited succession rights and no statutory control over the rent. (See below for these different types of tenancy.)

Flats and apartments

5.36   The traditional way of creating a separate title to a flat or maisonette is a long lease, typically for 99 or more years, at a nominal rent which is sold at a premium. This enables mutual rights, covenants and repairing obligations to be enforced between the several flat owners in the building notwithstanding changes of ownership. An annual service charge may be payable as an addition to the rent. Where there are only two flats in a building there will usually be an exchange of freeholds so that the lower flat owner holds the freehold reversion to the upper flat and vice versa. When there are more than four flats in a building a management company can be formed which holds the freehold (including the common parts) and manages the scheme as lessor of all the flats. This is generally a company limited by guarantee with each of the flat owners being a member so there is democratic control of the flat scheme and an independent body to take the responsibility. The cost of this may not be justified for three or four flats so then one of the owners may have to take the responsibility of management.

Service charges

5.37   Lessees of flats have some statutory protection in respect of service charges. Only reasonably incurred amounts are payable for services and any work must be carried out to a reasonable standard. The lessee may insist upon receiving a written summary of relevant costs and may inspect the accounts. A surveyor or a manager may be appointed and disputes may be referred to a Leasehold Valuation Tribunal. Residents associations[46] also have some statutory rights, for example to be consulted when repairs are to be carried out and to demand and receive information.[47] More recent legislation gives enhanced protection for leaseholders of flats. Protection is afforded against unreasonable charges for administration and improvements, and landlords cannot insist that a particular property insurance company is used. Accounting requirements have been introduced and leaseholders may withhold service charges when certain information is not provided. There are restrictions on forfeiting a lease for non-payment of service charges where these have not been admitted or agreed or settled by a court or tribunal, and Leasehold Valuation Tribunals are given an extended jurisdiction.[48]

---

[45]   Landlord and Tenant Act 1954, Part I.
[46]   Federation of Private Residents' Associations: www.fpra.org.uk; Society of Retired Leaseholders: www.sorl.org.
[47]   Landlord and Tenant Acts 1985 and 1987; Housing Act 1996. For homes disposed of by the public sector see Housing Act 1985. Protection covers leases by housing associations but not local authorities.
[48]   Commonhold and Leasehold Reform Act 2002, Part 2.

Commonhold

5.38 Since September 2004 commonhold can be used for new property developments (including for mixed residential and business premises) and is also available for leasehold or freehold conversions where the owners unanimously agree.[49] It has many advantages over the leasehold system, conferring freehold ownership for units within the commonhold coupled with membership of a commonhold association which owns and manages the common parts. A residential unit may be let but only for a term of less than 7 years with no premium. There are detailed provisions for setting the amount of the annual 'service charge' which provide a degree of protection.

Forfeiture

5.39 Forfeiture is the right of a landlord to bring a lease to an end and bring possession proceedings when there has been a breach by the tenant. It only arises where there is an express term giving the landlord this right but may be relevant to housing cases. It occurs when there has been a breach of a condition or covenant in the lease but the lease is only avoided when there has been peaceful re-entry or service of appropriate proceedings on the tenant (any subsequent judgment dates back to this date). The landlord must serve a Notice before Forfeiture other than in rent arrears cases and the tenant can then apply for relief from forfeiture.[50] Where a person is lawfully residing in the premises it is unlawful to enforce a right of forfeiture or re-entry other than by court proceedings.[51]

5.40 A regulated tenancy can be forfeit but that only brings the contractual tenancy to an end thus avoiding the need to serve a notice to quit and a statutory tenancy then arises. Forfeiture cannot bring an assured tenancy to an end because the landlord must obtain an order for possession on one of the statutory grounds. It commonly arises where there is a long lease at a low rent which was not protected under the Rent Act. Protection is afforded provided that the lease is for more than 21 years with a rent less than two-thirds of the rateable value.[52]

Enfranchisement

5.41 Since 1967 the lessee of a house (but not of a flat) who has been the tenant for at least 2 years has had the right to purchase the reversion or extend the lease if the rateable value was below a certain level and the original term was at least 21 years.[53] In 1993 further rights were given to leaseholders of flats to collectively purchase the freehold of their scheme.[54] To qualify, at least two-thirds of the flats must be let on long leases at low rents and the leaseholders must agree to purchase the freehold. They have to pay the market value of the freehold but advantages of enfranchisement include control of the management of their own block of flats and the power to grant new leases to overcome loss of value as the terms near expiry. Some tenants who do not qualify are given the right to buy a 90-year lease from the end of their current lease.[55]

---

[49] Commonhold and Leasehold Reform Act 2002, Part 1; Commonhold Regulations 2004, SI 2004/1829.
[50] Landlord and Tenant Act 1925, s 146.
[51] Protection from Eviction Act 1977.
[52] Landlord and Tenant Act 1954, Part II. For leases commencing after 1 April 1990 see Local Government and Housing Act 1989, s 186 and Sch 10.
[53] Leasehold Reform Act 1967. Some of the restrictions have been removed by the Commonhold and Leasehold Reform Act 2002.
[54] Leasehold Reform, Housing and Urban Development Act 1993, Ch I; Housing Act 1996.
[55] See Ch II of the 1993 Act.

Tenancies – private sector

Background

5.42   Many older people reside in rented accommodation, either as tenants or with a partner or other family member who is a tenant. Matters of concern will be repairing obligations, rent, security of tenure and the ability to pass on the tenancy or acquire ownership of the property. The starting point must be to identify the date when the tenancy commenced and whether the tenancy is in the public or private sector. Even these apparently simple questions are not straightforward and some research may be needed because housing policies have changed over the years and involve considerable statutory intervention. The relevant commencement date may be that for a previous tenancy that the present tenancy replaced because a landlord cannot deprive a tenant of established rights simply by having a new agreement signed. Also there have been changes in what comprises the 'public sector' and indeed a public sector tenancy may be transferred to the private sector (with some qualification).

Registered social landlords

5.43   Registered social landlords largely comprise housing associations and may be regarded as belonging to the 'quasi-public sector' because they are registered with and supervised by the Housing Corporations.[56] Tenants have the benefit of a tenant's guarantee and other guidance issued from time to time by the Housing Corporation. Such landlords previously let on secure tenancies in the public sector (although in most cases there was no right to buy), but from 15 January 1989 this changed to assured tenancies in the private sector (see below) although existing tenancies remain unaffected and a transfer where requested by the landlord will retain secure tenancy status.[57]

5.44   Privatisation of public sector housing has been a feature of central government policy since the mid-1980s and following the bulk transfer of housing stock former tenants of local authorities may find themselves tenants of registered social landlords.[58] Their tenancies will now be in the private sector but carry over some features of public sector housing such as a preserved right to buy.

Types of private sector tenancies

5.45   Over the years there has been a shift from full protection of residential tenants to dependence on market forces, but this is not retrospective so tenants do not lose any existing rights and should seek to retain earlier protection wherever possible. When considering a tenancy the first step must therefore be to identify the regime under which it was created and continues. Protection takes the form of restriction or control over the maximum rent that can be charged coupled with some security of tenure, but regardless of the type of tenancy no eviction may take place without a court order (see below). The tenant has no general right to assign a tenancy but limited succession rights may be afforded. This is an extremely complex topic and only an outline can be offered here.

---

[56]   There is a Housing Corporation for England and one for Wales.
[57]   Housing Act 1988, s 35(2). A housing association may be prohibited from granting assured shorthold tenancies under the terms of its registration (see below) but this has become less common.
[58]   There are statutory procedures for consultation before this takes place.

Regulated tenancy

5.46   A residential tenancy of a separate dwelling within certain rateable value limits commenced before 15 January 1989 will generally be a protected tenancy or a protected shorthold tenancy unless the landlord was from the public sector.[59] Exceptions include tenancies at low rents, holiday and student lettings, agricultural holdings, licensed premises and cases where payment is made for board or attendance or there is a resident landlord.

5.47   Where a protected tenancy comes to an end and the tenant continues to occupy the premises as his residence, it becomes a *statutory tenancy* and remains protected if and so long as the tenant occupies the premises as his residence. The term *regulated tenancy* covers both protected tenancies and statutory tenancies although these are often referred to as 'Rent Act tenancies'. No new regulated tenancies could be created after 15 January 1989 unless pursuant to a contract entered into before then or replacing an earlier such tenancy (including situations where a court authorises a move to suitable alternative accommodation). Thus regulated tenancies are being gradually phased out although many elderly people still occupy under them and they provide the most extensive range of rights.

Assured tenancy

5.48   From 15 January 1989 new private sector and housing association tenancies that relate to the tenant's principal residence will generally be assured tenancies.[60] Exceptions include tenancies at low rents, holiday and student lettings, agricultural tenancies, licensed premises and cases where there is a resident landlord.[61] If one of the exceptions applies the tenant has no security of tenure and once a notice to quit has been served and has expired there is no statutory protection except the Protection from Eviction Act 1977 which requires court proceedings for eviction.

Shorthold tenancies

5.49   This is a variation of the normal form of tenancy which was introduced in 1980 for protected tenancies and continued when assured tenancies were introduced. There are thus protected shorthold tenancies and assured shorthold tenancies, although only the latter can now be created. By serving the appropriate notice before commencement of a tenancy for a fixed term of at least 6 months (and provided there was not a previous assured tenancy), the landlord retained a right to possession thereafter upon giving 2 months' notice, however long the tenancy actually continues.[62]

5.50   All assured tenancies granted after 28 February 1997 are assured shortholds (even if not granted for an initial fixed term of at least 6 months) unless they fall within one of the exceptions. These include tenancies succeeding former assured tenancies and those that contain a provision stating otherwise.[63] There is no incentive for a landlord to grant an ordinary assured tenancy, but registered social landlords may be under an obligation to do so under the terms of their registration with a Housing Corporation.

---

[59]   Rent Act 1977. Shortholds rarely now arise as most have come to an end.
[60]   Housing Act 1988, Part I.
[61]   Housing Act 1988, Sch 1.
[62]   The protected shorthold provisions were more complex.
[63]   Housing Act 1996. Alternatively prior notice may be given by the landlord or the tenant may sign a prescribed form converting this to an assured shorthold tenancy.

5.51 The assured shorthold tenancy, which may be for a fixed term or a periodic tenancy from its inception, has thus become the only form for a new private letting (with a few exceptions) and is popular because it can be for a limited time and a mandatory order for possession must follow if the landlord complies with the necessary formalities.

5.52 More than one-half of all tenancies are now assured or assured shortholds, but previous types of tenancy retain their status and must be dealt with accordingly where they arise. This is important for older tenants because the assured shorthold tenancies lack the security of tenure that they desire whereas younger people are more willing to be mobile. There has been a decline in the number of regulated tenancies and the majority of these tenants are now elderly people living alone.

Restricted contracts

5.53 Certain tenancies and licences excluded from these statutory controls also have no protection from termination. Exclusions include holiday and free tenancies and situations where a tenant shares any accommodation with his landlord or a member of the landlord's family and the landlord is resident in the building.[64] Even so, an order for possession is required and may be postponed for up to 14 days or, if there would be exceptional hardship, 6 weeks.

Rents

5.54 Rents under residential tenancies are far less regulated than they used to be, but many older tenants will be eligible for assistance with their rent through means-tested housing benefit.[65]

5.55 There is an obligation on all landlords to provide a rent book where the rent is payable weekly unless the rent covers board as well.[66] Failure to do so is an offence but does not invalidate the tenancy or prevent the recovery of rent although it may make it difficult for the landlord to satisfy the court that rent has not been paid where the tenant's evidence that rent has been paid in cash is credible.

Protected/regulated tenancies

5.56 A system of *fair rents* applied to these tenancies and it was not possible to contract out of this.[67] Rent officers fixed the rent at an artificially low level because the scarcity value of accommodation must be ignored, and there was a right of appeal to a Rent Assessment Committee.[68]

Assured tenancy

5.57 There is no control over the amount of the rent for an assured tenancy, and this is to be agreed between the parties on the assumption that it will be determined according to market levels. Rent increases cannot be made in the first year and thereafter can be

---

[64] Housing Act 1988, Sch 1 and s 30(1) amending Protection from Eviction Act 1977, s 3. Some limited protection applies to such tenancies created before 16 January 1989.

[65] This is covered in Ch 10.

[66] Landlord and Tenant Act 1985, s 4(1).

[67] Rent Act 1977 (as amended) and Housing Act 1980. There was previously a system of rent control with security of tenure under the Rent Act 1957 and earlier legislation, but most of these tenancies will since have been 'de-controlled'.

[68] The scarcity value may no longer apply resulting in substantial rent increases, though it is still possible to argue that housing suitable for elderly people is scarce.

examined by the Rent Assessment Committee if they are above market levels unless they have been fixed in accordance with a rent review system in the original agreement.[69] For tenancies after 28 February 1997 any reference to the Rent Assessment Committee must be made within 6 months.

5.58 It is assumed that rents charged by registered social landlords will be below market levels since such landlords are expected to let to the less well off. Their rents are generally 30% lower than market rents.

Shorthold tenancies

5.59 The tenant can apply to a Rent Assessment Committee within the first 6 months to determine the rent but of course the landlord may choose to terminate the tenancy if he is not satisfied with the outcome.

Repairs

Liability under the tenancy

5.60 Any tenancy agreement will set out express repairing obligations and the tenant will be responsible for maintaining the premises, but under a residential letting will not become liable for repairs to the main structure, exterior and services. There may be an express or implied obligation on the part of the landlord to put or keep the property in repair, and the tenant can enforce this in the county court. The tenant must give the landlord notice of any want of repair before any question of compensation can arise, unless the landlord already had notice of the defects. This principle extends to latent defects which could not have been discovered by anyone.[70]

5.61 In the case of residential tenancies commenced on or after 24 October 1961 for less than 7 years, the landlord must keep in repair the structure and exterior of a dwelling and the installations for the supply of water, gas, electricity, sanitation, space heating and water heating.[71] This will only extend to the common parts of a building where the tenancy commenced after 15 January 1989. For certain tenancies at a very low rent there is an implied term that the premises are fit for human habitation at the commencement of the tenancy and will be kept fit, despite any stipulation to the contrary.[72] Even where these statutory obligations do not apply (for example a tenancy granted before 24 October 1961) the courts may imply obligations into the tenancy.

5.62 The standard of repair is determined by what is deemed appropriate to the age, character and prospective life of the dwelling and the locality. The landlord's obligation does not extend to improvements or to a design defect in the building.[73] It has been held that remedial work to deal with the consequences of damp are the landlord's responsibility, but not adding a comprehensive damp-proof system in a property that did not previously have one as this would turn the property into a different one from that which was let.[74] The distinction between repairs and improvements may not be easy to make. The courts are only inclined to enforce obligations to 'put and keep' in repair when the premises can be made fit at reasonable expense.

---

[69] Housing Act 1988, ss 13 and 14. Housing benefit for the tenant will be restricted to a market rent.
[70] *O'Brien v Robinson* [1973] AC 912.
[71] Landlord and Tenant Act 1985, s 11. This means 'put and keep in repair'.
[72] Landlord and Tenant Act 1985, s 8.
[73] *Liverpool City Council v Irvine* [1977] AC 239, [1976] 1 All ER 39, HL.
[74] *Eyre v McCracken* (2000) 80 P&CR 220, CA.

Liability in tort

5.63 A landlord may have a liability at common law in negligence if he lets premises that are not fit for occupation at the commencement of the tenancy, or if he built the premises negligently with defects that subsequently cause damage. The Defective Premises Act 1972 imposes liability on the landlord to anyone who suffers loss as a result of his failure to carry out repairs and maintenance to the premises where he knew or ought to have known of the defects. The landlord may also be liable under the Occupiers Liability Act 1957 in respect of defects in the common parts of a building which result in injury to a visitor.

Public law remedies

5.64 In addition there are certain public law remedies available. The first involves a *statutory nuisance*. Where premises are in such a state as to be prejudicial to health or a nuisance, then the occupier or the local authority environmental health officer may take action to require the owner to abate the nuisance.[75] Once a local authority is satisfied that a statutory nuisance exists it is obliged to take action.

5.65 A local authority must also take some action where housing is declared unfit for human habitation.[76] The statutory definition of 'unfit' takes into account such matters as stability, serious disrepair, dampness, ventilation, natural lighting and inadequate services, and the state of one room may be sufficient to render the home unfit. The powers and duties of the authority have been diluted by the Housing Grants, Construction and Regeneration Act 1996 but an older tenant unable to contemplate bringing county court proceedings may still be able to provoke an inspection by making a complaint to the local Environmental Health department.

5.66 Under the 1996 Act the local authority may now decide not to take immediate action in relation to an unfit dwelling by serving a deferred action notice. This must be reviewed every 2 years. A repairs notice may be served on the owner of the property,[77] or a closing order or demolition order may be made. There are rights of appeal built into these procedures. It follows that if a tenant complains to the local authority about the condition of a tenanted home the outcome may be re-housing rather than the repair of that home.

Succession rights

5.67 A spouse, civil partner or cohabitee, or a member of the family living with the tenant for at least 2 years immediately prior to the death of the tenant, could succeed to a protected tenancy. Originally two successions were permitted (to a spouse and then to a member of the family) but this has been restricted since 1988 and a second succession is likely to convert the tenancy from protected to assured. The rules are complex and should be checked.[78]

5.68 Only a spouse, civil partner or cohabitee may have succession rights under an assured tenancy, and a second succession is not permitted.[79] This can cause problems

---

[75] Environmental Protection Act 1990, Part III.
[76] See generally Housing Act 1985, s 189.
[77] This may trigger eligibility for a housing grant which the authority will wish to avoid, hence the option of the deferred action notice.
[78] Rent Act 1977, s 2 and Sch 1 (as amended by Housing Act 1988).
[79] Housing Act 1988 s 17(2); Civil Partnership Act 2004.

when a widow or a widower who has succeeded to the tenancy remarries, because the second spouse will not have succession rights and may be obliged to vacate the home. The spousal relationship included 'living together as husband and wife' and may now extend to a same sex relationship as well as a civil partnership.[80]

5.69 In the case of a joint tenancy the surviving tenant will automatically succeed to the tenancy by survivorship but there can be no further transmission. Following the death of a tenant the landlord will have a mandatory ground for possession against a person who inherits under a will or intestacy provided that possession proceedings are brought within 12 months of the death (or later if the landlord only became aware of the death some time afterwards).

Termination

Regulated tenancies

5.70 In order to bring a regulated tenancy to an end the landlord must first serve a valid notice to quit to terminate the contractual tenancy (unless it is a statutory tenancy when no notice is required).[81] A possession order may only then be obtained on certain grounds which are discretionary (eg a breach of the terms of the tenancy such as non-payment of rent) or mandatory (eg the tenancy was originally created on a specific basis). The court may stay or suspend a possession order based on one of the discretionary grounds or postpone the date for possession (see below).

5.71 The *discretionary grounds* include unpaid rent, nuisance or annoyance, tenant having given notice to quit and unlawful assigning or sub-letting. They also enable the landlord to recover possession for another employee or for personal or family occupation (but a greater hardship test then applies and this ground is not available to a landlord by purchase).[82] A possession order will only be made if it is reasonable to do so and either one of these grounds has been made out or suitable alterative accommodation is available. If this latter basis applies the court has a discretion as to whether the new tenancy should be a statutory tenancy or an assured tenancy, but obviously an older tenant will want the former.

5.72 The *mandatory grounds* comprise a number of special situations such as lettings by owner-occupiers who have given notice of an intention to return, lettings for a period prior to retirement and lettings to persons employed in agriculture.

Assured tenancies

5.73 If a contractual fixed term assured tenancy is brought to an end, other than by an order of a court or by surrender, a periodic assured tenancy (called a 'statutory periodic tenancy') normally comes into existence. A periodic assured tenancy can only be brought to an end by a landlord obtaining an order of the court or by surrender. In order to bring the tenancy to an end the landlord first serves a notice of intention to seek possession specifying the grounds relied upon. This must be in the prescribed form and state that proceedings will not be commenced earlier than a specified date or later than 12

---

[80] *Ghaidan v Godin-Mendoza* [2004] UKHL 30. For the indicia of such a relationship that makes it equivalent to living as husband and wife see *Mark Nutting v Southern Housing Group Ltd* [2004] EWHC 2982, Ch.

[81] This must be in the prescribed form and give not less than four weeks' notice – Protection from Eviction Act 1977, s 5(1).

[82] Rent Act 1977, s 98 and Sch 15.

months.[83] The court has a limited power to dispense with service of this notice where it is just and equitable to do so (but not where defined arrears are relied upon).

5.74   The grounds are broadly similar to those for regulated tenancies save that 8 weeks' (or 2 months') rent arrears becomes a mandatory ground,[84] persistent failure to pay rent becomes a discretionary ground, and an intention by the landlord to demolish or reconstruct the property is a mandatory ground unless the landlord has purchased the property with that intention. Since 1996 anti-social behaviour has been a ground for possession.[85]

5.75   An assured tenancy cannot be brought to an end by the landlord except by obtaining an order of the court. The court will not make a possession order based on one of the discretionary grounds unless it is satisfied that it is reasonable to make the order and may stay or suspend the order or postpone the date for possession (see below).

Assured shorthold tenancies

5.76   Quite apart from the right to bring possession proceedings under the grounds mentioned above, and to seek a judgment for rent arrears where this is the basis for the application, an accelerated possession procedure is available for assured shorthold tenancies. This enables the landlord to serve a notice bringing the tenancy to an end[86] and in most instances to obtain an order for possession that takes effect within 14 days (or 42 days if exceptional hardship) without a court hearing.[87] This notice may be given before any fixed term expires or even at the beginning of the tenancy and need not be in any particular form, although it must be in writing. There is no power to dispense with service of the notice.

Tenancies – public sector

Background

5.77   We no longer talk of council house tenancies, but rather social housing rented accommodation provided by either a local authority or a registered social landlord. In many areas local authorities have transferred all their housing stock to registered social landlords in the form of housing associations which have their own housing allocation policies and there may be joint allocations policies with other such associations in the area. The local authority will continue to have a duty to advise homeless people how they can apply for social housing in the area and may also have specific responsibilities to some categories of homeless person. Other local authorities have transferred management of their housing stock to Arms Length Management Companies (ALMOs).

Allocation

5.78   There is no legal right to social housing and waiting lists are long, especially as the number of houses has decreased during recent years. Where a local authority has housing stock it has a discretion as to the manner in which it allocates tenancies, but

---

83   Housing Act 1988, s 8; Forms 3 and 4, Assured Tenancies and Agricultural Occupancies (Forms) Regulations 1988, SI 1988/2203 (as amended).
84   The 3-month period under the Housing Act 1988 was reduced by the Housing Act 1996.
85   Housing Act 1996, s 148.
86   The notice must comply with Housing Act 1988, s 21 and be of 2 months' duration terminating on a date when the tenancy can be brought to an end. Many of these notices in practice prove to be invalid.
87   Civil Procedure Rules 1998, rr 55.11–55.19.

must have an allocation scheme for determining priorities which is made public along with details of housing available and opportunity for applicants to express a preference.[88] The policy must give reasonable preference (amongst other considerations) to people who:

(1)   are homeless;

(2)   are living in unsatisfactory housing conditions;

(3)   need to move on medical grounds; and

(4)   need to move to a particular locality for reasons of hardship.

Financial resources available to meet housing costs may be taken into account as well as behaviour affecting suitability to be a tenant. Any attempt to impose a blanket condition that excludes consideration on the merits of a particular category of person or to discriminate on grounds of colour, race or sex is open to judicial review, but no general priority applies to elderly or disabled people.

5.79   An authority is deemed to allocate social housing when it grants a secure tenancy in relation to one of its own dwellings or a tenancy is granted by a registered social landlord under a nomination agreement with the authority. A 'qualifying person' is eligible for allocation of social housing and most older people will qualify and thereby be entitled to have their names on the housing register which the local authority is obliged to keep. An applicant on a waiting list is entitled to enquire how the application is proceeding and if dissatisfied with a decision (for example not to include him on the list or to remove him from the list) may seek an internal review of the decision which may be challenged by judicial review.

5.80   There is a tension between the allocation process and community care assessments that has yet to be resolved. Such assessment may reveal the urgent need for a different type of housing (for example a home without steps). The social services authority should seek to meet the assessed needs by providing services but cannot in so doing interfere with the allocation process of the housing authority. In a recent decision it was stated:

> 'It is not sufficient for the purposes of an assessment under [National Assistance Act 1948] merely to say that the claimant's housing needs can be dealt with by the housing department in accordance with its allocation policy.'

But it is unclear what else can be done. Section 21(8) of the 1948 Act provides that the Act does not 'authorise or require' a local authority to make any provision 'authorised or required to be made (whether by that or by any other authority) by or under any other enactment'. That would appear to prevent housing being provided under the 1948 Act,[89] but does not ensure that disability needs are adequately met by an allocations policy and appears to leave the disabled individual stranded between two distinct means of provision.

---

[88]   Housing Act 1996, Part VI (as amended by Homelessness Act 2002). Code of Guidance for Local Housing Authorities (2002); Choice Based Lettings: Code of Guidance for Local Authorities (2008); Fair & Flexible: Statutory Guidance on Social Housing Allocations for Local Authorities in England (2009).

[89]   See *Wahid v Tower Hamlets LBC* [2002] EWCA Civ 287, Hale LJ.

Types

Secure tenancies

5.81   Where the landlord is a prescribed public body such as a local authority[90] and (for tenancies created before 15 January 1989) a housing association, a *secure tenancy* may be created.[91] There are two prerequisites:

(1)   the property must be let as a separate dwelling (thereby excluding hostels where some accommodation is shared); and

(2)   the tenant must be one or more individuals occupying the property as their 'only or principal home'.

Security is not lost during temporary absence (eg in hospital) as long as there is an intention to return and some physical indication of continued occupation such as furniture or personal possessions remaining in the property. Sub-letting of the whole of premises means that any tenancy ceases to be secure but parting with possession is not to be inferred simply from the fact that another person has been allowed to use and occupy a tenant's home during his temporary absence.[92]

5.82   Contrary to the position as regards private sector tenancies, a licence to occupy may enjoy the same protection as a tenancy.[93] However, certain types of arrangement may not be secure tenancies, in particular long leases, short-term housing, business lettings and accommodation for homeless persons.[94] Security of tenure may be affected by any assignment or subletting that has taken place and the status of tenant may be lost where a possession order is made by a court.

Introductory tenancies

5.83   A local housing authority or housing action trust can elect to implement a scheme whereby all subsequent lettings by them (except to a former tenant) are introductory tenancies and not secure tenancies. This lasts for one year and then becomes a secure tenancy unless possession proceedings have been commenced. In that event and subject to the tenant's right to seek a review, the court has no discretion and if the notices are valid must make an order.[95]

5.84   The introductory tenancy is thus a 'probation period' with the tenancy only becoming a secure tenancy after that period. Introductory tenants have succession, assignment and repairing rights, but do not have the right to buy, take in lodgers, sub-let, improve or exchange.

---

90   Also an urban development corporation, housing co-operative or housing action trust.
91   Housing Act 1985, Part IV as amended by Housing and Planning Act 1986 and Housing Act 1988. Housing Associations now grant assured tenancies.
92   *Lam Kee Ying v Lam Shes Tong* [1975] AC 247, PC.
93   Housing Act 1985, s 79(3). The licence must not have been granted as a temporary expedient to someone who entered the premises as a trespasser.
94   Housing Act 1985, Sch 1.
95   The decision to terminate and the review are susceptible to judicial review during an adjournment of the possession claim – *Manchester City Council v Cochrane* [1999] 1 WLR 809, CA.

Terms

5.85 The landlord must set out the terms of the tenancy in clear and simple language and there are restrictions on the manner in which these terms can be changed in the absence of agreement between the parties. The landlord can serve a notice of variation and consultation is then required.

Rent

5.86 Local authorities may charge such reasonable rents as they may determine. The rent and any service charges can be increased by one month's notice without consultation, because these depend on housing policy rather than rent control. In practice the level of rents is influenced by government decisions as to the payment of subsidy to local authority housing revenue accounts. Also, under general administrative law principles they must act rationally, may not make perverse decisions and must take all relevant matters into account and not be influenced by irrelevant matters. The remedy for a breach would be judicial review.

State of repair

5.87 The landlord must keep the structure, exterior, services and installations in repair and working order regardless of the terms of any agreement, and if the landlord fails to do so a tenant who complies with certain procedural requirements may recover the cost of any qualifying repairs from the landlord.[96] Improvements to the property may only be carried out with the landlord's written consent but this must not be unreasonably refused.

5.88 A public sector landlord may become liable under the Defective Premises Act 1972 to anyone who suffers loss as a result of a failure to carry out repairs and maintenance to the premises and this may not depend on knowledge of the defects. A local authority was held liable to a visitor when a rotten floorboard in a council house collapsed, because the authority should have maintained reasonable arrangements for inspection of the premises when the defect would have come to light.[97]

5.89 Although the public law remedies mentioned above in respect of private sector tenancies are also available to council tenants, it is unlikely that a council will take itself to court. Where a *statutory nuisance* is alleged the tenant may apply to the magistrates' court, but legal aid is not available and there is a risk of a liability for costs if the tenant fails to discharge the burden of proof.[98] An alternative is for the tenant to ask a magistrate to declare the house unfit in which event the local authority will usually take some action though not obliged to do so.

Termination

5.90 Before the property is repossessed the landlord must first serve a notice of its intention to seek possession setting out the grounds on which the court will be requested to make an order. This notice is a prescribed form[99] and should contain sufficient information including the amount of the arrears if rent arrears are relied upon.[100] It

---

[96] Secure Tenancies (Right to Repair Scheme) Regulations 1985, SI 1985/1493.
[97] *Clark v Taff-Ely Borough Council* (1980) 10 HLR 44.
[98] The procedure is set out in Environmental Protection Act 1990, s 82.
[99] Secure Tenancies (Notices) Regulations 1987, SI 1997/775 (as amended).
[100] Housing Act 1985, s 83.

specifies a date after which proceedings may be brought which must not be earlier than the date on which the tenancy could otherwise be brought to an end by a notice to quit served by the landlord. The court has a limited power to dispense with service of this notice where it is 'just and equitable' to do so but will only do so in exceptional cases.[101]

5.91   If the problem is not then resolved, the landlord may apply to the local county court within 12 months for a possession order and justify this on one of 18 statutory grounds.[102] The grounds for possession fall into three groups:

(1)   those, including non-payment of rent or nuisance, where the court can only make the order if it considers it reasonable to do so;

(2)   those, including situations where there is overcrowding or the landlord needs possession of the building, where the court must make the order if satisfied as to the availability of suitable accommodation but must take into account certain factors; and

(3)   those where both these criteria apply because this group is intended to enable local authorities to manage their housing stock, for example by regaining possession of accommodation adapted for a disabled occupier which is no longer needed by the current tenant. Such proceedings must be commenced between 6 and 12 months after the death of the previous tenant, and the court must take into account the age of the tenant, the length of time the tenant has lived there and the financial and other support the tenant gave the previous disabled tenant.

5.92   It follows that no mandatory grounds exist, and the ground relied on must be stated and should be examined with care. Most applications are on the basis of non-payment of rent or nuisance, but in those cases the court may stay or suspend any possession order that is made and usually does so subject to conditions on the first occasion if the tenant wishes to remain in the property.[103] Official policy is:[104]

> '[Local authorities] should see that, where a tenant does have an arrears problem, there is an approved approach with officers giving warnings of graded severity, depending on the duration and scale of the arrears, building up to repossession of the dwellings as the final sanction.'

> 'Personal contact with tenants ... is important. As arrears often start with personal crises as an authority's initial response should be a sympathetic one, aimed at gaining if possible an understanding of the tenant's circumstances and tailoring the subsequent action to those specific circumstances ... the initial aim should be to help the tenant to avoid further arrears and to clear those already incurred.'

Passing on the tenancy

Assignment and subletting

5.93   The tenant has no general right to assign a secure tenancy. If a secure tenancy is assigned it ceases to be secure unless the assignment is made as part of a financial settlement following divorce or to a person with rights of succession. This need not be the person next entitled to succeed to the tenancy, so this option might be used to ensure

---

[101]   *Braintree DC v Vincent* [2004] EWCA Civ 415.
[102]   Housing Act 1985, Sch 2.
[103]   Housing Act 1985, ss 84 and 85.
[104]   Department of the Environment Circular 18/87, *Rent Arrears*.

that a child rather than a spouse succeeds to the tenancy. There are further provisions enabling a mutual exchange of secure tenancies to take place with the landlord's consent.[105]

5.94 Any subletting requires the written agreement of the landlord but this must not be unreasonably withheld or made subject to conditions. Failure to obtain consent could amount to a ground for possession. This does not apply to a lodger who is merely a licensee, and all secure tenants have the unconditional right to take in lodgers.[106] The distinction between a lodger and a sub-tenant is based upon control over the property and the degree of integration into the household.[107]

Succession

5.95 The spouse or civil partner of a deceased tenant, or another member of the family including a cohabitee, may be entitled to succeed to a secure tenancy where the tenanted property was that person's principal or only home at the date of the tenant's death.[108] In the case of a non-spouse or civil partner there is the further requirement that this person has lived in the tenanted property or in other public sector accommodation with the tenant for at least 12 months immediately prior to the tenant's death.[109] There can be only one succession, so if the tenancy has already passed to the spouse it cannot thereafter pass to a child and the survivor of a joint tenancy counts as having succeeded under the statute so a tenancy will rarely pass to the child of a couple.

Right to buy

5.96 Most secure tenants have the right to buy at a discount after 2 years under the Housing Act 1985, although certain types of property or tenancy may be excluded such as sheltered housing, properties particularly suitable for older people and most housing provided by charitable bodies. Those secure tenants whose tenancies have been transferred to registered social landlords have a preserved right to buy. Some assured tenants of registered social landlords have since been given a right to buy.[110]

5.97 Mortgages for the full amount payable can be obtained to cover the cost of the purchase and an interest only option may be available. The tenant may even nominate certain family co-residents to purchase the property jointly with the tenant, and if notice exercising the right to buy is served it may not be too late for a nominated person to proceed with the purchase after the death of the tenant.[111] The discount that is allowed on the property valuation depends upon the duration of the tenancy and can be up to 60% or even more in the case of a flat. Part of this discount is repayable in the event of a sale within 3 years of the discounted purchase but repayment is not required on the death of the tenant within that period.[112]

---

[105] Housing Act 1985, s 92.
[106] Housing Act 1985, s 93(1)(a).
[107] *Street v Mountford* [1985] 2 All ER 289, HL.
[108] Housing Act 1985, s 87; Civil Partnership Act 2004. This may now be to an assured tenancy (but not a shorthold).
[109] Housing Act 1985, s 113. *Waltham Forest LBC v Thomas* [1992] 3 All ER 244, HL.
[110] Housing Act 1996, s 16.
[111] *Harrow LBC v Tonge* (1992) 9 LGR 81, CA. In *Bradford MCC v McMahon* [1993] 4 All ER 237, CA it was held that the council tenant must remain a secure tenant until the conveyance. It was suggested that the tenant might have obtained an injunction before death requiring the council to convey the house.
[112] See Housing Act 1985, Part V, as amended by Housing and Planning Act 1986.

5.98 It will not always be beneficial for an elderly secure tenant to purchase the property even if a substantial discount is available. For those on a limited income, interest on any mortgage arranged for the purpose may be covered by income support but mortgage interest tax relief is no longer available and housing benefit cannot be claimed because the rent ceases. The owner will become responsible for property insurance, all repairing obligations and any service charges (as before).

5.99 Family members may offer to underwrite the mortgage and repair costs but serious problems arise if they later prove unable to do so. Some older people buy their council home with financial assistance from members of the family who do not reside therein. In each of these situations it is important to record the basis in a legal document (ie is it a gift or a loan, and if the latter, on what terms is the loan made) and to ensure that any inheritance expectations will be fulfilled, especially if there are other members of the family who are not involved in the arrangement.

Licences

Types

5.100 A licence may take many forms and will arise whenever an individual who is not an owner or tenant occupies a property or even part of a property. A written agreement is not necessary, although clearly it is desirable when regular payments of money are involved that the terms be recorded in writing. This may be in a specific document or some other standard document that is referred to, such as a brochure for the home.

5.101 A bare licence arises where the individual merely lives in the home of someone else by permission but without making any payment. A contractual licence exists where there is an arrangement which includes regular payments but the rights of occupation fall short of a tenancy, perhaps because there is not exclusive occupation of the facilities. A 'licence coupled with an interest' may be created when the occupier has made some payment or contribution in the expectation of being allowed to remain as part of the household but does not thereafter make regular payments. The test of whether an occupier has a tenancy or a licence is one of substance rather than form, and depends largely on whether there is exclusive possession with a rent being paid.

5.102 In many situations an elderly person merely has a licence to occupy the property or facilities that represent that person's home. This may be an exclusive licence where the accommodation is self-contained, a licence to occupy a private room where other essential facilities are shared or merely a licence to share a room and other facilities. In the latter case the only exclusive facility may be a bed, wardrobe and chest of drawers. Care services may also be provided on a formal or informal basis, and the individual may be dependent on these.

Arrangements with family

5.103 If the arrangement is within the family there may merely be an informal (or bare) licence to occupy the room or facilities and this is unlikely to have a legal basis although if the court is asked to exclude an informal licensee from a property it may postpone any order for a reasonable period to allow alternative arrangements to be made. If the elderly person makes regular payments a contract could arise but it will be difficult in the family context to interpret as a commercial payment what may merely have been a contribution towards the household expenses. On the other hand a licence coupled with an interest may arise where the occupier contributes towards the cost of buying, altering or improving the home. Whilst it may be possible to enforce the right to remain in the home, if personal care services have been provided by the family as well as the accommodation these will be less easy to enforce and the whole arrangement then becomes no longer be viable.

Arrangements with strangers

5.104 If the arrangement is with strangers and depends upon making regular payments there will at the very least be a contractual licence even in the absence of a written agreement or express terms having been agreed. This is the position where a person pays for a room in an hotel or a residential care home or becomes a lodger, and the terms of the contract should be complied with. Failure to recognise this is to deny the individual fundamental occupation rights and freedoms such as the right to a period of notice before changes are imposed or the arrangement is terminated. Not only may the court construe the terms of the contract and award damages for any breach, it may also refuse to allow eviction of the occupier in breach of those terms or grant an injunction to prevent such breach. The problem usually lies in determining what the terms are when they have not been reduced to writing or otherwise clearly spelt out.

Possession proceedings

Orders

5.105 An order of the local county court is required before a residential occupier may be evicted. Applications for possession orders are dealt with by district judges in their chambers in the local county court. There are pre-action Protocols for possession claims based on rent arrears and also for mortgage arrears and these must be followed by the landlord or lender.[113] The occupier should attend or arrange legal representation at the initial hearing and respond to the evidence then presented by the claimant. Many claims are disposed of at that stage by a possession order (which may be immediate, suspended or postponed) but there may be an adjournment and if the claim is genuinely disputed on grounds which appear to be substantial directions will be given for a full trial. A claim for mortgage or rent arrears may be dealt with at the same time.[114]

Mortgages

5.106 When payments under a mortgage (or legal charge) fall into arrears or the loan is otherwise called in, the lender can apply to the local county court for a possession order and also a judgment for the arrears or, if the terms of the deed so provide, the full amount of the loan. A hearing takes place in a matter of weeks and if a possession order is made this may be enforced by the bailiff under a warrant for possession. In the case of a repayment or endowment mortgage of a dwelling the court has power[115] to adjourn, stay or suspend if the arrears are likely to be paid during a 'reasonable period', which can mean the remaining term of the mortgage.[116] There is no such power where there are 'all moneys' charges securing, for example bank overdrafts which are repayable on demand.[117]

---

[113] These are available at: www.justice.gov.uk/courts/procedure-rules/civil/protocol.
[114] Civil Procedure Rules 1998, Part 55 and PD55.
[115] Administration of Justice Act 1970, s 36 or in some cases Consumer Credit Act 1974.
[116] *Cheltenham and Gloucester Building Society v Norgan* [1996] 1 All ER 449, CA.
[117] *Habib Bank v Tailor* [1982] 1 WLR 1218, CA.

5.107 The claimants are also entitled to a money judgment for the outstanding balance if they seek this, but if the possession order is suspended it is usual to suspend the money judgment on the same terms.[118] In the case of loans under the Consumer Credit Acts the court has extensive powers to make a 'Time Order' giving more time to pay or to intervene where there is an extortionate credit bargain. It is normal to order 'costs to be added to security' (ie added to the mortgage account) or to say nothing about costs and to leave the lender to rely upon the terms of the mortgage deed. The court may only order 'costs not to be added to security' if there has been unreasonable conduct by the lender.[119]

5.108 A suspended possession order is a common outcome, whereby possession is ordered within 28 days but the warrant cannot issue as long as the borrower pays the normal monthly subscriptions under the mortgage and also an additional sum calculated to clear the arrears before the end of the mortgage term (or a little longer if that date is approaching). If the borrower is seeking to sell the property the proceedings may be adjourned for a period to see what progress can be made or an order for possession may be made but postponed for a period to give the borrower a reasonable time to effect a sale. The approach of the court may be influenced by whether there is any equity in the property (because the lender is not then at risk), the amount of the arrears, the circumstances of the borrower and the conduct of the borrower in relation to the loan.

5.109 It is not unusual for possession proceedings to arise where there has been a problem with some arrangement within the family for the provision of a home for an elderly member. A mortgage may have been arranged in reliance upon the willingness or ability of a son or daughter to meet the monthly subscriptions, or the elderly person may have made substantial financial contributions towards a home owned by a son or daughter who has fallen behind with mortgage payments. The judge will be reluctant to make young children or elderly people homeless so these factors should be drawn to the attention of the court where they exist. An adjournment of the possession proceedings may be granted to allow further time for the family to sort out the financial problem, but at the end of the day the terms of the mortgage must be performed and the court only has a limited discretion to grant relief. It is always important to ascertain the date when the mortgage was completed, because an elderly person who was already in occupation of the house at that time and did not agree to the mortgage may have rights that take effect in priority to those of the lender. An immediate possession order would not then be granted.

5.110 Problems also arise where older people offer their homes as security for loans taken out by younger members of their family and the borrower defaults on the loan repayment. This can result in the prospect of the older person becoming homeless at a time of increasing dependency upon others. The circumstances in which the security was provided must then be scrutinised and it is relevant as to whether independent advice was provided.

Tenancies

5.111 In the case of a secure tenancy, or an assured tenancy where the landlord is relying upon a discretionary ground for possession such as rent arrears, the landlord must prove:

---

[118] *Cheltenham and Gloucester Building Society v Grattidge* (1993) 25 HLR 454, CA.

[119] See CPR, r 48.3, s 50 of the Costs Practice Direction and *Gomba Holdings (UK) Ltd v Minories Finance Ltd (No 2)* [1993] Ch 171, [1992] 4 All ER 588, CA.

(1)   the tenancy (normally by producing the tenancy agreement);

(2)   service of the requisite notice seeking possession or of intention to bring proceedings;[120]

(3)   the arrears or other ground for possession; and

(4)   that it is reasonable to make an order for possession.

This last requirement, which does not apply for a mandatory ground, means that even if the ground is proved, the court has a choice of orders – outright possession order, suspended order, adjournment to another fixed, general adjournment, adjournment on terms, no order or dismissal of the claim.

5.112 The possession order is frequently suspended on payment of the arrears by instalments and unlike mortgage possession proceedings, the court is not restricted to doing so only where the arrears are likely to be cleared within a reasonable period. Where an elderly tenant has become confused and needs help to get financial affairs in order or to sort out claims for state benefits or housing benefit, the court is likely to adjourn the hearing to a later date.

5.113 Where the landlord is relying upon a mandatory ground for possession the maximum period of time that can be allowed before a possession order takes effect is 14 days, unless exceptional hardship would be caused, in which case the maximum period is 6 weeks.[121] It was held that when considering whether it was reasonable to make a possession order based on the behaviour of a mentally disordered tenant, a higher threshold may be imposed by the Disability Discrimination Act 1995, but it was still possible to justify eviction.[122]

Warrants for possession

5.114 If a possession order is not complied with the claimant may issue a warrant of possession and the court bailiff then gives the occupier notice of the date for eviction. The occupier may apply to the court for the warrant to be suspended and the court has a discretion unless the possession order was made on a mandatory ground. Even then the judge may direct the bailiff to arrange a later date. The court when exercising its discretion on an application to suspend a warrant may take account of matters (eg breaches of the terms of the tenancy agreement or anti-social behavior) other than those relied upon as grounds for making the original possession order.[123]

5.115 Once the warrant has been executed, there is no jurisdiction to suspend unless the original possession order is set aside or the warrant has been obtained by fraud, oppression or abuse of process.[124]

---

[120]   Unless the court considers it just and equitable to dispense with that requirement.
[121]   Housing Act 1980, s 89.
[122]   See *North Devon Homes Ltd v Brazier* [2003] EWHC 574 (QB) and *Manchester City Council v Romano* [2004] EWCA Civ 834.
[123]   *Sheffield City Council v Hopkins* [2001] EWCA Civ 1023.
[124]   *Hammersmith and Fulham LBC v Hill* (1995) 27 HLR 368.

General

5.116 A court order is generally required before any person may be turned out of or excluded from accommodation that has become that person's home.[125] In those instances where the court has a discretion the age and state of health of the occupiers may be a factor to be taken into consideration. It has been held that the procedure for issuing warrants of possession by administrative request whereby a bailiff then performs the eviction is not a breach of the occupiers' human rights,[126] because those rights are determined when the possession order is made. However, concern was expressed that the occupier was not notified of the request and thereby given a realistic opportunity to challenge the eviction by a further application to the county court, so the bailiff must now deliver a Notice of Eviction (Form N54) to the property in advance of the eviction. This explains the procedure for applying for a suspension of the warrant.

Spousal rights

5.117 A spouse in occupation of the matrimonial home has a right not to be evicted during the marriage unless the court otherwise orders, and a spouse not in occupation has a right, with leave of the court, to enter and occupy the home.[127] These rights are independent of ownership and may be binding on third parties (such as mortgagees) in certain circumstances. In the case of a tenancy in the name of the husband, a wife's occupation and payment of rent is as good as if by the husband thereby preserving the tenancy, and on divorce the court can transfer the tenancy although it seems that unless prevented by an injunction any party to the tenancy can sabotage this by giving notice to the landlord.

5.118 Rights of occupation may be protected by an entry on the registered title of the home, but notice will automatically be given to the registered owner. Such rights may be enforced as part of an injunction by excluding from the home a spouse, including a co-owner, where this is necessary for the protection of the other party (an *ouster order*), although a bedroom exclusion order coupled with a non-molestation injunction may be sufficient.

Unlawful eviction

5.119 Residential occupiers, including most licensees as well as tenants, are protected against unlawful eviction to the extent that at least 4 weeks' notice is required to terminate a contractual tenancy and a court order is required before eviction can take place. An injunction may be applied for following threats of eviction to prohibit conduct making occupation difficult (such as cutting off services) or restore possession. Civil remedies are available and such conduct may even amount to an offence.

Damages claims

5.120 An action for damages may be brought for trespass or breach of contract (or covenant) where there has been unlawful eviction. This may seek general, specific, aggravated and exemplary damages.

---

[125] There are exceptions, such as where there is shared accommodation and a resident landlord, but it is prudent in any event to seek a court order.
[126] Ie does not breach Articles 6, 8 or 14 of the European Convention on Human Rights.
[127] Family Law Act 1996 (previously Matrimonial Homes Act 1983).

5.121 A statutory tort has also been created where a landlord (or someone acting on his behalf) either unlawfully deprives an occupier of premises or intends to do so or knowing that his conduct is likely to cause the occupier to give up occupation does acts calculated to interfere with the occupier's peace and comfort, as a result of which the occupier gives up occupation.[128] The measure of damages for this tort, in addition to any other damages awarded, is the difference in value of the premises with and without the occupancy. This could be a considerable figure for a tenant who had security of tenure at a restricted rent, but may not be significant in the present buy-to-let housing market.

Criminal offences

5.122 A landlord (or persons acting on his behalf) who harasses or evicts or attempts to evict an occupier may commit a criminal offence. It is an offence to harass a residential occupier with intent to cause that occupier to give up occupation (in whole or part) or any right or remedy, and the withholding or withdrawing of services may amount to harassment. The act must be likely to interfere with the peace and comfort of the occupier. It is sufficient if an offender 'knows or has reasonable cause to believe' that the conduct is likely to cause the occupier to leave and specific intent need not be proved.[129] Local housing authorities must employ an officer to investigate and prosecute cases of harassment.

Implications

5.123 An application to the court for a possession order in respect of the home of an elderly person may be the first indication that the individual is no longer coping and is in need of some support, so everyone involved should be alert to this possibility. The provision of community care services or assistance in dealing with financial affairs[130] may avoid the need for a possession order, and if it is no longer possible for the individual to remain in the home a different procedure for re-housing may be appropriate. Where the court recognises this situation the hearing may be adjourned to a later date for an investigation to take place.

5.124 When guidance is offered to a defendant occupier present at the hearing, doubts may arise as to whether that person is capable of taking effective action especially as this situation has been allowed to develop in the first place. The court will be concerned to ensure that at an adjourned hearing a different picture emerges. If the action relates to a council house the local housing authority will be a party and may be asked by the court to refer the tenant's needs to the social services department with a view to an assessment being made. In other cases the claimant may be invited to communicate with the social services department on this basis and the court can indicate that unless satisfied about this a possession order is unlikely even at the adjourned hearing. It is helpful if the adjournment notice expressly indicates the reason for the adjournment and the judge should be asked to provide for this. It is not the usual policy for courts to communicate direct with social services departments and they have no power to require the attendance of a representative from that department.

---

[128] Housing Act 1988, ss 27 and 28.
[129] Protection from Eviction Act 1977 (as amended by Housing Act 1988).
[130] See Chs 7 and 10 respectively.

SPECIAL PROVISION

Preliminary

5.125 The needs of an elderly person may be such that special provision relating to accommodation must be made to meet those needs. Such provision may not relate exclusively to older people and will not be needed by them all, but is of great importance to those for whom it is intended. The provision contemplated under this heading comprises accommodation for homeless persons, special housing for elderly or disabled persons and housing grants to enable an existing home to be made suitable for continued occupation.

Homeless persons

Background

5.126 For many years local housing authorities have been placed under a statutory duty to provide or arrange housing or accommodation for individuals for whom they were responsible who were actually and unintentionally homeless and had a priority need.[131] The authorities were not necessarily obliged to provide accommodation of a particular type or best suited to an individual's needs and, whilst most authorities sought to cater for special needs, the accommodation available might not be suitable. Moral pressure could be applied in such circumstances but there was no legal remedy unless perhaps it could be argued that the accommodation was so unsuitable that the individual could be deemed to be still homeless. If the applicant was also in need of care and attention the provision of residential accommodation[132] might be sufficient, but not where there was a personal carer living with the applicant. The authority could charge for the accommodation provided, but only a person who did not have the means to obtain accommodation was likely to turn to the local authority for housing.[133]

Intentionally homeless

5.127 Those who were both homeless and had a priority need were entitled to permanent accommodation unless classed as *intentionally homeless* in which event they would only be housed on a temporary basis. This term has been the subject of much litigation, but appears to mean having deliberately given up accommodation which there is a right to occupy or failing to do what is necessary to keep such accommodation. However, an act or omission should not be seen as deliberate where the applicant was incapable of managing his or her affairs because of old age or mental illness. In the event of an adverse decision the only legal remedies were a complaint to the ombudsman or application for judicial review, but an appeal procedure might be offered by the council and in that event this had to first be utilised.

Applications for assistance

5.128 A person who is homeless or threatened with homelessness may be eligible for some assistance from the local authority. The authority may have a duty to provide

---

[131] This duty was introduced by Housing (Homeless Persons) Act 1977 and replaced by Housing Act 1985, Part III and then Housing Act 1996, Part VII (as amended by Homelessness Act 2002).

[132] Under Part III of the National Assistance Act 1948 – see Chs 6 and 7.

[133] Where the request for help was due to the personal inadequacies of the individual rather than lack of financial resources it would be appropriate to involve social services.

temporary accommodation to an applicant who is actually homeless, eligible for assistance and has a priority need, and also has a duty to protect the property of a homeless person or one who is threatened with homelessness.[134] A person in inadequate accommodation could be deemed to be homeless, and this may be so where it is no longer reasonable for an elderly person to continue to occupy their existing home. A person who lacks mental capacity may not be able to make their own homelessness application and may depend upon the support of another person,[135] although in this situation the community care obligations of the local authority may arise.[136]

Priority need

5.129 Being homeless is not by itself sufficient unless the applicant can show a *priority need*. The defined categories include, in addition to having dependent children or being pregnant, being *vulnerable* as a result of 'old age, mental illness or handicap or physical disability or some other special reason'. An applicant who has such a person living with him or who might reasonably be expected to live with him will have a priority need. In this context vulnerable means 'less able to fend for oneself so that injury or detriment will result, when a less vulnerable man (or woman) will be able to cope without harmful effects'.[137] The authority must first ask whether the applicant is vulnerable and then decide whether this is a result of one of the factors specified above, so evidence in support of the application should spell out how and why age or disability makes the applicant vulnerable. Failure by the authority to consider this would amount to a breach of its obligations.

5.130 Old age alone is not sufficient for the applicant to be deemed vulnerable, but the *Codes of Guidance*[138] states that the authority should consider whether old age is a factor which makes an applicant less able to fend for himself. The guidance advises that applications from persons over 60 years of age must be carefully considered especially when the applicant is leaving tied accommodation. Each case must be considered on its individual circumstances.

Threatened homelessness

5.131 Homelessness can arise in various ways and may include being threatened with homelessness. A person can be considered to be threatened with homelessness if he will become homeless within 28 days. Accommodation can only be regarded as available if this would extend to someone such as a spouse (or carer) who normally resides with the individual.[139] It has been held that where a court ordered possession of accommodation occupied by a person, that person was threatened with homelessness from the date of the order, but became homeless from the date on which a warrant of possession was enforced. Where an application for housing assistance based on threatened homelessness was made to a local authority, the authority could not remain inactive and do nothing until eviction, but immediately had to undertake an inquiry to determine whether the applicant was eligible for assistance and what duty was owed to him, and take steps to

---

[134] Housing Act 1996, s 212.
[135] *R v Tower Hamlets LBC, ex p Begum* [1993] AC 509.
[136] See Ch 7.
[137] *R v Camden LBC, ex p Pereira* (1999) 31 HLR 317, CA.
[138] *Homelessness Code of Guidance for Local Authorities* (2006) and *Supplementary Guidance on Intentional Homelessness* (2009) issued by Secretary of State available at: www.gov.uk/government/uploads/system/uploads/attachment_data/file/7841/152056.pdf and 7842/1304826.pdf.
[139] Housing Act 1996, s 175.

secure accommodation where satisfied that the applicant was threatened with homelessness, eligible for assistance and in priority need.[140]

The modern approach

5.132 The Homelessness Act 2002 requires these authorities to take a more strategic, multi-agency approach to the prevention of homelessness and the re-housing of homeless households. It ensures that everyone accepted by housing authorities as unintentionally homeless and in priority need must be provided with suitable accommodation until they obtain a settled housing solution, but allows housing authorities greater flexibility to assist non-priority homeless households, principally through a power for housing authorities to secure accommodation for such households where they have scope to do so. It facilitates lettings policies which offer more choice to homeless people and others in housing need with the aim of helping to create sustainable communities, tackle social exclusion and make better use of the national housing stock. It abolishes the former duty on housing authorities to consider whether other suitable accommodation was available before they could secure accommodation themselves and provides additional circumstances in which the applicant can bring the main homelessness duty to an end by accepting an assured tenancy.

5.133 Applicants are entitled to seek review of decisions as to suitability of accommodation whether or not they have accepted accommodation, and have a right of appeal against a local authority's refusal to accommodate pending appeal. An appeal is to the county court and must be brought within 21 days of an applicant being notified of the decision but there is power to extend time for good reason.

Special housing

Sheltered housing

5.134 Housing restricted to and designed so as to be suitable for elderly people may be an option for those who want to live an independent life in their own home without all the responsibilities of home ownership.[141] Most of the provision that is available comprises apartments or bungalows, but physical disabilities may be catered for and alarm systems are often installed. Schemes include purpose-built or converted housing without a warden and warden-assisted or warden-controlled housing.[142]

5.135 There is also supportive housing where residents have their own room but use communal facilities and perhaps receive a cooked daily meal[143] and housing with care where meals and care services are provided. Residents remain entitled to community care services and the warden may play a key role in facilitating these.

---

[140] *R v Newham London Borough Council, ex p Khan* (2000) *The Times*, 9 May.

[141] Guidance is available at: www.ageuk.org.uk/home-and-care/housing-choices/sheltered-housing/. There is a Factsheet available.

[142] In 2005 there were 30,000 'almshouse' dwellings providing accommodation for over 36,000 people in the heart of the community for modest charges. The occupier is a beneficiary of the charitable trust rather than a tenant – *Gray v Taylor* [1998] 1 WLR 1093. See www.almshouses.org.

[143] Eg houses under the Abbeyfield scheme which has some 550 member societies providing accommodation for several people in their own rooms in large house with communal facilities and a resident housekeeper. See www.abbeyfield.com.

Purchased homes

5.136 Tenure may be freehold but shared ownership or shared equity arrangements exist, and also loan-stock schemes under which entitlement to housing arises upon the making of an interest-free loan to a trust (which may be a charity). There are opportunities to buy at a discount, though this usually involves selling at a discount,[144] or to buy a 'life-share' in the whole or part of a property. This is usually organised through a finance company, the price paid depending upon age, sex, marital status and the property value, and there will be no return on death, but an annuity (or capital sum) may be paid to those who cease to reside in the property. Alternatively tenure may be on the basis of a long lease at a premium with a service-charge rent, but enfranchisement may nevertheless be possible for some leasehold sheltered housing schemes.

5.137 Before entering into any such scheme it is important to ascertain the detailed terms of the purchase or lease. Questions to be asked include what are the warden's duties, what services are provided, what is the service charge liability and is there a 'sinking fund' for property repairs. The identity of the managers of the scheme should be ascertained[145] and also whether there is a residents' association recognised by the managers. Any restrictions on resale or assignment should be identified because problems have arisen over disposal of some homes following death. Further information on sheltered housing schemes is available from a number of sources.[146]

Rented homes

5.138 There may also be an ordinary tenancy at a rent. Where sheltered housing is provided by the private sector there may be no statutory protection if 'attendance' is included, and some residents may be little more than licensees. Such schemes in the public sector will be secure or assured tenancies.

5.139 Since April 2003 many of the services provided by sheltered landlords that were previously funded by housing benefit are now funded directly by the local authority through the *Supporting People Programme*, a government initiative to bring together the professionals involved in providing housing and welfare support to vulnerable people. Housing benefit remains available for the rent but landlords are funded directly for services such as emergency alarms and wardens although the local authority can reclaim the cost from residents on a means-tested basis.

Regulation

5.140 There is no specific legislation to regulate sheltered housing. Leaseholders have some rights regarding service charges and a residents association may be recognised and entitled to be consulted in certain circumstances. Registered house builders selling sheltered housing are to comply with a *Code of Practice* issued by the National House-Building Council[147] under which any legally binding management agreements must comply with a specified standard. A Purchaser's Information Pack (PIP) is supplied

---

[144] Under leasehold schemes for the elderly (LSE) run by a small number of housing associations, the resident buys at a discount (eg 70%) of the normal price and receives the same percentage of the value upon a sale. See: www.housingcare.org/jargon-leasehold-schemes-for-the-elderly-07285.aspx.

[145] It helps if they are members of the Association of Retirement Housing Managers which has issued a Code of Practice: see www.arhm.org.

[146] See in particular *A Buyer's Guide to Sheltered Housing*, published by AgeUK and *Shared Ownership*, a Housing Corporation leaflet.

[147] See www.nhbc.co.uk.

which contains useful information and must be kept up to date, and the managing agents must supply the pack to subsequent purchasers.

Homes for disabled people

5.141 The Housing Act 1988 changed the role of local authorities to that of strategic planner rather than direct provider and housing associations are now encouraged to increase their use of private sector finance with a commensurate decrease in reliance on the public sector. Special grants are available from the Housing Corporation for housing associations which provide houses for disabled people but the take-up on this has been below expectations. However, local housing authorities have a general duty to consider the housing needs of their district and must have particular regard for the special needs of chronically sick and disabled people.[148]

Adaptations

5.142 If a local authority[149] is satisfied that the home of a disabled person fails to meet special needs arising from the disability, it is under a statutory duty to ensure that those needs are met by arranging for any necessary adaptations to be made.[150] This applies whether the home is owner-occupied or tenanted. The authority may recover the cost, but cannot make the provision dependent upon prior payment though the disabled person will first wish to know the cost implications. Additional help from this source may not be provided to the extent that grants are available, but it should be considered by those who cannot cope with the means-testing implications of a grant and it is not clear whether the availability of a grant excludes entitlement to adaptations that are needed.

5.143 Building alterations are subject to value added tax, but many alterations in the homes of people with disabilities are zero-rated. These include constructing ramps and widening doors or passages to enable the person to enter or move within their home, and providing a bathroom, washroom or toilet for the first time on the ground floor, or extending or adapting an existing bathroom, washroom or lavatory where this is necessary because of the disabilities. Vertical lifts and distress alarm systems supplied to disabled people are also zero-rated.

Housing grants

5.144 A framework of grants for renovation, repair, improvement and adaptation of houses in England and Wales was introduced in July 1990[151] but was changed by further legislation in 1996.[152] Owners or tenants of properties may be able to have the whole cost of grant works paid for by the local authority if they have a low income and this will not affect any benefits being received. A range of grants is available including housing renovation grants, disabled facilities grants, home repair assistance, houses in multiple occupation grants, common parts grants and group repair schemes. Although an elderly person may be eligible for any of these, we only consider the grant that is specifically intended to cover the needs of disabled people. It may be possible to make a combined application for a disabled facilities grant and a renovation grant.

---

[148] See generally Ch 7.
[149] This will generally be the district or borough council.
[150] Chronically Sick and Disabled Persons Act 1970, s 2. The claimant need not be on the Register of disabled people.
[151] Local Government and Housing Act 1989, Part VIII.
[152] Housing Grants, Construction and Regeneration Act 1996.

Disabled facilities grants

5.145 Mandatory but means-tested grants are available for certain types of work which, after consultation with the social services department, are deemed necessary and appropriate to meet the needs of an occupier who is disabled.[153] The works include:

- facilitating access to and from the dwelling, or to the main family room or the disabled occupier's bedroom;

- facilitating access to or providing a room in which there is a lavatory, bath, shower or washhand basin, or facilitating the use of such facility;

- facilitating preparation/cooking of food by such occupier;

- improving any (or providing a suitable) heating system;

- facilitating the use of a source of power, light or heat by altering the position of the means of access to or control of that source or providing additional means of control; and

- providing facilities for carers.

If a grant is approved the disabled person will have to arrange and supervise the work within the limited funding available, but the local authority can refuse payment or require repayment if the work is not to a satisfactory standard and in accordance with its specification, and it must usually be completed within a year. This may be a real problem if the applicant is also mentally disabled, but home improvement agencies exist in many areas which can help with the application for a grant, and thereafter with arrangement and supervision of the work.[154]

5.146 A person is disabled for this purpose if registered (or eligible for registration) as disabled or if he has had welfare arrangements made under s 29(1) of the National Assistance Act 1948 or in the opinion of the social services department such arrangements might have been made. To establish this the housing authority which deals with the grant must consult the social services department. The housing authority must also be satisfied that it is reasonable and practicable to carry out the relevant works having regard to the age and condition of the dwelling or building. The disabled person must normally live in the dwelling but, so long as the work is intended for his benefit, does not have to be the owner or tenant, though a multiple means-test may then apply in establishing the joint borrowing capacity. The same means-test applies as for other types of grant and is based upon many factors so details are not set out here, but disability costs are not taken into account.

5.147 Although a decision should be made within 6 months there may be considerable delays in obtaining reports from surveyors and occupational therapists, and these reports may conflict.[155] A disabled facilities grant may be available for works to the common parts of a building containing one or more flats if the disabled occupant has power or is under a duty to carry out the works. Discretionary grants are available for other work for the purpose of making a dwelling suitable for the accommodation, welfare and employment of a disabled occupant.

---

[153] These grants have been the subject of many complaints to the ombudsman, usually on account of delay.

[154] These agencies receive their core funding from the Department of the Environment.

[155] Despite delay in obtaining occupational therapists reports it is believed that many local authorities will not rely upon reports obtained by a health authority. The ombudsman has said in an annual report that if professionals are in short supply authorities should find another way of discharging their functions.

SPECIAL ARRANGEMENTS

Preliminary

5.148 An older person living in their own home may wish or need to contemplate an arrangement relating to that home, either in order to be able to continue living in the home or with a view to preserving the home or its value for the next generation. Alternatively, the home may be disposed of and the older person may live with other members of the family, perhaps investing money in their home or making a gift to them. The legal implications of some of these arrangements are considered under this heading, but in all cases before making the arrangements the effect on state benefits and tax liabilities should be taken into account by both parties. Such arrangements may also have funding implications if the older person subsequently moves into a residential care or nursing home.

Sharing the home

Preliminary

5.149 Either financial circumstances or care needs may dictate that elderly people share their homes. This could involve allowing a relative or friend to move in, taking in a lodger, or employing a resident housekeeper or carer. Where the arrangement is with a stranger for payment it is essential to identify the understandings and assumptions on which it is based, from both points of view, and it is desirable that these should be recorded in writing.[156] A formal document is not necessary and an exchange of letters may be sufficient. When the arrangement is with a member of the family there is a danger that one party takes advantage of the other if the personal and financial arrangements are not openly discussed in advance.

Family arrangements

5.150 Frequently shared occupation arises without any planning where a son or (more often) a daughter remains at home with parent(s). Often the parties rely on assumptions and fail to discuss their hopes and wishes. Mother may actually desire to move into a residential care home but not wish to leave her daughter alone, whilst the daughter may yearn for freedom yet not wish to be seen to desert mother. Other children who have moved away, enjoyed their freedom and raised a family may be favoured whilst the dedicated child who has stayed at home and adopted a caring role is taken for granted.

5.151 In these situations the departure or death of the parent may result in the member of the family who has stayed at home and become a carer suddenly becoming homeless without any recompense. This situation should be anticipated in any will, and whilst the manner and extent to which this is done is a matter for personal choice, it is important that the reality of the situation is appreciated.

5.152 Sometimes a relative comes to stay in the home of an elderly person at a time of crisis, perhaps due to bereavement or ill-health, and the visit is prolonged or becomes permanent. The outcome is that the elderly person is able to continue living at home with minimum changes to an established pattern of life dictated solely by a decline in personal faculties. By contrast, the lifestyle of the caring relative will be radically

---

[156] For precedents see: *Living Together Precedents*, Bowler and Ors, Sweet & Maxwell.

changed, and yet the expectations of both parties will seldom be discussed. The new relationship may even give rise to suspicion amongst other relatives. It is suggested that a meeting be arranged for all concerned members of the family to discuss with the elderly person the nature of the new arrangements, the financial implications to all parties, the extent to which other members of the family will participate and the longer term intentions. Whilst it may be unrealistic to expect that a formal agreement would be drawn up, it does no harm for notes of the conclusions to be made and signed by all those present. In this way detrimental misunderstandings within the family may be avoided and the contributions of all members coordinated.

5.153 These issues have only tended to reach the courts in the past couple of decades, but in an early case it was held that where a carer who provided her services without charge was given assurances that she would be allowed to continue to live in the house for the rest of her life, the burden of proving that she acted to her detriment did not rest with her. In the absence of proof to the contrary it would be inferred that her conduct was induced by the assurances and she would be allowed to remain in the house as long as she wished.[157]

Subletting or taking lodgers

5.154 In law there is a fundamental distinction between subletting part of the home and taking in a lodger, but in practice this distinction may become blurred especially when an elderly person is involved. The physical layout of the house may be relevant in deciding whether an occupant is a lodger or a sub-tenant because the distinction is really between two households and one. A subletting involves the grant of a tenancy of specific accommodation and the tenant will have the exclusive right to occupy that accommodation even if other facilities must be shared. The normal attributes of a tenancy will apply even though there may be no security of tenure because there is a resident landlord. By contrast, a lodger merely has a contractual licence to occupy part of the premises and to share other facilities, and cleaning services and meals will usually be provided. Whatever the legal nature of the arrangement, the notice period and weekly or other payment to be made should be confirmed in advance (preferably in writing) and also what it covers (eg meals, laundry, light and heating, hot water, telephone).

5.155 Taking a lodger may produce an additional income and, if the relationship works out, provide company for the elderly person but it is a more personal relationship than merely subletting part of the premises. It is not likely to amount to a breach of the terms of any mortgage or tenancy under which the property is held. The treatment of the income from the arrangement will also be different for tax purposes although there is presently an HMRC concession for income from letting one room. The effect of the additional income on any means-tested state benefits should not be overlooked.

Employing a housekeeper or carer

5.156 If a housekeeper or carer is to live in this will be an employment situation, but by contrast living in the home of a carer may be classed as being a boarder. Employing a housekeeper involves all the responsibilities of being a small employer including the obligation to make a redundancy payment at the end of the arrangement[158] and the risk

---

[157] *Greasley v Cooke* [1980] 1 WLR 1306, CA, Denning MR.
[158] The statutory exclusion of domestic servants in a private household only relates to close relatives of the employer – Employment Rights Act 1996, s 161.

of claims for wrongful dismissal or unfair dismissal. If the weekly remuneration exceeds the threshold, PAYE tax and national insurance records must be kept. A statement of the basic terms of employment is required, but it is desirable to set out the terms on a more comprehensive basis. Additional insurances may be required but it is worth checking the household policy as this may cover the employment of a housekeeper or be extendable for a small additional premium.

Sharing another home

Preliminary

5.157 As an alternative, it may seem attractive for an elderly person or couple to share a home with relatives or friends.[159] This may involve breaking up the family home, and money from the home disposed of may be expended on alterations and improvements to the home of the relatives, or a gift may be made to them in anticipation of sharing their home. A larger home may even be purchased for the purpose of joint occupation, perhaps following the sale of two homes.

Moving in with family

5.158 Arrangements within the family sometimes prove unsatisfactory to one side or the other so it is important that all relevant factors are considered before it is too late. Experience shows that there may be an unacceptable loss of independence and privacy by the elderly individual and of freedom and privacy for the sharing family. The parties should consider how well they get on now and are likely to get on if living in close proximity, whether the home is physically suitable and would provide sufficient privacy and the effect on state benefits and community care provision. The implications of a decline in health and the need to provide care should not be overlooked, nor the effect upon any marriage and any children in the household. Hasty decisions should not be made following bereavement or a period of ill-health and the arrangement should be the choice of the elderly person rather than the family though it may be suggested by the family.

5.159 If the arrangement does not work it is seldom possible for the previous situation to be restored and, whilst a legal document cannot provide for personal relationships, a clear enforceable agreement is desirable if either party commits capital to the arrangement. The financial arrangements may need to be unscrambled in order to separate the personal relationships and it is better to discuss this before the parties are committed than after things have gone wrong, when the parties may not be talking anyway!

Granny flats

5.160 Where a Granny flat or annex is created for independent occupation within or adjacent to the family home, an issue may arise as to whether this is a separate dwelling for council tax purposes. It has been held that a valuation tribunal cannot treat the terms of a planning consent and its restrictions on the form of use as the sole factor in its decision. Also it could not use as a test the level of community living between this annex

---

[159] Cohabitation involving a more personal relationship is dealt with in Ch 4 at **4.47** et seq.

and the main house or the practicality of selling the annex separately to assist in its decision. The question was whether the annex was constructed or adapted for use as a separate dwelling.[160]

Financial contributions

How to make the contribution

5.161 A person who decides to contribute a substantial sum towards the cost of purchase or improvement of a home with the intention of residing there will need to decide whether to do so by way of shared ownership, loan or gift. The parties should make it clear what their intentions are, because the courts have been inconsistent in dealing with these situations, as the cases mentioned in the following (and previous) paragraphs show. This situation often occurs in families and the conflicting interests that arise should be recognised, with parties being separately advised. Factors to take into account, depending on circumstances, include:

- a gift has potential inheritance tax advantages but does not offer any security and the money may not be recoverable if subsequently needed;
- a loan creates vulnerability to means-testing if residential care is needed at a later date and could embarrass the other party if it needs to be repaid (eg if the relationship breaks down);
- joint ownership protects the elderly individual in the event that the relationship breaks down but may leave the other party vulnerable to having to move house and also is vulnerable to means-testing.

If a gift is to be made the sooner this is done the better as regards both inheritance tax and means-testing, but a new will may need to be made to compensate for the gift within the family.

5.162 If the money is spent on building a bungalow in the grounds of a larger house, or to create a self-contained flat within that house, it may be best for this to be conveyed into the name of the elderly person rather than to establish joint ownership of the entire property, but in that event the deeds should be properly split so that problems do not arise if arms-length transactions take place subsequently. It is never wise to assume that the spirit of co-operation subsisting when the property is divided will still subsist when one party wishes to dispose of their interest and circumstances beyond the control of the parties can result in diversification of ownerships.

Arrangements that go wrong

5.163 Where there is no documentation recording the agreement between the parties, or they have not received adequate advice and there has been undue influence which renders any agreement unenforceable, the court must consider whether to grant equitable relief. Case-law has developed in a hesitant manner.[161] In some cases the person making the financial contribution was held to have acquired an equitable interest in the property, but this depended upon the intention of the parties at the time. There might be an implied, resulting or constructive trust where there was evidence of an

---

[160] *Rodd v Ritchins, Gilbert v Childs, Batty v Burfoot, Batty v Merrimen* (1995) *The Times*, 21 June. This case concerned Council Tax (Chargeable Dwellings) Order 1992.
[161] This topic is also considered in Ch 4 at **4.56** in the context of cohabitation although different principles may apply in those circumstances.

agreement that the property is to be shared beneficially and the party seeking an interest has in reliance thereon acted to his detriment, or where a common intention can be inferred from the conduct of the parties. But although such intention might be inferred from a direct contribution to the purchase price it was unlikely that anything less would do.[162]

5.164 In other situations the equitable doctrine of a *proprietary estoppel* was invoked if certain criteria were met. These were that the person seeking relief had made a mistake as to his legal rights and expended money or done acts in reliance thereon, and that the party against whom relief was sought was aware of his rights and the mistake and yet encouraged the expenditure or acts.[163] When the doctrine applied it was necessary to identify the extent of the equity, and this essentially meant putting the person seeking relief in the position he expected to be in. Thus a widow was given a licence to occupy a house for life when her father-in-law to whom it belonged had encouraged her to believe that it belonged to her husband who had carried out extensive works to it at his own expense.[164]

5.165 Where a son purchased a property in his name with the assistance of a financial contribution from his mother he was refused an order for possession despite having adopted the device of appointing a co-trustee to receive the sale proceeds. It was held that he should apply for an order for sale, because the mother had been given two rooms to live in and there was a collateral purpose in buying the house of providing a home for the mother as well as the son. The court would then have a discretion as to the future of the parties.[165] However, any such collateral purpose will seldom survive the claims of creditors following the bankruptcy of a joint owner.[166]

5.166 In another case an elderly father gave up a secure tenancy to live with his son and family in a home purchased for the purpose by the son with the assistance of a mortgage and a substantial cash gift from the father who expected to live there rent free for life. There was a family dispute and the father left, being eventually rehoused by the local authority rent free because he was eligible for housing benefit. At first instance the father failed to establish a beneficial interest in the house but was awarded the return of his gift with interest to be charged on the house on the basis of an equitable estoppel. On appeal it was held that this was a wrong approach to that relief and that he had merely lost the right to rent-free accommodation for life, so damages were directed to be assessed on that basis.[167] Conversely, where a house was purchased in the name of a son with a substantial contribution from the elderly father who was to have exclusive use of it for life and the son went bankrupt, it was held on appeal that the presumption of undue influence applied because the transaction was manifestly disadvantageous to the father. Accordingly the transaction was set aside and the father was awarded his proportion of the sale proceeds (a much reduced sum in the circumstances) rather than the return of his original gift.[168] This was despite the fact that the father was not treated as a co-owner.

---

[162] *Lloyds Bank v Rosset* [1990] 1 All ER 1111, HL.
[163] *Wilmott v Barber* (1880) 15 Ch D 96; *Pascoe v Turner* [1979] 2 All ER 945, CA.
[164] *Matharu v Matharu* [1994] 2 FLR 597, CA.
[165] *Bull v Bull* [1955] 1 All ER 253, CA.
[166] *Re Citro (a bankrupt)* [1991] Ch 142.
[167] *Baker v Baker* [1993] 2 FLR 247, CA.
[168] *Cheese v Thomas* [1994] 1 All ER 35, 1 FLR 118. One wonders whether the outcome would have been the same had the house substantially increased in value.

5.167 A family dispute arose where a father sold the family home that he had owned in his own name when the daughter moved out and bought a smaller home in the sole name of the son who remained with him. This was apparently so that a mortgage could be obtained, but a declaration of trust drawn up by the solicitors whereby the house was to be held in equal shares by the father and son was never signed. Following the father's death the court found that the presumption of advancement[169] had been rebutted and that the house had been held for the father and son equally.[170]

Cohabitation

5.168 Since these earlier cases there have been many claims involving couples who have lived together and perhaps raised a family but never married. Although they may be described as 'unmarried couples' the 'common law marriage' is a myth: when such a relationship breaks up the courts have none of the powers to re-distribute property or provide maintenance that are available following a divorce, and general equitable principles must be relied upon. Some of these couples may now be elderly, but the legal principles that are emerging are not restricted to a quasi-marriage and may also apply where two people, whether or not of the same sex, have chosen to share a home for a significant period of time. The home may be owned by either or both of the parties and they may have contributed to the purchase or improvement of that home, or simply the household, in different ways over the years of shared occupation. A general explanation of the developing law in this area is given in Chapter 4.

Gifts of the home

Preliminary

5.169 Elderly people often contemplate transferring their home or a share in the home to their children even though, in some cases, they still intend to live there. The motivation for such transfer is usually the desire to ensure that the children benefit from the biggest asset of the family without suffering any reduction due to inheritance tax or various forms of means-testing, but the intentions and expectations of the donor and the donees do not always coincide. However happy the family relationships may be, it is important to recognise that this is a conflict of interest situation that presents great dangers to both parties and they should be independently advised.

Objectives

Certainty

5.170 The starting point must be to consider why the gift of the home is being contemplated and whether the objectives will in fact be achieved or could be achieved without making the gift. If the objective is to ensure that a particular child or children inherit the house rather than someone else, this can equally well be achieved by making a will. From the point of view of the child there then remains the danger that these testamentary intentions will change, but testators normally reserve the right to change their minds so the question is why there should be a departure from this approach in the present instance. There is a clear conflict of interest between the parties here, and whatever the other reasons put forward to justify the gift this 'certainty factor' is usually uppermost in the minds of the proposed donees.

---

[169] The presumption of advancement has been abolished by Equality Act 2010, s 199.
[170] *McGrath v Wallis* (1995) *The Times*, 13 April, CA.

Tax planning

5.171 A more compelling reason for giving the home to the children is the desire to avoid inheritance tax on the death of the parent, yet gifts are often contemplated in situations where there is little prospect of a tax charge on that death. The expressed reason thus disguises the certainty factor. A rough calculation should be made of the donor's likely estate and, if appropriate, other tax saving measures could be considered.[171] More options are available when both parents are still alive (and are married to one another) because there will be no inheritance tax on any assets passing between them. Having identified the possible tax saving by reason of a gift of an interest in the home, and the problems that arise when a benefit is reserved such as the right to continue living in the home, the parties should consider whether the prospect of this financial saving really justifies the risks of the arrangement which are dealt with below.

Welfare benefit planning

5.172 In recent years another reason has emerged for premature transfer of the home of an elderly person, namely the desire to avoid having to sell the home in order to meet the cost of residential or nursing home care. In past years elderly people who could no longer look after themselves tended to be looked after in the family or in geriatric wards of local hospitals, sometimes for many years at the expense of the state under the National Health Service. Now hospitals are being restricted to patients needing medical treatment and those merely in need of personal or basic nursing care which cannot be provided at home or within the family are looked after in a residential care home or nursing home increasingly in the private sector. The funding for this, when the individual is unable to meet the weekly fees from personal resources, comes from the social services department of the local authority and means-testing applies to both the income and the capital resources of the resident.[172] An awareness of this has resulted in many discussions within families about the 'need' to dispose of the 'family' home (in favour of the younger generation, of course) before residential care is required notwithstanding that the parent may intend to continue living in that home. But will the declared objective work, and what are the other risks involved in this artificial arrangement?

Implications

Advantages and disadvantages

5.173 Before making the gift the anticipated advantages and disadvantages should be considered. Possible advantages include a saving of inheritance tax, probate fees and costs following death and avoidance of means-tested contributions towards the cost of a place in a residential care or nursing home funded by the local authority or other care services provided by the authority. Disadvantages may be that the value of the home is still taken into account under means-testing rules,[173] the capital gains tax owner-occupier exemption will apply to the gift but will be lost thereafter, and there will be no capital gains tax revaluation of the home on the donor's death. There may be no inheritance tax saving whilst the donor continues to live in the home because of the 'reservation of benefit' rules,[174] yet there could be a liability to this tax if the donee dies before the donor.

---

[171] There are various schemes available but these are beyond the scope of this book.
[172] The funding arrangements and means-testing rules are dealt with in Ch 10.
[173] The 'notional capital' rules may result in the gifted home still being treated as a resource, and more recent statutory provisions enable a charge to be placed on the home in certain circumstances – see Ch 9.
[174] Various schemes exist to mitigate this but the artificiality of some has been attacked by HMRC.

5.174 Reference has already been made to the conflict of interest between the parties, and independent advice is needed to ensure that there is no undue influence or misunderstanding and that the donor was competent to make the gift at the time it was made. There can be no standard advice and all the circumstances must be taken into account, the dominant factor being the attitudes and wishes of the proposed donor. If the gift is made, the donor may be reassured by the fact that the family's major asset is now owned by the children or may become worried by the loss of control over this important asset.

5.175 This may be a gift by a widowed mother to an only daughter who is a spinster, has devoted many years to looking after her parents and will need the home for herself after mother's death, or it may be a gift to independent children who see little of their parents but are quick to point out the 'financial realities' from their point of view. Whilst if everything goes according to plan there may be worthwhile financial savings from a well-timed gift of the home, the lack of ownership reduces the independence of the donor and it is not unusual for this to sour relationships at a later date. One or both of the parties may later regret the gift and in some instances this has resulted in litigation within the family.

Vulnerabilities

5.176 Whether the declared objectives of the gift are achieved is only part of the problem, and the other risks involved may be illustrated by asking a few questions.

(1)   Is there a danger that due to the ageing process the donor will cease to understand the reasons for making the gift and become obsessed with the 'loss' of the home?

(2)   May a difference of opinion result in a request (which it would be difficult to fulfil) for the home to be given back?

(3)   Was there an understanding, express or implied, that the donee would 'see that the donor was alright' and may this result in unrealistic expectations?

(4)   Will other members of the family understand and accept the gift, and will they have unrealistic expectations of the donee?

(5)   What happens if, having received the home, the donee loses all interest in the donor?

(6)   Is there a danger that the donee may prematurely seek to move the donor into a residential care home in order to release the value in the home?

(7)   What if the donor subsequently wishes to move home or to get married?

(8)   What happens if a donee dies first without making suitable provision for the donor, or becomes divorced or insolvent?[175]

5.177 In order to protect the donor's future occupation of the gifted house, the donee may immediately grant a tenancy to the donor perhaps at a low or nominal rent. This could be for the life of the donor or for a term of years sufficient to outlast that life but with the right to terminate following death. This provides little flexibility for a donor who may later wish to move home. An alternative is for the donor to settle the house on trust for himself or herself for life with the reversion to the children. There would be no tax saving and the existence of the settlement draws attention to what has happened so

---

[175]   Upon the bankruptcy of the donee there is a risk that the donor will lose the home.

may encourage an attempt by the local authority to impose charges for subsequent residential care. Any income from the life interest would be vulnerable to means-testing in any event.

Duty of solicitor

5.178 When elderly people contemplate making a gift of their home to a son or daughter, or offering that home as security for a loan to a son or daughter, the same solicitor is often asked to act for both parties. There is no general rule of law that a solicitor should never act for both parties in a transaction where their interests might conflict, and the solicitor may do so provided that he obtains the informed consent of both of them. This means consent given in the knowledge of the conflict and that as a result the solicitor may not be able to disclose to each party all that he knows or to give advice to one party which conflicts with the interests of the other. It is only when the parties are happy to proceed on that basis that the solicitor can act for both. The solicitor should advise the parties to seek independent advice and should satisfy himself that they are both in full command of their faculties.[176]

Equity release

Preliminary

5.179 Many elderly people are short of income or spendable capital and have considerable equity tied up in their homes but are unwilling to move. It is tempting for them to live off the capital in their home especially if there is no-one to inherit it, and there are schemes that make this possible. Eligibility may depend upon age, value and tenure of the home and whether there are other secured loans. There are several different types of scheme and some are quite satisfactory, but others are risky and can result in the homeowner having to sell the home prematurely. The basic schemes are as follows but many variations exist.[177]

Types

Mortgage annuity schemes (Home Income Plans)

5.180 Capital raised by an interest only loan secured on the property is used to buy an annuity the income from which covers the interest and leaves a surplus.[178] The size of the loan is restricted by the value of the property and the amount of the annuity depends upon age, sex and whether it is for a couple, but a small cash sum can be taken rather than part of the annuity (although this may seriously reduce the remaining annuity).[179] The scheme continues until the applicant dies and the mortgage debt then has to be repaid but the house is retained. It is a safe and reliable way of producing a moderate increase in income without losing control of the home, and may be repeated at a later date, but the net income available may be limited.

---

[176] *Clark Boyce v Mouat* [1993] 4 All ER 268. See also *Mortgage Express Ltd v Bowerman & Partners* [1994] 34 EG 116.

[177] The main providers of these schemes in the UK have launched an initiative called SHIP (*Safe Home Income Plans*) and conform to a voluntary code of conduct which includes a 'no negative equity' guarantee. The website is: www.ship-ltd.org.

[178] This was more popular when tax relief was available on the interest because part of the annuity is tax free.

[179] The annuity may only be sufficient to provide an income after covering mortgage interest for those over 70 years of age (a combined age of 150 years for a couple).

Home reversion plans

5.181 The home, or a share in it, is sold to a reversion company for a capital sum which may then, if desired, be invested in an annuity. Continued occupation of the home is guaranteed by a written agreement with the reversion company, and liability for repairs remains with the occupier but a small rent may be payable. Much depends upon the valuation of the house, but the former owner only receives a proportion in cash (between 30–50% maximum) depending upon age and life expectancy, and the reversion company enjoys the benefit of any increase in value due to inflation. This approach has the advantage that there is no capital to repay and no interest payments, but it is only likely to be attractive to those with no family to inherit because the reversion company will ultimately take the house or the share that has been sold. Since April 2007 these plans have been regulated by the Financial Services Authority.[180]

Roll-up loans

5.182 An interest only loan is taken secured by a mortgage on the property and the interest payable is rolled up in whole or part (ie the amount is added to the mortgage debt). The capital sum thus released may be invested to produce an income or used for the purchase of an annuity or other purposes[181] and the intention is that the mortgage will be repaid when the house is sold, but interest on interest can escalate at an alarming rate and the extent that this may be offset by inflationary increases in property values is not easy to predict. Values may also fall so there is a risk that before the scheme comes to an end the loan may exceed the value of the property. For this reason only small interest only loans are normally accepted, and repayments may be required if the loan reaches a specified percentage of the value of the property. This would put the elderly person under financial pressure at a time when his financial situation may have deteriorated even further.[182]

Investment bond income schemes

5.183 A secured loan was arranged and the money put into an investment bond from which regular withdrawals were made on the basis of assumed growth, thereby covering the interest on the loan and providing surplus income. These bonds became popular in the 1980s during and immediately following a prolonged period of stock-market growth, but many ran into difficulties during the recession that followed. There was not sufficient growth in the bonds to meet loan interest without taking money from the bond itself, leading to a continuous reduction in the householders' capital. As a result of this adverse experience the then financial services regulators FIMBRA and LAUTRO[183] declared such schemes unsuitable for elderly people, and those who lost money on them were able to bring a claim against the firms that sold them and any advisers involved on the basis that there was inadequate warning of the risks.[184]

---

[180] For more information visit: www.fsa.gov.uk/pages/about/index.shtml.

[181] Perhaps for the cost of surgery or a visit to a relative far away.

[182] Income support will not be claimable on the interest. The remedy in an appropriate case may be to convert from a roll-up loan to a conventional mortgage.

[183] In July 1994 FIMBRA and LAUTRO merged into the Personal Investment Authority (PIA) but the Prudential Financial Authority has now taken over these responsibilities.

[184] Only a small proportion of those who were sold inappropriate schemes sought compensation and many struggled with mounting debt. Few cases went to court and most were resolved by negotiation and reference to the Insurance Ombudsman or Investors Compensation Scheme Ltd.

Implications

5.184 Those contemplating one of these schemes should first consider whether they really do need some available capital or extra income, and then whether it would be better to achieve this (and other benefits as well) by moving to a smaller and perhaps more suitable home. If the scheme is still seen as financially attractive it may be worth considering whether there is a member of the family who could provide comparable assistance on more satisfactory terms. The firm offering the scheme will be doing so for commercial profit, and it may be that a close member of the family has the financial resources to provide similar benefits thereby retaining that 'profit' within the family, but to avoid misunderstandings it is essential to arrange independent legal advice and draw up suitable documentation confirming what is agreed. If any such scheme is entered into it will often be necessary for the individual to make changes to his or her will.

5.185 Some of these schemes have had a disastrous outcome for those involved, either because of unrealistic expectations or a change in financial circumstances that was not anticipated. No-one should enter into one of these schemes without first taking proper advice from an independent person qualified to give that advice. A solicitor who acts for the elderly person in part only of the scheme (eg drawing up the mortgage) may be under a duty to enquire why the loan is required and then advise upon the merits of the whole scheme.

Factors to be considered when contemplating such a scheme include:

(1)   the effect of extra income on means-tested benefit or welfare services;

(2)   the implications of inflation;[185]

(3)   the effect on other occupiers or dependants;

(4)   whether it restricts the scope for moving in the future;

(5)   what happens if there is a need to sell the home and move into sheltered housing or residential care; and

(6)   the costs of the scheme.

5.186 Even if a scheme appears sound initially, one should take into account the risks that an increase in interest rates could reduce net income,[186] the capital may be exhausted too soon (this does not apply to all schemes) and if the scheme depends on property values these may go down as well as up. There will usually be a considerable loss of capital if the individual dies soon after taking out the scheme, so other options such as grants, additional state benefits, re-investment of savings or arrangements in the family should be considered. Finally, those determined to go ahead should remember that any scheme is lucrative business for those selling it and get several quotes as these may differ widely.

Inheritance tax planning

5.187 An equity release scheme can be used to reduce an ultimate inheritance tax liability with the released capital being given to the next generation, but this will only be fully effective if the donor survives the gift by 7 years.

---

[185]   The individual may again run short of money especially as these plans are not index-linked and future options are then reduced.

[186]   A fixed rate loan is advisable.

SPECIFIC SITUATIONS

Preliminary

5.188 Retirement is seen by some as an opportunity to expand horizons and make full use of the additional leisure time that becomes available. When coupled with greater financial freedom this may result in the acquisition of a second home, perhaps in another country. Much will depend upon the age and state of health of the couple (or individual) and the involvement of other members of the family wishing to share in or willing to support such activity, but the time comes when it may be better to encourage the elderly person to simplify his or her affairs rather than take on additional complications.

Park homes

5.189 The development of park home estates (generally comprising static caravans) and their physical standards are controlled through planning permission granted for use of land as a 'caravan site' and the site licensing system under the Caravan Sites and Control of Development Act 1960. All caravan sites must have a site licence issued by the local authority, and whilst there is no discretion as to whether to issue such a licence for a park with planning permission there is a discretion as to what, if any, conditions to apply. Model Standards are issued from time to time by the Secretary of State. Authorities have powers to prosecute failure to comply with the licence and can carry out works in default, but are not under a positive duty to inspect or monitor sites.

5.190 A fully-equipped caravan (or chalet designed so as to be classed as a caravan) may be purchased but this depends upon a fully serviced site being available. Such a site may be rented, usually on a mobile home park, but security of tenure is limited. The Mobile Homes Act 1983 applies to licences and contracts between site owners and owner occupiers. It requires a park owner to enter into a legal agreement with each individual occupier dealing with rights and responsibilities regarding increases in the site fees, the basis on which a caravan on a site may be sold or transferred (including the commission charged and approval of the new occupier by the park owner), any other charges that are made and termination of the agreement.[187]

5.191 Owner-occupiers of mobile homes on land forming part of a protected site[188] who use these as their only or main residence have the benefit of statutory terms set out in the 1983 Act. Where this is for year round occupation there is protection from harassment and the right to minimum notice of 4 weeks with the county court having power to suspend eviction orders for up to 12 months.[189]

Second homes

5.192 When considering the acquisition of a second home it is necessary to take into account not only the capital that will be tied up but also all the expenses involved and to remember that most of these will continue until disposal even if continuing use cannot be made of the property. The problems of management and maintenance should not be overlooked especially if the property is at a distance from the owner's principal home

---

[187] For further information see *Mobile Homes – A Guide to Residents* (DoE Housing Booklet No 30); *Buying a Mobile Home* and *Mobile Homes – An Occupier's Guide* published by Shelter. There is also a National Association of Park Home Residents – address in Appendix I.

[188] Ie sites that require a licence under Caravan Sites and Control of Development Act 1960.

[189] Caravan Sites Act 1968.

and there are no family or friends in close proximity who are able and willing to take on these responsibilities. The capital tied up in the investment may be needed in the event of a decline in personal health but will not be available during any delay in disposing of the property yet may be included in any means-testing for benefits or services. Capital gains tax will be payable on any profit realised if the exemption continues to be claimed in respect of the principal home.

Empty properties

5.193 Provisions were introduced in July 2006 whereby local authorities may, in certain circumstances, take over the management of private sector houses where the owners of these properties prove unwilling or unable to arrange for them to be occupied themselves.[190] An Empty Dwelling Management Order (EDMO) may be made. Of course many properties are empty for a relatively short period whilst being sold, let or renovated. These provisions are aimed at dwellings that remain unoccupied for more than 6 months and begin to have an adverse impact on the immediate surroundings thereby affecting the interests of other property owners, but the acute housing shortage in certain parts of the country was also a factor.

5.194 The EDMO bridges the gap between the powers of local authorities under compulsory purchase orders and the voluntary measures open to them. It should not relate to the home of an elderly person who remains in hospital or a residential home for a period, but could be applied where an elderly person neglected a dwelling that was held as an investment.

Timeshare

5.195 Instead of purchasing a second or holiday home the individual may prefer to acquire periods of time in holiday complexes perhaps with the option to exchange for other accommodation on a regular basis. There are various schemes available and we only consider here the situation of the older person. In addition to a capital payment there will be an annual charge for repair and maintenance which is payable until the 'time-share' is properly transferred to another person and is not waived if for some reason advantage cannot be taken of the accommodation one year. These 'time-shares' are not always easy to sell, especially if the developer is still marketing new properties in the same complex, so they may be more attractive to older people with families who are anxious to inherit them. In the absence of this they can prove to be a liability during periods of incapacity and may delay the winding-up of an estate.

Foreign properties

5.196 Before purchasing a property abroad it is essential to consult a qualified lawyer practising in the country concerned (or an English solicitor with professed knowledge and experience of the different legal system involved[191]) because each country has its own conveyancing procedures. Also inheritance laws of the particular country may apply on a basis quite different from those in this country. If the correct documentation is not entered into initially it can be expensive, and may not always be possible, to amend this at a later date. Disputes can arise as to the extent of the property or the beneficial ownership, and unexpected consequences may arise following the death of the owner even if the property is in the joint names of a couple.

---

[190] Housing Act 2004.
[191] The Law Society maintains a register of solicitors with recognised expertise in foreign jurisdictions.

5.197 Before moving abroad to live it is desirable to investigate continuing pension and state benefits entitlement, the availability of health care and any reciprocal arrangements that exist, and the income and capital taxes situation. The effect of a change of residence or domicile on testamentary provision and financial management when incapacitated should also be considered.

CHAPTER 6

RESIDENTIAL CARE: REGULATION, CHOICE AND CONTRACTS

Caroline Bielanska

'My home is not a place, it is people.'
Lois McMaster Bujold, 'Barrayar', 1991

Standards are laid down and must be maintained by those who deliver paid-for care in residential homes and these are policed with the potential for legal intervention. The contract may be entered into and funded privately or through the authorities. This chapter is divided into three parts. The first considers the legal arrangements required to operate a care home, which although are more relevant to providers, are also relevant to prospective and actual residents and their advisers, who may need to know what services should be provided and how, as any failure in the operation of the care home can have detrimental consequences. The second part covers choice of accommodation, where the individual lacks mental capacity or where the local authority are funding the placement. The third part sets out contractual issues, including common terms and conditions.

OVERVIEW

Role of the adviser

6.1 Self care, dignity and independence may be said to be the hallmarks of individual freedom in a free society. Older people and their advisers may have to contemplate circumstances where they will not be able to care for themselves in a way wholly consistent with those principles. Preserving the ideal whilst maintaining proper protection for the vulnerability or frailty which may come with advancing years is an essential benchmark of caring within a civilised society. It follows that the older individual may at some point have to think about moving into a care home, with consequential contracts and legal arrangements, ensuring it meets present and foreseeable needs. Not every care home will provide the same degree of care for each and every resident.

6.2 Older people within care homes are entitled to the same protection of the law and are subject to the same constraints of the law as other citizens in their daily lives. The law, as it applies to life in a care home, is applied in a different context from other areas of legal practice but the same principles apply, and older people and their advisers should make a point of approaching such problems first from one of legal principle and only as a matter of practical expediency in the correct legal context. A move into a care home may be traumatic for an older person, where the move is associated with a loss of independence. Once established in a care home, it is important to avoid unnecessary moves as this may cause distress and even bring about premature death of the resident. Special care should therefore be taken in relation to selecting a care home and advisers should remember that their advice is to the older client and not to relatives, sponsors, public agencies or proprietors of a particular care home.

THE REGULATORY FRAMEWORK

Legislation

6.3   The Care Standards Act 2000 (CSA 2000) came about following the publication in December 1998 of the Government's White Paper, *Modernising Social Services*.[1] The Department of Health commissioned a research study in July 2006[2] to support the development of the policy on regulation of health and adult social care, which was followed in November of that year by a consultation document, *The future regulation of health and adult social care in England* which announced the Government's intention to create a new single regulator responsible for regulating health care and adult social care, and monitoring the operation of the Mental Health Act 1983. Since then, the original single regulator in England has changed a number of times.[3] The Care and Social Services Inspectorate for Wales (CSSIW) regulates care services in Wales.

6.4   The Health and Social Care Act 2008 (the HSCA 2008), repealed the CSA 2000 on 1 October 2010, insofar as it applied to England and established the Care Quality Commission (CQC), which is responsible for the registration, review and inspection of certain health and adult social care services irrespective of whether provided by the NHS, local authorities, private companies or voluntary organisations. The CSA 2000 has been amended to bring CSSIW broadly in line with the functions of the CQC, and the legislation still applies to Wales. Any following reference to CQC or 'registration authority' applies equivalently to CSSIW unless otherwise stated.

6.5   It is important to ascertain whether the body operating the home is exercising its public functions within the meaning of the Human Rights Act 1998, s 6(3)(b) and so under a duty as a public body to act in a way which complies with residents' European Convention on Human Rights. The HSCA 2008, s 145 gives all local authority funded residents the protection of the HRA 1998, even if the care home is privately run.[4]

Regulations

6.6   The legislation is underpinned by regulations.

For England:

- Care Quality Commission (Registration) Regulations 2009[5] (2009 Regulations)

---

1   Cm 4169.
2   Independent Research Study: the Future of Health and Adult Social Care Regulation, published November 2006.
3   The National Care Standards Commission and then the Commission for Social Care Inspection and Commission for Healthcare Audit and Inspection.
4   The Health and Social Care Act 2008 (Commencement No 4) Order 2008, SI 2008/2994.
5   SI 2009/3112.

- Health and Social Care Act 2008 (Regulated Activities) Regulations 2010[6] (2010 Regulations).

For Wales:

- Care Homes (Wales) Regulations 2002[7]

- Registration of Social Care and Independent Health Care (Wales) Regulations 2002[8]

- Children Act 1989 and Care Standards Act 2000 (Miscellaneous Regulations) (Amendment) (Wales) Regulations 2002[9]

- Care Homes (Amendment) (Wales) Regulations 2003[10]

- Care Homes (Wales) (Amendment No 2) Regulations 2003[11]

- Care Standards Act 2000 and Children's Act 1989 (Amendment) (Wales) Regulations 2004[12]

- Registration of Social Care and Independent Health Care (Amendment) (Wales) Regulations 2003[13]

- Care Standards Act 2000 and the Children Act 1989 (Regulatory Reform and Complaints) (Wales) Regulations 2006[14]

- Care Homes (Wales) (Miscellaneous Amendments) Regulations 2011.[15]

Basic standards of care

6.7 The efficient and effective delivery of the regulation of care should ensure a basic benchmark to the public, older people and their advisers as to the adequacy of service, and provide confidence that that operator is providing at least a basic standard of care. The CSA 2000[16] introduced the concept of National Minimum Standards, which now only apply in Wales[17] and have been replaced in England by the more outcome focused guidance, *Essential Standards of Quality and Safety*[18] which are taken into account in regulatory decisions and provide consistent national indication to those concerned in any aspect of care as to what may reasonably be expected. In England registered providers must have regard[19] to the essential standards, whereas in Wales, meeting such standards is a regulatory requirement of the operation of any care establishment or agency.

6.8 Standards which have to be taken into account in relation to regulatory decisions are of a doubtful legal status. However, some standards support the legislation and as

---

6   SI 2010/781.
7   SI 2002/324.
8   SI 2002/919.
9   SI 2002/2622.
10   SI 2003/947.
11   SI 2003/1004.
12   SI 2004/2414.
13   SI 2003/2709.
14   SI 2006/3251.
15   SI 2011/1016.
16   CSA 2000, s 23.
17   The Welsh Assembly issued minimum standards in 2004, in respect of care homes for older people, domiciliary care and nurses' agencies.
18   'Compliance Guidance: Essential Standards of Quality and Safety' (March 2010) which follows closely the aims of the 2010 Regulations. The guidance is available from www.cqc.org.uk.
19   2009 Regulations, reg 24.

such have clear legal status, such as the requirement for the home to give to the resident the 'Statement of Purpose'.[20] Overall, however, the standards are aimed towards ensuring that the fitness of the premises, services and facilities are established and maintained.

England

6.9 Most relevant to care homes in England, underpinned by the 2010 Regulations are the following:

Outcome 1, reg 17 –	Respect and involve service users to ensure their dignity, privacy and independence is maintained and they are involved in decisions made about their care and treatment.
Outcome 2, reg 18 –	Consent to care and treatment.
Outcome 3, reg 19 –	Service users should know how much they are expected to pay, when and what service they will get for the amount paid.
Outcome 4, reg 9 –	People experience effective safe and appropriate care and treatment and support which meets their needs and protects their rights.
Outcome 5, reg 14 –	Meeting nutrition needs.
Outcome 6, reg 24 –	Co-operating with other providers, such as hospitals and emergency service providers.
Outcome 7, reg 11 –	Safeguarding service users from abuse.
Outcome 8, reg 12 –	Cleanliness and infection control.
Outcome 9, reg 13 –	Management of medicines.
Outcome 10, reg 15 –	Safety and suitability of the home.
Outcome 11, reg 16 –	Equipment must be safe, available and suitable for the service user's needs.
Outcome 12, reg 21 –	Workers should have the right qualifications, skills and experience.
Outcome 17, reg 19 –	Complaint process, handling and solutions.

---

[20] 2009 Regulations, reg 12; Care Homes (Wales) Regulations 2002, reg 4.

Wales

6.10   An older resident located in Wales, should expect:

(1)   Before moving in, have had their health and personal care needs assessed and been assured that these can be met by the care home, and following residency should be reviewed periodically. Prospective residents should be given an opportunity to visit and assess the quality, facilities and suitability of the home prior to moving in.

(2)   Residents, where appropriate, can remain responsible for their own medication, and are protected by the home's policies and procedures for dealing with medicines.

(3)   Residents should be made to feel they are treated with respect and their right to privacy is upheld, with particular regard to: the provision of personal care, such as washing and toileting; consultations with, and examination by, health and social care professionals; consultations with legal and financial advisers; maintaining social contacts; entering bedrooms, toilets and bathrooms; and following death.

(4)   Residents should have access to a telephone for use in private and receive their mail unopened.

(5)   They should wear their own clothes.

(6)   Staff should call the resident by their preferred name.

(7)   Medical examination and treatment should be provided in the resident's own room.

(8)   Screening must be provided to ensure that privacy is not compromised, where a resident shares a room with another person who is not their spouse.

(9)   Staff must treat deceased residents and their family with care with sensitivity and respect.

(10)   Their lifestyle in the home should match the resident's expectations and preferences, and satisfy their social, cultural, religious, and recreational interests and needs. The routines of daily living and activities made available must be flexible and varied to suit resident's expectations, preferences and capacities and residents should have the opportunity to exercise their choice in relation to leisure and social activities and cultural interests; food, meals and mealtimes; routines of daily living; personal and social relationships and religious observance.

(11)   Residents should be able to maintain contact with family, friends, representatives and the local community.

(12)   The resident should live in a safe, comfortable bedroom with their own possessions (if they wish) around them.

(13)   The resident should be able to control their own money, if they wish. Where the care home manages resident's money, the manager must ensure that the personal allowances are not pooled with other residents and that appropriate records and receipts are kept.

Information available to the prospective resident

6.11   The care home must produce a 'statement of purpose'[21] setting out its aims and objectives, the kinds of services it offers to residents, and the range of residents' needs which the service is intended to meet, location of care home, legal status and full name of the service provider and details of any registered manager. This should be freely

---

21   See para **6.23**.

available to prospective residents, their representatives and advisers. In Wales, it is a requirement that care homes provide a copy of their most recent inspection report as part of their 'Service User's Guide', which will assist the potential resident in making a decision about the standards of that home.[22]

6.12   The CQC and the CSSIW also publish their inspection reports on their websites and this provides insight into the quality of care, but at a fixed moment in time. For this reason, they should be construed taking this into account, as care quality may fluctuate.

What is a care home?

6.13   Care homes still refer to themselves as residential, nursing, elderly mentally infirm, or mental nursing homes although the CSA 2000, which only applies to Wales, refers to all such homes as 'care homes', which have different conditions attached to their registration. In contrast, the HSCA 2008, which applies to England has harmonised the regulation of the majority of care services and requires 'regulated activities' to be registered with the CQC. This has resulted in the provision of accommodation to be registered as a separate activity to the provision of nursing or personal care. The consequence of the HSCA 2008 is that all care homes, whether they are private or public funded, must be registered.

6.14   NHS trusts may also operate care homes for adults with learning or intellectual difficulties which are sometimes referred to as Community Support Units. In England, these are required to be registered by the CQC, whereas in Wales, the responsibility falls on the Healthcare Inspectorate Wales.

Definitions

6.15   The regulations and legislation are silent on many terms, which do not appear as part of the regulatory framework, but are often used by providers of services to describe what they provide and to whom, such as 'residential accommodation, board, elderly, ill or disabled'.

The key definitions are:

- *'personal care'* means:

  '(a)   physical assistance given to a person in connection with—
  (i) eating or drinking (including the administration of parenteral nutrition),
  (ii) toileting (including in relation to the process of menstruation),
  (iii) washing or bathing,
  (iv) dressing,
  (v) oral care, or
  (vi) the care of skin, hair and nails (with the exception of nail care provided by a chiropodist or podiatrist); or
  (b)   the prompting, together with supervision, of a person, in relation to the performance of any of the activities listed in paragraph (a), where that person is unable to make a decision for themselves in relation to performing such an activity without such prompting and supervision.'[23]

- *'Nursing care'* means:

---

[22]   Care Homes (Wales) Regulations 2002, SI 2002/324, reg 5.
[23]   2010 Regulations, reg 2.

'any services provided by a nurse and involving:

(a)   the provision of care; or
(b)   the planning, supervision or delegation of the provision of care,

other than any services which, having regard to their nature and the circumstances in which they are provided, do not need to be provided by a nurse.'[24]

- *'Registered manager'* means a person registered with the CQC as a manager in respect of a regulated activity carried out in a particular premises or of a care home in Wales.

- *'Registered provider'* means a person who carries out a regulated activity under the HSCA 2008 in England or carrying on the operation of a care home in Wales.

- *'Registered person'* means, the person who is the service provider or a registered manager in respect of the regulated activity.[25]

6.16   In Wales, a care home is defined as such under CSA 2000, s 3(1) if it provides accommodation with nursing or personal care[26] for persons:

- who are or have been ill;

- who are or have had a mental disorder;

- who are disabled or infirm; or

- who are or have been dependent on alcohol or drugs.

Distinguishing care homes from supported living or extra care housing schemes

6.17   'Supported living' or 'extra care housing' describe arrangements where the service user receives a domiciliary package of care in the home[27] and accommodation[28] separately, usually by the local authority. In many cases this occurs as a result of former care homes closing and instead providing individual tenancy agreements to the occupant of the room (the former resident) and a separate agreement (usually from a different provider) for the provision of domiciliary care. The Court of Appeal in *R (on the application of Moore) v Care Standards Tribunal and the National Care Standards Commission*,[29] considered whether a former care home was permitted to cancel their registration and instead become a supported housing provider. Upholding the CSA 2000, s 3 definition of a care home it was held that the provision of accommodation, together with nursing or personal care, is a key factor in determining whether an establishment is a care home. The separation of the accommodation provider from the care provider does not necessarily mean that it is not a care home and the existence of a tenancy agreement is not conclusive in determining whether there is a care home. A tenancy agreement can be in place without the establishment ceasing to be a care home. In that case there was a very close link between the companies providing the accommodation and the care.

---

24   Ibid and Health and Social Care Act 2001, s 49(2).
25   2009 Regulations, reg 2.
26   It must include assistance with bodily functions, where such assistance is required; CSA 2000, s 121(9).
27   Usually under the CSDPA 1970, s 2.
28   A tenancy agreement so it is not provided under the NAA 1948, s 21.
29   [2005] EWCA Civ 627.

6.18 In 2011, the CQC published guidance, *Supported living schemes: regulated activities for which the provider may need to register: guidance for providers*,[30] which sets out indicative factors for registration.

Registration

The registration authority

6.19 The Care Quality Commission (CQC) is the registration authority for England[31] and the Care and Social Services Inspectorate Wales (CSSIW) undertake this function on behalf of the National Assembly.[32] Throughout this publication both bodies will be referred to as the 'registration authority'.

6.20 The legislation delegates to the registration authority duties of registration, inspection and cancellation of registration.[33] The statutes delegate to the Secretary of State or National Assembly for Wales power to make rules and regulations as to registration and inspection and that power is not delegated to the registration authority.[34]

Requirement to be registered

6.21 Any person or organisation that carries on or manages a care home[35] must be registered.[36] Failure to do so is a criminal offence. In England, the service provider must be registered to carry out the regulated activity at each operative location. In Wales, each establishment should have a registered owner or proprietor. If the proprietor or service provider is not in day-to-day control of the home, a manager is required to be appointed who must also be registered by the registration authority.[37] For ease of reading, any reference throughout this chapter made to the registered person applies to the service provider, proprietor or manager.

6.22 If the registration authority is satisfied that all statutory requirements are being and will continue to be complied with in relation to the care home, it must grant registration.[38] Entitlement of registration is dependent on the applicant proving to the satisfaction of the registration authority that they have complied with the statutory requirements. Accordingly, registration is a matter of discretion rather than one of clear entitlement both in relation to operators and managers. However, if it is not so satisfied no discretion arises and refusal of registration is mandatory.

Statement of purpose

6.23 The applicant, as part of the application, should submit to the registration authority a 'statement of purpose', which consists of:

(1) the aims and objectives of the care home;

---

30 PoC1C 100832.
31 HSCA 2008, ss 1, 2(2).
32 CSA 2000, s 5(b).
33 HSCA 2008, Chs 2 and 3, ss 60 and 17; CSA 2000, s 8(3).
34 HSCA 2008, ss 16 and 20; CSA 2000, s 22.
35 In England this is by reference to it being a regulated activity.
36 HSCA 2008, s 10(1); CSA 2000, s 10(1).
37 HSCA 2008, s 13(3); CSA 2000, s 22.
38 HSCA 2008, ss 12, 15; CSA 2000, s 13(2).

(2)   a statement as to the facilities and services which are to be provided and the range of service users' needs which those services are intended to meet;

(3)   the full name of the service provider and of any registered manager, together with their business address, telephone number and, where available, email addresses;

(4)   the legal status of the service provider;

(5)   details of the location at which the care home is to be carried on; and

(6)   address(es) for service of documents for providers and any registered managers.[39]

6.24   In Wales,[40] the statement of purpose requires more detail, in particular:

(1)   the name, address, relevant qualifications and experience of the registered provider and of any registered manager;

(2)   the number, relevant qualifications and experience of the staff working at the care home;

(3)   the organisational structure of the care home;

(4)   the age-range and sex of the intended residents;

(5)   the range of needs that the care home is intended to meet;

(6)   whether nursing is to be provided;

(7)   any criteria used for admission to the care home, including the care home's policy and procedures (if any) for emergency admissions;

(8)   the arrangements for residents to engage in social activities, hobbies and leisure interests;

(9)   the arrangements made for consultation with residents about the operation of the care home;

(10)   the fire precautions and associated emergency procedures in the care home;

(11)   the arrangements made for residents to attend religious services of their choice;

(12)   the arrangements made for contact between residents and their relatives, friends and representatives;

(13)   the complaints process;

(14)   the arrangements made for dealing with reviews of the resident's care plan;

(15)   the number and size of rooms in the care home;

(16)   details of any specific therapeutic techniques used in the care home and arrangements made for their supervision; and

(17)   the arrangements made for respecting the privacy and dignity of residents.

This statement of purpose is used by the registration authority to determine the overall issue of fitness of the individual, the home and the services to be provided.

The service users' guide

6.25   In Wales, the application requires the submission of the 'service users' guide', which should contain the following information for intended residents:

(1)   a summary of the statement of purpose;

---

[39]   See Care Quality Commission (Registration) Regulations 2009, SI 2009/3112, reg 12 and Sch 3.
[40]   Care Homes (Wales) Regulations 2002, SI 2002/324 (W.37), Sch 1, reg 4.

(2)   the terms and conditions in respect of accommodation to be provided for service users, including as to the amount and method of payment of fees;

(3)   a standard form of contract for the provision of services and facilities by the registered provider to service users;

(4)   a summary of the complaints procedure;

(5)   the address and telephone number of the appropriate office of the registration authority.

Once registration is completed and inspections have commenced, a copy of the inspection report should be contained in the service users' guide.[41]

6.26   In England, since 1 October 2010, there is no longer a legal requirement to provide a service users' guide, although many care homes which were previously regulated under the CSA 2000 continue to provide such a guide for prospective service users.

Unfitness

6.27   The registration authority will not register a care home if:

•   the person running and managing the service is unfit to do so;

•   the premises are not fit for the purpose of the service to be provided; or

•   the services and facilities fail to meet legal requirements. The care home must also meet the essential standards of quality and safety or national minimum standards.

Fitness of the individual

6.28   Regulations[42] require that a person must not carry on a care home unless they are fit to do so. This is qualified to mean they are of good character; physically and mentally fit to manage the carrying on the care home; have the necessary qualifications, skills and experience to do so; and have provided full and satisfactory personal information.[43]

6.29   In Wales, in the case of the registered manager, regard is to be had to the size of the home, the statement of purpose, the number and the needs of the residents when considering their qualifications and their physical and mental fitness to manage the care home.[44] Furthermore, an undischarged bankrupt or person subject to a voluntary arrangement with creditors is also unable to run a care home.[45]

Fitness of the premises

6.30   Premises must not be used for the purposes of a care home unless they are fit for purpose.

---

41   Care Homes (Wales) Regulations 2002, SI 2002/324 (W.37), reg 5.
42   Care Quality Commission (Registration) Regulations 2009, Sch 1 and Health and Social Care Act 2008 (Regulated Activities) Regulations 2010, regs 4, 5 and 6 and Sch 3; Care Homes (Wales) Regulations 2002, Sch 2.
43   Care Quality Commission (Registration) Regulations 2009, reg 5, Sch 1; Care Homes (Wales) Regulations 2002, regs 7 and 9.
44   Care Homes (Wales) Regulations 2002, reg 9(2)(b).
45   Ibid, reg 7(5).

6.31   In England, this is determined by reference to risks associated with unsafe or unsuitable premises, because of the design or layout, security, maintenance, operation of the premises and use of any surrounding grounds.[46] Residents, staff and visitors should also not be placed at risk of harm from unsafe or unsuitable equipment, including medical and non-medical equipment, furnishings or fittings, which should be suitable for purpose, be properly maintained and used correctly and safely.[47] The premises must be suitable for the purpose of achieving the aims and objectives set out in the statement of purpose and its location must be appropriate for the needs of the residents.

6.32   Outcome 10 of the 'essential standards guidance', sets out generic prompts, which include:

(1)   Ensure the premises are free from preventable offensive odours.

(2)   Measures are in place to protect the personal possessions of residents.

(3)   Have safe and secure storage facilities, including storage for the private belongings of residents.

(4)   Have sufficient toilets, and where necessary bathroom and bathing facilities, which take into account people's diverse needs and promote their privacy, dignity and independence.

(5)   Have call alarm systems that enable residents to get help when their mobility is limited for whatever reason.

(6)   Have space for social, therapeutic, cultural, educational and play activities that meet the needs of residents.

(7)   Have space for a relative, carer or friend to be able to stay with the resident at the end of their life.

(8)   Bedrooms must be single occupancy except where two people have made a positive choice to share.[48]

(9)   Bedrooms should be of a size and shape that supports the resident's lifestyle, care, treatment and support needs and enables access for care, treatment and support and equipment.

(10) Bedrooms can be personalised and in residents can make choices about their environment, including temperature, furnishings and decor.

(11) For new build care homes and other care homes seeking to register for the first time, bedrooms should be no smaller than 12 square metres. For existing care homes, they should be no smaller than they were as at 31 March 2010.

6.33   The Welsh regulations[49] are similar but not identical to the outcome-focused English essential standards guidance. An asterisk identifies those not contained in the English guidance. In particular it should ensure that:

(1)   the physical design and layout of the premises meets the needs of the residents;

(2)   the premises are of sound construction and kept in a good state of repair, externally and internally;

---

[46]   2010 Regulations, reg 15.

[47]   2010 Regulations, reg 16.

[48]   Pre-existing care homes, which provided at least 80% of places in single rooms as at 16 August 2002, may continue to do so. Where they did not provide that percentage of places in single rooms as at that date, they provide at least the same percentage of places in single rooms as they provided as at 31 March 2002.

[49]   Care Homes (Wales) Regulations 2002, reg 24.

(3) equipment provided and used in the premises are maintained in good working order;

(4) all parts of the care home are kept clean and reasonably decorated;

(5) there is adequate private and communal accommodation for residents;*

(6) the size and layout of rooms occupied or used by residents are suitable for their needs;

(7) there is adequate sitting, recreational and dining space provided separately from the residents' own rooms;*

(8) the communal space provided is suitable for the provision of social, cultural and religious activities appropriate to the residents' circumstances;

(9) there are suitable facilities to meet visitors in communal and private accommodation, which is separate from the residents' own rooms;*

(10) there are appropriately located and sufficient numbers of toilets, wash-basins, baths and showers fitted with a hot and cold water supply;

(11) any necessary sluicing facilities are provided;*

(12) storage facilities are provided both for the care home and the residents;

(13) suitable adaptations are made, and such support, equipment and facilities, including passenger lifts*, as may be required are provided, for residents who are old, infirm or physically disabled;

(14) external grounds which are suitable for, and safe for use by, residents are provided and appropriately maintained; and

(15) ventilation, heating and lighting suitable for the residents is provided in all parts of the care home where the residents may be.*

6.34 The Welsh regulations[50] are also prescriptive as to the facilities to be provided, as the registered person must, having regard to the size of the care home and the number and needs of service users, provide:

(1) suitable telephone facilities, which include the making of arrangements for private use;

(2) adequate furniture, bedding and other furnishings, curtains and floor coverings, and suitable equipment and screens for the resident's needs, where necessary;

(3) so far as it is practicable, allow residents to bring their own furniture and furnishings for their own room;

(4) arrange for the regular laundering of linen and clothing;

(5) so far as it is practicable and if the residents wish, provide adequate facilities for residents to wash, dry and iron their own clothes and to make arrangements for their clothes to be sorted and kept separately;

(6) provide sufficient and suitable kitchen equipment, crockery, cutlery and utensils, and adequate facilities for the preparation and storage of food;

(7) provide adequate and safe facilities for the residents to prepare their own food;

(8) provide, in adequate quantities, suitable, wholesome and nutritious food which is varied and properly prepared and available at such time as may reasonably be required by the residents;

---

[50] Ibid, reg 16.

(9)   make suitable arrangements for maintaining satisfactory standards of hygiene in the care home;

(10)   keep the care home free from offensive odours and make suitable arrangements for the disposal of general and clinical waste;

(11)   provide a place for the safe depositing of residents' money and valuables, and provide written evidence of the return to them of any money or valuables so deposited;

(12)   consult residents about their social interests, and make arrangements to enable them to engage in local, social and community activities and to visit, or maintain contact or communicate with, their families and friends; and

(13)   consult residents about the programme of activities arranged by or on behalf of the care home, and provide facilities for recreation including, having regard to the needs of the residents, activities in relation to recreation, fitness and training.

Of course those advising older clients and older clients themselves will easily be able to determine from contemporary inspection reports, awareness of the required minimum standards, visits to premises and discussions with those associated with the home whether or not there are likely to be circumstances which could lead to a home or its registered person being characterised as unfit. No older client would wish to be accommodated in a home that might be unfit. Where there is doubt, caution should be exercised. Unfitness leading to cancellation of registration will lead to major disruption in the security and lifestyle of the particular older client.

Overview of the procedure

6.35   There is a common thread in the procedure to be followed for decisions to be made in relation to care home registration (including variation of condition or cancellation of registration).[51]

(1)   The applicant must submit a full application containing all information required to be supplied by law. The application will be supported by relevant documentation. The applicant will also be expected to have submitted a Disclosure and Barring Check (formerly Criminal Records Bureau) and submitted this with the application.

(2)   On receipt of the application, the application will be considered. In England it is not usual for either the care home or the applicant to be interviewed, unless there is an obvious concern. In Wales an inspector for the registration authority will make contact with the applicant to arrange a pre-registration interview. The purpose of the interview is to ensure that the applicant is suitable.

(3)   The registration authority must then grant such application and issue a certificate of registration unless the statutory requirements are not met and it decides to exercise its discretion to refuse registration.

(4)   If the registration authority decides to grant registration it should give written notice of the proposal and details of the conditions subject to which the registration will take effect unless the only conditions are those which the applicant has specified or which have subsequently been agreed.

---

[51]   HSCA 2008, Health and Social Care Act 2008 (Regulated Activities) Regulations 2010, SI 2010/781, Care Quality Commission (Registration) Regulations 2009, SI 2009/3112; CSA 2000, Registration of Social Care and Independent Health Care (Wales) Regulations 2002, SI 2002/919 (as amended).

(5) If the registration authority decides to refuse the application for registration, it should give notice of its proposal with reasons.

(6) If the registration authority decides to cancel registration, vary conditions or impose additional conditions, it should give notice of its proposal with reasons.

(7) The notice of proposal must state that the recipient has a right to make written representations to the registration authority on any matter which the person wishes to dispute within 28 days from the date of service of the notice of proposal.

(8) The proposal shall not then be determined until either:
    (a) written representations have been made;
    (b) 28 days have elapsed without the recipient of the notice having indicated that they wish to make representations; or
    (c) the recipient of the notice has indicated that they do not wish to make representations.

(9) Following a failure to make written representations, the registration authority shall decide whether or not to adopt the proposal.

(10) If the registration authority decides to adopt the proposal, the authority serves notice of its decision upon the applicant. There is no need for such notice to be accompanied by any reasons, as those will have accompanied the proposal. However, the registration authority must give to the applicant details of the full right of appeal to the First-tier (Care Standards) Tribunal.

(11) Any appeal lies within 28 days from the date of service of the notice of decision to the Secretary of First-tier (Care Standards) Tribunal.

(12) Where the applicant is content to accept the proposals, the decision shall take effect from the date the notice was served.

Conditions of registration

6.36 Following the completion of enquiries and investigations relating to the application, the registration authority will either register or reject the application. The registration authority issues a 'Notice of Decision', which gives the applicant 28 days to make representations,[52] following which a final 'Notice of Decision' is sent to the applicant. Where successful this is accompanied by the 'Certificate of Registration'.

6.37 There are no limits upon the conditions that may be imposed upon registration or during the course of operation of a care home.[53] A condition can be varied, removed or imposed at any time following the registration procedure.[54] Such a variation or imposition of a new condition may arise as a result of a request or application from the registered person. A decision to vary a condition of registration or impose a new condition is subject to the appeal process. However, criminally enforceable conditions of registration may only be imposed following legal regulatory procedures.

Position pending appeal

6.38 An appeal against a decision of the registration authority to the First-tier (Care Standards) Tribunal has the effect of suspending the operation of the decision until final determination of the appeal, ie where the decision was closure the home continues in operation providing care and achieving revenue. Failure at appeal is instant closure.

---

[52] HSCA 2008, s 28; CSA 2000, s 18.
[53] HSCA 2008, ss 12(3) and 15(3); CSA 2000, s 13(3).
[54] HSCA 2008 ss 13(5) and 15(5); CSA 2000, s 13(5).

Prudent advisors and their older clients will take steps by way of contingency plan to seek alternative premises, even if they really wish to remain in their established home for as long as possible.

Inspection

Purpose

6.39 The purpose of an inspection is to ensure that services meet the required standards and the needs of residents. Inspectors of care homes for older clients have significant powers of inspection. The inspector must be properly authorised by the registration authority for the purpose of the particular inspection or inspections generally and must produce a duly authenticated document showing their authority to exercise the power if required.

Powers of inspectors

6.40 The legislation sets out the wide powers of inspectors to:

(1) enter and inspect care homes(and in Wales, also those suspected of being unregistered care homes);

(2) examine the premises and management;

(3) inspect and take copies of documents;

(4) require the production of documents or records; and

(5) interview the manager, any employee, or any resident (with their consent) in private.[55]

Where the registered person is a medical practitioner or registered nurse and there is concern that a resident is not receiving proper care, the inspector can see the resident in private and examine the medical records.

Sanctions

6.41 Any person who intentionally obstructs an inspector or fails without reasonable excuse to comply with a requirement is guilty of a criminal offence and liable on summary conviction to a fine not exceeding level 4 on the standard scale.[56] People who obstruct the officers may be prosecuted without prior warning.

The inspection

6.42 The inspection can last between one and five days but varies depending on the size of the care home, the nature of the services and facilities provided and any concerns raised. The legislation authorises the inspector to require any person to afford them such facilities and assistance to enable them to carry out the inspection, which would usually include the use of the care home's photocopiers, telephone and facsimile.[57] The wide scope of the legislation[58] allows the inspector to inspect any record or document.[59] These include employment records of staff and details of the resident's care.

---

[55] HSCA 2008, ss 62, 63 and 64; CSA 2000, ss 31 and 32.
[56] HSCA 2008, s 63(7); CSA 2000, ss 31 and 32.
[57] HSCA 2008, s 63(6); CSA 2000, s 32(2)(a).
[58] HSCA 2008, s 63; CSA 2000, s 31.

6.43   In Wales, medical reports can only be inspected with the consent of the resident unless the registered person is a medical doctor or a registered nurse, in which case no consent is required.[60] In England, any record or document, including medical reports can be inspected, irrespective of the consent of the resident.[61] This provision is to prevent a medically qualified registered person stopping the detection of any failure in care in respect of the resident.

Timing of inspection

6.44   Inspections can be conducted at any time and are usually without notice. There is no prescribed time interval between inspections, but regularity is based on the level of risk, determined by the registration authority using factors such as their previous knowledge of the care home, previous inspections, significant changes that have occurred and analysis of any concern raised by third parties or residents.[62] Inspection may be scheduled, as part of a rolling programme, or in response when concerns are raised over a care home's compliance with the standards, or themed when reviewing a specific set of standards, for example looking at management of medication in a specific area.

Outcomes

Inspector's feedback

6.45   The legislation is not prescriptive about the process following inspection, but in practice the initial findings will be discussed with the registered person, which allows them the opportunity to clarify any issues or concerns raised. If the inspector judges the care home is non-compliant with one or more of the regulations, they will decide the level of impact on the service user to determine the appropriate action.

6.46   If any standards or regulations are not being met, the inspector will make this known and issue a warning notice, which may also be referred to as a 'compliance notice'. The registration authority publishes a summary of the warning notice in its compliance report (unless representations about publication of the notice are received and upheld). It does not publish the summary of a warning notice until the factual accuracy checking process is complete.

Publication of inspection reports

6.47   The registration authority must publish inspection reports.[63] The report will set out any requirements or recommended actions that should be taken within a specific time. If these are not done, legal action could be taken. Inspectors may also make recommendations as to suggested improvements to meet best practice. These are not legally enforceable.

---

59   In Wales this is limited to those which are required to be kept under Care Home (Wales) Regulations 2002, Schs 3 and 4.

60   CSA 2000, s 31(5) and (6).

61   HSCA 2008, s 63(2).

62   In England, the CQC consider the results of completion of Quality and Risk Profile for the care home, which includes those events that the care home is required to notify the CQC about, such as the death of a resident (2009 Regulations, reg 14) or serious injury occurring to a resident (2009 Regulations, reg 18).

63   Inspection reports are available on the CQC and CSSWI websites.

Complaints

6.48 Older clients are consumers of the service within care homes. If dissatisfied, they should complain. The regulations[64] provide that every resident should be informed as to the manner in which complaints may be made, and require all complaints to be fully investigated. Residents are also to be advised of the address of the registration authority to which complaints in respect of the home may be made. The registration authority does not investigate complaints but uses them to inform whether action should be taken. This lack of investigation has been criticised as the abuse and poor care has at times been overlooked, causing public outcry.[65] As such the CQC are consulting on how best to inspect care facilities in the future.

Enforcement

Resident's concerns

6.49 If warning that statutory offence, prosecution or cancellation proceedings are in hand, it is safe for older clients and their advisers to assume that there is a history of negative criticism of performance of the care home in question. They should seek full and complete clarification, with disclosure of documents from care home proprietors who are found to be in this position. Anything less than full and frank disclosure which allays all fears should set alarm bells ringing. This may cause them to review the long term placement. A delay may mean that decisions have to be taken in a hurry when the full range of appropriate options is not available and when a move may cause the greatest emotional and physical disruption to the elderly individual.

Procedures

Enforcement/warning notices

6.50 In most cases of poor facilities and services, no statutory prosecution will take place until a formal enforcement or warning notice has been issued. That notice specifies:

(1)   the statutory regulation alleged to be broken;

(2)   the manner in which it has been broken;

(3)   the remedy required; and

(4)   the time limit within which such remedy must be effected.

An offence is committed by failing to comply with the regulations, not by failing to comply with the notice, but such a detailed notice will give a clear indication as to the scope of criticism and enable the older client and their adviser to form a reasonably fair view, from their own knowledge, as to whether the complaint is either justified or sufficiently substantial to cause concern.

---

[64]   Health and Social Care Act 2008 (Regulated Activities) Regulations 2010, SI 2010/781, reg 19; Care Homes (Wales) Regulations 2002, SI 2002/324 (W.37), reg 23.

[65]   Abuse at Winterbourne View hospital and poor care at Mid Staffordshire Hospital and Morecombe Bay Hospital, have caused the CQC to review its procedures.

Statutory offences

6.51   The legislation sets out varied statutory offences, with the English offences being wider:

(1)   a failure to register;[66]

(2)   a failure to comply with a condition of registration;[67]

(3)   contravention of or failure to comply with any specified provision of the Regulations;[68]

(4)   using a false description of a care home with the intention to deceive;[69]

(5)   knowingly using a false or misleading statement in a material respect in an application for registration or the variation of any condition;[70]

(6)   in England only, carrying on or managing a care home whilst registration is suspended;[71]

(7)   in Wales only, failing to display a certificate of registration;[72]

(8)   obstructing an inspector during a visit;[73]

(9)   in England only, failure to provide documentation and information;[74] and

(10) in England only, failure to provide an explanation.[75]

Cancellation

6.52   The ultimate sanction for the regulation authority is cancellation of registration. When effected such cancellation cancels the licence to trade. The home may not lawfully be carried on, the proprietor is out of business and the older client (and their advisers) are faced with an immediate and worrying dilemma. Alternative accommodation must be found immediately.

6.53   Cancellation of registration may occur in one of two ways:

(1)   the ordinary procedure;

(2)   the urgent procedure.

---

[66]   HSCA 2008, s 10 and CSA 2000, s 11.
[67]   HSCA 2008, s 33 and CSA 2000, s 24.
[68]   HSCA 2008, s 35 and CSA 2000, s 25.
[69]   HSCA 2008, s 36 and CSA 2000, s 26.
[70]   HSCA 2008, s 37 and CSA 2000, s 27.
[71]   HSCA 2008, s 34.
[72]   CSA 2000, s 28.
[73]   HSCA 2008, s 63(7) and CSA 2000, s 31(9).
[74]   HSCA 2008, s 64(4).
[75]   HSCA 2008, s 65(4).

The ordinary procedure

6.54   Statutory cancellation provision in England and Wales is not identical:

(1)   if the registered person or manager is convicted of a relevant offence in Wales,[76] such as failure to comply with conditions without reasonable excuse, or in England providing false information in an application, or gave a false description of premises;[77]

(2)   the care home is not carried out in accordance with requirements;[78]

(3)   in England, failure to comply with a condition;[79]

(4)   in Wales, the registered person has failed to pay at the time prescribed the annual registration fee, or the establishment has ceased to be financially viable, or is likely to cease to be financially viable within the next 6 months;[80]

(5)   in England, failure to comply with essential standards of quality and safety;[81] or

(6)   in England, no one is registered as a service provider or registered manager.[82]

The decision to cancel registration takes effect immediately after the decision-making process has been concluded. Until that time the home remains open for business.

The urgent procedure

6.55   The legislation permits the registration authority to apply, without notice, to the magistrates' court for an emergency closure of a care home.[83] The Justice of the Peace may make the order if satisfied there will be a serious risk to a person's life, health or well-being. Such order is effective immediately and must be in writing.

6.56   As soon as practicable after the making of an application, the registration authority must notify the appropriate authorities of the making of the application. Where such an order is made, the registration authority shall, as soon as practicable after the making of the order, serve on the person registered in respect of the care home a copy of the order and notice of the right of appeal.[84]

Implications of urgent procedure

6.57   The order takes immediate effect and the home is closed, albeit that the registration will be revived should an appeal to the First-tier Tribunal Health, Education and Social Care Chamber be successful. The significant business of a registered care home of great value may, without warning or immediate opportunity of appeal, be terminated causing destruction of the livelihood and reputation of the proprietors and immense disruption of the personal lives of those who had come to regard the establishment as their home. The Local Authority Social Services Department will undertake measures to locate suitable accommodation and be involved in the transfer of

---

[76]   CSA 2000, s 14(1)(a) and (b), ss 24–28 and 31; Registration of Social Care and Independent Health Care (Wales) Regulations 2002, SI 2002/919, reg 14.

[77]   HSCA 2008, ss 33, 37 and 36.

[78]   HSCA 2008, s 17(1)(c); CSA 2000, s 14(1)(c).

[79]   HSCA 2008, s 17(1)(d).

[80]   Registration of Social Care and Independent Health Care (Wales) Regulations 2002, reg 14.

[81]   HSCA 2008, s 17(1)(e); 2010 Regulations, reg 27.

[82]   HSCA 2008, s 17(2).

[83]   HSCA 2008, s 30; CSA 2000, s 20.

[84]   Conferred by HSCA 2008, s 32 or CSA 2000, s 21.

residents, irrespective of whether the resident is privately funded.[85] The only test for the magistrate (and First-tier Tribunal Health, Education and Social Care Chamber on appeal) is whether there will be serious risk to life, health or well-being of residents unless the order is made.

Appeal from urgent procedure

6.58 There is a right of appeal to the First-tier Tribunal Health, Education and Social Care Chamber.[86] If the case has been without notice, the appeal will usually be dealt with quickly. For cases where the registered person had notice and as such was able to make representations to the court, the appeal will occur within the usual hearing time frame.

6.59 It is possible that the effects of such an order may be suspended by an immediate and urgent application to the High Court for an order of judicial review quashing the magistrate's order and seeking an injunction in the interim. To quash the magistrate's order it needs to be shown that it is bad in law, including grounds, that it was made in circumstances that no reasonable magistrate could have contemplated. In a case where such a procedure was used effectively,[87] notwithstanding that an injunction prevented the order taking effect for more than 15 months, the substantive hearing of the application for judicial review resulted in that application being roundly rejected, albeit after the then Registered Homes Tribunal had concluded its hearing and its decision was awaited. Such an application is only likely to succeed if:

(1) it can be established that facts placed before the magistrate are demonstrably inaccurate or at least subject to very substantial objective criticism;

(2) the facts and circumstances placed before the magistrate are such upon which no reasonable magistrate could possibly make the order;

(3) the application to the magistrate has been dishonest to the extent that it is less than full and frank about the state of relations between the registration authority and the home;[88] or

(4) that there is an unreasonable delay in making the application.[89]

As the test is whether or not there will be a serious risk to health, life and well-being if the order is not made, any evidence that the registration authority knew of the circumstances and allowed care to continue for a significant period of time supports the proposition that no reasonable magistrate could come to the conclusion that an urgent order was necessary, given that the authority themselves had tolerated continuation of care in circumstances that they now say justify instant cancellation. Applications made without notice to or a prior interview of the registered person are not the norm. The difficulty is that the action may be justified in circumstances where older people are physically or emotionally at risk. Older people and their advisers should regard any such action (whether or not successful) with great concern. If such action is mooted or has been taken, this is probably not a home in which to remain.

---

[85]   Provision will be made under National Assistance Act 1948, s 21.
[86]   HSCA 2008, s 32(1); CSA 2000, s 21(1)(b).
[87]   *R v Ealing, Hammersmith and Hounslow Health Authority, ex p Wilson* (1996) 30 BMLR 92.
[88]   Eg if the application makes it appear that a sudden crisis has arisen, whereas the circumstances have been known to both parties and the subject of discussion for a considerable period of time.
[89]   Probably such application should be made within single numbers of days.

The First-tier (Care Standards) Tribunal

Statutory framework

6.60 The Health, Education and Social Care Chamber of the First-tier Tribunal was established under the Tribunals, Courts and Enforcement Act 2007 and took over the work formerly undertaken by the Care Standards Tribunal. It is commonly referred to as, the 'First-tier (Care Standards) Tribunal'. Being a statutory tribunal, its practice and legal authority are defined by statute. In respect of older people, the tribunal hears appeals against decisions of the CQC or CSSIW in respect of registration of care homes and agencies under the HSCA 2008 or CSA 2000. It also deals with appeals against decisions of the General Social Care Council,[90] the Health and Care Professions Council[91] and the Care Council Wales in respect of an entry in the Register of Social Care for social care workers under CSA 2000.

6.61 The relevant statutory instruments are:

- First-tier Tribunal and Upper Tribunal (Chambers) Order 2008;[92]
- Tribunal Procedure (First-tier Tribunal) (Health, Education and Social Care Chamber) Rules 2008;[93]
- First-tier Tribunal and Upper Tribunal (Composition of Tribunal) Order 2008.[94]

HM Courts and Tribunals Service administer the jurisdiction, which is undertaken by the Secretariat offices based in Mowden Hall, Darlington.

6.62 To the extent that the tribunal either is convened or conducts itself outside its constitution as defined within the statutory framework, it will be acting ultra vires and, whether or not with the consent of the parties, its decisions will be of no effect. The parties may of course agree an extra-statutory procedure which will have the effect of an agreed mediation or perhaps arbitration, but any decision will be based upon the contract that has been made and not have statutory force. The tribunal cannot, even for its own convenience or that of the parties, invent rules of practice, as distinct from regulating its own procedure.

General purpose of the tribunal

6.63 The First-tier (Care Standards) Tribunal sits in the public interest to determine whether or not decisions of registration authorities to:

- exclude prospective applicants from care home ownership;
- cancel registration; or
- change conditions of registration

should take effect. The tribunal does not exist in any way to further the complaints or criticisms of individual residents or their family and advisers. However, the complaints,

---

[90] The General Social Care Council closed on 31 August 2012 but the tribunal continues to hear cases arising from GSCC decisions made before 31 July 2012.
[91] This now carries out the functions of the General Social Care Council.
[92] SI 2008/2684.
[93] SI 2008/2699.
[94] SI 2008/2835.

criticisms or support may have an effect upon the tribunal's decision insofar as the tribunal gives weight to the evidence that it hears from or on behalf of those persons.

Constitution of the tribunal

6.64   The constitution of the tribunal is contained in the First-tier Tribunal and Upper Tribunal (Composition of Tribunal) Order 2008.[95] The tribunal consists of members who are drawn from a panel of tribunal judges and panels of lay members. The Senior President of the tribunal has overall responsibility for governing the tribunal. The tribunal judge acts as chairman and is legally qualified and the two lay members are of 'appropriate expertise'. Where appropriate, more serious cases will be heard by two judges and one lay member.

Venue

6.65   The tribunal has no fixed venue, although there are 152 potential venues for a hearing, enabling local access. The permanent staff of the tribunal identify the most convenient venue and seek the appointment of a tribunal judge and work with him or her to appoint a tribunal.

6.66   Hearings are in public. Parties may represent themselves or may be represented by any form of advocate, whether legally qualified or not. The premises include a retiring room for the tribunal and in most cases should incorporate two exits. Special rooms for the appellant owners or applicants and the respondent authorities must be provided.

Procedure

6.67   Appeals are handled under the First-tier Tribunal (Health, Education and Social Care Chamber) Rules 2008, which set out the procedure.[96] Any appeal must be commenced within 28 days of the decision by the person who carries on or manages the care home filing an 'application notice' to the tribunal. They will need to send a copy of the order, whether made by a justice of the peace or the registration authority. Evidence that should be attached to the appeal is set out in rule 20.

6.68   When the appeal has been received, the applicant will be sent an acknowledgement and a copy of the appeal. Details will be sent to the respondent registration authority, which should respond within 21 working days of receiving it. They will also need to provide details of whether they are to oppose the application with reasons. The tribunal judge and members of the tribunal will be appointed and the parties notified in writing of the practice requirements and the date by which they are required to take certain procedural steps. The tribunal gives notice of the hearing, unless the applicant has requested in writing that the case be decided without a hearing. If it is decided to have a preliminary directions hearing the date fixed for the full hearing will have to take this into account. The parties receive written notice within a reasonable period of time before the fixed hearing date.

---

95   SI 2008/2835.
96   HSCA 2008, s 32; CSA 2000, s 21.

Directions

6.69 Regulation 5 sets out the tribunals' general powers for giving directions. These may extend to setting a timetable for the sending of witness statements and other documents and directing whether exchange of such material is to be simultaneous or sequential. Directions may be made on whether there should be:

- disclosure and inspection of documents;
- appointment of an expert to assist the tribunal;
- the exclusion from consideration of a document or evidence of a witness other than the applicant;
- the issue of witness summonses;
- the joining of case hearings, where two or more cases relate to the same person, establishment or agency; and
- a direction requiring a person who is not a party to the proceedings to disclose any document or other material to the applicant party.

The hearing date and time estimate will also be set for the full hearing.

The hearing

6.70 Regulations 23 to 28 govern the procedure at the hearing, although the tribunal may determine its own procedure. However, at the beginning the tribunal judge will explain the order of proceedings. In cases concerning care homes for older clients, the burden of proof will always lie upon the registration authority with the effect that the authority's representatives will open the case, call their witnesses first and make the final closing speech.

Evidence

6.71 Evidence may be admitted at the discretion of the tribunal judge, notwithstanding that it would not generally be admissible as a matter of law. In practice, tribunals tend to receive all evidence and then give it the appropriate weight when making their decision.

6.72 There is no reason why older people who are or have been residents at a particular care home should not give evidence in person or by affidavit or statement before the tribunal. Experience shows that tribunals tend not to be swayed by written or oral evidence of support for care home owners or criticism adverse to care home owners but rely upon their own objective assessment of the evidence that they received at the hearing.

Decisions

6.73 Under the ordinary procedure the care home will have remained licensed to trade throughout the whole course of the hearing and so the delivery of the written decision, if adverse, will immediately turn a lawful situation into an unlawful position. In order to avoid this some tribunal judges offer (with agreement of the parties) a preliminary indication of the tribunal's view in advance of publication of the written decision, giving the sensible caveat that the decision may always change. It rarely does and this is a sensible course as it enables the parties to order their affairs in the interests of vulnerable clients within the care home.

6.74 At the conclusion of the hearing the tribunal will adjourn to consider its position. Oral judgments are permitted.[97] Every decision of a tribunal is required to be in writing, with reasons and what order the tribunal has made as a result of its decision.[98] Decisions may be by a majority but are usually unanimous.[99]

Appeals to the Upper Tribunal

6.75 Each party to the proceedings is sent a copy of the decision and any order made, together with a notice explaining their right to appeal and right to a review of the decision and the time within which, and the manner in which, the review or appeal may be exercised.[100] Appeals are to the Administrative Appeals Chamber of the Upper Tribunal, but permission must first be obtained to appeal from the First–tier Tribunal. On receipt of an application, the First–tier Tribunal will either:

(1) decide to review the decision itself;

(2) refuse to give permission to appeal, in which case an application can be made direct to the Upper Tribunal; or

(3) grant the application and forward to the Upper Tribunal.

6.76 A review may be made on the grounds that the decision was wrongly made as a result of an error by the tribunal staff, there was an error in the decision, or a party (or their representative to the proceedings) failed to appear for good and sufficient reasons. There is no automatic right for the decision to be reviewed if the president or tribunal judge is of the opinion that there is no reasonable prospect of success. The same tribunal that made the initial decision can hear the case and has power after hearing the evidence to set aside, vary, substitute or uphold the original decision.

6.77 There is no right to continue to operate a care home pending an appeal. Such operation is unlawful and it would be inappropriate for any registration authority to permit such an arrangement to continue.

Legal force of decisions

6.78 Decisions of the tribunal are binding, with the Upper Tribunal being a court of record. Decisions are necessarily heavily based upon individual facts of individual cases. Many deal with similar issues but virtually none relate to exactly the same facts. All issues will be matters of fact and degree.

---

[97] Tribunal Procedure (First-tier Tribunal) (Health, Education and Social Care Chamber) Rules 2008, SI 2008/2699 and HSCA 2008, s 32; CSA 2000, s 21 sets out the time limit and scope of appeal.

[98] Tribunal Procedure (First-tier Tribunal) (Health, Education and Social Care Chamber) Rules 2008, r 30(2).

[99] First-tier Tribunal and Upper Tribunal (Composition of Tribunal) Order 2008, art 8.

[100] Tribunal Procedure (First-tier Tribunal) (Health, Education and Social Care Chamber) Rules 2008, r 30(2)(c).

MOVING TO A CARE HOME

Choice of care home

The right to choose

6.79   The individual with mental capacity has the right to choose whether or not to enter a care home and, if so, which care home they wish to enter. Clearly that choice will be affected by the willingness of the care home concerned to accept the person and its suitability as a care home. A care home cannot lawfully accept into care someone whose care needs are beyond the capacity of that home to supply. For example, a first class hotel style care home which is only registered for personal care cannot accept someone who needs nursing care beyond the scope provided by the community nursing organised through the GP. To offer or to agree to supply nursing care when not appropriately registered would be unlawful and almost certainly construed as a statutory offence of holding out premises as being a care home registered to provide nursing care when not so.[101]

6.80   Funding of residential accommodation as well as the availability of welfare benefit support is covered in Chapter 10 of this publication. If an older person has limited funds and wishes to move to a more expensive care home than the local authority will pay for, they will need to be financially supported by others, such as friends or relatives. There may be occasions where, although the older person has assets above the local authority means test threshold, they choose not to use all their resources to pay for the cost of care and rely on financial support from others. Those third party sponsors will have a greater role in the selection of the care home than that of mere advisers and cannot be compelled to contribute to the funding of a placement which they find unacceptable. Paradoxically it may be that the only choice for the older person is that which a third party is prepared to fund. What is not permitted is that the older person should be the subject of compulsion when they are choosing how they should spend their own money.

Consent to placement

6.81   A person with mental capacity may not be admitted to or detained in any care home without their consent unless the client has been made the subject of an appropriate order under the Mental Health Act 1983 (MHA 1983), or under informal arrangements under s 131 of that Act. It does not follow that a person subject to care and treatment under the MHA 1983 lacks mental capacity to make care and/or treatment decisions which are not covered by that Act.[102]

6.82   Under the Mental Capacity Act 2005 (MCA 2005) a move of a compliant but incapacitated person to a care home can be made by an attorney appointed under a registered health and welfare lasting power of attorney (LPA (H&W)). If the incapacitated person does not have an LPA (H&W) or the attorney is in agreement, another individual can move the incapacitated person. In all cases, the person making the decision must reasonably believe the person concerned lacks mental capacity to make the decision and it is in their best interests.[103] The person moving the individual is then protected from liability.[104]

---

[101]   HSCA 2008, s 36.
[102]   MCA 2005, s 1(2); *Re C (Adult: Refusal of Treatment)* [1994] 1 WLR 290.
[103]   MCA 2005, s 4.
[104]   MCA 2005, s 5; see also Ch 2.

6.83 Care however would need to be taken to ensure that the resident was not detained to such an extent that they were deprived of their liberty under Article 5(1) of the European Convention of Human Rights. The MCA 2005 contains a regime to authorise the deprivation of liberty, of mentally incapacitated and complicit adults, who do not meet the criteria for detention under the MHA 1983.[105]

Local authority placements

6.84 Where a social services local authority have assessed a person as requiring residential accommodation then it is obliged (subject to conditions being met) to make arrangements for accommodating that person at a place of their choice.[106] The right to exercise choice over accommodation extends not only to prospective residents, but also to existing residents who wish to move to different or more expensive accommodation. Mandatory guidance has been issued to support the directions.[107]

Conditions for preferred accommodation

6.85 The local authority must arrange and fund the placement at the person's preferred choice of care home, if the following conditions are satisfied:[108]

(1)   there is a place available;

(2)   the accommodation is suitable for the assessed needs;

(3)   it does not cost more than the local authority would usually pay for such accommodation ('the usual cost'); and

(4)   the home agrees to comply with local authority terms and conditions.

Usual cost

6.86 The guidance emphasises that it is the 'usual cost' that must be used for comparative purposes, and that in certain situations this may be the cost in another part of the country; ie there may be circumstances where a local authority might judge the need to move to another part of the country to be an integral part of the individual's assessed needs. The type of care may also affect the usual cost, for instance the cost a local authority might usually expect to pay for respite care might be different from its usual cost for permanent care.

6.87 Whilst these provisions enable an individual to opt for more expensive accommodation (and for a third party[109] to pay the difference), this only applies if the usual cost figure used by the local authority would genuinely secure the person a placement in a less expensive home which met their assessed needs.

6.88 Many local authorities limit what they will pay for residential care, so a third party top up is common. Consideration should be given as to whether there has been a real choice of accommodation, or whether what is on offer is so limited it does not meet the needs of the resident unless a third party makes a contribution. The usual cost of

---

[105]   Deprivation of liberty is considered in detail in Ch 8.
[106]   National Assistance Act 1948 (Choice of Accommodation) Directions 1992, Direction 2. (Wales made identical directions in 1993).
[107]   LAC(2004)20; NAFWC 46/2004.
[108]   National Assistance 1948 (Choice of Accommodation) Directions 1992. Similar Directions were made in Wales in 1993.
[109]   See **6.80**, **6.90** and **6.102**.

care should be set at a level that is sufficient to meet the assessed care needs of supported residents[110] which should not be set arbitrarily so that residents are required routinely to seek assistance from third parties.[111] They should be able to secure appropriate accommodation without having to rely on an additional payment and may indicate market inadequacies or commissioning failure by the local authority.[112]

6.89 If challenged a local authority would need to be able to demonstrate that its usual cost was sufficient to allow it to provide people with the level of service they could reasonably expect if the possibility of a third party contribution did not exist.

Third party top ups

6.90 Where the preferred accommodation is more expensive than the local authority's usual rate, the prospective resident may be able to choose that accommodation, provided an able and willing third party, (usually a family member or friend) agrees to top up the difference, and that third party can reasonably be expected to pay the sum for the duration of the proposed placement. The amount of 'top-up' is calculated as the difference between:

(1)   the local authority's usual cost for a person with those assessed needs, and

(2)   the full standard or contractual rate for the care home.

Resident top ups

6.91 A resident is only able to make a top up out of their own resources for the cost of their care where the resident has accessed the 12-week property disregard[113] or deferred payments agreement[114] scheme. Regulations set out the detail, which must be read with the mandatory guidance in *Charges for Residential Accommodation Guide* (CRAG) and choice of accommodation guidance.[115]

(1)   A resident subject to a 12-week disregard may top up from:
    (a)   Earnings disregarded by CRAG
    (b)   Income disregarded by CRAG
    (c)   Capital disregarded by CRAG (with the exception of the value of the resident's home which is subject to the 12 week disregard)
    (d)   Other capital resources, excluding their home, with the proviso that:
        (i)   they can only top up to the value of the lower capital limit;
        (ii)   and where the resources are used to top up by residents who have resources above the lower capital limit, the level of tariff income that applies during the 12 week period of topping up is the same as if it would be if the person were not using capital to top up.

(2)   Residents who have a deferred payments agreement may top up from:

---

[110]   Para 2.5.4 of the guidance.

[111]   Para 2.5.7 of the guidance.

[112]   Para 2.5.8 of the guidance.

[113]   The resident's home is fully disregarded for the first 12 weeks of permanent admission to a care home, if their main asset is their home and they have limited other resources.

[114]   A local authority may place a charge over the resident's home if they are unable to pay the assessed fees and do not wish to or are unable to sell their home.

[115]   Health and Social Care Act 2001 (Commencement No 2) (England) Order 2001, SI 2001/3167; National Assistance (Residential Accommodation) (Additional Payments and Assessment of Resources) (Amendment) (England) Regulations 2001, SI 2001/3441. Identical Regulations were issued in Wales in SI 2003/931 (W.121) and guidance LAC(2004)20: NAFWC 46/2004.

(a)   Earnings disregarded by CRAG
(b)   Income disregarded by CRAG
(c)   Capital disregarded by CRAG
(d)   Other capital resources, including the value of their home, which is subject to the deferred payment agreement, with the proviso that the resident must be left with the total capital resources under the means-test to the value of the lower capital limit. When the value of the property is used as 'collateral' for top ups, the amount of the top up is added to the sum accruing under the deferred payment agreement.

Explanations and agreements

6.92   There is a duty on local authorities to explain to residents and prospective residents (and their carers) their rights under the choice of accommodation directions. Third party contributors are usually required to enter into a written agreement with the local authority and sometimes with the care home. The agreement will usually specify:

(1)   that failure to keep up payments will normally result in the resident having to move to other accommodation;

(2)   that an increase in the resident's income will not necessarily lessen the need for a contribution, since the resident's own income will be subject to charging by the local authority in the normal way;

(3)   that a rise in the accommodation fees will not automatically be shared equally between the local authority and third party;

(4)   that if the accommodation fails to honour its contractual conditions, the local authority must reserve the right to terminate the contract.

Choice of care and NHS continuing health care

6.93   The National Assistance 1948 (Choice of Accommodation) Directions 1992[116] and the equivalent Welsh 1993 Directions,[117] which apply to local authority provision, do not apply to NHS funded placements. As such providing the NHS is offering care which is clinically suitable, the patient does not have the right to choose where they receive that care. It will not usually be permissible for individuals to pay for higher-cost services and/or accommodation (as distinct from purchasing additional non NHS services).

6.94   However, the National Framework[118] for NHS continuing health care in England[119] provides guidance on the NHS paying more for the care:

(1)   where the person's need is for an identified clinical reason (for example, an individual with challenging behaviour wishes to have a larger room because it is identified that the behaviour is linked to feeling confined, or an individual considers that they would benefit from a care provider with specialist skills rather than a generic care provider);[120]

---

[116]   LAC (2004) 20.
[117]   WHC (2004) 066.
[118]   National Framework for NHS Continuing Healthcare and NHS-funded Nursing Care (DoH, November 2012); Welsh Assembly Government Circular: 015/2010.
[119]   The Welsh National Framework is silent on this.
[120]   NF Practice Guide, para 99.2–6.

(2)   where the resident was self-funding their care or a third party was topping up the cost of care and the resident is frail, has mental health needs or other relevant needs, a move to other accommodation could involve significant risk to their health and well-being; or

(3)   where an individual in an existing out of area placement becomes entitled to NHS continuing health care and where, although the care package is of a higher cost than the responsible Clinical Commissioning Group (CCG) would usually meet for the person's needs, the cost is reasonable taking into account the market rates in the locality of the placement. It may be reasonable for the CCG to fund because the location of the placement is close to family members who play an active role in the life of the individual or because the individual has resided in the placement for many years so that they have strong social links with the area and it would be significantly detrimental to the individual to move them.

Care contracts

Funding of accommodation

6.95   How the care home is funded dictates the parties to the contract. Care home accommodation can be funded by:

(1)   the local authority (whether or not supported by a third party top up); or

(2)   the NHS and/or local authority as aftercare services under the MHA 1983, s 117; or

(3)   the NHS, for those who meet the continuing NHS health care eligibility criteria; or

(4)   the resident's own resources (including any contribution from a third party).

Care home provision arranged by the local authority is not free to the resident. Whilst the local authority is primarily responsible for discharging liability for the provision of the accommodation for those who are eligible for such service, it is entitled and expected to recover from the resident (subject to their means), a contribution towards the cost of accommodation.[121] This is covered more extensively in Chapter 10. Chapter 7 sets out how people can obtain local authority support for their care.

6.96   In contrast, it is a right under the NHS that each and every citizen is entitled to equal access to a health service which is to be supplied free of charge.[122] However it does not entitle any citizen to demand a particular health service. The NHS must make available such services as it considers necessary to meet reasonable requirements. This extends to the provision of accommodation, both within and outside of a hospital.[123]

6.97   Individuals are not specifically owed the duty under the legislation[124] and as such the availability and demands of resources can be taken into account when deciding NHS policy. However, the level of service provision should be justifiable within local priorities and resources.[125] This is covered more extensively in Chapter 10.

---

[121]   National Assistance Act 1948, ss 22, 26 and 56.
[122]   NHSA 2006; NHS(W)A 2006, s 1(3).
[123]   NHSA 2006; NHS(W)A 2006, s 3(1)(a) and (b).
[124]   NHSA2006; NHS(W)A 2006, s 3.
[125]   *R v Secretary of State for Social Services ex p Hincks* [1980] BMLR 93); *R v Cambridge Health Authority ex p B (A Minor)* [1995] 1 FLR 1055; *R v Central Birmingham Health Authority ex p Walker* [1987] 3 BMLR 32.

Local authority care contracts

6.98   Where the local authority has assessed the person to be in need of residential accommodation,[126] they are bound to provide such care. The local authority may provide this from its own accommodation or by making arrangements with the voluntary or private sector.[127] Subject to a means test, the resident must make a contribution to the local authority (or if the resident agrees, directly to the care home proprietor) for the cost of residential accommodation.[128] If the resident has insufficient resources, the local authority will pay the shortfall.

6.99   Where the local authority arranges a contract, they agree with the care home provider to pay a sum of money for the whole of the personal care and accommodation so that the resident can be confident that care will continue irrespective of financial difficulty on the part of the resident or any third party contribution. It is not open to the care home proprietor to extract a further sum of money from anyone for provision for the same level of care.

6.100   The resident is allowed to keep a weekly sum for their own use, known as the 'personal expense allowance' (PEA). This can be spent by the resident as they see fit (on additional items and services, such as hairdressing and entertainment). It may not legitimately be claimed by the care home proprietor as a top up to meet what is said to be inadequate funding. The issue is one of pure contract law. If a complete service has been contracted for an agreed fee, then there no further fee can be requested for provision of the same service.

6.101   If, in the case of preferred accommodation under the Choice of Accommodation Directions,[129] a third party is to make a contribution (known as 'a third party top up') to the cost, then the local authority is entitled to satisfy itself that the third party has sufficient resources to meet that obligation for the duration of the arrangements.

6.102   The third party under a 'top-up' arrangement has the right to withdraw from the arrangement at any time, as the local authority will be committed to paying the whole cost.[130] The local authority will usually require the third party to enter into an agreement with them to secure the payment, with provision for recovery in the event the third party fails to make a contribution. That agreement should include provision for the third party to give notice that they will not be able to continue to make payments. The local authority will then need to reassess the resident to ascertain their needs. It could result in the resident having to move to another care home that is priced within the local authority's usual fee rate.

NHS nursing care provided by a registered nurse

6.103   Since the introduction of the Health and Social Care Act 2001, nursing care provided by a registered nurse in a care home registered for nursing care, is provided at the expense of the local NHS commissioning body.[131] There will be two contracts in respect of the same resident. The first is where the local NHS commissioning body will

---

[126]   Pursuant to National Assistance Act 1948, s 21.
[127]   National Assistance Act 1948, s 26.
[128]   National Assistance Act 1948, s 26(3A).
[129]   National Assistance Act 1948 (Choice of Accommodation) Directions 1992. Equivalent Directions were issued in Wales in 1993 in WOC12/93.
[130]   Including a cost which the local authority does not consider to be justified ex hypothesi.
[131]   This is the Clinical Commissioning Group (CCG) in England or Local Health Board in Wales (LHB).

contract with the care home proprietor to pay a flat sum of money, calculated on a weekly basis. The second contract is between the proprietor and whichever person or body is entering into the contract on behalf of the resident or the resident themselves (the 'resident's contract').

6.104 The resident's contract should specify separately the fee payable for accommodation and food; personal care; and nursing. The care home receives the sum for the nursing care provided by a registered nurse and will usually keep this, rather than pay it over to the resident. The resident's contract is usually for the gross amount, including nursing care by a registered nurse, but a deduction is made equal to the amount paid by the local NHS commissioning body.

6.105 The local NHS commissioning body is not obliged to make the contribution in the event that the resident needs to go into hospital, as arguably the resident would be receiving public funding twice for the same care; once when in hospital and once for their care home bed. If the care home proprietor insists on the payment being made by the resident, who has contracted for the gross amount, contact should be made to the local NHS commissioning body who have discretion to continue to make a payment to avoid the risk to the resident's security.

Self-funding client

6.106 Care contracts for self-funded residents are usually between the resident or their attorney[132] or court appointed deputy,[133] if they have one, and the care home. If the resident is to be financially supported by another person, the care home may wish that person to also be party to the contract. More frequently, care home owners require another person to guarantee payments. Guarantees may be appropriate for peace of mind, where there is concern that the older person may use up such funds that they may need to seek financial support from the local authority, in which case an unwanted move to another care home may be likely. It is unwise for professional advisers to give personal guarantees.

6.107 Some care home owners may seek to contract directly with a representative, rather than the resident. The representative will be fully and personally liable, as a principal contractor and does not have to be acting as an attorney or deputy. The care home owner can seek to enforce payment immediately without calling on any guarantee. This leaves the resident powerless, without any say in the performance of the contract, so they cannot terminate the contract if they wish to move or have a say in the alteration of any terms. This would apply even where the contract is made for the benefit of the resident. As a matter of practice, there should always be provisions for the resident to enforce the contractual obligations by direct action.

Terms of the contract

6.108 Care home proprietors formulate standard forms of contract to represent the provision of care in their care homes, and so are varied. Local authorities formulate standard forms of contract upon which they are prepared to contract with private sector

---

[132] Under an ordinary, enduring or financial lasting power of attorney.
[133] Where the resident lacks mental capacity to manage their finances, the Court of Protection can appoint a deputy to act on their behalf.

providers. The older person's adviser can have important influences on some vital constituents of these agreements so as to give them force and effect.[134]

(1) **Individual terms of contract**
   Matters to be considered include:
   (a) Who are the parties?
   (b) Can the resident enforce the terms of the contract effectively?
   (c) Who is liable to pay what?
   (d) Care home charges.

(2) **Charges**
   How much is to be charged, whether it is calculated at a daily or weekly rate and what is embraced by the charge should be clearly stated, including whether or not it is inclusive of VAT. There have been reported cases of some care homes charging a one-off placement fee of several thousands of pounds in addition to the first month's fees, merely for accepting the resident. This may sometimes be called, 'an administrative fee' to cover the cost of setting up a care plan, carrying out risk assessments and establishing their financial arrangements for the resident. There is strong argument that this should be part of the service they are required to provide as an operating cost and should not be charged separately to the resident.[135]

   Many contracts charge interest on arrears of fees. However, the rates vary, from the Bank of England base rate to significantly higher. It should be clear how interest is to be calculated, whether annually, monthly or daily.

   It should also be made clear what services are subject to an additional charge. For example, most will make an additional charge for hairdressing and chiropody and others may make a charge for laundry services. Extras should be subject to prior approval by the resident or their representative. Pre-determined use of the resident's PEA on the basis that it is bound to be consumed in hairdressing, chiropody, etc should not be permitted by the local authority, where they are contractors.

(3) **Increases in charges**
   The contract can be of long duration. Inevitably, there will be price increases. How such increases are to be negotiated should be reflected in the contract. At the least, the resident should have the right to have sufficient time to seek an alternative home before increases in charges take full effect.

(4) **Exclusivity of occupation**
   Although the resident will want to know the room they move into will be exclusively theirs for the duration of their stay, care home owners want the right to move residents to deliver effective care, as needs change. For example, a person who has dementia might need more care as their condition deteriorates. This could mean they must be moved to a unit, exclusively for dementia care, where there are more staff. In practice, there is less difficulty than may be perceived in theory.

(5) **Notice of termination**
   Both sides are committed to a long-term relationship. A reasonable notice is required by the home owner or by the resident to terminate that relationship. The home owner will need to be able to have enough time to find an alternative resident and the older person will need sufficient time to find alternative accommodation. There should be provisions entitling that notice period to be

---

[134] Office of Fair Trading's '*A Guide on Unfair Contract Terms in Care Home Contracts: a guide for professional advisers*', published October 2003.
[135] Office of Fair Trading, *Guidance on unfair terms in care home contracts – A guide for professional advisers*, published October 2003.

shortened in cases of genuine emergency – perhaps a dramatic change in the care requirements of the older resident, putting their needs beyond the resources of the particular home, or perhaps a dramatic breach by the home of its obligations making it impossible for the older person to remain.

The contract should specify how notice is to be effective; is an oral statement sufficient or must it be in writing and if so is this to be by hand or post. Can it be via electronic means? When is it to be presumed that the notice has been delivered? For example, it could be two working days after post or on actual delivery.

The contract should provide clear rights of termination if service needs change or if service delivery ceases to meet expectations. In the event of death or leaving the home, some contracts contain a 'no refund' clause. This is unfair as it may deny the individual a refund even if the home is in breach of contract. Where the resident has been justified in cancelling the contract, they should be entitled to a pro-rata refund and provision should be made in the contract.

(6)   **Death of the resident**
The resident's death will terminate the contract. However, care home owners usually expect a reasonable period of time in order to be able to re-prepare and re-let the accommodation.

Periods for payment following death vary in practice. The least is usually the balance of the week during which death occurs and the longest is six weeks – some compromise in the middle is probably right. Local authority contracts commonly end the day after the resident has died and so they will not pay beyond this period, unless it is a pre-agreed contractual term.

Some residents, particularly those who fail to apply for public assistance or have always been dependent on state support may die insolvent.[136] If the resident has applied for local authority support, they will be able to keep a minimum capital sum[137], although there will always be people who have never had any savings.

Who will pay the funeral expenses? The care home owner may find himself left with a difficult problem. They may seek to take a deposit. Some care home owners accept the responsibility themselves, although this is hardly fair. Some will no doubt 'price in' for such provision if they are able to test the market appropriately. Funeral expenses which may be discharged by others will be a preferential claim on the insolvent estate. Unpaid Social Security benefits to the date of death, with which a home owner might expect to discharge outstanding fees, may be taken in preference to meet funeral expenses incurred by relatives or financial supporters.

Local authorities are obliged to arrange burial for those where no other arrangements are available (including those accommodated under Part III of the 1948 Act) but may reclaim costs from the estate, so taking advantage of the preferred claim.[138] Most care home proprietors will have arrangements with local firms of funeral directors but this is no substitution for having had the foresight to make suitable arrangements in the contract.

(7)   **Services**
The contract should identify the exact services, which are to be provided, showing which are standard and those that are extra. This is probably the area that receives least attention in any form of negotiation. Older residents and their advisers might wish to consult with nurses, doctors and social workers to ensure that the contract reflects the resident's needs. It may avoid unplanned and

---

[136]   Insolvency Act 1986, ss 328–330.
[137]   £14,250 in England and £23,750 in Wales for 2013/14.
[138]   Public Health (Control of Disease) Act 1984, s 46(2).

unidentified financial extras causing later difficulties, or discovering the care home cannot really cope or needing to provide extra support should the care services be inadequate.

Some care homes attempt to exclude liability for failure to carry out the service it provides with reasonable care and skill. Often this is for failure related to the care of the resident or care of the resident's possessions and clothing, including when the resident goes into hospital. If the care home were in default of its obligations, where it has acted unreasonably or negligently, then this would seem unfair. It is not possible to exclude liability for death or personal injury caused by negligence as such terms are always void under the Unfair Contract Terms Act 1977, s 2, although such terms can appear in care contracts and so mislead residents and their family. Terms stating that the administration of medicines is at the resident's risk are also unfair as the home is under a duty to ensure the safe administration of medicines.

The contract should specify exactly and clearly what is extra. Each and every older resident is entitled to receive NHS services, whether in a care home providing personal or nursing care or living in the community, in accordance with the way in which those facilities are made available nationally or through locally implemented policies purchased by local NHS commissioning bodies. Some services should not be charged for, such as incontinence supplies, feeding equipment or seeing a GP, which are available free of charge from the NHS. Older people are also entitled to free drugs on prescription in accordance with the usual rules, and appropriate access to community health, physiotherapy, chiropody and other services.

The older resident is entitled to the choice of their own doctor. However, the doctor will only be obliged to provide a free medical service in accordance with their standard policy and practice in their NHS practice. They cannot be required to attend the care home, save as they would normally be required for a patient in the community. A dilemma may be faced because the NHS doctor is not entitled to charge a private fee to a patient unless that patient registers as a private patient – which may be beyond the means of the resident. Further, paradoxically, the NHS doctor is not entitled to take an additional fee from a third party for providing NHS medical services (ie the nursing home cannot pay a retainer for treatment of NHS patients).

If the local NHS GP requires attendance at their surgery, or the resident requires hospital visits, it is usually classed as an 'extra', and added to the bill.

(8) **Insurance**

It is unlikely that care home owners will have more than basic insurance to cover the property and valuables of older clients within their care. If there is such insurance, it may be limited to those items which are kept in safekeeping within the care home safe or elsewhere in a secure position. Care home owners will certainly carry insurance for public liability and should carry liability for nursing or care malpractice. The extent and existence of such insurance cover should be carefully checked and should be a contractual provision. If in doubt as to the existence of such insurance and particularly in relation to older resident's own property or valuables (jewellery, money, etc) then those advising must ensure that proper policies of insurance are taken out.

(9) **Valuables and money**

Older clients' money may be a greater issue than envisaged, even in those homes catering for publicly assisted clients. If the older client receives pensions or other Social Security benefits, then that money belongs to the older client. It cannot be allocated, even where intended for payment of fees, without proper sanction from the client and proper recording of its credit to the older clients' account in the care home records and its use to discharge the appropriate liability. In any event, the individual should have their PEA to use as they choose. This may be obvious, but it has been found to be overlooked many times in practice. Undocumented and unapproved use of older clients' money for care home purposes is at best foolish and at worst theft.

Care Homes will keep a record of resident's money which they hold and manage on behalf of the resident. In England this is expected to be part of the general records they keep relating to a resident, whereas in Wales it is a specific legal requirement.[139]

(10) **Furniture and personal belongings**

Older clients are frequently encouraged to bring personal items and furniture into a care home. Such items may often be very valuable. The contract should identify what items have been brought to the home and when they are taken away and if there are any additions, how those additions are to be recorded. Large items of furniture are still the older clients' property, even if they have furnished a care home for many years.

(11) **Gifts to and from staff**

Residents may wish to favour members of staff who provide them with the service for care upon which they depend. Properly drawn contracts of care should make it quite clear that gratuities will not be sought by staff or care home managers, nor should they be given. Incidents of request for gratuities or offers to perform extra services for extra payment should always be reported by older clients to the most senior officers responsible for the operation of the care home. Such soliciting or receipt of gratuities is usually a disciplinary offence under the contracts of employment of care home staff.

Older clients should be advised as to the importance of taking clear, independent advice before giving any gratuities or valuable items to care home staff either during their lifetime or effected by their will. A well organised care home will have an arrangement for a general pool of gratuity monies for distribution among staff on a regular basis and older clients in a reputable home should be advised, should they so wish, to make contributions for such a fund for general distribution.

(12) **Dispute solving**

It is sensible to arrange for a method whereby disputes, large or small, can be solved. Of course, courts of law exist to govern these situations as well as more usual commercial arrangements. However, access to county court or High Court may be of illusory benefit to a frail and vulnerable older client. Some form of mediation or arbitration to solve matters by reference to predetermined individuals who enjoy the confidence of both sides is likely to cause the relationship to prosper and lead to ready resolution of complaints, the festering of which can only work to the disadvantage both of the older client and their new home.

(13) **Complaints procedure**

Every care home must have a complaints procedure and must investigate complaints. A well-drawn contract will deal with the issue of the complaints procedure and identify quality assured goals for a complaints procedure.

---

[139] Care Homes (Wales) Regulations 2002, SI 2002/324, reg 17(2), Sch 4, para 9.

CHAPTER 7

COMMUNITY CARE

Caroline Bielanska

'Before you contradict an old man, my fair friend, you should endeavour to understand him.'
George Santayana (1863–1952)

The law has assumed an overseeing regulatory role in the provision of care services but these largely depend on policies which may be local and depend upon the availability of funding. In this chapter we start by explaining the policy of community care and the statutory environment. Then we look at the role of the authorities, the concept of 'ordinary residence' and strategic planning before examining the duties of local authorities in regard to vulnerable adults. Finally we deal with assessment, eligibility criteria and provision of services.

INTRODUCTION

7.1   The emphasis in this chapter is upon the statutory authority under which local authorities provide care services to older people and the procedures which they should adopt, because the individual has few personal rights to these services. Any obligation to provide specific services is likely to be of a general nature and not enforceable in a particular instance, and in many cases the authority merely has a discretion to provide services. Where legal action can be taken it is usually because the authority has not adopted or followed appropriate procedures or has failed to make a decision. The problem is usually lack of resources, with the result that even if the authority has the will to provide services it does not have the means. In consequence it may appear that many authorities operate on the basis of crisis management rather than forward planning, and the picture of care provision painted by policy documents may not be reflected in reality.

7.2   Local authorities are not alone in being required to provide services to people who need them. Housing authorities and health authorities must also do so and should participate in the assessment process. It is the social services department of the local authority that has the role of coordinating these services, yet that authority cannot insist upon other authorities doing anything so an integrated package of services cannot be guaranteed. Older people are not the only ones who may be entitled to these services. Children and those who are mentally ill or physically disabled or learning disabled are other categories, as are drug and alcohol misusers.

7.3   We identify first the policies that have come to be known as the community care reforms, the legislation that implements those policies and the sources of funding that enable them to be carried into effect. This is followed by a summary of how local authorities operate and the responsibilities imposed upon them. Then we consider the types of services that are provided and the detailed statutory provisions involved, and finally the procedures for deciding who should benefit from these services and how the services should be delivered. Complaints procedures and other methods of challenging the decisions (or lack of decision) of the authorities are dealt with in Chapter 9, and the bases upon which individuals are charged for community care services and residential care are summarised in Chapter 10.

THE POLICY

7.4   Community Care is not a new concept but has been the reality for profoundly disabled and infirm people for generations in the form of care in the community. It meant living alone or being cared for by family with little support from the state in an indifferent society. If helpful services were available advantage might be taken of them, but there was no attempt to structure these according to the needs of the individual. When the individual or family could no longer cope the only alternative was institutionalised care in a hospital geriatric ward or a residential care home. This meant being hidden away from society where standards might not have been what society would have wished.

7.5   The need became apparent to reduce institutional care and provide alternative services in a community setting, and increasing pressure from concerned people and organisations to recognise the rights and freedoms of people who needed care or support found expression in policies which become known as community care. Much was heard about bringing mentally ill or learning disabled people out of hospitals and enabling them to live in the community, but it was recognised that this meant more than just the provision of a home in the community for former hospital patients; a whole range of support and services had to be provided for all persons needing care, including those already living in their own homes.

7.6   In regard to older people the emphasis has been upon enabling them to remain in their own home or otherwise in the community when they, their family and friends could no longer cope without support. There developed a growing awareness that the alternative of institutionalised care was not always appropriate or suitable, and that many older people could remain living in their own community with services provided in their homes or those of their carers.

What is 'Community Care'

7.7   There is no precise definition for Community Care and it has tended to mean different things to different people. The phrase is commonly, if inaccurately, used to identify policy changes which took effect in April 1993. Specific interpretations are set out in the following paragraphs. Regrettably, but perhaps inevitably, the policies and such law as exists emphasise the provision of services rather than the right of the individual to benefit from those services.

Reports

7.8   The Social Services Committee initially referred to the provision of care for individuals in such a way as to enable them to lead as normal an existence as possible given their particular disabilities and to minimise disruption of life within their community.[1] The disruption element did not feature in later interpretations though it might be implicit. There has always been a tension between protection of the individual and the protection of the community, especially in regard to those who are mentally ill. During the 1989–90 session the committee produced a series of reports on aspects of community care, tackling the issues of funding, carers, quality and services.

7.9 In 1986 the Audit Commission carried out a review of community-based care services and identified many problems which needed to be tackled. Resources, staffing and training were all directed towards the more institutional forms of care, organisation was fragmented, and there was a lack of effective joint working and planning between the different agencies involved in the provision of services. The Commission regarded community care as providing clients with a full range of services, and a wide range of options; bringing services to people, rather than people to services; the adjustment of services to meet the needs of people, rather than the adjustment of people to meet the needs of services.[2]

7.10 A further review, *Community Care: Agenda for Action*, was published in 1988.[3] Commonly referred to as 'the Griffiths Report' this acknowledged the need to promote 'the provision of services to individuals, developed from a multi-disciplinary assessment of their needs and made with proper participation of the individuals concerned, their families and other carers'. Policies were proposed aimed at improving social care services by ensuring that they were properly tailored to the needs of individuals. It was pointed out that this required a clear, locally determined set of priorities and effective collaboration between public, private and voluntary agencies. The proposals were linked to changes in the financial arrangements for people needing public support in residential care and nursing homes, with local authorities to take over a new responsibility to assess the needs of people and meet the costs of residential or domiciliary care. A specific (or ring-fenced) community care grant was recommended.

7.11 This was followed in 1989 by the publication of a White Paper *Caring for People: Community Care in the Next Decade and Beyond* in which it was stated:

'Community care means providing the services and support which people who are affected by problems of ageing, mental illness, mental handicap or physical or sensory disability need to be able to live as independently as possible in their own homes, or in homely settings in the community.'

The White Paper went on to state that social services authorities would be responsible for:

'... carrying out an appropriate assessment of an individual's need for social care (including residential and nursing home care), in collaboration as necessary with medical, nursing and other agencies, before deciding what services should be provided.'

Implementation

7.12 The recommendations in the Griffiths Report were largely accepted and this resulted in the passing of the National Health Service and Community Care Act 1990 ('the 1990 Act' or 'NSCCA 1990'). The new policies were intended to come into effect

1   Second Report to the House of Commons, Session 1984–85 para 11.
2   *Making a Reality of Community Care* (Audit Commission Report of 1986).
3   Report to the Secretary of State for Social Services by Sir Roy Griffiths.

from April 1991, but to give local authorities time to prepare for their substantial new responsibilities and also due to the problems then being caused by the community charge, they were phased in. In April 1991, the inspection units within local authorities and complaints procedures were introduced, with development continuing on the new procedures and responsibilities within social services departments. In April 1992 the new planning arrangements for local authorities and health authorities became effective with the new system, including the new benefit arrangements to meet the costs of those entering residential or nursing homes, being fully implemented from April 1993. It was recognised that local authorities would need adequate resources to enable them to discharge their new responsibilities, and the monies which would otherwise have been provided to finance care through social security payments to people in residential and nursing homes were transferred to those authorities.

7.13   Subsequent reviews of the policies adopted and the role of social services resulted in the White Paper *'Modernising Social Services, the Royal Commission Report with Respect to Old Age: Long Term Care: Rights and Responsibilities'* (March 1999)[4] and a Department of Health Report *'Modernising Mental Health Services December'* (1998). The policies then adopted are to be found in:

- 'The NHS Plan' (July 2000);[5]

- 'Delivering the NHS Plan' (July 2002);[6]

- 'Shifting the Balance of Power within the NHS: Securing Delivery and Involving Patients and the Public in Healthcare' (July 2001);[7]

- 'Our health, our care, our say: a new direction for community services', White Paper, Department of Health, (2006);[8]

- 'Putting People First: A shared vision and commitment to the transformation of Adult Social Care', HM Government, (December 2007);

- 'A Strategy for Social Service in Wales over the Next Decade: Fulfilled Lives, Supportive Communities', Welsh Assembly, (February 2007).

More recently the Law Commission's report on the reform of social care[9] and the Dilnot Commission's report, 'Fairer Care Funding' (July 2011), resulted in the publication of the White Paper, 'Caring for Our Future: Reforming Care and Support' (July 2012)[10] and the Care Bill, currently making its way through Parliament.

7.14   The trend is towards more co-operation between, and the joint commissioning of services by, health authorities and local authorities responsible for social services. There is to be more choice and autonomy for the 'consumer' of services, although funding constraints still dominate and there remains an uneasy relationship with the private commercial and not-for-profit sectors. There remain gaps and overlaps in the provision of services with the potential for buck-passing between the service providers each of whom seeks to protect its own budgets.

---

4   The recommendations as to fundamental changes in funding arrangements have not been implemented.
5   Available at: www.nhsia.nhs.uk/nhsplan/.
6   Available via: www.dh.gov.uk/en/index.htm.
7   Available at: www.dh.gov.uk/prod_consum_dh/groups/dh_digitalassets/@dh/@en/documents/digitalasset/dh_4076522.pdf.
8   White Paper, Cm 6737.
9   Law Com No 326.
10   Cm 8378.

Legislation

Background

7.15 Social care, often referred to as 'community care' law is a patchwork of legislation dating back to 1948, with each statute reflecting different philosophical attitudes of its time. The two unifying themes (to which there are exceptions) of such statutory provisions are:

(1) they concern non-financial, non-medical services; and

(2) the local authority's social services department has the lead responsibility for ensuring services are provided.

National Assistance Act 1948

7.16 Part III of the National Assistance Act 1948 (NAA 1948) is concerned with the needs of vulnerable people for both residential accommodation and domiciliary-based services.

7.17 Section 21 obliges authorities to provide residential accommodation for people who are elderly, ill or disabled.[11] These obligations have changed little since 1948; it is still the statutory basis for the vast majority of local authority residential accommodation placements. It has been subject to several amendments: the National Health Service and Community Care Act 1990 (NHSCCA 1990) allowed for care beds to be arranged in care homes providing nursing services and the Immigration and Asylum Act 1999[12] and Nationality Immigration and Asylum Act 2002,[13] limited provision for asylum seekers and others from abroad who are disqualified from means-tested benefits and housing, as homeless persons seeking such assistance on the grounds of their poverty.

7.18 Section 29[14] empowers local authorities to provide general non-residential services for disabled people, including:

• advice and guidance;

• the maintaining of registers;

• the provision of occupational activities, such as workshops; and

• the provision of facilities which assist in overcoming limitations of communication or mobility.

These services are only available to disabled people,[15] namely 'persons aged 18 or over who are blind, deaf or dumb or who suffer from mental disorder[16] of any description and other persons aged 18 or over who are substantially and permanently handicapped by illness, injury, or congenital deformity'. This section does not therefore include people whose need arises merely because they are frail or temporarily incapacitated. Section 29

---

[11] See **7.161–7.170**.
[12] Immigration and Asylum Act 1999, s 116.
[13] Nationality Immigration and Asylum Act 2002, ss 10, 54 and Sch 3.
[14] See **7.181**.
[15] As defined in NAA 1948, s 29(1), which reflect the post-war period where many former soldiers were left with disabilities.
[16] Mental Health Act 1983, s 1.

services cannot be provided to a person if the same service has been required to be provided under the National Health Service Act 2006 (NHSA 2006) or the National Health Service (Wales) Act 2006 (NHS(W)A 2006).[17]

Health Services and Public Health Act 1968

7.19 Section 45 of the Health Services and Public Health Act 1968 (HSPHA 1968) created a general power for local authorities to make arrangements specifically for promoting the welfare of old people.[18] There is no requirement for the older person to be substantially or permanently disabled. The services which can be provided under s 45 are not listed in the Act, however guidance[19] sets out the types of services covered. These are similar to those set out in the NAA 1948, s 29. The Act does not set out any definition of who is 'old', but as it is merely a power, with limited budgets, services provided under this provision are rare.

Chronically Sick and Disabled Persons Act 1970

7.20 Section 2 of the Chronically Sick and Disabled Persons Act (CSDPA 1970) creates an absolute duty to provide prescribed services under NAA 1948, s 29 when the local authority is satisfied it is necessary to meet the disabled person's needs. The Act did not require the local authority to undertake an assessment of the disabled person's needs, and so it was quite possible until the introduction of the NHSCCA 1990, for no service to be provided as no assessment was obliged to be conducted.[20]

Mental Health Act 1983, s 117

7.21 During the late 1970s and the 1980s, the closure of long stay hospitals gathered pace, such that community care became linked in the public mind with the care of people with mental health difficulties in the community rather than by incarceration in isolated hospitals. Section 117 of the Mental Health Act 1983 (MHA 1983) creates a joint duty on local authorities and local NHS bodies[21] to arrange aftercare services (in co-operation with relevant voluntary bodies) for those who were detained under ss 3 (treatment), 37 (hospital order) 45A (hospital direction), 47 or 48 (transfer direction) and then cease to be detained, until satisfied that the patient no longer needs aftercare services. Aftercare is not defined in the legislation, however case-law[22] has confirmed it would normally include social work support, support in helping the ex-patient with problems of employment, accommodation or family relationships, the provision of domiciliary services and the use of day centres and residential facilities. Local authorities are not allowed to charge for the provision of aftercare services.[23] Chapter 8 covers this in more detail.

7.22 Most people with mental health problems receive their community care services under CSDPA 1970, s 2 or NHSA 2006, Sch 20 or NHS(W)A 2006, Sch 15.

---

[17]   NAA 1948, s 29(6).
[18]   See **7.173**.
[19]   DHSS 19/71.
[20]   See **7.1180** and **7.182**.
[21]   In Wales the responsible NHS body is the local health board; in England it is local Clinical Commissioning Groups; Health and Social Care Act 2012, s 40.
[22]   *Clunis v Camden and Islington Health Authority* [1998] QB 978, at 992.
[23]   *R (Stennett) v Manchester City Council* [2002] UKHL 34.

Health and Social Services and Social Security Adjudications Act 1983

7.23   The Health and Social Services and Social Security Adjudications Act 1983 (HASSASSAA 1983) gave power for local authorities to recover charges for services they provided and created mechanisms for placing charges on land in England and Wales.[24] In addition, Sch 9, Part II gave district councils, Welsh county councils and county borough councils power to provide meals and recreation for old people, when such councils did not have social services responsibility.

Disabled Persons (Services, Consultation and Representation) Act 1986

7.24   The Disabled Persons (Services, Consultation and Representation) Act 1986 (DP(SCR)A 1986) strengthened the legislation laid down in CSDPA 1970. It created a duty on local authorities to assess the need for services under CSDPA 1970, s 2(1) when requested by a disabled person,[25] their unpaid carer or representative.[26] Where assessments are conducted under s 4, the local authority must provide a written statement, which sets out the needs of the disabled person, which they should provide, and their proposals as to how they will meet those needs. The assessment must take into account the ability of an informal carer to carry on caring when deciding to provide services.[27]

National Health Service and Community Care Act 1990

7.25   The duty on a local authority social services department to provide a service only arises when the department is satisfied that the service is necessary. The need to be assessed is a prerequisite to the provision of services. Section 47 of NHSCCA 1990 obliges social services to assess potential service users for their possible need for 'community care services'.[28] For the purpose of this Act the phrase means:

> 'Services which a local authority may provide or arrange to be provided under any of the following provisions:
>
> Part III of the National Assistance Act 1948;
>
> Section 45 of the Health Services and Public Health Act 1968;
>
> Section 254 of, and Schedule 20 to the National Health Act 2006 and section 192 of, and Schedule 15 to, the National Health Service (Wales) Act 2006; and
>
> Section 117 Mental Health Act 1983'.[29]

Although, the definition does not list services provided under CSDPA 1970, s 2 as a community care service, provision is made under Part III of the NAA 1948, s 29.[30]

---

[24]   HASSASSAA 1983, s 22.
[25]   NAA 1948, s 29 defines a disabled person.
[26]   DP(SCR)A 1986, s 4.
[27]   DP(SCR)A 1986, s 8.
[28]   See **7.107–7.128** for detail of the assessment.
[29]   NHSCCA 1990, s 46(3).
[30]   *R v Powys County Council ex p Hambridge (No 1)* [1998] 96 LGR 627.

Carers (Recognition and Services) Act 1995

7.26 The NHSCCA 1990 provided no practical support for carers until the Carers (Recognition and Services) Act 1995 (C(RS)A 1995). In cases where the local authority are carrying out an assessment under the NHSCCA 1990 for community care services and a carer provides or intends to provide substantial and regular care for the potential service user, the carer may request an assessment of their ability or continued ability to provide care. The results of the assessment must be taken into account by the local authority in deciding what (if any) services to provide to the potential service user.[31] A carer specifically excludes anyone who is employed to care or volunteers for a voluntary organisation.[32]

7.27 The Act was amended by the Carers (Equal Opportunities) Act 2004, with the effect that the local authority must tell the carer of their right to an assessment[33] when undertaking an assessment of a potential service user and to prevent the carer's social isolation the assessment must take into consideration of whether the carer works or wishes to work, is undertaking or wishes to undertake education, training or any leisure activity.[34]

Human Rights Act 1998

7.28 The Human Rights Act 1998 (HRA 1998) has incorporated the European Convention of Human Rights into domestic law. Its application occurs in respect of the acts of a public body, such as the local authority and has been invoked in numerous community care judicial review decisions.[35] Following the case of *YL v Birmingham County Council*,[36] the Health and Social Care Act 2008, s 145 was passed, which provides that a service user who is placed in an independent care home under Part III of the NAA 1948 by a local authority is entitled to the same human rights as a resident placed in a local authority run home. In all other respects, independent home care providers continue to fall outside the Human Rights Act 1998.

7.29 It is arguable that a preference by a disabled person (and/or their family) for domiciliary care should be followed unless the provision of residential care as an alternative is a necessary and proportionate interference with Article 8 rights (the right to respect private and family life). This enables a court to consider whether the cost of domiciliary care is significantly more than residential care that it is necessary and proportionate to contravene Article 8 rights. The need to balance cost and administrative efficiency with the infringement of Article 8 rights was established in *R v North East Devon Health Authority, ex p Coughlan*,[37] with the court finding a promise made that the care facility would be the claimant's for life was sufficient to breach her right to her home under Article 8. Local authorities have been successful in establishing that their resources and the needs of other service users are relevant factors when considering whether an infringement of Article 8 rights is justified under Article 8(2).[38]

---

31 See **7.129–7.136** for more detail on carers' assessments.
32 C(RS)A 1995, s 1(3).
33 C(RS)A 1995, s 1(2B).
34 C(RS)A 1995, s 1(2C).
35 See Ch 1, at **1.66–1.92**.
36 [2007] UKHL 27.
37 [2000] 3 All ER 850, at [90]–[93].
38 *R (Haggarty) v St Helen's Borough Council* [2003] EWHC 803, para 60-61; *R (Mcdonald) v Kensington & Chelsea Royal London Borough Council* [2011] UKSC 33.

7.30 Article 6 (the right to a fair hearing) will be engaged where community care services derive from statute and affect a person's means of subsistence.[39] They may not be engaged when the services are in the gift of the state.[40] Where Article 6 is engaged a speedy resolution of disputes over welfare provisions is likely to be required.[41] The lack of Article 6 independence and impartiality found in many local authority decision-making procedures may be remedied by the availability of judicial review. The statutory context and the nature of the rights at play are important.[42]

7.31 Article 5 (the right to liberty and security of the person) is directly relevant to the area of mental health, expressly subject to the right to detain 'persons of unsound mind'.[43] Article 5(1) sets out a long list of circumstances which give rise to a right to detail which are narrowly interpreted in Convention case-law. It must be reliably established, through objective medical expertise, that the person detained has a true mental disorder of a kind or degree that warrants compulsory confinement and the validity of continued confinement depends upon the persistence of such a disorder. It does not permit the detention of a person simply because his views or behaviour deviate from the prevailing societal norms.[44] Any measure which deprives a person of their liberty should issue from and be executed by an appropriate authority and should not be arbitrary.[45] The Mental Capacity Act 2005 (MCA 2005) provides for a regime[46] to authorise the deprivation of liberty of persons who suffer from a mental disorder but do not meet the criteria for detention under the MHA 1983.

7.32 Article 2 (the right to life) is often triggered in relation to end of life care; whether particular treatment should be given or withdrawn.[47] It has also been unsuccessfully argued in challenges involving care home closures, with a connected claim that Article 3 (right not to be subjected to torture, inhuman or degrading treatment) has been breached.[48] The obligation on the local authority to take measures to protect citizens from breaches of Articles 2 and 3 is limited, as the obligation must not impose an impossible or disproportionate obligation on authorities.[49] Article 3 may be breached if the local authority fails to use their powers to protect vulnerable adults from abuse.[50]

7.33 Article 14 (right not to suffer discrimination) does not stand alone and can only be invoked in combination with another article. Discrimination will be permitted, if it is established that the act has an objective and reasonable justification that is proportionate.

---

[39] *Salesi v Italy* (1993) 26 EHRR 187.

[40] *Lombardo v Italy* (1996)] 21 EHRR 188.

[41] *FM v Italy* (1994)] 18 EHRR 570.

[42] *R (Alconbury Developments) v SSETR* [2001] UKHL 23 (Planning) and *R (Beeson) v Dorset County Council* [2002] EWCA Civ 1812 (community care means assessment).

[43] Article 5(1)(e).

[44] *Winterwerp v The Netherlands* (1979) 2 EHRR 387.

[45] *Winterwerp v The Netherlands* (1979) 2 EHRR 387; *R (KB) MHRT* [2003] EWHC 193 (Admin); *HL v United Kingdom* (45508/99) (2005) 40 EHRR 32.

[46] MCA 2005, Schs 1A and A1; ss 4A and 4B, 16A.

[47] *W (By Her Litigation Friend B) v A NHS Primary Care Trust* [2011] EWHC 2443 (Fam).

[48] *R (Dudley and others) v East Sussex County Council* [2003] EWHC 1093 (Admin); *R (Thomas) v Havering London Borough Council*; *R (W) v Coventry County Council* [2008] EWHC 2300 (Admin); *R (Haggarty) v St Helen's Borough Council* [2003] EWHC 803.

[49] *Osman v United Kingdom* (2000) 29 EHRR 611.

[50] *Re F (Adult: Court's Jurisdiction)* [2000] 3 WLR 1740.

Carers and Disabled Children Act 2000

7.34 The Carers National Strategy document 'Caring about Carers', published on 8 February 1999 highlighted the need for legislation to enable local authorities with social service responsibilities to provide services direct to carers. The Carers and Disabled Children Act 2000 (CDCA 2000) gives local authorities this power following an assessment. It also enables a carer's assessment to take place even where the person cared for has refused an assessment for, or the provision of, community care services. As with the C(RS)A 1995, the carer must not be paid or working for a voluntary organisation and must be providing or intending to provide substantial and regular care for someone for whom the local authority might provide or arrange community care services. The Act was amended by the Carers (Equal Opportunities) Act 2004 and so consideration must also be given to whether the carer works or wishes to work, or is undertaking or wishes to undertake education, training or any leisure activity.[51]

Local Government Act 2000

7.35 A local authority has a general power to do anything that it considers is likely to promote or improve the social well-being of its area. The power may be general or for a specific individual. The power extends to providing accommodation to any person.[52] Local authorities are required to have regard to guidance issued by the Secretary of State.[53] Guidance was last issued in 2009, by the Department for Communities and Local Government, entitled *Power to promote well-being of the areas: statutory guidance for Councils*.

7.36 Local authorities can charge for such services but this is limited by the restrictions that the recipient must agree to the provision of the service; when taking one financial year with another income does not exceed costs; and it cannot be used to charge for services that the authority is under a duty to provide.[54] Guidance was issued in 2003 by the Office of the Deputy Prime Minister, entitled *General Power for Best Value Authorities to charge for Discretionary Services – Guidance on the Power in the Local Government Act 2003*, with similar guidance being issued by the Welsh Assembly in 2004.

Health and Social Care Act 2001

7.37 The provision for direct payments in the Community Care (Direct Payments) Act 1996 was a reflection of the desire to promote autonomy and choice for those in need of services in how they arrange services, rather than depending on the local authority to arrange the service. This provision was repealed and replaced by the Health and Social Care Act 2001 (HSCA 2001), s 57. This brought into effect a payment by the NHS for those who were in receipt of nursing care provided by a registered nurse in a nursing home[55] to remedy the disparity that had the resident been in a hospital receiving care, there would have been no charge.

---

51 Carers and Disabled Children Act 2000, s 1(3A). For more detail, see **7.132–7.137**.
52 Carers and Disabled Children Act 2000, s 2(4)(f) and *R (on the application of J) v Enfield London Borough Council* [2002] 5 CCL Rep 434.
53 Carers and Disabled Children Act 2000, s 3(5).
54 Local Government Act 2003, s 93.
55 HSCA 2001, s 49.

7.38 The HSCA 2001 importantly created the power for local authorities to place a charge on a resident's property where they did not wish to sell their home to pay for care and otherwise had limited resources. The introduction of the deferred payment agreement[56] ensured that care would be provided, with the knowledge that the local authority would not pursue payment of care fees until the property was sold or the resident died, as distinct from similar recovery under HASSASSAA 1983, s 22. If the resident wished to live in more expensive accommodation that the local authority would provide, the resident's home could be used as collateral to fund the difference.[57]

Community Care (Delayed Discharges etc.) Act 2003

7.39 The Community Care (Delayed Discharges etc.) Act 2003 (CC(DD)A 2003) places a duty on local authorities and the NHS in England to work together to ensure the safe hospital discharge of people with social care needs. Where a person remains in hospital because a local authority has not provided the assessment or services that the person needs to be safely discharged, the local authority is liable to pay the relevant NHS body a charge per day of delay.

National Health Service Act 2006, Sch 20 or National Health Service (Wales) Act 2006, Sch 15

7.40 The NHSA 2006 and its Welsh equivalent (NHS(W)A 2006) are consolidating Acts. Schedule 20 was originally enacted in the National Health Service Act 1977,[58] and grants local authorities discretionary power to make arrangements[59] to prevent illness or mental disorder or care for people suffering from illness[60] and assist in their aftercare. As such it is aimed at those who do not qualify for assistance under CSDPA 1970, s 2 or the NAA 1948, s 29, as they are not permanently impaired. It extends to the provision or arrangement of home helps and laundry facilities to the household.[61]

Regulations

7.41 The bulk of the statutory control over the way community care services operate is exercised by regulations, rules and orders, providing greater explanation of a duty or power imposed by the primary legislation. By way of example, in relation to charges for residential accommodation, NAA 1948, s 22(1) requires local authorities to charge for accommodation and s 22(5) authorises the Secretary of State to issue regulations detailing how this should be done. This was done in 30 November 1992 with the making of the National Assistance (Assessment of Resources) Regulations 1992.[62]

---

[56] HSCA 2001, s 55. See also Ch 10.
[57] HSCA 2001, s 54.
[58] National Health Service Act 1977, s 21: Sch 8, para 2(1).
[59] NHSA 2006, s 254.
[60] Defined in NHSA 2006, s 275(1) and NHS(W)A 2006, s 206(1) to mean 'mental disorder within the meaning of the MHA 1983 (c. 20) and any injury or disability requiring medical or dental treatment or nursing'.
[61] NHSA 2006, Sch 20, para 3(1).
[62] SI 1992/2977 (as amended).

Directions and guidance

General

7.42   The administrative control of the community care system is exercised primarily by the Department of Health in England and the National Assembly in Wales issuing directions or guidance. Social services departments are run under the general supervision of the Secretary of State in England and the National Assembly Government in Wales.[63]

Directions

7.43   Directions are mandatory and are usually phrased as such. Concern has been raised that the ministerial direction can be withdrawn at any time without recourse to Parliament.[64] There may be uncertainty as to whether the instruction is a direction or guidance, as a direction could be contained within a circular, although a circular's wording may not be sufficient to be a direction.[65]

7.44   They are usually published separately although they may appear as appendices to local authority circulars. In this context important community care directions were issued as appendixes to LAC (93) 10[66] and DHSS Circular 19/71.[67] Other important separate directions issued are:

- National Assistance Act (Choice of Accommodation) Directions 1992 in England and identical Directions were issued in Wales in 1993;
- Community Care Assessment Directions 2004.[68]

Guidance

7.45   Guidance can take many forms, often in the form of local authority circulars (LAC) or National Assembly for Wales Circular (WOC) issued by the Department of Health or the Welsh Government. There are two basic types of social services guidance:

(1) *Policy Guidance* issued under the Local Authority Social Services Act 1970 (LASSA 1970), s 7(1) is clearly labeled as such and must be followed unless there are good reasons not to.[69] Failure to follow such guidance will be a breach of administrative law and may result in the court being prepared to set aside the decision.[70]

(2) *Practice Guidance* being advice that a local authority should have regard to when implementing or interpreting a particular statutory responsibility but it does not have to be followed.[71] Failure to have regard to such guidance (rather than a

---

63   Local Authority Social Services Act 1970, ss 7(1) and 7(1A).
64   *Godbold v Mahmood* [2005] EWHC 1002 (QB), at [24]–[26].
65   *R v North Derbyshire Health Authority, ex p Fisher* [1997] 1 CCL Rep 150.
66   LAC stands for 'Local Authority Circular', followed by the year it was issued in brackets and the series number. Concerns NAA 1948, Part III services and NHS Act 1977 Sch 8, which is now contained in NHSA 2006, Sch 20; NHS (W) A 2006, Sch 15. The Welsh equivalent has been published as Welsh Office Circular (WOC 35/93).
67   Concerning Health Services and Public Health Act 1968, s 45.
68   No equivalent Direction has been issued in Wales.
69   *R v Islington London Borough Council, ex p Rixon* (1997–98) 1 CCL Rep 119.
70   *R v North Yorkshire County Council, ex p Hargreaves* (1997) 1 CCL Rep 104 as an example of when the court set aside a decision which had been in breach of policy guidance.
71   Ie not issued under the Local Authority Social Services Act 1970, s 7.

failure to follow it), which is required by administrative law, may mean the local authority has failed to have regard to all material factors when reaching a decision and may result in the subsequent decision being set aside.

It is often said that policy guidance tells the local authority what it must do, whereas practice guidance suggests how it might go about doing it.

ROLE OF THE AUTHORITIES

Local authorities

7.46 Local authorities' social services departments are the primary gatekeeper to the delivery of community care services. They are responsible for strategic planning, information dissemination,[72] assessment and service delivery. Other authorities also have an important role in the overall provision of community care services to those in need of such assistance, notably the NHS and local authority housing departments and to a lesser extent their environmental health departments.

7.47 Social services functions are exercised by County Councils and unitary authorities.[73] Housing and environmental health functions are exercised by District Councils, as well as by unitary authorities.

7.48 Social services departments were created by the LASSA 1970, and brought together various welfare departments as recommended by the 1968 Seebohm Report.[74] As statutory bodies, social services departments have no inherent powers and are obliged to restrict their activities to actions specifically authorised by statute. Their functions are set out in LASSA 1970,[75] which also outlines the general framework within which social services must operate. It deals with the establishment, appointment and membership of social services committees and sub committees and the appointment of[76] the Director of Social Services, and the committee's obligation to provide adequate staff to assist the director in the discharge of the department's functions.[77] The lack of precision in LASSA 1970 as to how social services are to be organised and run, is addressed in general terms by provisions[78] which give to the Secretary of State in England various supervisory powers and specifically empower him to issue directions or guidance concerning the way particular functions are to be applied.

7.49 In 2008, the Secretary of State compelled all English social services departments to create the role of Director of Adult Social Services, alongside the Director of Children's Services post,[79] as part of the Government's vision for modernising community services as set out in the White Paper *Our health, our care, our say: a new direction for community services.*[80]

---

[72] CSDPA 1970, s 1.
[73] These include Metropolitan and London Borough Council.
[74] Report of the Committee on Local Authority and Allied Personal Social Services (Cmnd 3703).
[75] LASSA 1970, Sch 1.
[76] LASSA 1970, s 6(1).
[77] LASSA 1970, s 6(6).
[78] LASSA 1970, ss 7C–7E and see LGA 2000, s 102.
[79] Children Act 2004 required all local authorities with responsibility for educational and social services to appoint a Director of Children's Services with responsibility for coordinating and managing the provision of

The National Health Service (NHS)

7.50   The NHS is the responsibility of the Secretary of State for Health in England and the National Assembly Government in Wales.[81] The regional management of NHS in England is the NHS Commissioning Board (NHS CB), which is responsible for the management of the NHS budget, and allocates money to Clinical Commissioning Groups (CCGs) for them to locally manage the commissioning of care.[82] There are 27 Local Area Teams (LATs) of the NHS CB that are in charge of commissioning dental, pharmacy, optometry and some specialist services. The NHS CB ensures all CCG's operate to the same commissioning model.

7.51   All NHS Trusts, hospitals, mental health and care trusts are going through the process to become NHS Foundation Trusts by 2014. Foundation Trust status gives hospitals more financial autonomy. They are more accountable to local people, who can become members and governors. See Chapter 8 for more detail on the structure of the NHS.

Health and Wellbeing Boards

7.52   Local Health and Wellbeing Boards, established under the Health and Social Care Act 2012, bring together local authorities, CCGs and Healthwatch to work to ensure services are joined up and patients receive consistency in care. The Board undertakes a Joint Strategic Needs Assessment (JSNA) and develops a joint strategy, including recommendations for joint commissioning and integrating services.

Healthwatch

7.53   Healthwatch[83] is an independent body, introduced by the Health and Social Care Act 2012 with a statutory remit to collate evidence of service shortfalls and national issues to ensure regulators, other arms-length bodies and Government departments respond accordingly. Local Healthwatch groups are established to feed into the national Healthwatch England.

Ordinarily resident

Relevance

7.54   In almost all cases where a social services local authority is under a duty[84] to provide community care services, that duty is restricted to persons who are ordinarily resident in its area. The basic rules for determining a person's ordinary residence for residential accommodation provided under NAA 1948, s 21 are outlined in s 24. The concept of being ordinarily resident is the subject of interpretative guidance, first issued

---

local children's services across education, health and social services. This lead to the need to establish a separate role for a Director of Adults Social Services, who works under mandatory guidance issued by the Secretary of State.

80   Cm 6737, January 2006.

81   The Government of Wales Act 1998 and the National Assembly of Wales (Transfer of Functions) Order 1999, SI 1999/672, transferred NHS law making functions in Wales to the Welsh Assembly.

82   Strategic health authorities were abolished in April 2013 and primary care trusts transferred their commissioning responsibilities to Clinical Commissioning Groups, run by groups of local GPs in April 2013. These changes were brought about by the Health and Social Care Act 2012.

83   The role was previously undertaken by LINks (Local Involvement Networks).

84   As opposed to power.

in 1993.[85] The Department of Health replaced the 1993 guidance with more detailed guidance in 2010, which has since been updated.[86] The guidance should be read in conjunction with a number of Directions.[87] The Welsh Assembly Government has not updated its 1993 guidance. The guidance clarifies how local authorities should determine whether a person is ordinary resident in their area.

7.55 The ramifications are wide for people moving between areas: it determines which local authority funds the cost of residential care, domiciliary care, deprivation of liberty processes, delayed discharge processes and responsibility for aftercare services under MHA 1983, s 117. It is also relevant to NHS bodies when exercising partnership arrangements with local authorities.

Meaning

7.56 There is no statutory definition of the term 'ordinary resident', although it should be given its ordinary and natural meaning, subject to interpretation by the courts.[88] The concept involves questions of fact and degree and that factors such as time, intention, and continuity (each of which may be given different weight according to the context) have to be taken into account.[89] Generally a person's ordinary residence will be the place where their normal residential address is to be found. The House of Lords held in the *Shah* case[90] that in determining a person's ordinary residence that person's long term future intentions or expectations are not relevant; the test is not what is a person's 'real home' but whether a person can show 'a regular, habitual mode of life in a particular place, the continuity of which has persisted despite temporary absences'. A person's attitude is only relevant in two respects:

(1) the residence must be voluntarily adopted; and

(2) there must be a settled purpose in living in the particular residence.

'Ordinary residence' is to be given its 'ordinary and natural meaning', namely 'a man's abode in a particular place or country which he had adopted voluntarily and for settled purposes as part of the regular order of his life for the time being, whether of short or long duration'.

Implications of mental incapacity

7.57 The issue of whether a person has adopted a place voluntarily raises an issue for people who lack mental capacity to decide where to live. In *R v Waltham Forest LBC, ex p Vale*,[91] Taylor J set out two approaches, which are:

(1) The first approach applies where the person is so severely handicapped as to be totally dependent upon a parent or guardian. Taylor J stated that such a person (in

---

85 LAC (93)7 in England and WOC 41/93 in Wales.
86 The most current update was in March 2013.
87 Ordinary Residence Disputes (National Assistance Act 1948) Directions 2010; Ordinary Residence Disputes (Community Care (Delayed Discharges etc Act 2003) Directions 2010; Ordinary Residence Disputes (Mental Capacity Act 2005) Directions 2010.
88 Para 18, 2011 Guidance.
89 Para 19, 2011 Guidance.
90 *Shah v Barnet London Borough Council* [1983] 1 All ER 226.
91 (1985) *The Times*, 25 February.

that case it was a 28-year-old woman) is in the same position as a small child and her ordinary residence is that of her parents or guardian 'because that is her base'.

(2) The second approach, considers the question as if the person is of normal mental capacity, taking account of all the facts of the person's case, including physical presence in a particular place and the nature and purpose of that presence as outlined in *Shah*, but without requiring the person himself or herself to have adopted the residence voluntarily.

Taylor J further held that a person's ordinary residence could result after a stay in one place of only short duration and that there was no reason why one month should be adjudged too short.[92] Guidance advises to adopt a cautious approach to using the first *Vale* approach, as its relevance will vary according to the ability of the person to make their own choices and should only be applied to cases where there are similar material facts to those of *Vale*.[93]

Assessments

7.58 An individual who may be (or is about to be) in need of community care services does not need to be ordinarily resident to be assessed for services.[94]

Residential accommodation

7.59 Where an out of area placement is arranged, 'deeming provisions' are triggered;[95] the placing local authority remains responsible for provision of care in another local authority area. This applies when the person has been assessed and the local authority has accepted responsibility to provide. Likewise where a person is in NHS care they are deemed to be ordinarily resident in the area in which they were ordinarily resident immediately before admission as a patient to the NHS facility.[96] Where a person was not ordinarily resident in any area prior to admission, then the responsible social services local authority will be the one in whose area the person is at that time.[97] This applies even if the former local authority only provides advice and information about the move.

7.60 Where there is a break in local authority provision, for example a person who qualifies for their home to be disregarded during the first 12 weeks of a permanent admission to a care home and then becomes self-funding, but later seeks local authority support, the placing local authority is responsible during the initial 12-week period but the receiving local authority is responsible following the break in provision.

Non-residential services

7.61 The deeming provisions do not apply to non-residential care services, so the person should apply to the receiving local authority for support. Non-residential care

---

92 See also *R v Redbridge London Borough Council. ex p East Sussex County Council* (1992) *The Times*, 31 December.
93 2011 Guidance, para 33; *R (on the application of Cornwall County Council) v Wiltshire County Council* [2012] EWHC 3739 (Admin).
94 *R (on the application of B) v Camden London Borough Council* [2005] EWHC 1366 (Admin).
95 NAA 1948, s 24(5).
96 NAA 1948, s 24(6).
97 NAA 1948, s 24(3).

services include people in supported living schemes and adult placement/shared lives schemes as they do not usually amount to residential accommodation under NAA 1948, s 21.

Carers' services

7.62 Under the CDCA 2000, local authorities have a duty, when requested, to independently assess carers who provide or intend to provide a substantial amount of care to another adult on a regular basis. Practice guidance issued[98] sets out that where a carer is ordinarily resident in a different local authority to the cared-for person, and the cared-for person is eligible for social care support, it is the local authority in whose area *the cared-for person* lives that is responsible for carrying out the carers' assessment. The cared-for person's local authority is also responsible for the provision of any services to the carer, even where such services need to be provided in the carer's own local authority area. In this situation, there is an expectation in such cases both local authorities should work together.

Mental Health Act 1983, s 117 aftercare services

7.63 Responsibility for the provision of such services falls to the local authority and local NHS commissioning body for the area in which the person was 'resident' before being detained in hospital, even if the person does not return to that area on discharge. As such the concept of being 'ordinary resident' does not apply, as the circumstances on which aftercare provision arises are very different to NAA 1948 provision. The term 'resident' is not defined in the legislation, and so the term should be given its ordinary and natural meaning subject to any interpretation by the courts. If no such residence can be established, the duty falls on the authority where the person is to go on discharge from hospital.[99]

7.64 Disputes arising in connection with s 117 cannot be referred to the Secretary of State or Welsh Ministers for determination under NAA 1948, s 32(3). If a dispute cannot be resolved locally, it would be necessary to seek a court decision.

No settled residence

7.65 People of no settled residence or in urgent need should be treated as being ordinarily resident in the local authority area where they are present.[100] Local authorities will be cautious to consider whether the person has lost an ordinary residence in one area and acquired one in another area, so will look at the circumstances very carefully.[101] However, the local authority where the person is present should agree to take responsibility until the matter is resolved.

NHS Continuing Health Care

7.66 When a person has a primary health need (in addition to any social care needs) and is assessed as being eligible for NHS Continuing Healthcare (NHSCHC) under the

---

[98] Paras 24–27.
[99] MHA 1983, s 117(3); *R v Mental Health Review Tribunal, ex p Hall* [1999] 4 All ER 883; *R (on the application of Sunderland City Council) v South Tyneside Council* [2012] EWCA Civ 1232.
[100] *R v London Borough of Redbridge, ex p East Sussex County Council* (1992) *The Times*, 31 December.
[101] *R (on the application of Greenwich LBC) v Secretary of State for Health* [2006] EWHC 2576 (Admin).

National Framework for NHS Continuing Healthcare and NHS-funded Nursing Care[102] and the National Health Service Commissioning Board and Clinical Commissioning Groups (Responsibilities and Standing Rules) Regulations 2012,[103] the NHS must provide a package of care for their assessed health and social care needs. This care package may be provided in a number of settings including hospitals, care homes or the person's own home.

7.67   Problems arose as to which local authority was responsible where a person was receiving NHSCHC and then ceased to do so. In determining the ordinary residence of someone who went into NHSCHC accommodation on or before 18 April 2010 and continued to be there after that date, the ordinary residence rules that applied on the day they went into care should be applied – i e the dispute must be resolved in the light of the specific circumstances and not the deeming provisions. After this date, the deeming provisions apply.

Discharge under Community Care (Delayed Discharges etc.) Act 2003

7.68   In England, before discharging a person under the CC(DD)A 2003, NHS bodies are required[104] to take reasonable steps to ensure that eligibility for NHSCHC is assessed in cases where it appears that the person may have a need for such care, in consultation, where it considers it appropriate, with the local authority appearing to the NHS body to be the authority in whose area the patient is ordinarily resident.

7.69   If a local authority disputes responsibility, the NHS body is to be informed immediately. If the NHS body does not agree that the person is ordinarily resident elsewhere, the notified local authority must proceed with carrying out the assessment and arranging for the provision of any necessary services, in accordance with its duty to do so and challenge the matter in accordance with directions.[105]

7.70   Where there is no eligibility for NHSCHC but there is a likely need for community care services upon the person's discharge from hospital, CC(DD)A 2003, s 2 requires the NHS body to notify a person's local authority of this. It is the local authority in which the person appears to the NHS body to be ordinarily resident that must be notified by the NHS body.

Deprivation of Liberty Safeguards

7.71   The MCA 2005 provides for a framework for the deprivation of liberty (DoLs) of people who lack the capacity to consent to arrangements made for their care or treatment (in either a hospital or care home) but who need to be deprived of liberty in their own best interests, to protect them from harm.

---

[102]   Department of Health, November 2012.
[103]   SI 2012/2996, Part 6, reg 21.
[104]   National Framework for NHCCHC (November 2012), para 63; National Health Service Commissioning Board and Clinical Commissioning Groups (Responsibilities and Standing Rules) Regulations 2012, SI 2012/2996, Part 6.
[105]   Delayed Discharges (England) Regulations 2003, SI 2003/2277, reg 18. A determination from the Secretary of State can be sought under s 8 of the CC(DD)A 2003 as a last resort: local authorities should take all steps necessary to resolve the disputes themselves first, in accordance with the Ordinary Residence Disputes (Community Care (Delayed Discharges etc.) Act 2003 Directions 2010.

7.72 Under DoLs, hospitals and care homes ('managing authorities') must seek authorisation from the local NHS commissioning body[106] or local authority (a 'supervisory body') if they believe they can only care for a person in circumstances that amount to a deprivation of liberty. Where a person needs to be deprived of liberty in a care home, the DoLs provides that the supervisory body is always the local authority in which the person is ordinarily resident.

Disputed ordinary residence

7.73 Where local authorities fall into dispute over a person's ordinary residence, and that dispute cannot be resolved locally, the local authorities concerned may request a determination from the Secretary of State or Welsh Ministers.[107] This is seen as a last resort. Where there is a dispute between local authorities, one of those authorities is under a duty to provide any community care services required pending resolution of the issue. The Welsh guidance contains little detail on how to resolve the matter between local Welsh authorities. The English directions determine the relevant local authority in the following manner:

(1) if the person is already in receipt of services, the local authority providing them should continue to do so;

(2) if the person is not in receipt of services, the local authorities in dispute may agree which of them will provide services pending the resolution of the dispute;[108]

(3) if the local authorities in dispute cannot agree, the local authority in which the person is living must provide the services; and

(4) if the person is not living anywhere, the local authority in whose area the person is physically present (known as the 'local authority of the moment') must do so. This means where the person is situated.

Local authorities must agree a written statement of facts, signed by all the authorities involved and sent with the application for determination. The English directions set out the documents that must be submitted to the Secretary of State. Applications should be submitted within 28 days of the end of the period of 4 months during which local authorities have attempted to resolve the dispute themselves.

Cross-border arrangements between England and Wales

7.74 NAA 1948, s 32(4)[109] provides that arrangements for determining cross-border disputes between England and Wales must be made and published.[110] These arrangements set out that where the dispute involves a person who is living in England at the time the dispute is referred, the Secretary of State will determine the dispute, and where the person is living in Wales when the dispute is referred, the Welsh Ministers will determine the dispute. Each agrees to notify the other when such a dispute arises and will agree with the outcome reached.

---

[106] In England this is always the local authority and in Wales, the Local Health Board.

[107] Determinations can be sought under NAA 1948, s 32(3) (services under Part III of the NAA 1948 or in relation to services provided under CSDPA 1970, s 2); the Community Care (Delayed Discharges etc.) Act 2003, s 8 (in relation to England only) and para 183(3) of Sch A1 to the MCA 2005 (Deprivation of Liberty Safeguards); NAA 1948, s 32(3).

[108] WOC:41/93, para 32 is the only requirement in Wales.

[109] As inserted by the Health and Social Care Act 2008, s 148.

[110] Guidance, 'Arrangements under s 32(4) National Assistance Act 1948 between the Secretary of State and the Welsh Ministers', was published in March 2010.

Cross-border disputes between England and Scotland

7.75   Where an ordinary residence dispute arises between local authorities about care that has been arranged across the England/Scotland border, there is no mechanism for quickly agreeing which Minister is responsible for making a determination, or for recognising each other's determinations. As such both governments have agreed a Memorandum of Understanding[111] which provides clarification on which government department is responsible for determining cross-border ordinary residence disputes involving English and Scottish local authorities. It does not set out how the matter will be determined, merely which body will be responsible. Unlike the Welsh guidance, it is determined by which government is seeking reimbursement of expenditure.

Strategic planning

Government strategies

7.76   The English government has set overarching strategies in which more detailed policy is set, and to which local authorities must have regard when developing local policy, including:

- Putting people first: A shared vision and commitment to the transformation of adult social care[112]

- A vision for adult social care: Capable communities and active citizens[113]

- Shaping the Future of Care Together[114]

- Valuing people now: A new three-year strategy for people with learning disabilities[115]

- National Carers Strategy[116]

- Independent Living Strategy[117]

- National Dementia Strategy[118]

- Fulfilling and rewarding lives: the strategy for adults with autism in England[119]

- End of Life Care Strategy – promoting high quality care for all adults at the end of life[120]

- Fairer contributions guidance: Calculating an individual's contribution to their personal budgets[121]

- No health without mental health: a cross-government mental health outcomes strategy for people of all ages[122]

---

[111]   'Memorandum of Understanding between the Secretary of State and Scottish Ministers', April 2011: www.scotland.gov.uk/Resource/0040/00402946.pdf.

[112]   10 December 2007.

[113]   November 2010, Gateway reference 14847.

[114]   Green Paper, Cm 7673.

[115]   January 2009, Gateway reference 10531.

[116]   Recognised, valued and supported: next steps for the Carers Strategy: Gateway reference 15179, November 2010.

[117]   Office for Disability Issues, 2008.

[118]   Living well with dementia: A national dementia strategy, February 2009, Gateway reference 11198.

[119]   March 2010, Gateway references 13521 and 14307.

[120]   July 2008, Gateway reference 9840.

[121]   Gateway reference 15025.

[122]   February 2010, Gateway reference 14679.

- Caring for our future: reforming care and support[123]
- Adult Social Care Outcomes Framework; Public Health Outcomes Framework; NHS Outcomes Framework.[124]

The Welsh Assembly Government has strategic policies for carers, those with dementia, learning disabilities, autism and end of life care.

Registers of disabled people

7.77   Local authorities are empowered to make arrangements for compiling and maintaining classified registers of disabled adults.[125] Directions made under this provision oblige authorities to keep such registers for disabled adults ordinarily resident in their area.[126] The planning obligations on local authorities have been extended so as to require such authorities to inform themselves of the number of disabled people in their area.[127]

7.78   The planning purpose underlying this further provision[128] requires social services authorities to ensure that they are adequately informed of the numbers and needs of substantially and permanently handicapped persons in order that they can formulate satisfactory plans for developing their services. A disabled person is not required to be on the register to seek and obtain community care services.[129]

Strategic plans

7.79   The duty to produce an annual plan was introduced by the NHSCCA 1990.[130] However, following consultation in 2001 the English government ended the requirement to prepare community care plans due to an increased emphases on joint planning between the NHS and local authorities. The duty to prepare such plans was repealed in 2003.

7.80   In Wales, the duty remains to produce community care plans as part of its 'Health, Social Care and Well-Being Strategies' that local authorities and local health boards (LHBs) must produce.[131] Such strategy should set out how services will be jointly planned, developed and managed to improve integration, elimination of waste, duplication and confusion; minimise the likelihood of harm resulting from poor coordination of care; and how they will measure outcomes of care and improve them over time.[132]

7.81   In England, the Local Government and Public Involvement in Health Act 2007[133] requires local authorities and CCGs to prepare and publish a Joint Strategic Needs

---

123   White Paper, July 2012, Cm 8378.
124   December 2012.
125   NAA 1948, s 29(4)(g).
126   LAC (93)10, para 2(2) of Appendix 2.
127   CSDPA 1970, s 1.
128   DHSS Circular, LAC 12/70.
129   LAC (93)10 Appendix 4, para 3.
130   NHSCCA 1990, s 46.
131   NHS(W)A 2006, s 40; Health Social Care and Well-Being Strategy Guidance 2011–12 to 2013–14.
132   Page 19 of Welsh guidance.
133   Local Government and Public Involvement in Health Act 2007, s 116.

Assessment (JSNA) of the care needs of the people in their local area. They must involve their local Healthwatch organisation and local people.[134]

7.82   Each local authority and CCG must also prepare a 'joint health and well-being strategy',[135] which is the commissioning strategy they propose to adopt to meet the JSNA for their area. Consideration must be given as to the extent to which the needs could be met more effectively by sharing resources.[136] When exercising its functions, the local authority and the CCG must have regard to the JSNA and well-being strategy.[137]

7.83   The Public Sector Equality Duty (PSED) was created by the Equality Act 2010 (EA 2010) and replaces the race, disability and gender equality duties. Following the coming into force of the EA 2010[138] all public bodies must in the exercise of its functions have due regard to the need to:

(1)   eliminate discrimination, harassment, victimisation and any other conduct that is prohibited under the Act;

(2)   advance equality of opportunity between persons who share a relevant protected characteristic and persons who do not share it; and

(3)   foster good relations between persons who share a relevant protected characteristic and persons who do not share it.[139]

A 'relevant protected characteristic' is defined in Chapter 1 of the EA 2010, and includes age, gender and disability.[140]

7.84   The Equality and Human Rights Commission has published a statutory Code of Practice on Services, Public Functions and Associations and produced technical guidance to explain the needs of the PSED, outline the requirements of the EA 2010 and the specific duty regulations and provide practical approaches to complying with the PSED in England and Wales. The effect of this is that any plan should take the PSED into account, and where there is an adverse impact on the goals of the EA 2010, then the local authority must consider what action it should take to mitigate the situation.

The private sector

7.85   One of the key objectives of the community care reforms, detailed in the White Paper '*Caring for People*' (1989) was the promotion of a flourishing independent sector, with social services local authorities making maximum possible use of private and voluntary providers. In furtherance of this aim Treasury funding support for social services and social security benefits for community care users has been weighted in favour of the independent sector. Sir Roy Griffiths in his report which precipitated the community care reforms envisaged independent sector services existing alongside good quality public services.

---

[134]   As amended by s 192(5) of the Health and Social Care Act 2012.
[135]   Local Government and Public Involvement in Health Act 2007, s 116A.
[136]   Arrangements under NHSA 2006, s 75.
[137]   Local Government and Public Involvement in Health Act 2007, s 116B.
[138]   April 2011.
[139]   EA 2010, s 149.
[140]   EA 2010, s 6 defines a disability if (a) the person has a physical or mental impairment, and (b) the impairment has a substantial and long-term adverse effect on a person's ability to carry out normal day-to-day activities.

7.86   So significant, however, have the government's funding incentives for independent services been that a number of authorities have all but abandoned publicly provided community care services. Despite guidance suggesting that authorities should retain some public services[141] the House of Lords has confirmed this is not the case provided there is sufficient private or independent provision available.[142] In 1990 there were about 115,000 local authority supported residents. Almost all were in local authority staffed accommodation. At the peak in 2000 there were 250,000 such residents of whom less than 50,000 were in local authority staffed accommodation. By 2001 only 16% of supported residents were in local authority staffed homes.[143]

7.87   Although the independent care home sector has grown, many homes struggle to make a profit if they are too reliant on state supported residents. Research undertaken by Laing and Buisson found that at September 2012 of the total capacity of 487,800 care beds operating in the UK, those owned and run by the state was only 38,800.[144] 175,000 older residents (43.4%) paid the full costs of their long-term care fees. A further 56,000 (14%), while being supported by local authorities, also relied on 'top-ups' from family or friends. The remaining 43% of residents either had their fees paid in full by councils (143,000) or by the NHS under the continuing healthcare programme (29,000).

7.88   Payments which local authorities are willing to make for care home places for older people have slipped even further away from the levels deemed 'fair' to cover the costs involved and to give care home operators a reasonable rate of return on their investment.[145] Local authorities have on numerous occasions been successful in resisting price rises or attempts by the private sector to secure block payments to cover vacancies.[146]

Safeguarding vulnerable adults

Local authorities safeguarding role

7.89   In March 2000, the Department of Health published guidance[147] to local agencies, such as local authorities and police forces that have a responsibility to investigate and take action when a vulnerable adult is believed to be suffering abuse. It sets out a structure and content for the development of local inter-agency policies, procedures and joint protocols. Similar guidance[148] was published by the National Assembly of Wales. The guidance applies to all adults and not just elderly people. It defines abuse in terms of vulnerability as:

> 'A vulnerable person is one who is or may be in need of community care services by reason of mental or other disability, age or illness; and who is or may be unable to take care of him or herself or unable to protect him or herself against significant harm or exploitation.'

---

141   See for instance LAC(93) 10, para 4.
142   *R v Wandsworth London Borough Council, ex p Beckwith* [1996] 1 WLR 60, HL.
143   National Statistics Bulletin September 2003 for Community Care Statistics 2001.
144   Care of Elderly People UK Market Survey 2012–13.
145   Laing & Buisson's Fair Price for Care Toolkit 2012.
146   *R (on the application of Haggarty) v St Helens BC* [2003] EWHC 803 (Admin), at [60]–[61] (CTLR 30 April 2003); *R (on the application of Bevan & Clarke LLP) v Neath Port Talbot County Borough Council* [2012] EWHC 236 (Admin); *R (on the application of South West Care Homes Ltd) v Devon County Council (Defendant) & Equality And Human Rights Commission (Intervener)* [2012] EWHC 2967 (Admin).
147   'No Secrets Guidance on Developing and Implementing Multi-Agency Policies and Procedures to Protect Vulnerable Adults from Abuse'. A Statement of Principles to benchmark multi agency safeguarding processes was published on 16 May 2011 (Gateway reference: 16072).
148   'In Safe Hands: Implementing adult protection procedures in Wales'.

The consequence of the policy guidance is that local authorities will have allocated adult protection officers who will coordinate the implementation of local protocols. Such officers should be contacted when there is a concern about a vulnerable adult.

Removal from home under National Assistance Act 1948

7.90   Section 47 of the NAA 1948,[149] authorises the local authority's 'Proper Officer', (who will usually be person from the Environmental Health Department) to remove a person to a place of care where such a person is:

(1)   suffering from a grave chronic disease or, being aged, infirm, or physically incapacitated, is living in unsanitary conditions; and

(2)   is unable to devote to him/herself, and is not receiving from other persons, proper care and attention; and

(3)   refuses to go into hospital or an institution even though a bed is available.

Social services will be closely linked in the application, as will the person's medical GP. They must have tried without success to obtain the person's agreement to receive help and assistance.

7.91   The application is made by the Proper Officer in writing with medical support to the magistrates' court certifying that they are satisfied after a thorough inquiry and consideration that it is necessary to remove the person from the premises in which they are residing because:

(1)   it is in that person's interests; or

(2)   it is to prevent injury to the health of, or serious nuisance to other persons; or

(3)   to prevent serious nuisance to other persons.

The order can last up to 3 months and is renewable with no right of appeal. Alternatively in an emergency it is possible to obtain immediate removal without giving notice to any person involved, which lasts only 3 weeks, provided it is established by the Proper Officer that it is in the person's interest. As with less urgent applications there is no appeal and it is extremely doubtful if this procedure is compliant with the European Convention on Human Rights and as such is rarely used. It is likely that the power will be abolished by legislation in due course.[150]

Duty to protect property under the National Assistance Act 1948

7.92   The local authority is under a duty under NAA 1948, s 48 to take reasonable steps to prevent or mitigate loss or damage to the person's property when they have been admitted to hospital, residential accommodation under s 21 or removed under s 47 powers, where there is a danger of loss or damage to the property and no other suitable arrangements have been made to protect it. Any reasonable expenses incurred in doing such are recoverable from the person concerned.[151] A person's property is not defined and in practice this provision is used to remove loved pets from a person's property.

---

[149]   As amended by the National Assistance (Amendment) Act 1951.
[150]   See the draft Care and Support Bill as recommended by the Law Commission in its report on Adult Social Care in 2011 (No 326, HC941), now the Care Bill 2013 introduced into Parliament on 9 May 2013.
[151]   NAA 1948, s 48(3).

Guardianship under the Mental Health Act 1983

7.93   There are powers under the MHA 1983[152] to appoint a guardian with limited powers over the individual. A social worker from the relevant local authority will be involved. This is covered in more detail in Chapter 8.

Place of safety under the Mental Health Act 1983

7.94   Further powers in the MHA 1983[153] enable a person with a mental disorder to be removed from specific premises or a public place to a place of safety, which might be residential accommodation, a hospital or even a police cell. An application may be made by an approved mental health professional (usually these are social workers) to a magistrate where it is believed that the individual has been or is being neglected, ill-treated or not kept under control. This is covered in more detail in Chapter 8.

High Court's inherent jurisdiction

7.95   The exercise of the High Court's inherent jurisdiction may also be used to obtain appropriate orders, where the person is vulnerable, even if not incapacitated by mental disorder or mental illness, or is reasonably believed to be, either: (i) under constraint; or (ii) subject to coercion or undue influence; or (iii) for some other reason deprived of the capacity to make the relevant decision, or disabled from making a free choice, or incapacitated or disabled from giving or expressing a real and genuine consent.[154] The inherent jurisdiction is not to be used in the case of capacious adults to impose a decision upon them, but to facilitate the process of unencumbered decision making by those who had been determined to have capacity free of external pressure or physical restraint in making those decisions.[155]

7.96   Munby J has described a 'vulnerable adult' (rather than defined) as:

> 'someone who, whether or not mentally incapacitated, and whether or not suffering from any mental illness or mental disorder, was or might be unable to take care of him or herself, or unable to protect him or herself against significant harm or exploitation, or who was substantially handicapped by illness, injury or congenital deformity.'[156]

7.97   As local authorities have no automatic right to access an adult's home without a court order, they are often limited as to how they obtain sufficient and substantive evidence that the person is indeed vulnerable. It often requires a degree of co-operation from the vulnerable adult or existing knowledge of the circumstances, such as care being provided by the local authority. The Care Bill 2013 (if passed and enacted) will create a new adult safeguarding power for the local authority to make enquiries and take appropriate action where they have reasonable cause to suspect a person may be in need of care and support and is experiencing or at risk of abuse or neglect.[157]

---

[152]   MHA 1983, ss 7–10.
[153]   MHA 1983, ss 135–136.
[154]   *DL v A Local Authority* [2012] EWCA Civ 253.
[155]   *L v J* [2010] EWHC 2665 (Fam), [2011] 1 FLR 1279.
[156]   *SA (Vulnerable Adult with Capacity: Marriage)* [2006] 1 FLR 867.
[157]   Clause 42.

Restraint and deprivation of liberty

7.98 Whilst proportionate restraint is acceptable to prevent serious harm occurring to a vulnerable person, anything that exceeds this or amounts to a deprivation of the person's liberty without proper authority is unlawful.[158] Positive duties are imposed on a local authority to protect vulnerable persons against interferences with liberty carried out by private persons.[159] As such, they must take reasonable steps to prevent or seek court authorisation for a deprivation of liberty which they are aware of, or which they ought to be aware of. This includes investigating whether there is a deprivation of liberty, monitoring the situation if appropriate, and taking steps to end the deprivation of liberty, for example by providing additional support services or, if that is not possible, bringing the matter to court. However, the local authority must seek the assistance of either the Court of Protection or the High Court 'before it embarks upon any attempt to regulate, control, compel, restrain, confine or coerce a vulnerable adult'.[160]

7.99 The local authority has a vital role in the authorisation of deprivation of liberty, where the person does not qualify for detention under the MHA 1983 but lacks mental capacity to consent to their deprivation of liberty, which is explained in detail in Chapters 2 and 8.

Independent Mental Capacity Advocates and accommodation decisions

7.100 Independent mental capacity advocates (IMCAs) operate as a safeguard for those who are mentally incapable of making a decision about a long term stay[161] in a care home or hospital[162] and are unbefriended.[163] Urgent moves and short stays are not covered. Where the local authority believes that there is no person, available or willing[164] to be consulted, other than those paid or professionals providing care and treatment, they must instruct an IMCA to determine what would be in the incapacitated person's best interests.

7.101 The IMCA's role is to represent and support the person and not impose their own view of what they think is in the person's best interests. Regulations[165] set out who can be an IMCA and how they go about their role.[166]

7.102 The local authority must take into account the advice that is given by the IMCA when making the decision. The IMCA can directly challenge or assist the incapable

---

[158] Such as detention under the MHA 1983; an order from the Court of Protection under the MCA 2005, s 16A or 15; or authorisation under the Deprivation of Liberty Safeguards under MCA 2005, Sch A1.

[159] *Storck v Germany* (2005) 43 EHRR 96.

[160] *Re BJ (Incapacitated Adult)* [2009] EWHC 3310 (Fam), [2010] 1 FLR 1373, at [21]–[22], and *Re Z (Local Authority: Duty)* [2004] EWHC 2817 (Fam).

[161] For stays in care home a long stay is 8 weeks or over and in hospital a stay for over 28 days.

[162] See **8.98** for details of IMCAs when serious medical treatment is proposed. Also **2.157–2.158** for the role of advocacy.

[163] MCA 2005, ss 35–41.

[164] MCA Code, Chapter 10.

[165] Mental Capacity Act 2005 (Independent Mental Capacity Advocates) (General) Regulations 2006, SI 2006/1832 and Mental Capacity Act 2005 (Independent Mental Capacity Advocates) (Expansion of Role) Regulations 2006, SI 2006/2883 (Expansion Regulations); Mental Capacity Act 2005 (Independent Mental Capacity Advocates) (Wales) Regulations 2007, SI 2007/852, which have incorporated the expansion of the role of the IMCA.

[166] MCA 2005, s 35(3)(b).

person to challenge the local authority.[167] The MCA 2005 does not permit the IMCA to make an application to the Court of Protection as of right; the advocate would have to seek permission to make an application. The court however does have wide powers[168] to consider applications from other parties on behalf of the person.

IMCAs *and care reviews and adult protection cases*

7.103 The role of the IMCA extends at the discretion of the local authority, if they think it will be of particular benefit, in case reviews of unbefriended people where the local authority have made the arrangement for accommodation or where the person is the subject of adult protection measures (usually because they have been abused or neglected) irrespective of whether there are others who are available to be consulted.[169] The local authority should have drawn up a policy statement outlining the criteria to be applied when deciding for each eligible individual having an accommodation review or a review of those in receipt of adult protection measures as to whether they would benefit from having a review. Where the person satisfies the criteria a review must be undertaken. The arrangements must follow the procedures contained in the English 'No Secrets Guidance' or the Welsh 'In Safe Hands' guidance.[170]

GETTING ASSISTANCE

Gate-keepers

7.104 The NHSCCA 1990 contains an assessment process for people whose needs extend beyond health care into social care and support. The NHS and housing authorities are responsible for investigating the circumstances of people whose needs are exclusively medical or housing. Where a person's need includes the provision of social care and support, the social services department is charged with carrying out a community care assessment (and a duty to refer to the housing or health authority any collateral medical or housing need).[171] It is for this reason that social services are described as being the 'gate-keepers' for community care: individuals cannot access community care services without first having been assessed by social services, except in the case of urgency.

Objective

7.105 Community care assessments apply both to people seeking domiciliary and day-care services, and to people seeking admission to residential and nursing home care. Assessments should focus positively on what the individual can and cannot do, and could be expected to achieve, taking account of their personal and social relationships. Assessment should not focus only on the person's suitability for a particular service. The aim should be first to review the possibility of enabling the individual to continue to live at home even if this means arranging a move to different accommodation within the local community, and if that possibility does not exist, to consider whether residential or nursing home care would be appropriate.

---

[167] MCA Code of Practice, paras 10.31–10.39; Mental Capacity Act 2005 (Independent Mental Capacity Advocates) (General) Regulations 2006, SI 2006/1832, reg 7(2).
[168] MCA 2005, ss 50(2) and 50(3).
[169] MCA 2005, s 41; Code of Practice, para 10.2.
[170] Expansion Regulations, reg 4.
[171] NHSCCA 1990, s 47(3).

The context of an assessment

7.106 The policy guidance[172] which accompanied the introduction of the legislation stated that an assessment, 'does not take place in a vacuum: account needs to be taken of the local authority's criteria for determining when services should be provided, the types of services they have decided to make available and the overall range of services they have decided to make available and the overall range of services provided by other agencies, including health authorities. The individual service user and normally, with his agreement any carers should be involved throughout the assessment and care management process.'[173]

Assessment for services

Duty to assess

7.107 Local authorities are obliged to carry out an assessment under NHSCCA 1990, s 47(1) where:

(1) the individual's circumstances have come to their knowledge;[174]

(2) the individual appears to be a member of one of the client groups for whom community care services can be provided; and

(3) the individual may be in need of such services.[175]

The duty to assess therefore arises regardless of a specific request for an assessment. A local authority must carry out an assessment even if it considers it unlikely that the assessed person will be entitled to any services.[176] The provision creates a duty to assess (not a duty to provide), once there is the possibility that the individual may need community care services, irrespective of whether the person is ordinarily resident in the local authority area or whether the local authority has the legal power to provide or arrange services.[177]

7.108 To be within the scope of s 47(1) as a person who *'may be in need of any such services'*, the potential service user has to show there is a sufficiently concrete and likely prospect of them being in a position where community care services may need to be provided to them. The words *'may be in need'* are in the present tense and do not import a flavour of coverage of possible needs which may arise in the future. The word *'may'* indicates that there has to appear to the relevant local authority a significant possibility that the person in question might have a present need for community care services to be provided to him by that local authority and it is that possibility which then has to be investigated by means of the assessment under s 47(1)(a).[178]

---

[172] Community Care into the Next Decade and Beyond: Policy Guidance (1990).

[173] Paras 3.15–3.16.

[174] Ie he appears to be disabled, elderly or ill.

[175] Whether or not provided by the assessing authority: *R v Berkshire County Council, ex p P* (1998) 1 CCL Rep 141.

[176] *R v Bristol City Council, ex p Penfold* [1998] 1 CCL Rep 315.

[177] *R v Berkshire CC, ex p P* [1996] 1 CCL Rep 141.

[178] *R (on the application of NM) v Islington LBC* [2012] EWHC 414 (Admin).

7.109 However, in a number of situations, such as:

- release from a mental hospital;[179]
- discharge from hospital;[180]
- release from prison;[181]

it may be sufficiently clear that a person is likely in the very near future to be present in the area of the local authority and, when they are, may then be in need of community care services, so that the obligation of assessment under s 47(1)(a) arises before the person actually arrives.[182]

Assessment of a disabled person

7.110 If during the needs assessment it appears to the local authority that the person assessed is a disabled person,[183] they must make a decision as to the services[184] the disabled person requires under DP(SCR)A 1986, s 4. The duty extends to providing a written statement, which sets out the needs of the disabled person, which the local authority should provide, and their proposals as to how they will meet those needs.[185]

Getting an assessment

7.111 There is no need to request an assessment but the fact that a person may need community care services will have to be brought to the attention of the local authority, before they will assess that person's needs. This can be by direct contact from the potential service user or someone on their behalf to the local authority's social services department or by being referred from another local authority department, such as the housing department.[186]

7.112 It has been held that the local authority could not discharge its obligation to potential service users (who had in fact previously received services) simply by writing to them asking them to reply if they wanted to be considered for assessment. The court stated that 'the obligation to make an assessment for community care services does not depend on a request, but on the "appearance" of need'.[187] The threshold for appearing to need community care services is a low one,[188] although inevitably due to demand for assessments, social services operate a screening process to ascertain whether the individual seeking help may be someone whom they have a duty to assess.

---

[179] As contemplated in *R (on the application of B) v Camden LBC* [2005] EWHC 1366 (Admin).
[180] As in *R v Berkshire County Council, ex p P* [1998] 1 CCL Rep 141.
[181] As in *R v Mid Glamorgan CC, ex p Miles* 16 November 1993 (Unreported).
[182] *R (on the application of B) v Camden LBC and Camden and Islington Mental Health and Social Care Trust* [2005] EWHC 1366 (Admin) that the words 'a person ... may be in need of such services' refer to a person who may be in need at the time, or who may be *about to be* in need.
[183] 'A disabled person' is defined under s 29 of the NAA 1948, as persons aged 18 and over who are blind, deaf or dumb or suffer a mental disorder of any description and other persons who are substantially and permanently handicapped by illness, injury, congenital deformity and other disabilities as may be prescribed.
[184] Services are provided under CSDPA 1970, s 2(1).
[185] NHSCCA 1990, s 47(2).
[186] *R (on the application of P) v Newham LBC* (2000) 4 CCL Rep 48.
[187] *R v Gloucestershire County Council, ex p RADAR* [1996] COD 253.
[188] *R v Bristol CC ex p Penfold* [1998] 1 CCL Rep 315.

Health or housing needs

7.113 If it appears to the local authority that the person being assessed has health or housing needs the local authority must notify the appropriate CCG, LHB, or housing authority, and invite them to assist in the assessment, to such extent as is reasonable in the circumstances.[189] There is no duty on the approached authority to co-operate with the assessment and if there is a refusal to assist, in practice social services will have to make its own assessment as best it can.

Duration

7.114 The assessment process commences with the potential service user coming to the notice of social services and ends with a decision as to whether or not the individual is entitled to services. If services are required then the next stage is the preparation of a care plan detailing and quantifying the services and how they are to be delivered.

Mode of assessment

7.115 Legislation[190] empowers the Secretary of State to give directions as to the form assessments should take. Assessments are to be carried out in such manner and take such form, as the local authority consider appropriate. The Community Care Assessment Directions 2004[191] apply to every local authority in England. The brief Directions provide that in assessing needs under s 47(1) a local authority must:

(1)   consult the person being assessed and, where appropriate, any carer;

(2)   take all reasonable steps to reach agreement with the person and, where appropriate, any carer, on the community care services which they are considering providing to him; and

(3)   give details of charges for those services for which the assessed person and where appropriate, any carer would be liable.

However an assessment is conducted, enough information should be obtained to ascertain what the presenting needs are.

7.116 No equivalent Directions have been issued in Wales.

7.117 *The Single Assessment Process for Older People,* (SAP)[192] applicable to England and the Welsh equivalent, *the Unified and Fair System for Assessing and Managing Care* (UFSAMC) sets out a description of types of assessment that can occur, although they should not be prescriptive and therefore allow for flexibility:

(1)   **The Contact Assessment**
          This refers to the initial contact between the person and the department agencies, where basic information is obtained and the nature of the problem established with wider issues possibly being explored. The initial contact should look beyond the presenting problems and should establish seven key issues:
          (1)   the nature of the presenting need;

---

[189]   NHSCCA 1990, s 47(3).
[190]   NHSCCA 1990, s 47(4) and the C(RS)A 1995, s 1.
[191]   LAC (2004) 24.
[192]   March 2001, Department of Health.

(2)   the significance of the need for the older person;
(3)   the length of time the need has been experienced;
(4)   potential solutions identified by the older person;
(5)   other needs experienced by the older person;
(6)   recent life events or changes relevant to the problem(s);
(7)   perceptions of the family and carers.

Where the individual has indicated that there are no other problems or issues and the request is straightforward then there is no need for a wider assessment.

(2)   **The Overview Assessment**

This will be carried out if a more rounded assessment needs to be undertaken and may be apparent immediately. The overview assessment can occur after the contact assessment or may be relevant during an in-depth assessment of a specific problem. The detail of the assessment will depend on the judgment of the assessor and their ability to recognise the signposts that other issues need to be explored and whether they are using any assessment tools to guide them in the process.

(3)   **The In depth/specialist assessment**

Qualified and experienced professionals will be involved in this assessment, such as occupational therapists, registered nurses, and physiotherapists and will explore specific problems in detail.

(4)   **The Comprehensive Old Age Assessment/Comprehensive Assessment or Comprehensive Geriatric Assessment**

The assessment will involve an in-depth assessment of all or most of the domains of needs and should be completed for people, where the level of support and treatment likely to be offered is intensive or complex, including permanent admission to a care home, intermediate care services or intensive home care packages.

Practice and policy guidance

7.118   There is now a range of different practice and policy guidance issued in respect of assessments. Table 7.1 applies to England unless indicated otherwise in the footnotes. The guidance unique to Wales is set out in Table 7.2.

Table 7.1 Guidance in England

General Guidance for Adults	Carers Guidance	Specific user groups
Community Care – Community Care in the Next Decade and Beyond[193]	The Carers and Disabled Children Act 2000: A Practitioners Guide to Carers' Assessments[194]	Older People

---

[193]   Policy Guidance 1990.
[194]   March 2001 published by the Department of Health; August 2001 published by the Welsh Assembly Government.

General Guidance for Adults	Carers Guidance	Specific user groups
Care Management and Assessment: Practitioner's Guide[195]	Carers and Disabled Children Act 2000 and Carers (Equal Opportunities) Act 2004 Combined Policy Guidance[196]	National Service Framework for Older People[197]
Prioritising Need in the Context of Putting People First: A Whole System Approach to Eligibility for Social Care[198]	Social Care Institute for Excellence Practice Guide 5: Implementing the Carers (Equal Opportunities) Act 2005	Single Assessment Process Policy Guidance[199]
		Mental Health Users
		National Service Framework for Mental Health[200]
		Effective Care Co-ordination in Mental Health Services – Modernising the Care Programme Approach[201]
		Refocusing the Care Programme Approach: Policy and Positive Practice Guidance[202]
		Learning Disabled
		Valuing People: A New Strategy for Learning Disability in the 21st Century[203]
		Valuing People: Implementation Guidance[204]
		Deafblind
		Social Care for Deafblind Children and Adults[205]

---

[195] 1991, issued by the Social Services Inspectorate.
[196] August 2005, Department of Health.
[197] March 2001, Department of Health.
[198] February 2010, Department of Health.
[199] January 2002, Department of Health; LAC (2002) 1.
[200] September 1999, Department of Health; April 2002 National Welsh Assembly.
[201] 1999, Department of Health.
[202] March 2008, Department of Health.
[203] March 2001, Department of Health.
[204] LAC (2001) 23.
[205] LAC (2009) 6: NAWC 10/01 and supplementary guidance WAG 2008.

Table 7.2 Guidance in Wales

General Guidance for Adults	Carers Guidance	Specific user groups
The Unified and Fair System for Assessing and Managing Care (UFSAMC)[206]	Carers (Recognition and Services) Act 1995[207]	Adult Mental Health Services in Wales: Equity, Empowerment, Effectiveness, Efficiency: A Strategy Document[208]
		Mental Health Policy Wales Implementation Guidance: The Care Programme Approach for Mental Health Service Users[209]
		Adult Mental Health Services: Stronger in Partnership[210]
		Delivering the care programme approach in Wales: interim policy implementation guidance[211]

Assessing need

7.119 The areas (or domains), which may be assessed, are contained in annexes F and I of the English, SAP and 4.24 of the Welsh, UFSAMC. It includes such things as, activities of daily living, carer's perspective, service user's perspective, mental health needs, and safety. The Welsh guidance contains more detail and has a number of additional domains. Not all the domains have to be assessed, as it will depend on the potential service user's presenting needs.

7.120 Once the local authority has gathered together all the evidence it considers necessary[212] it is obliged to decide what the individual's community care needs are. The local authority is not required to assess an individual's *'needs'* but their *'need for community care services'*.[213] The assessment process may reveal many services or other items, which would enrich the individual's life; the local authority's statutory obligation is, however, initially limited to identifying those community care services which the individual *'needs'*. This distinction is important because even if the assessment identifies a person as having a need for community care services it does not follow that these services must be provided; the local authority must make a separate decision[214] as whether all or some of the assessed needs call for the provision of any community care

---

[206] NAFWC 09/02 WHC (2002) 32.

[207] WOC 16/96: WHC (96) 21.

[208] September 2001, National Assembly of Wales.

[209] 2003, National Assembly of Wales.

[210] 2004, National Assembly of Wales.

[211] 2010, National Assembly of Wales; at the time of writing, the Welsh Assembly government are planning to finalise this guidance.

[212] Using reports, interviews with the service user and any carer often using the SAP policy guidance, Annex F or para 4.24 of UFSAMC.

[213] NHSCCA 1990, s 47(1)(a).

[214] NHSCCA 1990, s 47(l)(b).

services. However, the assessment must investigate all potential care needs and not restrict what is included because of policy or financial reasons.[215] The assessment obliges social services to identify those needs which could potentially be satisfied by the provision of a community care service.

7.121 For example, someone who is no longer able to cook for themselves and is at risk of falling and suffering injury may be in need of the provision of meals at home or elsewhere, the provision of practical assistance in the home or a place in a residential care home; all of which are community care services. On the other hand, if the assessment suggests that a person may benefit from medical or non-residential housing assistance then these are requirements which are not capable of being satisfied by the provision of community care services and accordingly not 'needs'.

The meaning of 'need'

7.122 The individual's presenting needs should be assessed, i e the issues and problems that are identified when adults contact or are referred to social services for assistance. These are then compared to the local authority's eligibility criteria, which requires an analysis of the risk of harm to the person's independence and well-being to establish which presenting needs fall within the eligibility criteria.[216]

7.123 Psychological needs should not be overlooked. In *R v Avon County Council, ex p M*[217] the applicant had Down's Syndrome and a symptom of this was that he had formed an entrenched view that he wanted to go to a particular residential home even though an alternative, cheaper home, objectively catered for all his other needs. The authority, in deciding what accommodation he needed, had regard to a psychologist's report which stated that M's entrenched position was typical of and therefore a symptom of his Down's Syndrome. The authority refused to fund the more expensive home on the ground that it would set a precedent by accepting psychological need as being part of an individual's needs which could force it to pay more than it would usually expect to pay in such cases. Rejecting this argument, Mr Justice Henry held:

> 'The law is clear. The council have to provide for the applicant's needs. Those needs may properly include psychological needs. Where they do, it is not right to describe the payment in meeting those needs as "forcing the authority to pay more than the usual amount it would be prepared to pay for the individual concerned". The authority would simply be paying what the law required, and not being forced to pay more. So the introduction of the question of precedent in this context is, in my judgment, potentially misleading ...
>
> The [local authority's report] ... proceeds on the basis that the psychological need can simply be "excluded" ... M's needs are thus arbitrarily restricted to the remainder of his needs, which are then described as "usual". Meeting his psychological needs is then treated as mere "preference", a preference involving payments greater than usual.'

Time scale for an assessment

7.124 There is no statutory timescale within which an assessment must be carried out. As a matter of statutory interpretation, where a provision is silent as to the time for compliance the law implies that it be done within a reasonable time, and that what is a 'reasonable time' is a question of fact depending upon the nature of the obligation and

---

215 *R v Haringey LBC ex p Norton* (1997–1998) 1 CCL Rep 168, QBD.
216 Prioritising Needs Guidance, para 47; UFSAMC, 5.16.
217 [1994] 2 FLR 1006.

the purpose for which the computation is to be made.[218] Local authorities should publish time scales.[219] It would be reasonable for the assessment to occur between 4 and 6 weeks from the date of the initial request.[220]

7.125 Priority is given to assessments on hospital discharge in accordance with the Community Care (Delayed Discharges etc) Act 2003, so that assessments in the community may be subject to extreme delays.[221]

Delay

7.126 Where there is unreasonable delay in assessing[222] the potential service user or their representative should make a written complaint about the failure to assess, setting out the impact.[223] The effect of this, in England, is that social services must acknowledge receipt within 3 working days and offer to discuss how the complaint will be handled.[224] The complaint must then be investigated in an appropriate manner and hopefully this should ensure a rapid acceleration in the assessment process.[225]

7.127 In Wales, social services should attempt to resolve the complaint locally within 10 working days of the complaint being made, although this can be extended for a further 10 working days with the complainant's agreement.[226] At the end of this period, the complainant has the right to have the matter formally considered within 30 days of the complaint being first made.

Urgent cases

7.128 In an emergency, it is possible for the local authority to provide community care services, even if an assessment has not been carried out.[227] Provision will be made subject to a full assessment being conducted at a later date, which depending on the outcome, the service may continue, be reduced, altered or withdrawn.

Carers assessments

General

7.129 The legislation[228] contains a statutory right for carers who provide regular and substantial amounts of care to be involved in the assessment process. All carers, regardless of the amount of care provided, should be consulted where appropriate when social services are undertaking a community care assessment of the cared for person.[229]

---

[218] *Re North, ex p Hasluck* [1895] 2 QB 264; *Charnock v Liverpool Corporation* [1968] 3 All ER 473.

[219] Prioritising Needs guidance, para 80, although UFSAMC is silent.

[220] Local Government Ombudsman (2001) fact sheet, 'Complaints about councils that conduct community care assessments'.

[221] See Ch 8 for more detail.

[222] Or in intimating that there will be an assessment.

[223] Local Authority Social Services and National Health Service Complaints (England) Regulations 2009, SI 2009/309 (as amended by SI 2009/1768); Listening, responding, improving: a guide to better customer care (Department of Health, February 2009); Social Services Complaints Procedure (Wales) Regulations 2005, SI 2005/3366 (W.263).

[224] SI 2009/309, reg 13.

[225] See Ch 9 for details on the complaint's process.

[226] SI 2005/3366, reg 18.

[227] NHSCCA 1990, s 47(5).

[228] DP(SCR)A 1986, s 8; C(RS)A 1995, s 1; CDCA 2000, s 4.

[229] Community Care Directions 2004, Direction 2.

This must be done where the service user lacks mental capacity to make necessary decisions.[230] The following guidance has been issued:

- Carers (Recognition and Services) Act 1995: Policy and Practice Guidance;[231]
- Carers and Disabled Children Act 2000 Practice Guidance;[232]
- Carers and Disabled Children Act 2000 and Carers (Equal Opportunities) Act 2004 combined policy guidance;[233]
- Practitioners Guide to Carers Assessments;[234]
- Practice Guidance on the Carers (Equal Opportunities) Act 2004.[235]

The C(RS)A 1995 contains the core statutory responsibility for a carers assessment as opposed to the obligation imposed by the DP(SCR)A 1986 to merely 'have regard to' the ability of the carer to care when carrying out a community care assessment of a cared for person. The views and interests of carers who do not provide regular and substantial care should nevertheless be taken into account when an assessment is undertaken. In general terms, it is the cared for person's local authority's social services department who will be responsible for the assessment.[236]

7.130 Carers must be told of their right to an assessment of their own needs for services, when an assessment of the cared for person is being carried out, or has not yet been carried out because the cared for person is refusing an assessment.[237] The carer must make a request for an assessment, if they wish support. The carer does not have to be living with the person they care for, nor do they have to be the sole carer in order to ask for an assessment. There may be more than one carer providing substantial and regular care in the household, each of whom is entitled to an assessment. Carers should have the opportunity to be assessed in private to allow a candid expression of view.[238] It should never be assumed that the carer wants or is expected to continue to provide care. Nor should it be assumed that the cared for person wants to continue to receive care from this carer.

Linked carer's assessment

7.131 The C(RS)A 1995 provides recognition for carers by requiring the local authority (if so requested) to carry out a separate assessment of the carer at the same time as it assesses the person for whom the care is provided. The carer can be of any age. In order to qualify for an assessment under the Act, a carer must satisfy the following criteria:

(1)   a community care assessment (or reassessment) of the person for whom they care must be in the process of being carried out;

---

230   *R (on the application of W) v Croydon London Borough Council* [2011] EWHC 696 (Admin); MCA 2005, s 4.
231   LAC (96)7; WOC/16/96; WHC (96) 21.
232   2001, Department of Health.
233   August 2005, Gateway reference 5026.
234   March 2001, Department of Health and August 2001, Welsh Assembly Government.
235   Social Care Institute for Excellence, Practice Guide 5 and has the same status as Department of Health Practice Guidance: confirmed by Liam Byrne, Parliamentary under Secretary of State for Care Services in HC Debates col 722W, 11 July 2005.
236   Paras 24–27 of 2001 practice guidance; para 4.3 of the Welsh guidance.
237   C(RS)A 1995, s 2(b) and CDCA 2000, s 6(A).
238   2001 practice guidance, para 59 and Welsh policy guidance at para 3.11.

(2)   the carer must be providing (or intending to provide) a substantial amount of care on a regular basis. People who provide the care as a result of a contract of employment or as a volunteer placed by a voluntary organisation are excluded.[239]

Independent carer's assessment

7.132   The CDCA 2000 gives unpaid adult carers who provide substantial and regular care the right to request an assessment independent of any assessment of the cared for person.[240] It is particularly useful where the cared for person has refused a needs assessment under the C(RS)A 1995. It also gives local authorities power to provide carers' services to meet the carer's needs and help the carer to care. Carers' services are not specifically defined in the Act, although they are those services which the local authority sees fit to provide and will help the individual care for the cared for person and can be any form of support.[241] It cannot generally be any service of an intimate nature, unless the service user is in agreement or it is an emergency.[242] This is because the service is for the carer and not the cared for person. If the service is for the cared for person, the service is usually being provided under CSDPA 1970, s 2.

The assessment

7.133   The object of a carer's assessment is to identity their ability to provide or continue to provide care, which in essence requires the assessor to focus attention on the sustainability of care and what the carer would want to help them in their caring role and maintain their health and well-being.[243] In addition it must consider whether (a) the carer works or wishes to work; and (b) is undertaking or wishes to undertake education, training or any leisure activity.

Interpretation of 'substantial and regular'

7.134   There is no definition in the legislation of 'substantial and regular care'. It should be given a wide interpretation which takes full account of individual circumstances.[244] It is for the assessor to identify the impact of the caring role on the carer, in light of the carer's age, health, employment status, interests and other commitments. The policy guidance refers to the process of assessing and determining whether the care is regular and substantial by considering:

(a)   the key factors relevant to sustaining the chosen caring role; and

(b)   extent of the risk to the sustainability of that role.[245]

Recognition should be given not only to the time spent but the impact on carers, such as stress and their other responsibilities.

---

[239]   C(RS)A 1995, s 1(3).
[240]   CDCA 2000, s 1.
[241]   CDCA 2000, s 2(2).
[242]   CDCA 2000, s 2(3).
[243]   Practitioners Guide to Carers' Assessments, para 29, and Welsh guidance, para 3.6.
[244]   LAC (93)10, Appendix 4, para 8.
[245]   Paras 48–49 and para 4.11 of the Welsh 2000 Act guidance.

Sustainability

7.135 The English practice guidance,[246] provides that in deciding the impact of the caring role on the carer, the practitioner will need to address the following questions:

(a)   Is the caring role sustainable?

(b)   How great is the risk of the caring role becoming unsustainable?

The extent of risk to the sustainability of the caring role is the degree to which a carer's ability to sustain that role is compromised or threatened either in the present or in the foreseeable future by the absence of appropriate support.[247] Local authorities must consider the level at which they fix eligibility for services in relation to sustainability of the caring role in the light of the following bands of risk:[248]

Critical risk to sustainability of the caring role arises when:

- their life may be threatened;

- major health problems have developed or will develop;

- there is, or will be, an extensive loss of autonomy for the carer in decisions about the nature of tasks they will perform and how much time they will give to their caring role;

- there is, or will be, an inability to look after their own domestic needs and other daily routines while sustaining their caring role;

- involvement in employment or other responsibilities is, or will be, at risk;

- many significant social support systems and relationships are, or will be, at risk.

Substantial risk to sustainability of the caring role arises when:

- significant health problems have developed or will develop;

- there is, or will be, some significant loss of autonomy for the carer in decisions about the nature of tasks they will perform and how much time they will give to their caring role;

- there is, or will be, an inability to look after some of their own domestic needs and other daily routines while sustaining their caring role;

- involvement in some significant aspects of employment or other responsibilities is, or will be, at risk;

- some significant social support systems and relationships are, or will be, at risk.

Moderate risk to sustainability of the caring role arises when:

- there is, or will be, some loss of autonomy for the carer in decisions about the nature of tasks they will perform and how much time they will give to their caring role;

---

[246]   Para 68.
[247]   Para 99 Prioritising Needs guidance (2010).
[248]   Para 70, 2000 Act Practice Guidance.

- there is, or will be, some inability to look after their own domestic needs and other daily routines while sustaining their caring role;
- several social support systems and relationships are, or will be, at risk.

Low risk to sustainability of the caring role arises when:
- there is, or will be, some inability to carry out one or two domestic tasks while sustaining their caring role;
- one or two social support systems and relationships are, or will be, at risk.

Implications

7.136 If a carer's needs fall to be an eligible need, the local authority are not under duty to provide services to the carer; their duty is to provide support and services to address the risk.[249] If the service is provided to the cared for person, via the C((RS)A 1995 for community care services the carer should not be charged but if the service is for the carer, provided under the CDCA 2000, the carer can be charged.[250] Local authorities have a wide discretion to make reasonable charges for any non-residential services it provides in line with mandatory guidance.[251]

Eligibility criteria and the question of resources

Needs required to be provided

7.137 Once a local authority has assessed the needs of a potential service user[252] they are required to decide whether that person's needs are such that they '*call for the provision by [it] of any such services*'.[253] The local authority is obliged to '*have regard to*' the results of the assessment, rather than to provide services to meet all the identified needs.[254]

The concept of eligibility criteria

7.138 The House of Lords in the *Barry* case approved the concept of eligibility criteria in relation to community care services, stating:[255]

> 'It is possible to draw up categories of disabilities which could be experienced. Such a classification might enable comparisons to be made between persons with differing kinds and degrees of disability. But in determining the question whether in a given case the making of particular arrangements is necessary in order to meet the needs of a given individual it seems to me that a mere list of disabling conditions graded in order of severity will still leave unanswered the question at what level of disability is the stage of necessity reached. The determination of eligibility for the purposes of the statutory provision requires guidance not only on the assessment of the severity of the condition or the seriousness of the need but also on the level at which there is to be satisfaction of the necessity to make arrangements. In the

---

[249] Page 5 of SCIE Practice Guide 5.
[250] Health and Social Services and Social Security Adjudication Act 1983, s 7.
[251] 'Fairer Charging Policies for Home Care and Other Non Residential Social Services', October 2012; in Wales under NAFWC 28/02, 17/03, 32/03, and 10/2004; Carers Strategies (Wales) Measure 2010; Guidance 2011.
[252] Ie NHSCCA 1990, s 47(1)(a).
[253] Under s NHSCCA 1990, s 47(1)(b).
[254] *R v Bristol City Council, ex p Penfold* [1998] 1 CCL Rep 315.
[255] *R v Gloucestershire County Council, ex p Barry* [1997] AC 584, [1997] 2 All ER 1, HL

framing of the criteria to be applied it seems to me that the severity of a condition may have to be matched against the availability of resources. Such an exercise indeed accords with everyday domestic experience in relation to things which we do not have. If my resources are limited I have to need the thing very much before I am satisfied that it is necessary to purchase it.'[256]

Implications

7.139 The effect of the House of Lords' judgment is that social services local authorities can take their available resources into account, when coming to a decision as to whether or not a person has a 'need' for services. This principle is, however, subject to four significant constraints:

(1)   when such authorities tighten their eligibility criteria, existing service users must be the subject of a full individual community care reassessment before any decision can be taken as to the withdrawal of services;

(2)   the extent of a local authority's available resources can only be taken into account during the assessment process and in deciding whether it is necessary to provide the disabled person with the services they have been assessed as needing. Once, however, it has been decided that the service should be provided then it must be provided, regardless of resource constraints;[257]

(3)   resource availability alone cannot be 'determinative'; the actions in the *Barry* case[258] amounted to treating the cut in resources as the sole factor to be taken into account, and that was unlawful;

(4)   resource availability will not be a relevant factor where a disabled person would be at severe physical risk if the services were not provided.[259] In such a case, McCowan LJ held[260] that he could not 'conceive that an authority would be held to have acted reasonably if it used shortages of resources as a reason (for not providing the service)'.

Extent

7.140 The House of Lords decision concerned services under of CSDPA 1970, s 2. The judgment has been criticised which suggests it is limited to s 2 services.[261] However, the established general principle that local authorities are able to take into account the extent of their available resources, in constructing eligibility criteria for services, applies to all the community care statutory services. It is nevertheless constrained by the four factors detailed in **7.139**.

Eligibility criteria

7.141 Eligibility criteria are an administrative creation, designed to ensure that the resources available for community care services are applied fairly. A local authority

---

[256] Judgment of Lord Clyde.
[257] *R v Sutton London Borough Council, ex p Tucker* (1998) 1 CCL Rep 251.
[258] Ie of Gloucestershire County Council.
[259] *R v Birmingham City Council, ex p Killigrew* (2000) 3 CCL Rep 109.
[260] In the first instance decision upheld by the House of Lords (1994) LGR 593, (1997) 1 CCLR 7.
[261] *R v East Sussex County Council, ex p Tandy* [1998] 2 WLR 884 and *R v Birmingham County Council, ex p Mohammed* [1999] 1 WLR 33.

decides[262] whether the individual's assessed needs are such that services should be provided. In order to take this decision, the local authority has regard to 'eligibility criteria', based on a national framework.

7.142 Mandatory policy guidance was issued in England as Fair Access to Care Services (FACS)[263], and in Wales in The Unified and Fair System for Assessing and Managing Care (UFSAMC).[264] FACS has been updated in 'Prioritising need in the context of Putting People First: a whole system approach to eligibility for social care – eligibility criteria for adult social care' (Prioritising Needs Guidance).[265] The guidance aims to promote clarity and consistency in the way in which eligibility for adult social care is determined and covers how assessments and reviews should be carried out. In England, the Social Care Institute for Excellence has published practice guidance to assist decision makers.[266]

7.143 The eligibility framework is graded into four bands, based on the seriousness of the risk to independence if problems and issues are not addressed. Each local authority should use the framework to specify its criteria, taking into account its own resources, local expectations and local costs. It must also take into account any agreement with the NHS and agreements with local agencies.[267] An individual local authority should make similar decisions, which should ensure fairer decisions in their area, but this does not mean that every local authority should make identical decisions about eligibility or what services should be provided. The framework document makes no reference to age, gender, ethnic group, religion, disabilities, impairments or similar difficulties, personal relationships, location, living and caring arrangements, and similar factors.[268]

7.144 Paragraph 5.16 of UFSAMC uses slightly different wording to para 54 of the Prioritising Needs Guidance, which sets the following framework:

Critical – when

- life is, or will be, threatened; and/or
- significant health problems have developed or will develop; and/or
- there is, or will be, little or no choice and control over vital aspects of the immediate environment; and/or
- serious abuse or neglect has occurred or will occur; and/or
- there is, or will be, an inability to carry out vital personal care or domestic routines; and/or
- vital involvement in work, education or learning cannot or will not be sustained; and/or
- vital social support systems and relationships cannot or will not be sustained; and/or

---

[262] Under NHSCCA 1990, s 47(1)(b).
[263] LAC (2002) 13.
[264] NAFWC 09/02 WHC (2002) 32.
[265] February 2010, Gateway reference 13729.
[266] April 2010.
[267] Prioritising Needs Guidance, para 44, UFSAMC, para 5.19.
[268] Prioritising Needs Guidance, para 47; UFSAMC, para 5.16.

- vital family and other social roles and responsibilities cannot or will not be undertaken.

Substantial – when

- there is, or will be, only partial choice and control over the immediate environment; and/or

- abuse or neglect has occurred or will occur; and/or

- there is, or will be, an inability to carry out the majority of personal care or domestic routines; and/or

- involvement in many aspects of work, education or learning cannot or will not be sustained; and/or

- the majority of social support systems and relationships cannot or will not be sustained; and/or

- the majority of family and other social roles and responsibilities cannot or will not be undertaken.

Moderate – when

- there is, or will be, an inability to carry out several personal care or domestic routines; and/or

- involvement in several aspects of work, education or learning cannot or will not be sustained; and/or

- several social support systems and relationships cannot or will not be sustained; and/or

- several family and other social roles and responsibilities cannot or will not be undertaken.

Low – when

- there is, or will be, an inability to carry out one or two personal care or domestic routines; and/or

- involvement in one or two aspects of work, education or learning cannot or will not be sustained; and/or

- one or two social support systems and relationships cannot or will not be sustained; and/or

- one or two family and other social roles and responsibilities cannot or will not be undertaken.

Risk to independence

7.145 The potential service user's presenting needs[269] should be assessed, and their eligible needs[270] should be prioritised, according to the risks to their independence if help were not provided. Both a short-term and a longer-term view should be adopted, in

---

[269] 'Presenting needs' are defined in the guidance as 'the issues and problems that are identified when adults contact or are referred to social services for assistance'.

[270] 'Eligible needs' are defined as 'those needs that are assessed as falling within the eligibility criteria, which the local authority has a duty to meet'.

particular taking a preventative approach to avoid problems escalating.[271] Needs should be considered over a period of time, rather than at a single point, so that the needs of people who have fluctuating or long-term conditions are properly take into account.[272] People with hidden needs, such as those with autism or Asperger Syndrome should not be refused services on the basis that their IQ is too high.[273]

7.146 Risks to independence and well-being relate to all areas of life, (with the exception of life-threatening circumstances or where there are serious safeguarding concerns), there is no hierarchy of needs. Local authorities should make decisions within the context of a human rights approach, considering people's needs not just in terms of physical functionality but in terms of a universal right to dignity and respect.[274] Once the eligible need has been identified, the local authority must meet it taking into account the individual's aspirations and outcomes that they want from the service.[275]

Review of eligibility criteria

7.147 Local authorities should review their criteria at least annually, although if there are any major changes, financial or otherwise, criteria may be reviewed more frequently.[276]

7.148 In the event that criteria is more restrictive, service users need to be fully reassessed against the revised criteria and it must be concluded that they no longer need the service, the need is being met in another way or that they no longer meet the criteria before the service is withdrawn. However, services should not be withdrawn if it will leave the service user in serious risk.[277]

The written record of the assessment and the care or support plan

Form

7.149 There is no statutory format to assessments, although most local authorities have designed their own pro forma records.

Access to a copy

7.150 Current guidance is silent on the right for the service user to a copy of the assessment, although written reasons should be provided where the local authority decide not to provide any help or withdraw help following an assessment.[278] The 1991 practice guidance advised that a copy of the assessment of needs should normally be shared with the potential service user, any representative of that user and all other people who have agreed to provide a service. Despite this many local authorities do not appear to provide copies of assessments or care plans in the absence of a specific request. Where service users have difficulty obtaining a copy of their assessment and/or care plan they

---

[271] Prioritising Needs Guidance, para 35.
[272] Prioritising Needs Guidance, para 63.
[273] Prioritising Needs Guidance, para 64.
[274] Prioritising Needs Guidance, para 61.
[275] Prioritising Needs Guidance, para 53.
[276] Prioritising Needs Guidance, para 46: UFSAMC, para 5.22.
[277] *R v Gloucestershire CC, ex p Barry* [1997] 2 All ER 1; *R v Birmingham CC, ex p Killigrew* [2000] 3 CCLR 109.
[278] Prioritising Needs Guidance, para 106: UFSAMC, para 7.21.

can make a request, under the Data Protection Act 1998, for their file to be copied to them as these documents will be part of their social services file and therefore accessible via this process.[279]

The care or support plan

7.151 Once a local authority has made a decision that a person's need is such that community care services are called for, then they must make arrangements for those services to be provided. An appropriate care or support plan (also referred to as a support plan) can then be put together in collaboration with the individual.[280] A support plan is essentially a statement of the arrangements that are necessary in order that the services be delivered to the qualifying individual. The local authority should agree a written record of the support plan with the individual that should include the following:[281]

- a note of the eligible needs identified during assessment;
- agreed outcomes and how support will be organised to meet those outcomes;
- a risk assessment including any actions to be taken to manage identified risks;
- contingency plans to manage emergency changes;
- any financial contributions the individual is assessed to pay;
- support which carers and others are willing and able to provide;
- support to be provided to address needs identified through the carer's assessment, where appropriate; and
- a review date.

Reviews and re-assessments of service users

7.152 Service users' needs for community care services should generally be subject to an initial review after 3 months and thereafter they should be reassessed annually, unless their situation justifies more frequent reviews. The service user, service provider and other appropriate individuals or agencies, can request a review.[282] Reviews, like the initial assessment should focus on outcomes rather than services.[283]

7.153 The review may lead to confirmation of the current level of service, an amendment to the care plan or lead to closure, such as where the service user no longer needs the service, it can be met in another way or they no longer qualify for the service. Reasons should be provided, failing which the resulting care plan may be quashed.[284]

The service user's resources

7.154 Once an individual's needs, and carer(s) where appropriate, have been assessed and a decision made about the support to be provided, an assessment of the individual's

---

[279] See Ch 9 on accessing data.
[280] Prioritising Needs Guidance, paras 78 and 119.
[281] Prioritising Needs Guidance, para 121; UFSAMC, para 2.22; The SAP guidance contains a longer more detailed list which should apply to older people, but in practice local authorities apply the Prioritising Needs list to all potential service users (LAC (2002) 1).
[282] Prioritising Needs Guidance, para 144: UFSAMC, para 2.54.
[283] Prioritising Needs Guidance, para 142.
[284] *R v Birmingham CC, ex p Killigrew* [2002] 3 CCL Rep 109.

ability to pay charges should be carried out promptly, and written information about any charges or contributions payable, and how they have been calculated, should be communicated to the individual. This means that once a person has been identified as having an eligible need, local authorities should take steps to ensure that those needs are met, regardless of the person's ability to contribute to the cost of these services.

7.155 An assessment of the person's ability to pay for services should only take place after they have been assessed as having eligible needs. A person's ability to pay should only be used as a reason for not providing services in circumstances where a person has been assessed as needing residential accommodation, the person has the means to pay for it and if the person, or someone close to them, is capable of making the arrangements themselves.[285]

Choosing between care packages

Alternatives

7.156 The assessment process may identify needs which are capable of being met by two alternative care packages; for instance a frail elderly widow may be assessed as requiring almost 24-hour care assistance to help with meals, dressing, bathing and to ensure that she suffers no harm. This 'assessed need' could be met by the provision of 24 hour home care assistance or by her moving into a residential care home.

Implications of cost

7.157 Where the local authority can meet the assessed need by two or more different care packages, they are entitled to have regard to the comparative cost of the two options. The 1990 policy guidance advises:

'3.25 The aim should be to secure the most cost-effective package of services that meets the user's care needs, taking account of the user's and carers' own preferences. Where supporting the user in a home of their own would provide a better life, this is to be preferred to admission to residential or nursing home care. However, local authorities also have a responsibility to meet needs within resources available and this will sometimes involve difficult decisions where it will be necessary to strike a balance between meeting the needs identified within available resources and meeting the care preferences of the individual. Where agreement between all parties is not possible, the points of difference should be recorded. Failure to satisfy particular needs can result in even greater burdens on particular services, for example where a person becomes homeless as a result of leaving inappropriate accommodation which has been provided following discharge from hospital.'

The guidance goes on to emphasise that:

'the provision of services, whether or not the local authority is under a statutory duty to make provision, should not be related to the ability of the user or their families to meet the costs, and delegated budgeting systems should take this into account. The assessment of financial means should therefore, follow the assessment of need and decisions about service provision.'

---

[285] LAC (98) 19, paras 9 and 10), Prioritising Needs Guidance, paras 71 and 77.

Cheapest option

7.158 The Court of Appeal has approved the principle of local authorities being able to choose the cheaper option (when there are two equally suitable ways of meeting an assessed need).[286] It affirmed a decision by Hidden J in which he held:

> 'in so far as the Council had regard to the fact that the residential placement was a more cost effective means of meeting needs than 24 hour care in the home, it was entitled to do so. It was always aware that identified needs must be met, but that cost effective use of resources might be relevant to the type of service provision.'

In effect the local authority may decide to provide residential home care rather than 24-hour care in the home, provided that it is suitable to meet the assessed need;[287] one type of residential accommodation over another;[288] or continence pads to meet the need for assistance to urinate safely for a person who was not incontinent[289] or replacing a warden in a sheltered housing accommodation with a remote on call service.[290] Occasionally, the alternative will interfere with the person's dignity in the context of Article 8 of the European Convention of Human Rights, such as merely providing strip washing for a service user[291] or failing to provide suitable accommodation necessitating the service user to defecate or urinate on the floor.[292]

7.159 It is acceptable for budgetary purposes to operate a set level or ceiling on what the local authority will pay for a package of care, however they should only ever be used as a guide and not be inflexible. The local authority should spend above the cost ceiling where it will make a significant difference to the service user. Persistently sticking to cost ceilings fetters the local authority's discretion and is amenable to judicial review or a complaint to the Ombudsman.[293]

The need for real alternatives

7.160 Where the local authority chooses the cheapest option, it must meet the service users need[294] and is subject to the National Assistance (Choice of Accommodation) Directions 1992[295] where the service is accommodation in a care home[296] or the obligation to promote independent living.[297] The local authority must provide cogent reasons for rejecting the service user's preferred option for care[298] and have an identified and not hypothetical alternative package of support.[299]

---

[286] *R v Lancashire County Council, ex p RADAR* [1996] 4 All ER 421.

[287] *R v Lancashire CC, ex p Ingham and Whalley,* 5 July 1995 (Unreported); *Rahma Khana v Southwark LBC* [2002] LGR 15.

[288] *R v Kensington & Chelsea, ex p Kujtim* [1999] 4 All ER 161.

[289] *R (on the application of Elaine McDonald) v Kensington & Chelsea Royal Borough Council* [2010] EWCA Civ 1109.

[290] *R (on the application of Tiller) v Secretary of State for the Home Department* [2011] EWCA Civ 1577.

[291] Complaint against Bolsover District Council, 30 September 2003, Nos 02/C/8679, 8681 and 10389.

[292] *R (on the application of Bernard) v Enfield London Borough Council* [2002] EWHC 2282 (Admin).

[293] The Ombudsman found maladministration against *Liverpool CC* (96/C/4315).

[294] *R v Avon County Council, ex p M* [1999] 2 CCL Rep 185.

[295] See Ch 6 on choice of accommodation.

[296] LAC (2004) 20; WOC 12/93.

[297] *R v Sutton LBC, ex p Tucker* [1998] 1 CCLR 251; *R (on the application of B) v Cornwall County Council* [2009] EWHC 491 (Admin).

[298] *R (on the application of Alloway) v Bromley London Borough Council* [2004] EWHC 2108 (Admin).

[299] *R (on the application of LH and MH) v Lambeth London Borough Council* [2006] EWHC 1190 (Admin).

Provision of residential accommodation

Duty to provide under National Assistance Act 1948, s 21

7.161 Section 21 of the NAA 1948 provides:

> 'Subject to and in accordance with the provisions of this Part of this Act, a local authority may with the approval of the Secretary of State,[300] and to such extent as he may direct shall, make arrangements for providing residential accommodation for persons aged eighteen or over who by reason of age, illness, disability[301] or any other circumstances[302] are in need of care and attention which is not otherwise available to them.'

The duty applies to those who are ordinarily resident in the local authority area,[303] and are empowered (but not obliged) to provide such accommodation for persons not ordinarily resident in their area, and in urgent need.[304] Except in cases of urgency, the local authority will only provide such accommodation after it has carried out a community care assessment which has concluded that such a service is necessary.

7.162 Accommodation for asylum seekers is generally provided under Part XI of the Immigration and Asylum Act 1989, through the National Asylum Support Service (NASS). However, that obligation does not arise where the asylum seeker is entitled to accommodation under s 21.[305]

7.163 If the older person has been detained under certain sections of the MHA 1983, accommodation services in care homes can also be provided by the NHS and local authorities under s 117.[306]

Type of accommodation

7.164 The type of residential accommodation provided by a local authority will depend upon the extent of the person's assessed need: most frequently it will be in a care home but it is not limited to this.[307] Accommodation may be arranged under s 21(1)(a) without including either nursing or personal care. So the 'care and attention' which is needed under s 21(1)(a) is a wider concept than 'nursing or personal care'.[308] If a local authority assesses a person as needing supported lodgings, warden controlled accommodation or some other type of housing short of residential accommodation, then it is under a duty to contact the relevant housing department and ask for their involvement in the assessment process.

Care and attention

7.165 The Act contains no definition for 'care and attention' which Baroness Hale in *R (on the application of M) v Slough Borough Council*,[309] says at para 33:

---

[300] Direction was made in LAC(93)10 and WOC 35/93 which are identical.

[301] None of these terms are defined in the legislation.

[302] The Secretary of State's Direction does not limit the potential client group but refers to people who are or have been suffering from a mental disorder as well as the prevention of mental disorder as well as those who are drug or alcohol dependent.

[303] NAA 1948, s 24(1).

[304] NAA 1948, s 24(3).

[305] *R (on the application of Westminster City Council) v National Asylum Support Service* [2002] 1 WLR 2956.

[306] See **7.190–7.191** and **8.162–8.168**.

[307] *R v Bristol City Council, ex p Penfold* [1998] 1 CCLR 315.

[308] *R (on the application of M) v Slough Borough Council* [2008] 1 WLR 1808, at [32].

[309] [2008] 1 WLR 1808.

'... the natural and ordinary meaning of the words "care and attention" in this context is "looking after". Looking after means doing something for the person being cared for which he cannot or should not be expected to do for himself: it might be household tasks[310] which an old person can no longer perform or can only perform with great difficulty; it might be protection from risks which a mentally disabled person cannot perceive; it might be personal care, such as feeding, washing or toileting. This is not an exhaustive list. The provision of medical care is expressly excluded.'

Distinction is often made between medical needs and personal and other care needs, to determine entitlement. In *R (on the application of Nassery) v London Borough of Brent*[311] the court found the local authority had been lawful in deciding that the claimant's needs were medical due to his self-harming – he did not need help with activities that he could not carry out himself or only with great difficulty.

7.166 The Supreme Court found in *Westminster City Council v SL*[312] that care and attention can include personal care, or services 'of a close and intimate nature' but the words do not cover monitoring a person's condition to avoid a relapse, and arranging contact with counselling groups and befrienders. This approach divorces the concept of care and attention from the overall context of s 21(1)(a). It is wrong to elevate the words of Lady Hale in *Slough* that care and attention involves 'doing something for the person which he cannot or should not be expected to do for himself' into a compendious statement of all the elements of the 'care and attention' or 'looking after' concept. What is involved in providing 'care and attention' must take some colour from its association with the duty to provide residential accommodation. The care and attention must be accommodation-related.

7.167

It is not a pre-requisite of eligibility under section 21(1)(a) that a person was incapable of performing a domestic task themselves at any point, ie. the person's condition may fluctuate.

Otherwise available

7.168 The duty to provide residential accommodation only arises when the care and attention required by the person is not 'otherwise available'. Alternative options may include a package of domiciliary care services to enable the person to remain in their own home, and/or the provision of accommodation under the Housing Act 1996 or by the NHS for those who qualify for NHSCHC.

7.169 The interpretation of the phrase 'otherwise available' has been considered by the House of Lords[313] who held that for residential accommodation to be 'provided' by a local authority under s 21 it must either provide the person with accommodation in one of its own homes or the arrangement must include a provision for payments to be made by the local authority to the independent owner of the home. The court held that where a person is self-funding, the accommodation is not provided by the authority, even if it was instrumental in placing the resident in the home in the first place.

---

[310] The phrase may include, for example, household tasks and shopping, illustrated in *R (on the application of Mani) v Lambeth London Borough Council* [2004] BLGR 35 where the claimant had one leg shorter than the other, and although mobile, he needed help with bed-making, hoovering and carrying heavy shopping.
[311] [2011] EWCA Civ 539.
[312] [2013] UKSC 27.
[313] *Steane v Chief Adjudication Officer* [1996] 4 All ER 83, [1996] 1 WLR 1195.

7.170 The Court of Appeal has held[314] that 'care and attention' cannot be considered as otherwise available if the person concerned is unable to pay for it according to the means test regime.[315] This is now enshrined in s 21(2A).

7.171 Despite this, having capital in excess of the means test upper limit, does not in itself constitute adequate access to alternative care and attention. The local authority must satisfy themselves that the individual is able to make their own arrangements, or has others who are willing and able to make appropriate care arrangements for them. Where the person has a suitable advocate or representative, such as a close relative, local authorities only have to provide guidance and advice on the availability and appropriate level of services to meet the individual's needs. If there is no identifiable advocate or representative to act on the person's behalf, the local authority will be responsible for making the arrangements and contracting for the person's care.[316]

Self-funders becoming supported residents

7.172 Self-funding residents may find that their capital is depleted over time. Chapter 10 of this publication sets out more detail of the means testing regime for residential care. As soon as capital falls to the eligible level, the person should be entitled to local authority financial support. As soon as reasonably practical, the local authority should undertake an assessment of needs and if necessary take over arrangements so that the resident is not forced to use up all their capital. Local authorities should reimburse the resident for any payment made for the accommodation, which should have been met by the local authority pursuant to its statutory duties.[317]

Accommodation under Mental Health Act 1983, s 117

Duty to provide aftercare services

7.173 The duty to provide accommodation (and other community care services) under MHA 1983, s 117 is a quite separate community care service to the duty under NAA 1948, s 21 in that local authorities have no statutory basis to charge for such services and the cost should be met by the NHS and social services.[318] The duty only applies in respect of persons who are detained under MHA 1983, s 3 or admitted to a hospital under s 37 or transferred to a hospital in pursuance of a transfer direction made under ss 47 or 48 and then cease to be detained and (whether or not immediately after so ceasing) leave hospital. It is a joint duty between the local NHS body and the local authority, although in practice the responsibility for commissioning residential accommodation is carried out by the local authority. Chapter 8 covers this in more detail.

Non-accommodation (home or community based) services

Overview

7.174 Local authorities are empowered to provide community care services where the need arises through illness, disability or age. As a generalisation:

---

[314] *R v Sefton Metropolitan Borough Council, ex p Help the Aged* [1997] 4 All ER 532.

[315] The National Assistance (Assessment of Resources) Regulations 1992 (as amended) (SI: 1992/2977).

[316] LAC (1998) 19 at para. 10, Prioritising Needs guidance, paras 71 & 77 and WOC 27/98 para 9.

[317] LAC (2001) 25, para. 24.

[318] *R v Redcar & Cleveland BC, ex p Armstrong; R v Manchester City Council ex p Stennett R: Harrow London BC, ex p Cobham* [2002] 4 All ER 124: HSC (2000) 3: LAC (2000) 3.

- if the need exists because the person is a disabled person, then the services will be available under CSDPA 1970, s 2;
- if the need stems from illness then the services will be available under NHSA 2006, Sch 20 or NHS(W)A 2006, Sch 15;
- if the need is caused merely because age has made the person frail, then the services will be available under Health Services and Public Health Act 1968 (HSPHA 1968), s 45.

Although there is considerable overlap between these categories of people (and many older people will also have needs because of illness and/or disability) these distinct statutory provisions are considered separately below.

Services to promote the welfare of old people

7.175 Services provided under HSPHA 1968, s 45 are available to old people. This section provides that local authorities may, with the approval of the Secretary of State, and to such an extent as he may direct, shall make arrangements for the promotion of the welfare of old people. The only (and current) Directions that have been issued are contained in DHSS Circular 19/71. The Circular explains (at para 3) that the purpose of s 45 is to enable local authorities to make approved arrangements for the elderly who are not substantially and permanently handicapped, and thus to promote the welfare of the elderly generally and so far as possible to prevent or postpone personal deterioration or breakdown.

7.176 The Direction gives local authorities the discretion to provide:

- meals and recreation in the home or elsewhere;
- information on elderly services;
- travel assistance to participate in s 45 service;
- assistance in finding boarding accommodation;
- social work support and advice;
- home help and home adaptations;
- subsidy of warden costs;
- warden services.

Services to promote the welfare of ill people

7.177 Where a person needs community care services in order to avoid illness or because of illness or in order to recover from an illness, then these services are provided by social services local authorities primarily under the NHSA 2006, Sch 20[319] or NHS(W)A 2006, Sch 15.[320] Although it is primarily concerned with services connected with illness, it is not exclusively so, for instance, it also obliges local authorities to provide (in certain instances) a home help and laundry service for elderly and/or disabled people. Illness is defined as including mental disorder within the meaning of the MHA

---

[319] NHSA 2006, s 254.
[320] NHS(W)A 2006, s 192.

1983 and any injury or disability requiring medical or dental treatment or nursing.[321] Persons who are alcoholic or drug-dependent are also specifically included within the definition.[322]

7.178 These provisions do not authorise the provision of any services but leave to the Secretary of State or Welsh Ministers the power to specify in Directions what services may and what services must be provided. Directions in this respect were issued on 17 March 1993 as Appendix 3 to LAC (93) 10.[323] No subsequent separate Directions have been issued in Wales.

The duty to provide services to alleviate mental disorder

7.179 The Secretary of State's Directions oblige local authorities to make domiciliary care arrangements for the purpose of preventing mental disorder, as well as for persons who are or who have been suffering from mental disorder. The services are:

- centres (including training centres and day centres) or other facilities (including domiciliary facilities), whether in premises managed by the local authority or otherwise, for training or occupation of such persons; including the payment of persons engaged in suitable work at the 'centres or other facilities;

- social work and related services to help in the identification, diagnosis, assessment and social treatment of mental disorder and to provide social work support and other domiciliary and care services to people living in their own homes and elsewhere.

The power to provide services to alleviate 'illness'

7.180 The Secretary of State's Direction empowers (but does not oblige) local authorities to make the following domiciliary care arrangements:

- centres or other facilities for training such persons or for keeping them suitably occupied (and the equipment and maintenance of such centres) together with any other ancillary or supplemental services for such persons;

- meals at the centres referred to above, or at other facilities (including domiciliary facilities) and meals-on-wheels for house-bound people;

- social services (including advice and support) for the purposes of preventing the impairment of physical or mental health of adults in families where such impairment is likely, and for the purposes of preventing the break-up of such families, or for assisting in their rehabilitation;

- night-sitter services;

- recuperative holidays;

- facilities for social and recreational activities;

- services specifically for persons who are alcoholic or drug-dependent.

---

[321] NHSA 2006, s 275(1); NHS(W)A 2006, s 206(1).

[322] Appendix 3 to LAC (93) 10, para 3(g).

[323] Although this pre dates the 2006 legislation, the NHS (Consequential Provisions) Act 2006, s 4 and Sch 2, para 1(2) ensure they apply to the 2006 Act.

Home help and laundry services

7.181 Schedule 20, para 3[324] requires local authorities to provide a home help service for households where such help is required owing to the presence of a person who is (amongst other things) suffering from illness, aged or handicapped as a result of having suffered from illness or by congenital deformity. It also gives authorities a discretion to provide a laundry service for households where the power to provide a home-help exists.

Services for disabled people

7.182 Specific services for disabled people are available under the NAA 1948, s 29 and CSDPA 1970, s 2.[325] Local authorities are only obliged to provide services under both these provisions to persons in need who are ordinarily resident[326] in their area. The services available to disabled people under NAA 1948 are wide-ranging but general in nature. Conversely CSDPA 1970 spells out with great precision the services, which it requires to be made available.

National Assistance Act 1948, s 29

7.183 This provision does not in itself authorise the provision of any services but leaves to the Secretary of State the power to specify in Directions what services may and what services must be provided. The most recent Directions in this respect were issued on 17 March 1993 as Appendix 2 to LAC (93) 10.

- Services which local authorities are obliged to provide:
  - social work service, advice and support;
  - social rehabilitation/adjustment to disability including assistance in overcoming limitations of mobility or communication;[327]
  - compiling and maintaining registers;[328]
  - occupational, social, cultural and recreational facilities;
  - workshop and workshop hostel services.
- Services which local authorities have discretion to provide:
  - holiday homes;
  - free or subsidised travel for which concessions are available;
  - assistance in finding accommodation;
  - subsidy of warden costs;
  - warden services;
  - information on disability services.

Chronically Sick and Disabled Persons Act 1970, s 2

7.184 The underlying purpose of this provision was to convert the vaguely worded generally discretionary services[329] into a set of specific services to which individual disabled people had an enforceable right. Although it represents the most important community care provision, it is unfortunately beset with a number of interpretative

---

[324] NHS(W)A 2006 does not specifically contain this provision.
[325] See 7.18.
[326] They have a power to provide such services for persons not so resident.
[327] LACA (93) 10, appendix 2, para 2(1)(a).
[328] See 7.18.
[329] Ie those under NAA 1948, s 29.

difficulties. A local authority is only obliged to make a particular service available[330] when it is satisfied that the service is necessary in order to meet the needs of the disabled person.

7.185 The Act sets out the following specific services, expanded by LAC (93) 10 which the local authority must provide:

- practical assistance in the home;[331]
- wireless, TV, library, etc;
- lectures, games, outings and other recreational/educational facilities;
- assistance in travelling to community based services;
- home adaptations and disabled facilities;
- holidays;
- meals (at home or elsewhere);
- a telephone.

The Blue Badge Scheme

7.186 The CSDPA 1970[332] requires motor vehicle badges to be made available for the benefit of disabled people and for regulations to be issued concerning the operation of this scheme.[333] The scheme is the subject of guidance issued by the Department of Transport.[334] A similar scheme also operates in Wales and the Welsh Government issued guidance in 2012.

7.187 The regulations governing the Blue Badge scheme give local authorities the discretion to charge a fee on the issue of a badge, which cannot exceed £10. People who may be issued with a badge without further assessment (known as 'automatic') are those who are more than 2 years old and fall within one or more of the following descriptions:

- receive the Higher Rate Mobility Component of Disability Living Allowance;[335]
- are registered blind (severely sight impaired);
- receive a War Pensioner's Mobility Supplement;
- have been both awarded a lump sum benefit at tariffs 1–8 of the Armed Forces Compensation Scheme and certified as having a permanent and substantial disability which causes inability to walk or very considerable difficulty in walking.

People who may be issued with a badge after further assessment are those who are more than 2 years old and fall within one or more of the following descriptions:

---

[330] Ie under CSDPA 1970, s 2.
[331] Eg personal care, cleaning, and ironing.
[332] CSDPA 1970, s 21 (as amended).
[333] Disabled Persons (Badges for Motor Vehicles) (England) Regulations 2000, SI 2000/682 (as amended); Disabled Persons (Badges for Motor Vehicles) (Wales) Regulations 2000, SI 2000/1786 (W).
[334] Blue Badge Scheme local authority guidance (England), 29 February 2012.
[335] From April 2013, Disability Living Allowance is being phased out and will gradually be replaced by Personal Independence Payments (PIPs). In this regard the eligibility will change to include those who are in receipt of the higher rate of the mobility component of PIPs.

- drive a vehicle regularly, have a severe disability in both arms and are unable to operate, or have considerable difficulty in operating, all or some types of parking meter; or

- have a permanent and substantial disability that causes inability to walk or very considerable difficulty in walking.

Not all cases will require a mobility assessment as it may be apparent from the circumstances.

Disabled facilities

7.188 Local authorities are required to assist disabled persons in arranging for the carrying out of any works of adaptation in the home or by providing for them any additional facilities they may require which are designed to secure their greater safety, comfort or convenience.[336] This obligation is in two parts; one relating to adaptations[337] and the other to the provision of additional facilities.[338]

Adaptations

7.189 This includes such matters as stair lifts, ground floor extensions, doorway widening, ramps, wheel chair accessible showers and so on. Financial assistance may be available to assist in the funding of the proposed adaptation via a Disabled Facilities Grant.[339] A social services local authority's responsibility to assist with such adaptations under CSDPA 1970, s 2(1)(e) is independent of the question of whether the work qualifies for such a grant.[340] This does not prevent there being considerable delays[341] and confusion as to responsibility for provision, which has resulted in a considerable number of complaints to the Ombudsman. In the event that any grants awarded are inadequate, the local authority may meet any deficit by support provided under s 2(1)(e).

Community equipment services

7.190 This includes the provision of 'additional facilities' designed to secure the disabled persons greater safety, comfort or conveniences, This includes all manner of fittings and gadgets such as hand rails, alarm systems, hoists, movable baths, adapted switches and handles, and so on. Guidance on the provision of community equipment services has been issued.[342] All health and local authorities should have in place community equipment services, so that certain equipment is unified and provided irrespective of which public body has responsibility for provision and managed by a single operational manager.

7.191 Community equipment is defined as being 'equipment for home nursing usually provided by the NHS, such as pressure relief mattresses and commodes, and equipment

---

[336] This comes within the obligations under CSDPA 1970, s 2.
[337] Ie significant works possibly of a structural nature.
[338] Ie works involving the provision of fixtures, fittings and equipment.
[339] See Ch 5 on the availability of housing grants.
[340] Grants are provided under the Housing Grants, Construction and Regeneration Act 1996.
[341] As an example, a complaint (no 90/C/0336) against Redbridge LBC, 3 October 1991, the Ombudsman found maladministration where the claimant waited 9 months for an assessment by the Occupational Therapist.
[342] English guidance, HSC 2001/8: LAC (2001) 13 and 'Guide to Integrating Community Equipment Services'; Welsh guidance, 'Fulfilled Lives, Supportive Communities, Guidelines for Developing and Integrating Community Equipment Services in Wales' (WAG 2009).

for daily living such as shower chairs and raised toilet seats, usually provided by local authorities'.[343] It includes, but is not limited to:

- minor adaptations, such as grab rails, lever taps and improved domestic lighting;
- ancillary equipment for people with sensory impairments such as liquid level indicators, hearing loops, assistive listening devices and flashing doorbells;
- communication aids for people with speech impairments;
- wheelchairs for short-term loan, but not for permanent wheelchair users, as these are prescribed and funded by different NHS services;
- telecare equipment such as fall alarms, gas escape alarms and health state monitoring for people who are vulnerable.

Equipment is jointly funded by the local authority and the NHS, so service users are not changed.[344] Minor adaptations should not be charged for if the cost of making the adaptation is £1,000 or less, which sum includes the cost of buying and fitting.[345] Where the adaptation is over £1,000 then local authorities have discretion to make a charge.[346]

Services for mentally ill people

7.192 Most non-accommodation services that authorities provide for people with mental health difficulties are delivered under either CSDPA 1970, s 2[347] or NHSA 2006, Sch 20.[348] Anyone who receives services under MHA 1983, s 117 will also be entitled to the provision of services under the CSDPA 1970 and NHSA 2006.

7.193 Some people who receive community care services are entitled to them under MHA 1983, s 117. Such persons must have been detained for treatment either under s 3 or under one of the criminal/imprisonment sections.[349] Where such persons cease to be detained, s 117 requires the NHS and local authority to provide them with 'after-care services'. These services are potentially unlimited in nature and are services to which the user has specific individual legal rights. From a service user's perspective, the receipt of domiciliary services under s 117 has the added advantage that local authorities are not empowered to charge for them.[350]

Intermediate care and re-ablement services

7.194 Intermediate care is made up of services that help people stay in their own home or a care home instead of going into hospital, or more usually are provided to help the person get home after a hospital stay. Best practice guidance has been issued in England, and describes intermediate care as a service that:[351]

---

[343] Para 7 of the English guidance.
[344] NHSA 2006, s 75; NHS(W)A 2006, s 33.
[345] Community Care (Delayed Discharges etc.) Act (Qualifying Services) (England) Regulations 2003, SI 2003/1196 and LAC (2003) 14.
[346] Health and Social Services and Social Security Adjudications Act 1983, s 17.
[347] Services which are available to persons 'who suffer from a mental disorder of any description'.
[348] NHA(W)A 2006, Sch 15. These services are available to inter alia persons who are, or have been, suffering from an illness.
[349] MHA 1983, ss 37, 47 or 48.
[350] *R v Richmond London Borough Council, ex p Watson* (1999) 2 CCLR 402, LAC (2000) 3.
[351] Intermediate Care-Halfway Home: updated guidance for the NHS and local authorities, Department of Health (2009).

- is targeted at people who would otherwise face unnecessary prolonged hospital stays or inappropriate admission to acute in-patient care, long term residential care or continuing NHS in-patient care;

- is provided on the basis of a comprehensive assessment, resulting in a structured individual care plan that involves active therapy, treatment or opportunity for recovery;

- has a planned outcome of maximising independence and typically enabling the patient/user to resume living at home;

- is time limited, normally no longer than 6 weeks and frequently as little as 1–2 weeks or less; and

- involves cross-professional working, with a single assessment framework, single professional records and shared protocols.

It is defined in England by regulations as:[352]

> 'a qualifying service which consists of a structured programme of care provided for a limited period of time to assist a person to maintain or regain the ability to live in his home.'

Wales has no such regulations, however they operate a similar scheme, which is set out in guidance.[353]

7.195 Re-ablement is essentially a form of intermediate care and defined as:[354]

> 'an active period typically of up to 6 weeks of intense activity and support designed to promote people's independence. This is a preventive measure that can reduce people's need for both acute hospital care and can help people to continue living at home for longer.'

Intermediate care is usually provided by a stay in a residential rehabilitation unit or nursing and care services to support the person in their own home after discharge. Depending on their needs, intermediate care can last for a few days or weeks. Local authorities which arrange the service cannot charge the person for the first 6 weeks after discharge from hospital.[355] Some local authorities have erroneously charged for the provision of re-ablement services on the basis that they are not intermediate care services and should repay any amount that may have been wrongly charged.[356]

7.196 To reduce emergency readmissions to acute hospital services, the English government have a policy that the NHS will be responsible for the patient for the first 30 days following discharge. This is provided as re-ablement services under NHSA 2006 (NHS(W)A 2006), ss 2 or 3 and cannot be charged for. They are not qualifying services so the person will get 30 days of free NHS care followed by up to 6 weeks of free intermediate care.

---

[352] Community Care (Delayed Discharges etc) Act (Qualifying Services) (England) Regulations 2003, SI 2003/1196.

[353] Intermediate Care Guidance WHC (2002) 128 NAFWC 43/02.

[354] Changes to the tariff for post discharge support and additional funding for re-ablement in 2010–11 and future years, Appendix 3. Department of Health (2011).

[355] Community Care (Delayed Discharges etc.) Act 2003, s 15 and the Community Care (Delayed Discharges etc) Act (Qualifying Services) (England) Regulations 2003, SI 2003/1196, reg 4(2).

[356] LAC (DH) (2010) 6: Charging for re-ablement.

REFORM TO SOCIAL CARE

The Care Bill 2013

7.197 Following the Law Commission's report, Adult Social Care,[357] and the Dilnot Report,[358] the government set out its vision to reform the care and support system in its White Paper, 'Caring for our future: reforming care and support'.[359] This contains a draft Care and Support Bill to create a single modern piece of law for adult care and support, replacing complex and outdated legislation. It was subject to pre-legislative scrutiny in Parliament, and laid before Parliament as the Care Bill 2013 on 9 May 2013. If passed, the main provisions will be brought into force by April 2015.

7.198 The key features of the Bill are:

- It consolidates the current piecemeal legislation into a unified adult social care statute.

- The primary legislation sets out the duties imposed and powers conferred on local authorities, avoiding the need to use directions and approvals. Regulations will provide the detail.

- It establishes core responsibilities to help guide decision making under the legislation and promote a consistent application of the legislation, such as the duty to promote the adults well-being whenever it exercises a social care function.

- The duty to undertake a community care assessment is triggered where a person appears to the local authority to have social care needs that can be met by the provision of community care services (including a direct payment in lieu of services) and where a local authority has a legal power to provide or arrange for the provision of community care services (or a direct payment) to the person.

- The duty to undertake a carer's assessment applies to all carers who are providing or intend to provide care to another person, not just those providing a substantial amount of care on a regular basis.

- The duty to assess a carer is triggered where a carer appears to have, or will have upon commencing the caring role, needs that could be met either by the provision of carers' services or by the provision of services to the cared-for person, ie there is no need to request an assessment.

- Services will be portable by the introduction of (1) an enhanced duty to co-operate when service users move areas; and (2) a national portable needs assessment and national eligibility criteria.

- Community care services and carers' services will be undefined and there will not be a central definition of a disabled person or service user as the right to assessment and services will be based on a person's needs for support.

- There will be a duty on local authorities to produce a care plan for people who have assessed eligible needs. Regulations will set out the form and content that the care plan should take.

- Direct payments will be extended to cover residential accommodation to give greater choice and control.

---

[357] Law Com No 326 (10 May 2011).
[358] Farer Care Funding: July 2011, Commission on Funding of Care and Support.
[359] Cm 8378 (July 2012).

- The choice of accommodation directions will be placed in statute law and extend to MHA 1983, s 117 aftercare services.
- NAA 1948, s 47 will be repealed as it is not Human Rights Act 1998 compliant.
- Each social services authority will be under a duty to establish an adult safeguarding board and should specify the functions and membership of the board, the requirement to share information and a duty to contribute to serious case reviews.
- National and consistent framework for charging for all services.
- Local authorities will be obliged to offer deferred payment agreements.
- A financial cap on what people will pay for their care. The Bill does not set out the limit, but it is said to be £72,000. This however is for assessed and eligible care needs and will not cover the cost of board and lodging for those being cared for in a care home and costs accrued before the commencement date will not count towards the cap. People with assets of £118,000 or under will be entitled to means-tested help with residential care costs. This provision will be brought in a year later, in April 2016.

CHAPTER 8

HEALTH CARE

Caroline Bielanska

'Health is worth more than learning.'
Thomas Jefferson (1743–1826)

The right to receive – and to refuse – medical treatment has increasingly come under legal scrutiny and a new approach to compulsory mental health legislation has proved difficult to formulate. In this chapter we consider first the structure of the National Health Service and NHS continuing healthcare and community healthcare. This is followed by medical treatment including consent to treatment, treatment without consent and the role of the Independent Mental Capacity Advocate. Advance decisions, lasting powers of attorney and the withholding or withdrawal of treatment are then addressed before finally we provide an overview of mental health law.

INTRODUCTION

8.1   Under community care policies the role of health authorities is restricted to the provision of health care. In this chapter we first consider the structure of the National Health Service (NHS) and the provision of medical treatment with reference to the needs and problems of older people. Although their rights to health care and treatment are the same as other members of the community, their needs may differ. Problems arise in regard to consent to treatment and the type or extent of treatment that should be given, and this topic is considered next along with end of life decisions.

8.2   We then summarise aspects of mental health legislation that involve health authorities and may be relevant to people as they become older. The registration and control of nursing homes in the private sector is dealt with in Chapter 6 in the context of care standards and the registration requirements.

THE NATIONAL HEALTH SERVICE

Preliminary

8.3   We consider here the services provided under the NHS and the manner in which they are provided. Complaints about medical treatment or the delivery of health care, including the right to inspect medical records, are considered in Chapter 9. Financial implications are dealt with in Chapter 10 but it should not be overlooked that the provision of hospital care can affect entitlement to state benefits.

Structure and services

Aim of the NHS

8.4   The National Health Service Act 1946 created the National Health Service (NHS), to provide a publicly funded comprehensive range of health care services, based on people's needs. It has been subject to structural reorganisation numerous times, but the ethos to provide health services free of charge unless expressly provided for by statute, remains unchanged.[1] The structure of the NHS in both England and Wales operates independently and is politically accountable to the Secretary of State for Health in England[2] and the Minister for Health for the Welsh Assembly Government.[3] Although they have separate legislation, it is broadly the same. References are to the English Act, unless otherwise stated.

8.5   Legislation does not give patients the right to receive services, rather it creates a target duty on the Secretary of State to continue to promote a comprehensive health care service, designed to secure improvement in the physical and mental health and in the prevention, diagnosis and treatment of illness to patients.[4] As individuals are not specifically owed a duty to receive a particular service, and as such available resources and the demands on those resources can be taken into account when deciding NHS policy, so services can be rationed or not provided at all. However, the level of service provision should be justifiable within local priorities and resources.[5]

8.6   Rarely can an action be brought for breach of statutory duty in regard to the delivery of health care or medical treatment but normal principles of negligence apply. Hence the existence of claims for clinical negligence, which arise where there is a breach of the duty of care to the patient and injury or damage results.

8.7   Services which can be provided are those which the Secretary of State considers appropriate to discharge the target duty,[6] but in particular must provide the following, to the extent he considers necessary to meet all reasonable requirements:

(1)   hospital accommodation;

(2)   other accommodation;

(3)   medical, dental, opthalmic, nursing and ambulance services;

(4)   services and facilities for the diagnosis and treatment of illness; and

(5)   appropriate services and facilities for the prevention of illness, the care and after care of people who suffer or have suffered from an illness.[7]

The provision of pharmaceutical services is the responsibility of the Local Area Teams (LATs) of the NHS Commissioning Board.[8]

---

1   National Health Service Act 2006 (NHSA 2006), National Health Service (Wales) Act 2006, (NHS(W)A 2006), s 1(3).
2   NHSA 2006, ss 1–3.
3   NHS(W)A 2006, ss 1–3.
4   NHSA 2006, s 1(1).
5   *R v Secretary of State for Social Services, ex p Hincks* [1980] BMLR 93; *R v Cambridge Health Authority, ex p B (A Minor)* [1995] 1 FLR 1055; *R v Central Birmingham Health Authority, ex p Walker* [1987] 3 BMLR 32.
6   NHSA 2006, s 2(1).
7   NHSA 2006, s 3(1).
8   NHSA 2006, s 126, Part 7, Chapter 1.

The NHS in England

Structure

8.8   Significant reform of the NHS in England took effect on 1 April 2013. In summary the following organisations form part of the NHS structure:

- **The Department of Health:** which is responsible for strategic leadership of both the health and social care systems.

- **The NHS Commissioning Board:** often referred to as 'NHS England' or 'the NHS Board' which is an independent body (but operating though LATs) whose functions include allocation of resources to and overseeing the operation of localised clinical commissioning groups (CCGs). The LATs have commissioning responsibilities for GP services, dental services, pharmacy, and certain aspects of optical services, while 10 LATs lead on commissioning specialised services across England. A smaller number of LATs carry out the direct commissioning of other services, such as military and prison health. It is the NHS Board through their LATs which is responsible for operating independent review panels of NHS continuing health care appeals from CCGs.[9]

- **Clinical commissioning groups (CCGs):** includes all GP practices in local areas that commission most services, including, planned hospital care, rehabilitative care, urgent and emergency care (including out-of-hours), most community health services, mental health and learning disability services. The service can be commissioned from NHS hospitals, as well as social enterprises, charities or private sector providers.

- **NHS Trusts and Foundation Trusts:** There are a wide range of NHS health trusts managing ambulance services and NHS hospital care in England, including hospital trusts and acute trusts, which can be regional or national centres for more specialised care and can also provide services in the community, for example through health centres, clinics or in people's homes; care trusts, which are set up when local social services and the NHS decide to provide some services jointly; and mental health trusts providing health and social care services.

- **Health and wellbeing boards:** a forum for local commissioners across the NHS, social care, public health and other services to strengthen working relationships between health and social care.

- **Public Health England:** which aims to coordinate a national public health service to support public health.

- **Other NHS bodies which support the health care system:** such as The National Institute for Health and Care Excellence[10] (NICE) which provides national guidance and advice to improve health and social care; NHS Blood and Transplant, which manages the national voluntary donation system for blood, tissues, organs and stem cells; The Health and Social Care Information Centre which provides data, information and technology resource for the health and care systems; the National Institute for Health Research and its Clinical Research Networks; the NHS Litigation Authority, which manages negligence claims against the NHS; and the NHS Business Services Authority which provides a range of central services to NHS organisations, NHS contractors, patients and the public, including the administration of the Low Income Scheme, Medical and Maternity

---

[9]   This is dealt with in Ch 9.

[10]   It is NICE which set recommendations for treatment options, that CCGs will refer to when setting their budgeting strategy.

Exemption Schemes, Tax Credit NHS Exemption Cards, and Prescription Pre-payment Certificates and European Health Insurance Card (EHIC) cards.

8.9 The Trusts obtain most of their income through contracts with CCGs or LATs which set out the treatment or services the trust agrees to provide for the purchaser. All NHS trusts are expected to become foundation trusts by 2014 and the NHS Trust Development Authority is tasked with assisting in this transition. There are already hospitals run as foundation trusts, which are self-governing and accountable to local people. Foundation trusts are authorised to deliver services under terms set by the independent regulator, Monitor.

Regulation

8.10 Responsibility for regulating particular aspects of care is shared across a number of different bodies, such as:

- **The Care Quality Commission (CQC):** which regulates all health and adult social care services in England, including those provided by the NHS, local authorities, private companies and voluntary organisations.

- **Monitor:** assesses NHS trusts for foundation trust status and licenses foundation trusts to ensure they are well led, in terms of both quality and finances. It also grants licenses to all providers of health care services (and so has a regulatory role) and aims to promote competition and regulate prices.

- **Healthwatch:** functions as an independent consumer champion, gathering and representing the views of the public about health and social care services in England. Healthwatch reports local views, experiences and concerns to Healthwatch England, which works as part of the CQC.

The NHS in Wales

8.11 The reorganisation of NHS Wales came into effect on 1 October 2009, which created single local health organisations that are responsible for delivering all health care services within a geographical area, rather than the Trust and Local Health Board system that existed previously. The National Delivery Group is responsible for overseeing the development and delivery of NHS services across Wales and its chair is also the Chief Executive of NHS Wales, with responsibility for providing policy advice to the Minister and for exercising strategic leadership and management of the NHS.

8.12 In summary the following organisations form part of the NHS Wales structure:

- **Seven Local Heath Boards (LHBs):** which plan, secure and deliver health care services in their areas. It is the LHB to which reviews of NHS continuing health care are made. They commission the provision of GP care, hospital care, dentists, opticians and pharmacies.

- **The Welsh Ambulance Services Trust:** for the delivery of pre- hospital care throughout Wales.

- **Velindre NHS Trust:** offers specialist services in cancer care and a wide range of support services, such as bowel screening, cardiac networks and artificial limbs.

- **Public Health Wales:** the unified public heath organisation in Wales, which includes providing and managing a range of public health, health protection, health care improvement, health advisory, child protection and microbiological laboratory services and services relating to the surveillance, prevention and control of communicable diseases.

- **Community Health Councils:** statutory lay bodies that represent the interests of the public in the health service in their district.

- **The NHS Wales Shared Services Partnership:** an independent organisation, owned and directed by NHS Wales, which provides support through the provision of a comprehensive range of high quality, customer focused support functions and services.

Relationship with local authorities

Co-operation

8.13 Since 1974, joint planning by local authorities and health bodies has been encouraged, from the development of common policies and strategies to the production of operational plans. In more recent legislation, that encouragement to co-operate has now become a positive duty. In exercising their respective functions, NHS bodies (on the one hand) and local authorities (on the other) must co-operate with one another in order to secure and advance the health and welfare of the people of England and Wales.[11] This co-operation is particularly important in regard to groups such as the mentally ill, disabled and older infirm.

Joint commissioning

8.14 NHS bodies and local authorities have the ability to make payments[12] to each other, pool resources[13] and work together to improve existing services and develop new services. This enables each public body to lose their identity, taking the lead on commissioning a service and creating integrated provision; the aim is to deliver a seamless service.

NHS Constitution in England

8.15 The NHS Constitution was first published on 21 January 2009 and arose from Lord Darzi's report, *High Quality Care for All*. The current edition was published in March 2013. The purpose of the constitution is to set out in one place what staff, patients and the public expect from the NHS. The constitution takes the form of a series of rights and pledges to which patients, public and staff are entitled.

8.16 All NHS bodies, private and third sector providers supplying NHS services are required by law to take account of the constitution in their decisions and actions. It is accompanied by a Handbook which explains the rights, pledges and responsibilities set out in the NHS constitution in more detail and a public health supplement for local authorities and Public Health England.

---

[11]   NHSA 2006, s 82.
[12]   NHSA 2006, ss 256–257 and s 76; NHS(W)A 2006, ss 194–196 and s 34.
[13]   NHSA 2006, s 75; NHS(W)A 2006, s 33.

The National Service Framework for Older People

8.17 The National Service Framework for Older People was published by the Department of Health in March 2001 and includes eight standards of care for older people's services. The Welsh Assembly Government published a similar strategy in 2003.[14] Each one contains key milestones:

(1) *Rooting out age discrimination* aims to ensure that older people are never unfairly discriminated against in accessing NHS or social care services.

(2) *Person-centred care* aims to ensure that older people are treated as individuals and that they receive appropriate and timely packages of care which meet their needs as individuals, regardless of organisational boundaries.

(3) *Intermediate care*[15] aims to provide integrated services to promote faster recovery from illness, prevent unnecessary acute hospital admission, support timely discharge and maximise independent living.

(4) *General hospital care* aims to ensure that older people receive the specialist help they need in hospital and that they receive the maximum benefit from having been in hospital.

(5) *Stroke* aims to reduce the incidence of stroke in the population and ensure that those who suffer a stroke have prompt access to integrated stroke services. This standard provides guidance on a care pathway for stroke care for all ages.

(6) *Falls* aims to reduce the number of falls that result in serious injury and ensure effective treatment and rehabilitation for those who have fallen.

(7) *Mental health in older people* aims to promote good mental health in older people and to treat and support those older people with dementia and depression.

(8) The promotion of health and active life in older age aims to extend the life expectancy of older people.

NHS continuing health care

The legal context

8.18 Legislation requires the promotion of a comprehensive health service, designed to secure improvement in (i) the physical and mental health of people and (ii) the prevention, diagnosis and treatment of illness and to provide services, as are necessary, to meet all reasonable requirements.[16] Although not defined in the legislation, it is within this context that the NHS can provide NHS continuing health care (NHSCHC). This means a package of ongoing care that is arranged and funded solely by the NHS where the individual has been found to have a 'primary health need'. Such care is provided to an individual aged 18 or over, to meet needs that have arisen as a result of disability, accident or illness.[17]

---

[14] The strategy for older people in Wales, updated in 2005 in 'Raising the standard: the revised adult mental health national service framework and an action plan for Wales'.

[15] See **7.192**.

[16] NHSA 2006 and NHS(W)A 2006, ss 1 and 3.

[17] National Framework for NHS continuing health care and NHS funded care, para 13 in England, (Department of Health, November 2012) and para 2.1 in Wales (Welsh Assembly Government, 2010).

8.19   Case-law has attempted to clarify the point at which a chronically sick and disabled person is the responsibility of the local authority, and so subject to the means test, so that nursing services can only legally be provided by the local authority if the totality of the person's care needs are:

(1)   merely incidental or ancillary to the provision of the accommodation which a local authority is under a duty to provide under the National Assistance Act 1948; and

(2)   of a nature that a local authority could be expected to provide.[18]

In contrast, where a person's primary need is a health need, the NHS is regarded as responsible for providing for all their needs, including accommodation, if that is part of their overall need. Anyone eligible should receive that care free and not be subject to any financial charge. The boundary between the local authority and NHS is a grey area, which the National Framework (NF) attempts to address.

The National Framework

8.20   Guidance on eligibility for NHSCHC was initially introduced in 1995, and has undergone a number of revisions, but following various legal challenges[19] and complaints to the Ombudsman, both the English and Welsh Government have published a *National Framework for NHS Continuing Healthcare and NHS-funded Nursing Care.*[20] The NF document focuses on the process for establishing eligibility, the principles of care planning and dispute resolution relevant to that process. The English NF incorporates, practice guidance, frequently asked questions and refunds guidance. It must also be read in conjunction with the National Health Service Commissioning Board and Clinical Commissioning Groups (Responsibilities and Standing Rules) Regulations 2012, which requires the relevant assessment tools to be used and sets out the requirement to have panels to consider disputes.[21]

8.21   It is to be read in conjunction with the national tools to support decision-making: the *Decision Support Tool* (DST), and the *Fast Track* and *Checklist Tool.* Separate user notes, to clarify how to apply the tools, are attached to the tools themselves. In Wales, only the DST has been adopted, and forms part of the NF document, although locally agreed Fast Track protocols can be developed.

Characteristics of eligibility

8.22   Certain characteristics[22] of need, and their impact on the care required to manage them are used by those deciding eligibility to help determine whether the 'quality' or 'quantity' of care required is more than the limits of the local authority's responsibilities, which are:

•   **Nature:** the type of needs, and the overall effect of those needs on the individual, including the type ('quality') of interventions required to manage them;

---

18   *R v North & East Devon Health Authority, ex p Coughlan* [2000] 3 All ER 850.

19   *R v North & East Devon Health Authority, ex p Coughlan* [2000] 3 All ER 850; *R (on the application of Grogan) v Bexley NHS Care Trust (1) South East London Strategic Health Authority (2) Secretary Of State for Health* [2006] EWHC 44 (Admin).

20   National Framework for NHS Continuing Healthcare and NHS-funded Nursing Care (DoH November 2012); Welsh Assembly Government Circular: 015/2010: now referred to as NF in these footnotes.

21   SI 2012/2996.

22   NF, para 35 in England and para 4.2 in Wales.

- **Intensity:** both the extent ('quantity') and severity (degree) of the needs, including the need for sustained care ('continuity');
- **Complexity:** how the needs arise and interact to increase the skill needed to monitor and manage the care;
- **Unpredictability:** the degree to which needs fluctuate, creating difficulty in managing needs; and the level of risk to the person's health if adequate and timely care is not provided.

Each of these characteristics may, in combination or alone, demonstrate a primary health need, because of the quality and/or quantity of care required to meet the individual's needs.

What does not determine eligibility?

8.23 Eligibility (and conversely ineligibility) should not be based on:[23]

- the setting of care;
- the ability of the care provider to manage care. Only where the successful management of a healthcare need has permanently reduced or removed an ongoing need will this have a bearing on eligibility;
- the use (or not) of NHS employed staff to provide care;
- the individual's own financial position;
- the need for/presence of 'specialist staff' in care delivery;
- a need is well managed;
- the existence of other NHS-funded care; or
- any other input-related (rather than needs-related) rationale.

In Wales the following are included in the list:

- the number of staff delivering the care;
- the cost of the care package; or
- changes made to an existing package of care.

Fast tracking terminally ill people

8.24 Where a person has a rapidly deteriorating condition, which may be entering a terminal phase, they may need NHSCHC funding to enable their needs to be urgently met (eg to allow them to go home to die or to allow appropriate end of life support to be put in place). It is a primary health need because of the rate of the deterioration. Such individuals will require fast tracking[24] for immediate provision of funding and as such the Fast Track tool[25] may be used by a senior clinician such as a nurse, consultant or a GP to outline the reasons for the fast-tracking decision. This may be supported by a prognosis, if available, but strict time limits are not relevant for end of life cases and should not be imposed. If possible and appropriate, the initial fast-tracking decision

---

23   NF, para 58 in England and para 4.4 in Wales.
24   NF, paras 97–107.
25   Fast track tool for NHSCHC, Department of Health, November 2012.

should be followed by a full assessment of need. Where a recommendation is made for an urgent package of care via the fast-track process, this should be accepted and actioned immediately by the CCG.

8.25   In Wales those who are terminally ill are cared for in accordance with the Welsh Assembly's *end of life care pathway*.[26]

Rehabilitation

8.26   At the point of discharge from hospital, consideration should be given as to whether further NHS-funded therapy and/or rehabilitation might make a difference to the potential of the individual, and if so, the patient should be transferred to the appropriate NHS service. It might also include intermediate care[27] or an interim package of support in an individual's own home or in a care home. In such cases a decision should be made, and recorded, to undertake a full consideration of eligibility once all treatment and rehabilitation has been completed.

The Checklist (applicable to England only)

8.27   The first step for most people will be a screening process, using the Checklist. Its purpose is to identify only those people who may be eligible for NHSCHC to avoid unnecessary and costly fuller assessments. A nurse, doctor, other qualified healthcare professional, or social worker could apply the Checklist to refer individuals for a full consideration of eligibility for NHSCHC. Whenever an individual outside a hospital setting is having their health or social needs assessed or reviewed by a CCG or a local authority, consideration should always be given to whether their needs suggest that it might be appropriate to use the Checklist to identify whether or not there is potential eligibility for NHSCHC.

8.28   Paragraph 22 of the Checklist document advises a full assessment if the person has two or more high care needs (Level A), five or more moderate or one high and four moderate (Level A and B) or one priority domains of care. However, in practice many people fail to be assessed, and in such cases consideration should be given as to whether the local authority failed in its duty[28] to refer the health need when undertaking an assessment of the person's needs.[29] An adverse decision may be pursued by asking the CCG to reconsider it. This should include a review of the original Checklist and any new information available, and might include the completion of a second Checklist. If the person or their representative remains dissatisfied they can pursue the matter through the usual social services complaints process.

The Decision Support Tool

8.29   Once an individual has been referred for full consideration for NHSCHC, an individual, or individuals should be identified by the CCG in England or in Wales as part of the unified assessment, to coordinate the process. The person coordinating the assessment process and eligibility consideration will liaise with the multidisciplinary team members themselves to complete the Decision Support Tool (DST), matching, as far as possible, the individual's level of need with the description that most closely relates to their specific needs.

---

[26]   WHC (2006) 030 *End of Life Care – All Wales Care Pathway for the Last Days of Life.*
[27]   See **7.192.**
[28]   NHSCCA 1990, s 47(3).
[29]   See Hertfordshire County Council (00/B/16833).

8.30   The DST is designed to ensure that the full range of factors which have a bearing on an individual's eligibility are taken into account in making the decision. The tool provides a framework to bring together and record the various needs in 'care domains', or generic areas of need. The domains are sub-divided into statements of need; representing low, moderate, high, severe or priority levels of need, depending on the domain. The care domains are:

(1)   Behaviour

(2)   Cognition

(3)   Communication

(4)   Psychological/Emotional Needs

(5)   Mobility

(6)   Nutrition – Food & Drink

(7)   Continence

(8)   Skin (including tissue viability)

(9)   Breathing

(10) Drug Therapies & Medication: Symptom Control

(11) Altered States of Consciousness

(12) Other significant care needs

8.31   The Welsh DST is similar but not identical to the English Tool, and is an annex to the main NF document. The 'Psychological' and 'Continence' domains have an additional band of need.

The decision

8.32   Decisions and rationales relating to eligibility should be transparent from the outset. The result of completing the DST should be an overall picture of the individual's needs, which captures their nature, and complexity, intensity and/or unpredictability and the quality and/or quantity (including continuity) of care required to meet the individual's needs. Once the multidisciplinary team has reached agreement, they should make a recommendation about eligibility to the CCG.

8.33   A clear recommendation of eligibility would be expected if after completion of the tool it identified:[30]

(1)   a level of priority needs in any one of the four domains that carry this level; or

(2)   a total of two or more incidences of identified severe needs across all care domains.

If there is one domain recorded as severe, together with needs in a number of other domains, or a number of domains with high and/or moderate needs, this can also indicate a primary health need. In these cases, the overall need, the interactions between needs in different care domains, and the evidence from risk assessments, should be taken into account in deciding whether a recommendation of eligibility for NHSCHC should be made.

---

[30]   The DST at para 31 in England and in Annex 6, para 31 of the NF in Wales.

8.34 It is not possible to equate a number of incidences of one level with a number of incidences of another level, for example 'two moderates equals one high'. Where an assessment for NHSCHC has been carried out the assessed person or their representative should be notified in writing of the decision made, the reasons for that decision and if unsuccessful, how to apply for a review.[31]

Time scales

8.35 The time that elapses between the Checklist (or, where no Checklist is used, other notification of potential eligibility) being received by the CCG and the funding decision being made should not exceed 28 days. When there are valid and unavoidable reasons for the process taking longer, timescales should be clearly communicated to the person and (where appropriate) their carers and/or representatives.[32]

8.36 In Wales, the time taken for assessments and agreeing a care package should be completed in 6 to 8 weeks from initial trigger to agreeing a care package.[33]

Reviews

8.37 In England, regular reviews should be carried out, no later than 3 months following the initial decision, and then at least once a year after that. Some people will need more frequent reviews. When reviewing the need for registered nursing care for residents in care homes registered for nursing care, potential eligibility for NHSCHC should always be considered and a full assessment carried out, where necessary.

8.38 In Wales, as a minimum there should be an initial review of the care plan within 6 weeks and a further review at 3 months of services first being provided. Thereafter reviews should be at least annually.

Community health care

General practitioners

8.39 General practitioners, or GPs, are independent contractors who provide their services in medical practices under a contract with the LATs to patients who register with them. People who are ordinarily resident in the UK, including people from other EEA countries and abroad, have the right to be registered with a GP of their choice. The chosen GP surgery must accept an individual unless there are good reasons for not doing so; for example, they live outside their commissioning boundaries.

8.40 Patients have the right to see a GP (not necessarily their own) at the surgery at any time during surgery hours. Outside normal surgery hours, patients can still phone their GP surgery, but will usually be directed to an out-of-hours service. Alternatively, patients can call NHS 111 for non-emergency advice or seek advice from the NHS Direct website. Home visits cannot be insisted upon and are at the doctor's discretion, but should be available to patients who genuinely need them. Patients away from home for up to 3 months can ask to be treated as a temporary patient by another GP and even if not accepted, that GP must give any treatment immediately necessary.

---

[31] See Ch 9 for how to challenge an adverse decision.
[32] NF, paras 95–96 (England).
[33] NF, paras 5.44–5.46 (Wales).

Type of out-of-hours care

8.41   Out-of-hours cover may include some or all of the services below:

- GPs working in Accident & Emergency departments, NHS walk-in centres or minor injuries units (MIUs).

- Teams of health care professionals working in primary care centres, A&E departments, MIUs or NHS walk-in centres.

- Health care professionals (other than doctors) making home visits, following a detailed clinical assessment.

- Ambulance services moving patients to places where they can be seen by a doctor or nurse, to reduce the need for home visits.

Continence services

8.42   The NHS funds incontinence products wherever the person is cared for.[34] What is available varies from region to region: each NHS commissioning body has its own eligibility criteria and contract to supply continence products. If the person meets the eligibility criteria, they should be told which ones they will need and given details of how to receive regular supplies, which should be provided promptly. If the NHS body imposes a maximum number of pads they will supply over a set period of time, this is likely to be unlawful if challenged, as it fetters their discretion, contrary to guidance and could constitute maladministration. If the person is eligible to receive long-term continence supplies they should be re-assessed at least annually, which allows needs to be reviewed and enables any new or more suitable products to be considered.

8.43   The All Wales Continence Bundle provides nurses with tools to support the improvement of the patient experience and dignity in care. It includes assessment tools to identify immediate needs and the need for support in the longer term, an audit tool to measure how well staff are responding to patient needs and a questionnaire to be used to get feedback about patient experience.

Other common community health services

8.44   District nurses, also known as community nurses, provide nursing care for patients in non-hospital settings. They may work in the patient's own home, GP surgeries, health centres and care homes that are registered to provide only personal care. They are usually employed by the CCGs or LHB to provide nursing care such as palliative care, wound dressing and administering medication in a variety of settings. They work closely with GPs, social workers, and occupational therapists.

8.45   Community psychiatric nurses and community mental health nurses are nurses with specialist mental health training, and may be employed by the CCG/LHB or hospital trust. Access to the service is either by a referral from the GP or from a psychiatrist who may be community- or hospital-based. Their role is to assess, counsel, manage and support people in the community who have mental health problems and support their family and carer(s) in providing care. They also assist with monitoring and administering psychiatric drugs to patients in the community.

---

[34]   Good practice in continence services: Department of Health, April 2000.

Hospital care

Access

8.46   Generally patients cannot receive NHS hospital treatment without a GP referral, unless they need urgent medical attention in an emergency. In England, if a patient is referred for a first outpatient hospital appointment, the patient can choose to go to any NHS hospital that provides a service or where there are arrangements, a private hospital. This may not apply to all services such as mental health or urgent services.

8.47   For patients receiving treatment in hospital under the NHS there is no right to a second opinion but one should be obtained on request if there is any doubt. Patients have the right to be examined and treated without medical students present if they so wish.

Discharge

8.48   Once a patient is clinically fit to be discharged, they do not have the right to occupy an NHS bed indefinitely and are free to leave. 'Clinically fit or ready for discharge' does not mean the patient is healthy or recovered, merely that they are stable and no longer require acute health services.

8.49   At the point of discharge importance decisions are often required to be made, particularly if the patient has any ongoing health or social care needs. A ward-based care coordinator should be designated to coordinate care and ensure a smooth discharge planning process, although in practice it does not always occur. Consideration should be given as to whether:

(1)   the patient is eligible for NHSCHC;[35]

(2)   the patient is eligible for nursing care provided by a registered nurse in a nursing home;[36]

(3)   the patient qualifies for aftercare services under MHA 1983, s 117;[37]

(4)   the patient has a legitimate expectation that the NHS will fund their accommodation because they have been in an NHS facility for a prolonged period of time or because they have been promised the facility would be their home for their lifetime;[38]

(5)   the patient needs intermediate, recuperation or re-ablement services to assist their recovery to maximum independence;[39]

(6)   the patient needs to be referred for community health services, such as continence, nutrition, speech and language or mental health services;

(7)   the patient needs to be referred for community equipment services, to enable them to be safely discharged and mobilised back home, whether or not this is their own home or a care home;[40]

---

[35]   See **8.18–8.34**.
[36]   See **6.80–6.81**.
[37]   See **8.162–8.166**.
[38]   European Convention on Human Rights, Article 8; *R v North & East Devon Health Authority, ex p Coughlan* [2000] 2 WLR 622; *Gunter v South West Staffordshire PCT* [2005] EWHC 1894 (Admin).
[39]   See **7.192**.
[40]   See **7.188–7.189**.

(8)   the patient is approaching the end of their life and they wish to return with dignity to die in the place of their choice, with support from community palliative care services;

(9)   the patient (and any carer) needs a community care needs assessment or carer's assessment from the local authority for services to meet their social care needs;

(10) the patient needs to self care and manage and knows what to expect for their condition;

(11) the patient needs to move to alternative accommodation, and may also require adaptations or additional support;

(12) the patient needs long term care in a registered care home, for which they will self-fund.

Guidance

8.50   Good practice guidance, *Ready to go?*,[41] a safe discharge protocol, *Definitions – Medical Stability and Safe to Transfer*[42] and *The Community Care (Delayed Discharges etc) Act 2003 Guidance for Implementation*[43] has been issued in England. In addition there is guidance for people being discharged from mental health settings, *A positive outlook – a good practice toolkit to improve discharge from inpatient mental health care*, published by the Care Services Improvement Partnership.[44] The Department of Health have published a toolkit, *Achieving timely 'simple' discharge from hospital* for the 80% of patients who have simple discharge needs.[45]

8.51   In Wales, the National Assembly have published the *Hospital Discharge Planning Guidance*[46] and best practice guidance, *Passing the Baton 2009*.[47]

8.52   The *Ready to go* guidance sets out 10 steps to be taken for an effective discharge from hospital:

(1)   Start planning for discharge or transfer before or on admission.

(2)   Identify whether the patient has simple or complex discharge and transfer planning needs, involving the patient and carer in the decision.

(3)   Develop a clinical management plan for every patient within 24 hours of admission.

(4)   Coordinate the discharge or transfer of care process through effective leadership and handover of responsibilities at ward level.

(5)   Set an expected date of discharge or transfer within 24–48 hours of admission, and discuss with the patient and carer.

(6)   Review the clinical management plan with the patient each day, take any necessary action and update progress towards the discharge or transfer date.

(7)   Involve patients and carers so that they can make informed decisions and choices that deliver a personalised care pathway and maximise their independence.

---

[41]   12 March 2010.
[42]   (2003).
[43]   LAC (2003) 21; HSC 2003/009.
[44]   (2007).
[45]   (2004).
[46]   NAFWC 17/2005: WHC (2005) 035.
[47]   Available on NHS Wales website.

(8) Plan discharges and transfers to take place over 7 days to deliver continuity of care for the patient.

(9) Use a discharge checklist 24–48 hours prior to transfer.

(10) Make decisions to discharge and transfer patients each day.

8.53 The following operating principles should apply:

(1) Discharge and transfer planning starts early to anticipate problems, put appropriate support in place and agree an expected discharge date.

(2) A person-centred approach treats individuals with dignity and respect, and meets their diverse or unique needs to secure the best outcomes possible.

(3) The care planning process is coordinated effectively.

(4) Communication creates strong and productive relationships between practitioners, patients and carers.

(5) The multi-disciplinary team works collaboratively to plan care, agree who is responsible for specific actions and make decisions on the process and timing of discharges and transfers.

(6) Social care is involved, where discharge is to be by the delayed discharges process.[48]

(7) Patients and carers are involved at all stages of discharge planning, given good information and helped to make care planning decisions and choices.

(8) Patients who do not have capacity to make decisions are given their rights and obligations under the Mental Capacity Act 2005 (MCA 2005).

(9) Carers are offered an assessment to identify any services they may need to support them in their caring role, if appropriate.

(10) A person's eligibility for NHSCHC is assessed where appropriate.

Discharge under the Community Care (Delayed Discharges etc) Act 2003

8.54 The Community Care (Delayed Discharges etc) Act 2003 applies only in England and provides a financial incentive for local authorities with social services responsibilities to provide community care services for a patient and/or their carer which are needed for the patient's safe transfer to a more appropriate setting. Social services who fail to undertake assessments and/or fail to put into place services to effect a transfer from hospital are fined for each day the patient remains in an acute hospital bed.

8.55 NHS bodies are required to make two notifications to social services in order to trigger a claim for reimbursement. The first (assessment notification: Section 2) gives notice of the patient's possible need for services on discharge. Following this notification, social services have a minimum period of 3 days to carry out an assessment and arrange services. The second (discharge notification: Section 5) gives notice of the day on which it is proposed that the patient is discharged. Reimbursement liability commences on the day after the minimum three-day period (Section 2) or the day after the proposed discharge date (Section 5) – whichever is the later.

---

[48] See 8.54.

8.56   Prior to serving the Section 2 notice, the NHS body should consult the patient and their carer (if any).[49] This is to allow a patient who want to arrange their own care to do so and prevents the NHS initiating assessments that are not required.

8.57   Under the National Health Service Commissioning Board and Clinical Commissioning Groups (Responsibilities and Standing Rules) Regulations 2012, reg 21(2)[50] the NHS body must take reasonable steps to ensure that an assessment of eligibility for NHSCHC is carried out on a patient where it appears to them that the patient may be in need of such care. This should be considered before a Section 2 notice is issued to social services.[51]

8.58   Despite any reimbursement issues which may arise between the NHS and social services, the patient cannot be forcibly removed against their wishes without a court order. However, it has been known for those who are mentally incapable of consenting to their removal to be transferred to another facility on the grounds of 'necessity'; relying on the statutory protection from liability afforded by the MCA 2005.[52] Statutory protection may not be applicable if the care and treatment decision makers move the client against the specific consent of the patient's health and welfare attorney, as they may not be acting in accordance with a best interests determination.[53]

MEDICAL TREATMENT

Consent to treatment

The requirement for consent

8.59   The general principle is that no medical treatment should be given without the consent of the patient. However, consent may be implied, for example the patient seeks the treatment. Provision of basic nursing care such as cleaning up a protesting patient may be excusable in the absence of express consent, but not intrusive medical treatment. For consent to be valid the patient must:

(1)   have the capacity to give consent;

(2)   be given appropriate information prior to consent;

(3)   consent to the particular treatment that is given; and

(4)   give consent voluntarily.

Evidence of consent

8.60   Consent may be in writing and usually comprises a signed form, but can be verbal or implied by conduct. A signature on a form is merely evidence of consent which may be rebutted, and so the issue is whether the patient decided to have the treatment, not whether the patient signed the consent form. However, if there is a dispute, the court has held that it is not up to the doctor to prove consent; the patient must prove they did not consent.[54]

---

49   Community Care (Delayed Discharges etc) Act 2003, s 2(4).
50   SI 2012/2996.
51   NF, paras 62–67.
52   MCA 2005, s 5.
53   MCA 2005, s 4(7)(c).
54   *Freeman v Home Office (No 2)* [1984] 1 All ER 1036, CA.

8.61 The General Medical Council (GMC) has published guidance, *Consent: patients and doctors making decisions together.*[55] It includes the following:

(1) the patient's consent should be obtained in complex or high risk cases;

(2) some treatments legally require written consent, such as organ donation;

(3) express consent is required where treatment is part of research programme or is an innovative treatment designed specifically for their benefit;

(4) in an emergency, oral consent can be relied upon provided the patient has been given information to make the decision, which should be recorded in their notes.

Informed consent

8.62 The patient should be informed of anything which might influence their decision whether to go ahead or not with the treatment.[56] The patient's decision may be for rational or irrational reasons or for no reason. They are not to be treated as lacking mental capacity merely because others think it is unwise.[57] The GMC guidance to doctors on consent states:[58]

'You must give patients the information they want or need about:

a. the diagnosis and prognosis
b. any uncertainties about the diagnosis or prognosis, including options for further investigations
c. options for treating or managing the condition, including the option not to treat
d. the purpose of any proposed investigation or treatment and what it will involve
e. the potential benefits, risks and burdens, and the likelihood of success, for each option; this should include information, if available, about whether the benefits or risks are affected by which organisation or doctor is chosen to provide care
f. whether a proposed investigation or treatment is part of a research programme or is an innovative treatment designed specifically for their benefit
g. the people who will be mainly responsible for and involved in their care, what their roles are, and to what extent students may be involved
h. their right to refuse to take part in teaching or research
i. their right to seek a second opinion
j. any bills they will have to pay
k. any conflicts of interest that you, or your organisation, may have
l. any treatments that you believe have greater potential benefit for the patient than those you or your organisation can offer.'

8.63 The patient must be able to assess any risk involved with the procedure to understand the benefits and to appreciate the consequences of not proceeding. The higher the risk involved and the more serious the potential consequences, the higher the duty to explain risk, which would affect the judgment of a reasonable person.[59] The relevant test is the test of a reasonable practitioner and what information they would give the patient given the circumstances.[60] The test of a 'reasonable practitioner' is no longer assessed uncritically by considering what a body of professional opinion

---

[55] (2008).

[56] *Sidaway v Board of Governors of the Bethlem Royal and the Maudsley Hospital* [1984] 1 All ER 1018, CA; affd [1985] 1 All ER 643, HL.

[57] MCA 2005, s 1(4).

[58] General Medical Council Consent: patient and doctors making decisions together (2008) para 9.

[59] *Pearce v United Bristol Healthcare NHS Trust* [1998] 48 BMLR 118.

[60] *Bolam v Friern Hospital Management Committee* [1957] 2 All ER 118.

demonstrates is reasonable. The House of Lords indicated that the court should consider whether a body of opinion is capable of 'withstanding logical analysis'.[61]

8.64 A patient must be given the necessary information in a non-technical and easily understood format. Patients must be told of material risks that a reasonable person would regard as significant, but it is up to the health care professional to determine in each case how much information should be disclosed. When a patient asks questions about risks, the doctor's duty must be to answer truthfully and as fully as the questioner requires.[62]

8.65 If the health care professional believes that disclosure of certain information to a patient will cause serious damage to the mental (or physical) health of the patient, then such information may be withheld. There is a high duty to show that they reasonably believe that communication to the patient of the existence of the risk will cause serious harm; in this context 'serious harm' means more than the patient might become upset or decide to refuse treatment. A full explanation must be given in the records to justify any such decision.

Consent to particular treatment

8.66 The patient must give consent to the particular treatment. It is not generally justified to treat a non-urgent second condition during the treatment of a primary condition, unless this has been agreed in advance. Therefore consideration should be given to whether the patient has given consent to the treatment in general terms or only if performed by a particular doctor.

Voluntary consent

8.67 Consent must be freely given and no threat or implied threat should be used to obtain the consent.[63] Threats such as the use of compulsory detention under the Mental Health Act 1983 (MHA 1983) if treatment is not accepted or that discharge may result from failure to agree to treatment would nullify the consent. Whether consent is voluntary will depend on what information is given to the patient and how this is presented.

Capacity to consent

8.68 Consideration must be given as to whether the patient is competent to consent to the proposed treatment (function specific) at the time (time specific) when the decision is to be made.[64] If the patient has the requisite capacity, the doctor is bound by the patient's decision. Questions of a patient's mental capacity must be considered in the context of the MCA 2005. Detailed guidance is provided in the mandatory Code of Practice, to which health professionals have a duty to have regard. The general issue of mental capacity has been considered in Chapter 2.

---

[61] *Bolitho v City and Hackney Health Authority* [1998] AC 232; *Pearce v United Bristol Healthcare NHS Trust* (1998) 48 BMLR 118.

[62] *Sidaway v Board of Governors of the Bethlem Royal and the Maudsley Hospital* [1984] 1 All ER 1018, CA; affd [1985] 1 All ER 643, HL.

[63] *Re T (Adult: Refusal of Medical Treatment)* [1993] Fam 95, [1992] 4 All ER 649, CA.

[64] *Re T (Adult: Refusal of Medical Treatment)* [1993] Fam 95, [1992] 4 All ER 649, CA, Donaldson MR; MCA 2005, s 2 and see **2.19–2.20**.

8.69 No one is able to give consent on behalf of an adult who lacks the capacity to give consent for themselves unless they are doing so by the authority of a registered health and welfare lasting power of attorney (LPA (H&W)) or as a court-appointed deputy. One of the basic principles of the MCA 2005 is that a person must be assumed to have capacity unless it is established that they lack capacity.[65] Capacity may be permanent, temporary, or fluctuating. Under MCA 2005, s 2, a patient will be deemed to lack capacity to consent to treatment if at the time the treatment needs to be given, they are unable to make the decision because of an impairment of, or disturbance in the functioning of, the mind or brain. The person assessing mental capacity must not make unjustified assumptions based on discriminatory beliefs.[66]

8.70 A patient may have capacity to consent where the issues are straightforward, but lack capacity to consent where the issues are more complex, or they may have good days and bad days where capacity is better at times and worse at others. Capacity in older people can be compromised by conditions such as dementia or stokes. In a medical context, capacity can be affected by a number of other factors such as unconsciousness, infections, the effects of shock, severe fatigue, pain or drugs being used in the treatment.

The functional test

8.71 The MCA 2005 adopts a functional test to determine whether the patient has mental capacity to consent to the treatment, which means they must be unable:

(a) to understand the information relevant to the decision;

(b) retain that information;

(c) use or weigh that information as part of the process of making the decision; or

(d) communicate the decision (whether by talking, using sign language or any other means).[67]

Medical professionals should use appropriate means to enable the patient to understand the relevant information using simple language, visual aids or any other means.[68] The fact that a patient is only able to retain the relevant information for a short period does not prevent them from being regarded as able to make the decision.[69]

8.72 The question is whether the patient can understand in broad terms what they are consenting to and extends to:

(1) the nature, purposes and benefits of the proposed treatment;

(2) any alternatives to the proposed treatment;

(3) the risks of the proposed treatment; and

(4) the consequences of not having the treatment.

This may amount to being able to undertake a risk/benefit/consequence analysis of what is proposed and what is likely to happen if the treatment is not undertaken. The extent

---

[65] MCA 2005, s 1(2).
[66] See **2.20**.
[67] MCA 2005, s 3(1).
[68] MCA 2005, ss 1(3) and 3(2).
[69] MCA 2005, s 3(3).

of understanding is in direct proportion to the severity and risk of the treatment, or in inverse proportion to the risk of not having the treatment.

Assessment of capacity

8.73   The assessment of a patient's ability to consent will usually be made by the doctor proposing the treatment. The capacity decision is a matter for clinical judgment guided by professional practice[70] and taking into account the advice on assessing capacity in the MCA 2005 Code of Practice. A judgment must be formed of the patient's understanding of the particular treatment concerned and information provided by the doctor. The complexity of the proposed treatment and the degree of understanding required will be different in each case and capacity should therefore be assessed on each occasion and be continually reassessed with each particular treatment and at each stage of treatment. In difficult cases it is appropriate to set up a multidisciplinary team to undertake this assessment involving other healthcare professionals and possibly assistance from psychiatric colleagues.

Clinical trials and research

8.74   The law and governance arrangements that apply to medical research are complex and vary depending on the type of research, the participants involved, how it is funded and where in the UK it is undertaken. GMC guidance states:

> 'Seeking consent is fundamental in research involving people. Participants' consent is legally valid and professionally acceptable only if they have the capacity to decide whether to take part in the research, have been properly informed, and have agreed to participate without pressure or coercion.'[71]

When considering adults who lack capacity, the law differentiates between clinical trials of 'investigational medicinal products' (generally research involving the testing of new drugs) and other types of research. Clinical trials of the former are governed by the Medicines for Human Use (Clinical Trials) Regulations 2004 (the 2004 regulations).[72] The regulations set out good clinical practice in the conduct of clinical trials on investigational medicinal products, including trials for adults who lack capacity.[73] The MCA 2005 governs other research involving people over 16 who lack capacity.

8.75   The general principles under both the 2004 regulations and the MCA 2005 are that research should only involve adults who lack capacity if it relates to their incapacity and treatment and if the research is expected to provide a benefit which outweighs the risk. Research not involving the testing of drugs can involve adults who lack capacity if the research may lead to an indirect benefit to them or others who lack capacity and the risks are minimal.

8.76   The views of those close to the incapacitated adult must be sought and in particular for drug trials, consent must be sought by the patient's legal representative defined under the 2004 Regulations as an adult independent of the trial who by virtue of their relationship with the patient is suitable to act as such.[74] If there is no such suitable

---

70   General Medical Council *Consent: patient and doctors making decisions together* (2008), paras 71–74.
71   General Medical Council *Supplementary guidance: consent to research* (2010), para 1.
72   SI 2004/1031.
73   SI 2004/1031, Sch 1, Parts 1 and 5.
74   Ibid, reg 2(a), Sch 1, Pt 2.

person, an independent doctor, preferably one who is primarily responsible for the patient's treatment, should be approached. Under the MCA 2005, a consultee should be approached and consulted about their opinion as to whether the patient should take part and their view about the patient's wishes if they had capacity to decide for themselves.[75]

Removed tissue

8.77 The Human Tissue Act 2004 (HTA 2004) established the Human Tissue Authority to regulate activities concerning the removal, storage, use and disposal of human tissue. Consent is the fundamental principle of the legislation and underpins the lawful removal, storage and use of body parts, organs and tissue. Different consent requirements apply when dealing with tissue from the deceased and the living. The HTA 2004 lists the purposes for which consent is required.

8.78 The HTA 2004 does not specify the criteria for considering whether an adult has capacity to consent and as such the MCA 2005 should be considered together with general principles governing capacity to consent to medical procedures.

Consequences of lack of consent

8.79 It is a criminal and tortious assault to perform physically invasive medical treatment without the patient's consent.[76] The effect of valid consent is to protect the doctor from a claim for damages, but it will not necessarily prevent a criminal prosecution because a patient cannot consent to any form of physical harm.

Statutory protection against liability

8.80 MCA 2005, s 5 provides protection from liability for people who need to provide care or treatment for people who lack capacity, where the treatment is reasonably believed to be in the patient's best interests.[77] The provision does not define the limits of care and treatment nor does it provide authority to make the decision on behalf of the patient. However, a person will not be afforded the statutory protection where:

(1) the proposed decision conflicts with a decision of an attorney (LPA (H&W)) or deputy; or

(2) the medical treatment is serious and requires an order from the court before it can be given.[78]

8.81 When it comes to advance decisions to refuse treatment the MCA 2005, s 26 provides the following protection from liability:

'(2) A person does not incur liability for carrying out or continuing the treatment unless, at the time, he is satisfied that an advance decision exists which is valid and applicable to the treatment.

(3) A person does not incur liability for the consequences of withholding or withdrawing a treatment if, at the time, he reasonably believes that an advance decision exists which is valid and applicable to the treatment.'

---

[75] MCA 2005, s 32.
[76] *Collins v Wilcox* [1984] 1 WLR 1172, per Goff LJ at 1177.
[77] See **2.38–2.48**.
[78] Practice Direction 9E.

The MCA 2005 also provides that nothing in an apparent advance decision stops a person providing life-sustaining treatment, or doing any act they reasonably believe to be necessary to prevent a serious deterioration in the patient's condition while a decision as respects any relevant issue is sought from the court.

Claims for damages

8.82   Lack of consent may result in an action for damages based on a tort. The tort of trespass to the person, or assault and battery, depends upon physical contact but may be brought without proof of damage. Any touching of the individual against his wishes is a battery and may justify an award of damages.

8.83   In a situation where medicines have been administered without consent, the claim may have to be in negligence because there may have been no physical contact. Problems of causation then arise, because proof of damage is required in consequence of the breach of duty of care; for example, can the patient prove that they would have been better off without the treatment and if the doctor saves the patient's life will the court really compensate the patient with money? The real risk comes if the treatment goes wrong because liability may be absolute in the absence of consent.

Doubtful consent

8.84   Wrong or misleading information may give rise to an action in negligence if this breach of duty causes an injury directly resulting from the failure to inform. The patient must show that they would not have consented to the treatment had they been properly informed and that the damage directly resulted from this failure to inform and the subsequent treatment.

8.85   A different approach may apply in the private sector where treatment is based upon contract. If the consultant or medical practitioner departs from the terms of the agreement, a claim for breach of contract may arise with damages based upon the consequence of the breach. However, a court may still decide that the patient would have agreed to the treatment had the matter been fully considered.

Powers of the court

8.86   The courts do not only award damages; they may also grant an injunction to prevent treatment or a declaration as to the legality of treatment. For example, a patient obtained a High Court injunction to prevent any doctor from amputating his leg despite gangrene of the foot.[79]

Declarations

8.87   The Court of Protection has jurisdiction to make declarations under MCA 2005, s 15 which is considered at **2.99**. Under ss 16 and 17, the court can make decisions regarding the incapacitated patient's welfare including specific authority to give or refuse consent to health care treatment. Under s 26, there is also power to declare whether an advance decision is binding or not. Most care and treatment decisions can be made relying on the statutory protection of s 5, so the court should be seen as a court of last resort, and generally only those that fall under the remit of the practice direction on serious medical treatment, appeals against deprivation of liberty authorisations, or those where they cannot otherwise be resolved should be brought to the court.

---

[79]   *Re C (Adult: Refusal of Medical Treatment)* [1994] 1 All ER 819.

8.88   The practice direction states that the following should be regarded as serious medical treatment and should be brought to the court:

(1)   decisions about the proposed withholding or withdrawal of artificial nutrition and hydration from a person in a permanent vegetative state[80] or a minimally conscious state;

(2)   cases involving organ or bone marrow donation by a person who lacks capacity to consent; and

(3)   cases involving non-therapeutic sterilisation of a person who lacks capacity to consent.

Examples of serious medical treatment may include:

(a)   certain terminations of pregnancy in relation to a person who lacks capacity to consent to such a procedure;

(b)   a medical procedure performed on a person who lacks capacity to consent to it, where the procedure is for the purpose of a donation to another person;

(c)   a medical procedure or treatment to be carried out on a person who lacks capacity to consent to it, where that procedure or treatment must be carried out using a degree of force to restrain the person concerned;

(d)   an experimental or innovative treatment for the benefit of a person who lacks capacity to consent to such treatment; and

(e)   a case involving an ethical dilemma in an untested area.

Treatment without consent

8.89   Lawful authority to give medical treatment without the consent of the patient (or the consent of the court, or a health and welfare attorney on behalf of the patient) is provided by either common law or statute in certain circumstances. It means treatment to some extent can be given where the patient is:

(1)   unconscious – emergency treatment can then be given to save the patient's life;

(2)   not competent to give consent – treatment considered by the treating doctor to be in the patient's best interest[81] may be given. It may also apply to routine measures such as dressing and undressing such patients;

(3)   detained under the treatment provisions of the MHA 1983 – certain treatment for a mental disorder can (subject to safeguards) be given without the patient's consent;

(4)   suffering from a mental disorder and their behaviour may be a danger to themselves or others. In this situation the common law defence of self-defence and use of reasonable force is warranted.

Necessary treatment

8.90   In an emergency the doctor responsible for a patient who is unable to give or refuse consent to treatment should act in accordance with good medical practice and give treatment which is designed to preserve the life of the patient, assist recovery and

---

[80]   *Airedale National Health Service Trust v Bland* [1993] 1 All ER 821, [1993] 1 FLR 1026, HL.

[81]   MCA 2005, s 4 sets out the process for determining best interests.

ease suffering but limited to treatment that is necessary and reasonable.[82] This is often referred to as the principle of necessity, which can be justified on the basis of implied or constructive consent. The doctor should do no more than is justified by the emergency; if it is possible to postpone treatment until the patient is in a position to give consent, this option should be taken.[83]

8.91 An advance decision to refuse medical treatment could rebut this presumption, if it is found to be valid and applicable to the actual situation that has then arisen.

Consultation with others

8.92 If a person lacks capacity to consent and a decision must be made on their behalf, it is necessary for the medical professionals to consult those who are engaged in caring for the patient or interested in their welfare about the proposed treatment to determine if it is in the patient's best interests.[84] This allows for those close to the patient, no matter what their formal relationship to be consulted.

Best interests

The process for determining best interests

8.93 The decision in *R (on the application of Burke) v General Medical Council*[85] makes clear that doctors are under no legal or ethical obligation to agree to a patient's request for treatment if they consider the treatment is not in the patient's best interests. However, having decided that the treatment could be given for a mentally incompetent adult, doctors will need to consider whether giving the treatment is in the patient's best interests.

8.94 MCA 2005, s 4 sets out the process to go through to determine whether the treatment is in the best interests of the patient who lacking capacity and is considered generally at **2.29–2.37**.

Patient's views

8.95 Ascertaining the patient's wishes is core to establishing what might be in their best interests.[86] If it is reasonably ascertainable doctors must try and establish the patient's past and present wishes and feelings as well as their beliefs and values. Doctors will be bound by any valid and applicable advance decision, and must follow this even if they consider withdrawal or not giving the specified treatment would be in the patient's best interests. If it is not valid and applicable then the advance decision may be used to establish the patient's wishes.[87]

8.96 It is good practice to ascertain the patient's wishes at an early stage when the patient still has capacity to express these. These may be contained in guidance contained in the LPA (H&W). Doctors should:

---

82   *Bolam v Friern Hospital Management Committee* [1957] 2 All ER 118.
83   General Medical Council *Consent: patients and doctors making decisions together* (2008) para 79.
84   MCA 2005, s 4 sets out how to determine best interests.
85   [2005] EWCA Civ 1003.
86   MCA 2005, s 4(6).
87   *An NHS Trust v D* [2012] EWHC 885 (COP); [2012] EWHC 886 (COP).

(1) discuss treatment options in a place and at a time when the patient is best able to understand and retain the information;

(2) ask the patient if there is anything that would help them remember information, or make it easier to make a decision; such as bringing a relative, partner, friend, carer or advocate to consultations, or having written or audio information about their condition or the proposed investigation or treatment;

(3) speak to those close to the patient and to other health care staff about the best ways of communicating with the patient, taking account of confidentiality issues; and

(4) record any decisions that are made, wherever possible while the patient has capacity to understand and review them.

Whom to consult

8.97   If a patient lacks capacity, in establishing what decision is in the best interests of the patient, the views of the following must be taken into account (if it is practicable and appropriate to consult them):[88]

(1) anyone named by the person as someone to be consulted on the matter in question or on matters of that kind;

(2) anyone engaged in caring for the person or interested in his welfare;

(3) any attorney of a lasting power of attorney granted by the person; and

(4) any deputy appointed for the person by the court.

Independent Mental Capacity Advocate (IMCA) and serious medical treatment

8.98   The MCA 2005 created the Independent Mental Capacity Advocate (IMCA)[89] service as a safeguard so that there is someone independent to represent and support mentally incapacitated people at times when critical decisions are being made about their health or care and there is no one appropriate to consult.

8.99   If an NHS body is proposing to provide serious medical treatment for a person who lacks capacity to consent to the treatment, and there is no person other than one professionally engaged in providing care or treatment for that patient whom it would be appropriate to consult in determining what would be in the patient's best interests, then before the treatment is provided the NHS body must instruct an IMCA to represent and support the patient, and take their views into account.[90]

8.100   'Serious medical treatment' involves providing, withholding or withdrawing treatment in circumstances where:

(a) in a case where a single treatment is being proposed, there is a fine balance between its benefits to the patient and the burdens and risks it is likely to entail for them;

---

[88]   MCA 2005, s 4(7).
[89]   See **7.100** on the IMCA's role in supporting unbefriended adults when long term accommodation stays are to be decided.
[90]   MCA 2005, s 37.

(b) in a case where there is a choice of treatments, the decision as to which one to use is finely balanced; or

(c) what is proposed would be likely to involve serious consequences for the patient.[91]

Extent of treatment

8.101 How far should the doctor go when treating an incompetent patient? Short-term incompetence is of less significance than long-term because the minimum necessary treatment can be given until the patient recovers and can express wishes in regard to further or more drastic treatment. The doctor must consider whether it is likely that the person will at some time have capacity and, if it appears likely that they will, when that is likely to be.[92]

8.102 A person who is likely to remain incompetent is entitled to more than minimum treatment, but it may be difficult to decide whether further treatment is in the patient's best interests and if so which form of treatment should be adopted. Before a decision is made on behalf of a person who lacks capacity, regard must be had to whether the purpose for which it is needed can be as effectively achieved in a way that is less restrictive of the person's rights and freedom of action.[93] Decisions may also need to be taken as to whether it is appropriate to change the emphasis from preserving the patient's life to allowing the patient to die whilst preserving comfort and dignity.[94]

Advance decisions

Distinguishing an advance decision

8.103 Advances in medical science together with our ageing population mean that many people may be kept alive for long periods by medical treatment which, if they remained competent to make a decision, they might refuse. It is a basic principle of English law that a mentally competent adult can refuse medical treatment even if this is certain to lead to their death.[95] A decision to refuse treatment made at a time when the patient has capacity to take effect in the future when they lack capacity, is an extension of that basic principle.

8.104 The common law has recognised that such decisions can be binding on medical professionals in certain circumstances.[96] The MCA 2005[97] codified the common law regarding advance decisions, allowing people over the age of 18, with mental capacity to refuse treatment in specified circumstances at a future time when they may then lack mental capacity to refuse consent to such treatment. Such wishes are binding if they are valid and applicable.

8.105 An advance decision specifically relates to the refusal to have a specific treatment, and does not allow for the patient to demand a particular treatment to be given, although the patient may set out their wishes, within the advance decision or separately

---

[91] Mental Capacity Act 2005 (Independent Mental Capacity Advocates) (General) Regulations 2006, SI 2006/1832, reg 4.
[92] MCA 2005, s 4(3).
[93] MCA 2005, s 1(6).
[94] See 8.118.
[95] *Re B (Adult, Refusal of Medical Treatment)* [2002] 2 All ER 449.
[96] For example, *HE v A Hospital NHS Trust* [2003] 2 FLR 408.
[97] MCA 2005, ss 24–26.

(known as an advance directive or advance statement), for treatment that they are prepared or would like to receive.[98] An advance directive or statement is not binding but could be useful information for medical professionals when establishing what is in the best interests of the patient. For example, some religious beliefs have important implications in relation to care and treatment options.

8.106 An advance decision is distinguished from a LPA (H&W), in particular it must be followed, if valid and applicable, even if those treating the individual believe the refusal is not in the best interests of the patient, whereas an attorney is required to make the decision in the patient's best interests.

Definition

8.107 MCA 2005, ss 24–26 set out the statutory framework for advance decisions. Section 24(1) defines an advance decision in the following way:

> '"Advance decision" means a decision made by a person ("P"), after he has reached 18 and when he has capacity to do so, that if –
>
> (a) at a later time and in such circumstances as he may specify, a specified treatment is proposed to be carried out or continued by a person providing health care for him, and
> (b) at that time he lacks capacity to consent to the carrying out or continuation of the treatment, the specified treatment is not to be carried out or continued.'

Form of decision

8.108 There is no prescribed form for an advance decision. It can be expressed in layman's terms, and may be found to be applicable even if the treatment to be refused is not the treatment specified, provided it is clear as to the treatment the patient intended to refuse.[99] An advance decision can be made orally or in writing; however, if it relates to the refusal of life sustaining treatment then it must:

(1) be in writing;
(2) be signed by the patient and witnessed. If the patient is unable to sign, it can be signed by another in their presence at their direction;
(3) contain a statement that life sustaining treatment is refused even if life is at risk.

Life sustaining treatment is defined as 'treatment which, in the view of a person providing health care for the person concerned, is necessary to sustain life'.[100]

8.109 An advance decision may be withdrawn or altered at any time when the patient has capacity to do so. A withdrawal need not be in writing, although an alteration need not be in writing unless the decision resulting from the alteration is one relating to the withdrawal of life sustaining treatment.

8.110 The MCA 2005 was amended by statutory instrument[101] to allow some advance decisions signed before the Act came into force to be treated as valid in relation to a refusal of life sustaining treatment even if they did not comply with the conditions laid

---

[98] *R (on the application of Burke) v General Medical Council* [2005] EWCA Civ 1003.
[99] *X Primary Care Trust v XB* [2012] EWHC 1390 (Fam).
[100] MCA 2005, s 4(10).
[101] Mental Capacity Act 2005 (Transitional and Consequential Provisions) Order 2007, SI 2007/1898.

down in the Act in this respect. Such advance decisions may still be valid if the decision was in writing and there was a reasonable belief that the decision was made before 1 October 2007 (when the MCA 2005 came into force) and there was a reasonable belief that the person lacked capacity since then to comply with the terms of the MCA 2005 in this respect.

When are advance decisions binding?

8.111 The fundamental problem with advance decisions is that they are by definition made in advance of a particular situation and before the exact circumstances of a patient's treatment can be known. In many cases in the absence of a specific diagnosis, patients have to second guess the treatments they may be offered and try to anticipate how they might feel in that situation. In order for an advance decision to be binding on medical practitioners they need to consider whether the decision was validly made, whether the patient intended it to apply to the particular circumstances in which they now find themselves, and whether they may have changed their mind in the interim.

8.112 If the patient has made an advance decision which is both valid, and applicable to a treatment, the decision has effect as if the patient had made it, and had had capacity to make it, at the time when the question arises whether the treatment should be carried out or continued.[102]

Validity

8.113 An advance decision is not valid[103] under s 25 of the Act if:

(1) the patient was not mentally competent when it was made or was coerced into making it;[104] or

(2) authority has subsequently been granted to someone under a LPA (H&W) which confers authority on that person to give or refuse consent to the treatment to which that advance decision relates;[105] or

(3) it has been withdrawn;[106] or

(4) the patient has done something which is clearly inconsistent with the advance decision being his fixed decision.[107]

Applicability

8.114 Under s 25, an advance decision is not applicable[108] to the treatment in question if at the material time:

(1) the patient has capacity to give or refuse consent to the treatment;[109]

(2) the treatment is not the treatment specified;[110]

---

[102] MCA 2005, s 26.
[103] See MCA Code of Practice, para 9.40.
[104] *Re T (Adult refusal of treatment)* [1992] 4 All ER 649.
[105] MCA 2005, s 25(2)(b).
[106] MCA 2005, s 25(2)(a).
[107] *HE v A Hospital NHS Trust* [2003] 2 FLR 408.
[108] MCA Code of Practice, paras 9.41–9.44.
[109] MCA 2005, s 25(3).
[110] MCA 2005, s 25(4)(a).

(3)   any circumstances specified are absent;[111] or

(4)   there are reasonable grounds for believing that circumstances exist which the patient did not anticipate at the time of the advance decision and which would have affected their decision had they anticipated them (for example advances in medical science which change the treatment options available).[112]

An advance decision to refuse treatment for a mental disorder can be overruled if the patient is detained in hospital for treatment under the MHA 1993, when that treatment is to compulsorily be given under Part 4 of that Act.[113] Other treatment can be refused.

8.115   From a practical point of view, advance decisions should be regularly reviewed to avoid the suggestion that the decision was withdrawn, or that circumstances now exist that were not anticipated at the time which would have affected the decision. It is not advisable however, to unintentionally include a review date in the document.[114] It is a good idea for patients to discuss their decisions with their doctor, family and close friends.

Health and welfare lasting powers of attorney

Appointing others to make decisions

8.116   The LPA (H&W) created the legal mechanism to allow the delegation of health and welfare decisions to others (known as 'attorneys' but sometimes referred by the medical profession as 'proxies') when the donor lacks capacity. The donor may give their attorney the authority to give or refuse consent to life-sustaining treatment. Chapter 2 contains general detail about the creation and registration of LPAs.

Interrelationship of advance decisions and health and welfare lasting powers of attorney

8.117   Insofar as an advance decision and a LPA (H&W) cover the same decision, the later document to be created takes effect. They cannot operate together in respect of the same decision, although with careful drafting it is possible to make one subject to the other so there is no overlap. For example, a Jehovah's Witness may refuse a blood transfusion by an advance decision and make a LPA (H&W) subject to that advance decision, with the effect that the attorney can give or refuse consent to life-sustaining treatment for everything, with the exception of the blood transfusion.

Allowing the patient to die

End of Life Care Strategy

8.118   As people live longer, more wish to have active involvement and control over the end of their lives. In 2008 the Department of Health published the *End of Life Care Strategy* which aimed to set out a strategy to enable people to die in accordance with their wishes. The strategy aims to provide patients with the following vision:

---

[111]   MCA 2005, s 25(4)(b).
[112]   MCA 2005, s 25(4)(c).
[113]   MCA Code of Practice, paras 9.37, 13.33, 13.35–13.37.
[114]   *X Primary Care Trust v XB* [2012] EWHC 1390 (Fam).

'1. The opportunity to discuss your personal needs and preferences with professionals who can support you. You will have the opportunity for these to be recorded in a care plan so that every service which will be involved in supporting you will be aware of your priorities. Your preferences and choices will be taken into account and accommodated wherever possible:

- All health and social care staff will be trained in communication regarding end of life care;
- Health and social care professionals will be trained in assessing differing requirements; and
- A care plan will be offered to every patient and carer, to help ensure services are provided to meet their needs and preferences.

2. Coordinated care and support, ensuring that your needs are met, irrespective of who is delivering the service to you:

- Every organisation involved in providing end of life care will be expected to adopt a coordination process, such as the Gold Standards Framework (www. goldstandardsframework.nhs.uk);
- Local end of life care coordination centres will be established to coordinate care across organisational boundaries; and
- End of life care registers will be piloted and established to ensure that every organisation which will be involved in care is aware of a patient's wishes.'

Preserving life

8.119 Doctors have a legal duty to protect the life and further the health of patients. An act by which the doctor's primary intention[115] is to bring about a patient's death would be unlawful.[116]

8.120 In July 2010, the GMC issued new guidance for doctors, *Treatment and care towards the end of life: good practice in decision making*. The guidance states as one of the basic principles that treatment must not be motivated by a desire to bring about the patient's death and must start from a presumption in favour of prolonging life. That presumption will normally require a doctor to take all reasonable steps to prolong a patient's life. However there is no absolute obligation to prolong life irrespective of the consequences for the patient, and irrespective of the patient's views.[117]

Withholding and withdrawing of life-prolonging treatment

8.121 In the cases of adults with capacity, a patient has the right to refuse medical treatment even if that is certain to lead to death.[118]

8.122 An attorney acting under a LPA (H&W) can give or refuse consent to life-sustaining treatment on behalf of the mentally incapacitated patient for whom they act, where the power includes such authority. In contrast, a deputy who may be given authority by the court to give or refuse consent to general health care treatment cannot be given authority to refuse life-sustaining treatment.[119] The rationale for difference is that it is the patient who decides that they wish to delegate that important decision

---

[115] *R v Cox* (1992) 12 BMLR 38.

[116] For a very rare exception in the case of conjoined twins see *Re A (Children) (Conjoined Twins: Surgical Separation)* [2000] 4 All ER 961.

[117] Para 10 of the guidance.

[118] *Re T (Adult: Refusal of Treatment)* [1992] 4 All ER 649; *B (Consent to Treatment: Capacity)* [2002] EWHC 429 (Fam).

[119] MCA 2005, s 20(5).

under a LPA, but the court does not presume to do that on their behalf. The attorney and deputy are considered to be legal proxys.

8.123 If a patient lacks capacity, in the absence of an attorney with the authority to make a decision, or a binding advance decision, a decision to withdraw life-prolonging treatment can be made in their best interests, with the medical professionals relying on the statutory protection afforded by s 5.[120]

The decision-making model

8.124

(1) The doctor, with the patient (if they are able to contribute) and the patient's carer, make an assessment of the patient's condition taking into account the patient's medical history and the patient and carer's knowledge and experience of the condition.

(2) The doctor uses specialist knowledge, experience and clinical judgment, together with any evidence about the patient's views (including advance statements, directives or non-valid or applicable advance decisions), to identify which investigations or treatments are clinically appropriate and are likely to result in overall benefit for the patient.

(3) If the patient has made an advance decision to refuse a particular treatment, the doctor must make a judgment about its validity and its applicability to the current circumstances. If the doctor concludes that the decision is legally binding, it must be followed in relation to that treatment. Otherwise it should be taken into account as information about the patient's previous wishes.

(4) If an attorney or deputy has been appointed to make health care decisions for the patient, the doctor should confirm the authority, explain the options (as they would do for a patient with capacity), setting out the benefits, burdens and risks of each option. The doctor may recommend a particular option which they believe would provide overall benefit for the patient. The doctor should offer support to the legal proxy in making the decision, but must not pressurise them to accept a particular recommendation. The legal proxy should weigh up these considerations and any non-clinical issues to make the decision to give or refuse consent.

(5) In circumstances in which there is no legal proxy with authority to make a particular decision for the patient, and the doctor is responsible for making the decision, the doctor must consult with members of the health care team and those close to the patient (as far as it is practical and appropriate to do so) before reaching a decision. When consulting, the doctor will explain the issues; seek information about the patient's circumstances; and seek views about the patient's wishes, preferences, feelings, beliefs and values. The doctor may also explore which options those consulted might see as providing overall benefit for the patient, but must not give them the impression they are being asked to make the decision. The doctor must take the views of those consulted into account in considering which option would be least restrictive of the patient's future choices and in making the final decision about which option is of overall benefit to the patient.

(6) In England and Wales, if there is no legal proxy, close relative or other person who is willing or able to support or represent the patient and the decision involves

---

[120] See **8.80.**

serious medical treatment, the doctor must approach their employing or contracting organisation about appointing an IMCA. The IMCA will have authority to make enquiries about the patient and contribute to the decision by representing the patient's interests, but cannot make a decision on behalf of the patient.

(7)   Following withdrawal of life-prolonging treatment, any subsequent treatment given should be for the sole purpose of enabling them to end the patient's life in dignity and free from pain or suffering.

(8)   When death occurs, its cause will be attributed to the natural and other causes of their present state and those treating will not be subject to any civil or criminal liability.

Assisted suicide

8.125   A decision to refuse treatment which subsequently leads to a patient's death is not suicide. There is no question of a competent patient refusing medical treatment being seen as committing suicide. However some patients with a terminal diagnosis wish to control the manner and timing of their death and often need the assistance of others to do that. Although suicide itself is now decriminalised, assisting suicide is still an offence and cases have been brought to try and force the courts to declare that in particular cases those assisting the individual will not be prosecuted.

8.126   In April 2002, Diane Pretty,[121] terminally ill with motor neurone disease, unsuccessfully challenged the House of Lords' decision in the European Court of Human Rights, that no right to assisted suicide is guaranteed by Articles 2,[122] 3,[123] 8,[124] 9[125] and 14[126] of the European Convention on Human Rights. The Director of Public Prosecutions had refused to undertake not to prosecute Mrs Pretty's husband if he were to assist her in taking her life. As such she could not be helped and allowed to die with the assistance of her husband.

8.127   However in the 2009 case of *R (on the application of Purdy) v the Director of Public Prosecutions,*[127] the House of Lords required the Director of Public Prosecutions to promulgate an offence specific policy which would identify the facts and circumstances which would be taken into account when deciding whether to bring a prosecution against an individual who assisted the suicide of another. New policy guidance was issued in February 2010, which makes a distinction between people acting with compassionate motives who are less likely to be prosecuted, and those who are acting with malicious encouragement or assistance of suicide, which will be prosecuted. Prosecution is more likely if the person committing suicide lacked the mental capacity to reach an informed decision to end their life or if they were physically able to undertake the act without assistance.

8.128   End of life issues are undoubtedly some of the hardest issues that face us. Many people struggle with the fine distinction between the legal refusal of medical treatment which an adult with capacity is able to do in the knowledge that this will bring about

---

[121]   *R (on the application of Pretty) v Director of Public Prosecutions* [2001] UKHL 61.
[122]   The right to life.
[123]   Freedom from torture and inhuman and degrading treatment.
[124]   Respect of home and family life and privacy.
[125]   Freedom of thought, conscience and religion.
[126]   Prohibition of discrimination.
[127]   [2009] UKHL 45.

their death, and the crime of assisted suicide which would be committed by the loved one of a mentally competent adult with a terminal illness who asks for their help.

MENTAL HEALTH

The scope of mental health law

Mental health in context

8.129 One in four people will develop a mental health problem at some point in their life.[128] As such older people may have the same mental health needs and suffer the same mental health problems as anyone else. However, some mental illnesses, such as depression and dementia, are more common in older people. Depression, in particular, is under-diagnosed, partly because many older people live alone. It is thought that at any one time, some 10–15% of those aged over 65 will have depression and 3–5% severe depression. There are over 820,000 people in the UK with dementia. It is estimated that by 2021 there will be one million people with dementia in the UK.

8.130 The mental health problems of older age are sometimes seen as the inevitable result of the ageing process and not as health problems that will respond to treatment. Furthermore, older people may experience direct discrimination in the provision of health care, particularly if they are from black or minority ethnic communities, or if they have learning difficulties.

8.131 Mental health law in England and Wales is primarily concerned with the compulsory detention and compulsory treatment of people with mental disorder. Such patients are commonly said to have been 'sectioned'. The law has less to say about people with mental health problems who enter hospital voluntarily and who, as a result, may not be detained and are free to come and go as they please. These 'informal' patients are in the majority, while an even larger group of people with mental health needs live outside hospital in 'the community'.

Source of law

The Mental Health Act 1983

8.132 The Mental Health Act 1983 (MHA 1983) is the principal piece of mental health legislation. It was amended by the Mental Health Act 2007 (MHA 2007) which also made amendments to the MCA 2005 and introduced Deprivation of Liberty Safeguards. It is supported by numerous Regulations and a Code of Practice[129] which provides detailed guidance on the Act. Professionals are required to have regard to the Code when carrying out their relevant functions under the Act and should only depart from it, if they have cogent reasons for doing so.[130] The MHA 1983 applies to England and Wales, but is applied to Northern Ireland by Order.[131] There is separate legislation for Scotland.[132]

---

[128] 'No health without mental health: a cross-government metal health outcomes strategy for people of all ages', Department of Health (2011), p 10.
[129] Department of Health *Mental Health Act 1983 Code of Practice* (2008) London, TSO.
[130] *R (on the application of Munjaz) v Ashworth Hospital Authority* [2005] UKHL 58.
[131] Mental Health (Northern Ireland) Order 1986.
[132] Mental Health (Care and Treatment) (Scotland) Act 2003.

8.133 The key features of MHA 2007 are as follows:

(1)   It has a much broader definition of 'mental disorder', which replaced the four old classes with a single definition.[133]

(2)   Compulsion is possible beyond hospital, with some patients being placed on Supervised Community Treatment and made subject to Community Treatment Orders (CTO) with the possibility of their being recalled to hospital.[134]

(3)   Compulsion may be justified even if a patient is not 'treatable'.[135] It is not necessary to show that treatment will alleviate or prevent a deterioration of a patient's mental disorder. It is simply necessary to show that medical treatment is available, that is appropriate to their mental disorder and the other circumstances of their case, with the proviso that its purpose is to alleviate or prevent a worsening of the disorder or one or more of its manifestations.[136] It is not enough for treatment to exist 'in theory' if it cannot actually be offered or accessed.[137]

(4)   A trained 'Approved Mental Health Professional' (AMHP), acts independently to bring an alternative perspective to the medical view.[138] The AMHP can be from a wide range of health professions such as a social worker, nurse or an occupational therapist.

(5)   The Responsible Clinician (RC) has the role of seeking detention when the patient meets the criteria. It does not need to be a psychiatrist or even a doctor.[139] In fact, it is possible that a patient's RC will be a psychiatrist or a psychologist, or even a nurse, social worker or occupational therapist (but not one that is also the AMHP).

(6)   A patient under MHA 1983 may apply for the displacement of their nearest relative, as their representative[140] and there is a ground for displacement of the nearest relative if they are not a suitable person to act as such.[141]

European Convention on Human Rights

8.134 The Human Rights Act 1998 (HRA 1998) introduced the European Convention on Human Rights (ECHR) into domestic law, with the effect that every public body must ensure that their acts and their interpretations of domestic law are compatible with the ECHR and the cases decided under it. This is considered in Chapter 1.

Mental health government policies

8.135 In addition to the strategy document, 'National Service Framework (NSF) for older people',[142] which is explained at **8.17**, the Department of Health also published a NSF for Mental Health.[143] It is equally relevant to older people with mental health problems and covers:

---

[133]   MHA 1983, s 1(2).
[134]   MHA 1983, s 17A–17G.
[135]   MHA 1983, ss 3(2)(b) and 20(4)(b).
[136]   MHA 1983, ss 3(2)(d), 145(4).
[137]   Department of Health Briefing sheet A2: Criteria (April 2006), p 2.
[138]   MHA 1983, ss 114 and 115.
[139]   MHA 1983, s 34(1).
[140]   MHA 1983, s 29(2)(za).
[141]   MHA 1983, s 29(3)(e).
[142]   (2001). See also: Department of Health National Service Framework for Older People: A report of progress and future challenges (2003).
[143]   (1999), A national service framework for mental health: modern standards and service models.

(1)   mental health promotion;

(2)   primary care and access to services;

(3)   effective services for people with severe mental illness;

(4)   caring about carers; and

(5)   preventing suicide.

The NSF do not give individuals legally enforceable rights to services or to a particular level of service. However, they do help to establish best practice and to identify factors that health bodies and social care bodies should take into account when they are planning and developing their services. In July 2005, the Department of Health published an initiative, *Securing better mental health for older adults*, which aimed to coordinate mental health services and older people's services. There followed a service development guide, which aimed to improve front line practice,[144] and in 2006, as part of a more general review, the government published a report reflecting on the next steps to be taken in implementing the NSF.[145]

Mental health assessments

The Care Programme Approach

8.136   As well as the NSF, there is the Single Assessment Process (SAP),[146] which aims to ensure that older people's care needs are assessed thoroughly and accurately, but without duplication. In 2008 the Department of Health implemented an updated and refocused version of what is known as the Care Programme Approach (CPA), a specific assessment process for those who fall under the MHA 1983.[147] Similar guidance[148] exists in Wales, although the intention is that it is integrated into the community care assessment process.[149]

8.137   The CPA is focused on the assessment, review and care management of patients who have complex needs, require multi-agency input and are at higher risk. In England, there is no automatic entitlement to a CPA, although people subject to a community treatment or guardianship order will generally be subject to one.[150] The minimum requirement is that a statement of agreed care should be recorded in the relevant clinical or practice notes (the care plan). In most cases, where agencies are helping older people who have mental illness, they will use the SAP[151] rather than the CPA.[152]

---

[144]   Care Services Improvement Partnership & Department of Health Everybody's business. Integrated mental health services for older adults: a service development guide (2005).

[145]   Department of Health *A new ambition for old age: Next steps in implementing the National Service Framework for Older People* (2006).

[146]   See **7.117.**

[147]   Department of Health *Refocusing the Care Programme Approach: Policy and Positive Practice Guidance* (2008). There have been a number of revisions of the original 1990 policy in HC (90) 23; LASSL (90) 11.

[148]   Welsh Assembly Government: *Mental health policy Wales implementation guidance: the care programme approach for mental health users* (2003); *Adult mental health services: stronger in partnership* (2004); *Delivering the care programme approach in Wales: interim policy implementation guidance* (2010).

[149]   Usually referred to as the unified assessment process.

[150]   2008 CPA, pp 14–15.

[151]   Department of Health Guidance on the Single Assessment Process for Older People, HSC 2002/001, LAC (2002) 1.

[152]   *Care management for older people with serious mental health problems* (2002).

The European Convention on Human Rights and persons of unsound mind

8.138 In certain circumstances the ECHR permits 'persons of unsound mind' to be deprived of liberty,[153] where there is reliable objective medical evidence that the person has a mental disorder of a kind and degree which warrants their compulsory confinement.[154]

Definitions

Mental disorder

8.139 The MHA 1983 is concerned with the 'reception, care and treatment of mentally disordered patients, the management of their property[155] and other related matters'.[156] A 'patient' is defined as 'a person suffering or appearing to be suffering from mental disorder',[157] which is any disorder or disability of the mind.[158] However, dependence on alcohol or drugs is not considered to be a disorder or disability of the mind.[159] A person with a learning disability must not be deemed to suffer from mental disorder because of that disability alone, unless it is associated with abnormally aggressive or seriously irresponsible conduct on their behalf.[160]

Medical treatment

8.140 The term 'medical treatment' includes nursing, psychological intervention and specialist mental health, habilitation, rehabilitation and care.[161] To be covered by MHA 1983, however, its purpose must be to alleviate, or prevent a worsening of, the patient's mental disorder or one or more of its symptoms or manifestations.[162] The High Court has expressed the view that 'the concept [of treatment] is a very wide one'[163] and the House of Lords that its purpose 'may extend from cure to containment'.[164]

Managers

8.141 It is the hospital mangers who have the overall responsibility to detain and discharge patients under the MHA 1983. Depending on where the patient is detained, these will be the managers of the CCG, NHS Board, NHS Trust, NHS Foundation Trust, LHB, Special Health Authority or the independent mental health hospital's registered manager.[165]

---

[153] ECHR, Article 5(1)(e).
[154] *Winterwerp v The Netherlands* (1979) 2 EHRR 387.
[155] The property and affairs aspect is now dealt with under MCA 2005.
[156] MHA 1983, s 1(1).
[157] MHA 1983, s 145(1).
[158] MHA 1983, s 1(2).
[159] MHA 1983, s 1(3).
[160] MHA 1983, s 1(2A).
[161] MHA 1983, s 145.
[162] MHA 1983, s 145(4).
[163] *R (on the application of Wheldon) v Rampton Hospital Authority* [2001] EWHC Admin 134, per Elias J.
[164] *Reid v Secretary of State for Scotland* [1999] 1 All ER 481.
[165] MHA 1983, s 145(1).

Nearest relative

8.142 The nearest relative is a creature of the MHA 1983, which gives the relative a number of significant powers and duties in relation to detention, discharge, being informed or consulted when certain actions have been taken under the MHA 1983 or when these are proposed. The nearest relative is distinct from the concept of 'next of kin', which is often used by health and social care professionals to mean the person the patient or service user chooses to be contacted if the person is unable to be consulted.

Admission to a hospital or care home

General

8.143 Most of the provisions in MHA 1983 that apply to hospitals apply with equal force to establishments such as independent hospitals.[166] If possible, admission to hospital should be voluntary.[167] Compulsory admission will be considered where a patient's mental state, together with reliable evidence of past experience, indicates a strong likelihood that they will have a change of mind about informal admission, either before or after they are admitted, with a resulting risk to their health or safety or to the safety of other people.

Admission for assessment (s 2)

8.144 Under MHA 1983, s 2, a patient may be admitted to hospital and detained there, for an assessment, or an assessment followed by treatment for up to 28 days, where the patient is suffering from a mental disorder of a nature or degree which warrants such detention and they ought to be detained in the interests of their own health or safety or with a view to protect others.[168] The application must be made by two medical recommendations, together with an application by the nearest relative or, more usually, an AMHP.[169] The AMHP must inform the nearest relative of the application and their power of discharge.[170]

8.145 During the assessment period an application may be made for their admission for treatment under s 3. Alternatively, the patient may be discharged by the RC;[171] discharged following a hospital managers hearing;[172] or transferred into guardianship.[173]

Admission for treatment (s 3)

8.146 A patient may be detained for up to 6 months[174] for treatment if they are suffering from a mental disorder of a nature or degree which makes it appropriate for them to receive available medical treatment in a hospital and it is necessary for their

---

[166] MHA 1983, s 34(2).
[167] MHA 1983, s 131(1).
[168] MHA 1983, s 2(2)(a) and (b).
[169] MHA 1983, s 11.
[170] MHA 1983, s 11(3).
[171] MHA 1983, s 23.
[172] MHA 1983, s 23: see **8.179**.
[173] MHA 1983, s 19(1) and Mental Health (Hospital, Guardianship and Consent to Treatment) (Wales) Regulations 2008, reg 7(3); see **8.159**.
[174] MHA 1983, s 20(1).

health or safety, or for the protection of others, that they should receive such treatment and it cannot be provided unless they are detained.[175]

8.147 The application should be made by two medical recommendations, together with an application by the nearest relative or more usually, an AMHP.[176] The AMHP must consult with the nearest relative,[177] unless it is not reasonably practicable or would involve unreasonable delay.[178] Where consultation has taken place, an application may not be made under s 3 if the nearest relative objects to it.[179] Detention may be renewed for a further period of up to 6 months,[180] and then for further periods of up to 12 months at a time.[181]

Application for emergency admission (s 4)

8.148 MHA 1983, s 4 applies in cases of urgent necessity, and enables an application to be made for a patient's admission for assessment, even though the full requirements of s 2 are not met. The criteria are the same as those for an admission for assessment under s 2. The application must be made by the nearest relative or an AMHP, together with one medical recommendation.[182]

8.149 Once an application has been properly made the patient may be taken to hospital (if they are not already there) and detained for a period of 72 hours.[183] This period is not renewable, although the admission may be converted into one for assessment under s 2 by providing a second medical recommendation.[184] A patient detained under s 4 may not apply to the Tribunal.

In hospital informally

Detention by a doctor

8.150 Under MHA 1983, s 5(2),[185] a hospital in-patient may be detained for up to 72 hours, where it appears that an application ought to be made for the patient's admission to hospital. The application is made by the doctor or the approved clinician in charge of their treatment (or by that doctor's nominated deputy) which enables the patient to be held while they are assessed for possible detention under s 2 or 3.

Detention by a nurse

8.151 Under MHA 1983, s 5(4),[186] a hospital in-patient who is receiving treatment for mental disorder may be detained for up to 6 hours by a nurse, if it appears that the patient is suffering from mental disorder of a degree that it is necessary for their health or safety, or for the protection of others, for them to be immediately restrained from

---

[175]　MHA 1983, s 3.
[176]　MHA 1983, s 11.
[177]　MHA 1983, s 11(4).
[178]　Ibid.
[179]　Ibid.
[180]　MHA 1983, s 20(2)(a).
[181]　MHA 1983, s 20(2)(b).
[182]　MHA 1983, s 12.
[183]　MHA 1983, s 4(4).
[184]　MHA 1983, s 4(4)(a).
[185]　Guidance on the use of s 5(2) is given in the MHA 1983 Code of Practice, paras 12.2–12.20.
[186]　Guidance on the use of s 5(4) is given in the MHA 1983 Code of Practice, paras 12.27–12.34.

leaving the hospital and it is not practicable for a doctor or clinician to detain the patient under s 5(2). This allows the doctor or approved clinician to examine the patient and decide whether they need to be further detained.

Community powers

Power to enter and inspect premises

8.152 In some circumstances, an AMHP may enter and inspect premises in which a mentally disordered person is living if they have reasonable cause to believe that the patient is not under proper care.[187] The AMHP may not force entry, restrain or remove the patient but may be used to enter a private house or other non-regulated premises.

Warrant to enter premises

8.153 Under MHA 1983, s 135(1), an AMHP may apply to a magistrate for a warrant authorising a police constable to enter private premises and remove someone to a 'place of safety'. The person is usually taken to a police station or hospital, but it may be a care home or other suitable place.[188] The person in question must be suffering from mental disorder and has been, or is being, ill-treated, neglected or kept otherwise than under proper control or is unable to care for themselves and living there alone.

8.154 In executing the warrant, a police constable may use reasonable force, and they must be accompanied by an AMHP and a registered medical practitioner.[189]

8.155 The purpose of a person's removal under s 135(1) is to consider whether they should be detained under MHA 1983, or whether other arrangements need be made for their treatment or care. Once the person has arrived at the place of safety, they may be detained there for up to 72 hours.[190] Within that period, they may also be transferred to another place of safety. The person may be given medical treatment with their consent, if they are mentally capable, or, where they are incapable, in their best interests.[191] Sections 5 and 6 of the MCA 2005 do not confer on police officers authority to remove persons to hospital or other places of safety for the purposes set out in s 135.[192]

Retaking patients

8.156 A magistrate may issue a warrant authorising the retaking of a patient who is already liable to be detained in hospital under MHA 1983.[193] This power may be used where that person is believed to be present within premises to which admission cannot be gained. An application under s 135(1) will be made by a police constable, or by anyone else who is authorised to retake the patient.[194] In executing the warrant, a police

---

[187] MHA 1983, s 115.
[188] MHA 1983, s 135(6).
[189] MHA 1983, s 135(4).
[190] MHA 1983, s 135(3).
[191] MCA 2005, s 4.
[192] *R (on the application of Sessay) v South London and Maudsley NHS Foundation Trust* [2011] EWHC 2617 (QB).
[193] MHA 1983, s 135(2).
[194] MHA 1983, s 18.

constable may use reasonable force, and they may be accompanied by a registered medical practitioner, or by anyone else who is authorised to retake the patient.[195]

8.157 Alternatively, where a patient who is absent without permission from the place where they are detained under s 3 for treatment is found otherwise than in private premises, they may be retaken and returned to the place of detention.[196] This power may be exercised by an AMHP, a police constable, an 'officer' of the hospital in question or anyone else authorised in writing by the managers of the hospital.[197] A similar power exists with regard to patients who are subject to guardianship.[198]

Mentally disordered persons found in public places

8.158 Under MHA 1983, s 136, where someone in a 'public place' appears to be suffering from mental disorder and to be in immediate need of care and control, a police constable may remove them to a place of safety for to 72 hours.[199] The purpose of such removal is to enable the person to be examined by a doctor and interviewed by an AMHP, and for any necessary arrangements to be made for their treatment or care.[200] The power will lapse once the assessment is complete. The person may be given medical treatment with their consent, if they are capable, or where they are incapable, in their best interests. Sections 5 and 6 of the MCA 2005 do not confer on police officers authority to remove persons to hospital or other places of safety for the purposes set out in s 136.[201]

Guardianship

8.159 An application for a person's reception into guardianship may be made where they suffer a mental disorder of a nature or degree which warrants guardianship and it is necessary and in the welfare of the patient or for the protection of other persons.[202] The guardian may be either a local social services authority or someone approved by that authority. The guardian will have power to require the patient to reside at a particular place; require the patient to attend a specified place for the purpose of medical treatment, occupation, education or training; and/or require access to the patient, where they reside, to be given to a specified person.[203]

8.160 There is power to take the patient to the place they are required to reside.[204] If they leave that place, they may be retaken under MHA 1983 and returned there.[205] However, if this happens repeatedly, or if the person resists the exercise of any other of the guardian's powers, it may be that guardianship is not the most appropriate way to provide care and the order should be discharged.[206]

---

[195] MHA 1983, s 135(4).
[196] MHA 1983, s 18(1).
[197] Ibid.
[198] MHA 1983, s 18(3).
[199] MHA 1983, s 136(2).
[200] MHA 1983, s 136(2).
[201] *R (on the application of Sessay) v South London and Maudsley NHS Foundation Trust* [2011] EWHC 2617 (QB).
[202] MHA 1983, s 7(2).
[203] MHA 1983, s 8(1).
[204] MHA 1983, s 18(7).
[205] MHA 1983, s 18(3).
[206] MHA 1983 Code of Practice, para 26.35. See also *C v Blackburn with Darwen BC* [2011] EWHC 3321 (Fam).

8.161 An application for a person to be received into guardianship may be made by their nearest relative or an AMHP.[207] Where the applicant is an AMHP, the nearest relative must still be consulted.[208] Every application must be supported by two medical recommendations, each of which must comply with MHA 1983, ss 11 and 123.[209] Guardianship will last for 6 months, which is renewable for one further 6-month period and then for periods of up to 12 months.[210] Guardianship may continue, even though a patient is admitted to hospital informally, or under MHA 1983, s 2 or 4. However, it will come to an end where a patient is detained under s 3 for treatment.[211]

Aftercare services under s 117

8.162 Under MHA 1983, s 117,[212] the relevant statutory bodies must provide aftercare services for patients who have been detained under a treatment section of the Act and are subsequently discharged and leave hospital. This duty falls upon NHS bodies, such as CCGs or the NHS Board in England[213] and LHBs in Wales and local authorities. This duty may be fulfilled through or in co-operation with voluntary organisations. The duty continues until the aftercare authorities are satisfied that a patient is no longer in need of those services.

The meaning of aftercare

8.163 'Aftercare' is not defined in the Act. The Code of Practice to MHA 1983 says that 'Aftercare is a vital component in patients overall treatment and care. As well as meeting their immediate needs for health and social care, aftercare should aim to support them in regaining or enhancing their skills, or learning new skills, in order to cope with life outside hospital'.[214] The High Court has suggested that aftercare services 'would normally include social work, support in helping the ex-patient with problems of employment, accommodation or family relationships, the provision of domiciliary services and the use of day centre and residential facilities'.[215]

8.164 This suggestion was accepted in the House of Lords.[216] The High Court expanded on this and said it must be a service that is necessary to meet a need arising from a person's mental disorder. It does not cover any and all services simply because those services do or may prevent deterioration of relapse of a mental condition. Employment and ordinary accommodation are common needs that do not arise from mental disorder, although mental disorder may give rise to a need for assistance in finding them.[217]

---

[207] MHA 1983, s 11.
[208] MHA 1983, s 11(4).
[209] MHA 1983, s 7(5).
[210] MHA 1983, s 20.
[211] Guardianship is considered in Chapter 26 of the MHA 1983 Code of Practice.
[212] Aftercare is discussed in Chapter 27 of the MHA 1983 Code of Practice.
[213] The Health and Social Care Act 2012 amended the NHS Act 2006 and created new NHS structures in England. CCGs have responsibility for commissioning primary medical services with the exception of services commissioned directly by the NHS Commissioning Board, such as high secure psychiatric services, specialised services and the majority of health services for prisoners/those detained in 'other prescribed accommodation' and members of the armed forces.
[214] MHA 1983 Code of Practice, para 27.5.
[215] *Clunis v Camden and Islington Health Authority* (1998) 1 CCLR 215, per Beldam LJ at 225.
[216] *R (on the application of Stennett) v Manchester City Council* [2002] UKHL 34, at [9].
[217] *R (on the application of Mwanza) v LB of Greenwich* [2010] EWHC 1462 (Admin).

8.165 The aftercare needs of a particular patient, and the services that are to be provided to meet them, should be identified through the CPA.[218] Aftercare planning is discussed in Chapter 27 of the MHA 1983 Code of Practice. Guidance on aftercare was also issued by the Department of Health in May 1994.[219]

Charging for aftercare

8.166 The House of Lords has ruled that s 117 gives a freestanding entitlement to services, which must be provided free-of-charge.[220] NHS bodies and local authority should establish jointly agreed local policies on s 117, setting out the criteria for identifying aftercare services and for deciding which of the responsible public bodies should finance them.[221]

The responsible authority

8.167 The NHS body and the local authority responsible for providing aftercare services will be the one for the area in which the patient was resident before they were detained.[222] This applies even if the patient never returns to that area.[223]

8.168 The term 'residence' in s 117 carries its everyday meaning and is not the same as 'ordinary residence' in the NAA 1948.[224] Those authorities will only lose their s 117 responsibility for the patient if they subsequently are satisfied that the patient is no longer in need of the aftercare services,[225] or if, having been detained again under MHA 1983, the patient acquires a fresh entitlement.

Supervised Community Treatment

8.169 Supervised Community Treatment (SCT) which is known as a Community Treatment Order (CTO), can help reduce stays in hospital and allows patients compulsorily detained in hospital for treatment to continue with their daily lives in the community while having treatment, with necessary and appropriate conditions placed upon them, and to be returned quickly to hospital if their mental state deteriorates.[226] A

---

[218] See: Department of Health *Building Bridges – A Guide to Arrangements for Inter Agency Working for the Care and Protection of Severely Mentally ill People* (1995); Department of Health *Effective Care Co-ordination in Mental Health Services: Modernising the Care Programme Approach* (1999); Department of Health *National Service Framework for Mental Health* (1999), Standard Five; Department of Health *Refocusing the Care Programme Approach: Policy and positive practical guidance* (2008).

[219] Department of Health *Guidance on the discharge of mentally ill people and their continuing care in the community* (1994), HSG(94)27.

[220] *R (on the application of Stennett) v Manchester City Council* [2002] UKHL 34.

[221] Department of Health *After-care under the Mental Health Act 1983: Section 117 after-care services* (2000), HSC 2001/003, LAC (2000) 3.

[222] *R v Mental Health Review Tribunal, ex p Hall* [1999] 3 All ER 132.

[223] Department of Health *After-care under the Mental Health Act 1983: Section 117 after-care services* (2000), HSC 2000/003: LAC (2000) 3.

[224] Department of Health *Ordinary Residence: Guidance on the identification of ordinary residence of people in need of community care services, England* (April 2013); WOC 41/93 in Wales. See *R (on the application of M) v Hammersmith and Fulham LBC* [2011] EWCA Civ 77.

[225] MHA 1983, s 117(2).

[226] MHA 1983, s 17A(2).

CTO will last initially for 6 months, but is renewable. However, it will come to an end if the patient is discharged,[227] they cease to be liable to be detained for treatment[228] or the CTO is revoked.[229]

Medical treatment

General

8.170 A patient detained under MHA 1983 may be given medical treatment for their mental disorder, if necessary, without their consent. However, not everyone who receives in-patient mental health treatment is detained under the Act; and some patients who are detained require treatment for purely physical conditions. In either of those circumstances, MHA 1983 is irrelevant and treatment may only be given with the patient's consent if they are capable, or under the MCA 2005, if they are not.

Powers

8.171 A patient who is detained for treatment may be given medical treatment for their mental disorder even though they do not consent to it.[230] It applies even if the patient would be capable of giving or withholding such consent.[231] However, a different position applies where the patient is capable and the treatment consists of Electric Convulsive Therapy (ECT).[232]

8.172 A patient who is detained under one of the short-term provisions in MHA 1983 (in other words, under s 4, 5, 135 or 136) or who, being in the community, is subject to SCT[233] or guardianship[234] may not be given medical treatment for mental disorder under the Act. In such a case, the patient may be treated with consent if they are capable, or under MCA 2005 if they are not. That is so, whether the treatment is for any general medical disorder or for the patient's mental disorder. Separate rules apply in the case of a patient who, being subject to SCT, has been recalled to hospital but has not yet had their CTO revoked.

The status of an attorney

8.173 An attorney cannot consent to or refuse treatment for a mental disorder for a patient under the MHA 1983. If the donor is made subject to a guardianship order under the MHA, the attorney cannot determine where the donor is to live, as any interference in the order may constitute a criminal offence. The restriction does not apply to people detained under ss 135 or 136 in a place of safety. In these situations the attorney will have authority to make the decision, subject to the Court of Protection making an alternative order.

---

[227] MHA 1983, s 17C(b).
[228] MHA 1983, s 17C(c).
[229] MHA 1983, s 17C(d).
[230] MHA 1983, ss 56 and 63.
[231] *R (on the application of B) v SS (Responsible Medical Officer, Broadmoor Hospital)* [2006] EWCA Civ 28; *R (on the application of Wilkinson) v Broadmoor Hospital* [2001] EWCA Civ 1545; *R (on the application of N) v M* [2002] EWCA Civ 1789; *R (on the application of PS) v G (Responsible Medical Officer)* [2003] EWHC 2335 (Admin).
[232] MHA 1983, s 58A.
[233] MHA 1983, s 17A–17G.
[234] MHA 1983, s 7.

Part IV safeguards

8.174 In most cases, a detained patient will consent to treatment, although those detained for treatment may be given medical treatment for their mental disorder without their consent. Part IV of the Act restricts this power and gives the patient a number of safeguards. A patient may not use an advance decision even one made when they were incontestably capable to prevent medical treatment for mental disorder being given under Part IV.[235]

The role of the Second Opinion Appointed Doctor (SOAD)

8.175 A second opinion appointed doctor (SOAD) may be appointed by the CQC when a second opinion is needed under either s 57 (for treatment, namely psychosurgery and the surgical implantation of hormones requiring consent *and* a second opinion) or s 58 (for treatment requiring consent *or* a second opinion to allow medication to continue to be given after the initial 3-month period). Urgent treatment may be given without the requirement for consent and/or a second opinion under MHA 1983, s 62.

Medicine for 3 months

8.176 In the case of 'medicine' administered to a detained patient the MHA 1983 safeguards apply once 3 months or more have elapsed since the first occasion when medicine was administered to them.[236] Therefore medicine may be administered within the first 3 months under MHA 1983, s 63 (and it may be administered without the patient's consent).

Medicine after 3 months

8.177 Once 3 months have elapsed since the medicine was first given to the detained patient, treatment may only be administered with the patient's consent[237] or if they are incapable or (being capable) withhold consent, a SOAD must certify that 'it is appropriate for the treatment to be given'.[238]

Discharge from MHA 1983 detention

Procedure

8.178 A patient will be discharged from the MHA 1983 detention where the period for which they were detained or subject to guardianship expires without being renewed or replaced by a new 'section'.[239] However, positive steps to the same effect may be taken at an earlier stage.

8.179 A patient may be discharged from detention under MHA 1983 by the RC, by 'the managers' of the hospital in which they are detained, or by their nearest relative.[240] A patient who is subject to guardianship may be discharged by the RC or the nearest relative, or by the responsible social services authority.[241]

---

[235] MCA 2005, s 28, Code of Practice, paras 13.35–13.37.
[236] MHA 1983, s 58(1).
[237] MHA 1983, s 58(3)(a).
[238] MHA 1983, s 58(3)(b).
[239] MHA 1983, s 20(1).
[240] MHA 1983, s 23(2)(a).
[241] MHA 1983, s 23(2)(b).

8.180 If the patient would be likely, when discharged, to act in a manner dangerous to other persons or to themselves, the RC may send the managers a report to that effect. In that event the nearest relative's discharge order will be of no effect and the nearest relative will be unable to make a similar order within the next 6 months.[242] The nearest relative must be notified when any such 'barring' order is made by the RC, and they will have the right to apply to the Tribunal.[243]

Managers' hearings

8.181 The 'managers' of the hospital in which a patient is detained have the power to discharge the patient and can decide whether to review a patient's detention. However, a review is usually held when the patient requests it or the RC issues a 'barring order', which prevents discharge, and a review *must* be held when a patient's detention is renewed.[244] The managers are not obliged to discharge a patient as they have an unfettered discretion.[245] However, if the managers fail to consider the criteria for detention, and as a result, they do not discharge the patient, the continued detention might be unlawful[246] and the patient might be entitled to damages.[247]

8.182 There is no particular test that the managers must apply when considering whether to discharge a patient under MHA 1983. However, it is widely accepted that they should look to the criteria for the patient's detention and consider whether they are still made out. Where they are considering a 'barring' order, made by the RC under MHA 1983, s 25(1) the managers should also ask whether the patient, if discharged, would be likely to act in a manner dangerous to other persons or to themselves?

Mental Health Tribunal

Nature

8.183 Technically, the Mental Health Tribunal is the First-tier Tribunal (Mental Health), and part of the Health, Education and Social Care Chamber. It covers the whole of England and is administered from offices in Leicester. There is a separate Mental Health Tribunal for Wales, which is based in Cardiff. For consistency, it will be referred to as the Mental Health Tribunal.

8.184 The Mental Health Tribunal is a court like any other. It hears cases involving people detained under MHA 1983 and has the power to discharge those people from detention. Each Mental Health Tribunal consists of three members, one of whom (the Tribunal Judge) is legally qualified, one of whom is a psychiatrist, and one of whom is a lay member with some relevant experience. The Tribunal is unique in that it does not have a fixed location for hearings but travels to the patient, sitting in hospitals and community settings throughout the country.

---

[242] MHA 1983, s 25(1).

[243] MHA 1983, s 66(1)(g) and (2)(d).

[244] MHA 1983 Code of Practice, para 31.1.1.

[245] *R (on the application of SR) v Huntercombe Maidenhead Hospital* [2005] EWHC 2361 (Admin).

[246] *R v Riverside Mental Health Trust, ex p Huzzey* (1998) 43 BMLR 167.

[247] *Gary Charles Alfred Huzzey v Brent, Kensington & Chelsea NHS Trust*, unreported, QBD (26 February 2001) Gray J.

Functions

8.185 The Tribunal is governed by MHA 1983,[248] and its procedures are laid down in the Tribunal Procedure (First-tier Tribunal) (Health, Education and Social Care Chamber) Rules 2008.[249] The jurisdiction of the Tribunal extends only to those patients who are compulsorily detained in hospital, or made subject to guardianship or to SCT, under MHA 1983.[250] Its principal function is to determine whether a patient should be discharged.

Applications and references

8.186 There are three ways in which the case of a patient who is detained under the civil provisions of MHA 1983 may come before a Mental Health Tribunal:

(1)   upon application by a patient or their nearest relative;

(2)   upon referral by the hospital managers (where the patient does not themselves apply within the relevant period);[251]

(3)   following a reference by the Secretary of State.[252]

Powers

8.187 The Tribunal has a general discretion to discharge a patient from detention or guardianship. However, it must discharge a patient detained under s 2 or 3 if the detention criteria is no longer satisfied.[253] If the patient is subject to guardianship it must order discharge if it is satisfied that the patient is not then suffering from mental disorder or that it is not necessary in the interests of the welfare of the patient, or for the protection of other persons, that the patient should remain under guardianship.[254]

8.188 Where the Tribunal application was made by a nearest relative whose discharge order has been barred by the RC, the Tribunal must order discharge unless it is also satisfied that the patient, if released, would be likely to act in a manner dangerous to themselves or to other persons.[255]

8.189 In the case of a patient who is subject to a CTO, the Tribunal must discharge them if the criteria is no longer satisfied.[256] Where the Tribunal application concerns a patient who is the subject of a CTO and was made by a nearest relative whose discharge order has been barred by the RC, the Tribunal must order discharge unless it is also satisfied that the patient, if released, would be likely to act in a manner dangerous to themselves or to other persons.[257]

---

[248]   MHA 1983, s 65 and Sch 2.
[249]   SI 2008/2699.
[250]   MHA 1983, s 68.
[251]   MHA 1983, s 68.
[252]   MHA 1983, s 67.
[253]   MHA 1983, s 72(1)(a), (1)(b): *Perkins v Bath DHA; R v Wessex MHRT, ex p Wiltshire CC* (1989) 4 BMLR 145.
[254]   MHA 1983, s 72(4).
[255]   MHA 1983, s 72(1)(b)(iii).
[256]   MHA 1983, s 72(1)(c).
[257]   MHA 1983, s 72(1)(c)(v).

8.190 In determining whether it is necessary for the RC to be able to recall the patient to hospital, the Tribunal must consider 'having regard to the patient's history of mental disorder and any other relevant factors, what risk there would be of a deterioration of their condition if they were to continue not to be detained in hospital'.[258]

8.191 The Tribunal may defer discharge of a patient to a future date specified in the direction,[259] in order to give time for aftercare arrangements to be made. However, where it is unlikely that those arrangements can be made, it will be unlawful to defer discharge, even for a very short period of time.[260]

8.192 If a Tribunal decides not to discharge a patient, it may recommend that:[261]

- the patient be granted leave of absence or transferred to another hospital (or into guardianship); or
- the RC considers making a CTO in respect of the patient.

If either recommendation is not complied with, the Tribunal may consider the case further.[262]

Monitoring detention

General

8.193 The CQC in England has the role of monitoring the detention of patients under the MHA 1983 and those who are deprived of their liberty under the MCA 2005. In Wales this function is carried out by the Healthcare Inspectorate Wales.

Functions

8.194 The three principal mental health-related functions of the CQC are:

(1) to monitor the operation of MHA 1983, to visit and interview detained patients in private, and to report any findings to the Secretary of State for Health;[263]

(2) to monitor the use of the deprivation of liberty safeguards in all care homes and hospitals in England, and provide advice and information on using them;[264] and

(3) to manage the SOAD scheme.

The CQC will visit hospitals and other places where patients are detained to monitor compliance with MHA 1983 and the Code of Practice. Commissioners will interview detained patients in private, scrutinising their records, and assess factors that might affect their care, treatment and quality of life. The CQC check on the use of the

---

[258] MHA 1983, s 72(JA).
[259] MHA 1983, s 72(3).
[260] *R (on the application of H) v Ashworth Hospital Authority* [2002] EWCA Civ 923.
[261] MHA 1983, s 72(3) and (3A).
[262] MHA 1983, s 72(3)(b) and (3A)(b).
[263] MHA 1983, ss 120(1) and (4).
[264] Mental Capacity (Deprivation of Liberty: Monitoring and Reporting; and Assessments – Amendment) Regulations 2009, SI 2009/827.

deprivation of liberty safeguards as part of its existing inspection programme, by visiting the places where they are used. The care services that seek authorisations must notify the CQC of the outcome.

8.195 In addition, the CQC has the statutory power to consider complaints in relation to detained patients. However, it will only decide to use this power if the complaint has progressed through the first two stages of the NHS Complaints Procedure (or the equivalent for independent providers).

8.196 The CQC receives notification of the deaths of detained patients and reviews all deaths from unnatural causes. This is so as to establish whether the Code of Practice has been followed and whether there are lessons for future practice and policy. In addition, the CQC gives expert advice and guidance to the Department of Health, to providers and to professionals on their responsibilities under MHA 1983.

Deprivation of liberty

Relevance

8.197 Large numbers of people, who lack mental capacity to consent, particularly older people and those with learning difficulties, have been accommodated in hospitals and care homes without being detained under the MHA 1983. It is the common law doctrine of 'necessity' that has provided the legal framework for this action. Unlike MHA 1983, 'necessity' does not consider whether a person is suffering from mental disorder; rather, it looks to their 'capacity'. Where a person is 'incapable' of giving valid consent, whether to medical treatment or more general care, 'necessity' allows those responsible to provide treatment or care that is in their 'best interests'. Those people undertaking such necessary acts, whilst not specifically authorised, are protected from liability,[265] provided they reasonably believe the person lacks mental capacity to make the care and treatment decision and what is proposed is considered to be in the person's best interests.

8.198 Because 'proportionate restraint' may be used to prevent likely and serious harm occurring to the person, some people admitted to a hospital or care home find the doctrine of 'necessity' being used to confine them there. The person undertaking the act of care and treatment will not be protected from liability if they restrict the person to the extent or degree that it amounts to a deprivation of their liberty.[266] Where a patient objects to the deprivation of their liberty, they should be detained under MHA 1983.

The need for safeguards

8.199 The European Court of Human Rights[267] (ECtHR) held that because the common law doctrine of necessity was too uncertain in its application and provided too few safeguards against an arbitrary detention, it should not be used as the basis for the detention of mentally incapable but compliant patients. Failure to have such a safeguard would breach Article 5 (ie right to liberty) of the ECHR.

---

[265] MCA 2005, s 5.
[266] MCA 2005, s 4A.
[267] *HL v United Kingdom* (45508/99) (2005) 40 EHRR 32 (5 October 2004).

Deprivation of Liberty Safeguard (DoLS)

8.200 The government decided the best way to safeguard those who were deprived of their liberty but not eligible for detention under the MHA 1983 was to create a framework known as the Deprivation of Liberty Safeguards (DoLS). This was incorporated into MCA 2005,[268] which is underpinned by a Code of Practice.[269] A mentally incompetent person can be deprived of their liberty:

(1) through the DoLS process;[270]

(2) through a welfare order made by the Court of Protection;[271]

(3) where vital acts or life sustaining treatment is being undertaken, pending a court order;[272] or

(4) by a declaration made by the Court of Protection under MCA 2005, s 15 which is wide enough to include permitting compulsory removal and detention for the purposes of medical treatment, if found to be in the best interests of the patient. Such an order would not be in breach of Article 5 of the ECHR, provided:

    (a) the court authorises detention before the detention commences;

    (b) there is evidence from an appropriate expert that the patient lacks mental capacity and that the proposed detention is appropriate; and

    (c) the order contains adequate reviews at reasonable intervals.[273]

Deprivation of liberty without authorisation is unlawful and may result in damages being award by the court.[274]

When can a person be deprived of their liberty?

8.201 A person may only be deprived of their liberty if:

(1) it is in their own best interests[275] to protect them from harm;

(2) it is a proportionate response to the likelihood and seriousness of the harm; and

(3) there is no less restrictive alternative.[276]

How can you tell if a person is being deprived of their liberty?

8.202 A significant body of case-law has developed as there is no easy test to identify whether a person is being deprived of their liberty. The ECtHR has established that when determining whether there is a 'deprivation of liberty' within the meaning of Article 5, three conditions must be satisfied:

(1) an objective element of a person's confinement in a certain limited space for a not negligible time;[277]

---

[268] MHA 2007, s 50 and Schs 7–9.

[269] MCA 2005, Schs A1 and 1A. See also: Ministry of Justice *Deprivation of Liberty Safeguards: Code of Practice* (2008) London, TSO. A Welsh version has also been issued by the National Assembly Government.

[270] MCA 2005, Sch A1.

[271] MCA 2005, ss 16(2)(a), 16A and 4A(3).

[272] MCA 2005, s 4(B).

[273] The conditions enumerated by Munby J in *Sunderland City Council v PS* [2007] 2 FLR 1083.

[274] An example of this see, *G v E* [2010] EWHC 621 (Fam).

[275] MCA 2005, s 4.

[276] MCA 2005, s 1(6).

[277] The key factor is whether the person is, or is not, free to leave (*HL v United Kingdom* (2004) 40 EHRR 761 at para 91).

(2)   a subjective element, namely that the person has not validly consented to the confinement;[278] and

(3)   the deprivation of liberty must be one for which the State is responsible.[279]

8.203 When determining whether the circumstances amount objectively to a deprivation of liberty, as opposed to a mere restriction of liberty, the court looks first at the concrete situation in which the individual finds themselves, taking account of a whole range of criteria, including the type, duration, effects and manner of implementation of the measure in question, bearing in mind that the difference between deprivation and restriction upon liberty is merely one of degree or intensity and not one of nature or substance.[280] In particular the court will look at the extent to which it can be said that the managers of the establishment, exercise complete and effective control over the person in his treatment, care, residence and movement.[281]

8.204 As Munby LJ observed in *Cheshire West and Chester Council v P* 'account must be taken of the individual's whole situation ... the context is crucial' and set out the following factors to consider:[282]

(1)   Mere lack of capacity to consent to living arrangements cannot in itself create a deprivation of liberty.

(2)   In determining whether or not there is a deprivation of liberty, it is legitimate to have regard both to the objective 'reason' why someone is placed and treated as they are and also to the objective 'purpose' (or 'aim') of the placement.[283]

(3)   Subjective motives or intentions have only limited relevance. An improper motive or intention may have the effect that what would otherwise not be a deprivation of liberty is in fact, a deprivation. But a good motive or intention cannot render innocuous what would otherwise be a deprivation of liberty. Good intentions are essentially neutral. At most they merely negative the existence of any improper purpose or of any malign, base or improper motive that might, if present, turn what would otherwise be innocuous into a deprivation of liberty. Thus the test is essentially an objective one.

(4)   In determining whether or not there is a deprivation of liberty, it is always relevant to evaluate and assess the 'relative normality' (or otherwise) of the concrete situation.[284]

(5)   The assessment must take account of the particular capabilities of the person concerned. What may be a deprivation of liberty for one person may not be for another.

(6)   The relevant comparator in Court of Protection cases, which deals with adults with disabilities, whose lives are dictated by their own cognitive and other

---

[278] Whether the person objects to their confinement: see paragraph 25 in *P and Q v Surrey County Council* [2011] EWCA Civ 190; *JE v DE* [2006] EWHC 3459 (Fam).

[279] *Storck v Germany* [2005] 43 EHRR 96, at paras 74, 76 and 77. It applies to all care, whether publicly or privately arranged.

[280] *Guzzardi v Italy* (1980) 3 EHRR 333, at para 92; *Nielsen v Denmark* (1988) 11 EHRR 175, at para 67; *HM v Switzerland* (2002) 38 EHRR 314, at para 42; *HL v United Kingdom* (2004) 40 EHRR 761, at para 89; and *Storck v Germany* (2005) 43 EHRR 96, at para 42.

[281] *DD v Lithuania* [2012] ECHR 254, at para 146 and *Kedzior v Poland* [2012] ECHR 1809 at para 57.

[282] [2011] EWCA Civ 1257, at paras 34–35 and 102.

[283] Ibid, paras 60–77 and 102 (vi) and (vii) read in the light of *Austin v United Kingdom* [2012] ECHR 459, as set out in *CC v KK* [2012] EWHC 2136 (COP) at paras 94–96, where detention may legally occur for the common good of society, such as the practice of 'kettling' to manage crowd control.

[284] *P and Q v Surrey County Council* [2011] EWCA Civ 190, at para 28.

limitations is an adult of similar age with the same capabilities as that person, affected by the same condition or suffering the same inherent mental and physical disabilities and limitations as them.[285]

(7)   Generally care in a domestic setting, such as being cared for by their parents, friends or relatives in a family home, if they are in a foster/adult placement or in specialist sheltered accommodation is unlikely to involve a deprivation of liberty.[286]

The Supreme Court is to consider the matter, as there is doubt as to whether it is in line with ECtHR judgments.

8.205 Practical guidance as to the objective element is given in Chapter 2, paragraph 2.5 of the DoLS Code of Practice 2008, which sets out a 'non-exhaustive' list of factors pointing towards there being a deprivation of liberty, namely where:

(1)   restraint is used, including sedation to admit a person to an institution where that person is resisting admission;

(2)   staff exercise complete and effective control over the care and movement of a person for significant periods;

(3)   staff exercise control over assessments, treatments, contacts and residence;

(4)   a decision has been taken by the institution that the person would not be released into the care of others, or permitted to live elsewhere, unless the staff in the institution consider it appropriate;

(5)   a request by carers for a person to be discharged to their care is refused;

(6)   the person is unable to maintain social contacts because risk of restrictions placed on their access to other people;

(7)   the person loses autonomy because they are under continuous supervision and control.

It is not necessary for every above factor to be present before Article 5 is engaged.[287]

Who is eligible for the safeguard?

8.206 In the event a hospital or a registered care home[288] ('the managing authority') identifies that a person who lacks capacity is being, or risks being, deprived of their liberty, they must apply to the 'supervisory body' for authorisation.[289] The supervisory body will be either:

(1)   the relevant local authority in England[290] or National Assembly for Wales via the LHB, if the person is in an NHS facility; or

---

[285] *Cheshire West and Chester Council v P* [2011] EWCA Civ 1257, at [38], [39] and [102](viii) to (xii).

[286] *Re A and C* [2010] EWHC 978 (Fam) who lived at home with their family; *LLBC v G* [2007] EWHC 2640 in respect of an older man in a care home; and *Re MIG and MEG* [2010] EWHC 785, which was later cited as the *P and Q* case, but the High Court found care in foster and analogous placements, and sheltered accommodation, did not amount to a deprivation of liberty.

[287] *A PCT v LDV, CC and B Healthcare Group* [2013] EWHC 272 (Fam).

[288] Registered under the Health and Social Care Act 2008 in England or Care Standards Act 2000 in Wales.

[289] MCA 2005, Sch A1.

[290] Prior to April 2013, the supervisory body for the NHS was the Primary Care Trust but these have been abolished. The local authority has taken over the role of being the supervisory body for all DoLS cases in England. Reference in the Code of Practice to PCTs should not be read to mean local authority.

(2)   the local authority, if the person is in a care home.[291]

In the event that the person needs to be deprived of their liberty in another setting or to transfer them to a hospital or a care home, then an order from the Court of Protection should be obtained as the DoLS process will not apply.

Taking someone to a hospital or a care home

8.207   Taking a person who lacks capacity to a hospital or care home will not usually amount to a deprivation of liberty,[292] even if there is an expectation that the person will be deprived of liberty within the hospital or care home. Sections 5 and 6 of the MCA 2005 do not confer on police officers authority to remove persons to hospital or other places of safety for the purposes set out in ss 135[293] and 136[294] of the MHA 1983. If the person meets the criteria for detention under the MHA 1983, and detention is urgent, s 4 procedure should be followed.[295]

8.208   However, if the person does not meet the criteria for detention under the MHA 1983, and it is necessary to do more than persuade or restrain the person for the purpose of transportation, or where the journey is exceptionally long, such action may amount to a deprivation of liberty, so it may be necessary to seek authority from the Court of Protection.

Eligibility

8.209   Where authorisation is being requested the managing authority should obtain assessments of the person concerned to establish the person meets the following qualifying requirements:[296]

(1)   the person is aged 18 years or over ('the age requirement');[297]

(2)   he is suffering from a disorder or disability of the mind (within the meaning of the MHA1983 Act, but disregarding any exclusion for persons with learning disability; ('the mental health requirement');[298]

(3)   the person lacks capacity to make the decision as to whether or not he should be a resident in the hospital or care home ('the mental capacity requirement');[299]

(4)   it is necessary and in the detained resident's best interests to be deprived of his liberty which is a proportionate response to prevent a likely and seriousness harm occurring to that resident ('the best interests requirement');[300]

(5)   the person meets the eligibility requirement as set out in Sch 1A ('the eligibility requirement'). The person will not be eligible if they are detained in hospital under the MHA 1983 and will continue to be at the time the authorisation is intended to take effect; or the authorisation would be inconsistent with an obligation placed

---

[291]   MCA 2005, Part 13, Sch A1.
[292]   Relying on the statutory protection afforded by MCA 2005, s 5.
[293]   See 8.153–8.155.
[294]   See 8.158.
[295]   *R (Sessay) v South London and Maudsley NHS Foundation Trust* [2011] EWHC 2617 (QB).
[296]   MCA 2005, Part 3, Sch A1.
[297]   MCA 2005, Sch A1, para 13.
[298]   MCA 2005, Sch A1, para 14.
[299]   MCA 2005, Sch A1, para 15.
[300]   MCA 2005, Sch A1, para 16.

on the person under the MHA 1983, for example if they are on leave of absence from detention or is subject to a guardianship order, supervised CTO or conditional discharge order;[301] and

(6) there must not be a valid and applicable advance decision refusing the treatment in question nor a refusal by a health and welfare attorney or deputy acting within the scope of their authority ('the no refusal requirement').[302]

If at any time the person does not satisfy any of the above requirements, no authorisation or order can be granted and if the situation changes to the point that any of the requirements are no longer satisfied then the authorisation ceases to have effect, for so long as the person is ineligible.[303]

The assessors

8.210 A mental health assessor must consider how (if at all) the person's mental health is likely to be affected by their being detained.[304] Such assessor must either be MHA 1983, s 12 approved, or a registered medical practitioner with over 3 years' post registration mental health experience and have undergone approved deprivation of liberty training.[305] They must be separate to the best interests' assessor.

8.211 A best interests assessor must assess the person who is to be detained as to whether the deprivation of liberty is in their best interests. Regulations[306] set out who can carry out the best interests assessment, including the training and qualifications of the assessor. The assessment must be independent of the mental health assessment.[307]

8.212 The best interests assessor is under a duty to follow MCA 2005, s 4, so in particular must take into account the views of the person concerned and anyone named to be consulted, any carer, any attorney under a lasting power or deputy. They should also make recommendations as to who would be the best person appointed to represent the person's interest. The best interests assessor can indicate conditions, including the duration of the authorisation that should be attached to any authorisation. The best interests assessor must consult the managing authority and must have regard to the conclusions of what the mental health assessor says is in the person's best interests, any relevant needs assessment, and health or social care plan.[308] This information will be contained in a report that is sent to the supervisory body.

8.213 Either the mental health assessor or the best interests assessor can carry out the capacity assessment.[309]

---

[301] MCA 2005, Sch A1, para 17; Sch A1 applies for the purpose of determining whether the person is ineligible to be deprived of his liberty under the MCA 2005.

[302] MCA 2005, Sch A1, paras 18–19.

[303] MCA 2005, s 16A and Sch A1.

[304] MCA 2005, Sch A1, para 36.

[305] Mental Capacity (Deprivation of Liberty: Standard Authorisations, Assessments and Ordinary Residence) Regulations 2008, SI 2008/1858.

[306] Mental Capacity (Deprivation of Liberty: Standard Authorisations, Assessments and Ordinary Residence) Regulations 2008, SI 2008/1858; and Welsh equivalent, SI 2009/783.

[307] MCA 2005, Sch A1, para 129(5).

[308] MCA 2005, Sch A1, para 39.

[309] SI 2008/1858, reg 6.

Types of authorisations

8.214 There are two types of authorisations:

(1) **A standard authorisation:** used in most cases, where it is likely that within the following 28 days the person will meet all the qualifying requirements.[310]

(2) **An urgent authorisation:** used if the deprivation is already occurring or about to occur. Urgent authorisation is given by the managing authority, which amounts to a 'self authorisation', and lasts a maximum of 7 days[311] with the potential for one extension of a further 7 days, which must be made to the supervisory body.[312] In any event a standard authorisation must be applied for.

The Mental Capacity (Deprivation of Liberty: Standard Authorisations, Assessments and Ordinary Residence) Regulations 2008 in England[313] and the Mental Capacity (Deprivation of Liberty: Assessments Standard Authorisations, and Disputes about Residence) Regulations 2009[314] in Wales, set out the content and time scales for completion of the assessments. The Department of Health and Welsh National Assembly Government have published standard forms, which are not compulsory to use.

The authorisation

8.215 If all the assessments conclude that the relevant person meets the requirements for authorisation, and the supervisory body has written copies of all the assessments, it must give a written standard authorisation.[315] The authorisation may contain conditions, which must be monitored by the managing authority.[316] A copy of this should be provided to the person and their representative.

How long will the authorisation last?

8.216 The supervisory body sets the duration of the authorisation, based on the recommendation of the best interests assessor, for a maximum period of 12 months, although this is subject to review and can be shortened. The period cannot be longer than the period recommended by the best interests assessor.[317] It is also possible to seek a renewal of the authorisation in the same manner as the original authorisation process. If at any time the person no longer meets the conditions for detention then the authorisation will cease during the period that the person is no longer eligible.

The requirement to appoint a representative

8.217 The supervisory body must appoint a willing representative to act in the person's best interest, and that person may seek a review or appeal the decision.[318] The representative should support and represent the person and maintain contact with them. The functions of the representative are in addition to, and do not affect, the authority of any LPA attorney, any deputy or any powers of the court. If no such person is available,

---

[310] MCA 2005, Part 4, Sch A1.
[311] MCA 2005, Sch A1, para 78(2).
[312] MCA 2005, Sch A1, paras 84 and 85.
[313] SI 2008/1858.
[314] SI 2009/783.
[315] MCA 2005, Sch A1, para 50.
[316] MCA 2005, Sch A1, para 53.
[317] MCA 2005, Part 10, Sch A1, para 103.
[318] MCA 2005, Part 11, Sch A1.

an IMCA will be appointed or another advocate to act as a representative on the person's behalf, until such time as another representative is appointed.[319] Regulations set out the process for the selection, appointment and termination of an appointment of the relevant person's representative.[320]

Independent Mental Capacity Advocates (IMCAs)

8.218 Where a person is subject to the deprivation of liberty safeguards and there is nobody appropriate for the best interests assessor to consult, other than paid or professional care and treatment providers, the managing authority must notify the supervisory body when it submits the application for the deprivation of liberty authorisation. The supervisory body must then instruct an IMCA straight away to represent the person. The IMCA has the right to make submissions to the supervisory body on the question of whether a qualifying requirement should be reviewed, or to give information, or make submissions, to any assessor carrying out a review assessment.

8.219 If the relevant person or their representative requests an IMCA, then the supervisory body must instruct one. The role of the IMCA includes assisting the relevant person and their representative to understand the effect of the authorisation, what it means, why it has been given, why the relevant person meets the criteria for authorisation, how long it will last, any conditions to which the authorisation is subject and how to trigger a review or challenge in the Court of Protection.

Reviews

Managing authority and supervisory body

8.220 Deprivation of liberty can be ended before a formal review. An authorisation only permits deprivation of liberty: it does not mean that a person must be deprived of liberty where the circumstances no longer make it necessary. When a person is deprived of their liberty, the managing authority has a duty to monitor the case on an ongoing basis to see if the person's circumstances change. This usually forms part of the care plan, which should set out clear roles and responsibilities for monitoring and confirm under what circumstances a review is necessary.

8.221 If the detained person is deemed to have regained mental capacity to decide about the arrangements made for their care and treatment, the managing authority must assess whether there is consistent evidence of the regaining of capacity on a longer-term basis. This is a clinical judgment which needs to be made by a suitably qualified person. This is to avoid those with short-term fluctuating mental capacity being subject to deprivation of liberty restrictions and then removed in a short space of time, only to be then subject to deprivation of liberty restrictions again.[321] Where there is consistent evidence of regained mental capacity on a longer-term basis, deprivation of liberty should be lifted immediately, and a formal review and termination of the authorisation sought.

8.222 A standard authorisation can also be reviewed at any time by the supervisory body.[322] It must be carried out if the request is from the relevant person, their

---

[319] MCA 2005, Part 11, Sch A1 and s 39C(5).
[320] Mental Capacity (Deprivation of Liberty: Appointment of Relevant Person's Representative) Regulations 2008, SI 2008/1315 (as amended by SI 2008/2368); Mental Capacity (Deprivation of Liberty: Appointment of Relevant Person's Representative) (Wales) Regulations, SI 2008/266 (W.29).
[321] DoLS Code, paras 8.22–8.23.
[322] MCA 2005, Sch A1, para 102(1).

representative or the managing authority or any of the qualifying requirements are no longer met.[323] The best interests requirement may also be reviewed if there has been a change to vary the conditions to which the authorisation is subject.[324] Standard letters are available for the relevant person or their representative to request a review. There is also a standard form available for the managing authority to request a review. Urgent authorisations are reviewed by an application to the Court of Protection, although it is expected that concerns (including those involving a standard authorisation) should initially be raised informally through the supervisory body's or managing authority's complaints procedure to avoid court proceedings.

8.223 If following the review any of the eligibility requirements are not met, then the authorisation must be terminated immediately.

Court of Protection

8.224 The patient or their representative is able to seek a review of the authorisation to the Court of Protection at any time, which extend to having power to terminate, vary conditions or authorise detention.[325] The Court can consider:

(1) whether the relevant person meets one or more of the qualifying requirements for deprivation of liberty;

(2) the period for which the standard authorisation is to be in force;

(3) the purpose for which the standard authorisation is given; or

(4) the conditions subject to which the standard authorisation is given.

8.225 Where an urgent authorisation has been given, the relevant person or certain persons acting on their behalf, such as a donee or deputy, has the right to apply to the Court of Protection to determine any question relating to the following matters:

(a) whether the urgent authorisation should have been given;

(b) the period for which the urgent authorisation is to be in force; or

(c) the purpose for which the urgent authorisation has been given.

The Court of Protection (Amendment) Rules 2009[326] inserts Part 10A which provides that Practice Direction 10A, applies to any application made to the Court of Protection under s 21A of the MCA 2005 and sets out the procedure to appeal a DoLS. Specific forms have been developed to ensure, amongst other reasons, they are dealt with promptly by the court administration.

8.226 A court fee is payable, and whilst non-means tested legal aid is available the applicant must first seek to obtain funding through any legal protection insurance they may have. The applicant will still have to show the case has merit before legal aid is granted.[327] Legal aid is not available for the relevant person or their representative for the local authorisation process.

---

[323] MCA 2005, Sch A1, paras 105–107.

[324] MCA 2005, Sch A1, para 107.

[325] MCA 2005, s 21A.

[326] SI 2009/582 amends the Court of Protection Rules 2007, SI 2007/1744.

[327] Community Legal Service (Financial) (Amendment) Regulations 2009, SI 2009/502.

CHAPTER 9

CHALLENGING THE AUTHORITIES

Gordon Ashton and Caroline Bielanska

'If you limit your choices only to what seems possible or reasonable, you disconnect yourself from what you truly want, and all that is left is a compromise.'
Robert Fritz

Increased involvement by the authorities in the lives of individuals despite a human rights culture has resulted in procedures for disclosure of information, complaining about conduct and challenging decisions. In this chapter we develop these topics including data protection, freedom of information and the role of the Ombudsman before concluding with legal remedies. We also comment on any difficulties encountered where the person concerned lacks capacity.

9.1   One should always seek to work with the authorities, but inevitably situations arise where it is deemed appropriate to challenge policies or decisions of the authorities, or persons in authority, that relate to or affect an individual. Before reaching that stage, or in order to pursue a matter, it may be necessary to obtain information and during recent years the freedom of information movement has achieved considerable success in establishing the rights of the individual in this respect. Increased awareness of this area of law and procedure on the part of lawyers, and a greater willingness to complain on the part of the public, has resulted in many developments. We consider in this chapter the present state of the law and the remedies and procedures that are available.

ACCESSING INFORMATION

9.2   There is a general duty of confidentiality imposed at common law, so information concerning an older person may only be disclosed to third parties in certain defined circumstances. There may also be times when information held by a public body, as part of the way it carries out its functions, may be required, for example to see whether a proper process has been followed. The obligations of public bodies, organisations and individuals in relation to the disclosure of information is governed by:

(1)   professional conduct rules and practices;

(2)   the common law;

(3)   Access to Medical Reports Act 1988;

(4)   Data Protection Act 1998; and

(5)   Freedom of Information Act 2000.

The common law duty of confidentiality

9.3   This common law duty of confidentiality has long been recognised as a right which everyone is entitled to.[1] However it is not absolute, particularly for doctors.[2]

General Medical Council (GMC) Guidance *Confidentiality* (2009) states as core principles:

> '6. Confidentiality is central to trust between doctors and patients. Without assurances about confidentiality, patients may be reluctant to seek medical attention or to give doctors the information they need in order to provide good care. But appropriate information sharing is essential to the efficient provision of safe, effective care, both for the individual patient and for the wider community of patients.
>
> 7. You should make sure that information is readily available to patients explaining that, unless they object, their personal information may be disclosed for the sake of their own care and for local clinical audit. Patients usually understand that information about them has to be shared within the healthcare team to provide their care. But it is not always clear to patients that others who support the provision of care might also need to have access to their personal information. And patients may not be aware of disclosures to others for purposes other than their care, such as service planning or medical research. You must inform patients about disclosures for purposes they would not reasonably expect, or check that they have already received information about such disclosures.'

The GMC has published a supplementary guide specifically relating to the issue of confidentiality.[3]

Implications of mental disability

9.4   In the case of mentally disabled people (which of course can include older people) the request for information may be made by a carer or another member of the family, and then difficulties arise over disclosure because the information does not relate to the person making the request. People may only have access to information about themselves, so a person with a mental disability who is not capable of making an application or considering such information is in effect precluded from having access to such information notwithstanding that he is more likely to feature in files maintained by the authorities.[4]

9.5   Information may genuinely be needed by those seeking to make arrangements for care or support, but the difficulty lies in identifying those who have a legitimate interest in obtaining the information because the right to confidentiality does not lapse by reason of lack of competence. Information should not be released freely to other persons, and it must not be assumed that members of a family are entitled to inspect information about each other. Being an attorney under a lasting power of attorney for personal welfare or a deputy appointed by the Court of Protection for personal welfare may now overcome the problem, but short of this there is no procedure whereby people may delegate in general terms for the future the right to seek information about them, so future incapacity cannot be anticipated.

---

[1]   *Prince Albert v Strange* [1849] 1 Mac and G 25.
[2]   *Hunter v Mann* [1974] 2 All ER 414. Compare the duty of the solicitor.
[3]   General Medical Council *Good Medical Practice* (2013).
[4]   The guidance circulars seem to envisage access by third parties in some circumstances.

9.6   An attorney, carer or next of kin can always ask for information from the health or social services authority and, although there may be no statutory obligation to provide this, the authority may recognise that it is in the best interests of the individual to do so. A climate of mutual co-operation is usually preferable to undue reliance upon legal rights.[5]

Exceptions for doctors

9.7   There are some circumstances where the doctor can disclose personal information. The General Medical Council Guidance Confidentiality (2009) states:

'8. Confidentiality is an important duty, but it is not absolute. You can disclose personal information if:

(a)   it is required by law
(b)   the patient consents-either implicitly for the sake of their own care or expressly for other purposes
(c)   it is justified in the public interest.'[6]

Clearly if the person consents to information being disclosed, the holder of the confidential information can disclose without worry, provided the consent relates to the specific disclosure involved.[7] Wherever possible questions of disclosure should be discussed with the person in advance and express consent obtained.

Disclosure to the patient

9.8   Sharing information with a patient is an essential part of the patient/doctor relationship and key to obtaining the necessary consent for treatment. Doctors are advised to be very open about information to enable good decision-making. A diagnosis should not be withheld from a patient just because it is unpleasant, although if there is reasonable doubt about the diagnosis the doctor may not wish to reveal the least attractive one prematurely. It is suggested that information may only be specifically withheld if disclosure would be likely to cause serious harm to the patient's physical or mental health.[8]

Disclosure between medical professionals

9.9   It is generally considered that most patients understand that information must be shared within the health care team in order for the patient to be effectively treated. Consent is generally implied here, although doctors are advised to do what they can to inform patients about the way their information will be shared. Doctors must respect the wishes of any patient who refuses consent to disclose within the team, unless it is justifiable in the public interest. It is recognised there are circumstances where consent cannot be obtained, such as in an emergency and then doctors are expected to pass information to those providing care.[9]

---

[5]   For guidance see Chapter 16 of the Mental Capacity Act *Code of Practice*.
[6]   For examples see *W v Egdell* [1990] 2 WLR 471, CA; *Woolgar v Chief Constable of Sussex Police* [2000] 1 WLR 25, CA; *Brent London Borough Council v SK and HK* [2007] EWHC 1250 (Fam).
[7]   As regards both the extent of the information disclosed and the persons to whom it is disclosed.
[8]   See General Medical Council Guidance *Consent: Patients and Doctors Making Decisions Together* (2008), in particular paras 3–6.
[9]   General Medical Council Guidance *Confidentiality* (2009) paras 24–29.

Disclosure to others

9.10   It is sensible to establish with the person what information they want to be shared, with whom and in what circumstances. If anyone close to a patient wishes to share concerns with a doctor about the patient's health, it is not necessarily a breach of confidentiality for the doctor to listen, but they must explain that they cannot guarantee that they will not tell the patient and doctors are asked to consider if the patient would consider that listening to the concerns of others is a breach of confidentiality.[10]

Disclosures about people who lack capacity to consent

9.11   Problems arise with older people if they are mentally incapable of giving consent to disclose. Disclosure can be given to attorneys with a relevant lasting power of attorney or a deputy appointed by the Court of Protection where their authority (even if not specifically stated) encompasses disclosure.

9.12   If no such authority exists, consideration needs to be given as to whether the disclosure would be in the best interests of the person, applying the best interests' checklist under s 4 of the Mental Capacity Act 2005.[11] Solicitors are prevented from disclosing information about a client who has since lost mental capacity by the Solicitors Regulation Authority Code of Conduct Rules,[12] unless advance consent has been provided by that client. But sufficient information may need to be provided to those who are interested in the information, to be in a position to make an application to the Court of Protection for an order to disclose.

9.13   GMC guidance allows doctors to disclose information about patients who lack capacity even if the patient refuses consent, if they are convinced it is in the patient's best interests to do so. The doctor should inform the patient before doing so and consider the views of an advocate or carer, if appropriate.[13]

9.14   It is accepted in the GMC guidance that it might be necessary to share information with a patient's relatives, friends or carers to assess the patient's best interests.

Statutory requirements for disclosure by doctors

9.15   There are certain statutory provisions under which a doctor must disclose information. Some of these relate to compulsory notification of certain highly infectious diseases, accidents at work, drug addiction and death. When a statute imposes a duty on 'any person' to answer police questions, this includes a doctor.[14] The only statutory protection[15] is that a search warrant to enter and search a surgery, hospital or clinic for medical records may only be granted by a Circuit Judge[16] who must weigh the public interest in disclosure against that of confidentiality. A number of bodies concerned with health administration[17] can also require information in the performance of their duties.

---

[10]   Ibid, paras 64–66.
[11]   See **2.29** for further detail.
[12]   (2011).
[13]   Ibid, paras 57–63.
[14]   *Hunter v Mann* [1974] 2 All ER 414.
[15]   Police and Criminal Evidence Act 1984, s 9 and Sch 1.
[16]   In most other cases a lay magistrate may authorise the warrant.
[17]   The Parliamentary and Health Service Ombudsman, The Public Service Ombudsman for Wales, Department of Health, Welsh Assembly Government, CCGs, The NHS Board, LHBs, and NHS Trusts.

Public interest disclosure by doctors

9.16 There may be occasions when it is in the public interest for a doctor to disclose information about their patient.[18] The GMC Guidance states:[19]

> 'There is a clear public good in having a confidential medical service. The fact that people are encouraged to seek advice and treatment, including for communicable diseases, benefits society as a whole as well as the individual. Confidential medical care is recognised in law as being in the public interest. However, there can also be a public interest in disclosing information: to protect individuals or society from risks of serious harm, such as serious communicable diseases or serious crime; or to enable medical research, education or other secondary uses of information that will benefit society over time.'

Personal information can therefore be disclosed if the public interests outweigh the patient's interests in keeping the information confidential. Doctors should still seek a patient's consent except in exceptional circumstances such as when seeking consent could put the doctor or others at risk of serious physical harm, or where there is an urgent need to control an infectious disease.

Unfitness to drive

9.17 Problems can arise if a person is medically unfit to drive but will not be persuaded to stop driving. For older people this can sometimes happen if a patient has impaired capacity and lacks the insight into the limits of their condition. The GMC has issued supplementary guidance on this issue.[20] Doctors are advised that it is the driver who has the legal responsibility for informing the DVLA about a condition or treatment that may now or in the future affect their fitness to drive.[21] Doctors are advised that they should explain a patient's responsibilities to them and take every reasonable effort to persuade them to stop driving. If a patient refuses to stop, the doctor should disclose relevant medical information in confidence to the DVLA medical adviser and inform the patient accordingly.

Court orders

9.18 Those holding confidential information must disclose that information if required to do so by a court. Doctors do not share the professional privilege that is generally afforded to lawyers. Doctors are not required to volunteer information but may be subpoenaed to give evidence and must answer questions in the witness box and may be required to produce their records. Judges have a discretion as to whether to require such evidence to be given and will try to preserve medical confidentiality, wherever possible.

Elder abuse

9.19 Those who are concerned that their patient, client or service user is suffering physical, emotional or sexual abuse within the home or a residential setting should advise and offer to introduce the person to sources of help, but if the person is particularly vulnerable, disclosure of concerns to an appropriate source may be appropriate. According to the GMC Guidance, doctors are advised:[22]

---

[18] An example of this is to be found in *W v Egdell* [1990] 1 All ER 835.
[19] General Medical Council Guidance *Confidentiality* (2009), para 36.
[20] Confidentiality: Supplementary Guidance-Reporting concerns about patients to the DVLA or the DVA.
[21] Road Traffic Act 1988, s 94.
[22] General Medical Council 2009 Supplementary Guidance *Confidentiality*, para 63.

'If you believe that a patient may be a victim of neglect or physical, sexual or emotional abuse, and that they lack capacity to consent to disclosure, you must give information promptly to an appropriate responsible person or authority, if you believe that the disclosure is in the patient's best interests or necessary to protect others from a risk of serious harm.'

9.20   Solicitors may be in breach of their Professional code of conduct[23] if they disclose information without the client's consent. However, they are also under a duty to act in the client's best interests and this must be balanced. Many safeguarding organisations accept information from whistleblowers to safeguard vulnerable people, such as the Office of the Public Guardian who will investigate concerns raised in relation to registered powers of attorney or deputyships on a confidential basis.

9.21   It can be difficult if a competent elderly patient is suffering persistent abuse but declines to allow disclosure. If it is apparent that the perpetrator is also abusing others, for doctors the public interest exception may be relevant, and if court proceedings are involved they may be obliged to reveal their knowledge. Moreover the doctor must use his judgment as to whether abuse of one patient might betoken the abuse of others.

Remedies

9.22   A civil action may be brought in the courts to restrain improper disclosure but if the disclosure has already taken place it may be difficult to establish a claim for damages. There will seldom be a financial loss, but instead merely the suffering of an indignity and distress which might result in an award of damages.[24] In most cases the remedy will be a complaint to the professional body of the person or the organisation that has breached the duty of confidentiality.[25]

Medical reports

9.23   Under the Access to Medical Reports Act 1988[26] a patient has an additional and separate right to see any medical report prepared after January 1989 relating to themselves which is to be (or has been) supplied for employment or insurance purposes by a medical practitioner who is or has been responsible for their care.

Procedures

9.24   Before applying for a report the employer or insurer must obtain the patient's written consent and explain that they have the right to see the report before it is sent to the employer or insurance company (or within 6 months thereafter). If the patient wishes to see the report the doctor is notified and must wait for up to 21 days before releasing it so as to allow for access. If no contact is made within this period the doctor is free to submit the report. There is no charge for inspecting a report but a reasonable charge may be made for a copy. If the patient believes that the report is incorrect or misleading they can ask the doctor to correct it and, if the doctor refuses, to attach a written statement of their own view about the disputed matter.

---

23   Solicitors Regulation Authority's Code of Conduct 2011.
24   A civil action for breach of confidence.
25   *Cornelius v de Taranto* [2001] EWCA Civ 1511, 68 BMLR 62 at 77, per Morland J (awarding damages of £3,750 for injury to feelings caused by a doctor wrongly disclosing a medical report).
26   The Act only applies to England, Wales and Scotland.

Withholding reports

9.25 Medical practitioners may withhold reports where disclosure would:[27]

(1) cause serious harm to the patient or others;

(2) indicate the doctors intentions in respect of the patient; or

(3) reveal information about (or the identity of) another.

The report may not then be disclosed without the patient's consent. The doctor must notify the patient if any information is withheld, and if it is felt that information is being wrongly withheld or that there is a breach of the statutory provisions an application can be made to the county court for an order to make the doctor comply.

Data protection

9.26 Under the Data Protection Act 1998 the *Information Commissioner*[28] keeps a register of users ('data controller') who hold personal information ('data') about individuals, held electronically and/or in a structured filing system and this register may be inspected by the public. The *Information Commissioner's Office* is an independent body that promotes access to official information and protects personal information.

9.27 The right of access to 'personal data' is set out in s 7 of the Act and includes the entitlement to be informed whether such data is being 'processed' on behalf of that data controller, a description of that data, the purposes for which the data is being processed and the recipients to whom the data are or may be disclosed.

9.28 Various guidance has been published:

- *Guide to data protection* (Information Commissioner 2009);
- Guidance for Access to Health Records Requests (Department of Health 2010);
- Confidentiality NHS Code of Practice (Department of Health 2003);
- *Data Protection Act 1998 guidance to social services* (Department of Health/Welsh Assembly Government 2000).

Procedures

9.29 A direct approach may be made to any person or organisation, which it is believed holds personal data about the individual. Applications are made in writing to the data controller and access must general be granted within 40 days. A fee may be charged.[29] Applicants can inspect the record in person or authorise a representative to do so, and have photocopies on payment of postage and copying costs. Any unintelligible terms should be explained and may be required to be transcribed.

Correcting information

9.30 There is a right to have incorrect or misleading information corrected or erased, and an individual who suffers damage because of inaccurate personal data held by a

---

[27] Access to Medical Reports Act 1988, s 7.
[28] The Office of the Information Commissioner, Wycliffe House, Water Lane, Wilmslow, Cheshire SK9 SAP. Information Commissioner's Office, 2nd Floor, Churchill House, Churchill Way, Cardiff, CF10 2HH.
[29] At 2013, £50 maximum on a sliding scale (to include all radiographs, scans and test results).

data controller is entitled to seek compensation through the courts. It is a defence for the data controller to prove that all reasonable care was taken to ensure the accuracy of the information held. If no agreement can be reached as to whether the record be altered, it is good practice to allow the person to include a statement within their record that they disagree with the content. If a person is dissatisfied they can take this further under the organisation's complaints procedure.

Refusal of access

9.31   Information may be withheld from an individual, where in the opinion of the data controller it is likely to:[30]

(1)   cause serious harm to their physical or mental health;[31] or

(2)   disclose the identity of another person other than those acting as a professional in their capacity as a data processor.

Remedies

9.32   An applicant who considers that a data controller is failing to comply, for example by improperly withholding information, refusing to correct information which is inaccurate or acting on the basis of a wholly unreasonable opinion, should first make a complaint under the organisation's complaints procedure. If still dissatisfied, an application may be made to the court[32] to order compliance or enforcement by the Information Commissioner leading on non-compliance to an offence.

Access by others

9.33   Access to records may be obtained, not only by the person to whom it relates, but also by (amongst others):

(1)   a person authorised in writing to make the application on the person's behalf;[33]

(2)   deputies and attorneys if the information sought applies to decisions they have the legal right to make;[34] and

(3)   where the person has died, their personal representatives and any person who may have a claim arising out of the deceased's death.

These statutory provisions provide specific rights of access and are not intended to restrict the circumstances in which disclosure of information might otherwise be appropriate. Difficulties arise when the information is requested in respect of a mentally incapable individual, and no relevant deputy or attorney has been appointed. It is necessary to look at the purpose for which the records are held and the general duty of confidentiality. A carer, relative or friend can always ask for information, although there may be no statutory obligation to provide this, so it should be recognised that it may be in the best interests of the individual to do so.[35]

---

[30]   Data Protection (Subject Access Modification) (Health) Order 2000, SI 2000/ 413 and Data Protection (Subject Access Modification) (Social Work) Order 2000, SI 2000/415.

[31]   Ibid.

[32]   Either the county court or the High Court.

[33]   The authority may cease if the person who gave it now lacks capacity.

[34]   Department of Health Best Practice Guide *Guidance for Access to Health Records Requests* page 27.

[35]   MCA 2005, s 4.

9.34 A balance has to be reached between the public interest and the individual's private interests in maintaining confidentiality and the public and private interest in disclosing. Guidance was given on this point in the case of *R (on the application of S) v Plymouth County Council*, which established '... a clear distinction between disclosure to the media with a view to publication to all and sundry and disclosure in confidence to those with a proper interest in having the information in question'.[36] It is up to the data controller to consider whether it is in the best interests of the person to whom the information relates to discuss relevant matters with others. A balance needs to be struck between the individual's right to confidentiality and the rights of others who need the information to be able to exercise their responsibilities.[37]

9.35 Chapter 16 of the Mental Capacity Act *Code of Practice* gives guidance relating to the sharing of information when a person lacks capacity and deciding disclosure is in the best interests of the person.

Health records of deceased patients

9.36 The Access to Health Records Act 1990 has been substantially repealed by the Data Protection Act 1998, but still applies to access by personal representatives to the records of a deceased patient.

Freedom of Information Act 2000

9.37 The Freedom of Information Act 2000 (FOIA 2000) makes provision for the disclosure of information which is held by public authorities and those who provide services to public authorities. The Act is not intended to allow people to gain access to private sensitive information about themselves or others. Those wishing to access personal information about themselves should apply under the Data Protection Act 1998.

Principles

9.38 The FOIA 2000 gives individuals the right to ask any public authorities for all the information they have on any subject. For example, at the time of writing a request has been made to the DWP, and is to be responded to, as to the annual saving to the NHS due to pensioners retiring abroad where no indexing is given. Unless there is a good reason, the organisation must provide the information within 20 working days. Some information might be withheld to protect various interests which are allowed for by the Act. If this is the case, the public authority must state why they have withheld information.

9.39 Most requests are free but there may be a fee for photocopies or postage. If the public authority thinks that it will cost them more than £450 (or £600 for central government) to find the information and prepare it for release, they can turn down the request.

Enforcement

9.40 If a FOIA 2000 request for information is refused, it is possible to ask the public authority to review their decision. If this does not settle matters, it is possible to appeal

---

[36] [2002] EWCA Civ 388, at [49].
[37] See **9.20** relating to solicitors.

to the Information Commissioner's Office (ICO).[38] If information has been wrongly withheld, the ICO can order it to be released. There is a further right of appeal to the First-tier Tribunal (Information Rights) or the Upper Tribunal of the General Regulatory Chamber.[39]

COMPLAINTS PROCEDURES

Background

9.41   The increased role of the local authority in regard to community care provision and services has resulted in an enhanced need for complaints and appeal procedures, and applications have been made to the courts where these procedures are inadequate or have not worked properly. The impression may be gained that a local authority has a duty to provide certain services and that an individual may enforce these duties. It is not as simple as this. A distinction has to be drawn between those duties which create rights that may be enforced by individuals, and those which are expressed in general terms and not enforceable other than, perhaps, in the event of a total failure to perform them. It is then necessary to consider whether any duty is qualified in its terms so that an authority may be excused from performance if, for example, there is a lack of resources.

9.42   Even when an authority is obliged to make some provision they are not specifically directed to make adequate provision. It could be argued that by implication the provision made must be sufficient, but if the matter were tested in the courts it is likely that the authority would only be required to provide facilities within the resources available.[40]

Entitlement to services

9.43   Problems are bound to arise when the authority responsible for assessing needs and providing services is also responsible for funding such provision. An older person or a family carer is likely to ask whether there is entitlement to some service or provision that has been requested but is not being made available. This may relate to financial support, housing, domiciliary or day services, or residential care. There may be a procedure for resolving disputes as to entitlement. Assessments and case conferences form an essential part of the procedures involved in regard to services provided by the social services department, and good practices may be of more importance than legal rights. However, the particular provision involved may be outside the jurisdiction of the social services department (eg with the health or housing authority) even though it forms an essential part of a care package, and in that event the social services department cannot require the provision to be made although it may make a request which must then be considered.[41]

---

[38]   Information available at: www.informationcommissioner.gov.uk.

[39]   Tribunals, Courts and Enforcement Act 2007.

[40]   When interpreting the National Health Service Act 1977 Lord Denning added the words: 'such as can be provided within the resources available' and stated that the Secretary of State was not under an absolute duty to provide services but could take financial resources into account – *R v Secretary of State for Social Services, West Midlands RHA and Birmingham AHA, ex p Hincks* (1979) 123 Sol Jo 436.

[41]   See *R v Northavon District Council, ex p Smith* [1994] 2 AC 402, HL.

Inadequate provision or failure to act

9.44 Delay by an authority may be the most effective way of avoiding providing services when shortage of funds or lack of facilities make it difficult to fulfil a request. In regard to social services it is first necessary to consider whether an assessment of needs has been made in response to a request and if so what the needs are and whether they have been properly assessed. It is then appropriate to ascertain whether a decision has been made by the authority in regard to making provision to meet the assessed needs or whether the problem is that no decision has been made. If there has been no assessment or no decision has been made one should ascertain whether this is a request that the authority is obliged to consider, and if a decision has been made this may be vulnerable to challenge on the basis that there is a need for which the authority is obliged to provide. The statutory duty upon the authority may be general in nature and not enforceable by the courts in respect of an individual.

9.45 If an existing service is withdrawn or restricted there must have been a decision to do so, and this could only follow a re-assessment of the previously accepted needs of the individual or perhaps a new decision about provision based upon new threshold criteria. The change may be open to challenge if it does not follow a decision but has just happened. The authority may have raised its threshold levels for a particular service or provision due to lack of funding and this may be difficult to challenge, but automatic withdrawal should not follow and the authority must first make a new decision about meeting the assessed needs of the particular individual.

Complaining

9.46 People who feel that they are receiving inadequate services will wish to complain, but tactful handling of the matter at this stage may be more productive than single-minded reliance on legal rights. It is desirable to identify the authority which would be responsible for providing the service, and then to contact the officer who would make the decision, preferably in writing, with a carefully reasoned case. Whenever possible ask for a review of a decision and be prepared to accept a compromise, as this is usually quicker than adopting any complaints or appeal procedure and less damaging than an unsuccessful outcome. The legal position should however be checked at an early stage, especially in relation to any enforceable duties or time limits for taking action.

9.47 Complaints procedures are a form of alternative dispute resolution which are intended to avoid reference to the courts, but they may also be available in situations where there is no legal remedy. If there is a possibility of seeking legal redress it may not be appropriate to delay matters by pursuing a complaint. If it appears that a crime has been committed it may be necessary to report the matter to the police and in that event this should be done promptly. There is no legal justification for attempts to persuade complainants to waive legal rights before a complaint will be investigated, and the prospect of litigation will not arise in regard to most complaints.

9.48 In regard to older people, complaints are most likely to arise over treatment by the local authority or the health authority. We have already considered the role of the local authority in Chapter 7 as regards the provision of community care, but other responsibilities arise in relation to housing (Chapter 5), residential care (Chapter 6) and funding (Chapter 10). The role of the health authority is considered in Chapter 8. We now consider the complaints or appeal procedures that are available.

Monitoring officers

9.49   Local authorities must appoint a monitoring officer to report to the authority on any proposal, decision or omission made by the authority or any of its committees or officers which has given rise to or is likely to give rise to either a contravention of the law or any code of practice, or maladministration which could be referred to the ombudsman.[42] Any report must be prepared following consultation with senior officers and be circulated to those who have responsibility for the decision and then considered within 21 days. The original decision cannot be put into effect in the meanwhile.

9.50   A reasoned complaint to the monitoring officer might therefore be worth considering where the social services department is not complying with its duties in regard to the provision of services (eg withdrawing a service to an individual without first reassessing needs or deciding about provision).

Complaints in England

Health and social services

9.51   NHS bodies and local authority social services departments must follow the Local Authority Social Services and NHS Complaints (England) Regulations 2009[43] in resolving complaints. These regulations provide that each NHS body and local authority (responsible body) must appoint a complaint's manager and make arrangements for dealing with complaints to ensure that:

(1)   complaints are dealt with efficiently;

(2)   complaints are properly investigated;

(3)   complainants are treated with respect and courtesy;

(4)   complainants receive, so far as is reasonably practical:
  (i)   assistance to enable them to understand the procedure in relation to complaints; or
  (ii)   advice on where they may obtain such assistance;

(5)   complainants receive a timely and appropriate response;

(6)   complainants are told the outcome of the investigation of their complaint; and

(7)   action is taken if necessary in the light of the outcome of a complaint.

9.52   The NHS Constitution reinforces this as a 'right to complain':

'You have the right to have any complaint you make about NHS services dealt with efficiently and to have it properly investigated.

You have the right to know the outcome of any investigation into your complaint.

You have the right to take your complaint to the independent Health Service Ombudsman, if you are not satisfied with the way your complaint has been dealt with by the NHS.

You have the right to make a claim for judicial review if you think you have been directly affected by an unlawful act or decision of an NHS body.

---

[42]   Local Government and Housing Act 1989, s 5.
[43]   SI 2009/309 as amended by SI 2009/1768.

You have the right to compensation where you have been harmed by negligent treatment.

The NHS also commits:

- to ensure you are treated with courtesy and you receive appropriate support throughout the handling of a complaint; and the fact that you have complained will not adversely affect your future treatment (pledge);
- when mistakes happen, to acknowledge them, apologise, explain what went wrong and put things right quickly and effectively (pledge); and
- to ensure that the organisation learns lessons from complaints and claims and uses these to improve NHS services (pledge).'

The complainant

9.53 Under the Regulations a complainant can be someone who has used a service, or a person who is affected, or likely to be affected, by the action, omission or decision of the responsible body which is the subject of the complaint. A person can make a complaint on behalf of a person who has died and can make a complaint on behalf of someone who cannot make the complaint due to their physical or mental incapacity. The difficulty may be in deciding who should speak for the service user, especially where the complaint reflects disagreement between concerned people as to how the service user should be, or has been, dealt with. In such a situation, the complaints procedure may be useful in resolving that dispute and enabling decisions to be made for the service user.

9.54 Complaints can be about services provided by:

(a) the NHS, including where arrangements have been made through primary or independent providers;

(b) social services, including where the local authority has made arrangements with another person for the discharge of its adult social services functions or where services have been arranged under joint arrangements between the NHS and social services, in which case both responsible bodies must co-operate to resolve the complaint.

The process

9.55 Complaints should be made within 12 months from the date the complaint occurred or the date it came to the complainant's notice. Even if there has been a delay, the NHS or local authority may still consider the complaint if the complainant can show a good reason for not making the complaint earlier or it is still possible to investigate the complaint effectively and fairly.

9.56 The complaint can be made orally, in writing or by email. It must be acknowledged within 3 working days. The complainant must be provided with a copy of the complaint. The complaint can be discussed at a face-to-face meeting (if the complainant feels it is appropriate). The complaints manager can arrange for an independent conciliator or mediator to be brought in to help resolve the complaint.

9.57 A plan of action should be agreed, including timescales for when and how the complainant will hear back about their complaint. If the complainant is dissatisfied with the decision of the organisation concerned, it is possible to refer the matter to the Parliamentary and Health Service Ombudsman in respect of a complaint against the NHS or the Local Government Ombudsman for complaints against local authorities.

9.58 The complaint should be finalised within 6 months from the day when the complaint was received. If it is longer than this period, the complainant must be given written reasons why this has not been possible. Once any investigation is completed a written response explaining the outcome and what action has been taken should be sent.

Assistance and advice

The Patient Advice and Liaison Service

9.59 Hospital trusts and some larger community health centres in England, operate a Patient Advice and Liaison Service (PALS). PALS can give general advice on complaints and may be able to help resolve a less serious complaint by informal negotiation.

Independent Advocacy Services

9.60 Local authorities in England have the responsibility for commissioning independent Advocacy services, assisting with NHS and social care complaints.[44] In some areas, local HealthWatch[45] carry out these advocacy services, but where they do not they should be able to give general advice and support about complaints about the NHS and social care. In other areas, local authorities group together to commission the service at a regional level.

9.61 In Wales, the Community Health Councils may provide advocacy services in respect of NHS complaints.

Professional misconduct

9.62 Complaints about the professional misconduct of an NHS or social care practitioner should be made to their professional or regulatory body. Examples of professional misconduct include:

- practitioners who have a sexual relationship with a service user;
- practitioners who claim that they are competent to practice but are not;
- practitioners who falsely claim that they are qualified to practice;
- breaching confidentiality; and
- manipulating a service user's health or social care records.

The General Medical Council regulates doctors. The Health and Care Professions Council (HCPC) regulate health, psychological and social care professionals.

NHS discipline procedure

9.63 In December 2003, the Department of Health issued the document *High Professional Standards in the Modern NHS*,[46] a framework for the initial handling of concerns about doctors and dentists in the NHS. The framework consisted of two parts: Part I – Action when a concern arises; and Part II – Restriction of practice and exclusion.

---

44   Health and Social Care Act 2012, s 185.
45   Representatives from local HealthWatch organisations can request information from health and social care providers, who have a legal duty to respond. Providers of health and social care must reply in writing to reports and recommendations made by local HealthWatch within 20 days but in more complex cases, this time limit is 30 days.
46   HSC 2003/012.

In 2005, the Department agreed with the British Medical Association and British Dental Association the remaining three parts of the framework covering new disciplinary procedures for doctors and dentists employed in the NHS. These are: Part III – Conduct hearings and disciplinary matters; Part IV – Procedures for dealing with issues of capability; and Part V – Handling concerns about a practitioner's health. It was agreed with Monitor, the regulator of Foundation Trusts that the framework should be issued to NHS Foundation Trusts as advice.

9.64 For those who work outside of the NHS, in a private capacity, the provider of care should have a complaint's procedure and will fall to be regulated by the Care Quality Commission in England or the Healthcare Inspectorate for Wales.

Complaints in Wales

NHS complaints

9.65 The National Health Service (Concerns, Complaints and Redress Arrangements) (Wales) Regulations 2011[47] set out the common arrangements and duties that apply to NHS organisations in Wales in respect of the investigation and handling of complaints. Under the '*Putting Things Right*' arrangements, the NHS in Wales aim to 'investigate once, investigate well', ensuring that concerns are dealt with in the right way, the first time round.

9.66 They are similar but not identical to the English complaints process, with some notable differences:

(1) an acknowledgement to a complaint should occur within 2 working days of the complaint being received;

(2) an interim report should be provided within 30 days of the complaint being received, which may set out a plan of action to deal with the complaint;

(3) an investigation report (if part of the complaint plan) should be provided within 12 months of the complaint being received, although in exceptional circumstances this could be longer, but the complainant must be told of the reasons;

(4) Local Health Boards are able to investigate primary care complaints, rather than merely to facilitate resolution of complaints;

(5) a duty on NHS bodies in Wales to consider, when investigating a concern, whether there is a qualifying liability in tort[48] in respect of a service which they have provided, although it does not apply to concerns raised and investigated relating to primary care practitioners.

Social services complaints

9.67 The Social Services Complaints Procedure (Wales) Regulations 2005,[49] set out the process for complaints in Wales and applies to any social service provided by a local authority including any service that they are paying for. Policy guidance, *Listening and learning: a guide to handling complaints and representation in local authority social*

---

[47] SI 2011/704.

[48] Drawing on powers set out in the NHS Redress (Wales) Measure 2008.

[49] SI 2005/3366 (W.263).

services in Wales was published by the Welsh Assembly Government in 2006. In many respects it is similar to the English system, although it has three distinct stages and prescribed time limits for action:

- **Stage 1 – local resolution**
  The complainant raises concerns with the person running the services locally. They must try to resolve matters within 10 working days. The complainant (but not the local authority) can extend this by a further 10 days.

- **Stage 2 – formal consideration**
  The complainant has a right to ask the local authority for formal consideration of the complaint at any time. There is usually an investigation by someone not involved with the local service, but it could take some other form such as mediation or conciliation. A report with findings, conclusions and recommendations must be produced. The authority must respond to the complainant within 25 working days of the request to move to this stage. This can be extended only in exceptional circumstances.

- **Stage 3 – the independent panel**
  The complainant has a right to have an unresolved complaint considered by a panel hearing. They have the same right if the local authority has not responded after 3 months. Both the panel membership and the administrative arrangements are independent of the local authority. The panel must meet within 20 working days and make its report available within 5 working days. The local authority must respond within 15 working days. If the complainant remains unsatisfied they can take their complaint to the ombudsman.

THE OMBUDSMAN

General

9.68 The Ombudsman investigates and reports on complaints by members of the public about the way they have been treated by particular public bodies. Reference to an ombudsman may be a suitable way of seeking redress in situations where there is no legal remedy and, although it is not a rapid procedure and may not provide an adequate remedy, it may discourage similar administrative action in subsequent cases. The service is free and booklets are available giving an explanation of the procedures. Legal representation is not usually necessary but a solicitor may assist in presenting the complaint. The procedure is usually private but the resulting report may be published.

Types of Ombudsman

9.69 There are several Ombudsman services set up by the government and those of particular relevance to older people and their care are described below. In the fields of financial and legal services it has also been found helpful to establish ombudsmen, and where a dispute arises regarding the affairs of an older person it may be possible to refer this to the appropriate office. A search on the Internet will reveal the addresses of the Financial Ombudsman Service, the Pensions Ombudsman and the Legal Services Ombudsman, but other ombudsman-type services have been set up by particular industries.

Parliamentary and Health Service Ombudsman

9.70 Essentially two Ombudsman's roles combined into one organisation: the Parliamentary Ombudsman (or Parliamentary Commissioner for Administration) draws his powers from the Parliamentary Commissioner Act 1967, as since amended and The Health Service Commissioner (or Health Service Ombudsman) for England draws his powers from the Health Service Commissioners Act 1993.

9.71 The correspondence address is the Parliamentary and Health Service Ombudsman, Millbank Tower, Millbank, London SW1P 4QP Web site: www. ombudsman.org.uk.

Jurisdiction of the Health Service Ombudsman

9.72 The Health Service Ombudsman for England is empowered to investigate complaints against the NHS in England. He may investigate complaints of maladministration or of failure in, or to provide, a service, against NHS bodies, and others such as family health service providers and independent individuals or bodies providing a service on behalf of the NHS.

9.73 Complaints may be about attitude as well as actions of members of staff. In addition to the usual prerequisites, the ombudsman cannot investigate complaints within the clinical judgment complaints procedure unless they relate to the administration of that procedure.

Jurisdiction of the Parliamentary Ombudsman

9.74 The Parliamentary Ombudsman investigates qualifying complaints by members of the public about the way they have been treated by government departments and certain non-departmental public bodies in the UK, such as the Office of the Public Guardian and the Official Solicitor to the Supreme Court. A complaint may only be made through a Member of Parliament (MP), thus providing a barrier for trivial or inappropriate issues. The MP may try to sort the matter out by approaching the department concerned before referring to the Parliamentary Ombudsman.

Local Government Ombudsman

9.75 The Commissioner for Local Administration in England, generally known as the 'Local Government Ombudsmen' (LGO), was established by Part III of the Local Government Act 1974 (as amended). The LGO is empowered to investigate any local authority, as well as adult social care providers where people arrange or fund their adult social care. A complaint to the LGO may be more appropriate where the problem is an administrative matter rather than a legal issue such as a council taking too long to process an application, but it is important not to allow any time limit for commencing alternative legal proceedings to expire whilst awaiting the outcome.

9.76 The correspondence address is PO Box 4771, Coventry, CV4 0EH. Web site: www.lgo.org.uk.

The Public Services Ombudsman for Wales

9.77 The Public Services Ombudsman for Wales was established under the Public Services Ombudsman (Wales) Act 2005 and has powers to look into complaints about public services in Wales, ranging from NHS bodies, health and social care providers to local authorities, national and local government.

9.78 The correspondence address is 1 Ffordd yr Hen Gae, Pencoed CF35 5LJ. Web site: www.ombudsman-wales.org.uk.

Complaining to an Ombudsman

Advantages

9.79 There are many advantages in a complainant using the Ombudsman for redress, including the following:

(1) they are free to the complainant;

(2) they can result in the award of compensation;

(3) the responsible body is required to publicise the Ombudsman's report;

(4) the Ombudsman has access to all the relevant files and other records and can require the body to furnish additional information;

(5) the Ombudsman has the same powers as the High Court in respect of the attendance and examination of witnesses and in respect of the production of documents;

(6) complaints must be made within 12 months of the date on which the person aggrieved first had notice of the matters alleged in the complaint, although the Ombudsman has an overall discretion to extend time; and

(7) they are totally independent of the public body they investigate.

Limitations

9.80 The Ombudsman cannot investigate a complaint unless it has first been drawn to the attention of the relevant body and that body has been afforded an opportunity to investigate and reply to the complaint. If a remedy is available in the courts, the Ombudsman may only become involved if they consider in the particular circumstances it unreasonable to expect the complainant to go to court, and the cost is not normally regarded on its own as a good reason. In general before accepting a complaint, the Local Ombudsman will expect a person to have exhausted the relevant body's complaints procedure.

Disadvantages

9.81 The disadvantages of the procedure include:

(1) there is no obligation on the Ombudsman to accept a complaint;

(2) of those that are investigated most do not result in a final report;

(3) the investigation is conducted privately, so the complainant may feel 'in the dark'; and

(4) it is lengthy and can take well over a year or longer for an investigation to be completed.

Maladministration

9.82 The matters complained of must amount to maladministration, a term which refers to the way in which a matter has been handled rather than the actual merits of a decision and as a result the complainant has suffered injustice, such as disappointment, a lost opportunity or a serious financial loss. There is no power to question the merits of a decision where there is no maladministration. Although there is an overlap between the services of the ombudsman and judicial review (see below) in practice the ombudsman takes the view that judicial review is not a remedy that is available for most complainants but a complaint will not be dealt with if a court application has been made.

9.83 Maladministration is not defined although it is concerned with the manner in which decisions by the body are reached and the manner in which they are or are not implemented. The Health Services Commissioner has stated that maladministration includes, not only bias, neglect, inattention, incompetence, ineptitude, perversity, turpitude, arbitrariness but also:

(1) rudeness;

(2) unwillingness to treat the complainant as a person with rights;

(3) refusal to answer reasonable questions;

(4) neglecting to inform the complainant on request of their rights or entitlement;

(5) knowingly giving advice which is misleading or inadequate;

(6) ignoring valid advice or overruling considerations which would produce an uncomfortable result for the overruler;

(7) offering no redress or manifestly disproportionate redress;

(8) showing bias, whether because of colour, sex or any other grounds;

(9) omission to notify those who thereby lose the right of appeal;

(10) refusal to inform adequately of the right of appeal;

(11) faulty procedures;

(12) failure by management to monitor compliance with adequate procedures;

(13) cavalier disregard of guidance which is intended to be followed in the interest of equitable treatment of those who use the service;

(14) partiality: and failure to mitigate the effects of rigid adherence to the letter of the law where that produces manifestly inequitable treatment.

The complainant

9.84 Normally the complaint is made by the person who claims to have suffered injustice, but where they are for any reason unable to act for themselves it may usually be made by a member of their family or some body or individual suitable to represent them.

Procedure

9.85 The complaint must first be taken up with the appropriate body which should provide a leaflet explaining how to make complaints and how these are dealt with. Only if satisfaction is not gained in this way should the complaint be referred to the Ombudsman. There is a 12-month time-limit from the date when the grounds of complaint arose, though there is a discretion to allow a longer time.

9.86 The complainant must complete a complaint form, which is available from the relevant Ombudsman's website. The complainant must offer some evidence in support which shows they have personally been affected by bad administration, which usually involves producing correspondence and documents, though these will be returned when the investigation is over.

9.87 After considering the complaint the Ombudsman will either write to the complainant, or their MP if a complaint is to the Parliamentary Ombudsman, confirming that they have accepted it, or give reasons for not being able to do so. The Ombudsman will set out a summary of what is to be investigated, how they will go about investigating the complaint and what they will do next.

9.88 When the investigating officers have collected all the relevant information the Ombudsman considers the case and decides whether to uphold the complaint, in which event the body concerned is invited to offer a suitable remedy for the injustice caused. A written report is sent to the complainant or the MP referring the case if the complaint is to the Parliamentary Ombudsman, and if a complaint is upheld this will state whether the body has agreed to remedy any injustice or hardship caused, perhaps by offering an apology or agreeing to policy changes or new procedures.

9.89 The Ombudsman only makes recommendations and so has no power to compel the body to comply with those recommendations. However it is very rare for the recommendations to be ignored. There is no right of appeal against the Ombudsman's decision. The process is confidential and information is not given to the press or the public about particular cases in a way which would identify the complainant.

OTHER CHALLENGES

NHS continuing health care claims

9.90 There is a review process the purpose of which is to check that proper procedures have been followed in reaching decisions about the need for NHS continuing health care (NHSCHC) and the NHS services contributing to continuing health and social care and to consider the application of the eligibility criteria for NHSCHC to the facts of the client's care needs.[50]

9.91 The review procedure does not apply where individuals or their families and any carer wish to challenge:

(1) the content of the eligibility criteria;

(2) the type and location of any offer of NHS funded continuing care services;

(3) the content of any alternative care package which they have been offered; or

(4) their treatment or any other aspect of the services they are receiving or have received (this would properly be dealt with through the complaints procedure).

---

[50] Ch 8 contains details of eligibility for NHSCHC.

Procedure

Consent

9.92   A third party cannot give or refuse consent for an assessment of eligibility for NHSCHC on behalf of a person who lacks capacity, unless they have a health and welfare Lasting Power of Attorney or they have been appointed a welfare Deputy by the Court of Protection. It is, however, possible for an assessment to be carried out if the local NHS commissioning body believe it is in the patient's best interest, without the client's consent.[51]

Representation by lawyers

9.93   In England, the National Framework document makes clear if the individual chooses to have a legally qualified person to act as their advocate, that person would be acting with the same status as any other advocate nominated by the individual concerned. The process is fundamentally about identifying the individual's needs and how these relate to the Framework. Health and social care practitioners should be confident of their knowledge and skill in dealing with most queries that arise about the process and the appropriate completion of the Decision Support Tool. Where wider issues are raised by advocates (such as legal questions) they should, if appropriate, be asked to raise these separately with the Clinical Commissioning Group (CCG) outside the multidisciplinary team meeting.[52]

Timescales to challenging an adverse decision in England

9.94   Timescales, which apply to the review process for NHSCHC eligibility decisions are:

- an individual or their representative should seek a review of an adverse eligibility decision no later than **6 months** from the date they were notified of that decision;
- the responsible NHS body should deal with a request for a local review within **3 months** of receipt;
- an individual or their representative should request an Independent Review by the NHS Board no later than **6 months** following notification of the responsible NHS body's review decision; and
- the Independent Review should be conducted within **3 months** of the request.

The local review process

9.95   If there is a disagreement about a decision, or about who pays for care, the CCG in England or the Local Health Board in Wales (LHB), local resolution process will usually be the first step. The exact process is determined locally. However, local review panels should not be used as a gate keeping function or as a financial monitor. Because the final eligibility decision should be independent of budgetary constraints, finance officers should not be part of any decision-making panel.

9.96   In England, if an individual has been screened out from full consideration following use of the Checklist[53], they may ask the CCG to reconsider its decision and

---

[51]   MCA 2005, ss 4 and 5.
[52]   NF England, Practice Guidance, para 10.2.
[53]   This does not apply in Wales.

agree to a full assessment of eligibility. The CCG should give this request due consideration, taking account of all the information available. A clear and written response should be given to the individual and their representative together with details of the right to complain under the NHS complaints procedure, if they remain dissatisfied.

9.97   The CCG/LHB should deal promptly with any request to review a decision about eligibility for NHSCHC. A review should not proceed if it is discovered that the individual has not previously received a comprehensive assessment of needs.

The independent review

9.98   If the local review does not provide a satisfactory solution then the matter can progress to an independent review to consider:

(1)   if the correct procedure has been followed in reaching a decision as to the person's eligibility for NHSCHC; or

(2)   whether the National Framework has been correctly applied

and to make a recommendation to the local NHS commissioning body in the light of its findings.

9.99   The National Health Service Commissioning Board and Clinical Commissioning Groups (Responsibilities and Standing Rules) Regulations 2012[54] require the NHS Commissioning Board (the NHS Board) to maintain independent review panels. In Wales, The Community Health Council Independent Review Panel established by the Local Health Board undertakes the review. The chair of the Independent Review Panel (IRP) should be selected by the NHS Board/LHB following an open recruitment process. The appointment of representatives of NHS Board/LHB and local authorities will be on the basis of the nomination of those organisations. They should take account of the professional and other skills, which will be relevant to the work of the panel.

9.100   The key principles for the IRP, and for any dispute resolution process for NHSCHC are:

(1)   gathering and scrutiny of all available and appropriate evidence, whether written or oral, including that from the GP, hospital (nursing, medical, mental health, therapies etc), community nursing services, care home provider, Social Services records etc, as well as any information submitted by the individual concerned;

(2)   compilation of a robust and accurate identification of the care needs;

(3)   audit of attempts to gather any records said not to be available;

(4)   involvement of individual/carer as far as possible, including the opportunity for individuals to input information at all stages;

(5)   there should be a full record of deliberations at all review panels;

(6)   clear and evidenced written decisions to the individual setting out rationale for the panel's decision on their eligibility for NHSCHC on the basis of their needs only.

9.101   The IRP's role is advisory, but the decisions of the IRP should be accepted in all but exceptional circumstances by the local NHS commissioning body. If it decides not to

---

[54]   SI 2012/2996.

accept an IRP recommendation in an individual case, it should explain this in writing to the individual and the chair of the IRP, including its reasons for not accepting it.

9.102 If the individual is dissatisfied with this, the matter should be pursued through the NHS complaints procedure, and possibly on to the Ombudsman. It is suggested that judicial review is not worthwhile as they are generally unsuccessful.[55]

Representation at IRP

9.103 An individual may have a representative present to speak on their behalf if they choose, or are unable or have difficulty in presenting their own views. This role may be undertaken by a relative or carer or advocate acting on the individual's behalf.[56] The IRP must be satisfied that any person acting on behalf of the individual accurately represents their views and that their interests or wishes should not conflict with those of the individual.

9.104 In England, advocates should be provided where this will support the individual through the review process. The NHS Board and CCGs should ensure that there are agreed protocols as to how the provision of advocates will operate and the circumstances in which they are to be made available.[57]

Default powers

9.105 Many statutes vest supervisory powers in ministers (usually the Secretary of State) and *Codes of Guidance* may then be issued by the government department. Some statutes giving powers to or imposing duties on local authorities authorise the minister to make regulations prescribing how they shall exercise or perform these. A complaint may be made direct to a minister if the authority does not comply with his directions and the minister may exercise default powers. This might be appropriate where the authority unreasonably refuses to make an assessment or fails to provide services which are assessed as needed when it has the resources to do so. There can be no intervention in respect of the exercise of a mere discretion.

9.106 Under these powers the minister may call an authority to account for failure to exercise its functions and even transfer the powers of the defaulting authority to himself or to another authority.[58] It is rare for these powers to be exercised, but the threat to refer a matter to the minister may be a useful tactic and if the issue is the level of resources these default powers may be the only remedy available. In some circumstances ministers may declare a local authority to be in default and direct the authority to comply within time limits, and if the direction is not complied with it may be enforced by an order for mandamus from the High Court.

9.107 Thus there is a general power to declare local authorities in default if they fail to comply with their social services duties[59] and this may prove to be an essential ingredient of making community care work, fuelled by persistent complaints by disabled persons

---

55   *R (on the Application of Green) v South West SHA* [2008] EWHC 2576 (Admin); *R (on the application of St Helens BC) v Manchester PCT* [2008] EWCA Civ 931; *Jones v Powys LHB* [2008] EWHC 2562.
56   NF England, para 20 annex E; Wales, A 5.14.
57   NF England, para 9, annex E.
58   National Assistance Act 1948, s 36; Mental Health Act 1983, s 124; National Health Service Act 1977, s 85.
59   Local Authority Social Services Act 1970, s 7D, inserted by National Health Service and Community Care Act 1990, s 50. Similar powers exist as regards the provision of services for children – Children Act 1989, s 84.

about the performance of particular authorities. It may be more appropriate to deal with a general breakdown in some service provision rather than individual cases.

LEGAL REMEDIES

Preliminary

9.108 When negotiation and persuasion do not result in needs being met it becomes necessary to consider the legal remedies that are available. There may be a choice but equally none of the remedies may offer the certainty of results within an acceptable timescale. Nevertheless, the threat to use one of these remedies or the taking of the initial steps may be sufficient to create a further climate for negotiation. The following methods may be available of challenging an authority and enforcing its duties:

- civil action in the courts;
- judicial review;
- reference to a court outside this country.

The fact that the potential claimant is incapable of making decisions need not deprive the individual of the right to bring an action, because special procedures exist to enable people who lack capacity to be parties to proceedings with other people acting on their behalf.[60]

County court

9.109 A claim may be appropriate in the county court, and whilst this may not provide interim relief a successful outcome might discourage an authority from persisting in or repeating a breach of its obligations in the future. A claim for damages may be a possible remedy for failure by an authority to perform in a proper manner, or at all, an obligation it has accepted and the court also has power to award specific performance or an injunction. Such a claim would have to be based upon a recognised 'cause of action', typically breach of contract or the tort of negligence, although the possibility of a breach of statutory duty should not be overlooked.

Breach of contract

9.110 This might arise where an authority agrees to provide services which have been assessed as needed and are being paid for, but then fails to deliver those services.[61] The measure of damages might be based upon the cost of obtaining services from another source or making good inadequate provision.

9.111 It is not unusual for legally enforceable agreements to be entered into with the authorities, and an action may be brought for damages for breach of contract if there is a failure by the authority to perform the terms of such an agreement.[62]

---

[60]   See generally Ch 2 and Ch 3.
[61]   Query whether if the authority withdraws services without giving any reason the user may purchase replacement services commercially and then claim the cost.
[62]   Eg the provision of regular transport to a day care centre.

Negligence

9.112 Alternatively, where a common law duty of care can be established an action may lie in the tort of negligence based upon the manner in which the authority has performed (or failed to perform) a service,[63] the remedy sought being damages or an injunction. However, the fact that the service is provided under a statutory discretion may render the claim non-justiciable.[64] This may include employer's liability, and liability for the acts of an agent which the authority has expressly authorised or subsequently ratified,[65] but a duty of care owed to the individual may not be recognised.[66]

Breach of statutory duty

9.113 The courts will not allow individuals to bring actions for breach of statutory duty unless the legislation expressly or by implication enables this. It is necessary to establish that the statute imposes a duty upon the authority as distinct from merely conferring a power, that this is a specific duty towards the claimant rather than merely a general duty and that the damage caused is of the nature envisaged by the statute.[67] However, if an authority in the exercise of its statutory powers acknowledges that it will make some specific provision and then fails to do so, it is possible that an action may be brought for breach of statutory duty. Where an authority fails to discharge its general functions the remedy is to ask the Secretary of State to exercise his default powers (see above) and an action for breach of statutory duty is not appropriate.[68]

9.114 This is a complex and controversial area of law and many cases have reached the appeal courts.[69]

Small claims

9.115 If the claim is under £10,000 and does not raise legal complexities[70] it will normally be dealt with as a small claim before a district judge[71] thus minimising the risk of an adverse costs order and enabling the claimant to cope without legal representation or with the assistance of a friend as a lay representative. The procedure will no longer be adversarial and the judge may be persuaded to enquire into the failings of the authority if it appears that there is a legal basis for a damages claim. Repeated small claims can be brought if there is a continuing failure by the authority to provide the service, but the first award of damages is likely to have the desired effect.[72]

---

[63] *Barrett v Enfield LBC* [2001] 2 AC 550, HL.

[64] *D v East Berkshire Community Health NHS Trust* [2005] 2 AC 373.

[65] In *Phelps v Hillingdon London Borough Council* [2001] 2 AC 619 a local education authority was held to be vicariously liable for breaches by those whom it employed of a duty of care towards dyslexic pupils.

[66] *X (Minors) v Bedfordshire CC* [1995] 2 AC 633; *Stovin v Wise* [1996] AC 923. Local authorities were not liable for abuse of children in their care.

[67] *X (Minors) v Bedfordshire CC* [1995] 2 AC 633; *Stovin v Wise* [1996] AC 923.

[68] *Wyatt v Hillingdon LBC* (1978) 76 LGR 727, CA applying *Southwark LBC v Williams* [1971] 2 All ER 175, CA.

[69] For the distinction between claims brought in negligence and for breach of statutory duty see *Gorringe v Calderdale MBC* [2004] 1 WLR 1057.

[70] It is unlikely that a claim for breach of statutory duty would be allocated to the small claims track.

[71] Civil Procedure Rules 1998, Parts 26 and 27.

[72] The Civil Justice Council has produced *A Guide to Bringing and Defending a Small Claim* which is available at courts or can be downloaded at: www.judiciary.gov.uk/about-the-judiciary/advisory-bodies/cjc.

Judicial review

General

9.116 The High Court (sitting in the Administrative Court) may review the legality of a course of action by a public body.[73] These include inferior courts, tribunals and other public bodies such as health authorities and social services.[74] The court is concerned with the decision-making process rather than the merits of the decision and the applicant must have sufficient interest in the decision being challenged. The procedure may be used to force an authority to do something it is legally obliged to do or to prevent it from a particular course of action, but complicated rules have been developed to govern the circumstances in which the procedure is available.

9.117 Relief is available where the decisions are unlawful. They may be ultra vires (outside the powers of the body making it), contrary to the rules of natural justice, made in a way that is procedurally incorrect, based on a misinterpretation of the law or contrary to a legitimate expectation. A decision may also be challenged if it is unreasonable or irrational, and this would be the case if a material consideration had not been taken into account or matters had been taken into account which ought not to have been. The *Wednesbury principle* is often quoted:[75]

> 'a person entrusted with discretion must ... direct himself properly in law, he must call his own attention to the matters which he is bound to consider ... Similarly, there may be something so absurd that no sensible person could ever dream that it lay within the powers of the authority.'

In order to be upset on the irrational ground a decision must be 'so outrageous in its defiance of logic or of accepted moral standards that no sensible person who had applied his mind to the question to be decided could have arrived at it'.[76]

Procedure

9.118 The procedure is governed by the Civil Procedure Rules 1998.[77] The claim must be made promptly and in any event within 3 months of the ground arising unless time is extended by the court in its discretion. This would be exceptional and time cannot be extended by agreement between the parties. There is a *Pre-action Protocol* which requires the applicant to send a letter before action to the potential defendant identifying the decision or act that is being challenged and explaining the reason for the challenge.

Permission

9.119 Permission is required to bring the proceedings. This will be dealt with on paper by a High Court Judge but if refused the applicant may request reconsideration at an oral hearing.

---

[73]   Senior Courts Act 1981, s 31 (formerly the Supreme Court Act 1981).

[74]   The activities of 'private' bodies may involve a sufficient public element to render the exercise of their powers in certain contexts to be subject to judicial review. But see *R (on the application of Heather) v Leonard Cheshire Foundation* [2002] EWCA Civ 366.

[75]   *Associated Provincial Picture Houses Ltd v Wednesbury Corpn* [1947] 2 All ER 680, CA.

[76]   *CCSU v Minister for Civil Service* [1985] AC 374, HL, per Lord Diplock.

[77]   Part 54 and Practice Direction 54A.

9.120 The application for judicial review is generally the last resort and the applicant must normally have used any available alternative remedy before permission will be given including alternative dispute resolution procedures such as mediation. In relation to an application involving a local authority this will mean using any complaints procedure unless there is an urgent need for interim relief, and might even mean making an appeal to the Secretary of State but if he fails to act when asked to use his default powers and the authority has acted unlawfully it may be possible to seek judicial review of that failure.[78] A complaint to the local government ombudsman does not have to be pursued.

Urgent cases

9.121 Although it is intended to be a speedy remedy there may be long delays due to a large increase in the number of applications, but urgent cases can be expedited. Interim relief can be granted although an undertaking in damages is generally required and it is unlikely that relief would be granted before notice has been given to the public body thus providing an opportunity to make representations. In social welfare and housing cases which have less impact on third parties interim remedies appear to be granted more readily than in other cases. It may be appropriate to issue a judicial review application and then, perhaps after interim relief, have proceedings stayed pending alternative dispute resolution.

Remedies

9.122 There are several orders that can be made. A *mandatory order* requires the performance of a specific public duty imposed by law whereas a *prohibiting order* restrains a body from acting unlawfully. A *quashing order* may be used to review and if necessary quash an invalid decision and an *injunction* requires a party to do, or refrain from doing, a particular act. Finally, the court may make a *declaration* as to a finding on a question of law or rights, and this may be that a provision of legislation is incompatible with an ECHR right. These remedies may be linked. An interim injunction can be granted and this may be mandatory, but the court has no power to make an interim declaration.[79]

9.123 A claim for damages may be included in the application as a secondary remedy but breach of a public law right does not of itself give rise to a right for financial compensation. So if a person successfully challenges a decision not to provide him with services that would not of itself entitle him to damages even if he had paid for such services himself.

Discretion

9.124 Even if a case is made out, the relief is discretionary. The court will not grant relief if it considers that there is no need or it would be administratively inconvenient[80] or the applicant's conduct does not merit it. Relief may be refused if, by reason of delay, there may be substantial hardship or prejudice to another person or detriment to good

---

[78] See dicta of Simon Brown J in *R v Kent CC, ex p Bruce* (1986) *The Times*, 8 February, although the minister's default powers are not now usually an alternative to judicial review.

[79] *Riverside Mental Health NHS Trust v Fox* [1994] 1 FLR 614, CA.

[80] Lack of resources may prove an effective defence to a local authority in regard to its obligations to provide services, but will not necessarily be so.

administration.[81] The applicant must have sufficient interest in the matter (locus standi) but this may include action groups in appropriate circumstances.[82]

9.125 The court has proved reluctant to interfere with decisions of local and health authorities which involve allocation of scare resources.

European Court of Justice (ECJ)

General

9.126 The Court of Justice of the European Union comprises the Court of Justice (known in England as the European Court of Justice (ECJ)) and the General Court (previously called the Court of First Instance) along with its specialised tribunals. All the EU's judicial bodies are based in Luxembourg, separate from the political institutions in Brussels and Strasbourg.

Constitution

9.127 The ECJ was established in 1952 and is composed of one judge per member state – currently 28 – assisted by nine Advocates-General. The judges and Advocates-General are appointed by common accord of the governments of the member states and hold office for a renewable term of 6 years. The treaties require that they are chosen from legal experts whose independence is 'beyond doubt' and who possess the qualifications required for appointment to the highest judicial offices in their respective countries or who are of recognised competence. A President is elected from and by the judges for a renewable term of 3 years to preside over hearings and deliberations, directing both judicial business and administration. The Registrar is the court's chief administrator.

9.128 The General Court has a further 15 judges and was set up in 1989. It is an inferior court which handles certain cases including those brought against Community institutions by natural or legal persons.[83] There is a right of appeal to the full court. There are no Advocates-General but one of the judges may adopt this role.

Jursidiction

9.129 The ECJ is the highest court of the European Union in matters of European Union law, but not national law. It is tasked with interpreting EU law and ensuring its equal application across all EU member states. The ECJ also has judicial review powers over the actions of Community institutions[84] and can annul an institution's legal rights if it acts outside its powers. Decisions of the ECJ are binding upon the courts of the United Kingdom and are becoming increasingly important in shaping our law.

9.130 The European Commission may bring an action against a member state for failure to fulfil its obligations under the Treaty and another member state may also do so.[85] There was no sanction for failure to comply with a ruling of the ECJ until the Maastricht Treaty in 1994 which provides for penalties to be imposed on a member

---

[81] Senior Courts Act 1981, s 31(6).
[82] *R v Secretary of State for Social Services, ex p CPAG* [1989] 1 All ER 1047, CA.
[83] Articles 173 and 175 of the Treaty of Rome.
[84] Article 173.
[85] Article 169.

state. National governments are treated as responsible for the acts of local authorities and other public bodies, so instead of bringing a case in the local court an individual whose rights have been infringed by non-implementation of an EC directive can complain to the Commission which can investigate and bring a case before the ECJ which can award damages to the individual. There have been a number of references by pressure groups and more are likely in the future, especially in regard to discrimination on grounds of sex, age or disability.

References by national courts

9.131 It is not possible to appeal the decisions of national courts to the ECJ, but rather national courts refer questions of EU law to the ECJ. However, it is ultimately for the national court to apply the resulting interpretation to the facts of any given case. Where an issue of Community law arises before a national court, questions of interpretation or validity can be referred to the ECJ for a preliminary ruling.[86] The procedure is available to the national court rather than to the parties, and it is the court which decides the question to be referred although a party may make the initial request for a reference.

Procedure

General

9.132 The ECJ has its own Rules of Procedure. The procedure generally includes a written phase and an oral phase. The proceedings are in a language chosen by the applicant. The working language of the court, however, including the language in which the judges deliberate and the language in which preliminary reports and judgments are drafted is French.

Role of the Advocates-General

9.133 The Advocates-General are responsible for presenting a legal opinion on the cases assigned to them, generally when the court considers the case raises a new point of law. They can question the parties involved and then give their opinion on a legal solution to the case before the judges deliberate and deliver their judgment. The intention behind having Advocates-General attached is to provide independent and impartial opinions concerning the court's cases. Unlike the court's judgments, the written opinions of the Advocates-General are the works of a single author and in consequence are generally more readable and deal with the legal issues more comprehensively than the court, which is limited to the particular matters at hand. The Advocates-Generals' opinions are advisory and do not bind the court, but they are nonetheless very influential and are followed in the majority of cases.

Decisions of the court

9.134 The court acts as a collegial body: decisions are those of the court rather than of individual judges; no minority opinions are given and the existence of a majority decision rather than unanimity is never suggested. The court can sit in plenary session, as a Grand Chamber of 15 judges (including the president and vice-president), or in chambers of three or five judges. Plenary sittings are rare but are required in exceptional cases provided for in the treaties and the court may also decide to sit in full if the issues raised are considered to be of exceptional importance. Sitting as a Grand Chamber is more common and can happen when a Member State or a Union institution, that is a

---

[86] Article 177.

party to certain proceedings, so requests, or in particularly complex or important cases. Each chamber elects its own president who is elected for a term of 3 years in the case of the five-judge chambers or one year in the case of three-judge chambers.

European Court of Human Rights

Background

9.135 In 1950 the Council of Europe formulated the European Convention on Human Rights which sets out certain fundamental human rights concerned with liberty, natural justice, respect for privacy and freedom of expression and from discrimination. By Article 1 countries which ratify the Convention agree to secure to everyone within their jurisdiction the rights and freedoms contained therein, and various Protocols have followed some of which have been ratified by the United Kingdom. In England and Wales this is implemented by the Human Rights Act 1998.[87]

Constitution

9.136 The European Court of Human Rights is a supra-national or international court established by the Convention in 1959. It is based in Strasbourg, France. It is charged with ensuring the observance of the engagement undertaken by the contracting states in relation to the Convention and its protocols. In 1998 the court became a full-time institution and the European Commission of Human Rights, which used to decide on admissibility of applications, was abolished.

9.137 The court comprises a judge for every state which is a party to the Convention and is governed by Rules of Procedure. Protocol 14 amended the Convention so that judges would be elected for a non-renewable term of 9 years, whereas previously judges served a 6-year term with the option of renewal. The Convention requires that judges are of high moral character and have qualifications suitable for high judicial office. They are elected by majority vote in the Parliamentary Assembly of the Council of Europe from the three candidates nominated by each contracting state. The judges perform their duties in an individual capacity and are prohibited from having any institutional or other type of ties with the contracting state on behalf of whom they were elected.

9.138 A Committee is constituted by three judges, Chambers by seven judges and a Grand Chamber by 17 judges. The plenary court is an assembly of all of the court's judges but has no judicial functions. It elects the court's President, Vice-President, registrar and deputy registrar. It also deals with administrative matters, discipline, working methods, reforms, the establishment of Chambers and the adoption of the Rules of Court.

Jurisdiction

9.139 The court hears applications alleging that a contracting state has breached one or more of the human rights provisions set out in the Convention and its protocols. An application can be lodged by an individual, a group of individuals or one or more of the other contracting states. The jurisdiction of the court is generally divided into inter-state cases, applications by individuals against contracting states, and advisory opinions.

---

[87]   See Chapter 1.

Applications by individuals constitute the majority of cases heard by the court and can be made by any person, non-governmental organisation or group of individuals.

Procedure

General

9.140 By 2009 the court had become swamped with cases but it was realised that more than 90% of applications were declared to be inadmissible, and around 60% of decisions related to repetitive cases where the court had already found a violation or where well-established case-law existed. Accordingly Protocol 11 simplified the procedure and reduced the length of proceedings. However, the workload continued to increase, so in June 2010 Protocol 14 introduced further reforms to enable the court to focus on cases that raised important human rights issues. The court's filtering capacity was reinforced to deal with clearly inadmissible applications, new admissibility criteria were introduced so that cases where the applicant has not suffered a significant disadvantage would be declared inadmissible, and measures were introduced to deal more effectively with repetitive cases.

Applications

9.141 Although the official languages of the court are English and French, applications may be submitted in any one of the official languages of the contracting states. An application has to be made in writing and signed by the applicant or by the applicant's representative. It is a requirement that one or more of the fundamental rights have been violated, all available remedies in the member state concerned have been exhausted, and the application is made within 6 months of the final decision of the highest competent court or authority.[88] The application should contain a summary of the complaint, details of the Convention rights violated and of the remedies used or attempted, and a chronological history of the case. Details of all decisions of the courts or the authorities should be provided. Once registered with the court, the case is assigned to a judge rapporteur who can make the final decision that the case is inadmissible.

Admissibility

9.142 A single judge can now reject plainly inadmissible applications, and in cases of doubt may refer the application to the committee of the court. The three judge committee has jurisdiction to declare applications admissible and decide on the merits of the case if it was clearly well founded and based on well-established case-law. The court can declare applications inadmissible where the applicant has not suffered a significant disadvantage and which do not raise serious questions affecting the application or the interpretation of the Convention, or important questions concerning national law. The court should encourage the parties to reach a settlement at an early stage of the proceedings, especially in repetitive cases, and can issue advisory opinions.

Hearings

9.143 After the preliminary finding of admissibility the case is referred to a Chamber of the Court which communicates with the state against which the application is made, asking the government to present its observations. The court may undertake any investigation it deems necessary on the facts or issues raised in the application and contracting states are required to provide the court with all necessary assistance for this

---

[88] The fact that an applicant is mentally incapable of acting in person may be an acceptable reason for delay.

purpose. Hearings are required to be in public, unless there are exceptional circumstances justifying the holding of a private hearing, but in practice the majority of cases are heard in private following written pleadings and in many cases, a hearing is not held.

9.144 The state concerned is a party because the main issue is between the court and the state, to establish whether a violation has occurred, but the applicant may also on request be represented by an advocate being either a solicitor, barrister or advocate, or other person approved by the President. Cases which raise serious questions of interpretation and application of the Convention or which may depart from previous case-law can be heard in the Grand Chamber.

Judgments

9.145 The court's judgments are public and must contain reasons justifying the decision. Article 46 of the Convention provides that contracting states undertake to abide by the court's final decision. On the other hand, advisory opinions are, by definition, non-binding. In final judgments the court makes a declaration that a contracting state has violated the Convention, and may order the contracting state to pay material and/or moral damages and the legal expenses incurred in domestic courts and the Court in bringing the case.

9.146 Chambers decide cases by a majority and any judge who has heard the case can attach to the judgment a separate opinion which can concur or dissent with the decision of the court. The judgment of the Grand Chamber is final. Judgments by the Chamber of the Court become final 3 months after they are issued, unless a reference to the Grand Chamber for review or appeal has been made. If the panel of the Grand Chamber rejects the request for referral, the judgment of the Chamber of the Court becomes final.

CHAPTER 10

FINANCIAL AFFAIRS

Gordon Ashton and Caroline Bielanska

'It is pretty hard to tell what does bring happiness; poverty and wealth have both failed.'
Kin Hubbard (1868–1930)

Financial affairs have to be administered within a legal framework whether these comprise the management of wealth, the collection of state benefits or the securing of publicly funded support. In this chapter we first identify personal funding from various sources and then outline the different taxes that may be payable. Next we consider the welfare or state benefits that may be claimable by an elderly individual before summarising the appeal process. Finally we look at funding for community and residential care including the contribution that the individual may be required to make.

INTRODUCTION

10.1 The income of older people is derived from a wide variety of sources and may be more than enough for personal needs in which event it accumulates as capital, or it may be insufficient in which event some form of income supplement is required. Those with surplus income may choose to pass this, or some of the capital that produces the income, to the next generation but those with inadequate income may be supported by their family on a voluntary basis. The effects of inflation upon savings may result in individuals who were comfortably off initially upon retirement finding themselves in straightened circumstances during later years, and access to good investment advice is often needed on the transition to retirement and at later intervals.

10.2 In the event of physical disability or loss of mental capacity the emphasis may change from how much income the individual has to how the care and support that is needed can be funded. In the past hospital and other care provided under the National Health Service was free, but this is now being restricted by eligibility criteria for some medical treatments and health care services, and under community care policies those with social and personal care needs must contribute towards the cost which may exceed the income of the individual.

10.3 In many cases support is needed from outside sources, both for the individual and the family or carers, and a system of *social welfare* has built up. This does not only come in the form of cash benefits, such as from welfare benefits and direct payments from social services, but also includes a wide range of benefits-in-kind, such as community support and equipment services. Cash benefits can be enforced by the claimant with an appeal or complaints process for those who are dissatisfied. They can be targeted towards those most in need, either by reason of lack of resources or disability, but may not be spent for the purpose intended and do not necessarily secure the support that is required.

10.4 A less obvious way of giving support or incentives is through the tax system, with certain types of income being exempt from income tax and tax allowances being given to older or blind people. In recent years there has been a move away from tax reliefs towards more direct support through welfare benefits for infirm and disabled people and the provision of services under community care policies.

10.5 In this chapter we concentrate upon those sources of income that are of particular relevance to older people as distinct from other members of the community. Investment advice is beyond the scope of this book.[1] We also examine the available forms of income supplement and the extent to which the individual may be expected to pay for or contribute towards services and other provision that is required for personal care and support. We start by looking at personal sources of funding and then in turn consider funding by the state, the local authority and from other sources. The topic of managing these financial affairs during periods of incapacity is dealt with in the following chapter.

PERSONAL FUNDING

Preliminary

10.6 Remunerative employment may continue well beyond the 'normal' retirement age, but for most people this source of income ceases on or before reaching the state pension age either through choice or force of circumstances. The weekly or monthly wage will then be replaced by such pensions as may be available and these also will be paid weekly or monthly thus replacing earnings though almost inevitably at lower levels. A personal income may also be available from savings, perhaps supplemented by lump sum retirement benefits or the maturity of life policies, and a decision needs to be taken as to whether to invest solely for income or partly for capital growth with the prospect of increasing investment income at a later stage. Some state benefits based upon disability can continue to be paid in addition to the state pension which will arise at this stage, but there is the option to defer drawing this pension with a view to claiming an increased amount at a later date. Taxation will have an impact on most of these sources of income.

10.7 A minority of older people find that they are entitled to additional support from a trust or settlement, perhaps a life interest trust under the will of a deceased spouse or parent or a discretionary trust created by a deceased sibling.[2] Others will receive support as needed, financial and otherwise, from the immediate family on an informal basis and this may replace or supplement the support that would otherwise be available. For those whose personal income falls below a subsistence level or who need services that they cannot afford, support is available from a variety of sources and these are dealt with in later parts of this chapter.

---

[1] There are strict controls under the Financial Services and Markets Act 2000 upon the giving of investment advice. The Financial Services Act 2012, created the Prudential Regulation Authority managed by the Bank of England and the Financial Conduct Authority (www.fca.org.uk) to provide safeguards for consumers through more robust oversight.

[2] Those who set up these trusts will wish them to be supportive but not to deprive the beneficiary of funding that would have been available from other sources. This topic is considered in Ch 12.

Pensions

10.8   The state retirement pension will be a basic component in the weekly income of most older people and the main component for many. It is considered below in the context of state benefits. Under this heading we consider those pensions that people provide for themselves or may be entitled to following a period or periods of employment. There are tax incentives for individuals to provide for their own pensions in an appropriate manner, including income tax relief on contributions at the highest rate and tax relief from income tax and capital gains tax of the pension fund.[3] It may also be possible to take part of the pension as a tax-free lump sum. Most older people will be at the stage where they are drawing their pensions, but there may still be tax advantages for some in making further contributions and the potential growth in a pension or pension fund if the pension is deferred should not be overlooked.

Occupational

10.9   Occupational pensions are arranged by employers, an example being the company pension scheme whereby a separate trust fund is set up. Employees receive a booklet setting out the terms and the scheme may be contributory or non-contributory. Additional voluntary contributions (AVCs) are a way of saving for retirement through the pension scheme and full tax relief is available on these subject to limits.[4]

10.10   The Pensions Act 2008 introduced a new requirement for employers to automatically enroll any eligible employees into a workplace pension scheme and since October 2012, most employers are obliged to establish such a scheme for employees who work in the UK, earn above a prescribed amount and are aged between 22 years and the state pension age. Employers are required to provide a minimum employer contribution. It is open to employees to opt out of the scheme.

10.11   Employers may choose a defined benefit scheme to provide a minimum level of benefits or a defined contribution scheme such as The National Employment Savings Trust[5] (NEST) where employers will pay a minimum contribution.

10.12   By law men and women must now have the same pension age under a company scheme. In a preliminary ruling the European Court of Justice has held that the principle of equal pay for men and women[6] can be relied upon in the context of claims relating to benefits under occupational pension schemes against the trustees as well as employers, and at the instance of employees' survivors as well as employees themselves. However, the principle does not apply to inequalities in capital and substitute benefits paid by funded defined-benefit schemes as a result of actuarial factors varying between men and women, or to extra benefits for which employees pay voluntary contributions. Where an employee transfers to another scheme on a change of employment, the new scheme is bound to make good any discrimination under the earlier scheme but only for periods of service after 17 May 1990.[7]

---

[3]   The tax relief on contributions is capped and tax liabilities now arise in respect of substantial pension funds.
[4]   Since 1988 pension schemes must offer this facility. Free-standing additional voluntary contributions (FSAVCs) can also be made to independent pension plans offered by insurance companies.
[5]   An independently-run pension scheme backed by the Government.
[6]   Under Article 119 of the EC Treaty.
[7]   *Coloroll Pension Trustees Ltd v Russell* (1994) *The Times*, 30 November.

Benefits

10.13 Benefits normally include a pension at a specified age often with a lump sum, a death benefit for those who die before retirement and a widow's (or widower's) pension.[8] There may also be provision for enhanced benefit on early retirement through ill-health or redundancy. There are complex rules to register a pension scheme with HMRC and the Pensions Regulator.[9] However, all pension schemes must have flexibility including early retirement or withdrawal, preserved rights after two years in a scheme and transfer to another company scheme or to a personal pension.

10.14 There are various types of scheme. Under the *final salary* scheme the pension is a proportion of the salary for the last year (or average of the last few years) which is based on the number of years worked times a set fraction (eg 30/60th). It may be increased each year in line with inflation. The employer and sometimes the employee contribute an agreed proportion of the employee's salary towards the pension and the employee may be contracted out of Additional State Pension. Final salary schemes have tended to be restricted to public sector employees and big companies and many are being withdrawn due to the high cost. Transfer on a change of employment can be complicated and may result in a loss of benefits.

10.15 The trend now is for *money purchase* schemes. Under these, the pension depends upon the size of the contributions made by or in respect of the employee to an investment fund and the growth in that fund. All income is accumulated and the fund is exempt from taxation. Alternatively, under an *average earnings* scheme the pension is based upon average earnings calculated over the period of participation, and a set calculation is applied for the pension. Finally, as its name implies the *flat rate pension* is based on the number of years employed.

Personal pensions

10.16 Self-employed people, and also employees, may contribute to personal pensions although many older people who were employed will not have had this option. Employers may also contribute but there is no general obligation to do so. There are revenue restrictions on contributions, retirement age and benefits but policies may be with-profit, unit-linked, deposit or non-profit. Until July 1988 a different type of pension policy was available solely to the self-employed[10] and those then in existence may continue. Benefits come in the form of a lump sum and an annuity with some flexibility between the two, and on retirement it is often worthwhile taking the maximum permitted lump sum and investing this in other ways which may include the purchase of an annuity on the open market. The amount of the benefits depends upon the amount contributed and the performance of the pension fund.

10.17 For employees, contributions to personal pension policies may be instead of the additional state pension or an occupational scheme, and whilst an employee may switch many have been encouraged to do so when this was not beneficial to them. Claims for

---

8   Death-in-service benefits may be payable on a discretionary basis with the employee nominating a spouse or children as beneficiaries, and the money does not then form part of the employee's estate for inheritance tax purposes.

9   www.thepensionsregulator.gov.uk.

10   Section 226 pension policies (Income and Corporation Taxes Act 1970). The revenue restrictions were slightly different from the personal pensions.

compensation can be brought against those who gave inappropriate advice. An advantage of the personal pension is that a change of employment need not affect the pension arrangements.

Disputes

10.18 Pensions law is highly specialised, but there are information, conciliation and arbitration procedures which provide an alternative to litigation. The *Pensions Advisory Service* acts as a conciliation and information service for aggrieved members of occupational and personal pension schemes.[11] Its services are provided free, and it operates through a network of voluntary advisers throughout the country whose work is monitored by regional organisers.[12]

10.19 Since 1991 there has been a *pensions ombudsman* whose jurisdiction covers maladministration as well as breaches of trust.[13] He has power to require the production of papers and the giving of oral evidence, and can make orders without financial limit which are binding on employers and trustees as well as the complainant. Any appeal from his decisions is to the High Court on a point of law only, although judicial review would be available if he adopted inappropriate procedures or acted unfairly.

Taxation

Income tax

10.20 Income tax continues to be payable in the normal way throughout retirement, but there are various tax free allowances or reliefs available to taxpayers who have attained 65 years of age.[14] Income from state benefits may or may not be taxable depending upon its purpose, but other forms of support provided by local authorities and charitable organisations are generally not taxable. A taxpayer who is not capable of completing a tax return will usually be incapable of handling his affairs generally, and reference should be made to Chapter 10 for the procedures that are available for delegation of financial affairs.

Allowances and reliefs

10.21 Higher *personal allowances* apply at age 65 years and these are higher still at 75 years. Older married couples living together can claim a *married couple's allowance*. If the couple were married before 5 December 2005 with at least one spouse born before 6 April 1935, the husband can claim this. If the couple were married or entered a civil partnership after 6 December 2005, and at least one spouse or civil partner was born before 6 April 1935, the person with the higher income can claim. The tax bill is reduced by 10% of the *married couple's allowance* to which they are entitled. People who are certified blind and are on a local authority register of blind persons qualify for an additional tax free personal allowance.

10.22 Tax relief is available, subject to certain limits, on rent from furnished rooms in the owner's or tenant's home that are let.

---

[11] www.pensionsadvisoryservice.org.uk.
[12] These are pension professionals such as actuaries, auditors, pension administrators, fund managers, lawyers and pension consultants.
[13] www.pensions-ombudsman.org.uk. See Ch 9 for further information about the Ombudsman service.
[14] www.hmrc.gov.uk/incometax/allowance-relief.htm.

Planning

10.23 Some simple steps which may reduce the annual tax bill or assist with cash flow are worth considering. The most obvious is to ensure that all eligible allowances have been claimed, and if in doubt the taxpayer should complete and submit Tax Claim Form R40. This can be done at the end of the tax year (after 5 April) or when the overpayment reaches £50. It is also important to ensure that any Notice of Coding for PAYE on pension income is correct, and *taxed income relief* should be given if appropriate to secure the lower rate of tax on investment income. Steps can be taken to reduce or increase the income of a taxpayer who is 'caught in the margin' due to the fact that higher allowances reduce proportionately if income is more than a certain sum.[15]

10.24 In order to assist with cash-flow, investments may be rearranged so that income is received without deduction of tax where a repayment claim would otherwise be necessary. Non-taxpayers can apply on form R85 to receive gross interest on bank and building society accounts. Spouses or civil partners may wish to transfer investments between them in order to equalise income so that they each gain the full benefit of their personal allowances and the reduced rate band, any higher rate liability is minimised and neither party is caught in the margin as regards higher allowances.

Capital taxes

10.25 Under this heading we merely identify the basic features of our capital taxation. Many older people contemplate moving abroad on retirement but the implications of a change of domicile upon capital taxation in this country should first be considered. There are special dispensations in respect of capital gains tax and inheritance tax for certain trusts for the benefit of disabled beneficiaries, and these are dealt with in Chapter 12.[16]

Capital gains tax (CGT)

10.26 The gain in the value of an asset during a taxpayer's ownership is taxed on a disposal, which may be a sale or a gift, but the expenses of acquiring and disposing of the asset are deducted. The net gains, which means total chargeable gains less allowable losses, of the taxpayer in the tax year are taxed at the taxpayer's highest rates of income tax for the year, but an annual exemption reduces or eliminates the taxable gain. CGT is payable on 31 January following the tax year of the disposal.[17]

10.27 Certain assets are exempt, including an owner-occupied dwelling house. Only gains or losses since March 1982 are taken into account. Rollover relief may be available on qualifying business assets, including furnished holiday lets or gift hold-over relief on shares in a qualifying business, to postpone the payment of CGT.

10.28 There are various strategies that can be adopted to reduce potential CGT bills but the more sophisticated ones are beyond the scope of this book. Any losses may be realised prior to 5 April when a net taxable gain would otherwise arise in the tax year, and when cash is needed it may be possible to dispose of assets that do not create a gain. Where practicable a taxpayer should avoid making disposals that would produce a large

---

[15] This results in a high rate of tax being paid until the allowance is lost completely.
[16] Taxation of Chargeable Gains Act 1992, s 3 and Sch 1, para 1; Inheritance Tax Act 1984, ss 3(A)(1)–(3) and 89.
[17] www.hmrc.gov.uk/cgt/.

gain shortly before death because although all assets are valued on death for Inheritance tax purposes, CGT is not also then charged.

10.29 Independent taxation applies to CGT, so each spouse or civil partner has the benefit of the annual exemption but the losses of one spouse or civil partner cannot be set against the gains of the other. Transfers between spouses and civil partners are not treated as a disposal, so this leaves scope to plan ahead and minimise future tax liabilities. The couple can ensure that realisations that produce gains are by the partner with the lower rate of tax or that an asset is in joint names before disposal where one party's annual exemption or lower rates of tax would not otherwise be used up.

Inheritance tax (IHT)

10.30 The capital value of all net assets held at death is taxed, and life-time gifts will be included unless they are exempted under technical rules.[18] Certain types of asset such as business assets and agricultural property are exempt or valued on a beneficial basis. The excess above a threshold (known as the 'nil rate band') is taxed at a fixed rate.[19] There will be IHT on trusts created during a person's lifetime if the funds put into the trust are valued over the nil rate band, at 20% of the capital value over that threshold.

10.31 Potential IHT bills may be reduced by making regular gifts within the annual exemptions and making large gifts sooner rather than later. There is no tax on transfers between spouses and civil partners and each party is allowed their own nil rate band. Since October 2007 it is possible to transfer any unused nil rate band threshold from a late spouse or civil partner to the second spouse or civil partner when they die, so increasing the tax free threshold of the second spouse or partner. Tax planning generally is beyond the scope of this book.

Council tax

10.32 This is a tax on domestic properties with a personal element.[20] The amount of most bills depends solely on the value of the property but the tax assumes that two people live in a dwelling and some bills are reduced according to the number and status of the people living there. Much of the complexity of the tax arises from the concessions which are intended to assist disabled people and their carers. Appeals are to the Valuation Tribunal.[21]

Valuation bands

10.33 Properties are assessed in one of eight valuation bands, but disability reduction relief may apply to houses adapted for people with disabilities to reduce the value band. Parts of the home needed by someone with a disability which add to its value should be ignored in fixing the value band. If there are disabled facilities which detract from the value of the home the value band may be reduced under the 'material reduction' scheme. It is possible to challenge the band by appealing to the Valuation Office Agency.[22]

---

[18] These exemptions are summarised in Ch 12.
[19] The threshold is £325,000 until 2015. See www.hmrc.gov.uk/inheritancetax/.
[20] Local Government Finance Act 1992.
[21] www.valuationtribunal.gov.uk/Home.aspx.
[22] www.voa.gov.uk.

Discounts and exemptions

10.34 There is a discount of 25% for a sole resident, which disregards people who have paid live-in care or those who live with a person with severe mental impairment. Many older people may qualify for a full exemption including: unoccupied property where the person who lived there now lives in hospital, in a care home or with relatives due to their care needs; unoccupied property where the person who lived there has gone to care for someone else; property which is occupied only by people with severe mental impairment; or a self-contained 'granny flat' where the person who lives in it is a dependent relative of the owner of the main property.

10.35 A person is severely mentally impaired if they have a severe impairment of intelligence and social functioning, however caused, which appears to be permanent. This includes people with a mental illness such as dementia. To qualify for the discount the person must have a certificate of a registered medical practitioner to this effect and be entitled to one or more of certain benefits.[23]

Liability

10.36 The tax is charged on an adult resident in a dwelling which is that person's sole or main residence, but everyone is not liable for the tax.[24] People who live in the home of another person or in certain kinds of shared accommodation do not pay it directly. There is only one tax bill for each dwelling and where it is permanently occupied the occupier with the strongest legal interest is liable for the tax.[25] Joint owners, tenants or licensees are jointly and severally liable, and a heterosexual partner of someone liable to pay the tax is also jointly liable. A person who is severely mentally impaired will not be jointly liable to pay the tax with a person who is not so impaired but will be liable if occupying solely or only with other such people (unless exempt). Adult children living at home, boarders and sub-tenants do not have to pay the tax directly but may be expected to contribute by paying an increased amount for occupation.

10.37 An owner is liable for the tax in respect of unoccupied property (unless exempt) or one that has no permanent residents or is in multiple occupation.[26] Residential care homes, nursing homes and hostels are classified as dwellings so the owner is liable for the tax whether a local authority, voluntary organisation or commercial enterprise.

Implications

10.38 It follows that a retired couple living together have no discount but if the husband dies and the widow lives alone she receives a 25% discount. If the wife has a stroke and is looked after by her husband her personal liability for the tax ceases and a 25% discount applies, but if her husband has died and she is looked after by a paid carer it will be 50%. The problem with this is that the bill can vary with changes of personal circumstances, such as people moving in or out of the dwelling or the state of health of the occupants. These changes will have to be reported causing extra administration and possible confusion especially for elderly people who are likely to be affected but less able to understand the complications.

---

[23] These include employment and support allowance in the support group, attendance allowance, disability living allowance, and personal independence allowance.
[24] Council tax reduction helps those on low incomes.
[25] Owner-occupiers take precedence over tenants who take precedence over licensees.
[26] Council Tax (Liability of Owners) Order (as amended). It is not always easy to distinguish between a house in multiple occupation and a house divided into bedsits.

WELFARE BENEFITS

Overview

Introduction

10.39 There are many different benefits paid by the state to claimants through local Department of Work and Pensions offices, or certain central offices or the local authority. Most of these are periodic income payments, although others, from the social fund, consist of one-off capital grants or loans.

Department for Work and Pensions

10.40 The Department for Work and Pensions (DWP)[27] is divided into a number of executive agencies. Benefits for claimants of working age are dealt with by Jobcentre Plus,[28] and benefits for those over pension age by the Pension Service.[29] The Disability and Carers Service[30] deals with attendance allowance, disability living allowance, personal independence payments and carer's allowance. The National Insurance Contributions Office,[31] responsible for administering the National Insurance contributions system, is part of HM Revenue and Customs. The system is moving towards remote claims, by telephone or online, via a central website.[32]

Social Security Advisory Committee (SSAC)

10.41 The Social Security Advisory Committee (SSAC)[33] is an advisory body on all social security matters, except those relating to industrial injuries, war pensions and occupational pensions. Its functions, constitution and powers are set out in the Social Security Administration Act 1992. It is independent, expresses its views in objective terms, and on occasions has strongly opposed changes in policy.

10.42 Most regulations which reflect changes in benefit or contributions policy have to be submitted to the SSAC before they are passed, although it may waive such reference. However, there is a duty on the Secretary of State to give full information to the SSAC before they decide to waive the right to consider regulations.[34] If it decides to make a report it will consult organisations and individuals with relevant experience and the report is laid before Parliament with the regulations and a statement from the Secretary of State responding to any recommendations. The Secretary of State may lay regulations before Parliament before receiving a report if after the reference it appears to him that by reason of the urgency of the matter it is expedient to do so.[35]

---

[27] www.gov.uk/government/organisations/department-for-work-pensions.
[28] www.gov.uk/contact-jobcentre-plus.
[29] www.gov.uk/contact-pension-service.
[30] www.nidirect.gov.uk/disability-and-carers-service.
[31] www.hmrc.gov.uk/ni/.
[32] www.gov.uk.
[33] www.ssac.org.uk.
[34] See *Howker v Secretary of State for Work and Pensions* [2002] EWCA Civ 1623, where the Secretary of State wrongly told the SSAC that draft amendment regulations did not bring about any substantive change in the law.
[35] Social Security Administration Act 1992, s 173.

Entitlement

Habitual residence

10.43 Presence and habitual residence are important factors in determining entitlement to benefits. In order to satisfy the habitual residence test, a claimant must have a 'right to reside' in the Common Travel Area.[36] This is likely to be satisfied in many cases because the claimant is a British citizen, or because they have the right to reside under European law. The main people who are likely to be affected by the right to reside test are nationals from the A8 countries which acceded to the European Union on 1 May 2004[37] and from Bulgaria and Romania which acceded on 1 January 2007.

10.44 Assuming the claimant does have a right to reside, they must also comply with the test of being habitually resident. This applies to all claimants including British citizens who have been resident in the country for 2 years or less. This requires a settled intention to reside in the Common Travel Area.

Living abroad

10.45 A claimant moving to another country who qualifies for contributory benefits such as retirement pension may still be eligible to receive that benefit in that country, if Great Britain has a reciprocal agreement with the country, although annual upratings may not be paid.[38] There are reciprocal agreements in place with all European Economic Area (EEA) countries (except Greece) in addition to a number of non-EEA countries like New Zealand, Barbados and Jamaica, and the Isle of Man.[39] European law normally means that a person moving to another EEA country will continue to get their retirement pension paid in full, but note that if the pension is based on contributions paid in a third country the full benefit may not be paid.[40]

10.46 If a claimant who has been receiving benefits while resident in the UK goes abroad temporarily, the general rule is that entitlement to income-based benefits will cease after 4 weeks. Entitlement to disability benefits can continue for up to 26 weeks, as long as the claimant remains habitually resident in the UK.

Legislation

10.47 Primary legislation provides the authority for the payment of specific state benefits and the administration of the benefit system. The main statutes governing the social security system are the Social Security Contributions and Benefits Act 1992, which lays out the framework for particular benefits, and the Social Security Administration Act 1992, which deals with the administration of the system. There are a number of other statutes such as the Social Security Act 1998 and the Child Support, Pensions and Social Security Act 2000, which deal with specific aspects of the scheme. The last two of

---

[36] The United Kingdom, the Republic of Ireland, the Channel Islands and the Isle of Man.

[37] The A8 countries are Czech Republic, Estonia, Hungary, Latvia, Lithuania, Poland, Slovakia and Slovenia. Malta and Cyprus, which also acceded on 1 May 2004, are excluded as Commonwealth countries.

[38] *Carson & Reynolds v Secretary of State* [2005] UKHL 29.

[39] Full details of benefits available overseas can be obtained from the DWP International Pension Centre, Tyneview Park, Whitley Road, Benton, Newcastle Upon Tyne NE98 1 BA. See also www.dwp.gov.uk/international/.

[40] *Secretary of State for Work and Pensions v Burley* [2008] EWCA Civ 376 (23 April 2008).

these altered the decision-making and appeals system. In addition there is the Social Security Administration (Fraud) Act 1997 and the Social Security Fraud Act 2001, dealing with issues of social security fraud.

10.48 Other statutes introduce new benefits from time to time, for example, pension credit was introduced by the State Pension Credit Act 2002 and universal credit and personal independence payments was introduced by the Welfare Reform Act 2012.

Regulations

10.49 Statutes set out the general framework of the social security scheme, and the flesh is then added by regulations which provide the detailed rules for entitlement to particular benefits and regulate the claims, payments and appeals procedures. These are frequently amended, sometimes as uplifts to rates of benefits paid or to resolve a confusion or close a perceived loophole.

Directions

10.50 Sometimes even more flexibility is retained by reserving power to the Secretary of State to issue directions as to the manner in which particular claims are to be dealt with. These directions are issued to local DWP offices and treated as if they were regulations, but they are not published and can be amended from time to time with the minimum of formality, so that a claimant is sometimes unable to ascertain whether benefit should be payable and there is no appeal against an adverse decision. Whilst they may be a useful interim stage in the process of formulating regulations, all too often they continue in force for years without being converted into regulations.

Benefits

Categories

10.51 Benefits fall into three main categories:

(1) contributory benefits such as retirement pension, entitlement to which depends on a qualifying National Insurance Contributions (NIC) record, regardless of means;

(2) non-contributory benefits such as attendance allowance, entitlement to which depends on other qualifying conditions regardless of personal means; and

(3) income-based benefits such as pension credit, entitlement to which depends on a means-test.

Christmas bonus

10.52 A non-taxable Christmas bonus is paid to those receiving a qualifying benefit, such as attendance allowance, retirement pension or pension credit.

Contributory benefits

Retirement pension

Qualifying

10.53 A taxable pension is paid to those who attain state pensionable age[41] provided they qualify and make a claim. It is possible for a claimant to be working full-time and also receive a state pension. In order to qualify for the full pension the claimant must have a complete record of NICs, as an inadequate record will result in a reduced pension or no pension at all.[42]

10.54 Claimants who reach pension age on or after 6 April 2010 must have 30 years paid or credited contributions to receive a full pension. Anyone with fewer than 30 years contributions will be entitled to 1/30th of the state pension for each year of contributions. The reduced contribution paid by some married women does not count towards a pension. However claimants aged over 80 can claim a pension even if they have not paid any contributions, provided they were resident in England, Scotland or Wales for 10 years or more in any continuous period of 20 years, before they reached 80 years and were 'ordinarily resident'[43] in the UK, Channel Islands, Isle of Man, Gibraltar, a EEA country or Switzerland.

10.55 In respect of claimants who reached state pension age before 6 April 2010, women needed to have 39 years paid or credited contributions to get a full pension and men needed 44 years. To get the lowest amount of pension claimants need 10 or 11 qualifying years, depending on their state pension age. Any fewer qualifying years than this, and the claimant will not get any state pension.

Types

10.56 There are two principal types of pension:

(1)   Category A – earned by the claimant's own contributions. This can include the contributions paid by a former spouse or civil partner during the marriage or civil partnership;

(2)   Category B – claimed on the National Insurance record of the spouse or former spouse, or the civil partner or former civil partner. This is paid at a lower rate.

10.57 A person who has reached pension age and who has insufficient contributions of their own to claim a Category A pension will be able to claim a Category B pension on the contributions of their spouse or civil partner provided:

(a)   they were married or in a civil partnership when they reached pension age;

(b)   both partners are over pension age;

(c)   the partner satisfies the contribution conditions; and

---

[41]   At present 65 for men. From April 2010 the retirement age for women born between 6 April 1950 and 6 April 1955 is being increased in stages to 65. Their pension age will rise by one month every two months until 2018. By 2020 the retirement age for both sexes will rise to 66.

[42]   A comprehensive pension forecast by writing to the Future Pension Centre, The Pension Service, Tyneview Park, Whitley Road, Newcastle upon Tyne NE98 1BA, or online from www.gov.uk/state-pension-statement.

[43]   This term is explained in detail in Chapter 7.

(d)   the partner is entitled to a Category A retirement pension.[44]

For those born before that date, the old (more restricted) rules apply.

10.58 A widow, widower or surviving civil partner is entitled to a Category B pension where their late spouse or civil partner fulfilled the contribution conditions or died as a result of industrial injury or disease. This is paid at the same rate as a Category A pension. In addition, the claimant must fulfil one of the following conditions:

(a)   They had reached pension age when their partner died. A person who reaches pension age before 6 April 2010 cannot claim under this rule. If the survivor is a widower or a surviving civil partner, both parties must have reached pension age. This rule only applies to claimants reaching pension age before 6 April 2010.

(b)   They were entitled to a widows pension (or, if a man, would have been so entitled) because of the death of their late spouse. This rule only applies to those whose spouses died on or after 9 April 2001. It does not apply to a widower who reaches pension age before 6 April 2010.

(c)   The claimant has not remarried or cohabited since their partner's death and is entitled to a bereavement benefit as a result of their death.

10.59 The Pensions Bill 2013 plans to reform the state pension to make it simpler and fairer. It will create a single rate only available for those who have made a minimum level of NICs. Pension credit and other means-tested benefits will continue to provide a safety net, but the savings credit element of pension credit will be abolished.

Amount

10.60 The state pension is made up of three components, namely:

(1)   basic pension – a fixed weekly sum which is uprated annually;

(2)   additional pension – paid to those who qualify based on contributions made after April 1978 to the state earnings related pension scheme, (often called 'SERPS' or 'second state pension' both known as the additional state pension); and

(3)   graduated pension – paid to those who qualify based on contributions made between April 1961 and April 1975.

Additions

10.61 Those who were receiving additions for dependents including a spouse or civil partner before 6 April 2010 continue to do so, although no new entitlement exits after this date. An age addition of 25p per week is paid on reaching the age of 80.

Deferment

10.62 If the state pension is deferred for at least 5 weeks, the claimant will receive an extra payment. The rate is 10.4% for each year of deferral. Alternatively, provided they defer their pension for at least 12 months, the claimant can elect to receive a lump sum representing the unclaimed amount plus interest at 2% above Bank of England base rate, plus their weekly pension paid at the normal rate. The rules also provide for certain payments to be made to a surviving spouse or civil partner if the claimant dies before

---

[44]   'Partner' here means spouse or civil partner, but not cohabitee.

receiving their enhanced pension. Where the claimant elects to defer their pension, the amount deferred will not be treated as notional income for the purposes of the income-based benefits.

Bereavement benefits

Qualifying

10.63 Bereavement benefits are only payable to people below pension age, whose spouse or civil partner dies, where they have made sufficient NICs.[45] Women widowed before 9 April 2001 may continue to receive widow's benefits for as long as they qualify for them, but no new claims are possible.

10.64 For men whose wives died before 9 April 2001, there was no access to widow's benefits. This position has been repeatedly challenged, with the result that men with dependent children have been able to claim, but men without dependent children have not.[46]

10.65 Bereavement benefits will not be paid where the claimant is living with someone else as husband and wife, or as civil partners but without entering into a formal civil partnership or the claimant is in prison or legal custody.

Bereavement allowance

10.66 Bereavement allowance is a taxable benefit and is dependent on:

(1)   the NICs of the claimant's spouse or civil partner, although if death occurred because of an industrial injury or disease, their NICs do not matter;
(2)   the claimant being over the age of 45 at the date of death of the spouse or civil partner; and
(3)   the claimant not being entitled to widowed parent's allowance.

The rate of bereavement allowance may be reduced if the claimant's late spouse or civil partner did not pay enough NICs. The rate depends on the claimant's age when their spouse or civil partner died. It is only payable for 52 weeks following the date of death of the spouse or civil partner. If the claimant reaches state pension age before the end of the 52 weeks, they will no longer qualify.

Widowed parent's allowance

10.67 Widowed parent's allowance is a taxable benefit which includes a basic allowance for the claimant and any qualifying entitlement to additional related pension.

10.68 Entitlement requires the claimant to be in receipt of or entitled to child benefit in respect of any dependent child (or expecting a child of the claimant's late husband, with whom she was living at the date of his death, or pregnant as a result of artificial insemination and living with the deceased spouse or civil partner at the date of his death)

---

[45]   SSCBA 1992, ss 36–42; Social Security (Widow's Benefit and Retirement Pensions) Regulations 1979, SI 1979/642.
[46]   See R *(on the application of Hooper)* v *Secretary of State for Work and Pensions* [2005] UKHL 29; *Willis* v *United Kingdom* [2002] 2 FCR 743, [2002] 2 FLR 582; *Runkee and White v United Kingdom* (10 May 2007, Application Nos 42949/98 and 53134/99).

and the deceased spouse or civil partner having made sufficient NICs prior to death. This benefit is available to widowers, whose wife died prior to the introduction of this benefit.

Bereavement payment

10.69 Bereavement payment is a tax-free lump sum payment of £2,000 payable following the death of a spouse or civil partner. The payment may only be claimed where:

(1)   the deceased spouse or civil partner was under the state retirement pension age at the date of death; or

(2)   the claimant was under the state retirement pension age at the date of the spouse's death; and either
  (a)   the deceased spouse or civil partner had paid sufficient national insurance contributions prior to their death; or
  (b)   their death was caused by an industrial injury or disease.

A claim for a bereavement allowance must be made within 12 months of the death.

Jobseeker's allowance

Contributory Jobseeker's Allowance

10.70 Entitlement to contributory jobseeker's allowance (JSA) depends on having paid sufficient NICs. The amounts payable are based on age and it is not means-tested. Payments will last for a maximum of 6 months.

10.71 The claimant must be available for work and actively seeking work and must sign a jobseeker's agreement setting out what steps they are required to take to find work. It is possible to work part-time[47] while receiving JSA, any earnings in excess of £5 per week being deducted from the benefit. If the claimant receives any occupational pension exceeding £50.00 per week, their benefit will be reduced by the amount which their occupational pension exceeds that sum.

Income-based job seeker's allowance

10.72 Income-based JSA is payable to those under 60 who are outside the prescribed categories for income-based allowances. It is means-tested. The claimant must be available for employment and actively seeking employment and must have entered into a jobseeker's agreement. It may be paid as a top-up to contributory JSA during the first 6 months of a claim.

10.73 The Welfare Reform Act 2012 has made changes to income based JSA, which will be incorporated into the new Universal Credit being phased in throughout the UK. The aim is that Universal Credit will fully replace income based JSA from April 2014. Contributory JSA remains unaffected.

---

[47]   Up to 16 hours a week.

Incapacity benefit

10.74 Incapacity benefit is payable only to those people who were claiming it on or before 27 October 2008, when it was replaced by Employment and Support Allowance (ESA). All people who were receiving incapacity benefit are in the process of being transferred onto ESA, which should be completed by April 2014. This may involve a reconsideration of the person's right to benefit. This also applies to people who received severe disablement allowance prior to April 2001, when incapacity benefit was introduced.

Employment and support allowance

10.75 Employment and Support Allowance (ESA) replaced incapacity benefit for claims made on or after 27 October 2008. The benefit is a combined contributory (based on the amount of NICs made) and means-tested benefit, aimed at those under state pension age who are unable to work due to illness or disability and do not qualify for jobseeker's allowance.

10.76 For the first 13 weeks of a claim, the claimant will be in the 'assessment phase', with proof of incapacity demonstrated by completing a questionnaire and sometimes a work capability assessment. After 13 weeks of ESA the claimants are put into either:

(1)　a Work-Related Activity Group, where they must have regular interviews with an adviser, with financial sanctions for non-attendance, payments limited to a year for contributions based ESA, although the person may reapply.

(2)　a Support Group, where the claimant is severely disabled or has a severe health condition. They will not be expected to look for work and will get the extra support they need. They will not have to take up any work related support unless they want to and their claim is not limited to a year.

10.77 Changes brought about by the Welfare Reform Act 2012 mean that income-based ESA is to be subsumed into Universal Credit, from April 2014 but contributory ESA remains largely unchanged.

Non-contributory benefits

Attendance allowance

Entitlement

10.78 Attendance allowance is a non-taxable, non-means-tested benefit paid to those over 65 years of age.[48] It is available where disability begins:

(1)　at or after age 65 years; or

(2)　before that age but where the claim is not made until after age 65 years.

If the claimant has not yet reached the age of 65 a claim should be made for Personal Independence Payment.

---

[48]　See the Social Security Contributions and Benefits Act 1992, ss 64–67.

Qualifying

10.79 The claimant must be ordinarily resident in Great Britain and must either be a British national or satisfy certain other nationality criteria. No payment can be made while the claimant is an in-patient in a NHS hospital or is in local authority funded care for more than 28 days.[49] The idea is that claimants should not be entitled to payment for care needs when those needs are already being met by the State or a local authority.

10.80 There is a 6-month qualifying period and the disability must be expected to last for at least a further 6 months. However these periods do not apply if a claimant is terminally ill,[50] in which case payment can be made immediately. The benefit claim form must be sent with form DS1500, which is completed by the patient's doctor, specialist or consultant.

Rates

10.81 Attendance allowance is payable at two rates:

(1) the lower rate, which is for those who need attention or supervision either by day or by night; and

(2) the higher rate, which is for those who need attention or supervision both day and night or who are terminally ill.

'Attention' means actual physical help to do something, not just being there to keep an eye on someone. It might also include prompting or encouraging someone to perform an activity such as getting dressed; they might be physically capable of doing it without help but might, through lethargy or mental health problems (depression, confusion etc) be unlikely to do it if left to their own devices. It is attention which is reasonably required which counts, not that which is actually provided, so that a person struggling to cope alone without help could qualify.

10.82 'Supervision' is different from attention in that 'supervision' means keeping an eye on someone and being ready to intervene to reduce the risk of harm, whereas attention is actually intervening and assisting. Since elderly people can be frail, and thereby more likely to suffer injury when falling and less likely to be able to get up after a fall, it may be argued that if the claimant has a propensity to fall, eg because of dizzy spells, poor balance, stiffness etc, they reasonably require continual supervision during the day and thereby qualify for lower rate attendance allowance.

10.83 Quite often elderly people will try their best to cope with everyday living on their own, without help which they might well require, out of a sense of independence and pride, and also perhaps out of fear that if they are seen to be in need of help they may be forced out of their home and into residential care. It is therefore important to look beyond the stated needs, which may well be understated, and to consider what help is actually required. It is also essential to discount whatever help is in fact being given, by relatives or neighbours, and to consider instead how the claimant would cope if left entirely to their own devices.

---

[49] Social Security (Attendance Allowance) Regulations 1991, SI 1991/2740, regs 7 and 8. Note this does not apply to a non-publicly funded facility, eg a hospice.

[50] Ie expected to die within 6 months.

10.84 Difficulties can arise if the claimant's condition is variable, i e sometimes they need help but at other times, when their disability is not so bad, they can manage. In such cases, it may be necessary to look at quite a long period, perhaps of several months, to get an accurate assessment.

Duration

10.85 Once awarded, attendance allowance will continue to be paid irrespective of age for as long as the qualifying criteria continue to be satisfied. The benefit also serves as a passport to certain other benefits.[51] The benefit can be awarded either for a fixed period or for an indefinite period. Obviously if the claimant's condition is expected to improve, either naturally or because of treatment a fixed-term award will be appropriate, whereas if the condition is never likely to improve an award for an indefinite period (i e for life) could be made.

10.86 Attendance allowance can continue to be claimed for temporary trips abroad for up to 13 weeks (or 26 weeks if it is for medical treatment). For those who are habitually resident in an EEA country[52] or Switzerland they can continue to be eligible if the claimant has paid enough National Insurance to qualify for contribution-based benefits and is getting State Pension, Industrial Injuries Benefit, contribution-based ESA or bereavement benefits.[53]

Personal independence payments

Entitlement

10.87 From April 2013, personal independence payments (PIP) have replaced disability living allowance for all new applicants, aged 16 to 64 who are ordinarily resident in Great Britain. It is a non-taxable, non means-tested benefit. If a claimant or their partner receive PIP, they are exempt from the benefit cap.[54] Receipt of PIP is a route to carer's allowance and Motability.

10.88 There is a 3-month qualifying period and the disability must be expected to last for at least a further 9 months. However these periods do not apply if a claimant is terminally ill,[55] in which case payment can be made immediately. The benefit claim form must be sent with form DS1500, which is completed by the patient's doctor, specialist or consultant.

Qualifying conditions

10.89 PIP has two parts and two rates to each part:

(1) A person is entitled to the 'daily living component':
    (a) at the standard rate if the person's ability to carry out daily living activities is limited by the person's physical or mental condition; or

---

51 Social Security Contributions and Benefits Act 1992, ss 71–76.
52 EEA Countries are Iceland, Liechtenstein, Norway and all EU member countries.
53 Applications are via the Exportability Team Room C216, Pension, Disability and Carers Service, Warbreck House, Warbreck Hill Road, Blackpool, FY2 0YE.
54 Benefit cap has been introduced so that claimants cannot receive more than a set amount in benefits, even if their full entitlement would otherwise be higher. The cap is set at the average net earned income of working households.
55 Ie expected to die within 6 months.

(b) at the enhanced rate if the person's ability to carry out daily living activities is severely limited by the person's physical or mental condition.

(2) A person is entitled to the 'mobility component':
  (a) at the standard rate if the person's ability to carry out mobility activities is limited by the person's physical or mental condition; or
  (b) at the enhanced rate if the person's ability to carry out mobility activities is severely limited by the person's physical or mental condition.

Duration

10.90 Awards will be for a fixed term except in exceptional cases. At the end of the fixed period the person will have to re-apply.

The assessment

10.91 The assessment for PIP will look at how difficult the claimant finds activities of daily living and getting around when they are not at home. They are assessed on their ability to perform a list of activities concerning daily living, and activities concerning mobility, which are prescribed by the regulations.[56] Points are awarded based on the amount of difficulty they have doing each activity. If the claimant scores a total of between 8 and 11 points for daily living or for mobility they will be awarded the standard rate for that component. If they score 12 points or more they will receive the enhanced rate. If they do not qualify for at least the standard rate they will not qualify for PIP.

10.92 The assessment is usually a face-to-face meeting with an independent health care professional. On 5 March 2013 the regulations[57] were amended to make clear that, when assessing whether an individual can carry out an activity, the assessor must look at whether the claimant can carry out that activity: safely; to an acceptable standard; repeatedly and in a reasonable time period.

Motability

10.93 If a claimant is awarded higher rate mobility component for at least 12 months, they can exchange the award for a car under the Motability scheme, a registered charity, established in 1977. The claimant can use their allowance towards the costs of obtaining a car, via contract hire; hire purchase of a new car; or hire purchase of a used car.

10.94 The contract hire scheme is the most popular, and applicants will need at least a 3-year award from the date of expected delivery of the car. A relative or carer can be nominated to drive the car instead of the disabled person. There are about 500 approved vehicles and there are dealers throughout the country who are involved in the scheme. The benefit can be paid direct to the dealer. Under the contract hire scheme the applicant never actually owns the car but the costs of maintenance, insurance, servicing and breakdown assistance are all included in the payments. Adaptations to the car are restricted and excess charges will be incurred for mileage over 12,000 per year.

10.95 If the hire purchase route is followed the applicant will ultimately own the car but must pay all running costs. The car must be comprehensively insured, there are no

---

56 SI 2013/377.
57 Social Security (Personal Independence Payment) (Amendment) Regulations 2013, SI 2013/455 amending Social Security (Personal Independence Payment) Regulations 2013, SI 2013/377.

mileage charges and any adaptations may be carried out. A used car acquired on hire purchase must be AA inspected but AA membership is included as part of the agreement.

10.96 In addition to assisting with acquiring cars as above, Motability raises funds to help meet the cost of special equipment and adapted cars for those most severely disabled and administers the government's Mobility Equipment Fund which gives grants for specially adapted cars.

Disability living allowance

Entitlement

10.97 Disability living allowance (DLA) is a non-taxable and non-means tested weekly benefit paid to those who are severely disabled, aged under 65 years and who either cannot walk or need guidance or supervision while walking (the mobility component) or who need help to look after themselves or need supervision in the home (the care component).[58]

10.98 Claimants may qualify for either or both components, each of which is paid at three levels and the higher rates in each case may comprise a passport to certain other benefits.

Transition to Personal Independence Payment

10.99 No new applications can be received for adults, as it has been replaced by personal independence payment (PIP) although DLA remains available for children.

10.100 Payments will cease when the claimant is in a NHS hospital or local authority funded care for more than 28 days,[59] and will then need to reapply for PIP. If the individual reports a change in their condition or the fixed period comes to an end they must reapply for PIP.

10.101 DLA will continue to be paid for those:

(1) who are entitled to an indefinite award and their condition remains the same, although by 2015, the DWP will contact each claimant to apply for PIP as there is no automatic transition;

(2) who are aged 65 and over for as long as the qualifying criteria continue to be satisfied. Any changes in circumstances will be dealt with under the attendance allowance rules.

Carer's allowance

Entitlement

10.102 Carer's allowance (CA) is a weekly allowance with additions for dependants, paid to the carer of someone in receipt of attendance allowance; the middle or highest rate care component of disability living allowance or the daily living component of

---

58 Social Security Contributions and Benefits Act 1992, ss 71–76, Social Security (Disability Living Allowance) Regulations 1991, SI 1991/2890.
59 Social Security (Disability Living Allowance) Regulations 1991, reg 10.

personal independence payments.[60] It is also payable where the person being cared for is receiving constant attendance allowance (ie is entitled to an industrial disablement pension based on a 100% assessment and requires constant attendance). It is an earnings substitute, so is taxable but provides Class 1 NICs credits. The claimant must be 16 or over.

Qualifying

10.103 In order to qualify, the carer must be caring for the individual concerned for more than 35 hours a week. What constitutes 'caring' is not defined in the regulations. The carer is allowed to work while in receipt of CA but must not normally earn more than a prescribed earnings limit in a week.[61] If the earnings limit is exceeded in any one week, entitlement to CA ceases altogether for that week unless it is a week during which the carer is not caring for the disabled person.

10.104 If two individuals are being cared for it is not permissible to add the hours together to make 35, eg caring for one for 20 hours and the other for 15 hours will not suffice – the carer must spend at least 35 hours caring for one of them. Only one allowance can be claimed no matter how many persons are being cared for.

Effect on other benefits

10.105 CA overlaps with other benefits[62] so the claimant cannot receive both. It counts as an income resource for universal credit and pension credit but recipients under retirement age are not required to be available for employment and will receive the carer's premium. Married women may claim even if they would not otherwise have worked. However, if a woman claims, her husband cannot claim an addition for her in respect of any benefit he is claiming, and since CA is taxable, whereas a dependent increase is not, she may need to consider this carefully. A pension credit claimant is also entitled to an extra payment if they are receiving CA, or if they qualify for it but it is not in payment because it overlaps with their retirement pension.

10.106 Payment of the benefit will come to an end if either the disabled person's receipt of attendance allowance, disability living allowance, personal independence payments or constant attendance allowance ceases or the disabled person has been in hospital for 4 weeks.

National Insurance credits for carers

10.107 'The Home Responsibilities Protection Scheme' existed until 6 April 2010 but has been replaced with a scheme whereby, for the purposes of qualifying for Category A and Category B retirement pensions, widowed parent's allowance and bereavement allowance, a person is awarded national insurance credits for each week in which they are a carer. Entitlement under the old home responsibilities protection scheme is preserved by the new scheme.

---

[60] Social Security Contributions and Benefits Act 1992, s 70.

[61] £100 after tax per week for 2013/14.

[62] Ie Bereavement Allowance, contribution-based Employment and Support Allowance, contribution-based Jobseeker's Allowance, Incapacity Benefit, Industrial Death Benefit, Maternity Allowance, Severe Disablement Allowance, State Pension, Unemployability Supplement – paid with Industrial Injuries Disablement Benefit or War Pension, War Widow's or Widower's Pension, Widowed Mother's Allowance, Widowed Parent's Allowance or Widow's Pension.

10.108   A carer is classified as someone who is caring for at least 20 hours a week for someone who gets attendance allowance, constant attendance allowance or the middle-rate or highest-rate care component of disability living allowance, or the daily living component of personal independence payments.

Working tax credit

Eligibility

10.109   Working tax credit[63] is a means-tested but non-taxable benefit aimed at those who have a low income. The credit is administered by the HM Revenue and Customs (HMRC) and paid by the employer (in the case of employed claimants) or HMRC (in the case of self-employed claimants). It is being phased out with the introduction of universal credit.

10.110   Working tax credit is payable to claimants:

(1)   who are over 16 years of age and work at least 16 hours a week and either:
    (a)   have a dependent child;
    (b)   have a disability which puts them at a disadvantage in getting a job; or
    (c)   is aged 60 years or over.

(2)   who is aged over 25 years, work for at least 30 hours a week.

With effect from April 2012, the time for which a couple with children must work increases to 24 hours a week. The requirement to work these minimum hours continues throughout the claim and the claimant must notify the Revenue of any change which might affect entitlement. Changes to the claimant's circumstances or income must be reported within one month.

Components

10.111   There are basically four potential elements to the credit:

(1)   a basic element payable to all claimants;

(2)   an additional disability element;

(3)   an additional 30 hour element; and

(4)   an additional childcare element covering 70% of childminding costs, subject to maximum.

The exact credit varies depending on circumstances and income.

Industrial injuries disablement benefit

Entitlement

10.112   Industrial Injuries Disablement Benefit (IIDB) is a weekly non-taxable benefit payable to those who have been in employment and have:

---

[63]   Tax Credits Act 2002.

(1)   either suffered an accident at work or contracted a specific disease or medical condition (such as deafness)[64] while working in a prescribed occupation; and

(2)   been assessed as being more than 14% disabled (1% if the claimant has contracted byssinosis or even less than 1% if pneumoconiosis has been diagnosed). If the disability is assessed at less than these percentages then no payment is made (although if the claimant has a number of disabilities the percentages can be added together).

IIDB can be paid either for a fixed period or for life. IIDB will be taken into account as income if the claimant receives a means-tested benefit, such as pension credit. The amount paid depends on the age of the claimant and the extent of their disability.

Income based benefits

Pension credit

Introduction

10.113   Pension credit (PC) was introduced by the State Pension Credit Act 2002.[65] It is in two parts:

(1)   guarantee credit, which tops up income to an annually set minimum level; and

(2)   savings credit, a benefit for those aged at least 65, which rewards them for making provision for themselves in addition to the state retirement pension.

To claim guarantee credit, the claimant must at least have reached state pension age. As women's pension age increases from April 2010, the minimum age for pension credit increases with it. In the case of a couple, one or both must have reached pension age. To claim savings credit, the claimant (or his partner if any) must be 65 or over. It can be paid with guaranteed PC or on its own. A couple, whether of the same or different sexes, and whether married or not, make a single claim.

Guarantee credit

10.114   In order to claim guarantee credit, a person must:

(1)   be aged 60 or over;

(2)   be present in Great Britain, and satisfy the 'habitual residence' test;

(3)   not be subject to immigration control; and

(4)   has income below the minimum guarantee sum.

The assessment

10.115   Benefit is payable irrespective of the amount of capital, but there is a 'tariff income rule' whereby income is deemed to be received from any capital in excess of £10,000 at the rate of £1 a week for every £500 or part of £500. Thus capital of £12,500 attracts a tariff income of £5 and capital of £14,250 attracts a tariff income of £9.00 a week.

---

[64]   There are 70 different qualifying medical conditions. Details are available on the gov.uk web site.
[65]   State Pension Credit Act 2002; State Pension Credit Regulations 2002, SI 2002/1792.

10.116   The following are not included when calculating income: attendance allowance, Christmas bonus, disability living allowance, personal independence payments, housing benefit or council tax reduction.

10.117   Guarantee credit consists of the amount by which a person's income falls short of their requirements (the 'applicable amount'). Requirements are calculated by reference to a figure known as the 'standard minimum guarantee', which is increased annually and varies depending on whether the claimant is single or married and if married whether they have a polygamous marriage, with additional sum being added for each additional spouse.

10.118   Certain people are entitled to additions, namely:

* single people or couples who are severely disabled;[66]
* a carer[67] (whether single people or a couple);
* Housing costs, such as mortgage interest payments.

Savings credit

10.119   Savings credit is extra pension credit payable to reward those who have made provision for themselves, either by savings or by extra qualifying income such as a private pension. They are awarded 60p for every pound of qualifying income, subject to a maximum sum. Once income rises above a threshold, this figure diminishes until no more benefit is payable.

10.120   A claimant for savings credit must be at least 65. If they are a couple, at least one must be 65. In order to qualify for savings credit, a claimant must have qualifying income above the savings credit threshold. This is approximately the same as the state retirement pension.

Universal credit

Transition

10.121   Universal credit[68] (UC), is a new means tested single payment for people who are looking for work or on a low income and is introduced gradually from October 2013, so that by April 2014 all new claims will be for UC, instead of the benefits it replaces.

10.122   UC replaces income-based jobseeker's allowance, income-related employment and support allowance, income support, child tax credits, working tax credits and housing benefit. Pensioners will still be able to claim housing benefit up until October 2014. From the end of 2015 until October 2017 claimants receiving housing benefit will be transferred to UC on a local authority boundary basis.

---

[66]   Ie the claimant receives attendance allowance, the middle or higher rate care component of disability living allowance, constant attendance allowance, or daily living care component of personal independence payment; no non-dependant lives with the claimant; and nobody receives carer's allowance for looking after them.

[67]   Who is in receipt of carer's allowance.

[68]   Universal Credit Regulations 2013, SI 2013/376.

Eligibility

10.123   Claimants must be:

- over 18 years and under pension credit age;
- present in Great Britain;
- not in education; and
- accept a claimant commitment based on the group assigned.

If one of a couple does not meet any of the conditions, that person will be ignored for the purposes of calculating the UC maximum amount, although their savings/capital, income and earnings (with some disregards, such as the claimant's home) will be taken into account. If one member of a couple is over pension credit age, and the other one is under, both will have to claim UC unless they were already receiving pension credit when UC was introduced.

Conditionality groups

10.124   Those eligible are placed in a conditionality group based on their circumstances and capability, namely:

(1)   no work-related requirements;

(2)   work-focused interview requirement only;

(3)   work preparation requirement;

(4)   all work-related requirements; or

(5)   in work.

No work-related requirements

10.125   Claimants in this category have limited capability for work-related activity (LCWRA) either because they are earning above a specified threshold or are unable to meet any work-related requirements because of particular circumstances or capability, which includes carers who receive the carer's element or are providing care for a severely disabled person for at least 35 hours a week and those who have reached pension credit age (but are part of a UC claim because their partner has not).

Work-focused interview requirement only

10.126   Claimants in this category are required to attend regular work-focused interviews to discuss plans and opportunities for returning to work in the future. They are not required to apply for, or take up a job, or engage in work preparation activity as claimants are usually responsible for a child.

Work preparation requirement

10.127   Claimants in this group have limited capability for work (LCW) but are expected to attend training courses, prepare a CV or take part in the 'Work Programme', designed to assist claimants stay in touch with the job market. They are not required to take steps to apply for or take up work.

All work-related requirements

10.128 Claimants are required to look for and be available for full-time work of 35 hours a week but this can be less in certain circumstances, for example if the claimant has caring responsibilities or have physical or mental health problems.

In-work conditionality

10.129 Claimants whose income is below their earnings threshold, may still claim UC and may face conditionality requirements.

Calculation

10.130 The amount awarded depends on the income and circumstances of all the household members. There is a basic allowance with different rates for single people and couples and lower rates for younger people. There are additional amounts available for those with:

(1)   limited capability for work;

(2)   caring responsibilities;

(3)   housing costs;

(4)   minor children;

(5)   childcare costs.

Once this figure ('the work allowance') is ascertained, the claimant's earnings, other income, capital or savings are taken into account to work out the actual UC award. Earnings below the claimant's work allowance are ignored. Earnings over their work allowance is subject to a taper of 65%: meaning losing 65p of their maximum UC award for every £1 they earn over their work allowance.

10.131 Most unearned income[69] which the claimant could use to meet their living costs is taken into account in full, so their maximum UC award is reduced by £1 for every £1 of unearned income.

10.132 If the claimant's capital is below £16,000, the first £6,000 (£10,000 if they are in residential care) of their capital is disregarded when calculating entitlement, but thereafter the claimant is deemed to be receiving an income of £1 a week from each £250 (or part thereof) of the capital. This is known as 'tariff income'. The regulations set out what capital and income is to be disregarded in the means test and follow similar lines to the disregards applicable to the funding of residential care under the National Assistance (Assessment of Resources) Regulations 1992.[70]

The benefits cap

10.133 The UC benefit cap means that claimants cannot receive more than a set amount in benefits, even if their full entitlement would otherwise be higher. The cap is set at the average net earned income of working households.

---

[69]   Eg jobseeker's allowance (contributory), employment and support allowance, carer's allowance, bereavement allowance, widowed mother's allowance, widow's pension, industrial injuries benefit – excluding any increase where constant attendance is needed and for exceptionally severe disablement are taken into account.

[70]   SI 1992/2997.

10.134 If the claimant's total monthly income from the benefits included[71] in the cap is more than the benefit cap amount, and they are not covered by any of the exceptions[72] or earnings exception,[73] their UC will be reduced to bring them within the cap.

Income support

10.135 Income support is a means-tested benefit which is paid to those under 60 who are exempt from the requirement to register for work, eg because they are ill or disabled or have caring responsibilities.[74] It is possible for the claimant to work for up to 16 hours per week and for the claimant's partner to work up to 24 hours per week while receiving income support.

10.136 Where one of a couple is aged 60 or over and the other is aged under 60, the younger can claim income support for them both, or the elder can claim pension credit (subject to other qualifying conditions being met). The corresponding benefit for those who are required to sign on for work is income-based jobseeker's allowance.

10.137 Income support provides a basic weekly income for those of working age who have no other means of support or only a very limited income. If the claimant's capital is below £16,000, the first £6,000 (£10,000 if they are in residential care) of their capital is disregarded when calculating entitlement, but thereafter the claimant is deemed to be receiving an income of £1 a week from each £250 (or part thereof) of the capital. This is known as 'tariff income'. Those with over £16,000 will not qualify for income support.

10.138 Income support is being phased out between October 2013–April 2014 when it will be replaced by universal credit.

Eligibility

10.139 In order to qualify for income support a claimant must:

(1)   be resident in Great Britain and habitually resident in the Common Travel Area; and

(2)   have capital of less than £16,000;

(3)   not be in full time education; and

(4)   fall within one of the following groups:
    (a)   sick, disabled or pregnant;
    (b)   single parents with dependent children under the age of 7; or
    (c)   a carer in receipt of carers' allowance.

---

[71]   Benefits included in the cap are bereavement allowance, carer's allowance, contributory employment and support allowance (work related activity group – although there are some exceptions), contributory jobseeker's allowance, widowed mother's allowance, widowed parent's allowance and widow's pension.

[72]   The benefit cap does not apply if any member of the claimant's household receives the Limited Capability for Work Related Activity (LCWRA) element of universal credit, contributory employment and support allowance (support group), industrial injuries benefit, attendance allowance, a war pension, an armed forces and reserve forces compensation scheme payment, disability living allowance, or personal independence payment.

[73]   The claimant is exempt from the benefit cap for every month their earned income is £430 or more (2013/14).

[74]   Income Support (General) Regulations 1987, SI 1987/1967.

Calculation

10.140 The aim is to bring the weekly income up to an 'applicable amount' representing needs. Income support is calculated by deducting any income which the claimant and their spouse/partner may have from the applicable amount which is made up of three elements:

(1)   personal allowance – which depends on age and marital status;

(2)   premiums – based on age, disability and caring responsibilities;

(3)   housing costs-payable to claimants who have a mortgage.

Where the claimant has a partner and the claimant or their partner goes into a care home on a permanent basis, each member of the couple will be assessed for benefits individually. If the claimant or their partner goes into a care home for a temporary period, the couple's income and capital will be assessed jointly but their applicable amount will be either a couple's applicable amount under the normal rules or separate applications for a single person whichever is the greater.[75]

The social fund – reform

Overview

10.141 The Welfare Reform Act 2012 changed the discretionary Social Fund scheme from April 2013, which has resulted in the following reforms:

- Community Care Grants and Crisis Loans for general living expenses (including rent in advance) has been replaced by locally-based provision delivered by local authorities in England and devolved to the Welsh Assembly Government. Each local authority has discretion as to what type of help it provides in its area and how that will be funded.
- Crisis Loan Alignment Payments and other Crisis Loans which has been replaced by a national scheme of Short Term Benefit Advances, administered by the DWP.
- Budgeting Loans will continue to be available for claimants in receipt of legacy benefits until Universal Credit is fully rolled out by April 2014. It will be replaced by Budgeting Advances for Universal Credit recipients.

Discretionary Assistance Fund in Wales

10.142 The Welsh Government has set up the limited Discretionary Assistance Fund, administered by Northgate Public Services working in partnership with The Family Fund and Wrexham County Borough Council to provide Emergency Assistance Payments and Individual Assistance Payments.

The Individual Assistance Payment (IAP)

10.143 This is to help Welsh people on means-tested benefits and who are:

(1)   leaving an institution such as a hospital, care home or prison after having lived there for 3 or more consecutive months (or on a frequent or regular basis); or

---

[75]   Income Support (General) Regulations 1987, SI 1987/1967, reg 21 and Sch 7, para 9.

(2)   planning to care for someone leaving an institution as described above and neither the carer or leaver can afford to meet their needs; or

(3)   needing help that could stop admittance to an institution; or

(4)   part of a planned resettlement after a period of homelessness or leaving supported accommodation; or

(5)   experiencing exceptional and urgent pressures on their household, for example, due to domestic violence, chronic illness, disability or an accident; or

(6)   in need of help with a one-off or short-term travel expense which is essential to enable the claimant to continue to live independently.

The payment must be for items or services which are necessary to help the claimant live independently in the community. They are awards based on a single need, rather than a specific value or a regular on-going award. An IAP will generally not be awarded or the amount may be reduced, if the claimant or their partner have capital over £500, which is increased to £1000 where the claimant or their partner are of pension age.

The Emergency Assistance Payment (EAP)

10.144   This is to help Welsh people who are in financial need due to an emergency or a disaster and will otherwise suffer serious damage or risk to their family's health and safety, without EAP. The EAP can be used for such things as general living costs for day-to-day needs such as food, toiletries, heating or to obtain goods to replace things that have been stolen, damaged or destroyed. They are awards based on a single need, rather than a specific value or a regular on-going award.

Short-term Benefit Advances

10.145   Short-term Benefit Advances (STBAs) are only available, through the DWP, to people claiming any contributory or means-tested benefit, including universal credit and who can demonstrate there is a serious risk of damage to the health and/or safety of the claimant and/or their family because of their financial need. For example, it may be payable to pay for gas or electricity to avoid disconnection for people with health problems.

10.146   STBAs are dependent on the claimant being entitled to an eligible means-tested benefit, so for new benefit claims the decision maker will not make an advance unless they believe that the claimant is likely to be awarded the benefit once the claim has been processed. STBAs provide an advance payment of the claimant's future benefit award, with the advance being deducted from eventual benefit payments over a 3-month period, though this may be extended to 6 months in exceptional circumstances. There is no right of appeal against a refusal to offer a STBA or if awarded – the amount.

Budgeting loans/budgeting advances

10.147   Budgeting loans are being replaced by budgeting advances. Budgeting loans will still be available to those claiming the old means-tested benefits for at least 26 weeks until all remaining claimants have moved to universal credit. Thereafter they will be fully replaced by the budgeting advances.

10.148   The money, which is an interest-free loan can help pay for essential items like furniture, household equipment or clothing. It must be paid back within 2 years and the amount ranges from a minimum £100 to a maximum £1,500. At the time of writing, the amounts for budgeting advances is not yet set, but it should be repaid within one year, extendable to 18 months in exceptional circumstances.

10.149 Claimants are not eligible for a budgeting loan if they or their partner has more than £1,000 in savings. This amount is £2,000 if they or their partner is over state pension age. At the time of writing, the savings limit for budget advances has not been set.

10.150 Requests for a review of unsuccessful claims must be made in writing to Jobcentre Plus within 28 days of the decision, which can be further challenged, by asking the office of the independent case examiner to review the decision. This review should take no longer than 21 working days.

The regulated social fund

Overview

10.151 Payments from the regulated social fund are not discretionary but are payments which a claimant is legally entitled to receive provided they satisfied the qualifying eligibility rules. Accordingly the claimant has a right to request a review or to appeal to a First-tier Tribunal against any unfavourable decision made on their claim. The regulated social fund covers cold weather payments, winter fuel payments, funeral payments and maternity grants, and the first three are considered under the following headings.

Cold weather payments

10.152 These are automatically assessed by the DWP in periods of extreme cold weather, for those on certain means-tested benefits. Payments are at the standard rate of £25.00 per week for periods between 1 November and 31 March, when the average temperature in the claimant's area is forecast to be zero degrees centigrade or below for seven consecutive days.

Winter fuel payments

10.153 Claimants who are aged 60 or over will be entitled to a one-off non-taxable, non-means-tested, winter fuel payment, where on the qualifying date, being the third Monday in September each year, the claimant satisfies the following qualifying conditions of entitlement:

(1)   the claimant is aged 60 or over;

(2)   the claimant is not serving a custodial sentence, has not been receiving free in-patient treatment in a hospital for more than 52 weeks, and is not receiving pension credit, income-based employment and support allowance[76] or income-based jobseeker's allowance[77] and living in a care home;[78] and

(3)   the claimant is not subject to immigration control.

---

[76]   This will be replaced by universal credit by April 2014.
[77]   This will be replaced by universal credit by April 2014.
[78]   If the claimant meets all the other qualifying conditions save for being in a care home, they receive half the usual rate.

The claimant is entitled to a winter fuel payment[79] of £200 if they aged 60–79 inclusive and £300 if aged 80 or over. These figures have been temporarily increased in recent years to £250 and £400 respectively. Only one payment is made per household. Payments are automatic if the person is in receipt of state retirement pension, otherwise a claim needs to be made and thereafter future payments are automatic.

Funeral expenses payments

10.154 A funeral expenses payment[80] can be claimed via the DWP where the claimant or a member of their family takes responsibility for the cost of a funeral for a close family member and no other person could have taken primary responsibility for the cost of the funeral. The claimant (not necessarily the deceased person) must be in receipt of a qualifying benefit, which is one of the main income-based benefits.[81]

10.155 There is no fixed sum for a funeral payment. It covers necessary burial or cremation fees, certain other expenses like the cost of a journey to arrange the funeral and up to £700 for other costs such as the funeral director's fees, the coffin or flowers. However, only up to £120 can be paid in total if the person who died had a pre-paid funeral plan.

Housing benefit

Reform of housing benefit

10.156 The Welfare Reform Act 2012 introduced universal credit (commencing from October 2013, but being rolled out in phases) which will replace other means-tested benefits, includes housing benefit. Universal credit is calculated by way of a personal allowance and also housing costs; whether they consist of rent or of mortgage repayments. Housing benefit will disappear – eventually by November 2014. Universal credit will be administered by the DWP and local authorities will no longer be responsible for housing costs.

The regime

10.157 Housing benefit[82] can be claimed by people who have a low income and assists with paying rent for their home, whether or not they are in full-time work, and can be paid in addition to other benefits and occupational pensions. Claimants of income support or pension credit (guarantee credit) are 'passported' on to full housing benefit. It is paid by the local authority and claims must be made directly to the relevant local authority.

10.158 If the claimant is renting from the local authority, the benefit will in effect be a book entry in the local authority's accounts, and is known as a 'rent rebate', whereas if the claimant has a private landlord or is renting from a housing association the benefit will be called a 'rent allowance' and will involve an actual payment from the local authority.

---

[79] Social Fund Winter Fuel Payment Regulations 2000, SI 2000/729.
[80] Social Fund Maternity and Funeral Expenses (General) Regulations 1987, SI 1987/481.
[81] See *RM* v *SSWP* [2010] UKUT 220 (AAC) (1 July 2010).
[82] Housing Benefit Regulations 2006, SI 2006/213.

Eligibility

10.159 Housing benefit can be claimed by a person who:

(1)   has less than £16,000 capital, unless they are of pension age or over and receive guarantee credit;

(2)   is habitually resident or has the right to reside in the UK;

(3)   is not a full-time student;[83]

(4)   pays a commercial rent; and

(5)   is not getting income support where housing costs are included in the award.

Private tenants and Local Housing Allowance

10.160 Housing benefit which is paid to those who rent within the private sector is normally referred to as 'Local Housing Allowance' (LHA). The LHA rate is set based on rental prices in the local authority's area and the size of property the claimant is entitled to. This might mean that not all of the claimant's rent is covered by housing benefit because their home is larger than they are deemed to need or is too expensive. Some claimants are protected, for example, where one of the occupiers has died within the last 12 months, where rent will not be restricted for 12 months.

10.161 The claimant's rent will not include payments for fuel, food, or water charges. It can include certain service charges, provided their payment is a condition of occupying the property and not merely an optional extra. Eligible service charges include general management costs, gardens, areas for children, lifts, communal telephone costs, laundry facilities, and the cleaning of communal areas and windows. They also include the cleaning of the property being occupied where neither the claimant nor any member of their family can do it.

10.162 Where the claimant has lived in the property since before January 1996, the local authority must consider whether the accommodation is too large for the claimant, or the rent is unreasonably high. If it is, the local authority must consider whether the claimant or a member of their family is in a protected group, i e of pension age or over, incapable of work, or having a child living with them for whom they are responsible. Where the claimant is in a protected group, the local authority can restrict the rent, but only if there is suitable alternative accommodation available and it is reasonable for the claimant to move.

Pre-tenancy determinations

10.163 There is a scheme whereby the claimant can ask for a determination of rent to be made before entering into a tenancy agreement, to help to decide whether they can afford to take the tenancy. A rent assessment form is completed and signed by the claimant and the potential landlord and sent to the rent officer for determination.

10.164 If the claimant does not agree with the rent officer's assessment there is no right of appeal direct to the rent officer, nor to the First-tier tribunal. The claimant can ask the housing benefits office to request that the rent officer looks at the assessment again.

---

83   Partners of students, lone parents and disabled claimants are exempt from this rule.

Alternatively the claimant may seek judicial review of the rent officer's decision, and the court will set it aside if it is considered to be unreasonable.[84]

Social tenants

10.165　Local authority or housing association tenants of working age may have their housing benefit reduced if it is considered they have more bedrooms than they actually need, so that housing benefit is reduced by:

- 14% if the claimant has one spare bedroom;
- 25% if the claimant has two or more spare bedrooms.

Some households are protected from this reduction, including foster carers who have had a child placed with them, or have registered as a carer in the last 12 months, parents of a severely disabled child unable to share a room with a sibling and claimants over pension credit age.

Review

10.166　The claimant has the right to request that the housing benefit office review the claim if they are not happy with the decision made in respect of that claim. This request for a revision must be made within one month of the housing benefit office having sent their notification of benefit award to the claimant.

Discretionary housing payments

10.167　Discretionary housing payments (DHPs)[85] are administered by the local authority to assist in the provision of further financial assistance for those qualifying for housing and council tax benefit, where the benefit awarded is not sufficient to accommodate the claimant's housing costs. DHPs may be paid weekly, or can be a lump sum. The local authority can recover overpayment of a DHP but recovery cannot be made from any ongoing entitlement to housing benefit, council tax reduction or any other social security benefit. Any recovery must either be effected by agreement with the claimant, or by civil proceedings for debt in the county court.

10.168　There is no right of appeal to a tribunal in respect of DHP disputes, but the local authority must make provision for reviews internally.

Benefit cap

10.169　The benefit cap applies to people of working age and limits the total amount of benefit that they can receive each week. The limits are £500 for a couple or lone parent and £350 for a single person. The cap will be applied as a reduction in the amount of housing benefit awarded.

---

[84]　See, for example *R (on the application of Saadat) v Rent Service* [2001] EWCA Civ 1559.
[85]　Discretionary Financial Assistance Regulations 2001, SI 2001/1167, and the Child Support, Pensions and Social Security Act 2000, ss 69 and 70.

Council tax reduction

General

10.170   Local authorities set their council tax rate each year for each valuation band. The council tax bill may be reduced by the reduction scheme for disabled people, exemptions,[86] discounts,[87] council tax reduction or second adult rebate. The national council tax benefit scheme was abolished in April 2013 and is replaced by locally set council tax reduction (CTR).[88] Each local authority has its own CTR scheme, and so there is a postcode lottery on what the claimant will have to pay.

10.171   CTR can be claimed by people who have a low income and are liable to pay council tax. It can be claimed whether or not a claimant is in full time work and in addition to other benefits (including state pension) and occupational pensions.

Eligibility

10.172   A CTR award reduces the amount of council tax payable. People of working age are usually required to pay something towards their council tax bill, even if they were getting full council tax benefit before 1 April 2013. Pensioners with limited means are not affected, as they are entitled to the same level of CTR as they would have been if they were getting council tax benefit.

10.173   A pensioner getting the guarantee part of pension credit is entitled to a full reduction on council tax. However, if they have a non-dependent adult living in their household, the amount of CTR may be reduced. If they only get the savings part of pension credit but not the guarantee part, the local authority will use the Pension Service's calculation of income and capital to work out how much CTR they should get. CTR is not available if the claimant or their partner (regardless of age) has capital of over £16,000.

Second adult rebate in England

10.174   If the householder has a second adult living with them (who is not their spouse or partner) who is not liable to pay the council tax on the property, and that second adult has a low income or is on means-tested benefits,[89] the householder may claim a 'second adult rebate'. It is not possible to get a second adult rebate as well as CTR. The amount of rebate depends on the income of the second adult. Their capital is not taken into account. If the householder qualifies for both, the local authority should award the higher amount. The second adult rebate scheme does not apply to householders in Wales.

---

[86]   Eg where a property is unoccupied because the person who lived there now lives in a care home or has gone to care for someone else or property which is occupied only by people with severe mental impairment.

[87]   Commonly where the property is occupied by a sole person.

[88]   Council Tax Reduction Schemes (Default Scheme) (England) Regulations 2012, SI 2012/2886; Council Tax Reduction Schemes (Default Scheme) (Wales) Regulations 2012, SI 2012/3145 (W.317).

[89]   Income support, universal credit, pension credit, income-based jobseeker's allowance (jsa), income-related employment and support allowance (ESA).

Overpayments of DWP benefits

General

10.175 An overpayment of benefit may occur because the claimant has given incorrect information when making a claim, failed to report a relevant change in circumstances, the relevant office made an administrative error or the information was not taken into account correctly.[90] If the claimant has died, recovery can be effected from the estate provided there are duly appointed personal representatives, but not otherwise. The Welfare Reform Act 2012 makes recovery of overpayments easier by making most overpayments recoverable even if due to an official error. However the government has not set a date for when this provision will be brought into force.

10.176 If benefit has been obtained fraudulently a claimant can be prosecuted in the criminal courts, but so far as civil remedies are concerned an overpayment of a DWP benefit will only be recoverable in two situations:

(1)   where any person, whether fraudulently or otherwise, misrepresents or fails to disclose any material fact which it was reasonable for the claimant to have known and this results in the overpayment;[91]

(2)   if another benefit is subsequently paid to the claimant for the same period and the pension credit or income support or universal credit entitlement would have been less if the other benefit had been paid on time.[92]

Compensation for error

10.177 Claimants are entitled to compensation and interest if they are underpaid benefit as a result of clear error by the DWP and the delay in payment was more than 6 months. There is a guide used by the DWP, *Financial Redress for Injustice Resulting from Maladministration*. Requests for compensation should be sent to the office dealing with the claim and there is no appeal procedure, but if necessary a complaint could be made to the Parliamentary Ombudsman.

Challenging the DWP

Claims

10.178 The procedure for claims and appeals is dealt with in the Social Security Act 1998 and the Child Support, Pensions and Social Security Act 2000, as supplemented by regulations. The appropriate office must receive the relevant claim form, although many can be completed on line or with assistance over the telephone.

10.179 A decision on a claim should, if possible be made within 14 days although there is no sanction to enforce this directly. However, if no decision is made within a reasonable time consideration should be given to (i) lodging a complaint with the Parliamentary Ombudsman and/or (ii) applying for judicial review.

---

[90]   Social Security (Payments on Account, Overpayments and Recovery) Regulations 1988, SI 1988/664.
[91]   Social Security Administration Act 1992, s 71.
[92]   Social Security Administration Act 1992, s 74.

10.180   The Social Security Administration (Fraud) Act 1997 provides that a person who knowingly fails to disclose a change of circumstances is guilty of an offence and liable to prosecution. The information which must be disclosed is only that which would affect the amount of benefit.[93]

Backdating

10.181   In most cases the maximum period for which any benefit can be backdated is 3 months, but sometimes backdating is allowed in specified circumstances, for example[94] where qualification depends on the award of another benefit, backdating can be for a longer period. Retirement pension is the only benefit for which 12 months backdating is allowed.

Revisions and supersessions

10.182   It is open to the Secretary of State to revise the decision either on his own motion or on application by the claimant, within one month of the decision being given. From October 2013, applicants will have to ask for a 'mandatory reconsideration' before being allowed to appeal to the First-tier Tribunal against an unfavourable decision.[95]

10.183   Once the time for revision has elapsed a claimant can ask for supersession of a decision at any time, or the Secretary of State can supersede on his own initiative. The usual ground for a supersession is a change of circumstances (which may affect entitlement) since the original decision was made, but there are other grounds, usually where a decision is wrong in law or is based on a mistake as to the facts. Where the supersession is because of a new interpretation of the law by a commissioner or a court in a test case, arrears may not be backdated prior to that case, and where the case is decided after a decision which is being appealed the appeal tribunal cannot apply it in respect of any period which pre-dated it but must apply the law as previously understood.[96]

Appeals

Overview

10.184   Decisions of the Secretary of State, either as to entitlement or amount of benefit, can be challenged by appeal to the First-tier (Social Security and Child Support) tribunal (the First-tier Tribunal). The First-tier tribunal is administered by HM Courts and Tribunals Service, which is an executive agency within the Ministry of Justice. The process is governed by the Tribunal Procedure (First-tier Tribunal) (Social Entitlement Chamber) Rules 2008.[97] Financial assistance for legal representation at an appeal tribunal is not available.

10.185   Tribunals hearing appeals where capacity for work is in issue will consist of a judge sitting with a medical member. If the issue does not relate to the personal or work capability assessment but to some other aspect of these benefits such as an overpayment

---

[93]   *R v Passmore* [2007] EWCA Crim 2053.
[94]   Social Security (Claims and Payments) Regulations 1987, SI 1987/1968, reg 19(5)–(7).
[95]   These changes were brought in by the Welfare Reform Act 2012, s 102, but at the time of writing the operative details have not been published.
[96]   Social Security Act 1998, s 27(3).
[97]   SI 2008/2685.

or a failure to co-operate with the DWP, the appeal will be heard by a judge sitting alone. Tribunals hearing appeals relating to attendance allowance, disability living allowance or personal independence payments consist of a judge, a medical member and a person who is either disabled or has experience of people with disabilities. Tribunals hearing appeals against decisions relating to industrial injury benefits will consist of a judge sitting with either one or two consultants relevant to the appeal.

10.186 The tribunal can only consider the circumstances obtaining at the date of the decision appealed against,[98] and so any subsequent deterioration in the appellant's condition cannot be considered; the appellant will need to submit a new claim.

Mandatory reconsideration

10.187 From October 2013, it is mandatory to seek a reconsideration from the DWP office which made the decision, before being allowed to appeal to the First-tier Tribunal. The request for reconsideration must be made within one month of notification of the decision, or within 14 days of reasons for the decision being provided, if reasons were requested. This may be extended by up to 12 months if there are special circumstances which meant that a person could not apply for a reconsideration within one month.

10.188 There is no time limit for how long it should take for the matter to be reconsidered. Once the matter has been reconsidered, the claimant will receive a detailed 'Mandatory Reconsideration Notice' (MRN) that includes details of how to appeal directly to the First-tier Tribunal.

Appeals to the First-tier Tribunal

10.189 If the original decision is not superseded the claimant will need to make an appeal within one month, directly to HMCTS, SSCS Appeals Centre, PO Box 1203, Bradford BD1 9WP for cases in England and Wales, using form SSCS1, which must be completed and attach a copy of their MRN. The First-tier Tribunal will acknowledge receipt.

10.190 The relevant decision maker will send a 'decision maker's response', ie a bundle of documents which comprise a statement of the relevant facts, an explanation of the law involved and the reasons for the decision and copies of all relevant documents, including the reconsideration decision, within 28 days. The First-tier Tribunal will send the claimant an enquiry form (which must be returned to the tribunal within 14 days) to indicate whether an oral or a paper hearing (where all parties agree) of the appeal is required. Subject to any interlocutory issues that may need to be dealt with, eg as to further evidence or other directions required for an effective hearing, the appeal will be listed for hearing.

10.191 If the appellant has requested an oral hearing, at least 14 days' notice of the date, time and place of the hearing will be given to the appellant. The tribunal members will also be sent a copy of the decision maker's response in advance of the hearing. Withdrawal of an appeal can occur at any time before a final decision is made, even during the hearing itself. The procedure is to notify the clerk in writing if the hearing has not yet begun, or to notify the tribunal orally at the hearing.

---

[98] Social Security Act 1998, s 12(8)(b)).

10.192 Most appeal venues are now accessible to disabled people. In exceptional circumstances the hearing can take place in the appellant's home, where for example the appellant is too ill to travel at all, or where they suffer from a disabling condition such as agoraphobia.[99] Other methods of communication may be possible, such as video link.

The hearing

10.193 If an oral hearing has been requested, the appellant should attend in person if possible but the hearing may take place in their absence provided the appeal papers have been properly served at their last known address.

10.194 The procedure is informal and to a large extent determined by the judge although the rules of natural justice apply.[100] Formal representation is not strictly necessary, as the tribunal is inquisitorial in nature, not adversarial, and although impartial, regards itself as having an enabling role, ie by assisting an appellant to put forward their case in the best way they can. The judge must take a note, not a verbatim transcript, of the evidence given; evidence is not normally given on oath (although in appropriate cases it can be), and hearsay and documentary evidence are readily admitted.

Decisions

10.195 The decision of a two- or three-person tribunal can be either unanimous or by majority (in the case of disagreement in a two-person tribunal, the judge has the casting vote) and is usually notified at the conclusion of the hearing, with a summary written decision being handed out on the day. The tribunal has no power to award costs against the losing party. If either party wants a statement of reasons, they must request it within one month of receiving the summary decision (or 3 months if good cause for delay is established).

Correction, setting aside and supersession

10.196 Accidental errors or omissions in a tribunal decision can be corrected either by the clerk or by the judge. A party to the appeal can apply for the setting aside of a tribunal decision on the basis of a procedural error and a First-tier Tribunal can set aside a decision if it appears just to do so on the ground that:

(1)   a party or their representative was not present at the hearing; or

(2)   a relevant document was not received by a party or by the tribunal.

Applications to set aside must normally be made in writing within one month of notification of the decision, although a late application may be accepted for special reasons and the other party will be asked for comments on the application. The decision is usually made on the papers without any attendance by the parties, so should be accompanied by sufficient supporting information. There is no right of appeal to the Upper Tribunal against a refusal to set aside.

---

[99]   See *CIBJ2751/2002*, where the claimant suffered from agoraphobia, the judge allowed an appeal based in part on the Human Rights Act 1998.

[100]   Ie the right to be notified of the proceedings, the right to state your case and the right to be heard by an unbiased tribunal.

10.197 If new evidence comes to light which might have affected the decision, the Secretary of State has power to supersede the decision. A supersession should be asked for by the appellant in these circumstances (by writing to the relevant office). If given, it is treated as a new decision and carries a further right of appeal.

The Upper Tribunal

General

10.198 Appeals lie from First-tier Tribunal decisions, on points of law only, to the Upper Tribunal whose decisions are binding on First-tier Tribunals and the Secretary of State, so that such decisions comprise an additional source of law. The judges' decisions often contain a detailed analysis and interpretation of the law, and the most significant ones are reported. In complex cases a tribunal of three judges will be convened, otherwise the case may be dealt with by a single judge.

Grounds for appeal

10.199 The grounds for an appeal to the Upper Tribunal are:

(1) the decision was based on a mistaken interpretation of the law;

(2) inadequate reasons and/or findings of fact were recorded so that it is unclear how or why the decision was arrived at;

(3) the decision is not supported by any or any sufficient evidence and is therefore perverse; or

(4) there was a breach of the rules of natural justice.

Procedure

10.200 The appellant must seek leave to appeal from a First-tier judge, and request a full decision for evidence of an error on the face of the summary decision or a breach of the rules of natural justice. Most appeals are dealt with on written representations, although an oral hearing can be requested. Bundles of documents with submissions from both sides will need to be made, following which a judicial written decision will eventually be sent to the parties.

Decisions

10.201 The Upper Tribunal may:

(1) uphold the decision of the First-tier Tribunal;

(2) if the appeal is successful, make the final decision; or

(3) if the First-tier Tribunal did not determine all the material facts which are in dispute, send it back to another First-tier Tribunal with directions as to how it should be dealt with.

Courts

Appeal from the Upper Tribunal

10.202　Appeal lies from the Upper Tribunal, on a point of law only, to the Court of Appeal, but permission must be obtained from the Upper Tribunal within 3 months or, if refused, the court. Appeal lies from the Court of Appeal, also on a question of law only, to the Supreme Court.

Judicial review

10.203　An application may be made to the High Court or, sometimes, the Upper Tribunal, for judicial review in certain circumstances, but this is discretionary and will usually be refused if another remedy is available such as the normal appeal process.[101] Some benefit decisions are taken by the Secretary of State without a right of appeal so there is scope for judicial review where powers are improperly exercised, and excessive delay by the DWP in carrying out its statutory duties may also justify application.

European Court of Human Rights (ECtHR)

10.204　Any issue of law arising before a national court or tribunal concerning questions of interpretation or validity can be referred to the ECtHR for a preliminary ruling. Most benefit claims are brought under Article 14 (which provides that rights exercised under the Convention must be exercisable without discrimination). In order to bring a case under Article 14, the claimant must first show that one or more of his other rights under the Convention are being infringed.

10.205　A decision of the House of Lords[102] established that all benefits, whether contributory, non-contributory, or means tested, are possessions, and a claimant is entitled to enjoyment of his possessions under Article 1 of Protocol 1. However, it is still comparatively easy for the Secretary of State to argue that the discrimination in question is permissible because it is a proportionate means of achieving a legitimate (policy) aim.[103]

FUNDING COMMUNITY AND RESIDENTIAL CARE

Preliminary

10.206　Support provided or arranged by the local authority social services department are not necessarily free; means-testing applies to most forms of support provided by social services. There are two separate and distinct bases for levying charges and these depend upon whether the services comprise:

(1)　non-accommodation services, such as domiciliary care, home helps, meals-on-wheels etc; or

(2)　the provision of residential accommodation, usually in a care home.

---

[101]　*R v Chief Adjudication Officer, ex p Bland* (1985) *The Times*, 6 February.
[102]　*R (on the application of M) v Secretary of State for Work and Pensions* [2008] UKHL 63.
[103]　See for example *R (on the application of Carson) v Secretary of State for Work and Pensions* [2005] UKHL 37.

Free services

10.207 Local authorities are unable to change for certain services namely:

(1) social services support, advice, assessments and the administration associated with arranging and facilitating services;

(2) services provided as aftercare services under the Mental Health Act 1983, s 117;[104]

(3) intermediate care services, consisting of a time-limited, structured programme of care provided to assist a person to maintain or regain the ability to live in their home which must be provided free of charge for any period up to 6 weeks;[105]

(4) community equipment services (aids and minor adaptations costing less than £1,000);[106]

(5) services provided to a person with any form of Creutzfeldt Jacob Disease, or payments to people who have been infected with hepatitis C as a result of NHS treatment.

Charging for non-accommodation services

General

Power to charge

10.208 Local authorities have a discretionary power to charge for the non-accommodation services that they provide such as home help, meals-on-wheels and day centre placements. This power derives from the Health and Social Services and Social Security Adjudications Act 1983 (HASSASSAA 1983), s 17. In Wales the power to charge derives from the Social Care Charging Measure 2010.

10.209 The authorities are only empowered to charge for services provided under the statutes listed in the provision giving them this power. Although HASSASSAA 1983 does not specifically include services arranged under the Chronically Sick and Disabled Persons Act 1970, s 2 (the Disabled Persons Act), the Court of Appeal held that there is nothing in the Disabled Persons Act which has removed the right to charge for services provided under s 2, as such services are being 'provided under' the National Assistance Act 1948, s 29 which is listed in HASSASSAA 1983, s 17(2).[107]

10.210 Unlike the financial assessment for residential accommodation, it is not underpinned by regulations. Instead the Department of Health have issued mandatory guidance *(Fairer Charging Policies for Home Care and other non-residential Social Services)*, the current version of which was issued in June 2013. It is complemented by *The Fairer Contributions Guidance 2010: Calculating an individual's contribution to their personal budget*; the government's policy of personalisation, under which local authorities hand money over to those who qualify to enable them to buy in their own services. There is also Practice Guidance issued in 2002, that is no longer publicly available but which has not been officially superseded.

---

[104] See chs 7 and 8 of this publication for more detail.
[105] See ch 7 of this publication for more detail.
[106] See ch 7 of this publication for more detail.
[107] *R v Powys County Council, ex p Hambidge (No 1)* [1998] 1 FLR 643.

10.211 The Welsh Assembly issued policy guidance in 2011, *Introducing More Consistency in Local Authorities' Charging for Non-Residential Social Services*.[108] Where Welsh local authorities charge, it cannot be more than £50 per week and they cannot charge for transport to day care services where the transport is provided by or arranged by the local authority and the service user has been assessed as requiring the service to meet their needs.

Key Principles

10.212 The policy guidance includes a number of key principles, in particular:

- Flat rate charges are acceptable only in limited circumstances, such as for meals on wheels.

- Net incomes should not be reduced below the level of income support or guarantee pension credit plus 25% in England or 35% in Wales.[109]

- Where disability benefits are included as income, the local authority should assess the 'disability-related expenditure' of the service user, such as the cost of a private carer and community alarm. In Wales, this is set at 10% of the basic level of the disability benefit.

- Comprehensive welfare benefit advice should be provided to service users.

- The same savings disregard limits for residential care charges should be applied as a minimum.

- Earnings should be disregarded in assessments to encourage disabled people and their carers to work, where this is an option.

Means-testing assessable income and capital

10.213 Where a service user satisfies the local authority that they have insufficient means to pay the whole cost of the service, then the local authority must not charge that person (and not any other person) any more than it is reasonably practicable for him to pay.[110] The policy guidance reminds local authorities that they cannot require other members of an adult service user's family to pay anything towards the charges. Care must be taken where others hold assets which belong to the service user. If a spouse hold such assets, it may be appropriate for the local authority to ask the spouse to disclose the details of those assets. Local authorities should proceed on the basis of legal advice in such a case, but in the absence of disclosure they may be able to require the service user to pay the full cost on the basis that they are not satisfied that they have insufficient means to do so.

10.214 The value of the service user's home should not be taken into account, although other forms of capital may be, as set out in the *Charges for Residential Accommodation Guide (CRAG)*.[111] The effect of this is that if CRAG requires certain capital to be disregarded, the fairer charging policy requires the local authority to do likewise.[112]

---

[108] WAG10-12408, April 2011.
[109] At the time of writing Income support is being replaced by universal credit. It is envisaged that the guidance will be amended to reflect this change.
[110] HASSASSAA 1983, s 17(3); Section 7 of the Welsh Charging Measure.
[111] This is updated annually by the Department of Health and its Welsh equivalent by the National Assembly.
[112] *Crofton v NHS Litigation Authority* [2007] EWCA Civ 71, [2007] 1 WLR 923.

Means-testing state benefits

10.215 The current guidance does not reflect welfare reform changes and provides that the charging calculation must exclude earnings, working tax credit, child tax credit, savings credit, the mobility component of disability living allowance, war pensioners' mobility supplement, war widows' supplementary pension, and £10 per week of war disability pensions and war widows' pensions. It also excludes income received from the Independent Living (1993) Fund. Some of these benefits have been abolished and others are gradually being phased out.

10.216 The aim is that the service user's net income should not be reduced below the basic level of income support or guarantee pension credit, plus 25% in England or 35% in Wales. Income support is being abolished and gradually replaced by universal credit. There is no change to pension credit. The local authority may take disability-related benefits into account as income, but must offset against them the disability-related expenditure of the service user.

Disability-related expenditure

10.217 Available income may be dramatically reduced by disability costs. Any item where the service user has little or no choice other than to incur the cost in order to maintain their independence should be allowed to be deducted from assessable income and the practice guidance[113] provides it may include the following expenditure:

- community alarm;
- private care arrangements including respite care;
- specialist washing powders or laundry;
- special diets;
- clothing and footwear;
- additional bedding (eg because of incontinence);
- additional costs of special dietary needs of illness or disability;
- special clothing or footwear, if made or the nature of the disability causes greater wear and tear;
- extra heating or water (authorities must ignore winter fuel and cold weather payments);
- garden maintenance, cleaning and domestic help;
- purchase, maintenance and repair of disability-related equipment;
- personal assistance costs;
- other transport costs over and above the mobility component of disability living allowance.

However, disability-related expenditure must be calculated on a case-by-case basis, and not on the basis of general rules.[114] The local authority may not allow costs where there is a reasonable alternative available at a lower cost, such as the private purchase of incontinence pads as they are free on the NHS.

---

[113] Para 46 of the practice guidance.

[114] *R (B) v Cornwall County Council (Interested Party: The Brandon Trust)* [2009] EWHC 491 (Admin), affirmed by the Court of Appeal at [2010] EWCA Civ 55.

Direct payments in lieu of social care services

Personal budgets

10.218 As part of the government's personalisation agenda, service users may be allocated a personal budget to fund their care. In its most common form, it is paid as a direct payment, but it can also be:

- an account managed by the local authority, which is usually a 'virtual budget';
- an account held with a provider of care service but managed by the service user, such as an 'Individual Service Fund';
- an independent user trust also known as an 'independent living trust', which is managed by trustees on behalf of the service user.

Duty to make direct payments

10.219 Direct payments are an alternative to direct provision arranged by the local authority. The day-to-day control of the money and care package passes from social services to the service user, who contracts directly with the provider. This gives flexibility in choice and control in arranging services but for some creates a burden as they must negotiate contracts, set up tax records and pay tax, agree the level and detail of service and establish contingency plans in case arrangements break down.

10.220 Regulations[115] laid under the Health and Social Care Act 2001 (HSCA 2001), s 57 create a duty for local authorities to make direct payments to certain prescribed people who are assessed as needing community care services, or carers' services. Guidance has also been issued by the Department of Health in 2009[116] and by the Welsh Assembly in 2011.[117]

Eligibility

10.221 The local authority must offer a direct payment to anyone it has assessed as needing a care service, if that person is willing and able to manage the direct payment either alone or with assistance. This includes people who lack mental capacity to consent to receive them, so can be made to a willing and appropriate 'suitable person', who receives and manages the payments on their behalf.

10.222 Before making a direct payment for someone who lacks capacity, the local authority must first decide if it is appropriate to make a payment to a third party on behalf of the service user, and must consult and take into account the views of:

- anyone named by the service user to be consulted;
- anyone engaged in caring or interested in the service user's welfare;
- any deputy or attorney of the service user; and
- the service user.

---

[115] Community Care, Services for Carers and Children's Services (Direct Payments) (England) Regulations 2009, SI 2009/1887 and Community Care, Services for Carers and Children's Services (Direct Payments) (Wales) Regulations 2011, SI 2011/831 (W.125).

[116] Guidance on direct payments: for community care, services for carers and children's services, September 2009.

[117] Direct Payments Guidance Community Care, Services for Carers and Children's Services (Direct Payments) (Wales) Guidance 2011 with separate 'suitable person' guidance.

10.223 The guidance outlines the process to be followed for appointing a suitable person, the conditions to be met by them, how to resolve disputes, when advocacy may be appropriate and approaches to managing risk and safeguarding.[118] The process to establish who should be the suitable person is set out in the regulations, and is summarised as follows:

(1) Where the service user has an attorney acting with authority under a health and welfare lasting power of attorney or their deputy appointed by the Court of Protection whose powers relate to decisions about securing community care services to meet the person's needs, they can be the suitable person or veto the appointment of another suitable person.

(2) If the personal welfare attorney or deputy is unwilling or incapable of managing a direct payment or for some other reason the local authority consider them to be inappropriate to act as a suitable person, the local authority has discretion to choose an alternative person.

10.224 Direct payments cannot be made to people with a drug and/or alcohol dependency difficulty, who are subject to certain court orders or controls. However, people who have mental health problems and are subject to control under the Mental Health Act 1983 (MHA 1983) are not excluded from receiving a direct payment, but in such cases the local authority has a power and not duty to provide a direct payment.

Persons who cannot be providers

10.225 Certain categories of people will not be able to be paid to provide a service under the direct payment scheme, including:

(1) a spouse or civil partner of the payee;

(2) a person who lives with the payee as their spouse or civil partner (ie cohabitee);

(3) a person living in the same household as the payee who is the payee's:
    (a) parent or parent-in-law;
    (b) son or daughter;
    (c) son-in-law, daughter-in-law;
    (d) stepson or stepdaughter;
    (e) brother or sister;
    (f) aunt or uncle;
    (g) grandparent;

(4) the spouse, civil partner (or cohabiting as such) of any person specified in (a)–(g) above who lives in the same household as the payee.

The policy guidance states that even where the close relative is not living in the same household, they should still be excluded from the scheme unless the local authority 'is satisfied that that is the only appropriate way of securing the relevant services'.

Excluded services

10.226 Direct payments cannot be used for the purchase of permanent residential care, and any respite residential care purchased is limited to a cumulative total of 4 weeks in any 12-month period. However, in calculating the cumulative period only periods of

---

[118] Department of Health, September 2009; Welsh Assembly, 2011.

residential care less than 4 weeks apart are added together to make a cumulative total.[119] Direct payments cannot be used to purchase local authority provided services, although they may arrange some non-accommodation services for someone, as well as make direct payments.

10.227 The Care Bill 2013 proposes to extend direct payments to residential accommodation with the aim that, if passed, it will be brought into force by April 2016.

Amount of payment

10.228 The local authority has discretion as to the frequency of payments. The sum payable is the amount that the local authority determines (subject to a financial assessment of the individual), which is reasonable for the cost of the type of service needed. In estimating the cost, local authorities should include associated costs that are necessarily incurred in securing provision, without which the service could not be provided, or could not lawfully be provided, such as recruitment costs, National Insurance, statutory holiday pay, sick pay, maternity pay, employers' liability insurance, public liability insurance and VAT.

10.229 Individuals can adjust the amount they use from week to week and save any spare money to use as and when extra needs arise. So long as overall the payments are being used to secure the services they are for and the care plan objectives are met, the actual pattern of service does not need to be predetermined.

10.230 Local authorities commonly calculate the contribution based on a Resource Allocation System[120] (RAS), which provides an indicative amount to cover the cost of care. This will need to be reviewed and if necessary, it can be increased if it is insufficient to cover the cost of care. An inflexible or blanket approach to resource allocation will be unlawful.[121] As such, many local authorities adopt an 'Upper Banding Calculator' for those with exceptional needs. Ultimately the local authority will be arriving at a 'ball park' figure which they believe will be sufficient to purchase services to meet the assessed needs.[122] The local authority must give reasons to show how they have reached a decision about the sum allocated.[123]

10.231 If the recipient is unhappy with the amount of the direct payment or the assessed charge, then this should be resolved initially through discussion, failing which it should be pursued through the complaints procedure.

Charges for direct payments

10.232 Before the payment is made, the local authority will have undertaken a means test of the service user's resources. As such the service user may have to make a contribution towards the cost of their care. The direct payment will generally be the

---

[119]   Reg 13 of the English Regulations and reg 14 of the Welsh Regulations.
[120]   The Department of Health publication, 'Resource Allocation Tool 2: Step by Step Guide' (Gateway 9878, available at www.toolkit.personalisation.org.uk) which has as its sub-heading 'A practical guide to developing resource allocation systems for personal budgets' provides guidance on the different approaches on the allocation of resources.
[121]   *R (on the application of JL (A Child)) v Islington LBC* (2009) 12 CCLR 322.
[122]   Where the RAS tool and UBC is used, the process to arrive at the sum will be lawful – see *R (on the application of KM (By His Mother & Litigation Friend JM)) v Cambridgeshire CC* [2010] EWHC 3065 (Admin).
[123]   *R (on the application of Savva) v Kensington and Chelsea RLBC* [2010] EWHC 414 (Admin).

difference between the cost of care provision (as calculated by the RAS tool) less the amount the service user is assessed as being required to contribute.

Direct payments in lieu of health care services

10.233 The National Health Service Act 2006, s 12A gives CCGs the power to make direct payments to patients. It is underpinned by regulations.[124] The regime is identical to direct payments provided by local authorities, save that it is totally discretionary. The Welsh Assembly has no such plans to implement an equivalent scheme.

Paying for residential care

Meeting the charges

Fees

10.234 All care homes charge weekly fees to their residents, and the amount depends upon the nature and extent of the care provided as well as the quality and location of the particular home. The level of fees charged by homes providing nursing care is generally higher than those which provide solely personal care because of the cost of providing for those with greater needs.

10.235 Individuals who can afford to pay for a place in a home may arrange this independently with minimum formality.[125] Those who cannot meet the fees from their own resources must turn to their local authority for funding and this will depend upon an assessment of need for this type of care provider. Few homes are able to cater exclusively for private fee-paying residents, so the general level of fees tends to be dictated as much by what local authorities are prepared to pay as by market forces.

Charges and contributions

10.236 Those who enter a care home through an arrangement made by the local authority must pay for it, or contribute to the cost. Each local authority must fix a standard weekly charge for its own homes, which should represent the true economic cost of providing the accommodation and care. Where the local authority purchases a place from a home in the independent sector, the weekly charge should represent the cost of that place to the local authority.[126]

10.237 Residents are generally required to contribute in accordance with their resources up to the appropriate charge, but no one is required to pay more than this. The local authority either pays the agreed weekly fee to the home and collects the resident's contribution, or pays its share whilst the resident and (any third party)[127] pays the balance.

Homes of other authorities

10.238 A local authority may support a resident in the home of another authority outside its own area. The terms in such cases are agreed between the two authorities.

---

[124] National Health Service (Direct Payments) Regulations 2010, SI 2010/1000, Part 2.
[125] Chapter 6 sets out terms to consider when moving into a care home.
[126] NAA 1948, ss 22(2), 26(2).
[127] Chapters 6 and 7 sets out the role of the third party and top up payments.

The local authority managing the home should assess the resident's ability to pay in the usual way and collect the assessed contribution, accounting for this to the authority supporting the resident.[128]

Nursing by a registered nurse in a nursing home

10.239 Since the introduction of the Health and Social Care Act 2001 (HSCA 2001), nursing care provided by a registered nurse in a care home registered for nursing care, is provided at the expense of the local NHS commissioning body.[129] 'Nursing care by a registered nurse' is defined as:

> 'any services provided by a registered nurse and involving:
>
> (a)   the provision of care, or
> (b)   the planning, supervision or delegation of the provision of care,
>
> other than any services which, having regard to their nature and the circumstances in which they are provided, do not need to be provided by a registered nurse.'[130]

10.240 HSCA 2001, s 49 excludes the provision of nursing care by a registered nurse from community care services because this is not the responsibility of the local authority and so the local NHS commissioning body pays a flat fee directly to the care home proprietor. The resident may not notice any direct benefit. It should, however, be reflected in the care contract so that the resident is not paying for the nursing care provided by a registered nurse. The cost of personal and social care and accommodation is subject to the means test, and is paid for by the local authority where the resident has limited resources.[131]

NHS continuing health care payments

10.241 If the resident has a primary health care need, the NHS is responsible for the provision and funding of care.[132] Payments should be made in accordance with the guidance on refunds in Annex F of the National Framework in England. The Welsh National Framework document contains no detail about commissioning arrangements.

Delays on funding NHS continuing health care

10.242 Where the NHS Board or a CCG has unreasonably delayed reaching its decision on eligibility, and the individual has arranged and paid for services directly during the interim period, the Board or the CCG should make an ex-gratia payment in respect of the period of unreasonable delay.[133] Such payments should be made in accordance with the guidance for ex-gratia payments set out in the Treasury's guidance, *Managing Public Money*.[134] This sets out that, where public services organisations have

---

[128]   NAA 1948, ss 22(8), 21(4) and 32.
[129]   This is the Clinical Commissioning Group (CCG) in England or Local Health Board in Wales (LHB).
[130]   HSCA 2001, s 49(2).
[131]   See Chapter 6 at **6.98–6.102** for contract points.
[132]   Chapter 8 sets out the requirements for eligibility.
[133]   NF, Para 13, annex F (England).
[134]   http://www.hm-treasury.gov.uk/psr_mpm_index.htm.

caused injustice or hardship, they should provide remedies that, as far as reasonably possible, restore the wronged party to the position that they would have been in had matters been carried out correctly.[135]

Retrospective assessments for NHS continuing health care

10.243 The Department of Health introduced deadlines for people, living in England, who have never received an assessment but thought they were eligible for NHS Continuing Health Care. Retrospective assessments are only possible in exceptional cases. It is possible to make a complaint for failure to assess the person at the same time as seeking an assessment. The complaint can be for a period within the previous 12 months, and seek eligibility for that period. The assessment can deal with future eligibility, once determined.

Personal health budget for NHS continuing health care

10.244 The Department of Health intend from April 2014, that anyone in receipt of NHS continuing health care in England will have the right to ask for a personal health budget, including a 'direct payment'.[136] This will give those eligible greater choice and flexibility as to the delivery of their care. The Welsh Assembly has no such plans to implement an equivalent scheme.

Impact of NHS continuing health care on social security benefits

10.245 If a person receives a payment to reimburse them for money paid in care fees where they qualified for continuing NHS health care and during that period they were in receipt of state benefits, the payment will not cause them to have to reimburse the state for the benefits they received. However, such payment would then be taken into account for any future benefits entitlement.[137]

Means assessment

General

10.246 When the resident cannot afford the full charge, an assessment is made of their ability to pay in accordance with regulations[138] made under the National Assistance Act 1948, s 22(5). The regulations are regularly updated. Mandatory guidance is issued by the Department of Health and Welsh Assembly Government on the interpretation of the regulations in the *Charges for Residential Accommodation Guide*, commonly known as 'CRAG'.

10.247 The principle is that if the resident has capital above a set limit, they are required to pay the full cost of their accommodation. Where they have under the set limit, they are required to pay all their income above a personal expenses allowance towards the assessed charge. The assessment is reviewed annually but a resident may ask for reassessment at any time if this would be beneficial. Complaints about the level of charges or contributions levied by local authorities are subject to the usual social services complaints procedure.

---

[135] At para 4.12.4.
[136] NHSA 2006, s 12A. Applicable to England only.
[137] DWP guidance on payments for continuing NHS health care published on 26 May 2004: Decision Makers Guide Memo 08/04.
[138] National Assistance (Assessment of Resources) Regulations 1992, SI 1992/2977.

Assessment of capital and income

10.248　Residents are assessed on both their income and capital assets. However, those who have capital above the set limit are expected to fully fund their own care by using their income, and if this is insufficient, then using their capital. Local authorities are reminded[139] that they must satisfy themselves that individuals who have capital above the limit are able to make their own arrangements, or have others willing and able to do so for them. Local authorities should be proactive in aiming to ensure that self-funders, including those who may not have been through the assessment process, are aware of the right to an assessment and financial support.

10.249　The set limit for 2013/14 is £23,250 in England and £23,750 in Wales.

10.250　In England, the resident must still financially contribute using their capital towards their care, until the capital is reduced to the lower limit (set at £14,250 for 2013/14). The calculation produces a notional income, of £1.00 per week for every £250 or part thereof, between the higher and lower set amounts. The capital between these two levels will reduce rapidly until it reaches the lower limit.

10.251　There is no lower limit for Welsh residents, so residents are allowed to retain £23,750 of their capital.

Personal expenses allowance

10.252　The personal expenses allowance (PEA) is intended to be used by the resident for incidental expenditure of personal choice such as stationery, personal toiletries, treats and small presents for relatives or close friends. The sum is fixed annually by regulations.[140] The local authority has a discretion to increase the amount, but it should not be used to top-up the cost of more expensive accommodation.[141]

Assessment of spouses or civil partners

10.253　The financial assessment relates only to the means of the resident,[142] and there is no power to oblige a spouse or civil partner to take part. Jointly owned property may be deemed to be owned in equal shares, unless there is evidence to the contrary, such as a declaration of trust showing a different division of ownership. It is advisable to separate income and capital of the resident and their spouse or civil partner to avoid the non-resident using their own resources to fund the resident's care.

10.254　Where the resident is in receipt of an occupational pension, personal pension, or payment from a retirement annuity contract and has a spouse, or civil partner, who is not living in the same care home, 50% of that payment is disregarded providing the resident passes the sum on to their spouse or civil partner.[143] Residents who are not yet of retirement age may pay over their PEA to their spouse or civil partner, for their needs. The local authority has a discretion[144] to increase the PEA, although the spouse or civil partner will be required to seek welfare benefit support to prevent the local authority from exercising their discretion unnecessarily.

---

[139]　See amendment to CRAG in LAC (2000) 11.
[140]　2012/13, the personal expenses allowance in England is £23.90 and in Wales is £24.50.
[141]　NAA 1948, s 22(4).
[142]　CRAG, para 4.001.
[143]　National Assistance (Assessment of Resources) Regulations 1992, SI 1992/2977, Sch 3, para 10.
[144]　NAA 1948, s 22(4).

Disregarded capital and income

10.255 Certain types of capital and income are disregarded in the means assessment. This is largely in line with assessments for income-based benefits, though local authorities retain some discretion and there is no appeal procedures to an independent tribunal. An explanation of all disregards and when they should be applied are contained in CRAG.

10.256 Notable disregards include personal possessions,[145] surrender value of any life insurance policy[146] or annuity,[147] or the value of any cashing-in options rights for an investment bond written as a life insurance policy.[148] Of particular concern to older people and their families will be the treatment of the resident's own former home and any trust funds that have been set up to support the resident, so these types of asset are considered in the following paragraphs.

Assessment of the resident's home

10.257 The value of the resident's own home is disregarded:

(1)   during a temporary stay[149] in residential care;

(2)   for the first 12 weeks of a permanent stay in residential care, provided the resident does not have other assets sufficient to meet the cost;[150]

(3)   if it is occupied by a spouse or partner, or former partner (including a civil partner);

(4)   if it is occupied as their home by a relative or other family member who is aged 60 years or over;

(5)   if it is occupied as their home by the resident's child who is under 18 years; or

(6)   if it is occupied as their home by a relative or other family member who is incapacitated.[151]

It may be disregarded in the local authority's discretion if occupied by someone else, such as a person who has previously given up their own home to care for the resident but is not within the above disregards.[152] An elderly companion who has given up a home may also be considered. There is no effective appeal procedure in respect of the exercise of this discretion.

Assessment of trust funds

10.258 A beneficiary of a trust will only be assessed on their interest in the trust insofar as they are entitled to it.[153] It can be summarised as follows:

---

[145]   National Assistance (Assessment of Resources) Regulations 1992, SI 1992/2977, Sch 4, para 8.

[146]   Ibid, Sch 4, para 1.

[147]   Ibid, Sch 4, para 9.

[148]   See Sch 10, para 15 of the Income Support (General) Regulations 1987: *the Social Security Commissioners decision R (IS) 7/98* and CRAG 6.003-05.

[149]   Reg 2(1) defines 'temporary' as a stay which is unlikely to exceed 52 weeks, or in exceptional circumstances is unlikely to substantially exceed that period.

[150]   The qualifying conditions that can be found in para 12 of the Annex to LAC (2001) 10, National Assistance (Assessment of Resources) Regulations 1992, SI 1992/2977, Sch 4, para 2A. See also para 7.004 in CRAG.

[151]   Ibid, Sch 4, para 2; CRAG, paras 7003–7009.

[152]   Ibid, Sch 4, para 18: CRAG, para 7011.

[153]   See CRAG at section 10.

(1) where the resident has an absolute entitlement to income from the trust, the income they receive, or which would be available to them on an application is taken fully into account;

(2) the 'right' to receive income (which will have a value) from the trust is fully disregarded;[154]

(3) the reversionary interest (ie a future interest) in a trust is disregarded;[155]

(4) discretionary payments are disregarded;[156]

(5) where the capital is held in court, in trust or part of a structured settlement (which are disregarded locations), in consequence of a personal injury, both the capital and the capital value of any right to receive income are fully disregarded;[157]

(6) where the capital consists of any payment made in consequence of personal injury and a court has not specifically identified the payment as being to cover the cost of providing care, that capital is disregarded for a period of up to 52 weeks from the date of receipt of the first payment.[158]

(7) where the capital consists of any payment made in consequence of personal injury and a court has specifically identified the payment as being to cover the cost of providing care, that capital is taken into account. However, if the money is placed in a disregarded location such as a personal injury trust or is administered by a court the relevant disregards will apply;[159]

(8) periodic payments made in consequence of a personal injury pursuant to a court order or agreement are disregarded.[160]

Temporary stays

10.259 Admission to a care home may be merely for respite care or convalescence rather than on a permanent basis. The local authority need not carry out a means-test for stays of up to 8 weeks[161] but may charge what is reasonable for the resident to pay. For longer stays there must be a means-test.[162]

Selling the family home and buying another

10.260 The capital received from the sale of the resident's former home, will be disregarded for 26 weeks from the date of the sale, or longer (where appropriate), where the capital proceeds are to be used by the resident to buy another home for them to occupy.[163] If the property is sold and the resident's share of the proceeds is used towards the purchase of another property, which is to be occupied by the resident's spouse or civil partner, it would be unreasonable for the local authority to treat the resident as having deprived themselves of that capital in order to reduce their residential

---

[154] National Assistance (Assessment of Resources) Regulations 1992, SI 1992/2977, Sch 4, para 11.

[155] Ibid, Sch 4, para 4.

[156] CRAG, paras 8.051 to 8.057.

[157] National Assistance (Assessment of Resources) Regulations 1992, SI 1992/2977, reg 21(2), Sch 4, paras 10 and 19.

[158] CRAG, para 10.026.

[159] National Assistance (Assessment of Resources) Regulations 1992, SI 1992/2977, reg 21(2) and Sch 4, para 10A.

[160] Ibid, reg 21(2) and Sch 4, para 9; regs 16(5), 15(2) and Sch 3, para 10.

[161] NAA 1948, s 22(5A).

[162] National Assistance (Assessment of Resources) Regulations 1992, SI 1992/2977, Sch 4, para 1.

[163] Ibid, Sch 4, para 3; CRAG, para 6.032.

accommodation charge.[164] In these circumstances, it allows any proceeds of sale belonging to the resident to be used for the benefit of their spouse or civil partner.

Avoiding charges

Background

10.261 It has become the trend for some journalists to draw attention to the implications of means-testing for older people who may at some stage enter a care home, and to advise that they transfer their property to their children. Schemes are being marketed often by non-regulated lawyers which purport to avoid having the property taken by the state.[165] As a result many older people (and often their children who would be deprived of an inheritance which they may see as theirs by right) are asking solicitors to handle such transfers. In response the Law Society has produced specific guidance. The situation is far more complex than journalists would have us believe, and relatively few people decide to pass on ownership of their property after receiving comprehensive advice from a solicitor acting solely in their best interests.

Gifts of Assets Practice Note

10.262 Reference should be made to the Law Society's Practice Note *Making Gifts of Assets* (6 October 2011), which is available from their website.[166] This sets out professional conduct issues, advice that should be covered and sources of other help. The practice note expects advisers to be aware of public funded care, in particular:

(1) the eligibility criteria for NHS-funded continuing health care;
(2) charging and funding arrangements by local authorities for residential and domiciliary care;
(3) when care must be provided free of charge, eg aftercare under the MHA 1983, s 117 and registered nursing care by a registered nurse contribution;
(4) any means-testing criteria applied by local authorities which charge for care; and
(5) how local authorities can recover assessed charges.

Role of the solicitor

10.263 Before transferring a property in which there is a continuing intention to reside, the person should receive independent advice. It may be negligent for a solicitor to accept instructions to act in the transfer without giving such advice or ensuring that it has been obtained. The first step for any solicitor consulted in this situation is to identify the client and then to act solely in the best interests of that person. There is inevitably a conflict of interest between the prospective donor and donee, particularly where a substantial gift is contemplated, with the risk that the parties may fall out afterwards, perhaps because of a disparity of expectations.

10.264 The Solicitors' Regulation Authority's Code of Conduct 2011, allows a solicitor to act for two or more parties where there is a substantially common interest, but it is unwise to do so if one party is an older person as there may be unequal bargaining

---

[164] CRAG, para 6.069.
[165] The state, of course, does not take the home; it requires the resident to pay for their care, and the sale of the home may be the only means of raising the money. The likelihood of this is in fact low for those under 80 years and the risk of loss of the home to children if transferred may be greater.
[166] www.lawsociety.org.uk/advice/practice-notes/gifts-of-assets/.

power, or the adviser may be unable to act for all parties even handedly, or a party may be prejudiced by a lack of separate representation.[167] If the client is a child of the elderly person independent advice should be insisted upon for the parent and a transfer deed should not be prepared in the hope that the parent will sign it.

10.265   Solicitors are required to ensure their clients are in a position to make informed decisions about the services they need, how their matter will be handled and the options available to them.[168] This requires the solicitor to take instructions and during the course of the retainer, to have proper regard to the client's mental capacity or other vulnerability, such as physical incapacity or duress.[169]

Advising the donor

10.266   If the client is the older person, the solicitor should see them alone to ensure that:

(1)   it is their choice to make the gift;

(2)   they have sufficient mental capacity;

(3)   they are not being subjected to undue influence; and

(4)   they are aware of and understand the implications.

The solicitor should explain the realities of the proposed gift from the client's point of view but not comment on moral issues unless asked to do so. A practical approach is best, concentrating upon the potential benefits and risks of making the gift and the basis on which it is to be made (if it is to be made at all). Consider the client's objectives and whether these are likely to be achieved by making the gift or may be achieved in another way. Does the client realise that a gift passes ownership and all legal influence in respect of the property? Does the client expect that some rights or benefits will be reserved? Remember that the perceived problem (loss of the property or its value) does not arise if the client's income, including state benefits and investment income derived from the property or its sale proceeds, would be sufficient to cover the costs of care or if the property will not be means-tested because it remains occupied by another relevant person.

Reasons for transferring the property

10.267   There may of course be compelling reasons for the transfer by a person of their property, or an interest in that property, to another member of the family or even an outsider. The legal title may not have been vested in the appropriate person in the first place or may not reflect the present beneficial interests in the property. Another person may have made substantial financial contributions to the property which should be reflected in the ownership,[170] or may have provided care services over many years in reliance upon assurances that the property would continue to be available for occupation after the death of the present owner.[171]

---

[167]   Chapter 3 of the Code.

[168]   Solicitors Regulation Authority's Code of Conduct 2011 – Outcome 1.12.

[169]   Ibid, Indicative Behaviour 1.6.

[170]   *Nottingham City Council v Berresford and the Adjudicator to HM Land Registry* (2010/0577), 10 March 2011; *Cunningham v East Lothian Council* [2011] CSOH 185.

[171]   *Re Kumar (a Bankrupt)* [1993] 2 All ER 700: *Ellis v Chief Adjudication Officer* [1998] 1 FLR 184: CIS/242/1993.

10.268   In these (and other) situations it may be desirable to give effect to the transfer whilst the older owner can still make the decision so as to establish legal rights which all would wish to be acknowledged. On the other hand the gift may simply be contemplated to preserve the property for the next generation with vague assurances as to future use and occupation and, in some cases, as to the provision of personal care if needed. It is these situations that are of most concerns.

Transfer into trust

10.269   It is a concern that the older person is more likely to lose their home to their family following a transfer than by means-testing. In fact the state will not take the home; rather the owner will be disqualified for benefit or funding as a result of owning it, so that a sale may be the best option, but keeping it still remains a possibility.

10.270   There are steps that can be taken to minimise that alternative risk. Some advisers arrange a gift subject to a tenancy or a lease for life, but this ties the donor to that particular property. Another option is a settlement of the home with a life or other limited interest for the settlor but any income subsequently derived by the settlor from that settlement will be means-tested even if the capital is preserved. Alternatively the property may be settled into a discretionary trust; preserving both the income and capital. However, the transfer into any settlement is particularly vulnerable to the local authority's enforcement process, and the existence of the settlement may draw attention to the reason for the transfer of the property. If it is seen as a 'deliberate deprivation' the transfer will have failed to achieve its objective.

Tax implications

10.271   A gift of the property in which the donor continues to reside may be counter-productive so far as capital gains tax (CGT) and inheritance tax (IHT) are concerned. In respect of CGT, the owner occupier exemption may be lost as well as the tax-free revaluation on death. As regards IHT, the value of the property may still be included in the estate of a donor who continues to reside therein under the reservation of benefit rules notwithstanding that it is also included in the estate of the donee. Some advisers arrange a gift subject to a tenancy but this still results in the loss of those tax benefits associated with home ownership and will create a tax liability on any rent payable (pre-owned asset tax).

Anti-avoidance

10.272   Perhaps the most important question is whether the gift of the home will have the desired result. This may be a matter for speculation rather than legal advice because it depends largely on whether the local authority exercises the range of armory that it has at its disposal. In practice, few local authorities have been skilled or persistent in doing so, but with limited funds available to provide for community care, increased demands for residential care and more people who were home owners presenting themselves as having no assets, the determination of local authorities is likely to increase.

The realities

10.273   It is easy to become too preoccupied with the implications of means-testing, especially as this may be the reason for the proposal for the gift of the home. If residential care is not immediately contemplated the client may assume that a gift is merely a 'paper transaction' and expect to continue living there, without considering the terms. Who will pay for insurance, maintenance, repair and the mortgage (if there is one)? The client may never enter a care home or need means-tested funding, in which event the gift would be pointless and may even be detrimental; as they may not have the resources to downsize or release equity to fund care in their own home and so are forced by circumstance to move into a care home, but not one of their choice. Conversely, if the gift is made when the client contemplates entering a care home it is less likely to achieve its objective.

10.274 Those whose principal or only asset is the home are most vulnerable to the loss of that asset due to means-testing, but there are worse outcomes than this. A gift of the home may result in a loss of independence and even premature loss of the home. Human nature being what it is, once the gift has been made the home may be seen as belonging to the donees, who may become impatient to realise the capital that it represents and put pressure on the older relative to leave it and enter residential care. Even where there are good intentions a donee may die prematurely, or encounter financial difficulties or matrimonial problems, thereby causing control of the home to pass to others, notwithstanding any assurances given to the donor.

10.275 Artificial arrangements designed to avoid subsequent means-testing may be accepted by all concerned at the time but are not easy to justify to an older person at a later stage when periods of confusion arise, especially if there is resentment at having to leave the home and live in residential care, however necessary that may be. This is why independent advice is essential before transfer of the property, but it is also a reason for not transferring the property in the first place.

Enforcement provisions

Challenging charges

10.276 Where a service user wishes to challenge the charge, the usual procedure will be to pursue the matter through the local authority's complaints procedure. In respect of non-accommodation services, the service user should stress the local authority has power to reduce or waive charges, which is not limited to a consideration of their financial means. As the local authority has an overall discretion as to whether or not to levy any charges, it must retain a discretion to waive or reduce charges on any ground. Such an overall discretion might be used where, for instance, the service user lacked mental capacity and the services were put in without consent or they are at risk of serious and immediate harm if the services are not provided, but refuses to have the services if charged for them.

Withdrawal of services

10.277 Where the community care service is provided by the local authority in consequence of a statutory duty then the service cannot as a matter of law be withdrawn merely because the service user is refusing to pay for it.

10.278 The Department of Health's policy guidance, *Caring for People: Community Care in the next decade and beyond* (1990) states that 'the provision of services, whether or not the local authority is under a duty to make provision, should not be related to the ability of the service user or their families to meet the costs … . The assessment of financial means should, therefore follow the assessment of need and decisions about service provision'.[172] Local authorities should provide or continue to provide the service, while pursuing the debt through the court.

Recovery of charges

10.279 The local authority has certain statutory powers at its disposal. Any charge levied may, without prejudice to any other method of recovery, be recovered summarily as a civil debt.[173] The use of the phrase 'summarily as a civil debt' is a reference to provisions relating to the magistrates' courts.[174] Most would consider it more appropriate to pursue the debt through the civil county court. Routes for recovery are mainly aimed at those in residential care.

Imposing a legal charge

10.280 The local authority may impose a charge on any property belonging to the resident, with interest chargeable from the day after death.[175] Where the resident is unwilling to dispose of their property included in the means assessment and the local authority is reluctant to obtain a court order to compel the sale, it may impose a charge on the resident's interest in the property. As such, enforcement of the accruing debt is postponed. This may also be appropriate when a former carer still lives in the resident's home and the local authority has not exercised its discretion to disregard the value but does not wish to cause hardship to that person.

Deferred payment agreements

10.281 The local authority may take a charge on land in which the resident has a beneficial interest,[176] instead of a contribution towards the cost of care fees, by way of a 'deferred payment agreement'.[177] This discretionary power applies to residents who have had their permanent care arranged or provided[178] by the local authority or are proposing to do so and would be liable to pay the full rate or any lower amount if the property were sold.

10.282 It applies where the resident for whatever reason does not wish to sell their home or is unable to sell their home quickly enough to pay the care fees. Local authorities will be cautious where there is an outstanding mortgage on the property and will only agree to a deferred payment agreement if the resident can continue to meet the mortgage obligations and assessed contribution to care costs. The size of the weekly deferred contribution will be taken into account by the local authority when deciding whether to enter into an agreement. In the event that a resident has been refused a deferred payment, written reason should given to the resident with details of the complaint's procedure.

---

[172] At para 3.31.

[173] HASSASSAA 1983, s 17(4).

[174] NAA 1948, s 56; Magistrates' Courts Act 1980, s 58(1).

[175] HASSASSA 1983, ss 22 and 24.

[176] HSCA 2001, s 55; National Assistance (Residential Accommodation) (Disregarding of Resources) (England) Regulations 2001, SI 2001/3067, and National Assistance (Residential Accommodation) (Relevant Contributions) (England) Regulations 2001, SI 2001/3069 have been issued with similar Regulations in Wales in SI 2003/969 (W.131) and National Assistance (Residential Accommodation) (Additional Payments, Relevant Contributions and Assessment of Resources) (Wales) Regulations 2003, SI 2003/931 (W.121).

[177] Guidance has been published in LAC (2001) 25, LAC (2001) 29 and LAC (2002) 15 and in Wales in NAFWC 21/2003.

[178] Under Part III of the NAA 1948.

10.283 The deferred payment agreement does not apply during the mandatory 12-week disregard period as the property cannot be taken onto account during the first 12-week stay following a permanent admission to a care home nor does it apply during temporary stays.

10.284 Once the deferred payment agreement has been entered into no payment is required until 56 days after the resident's death or a specified earlier date or if the property is sold in the meantime, following which interest will start to accrue. The resident will be responsible for the cost of the Land Registry searches and legal fees.

Liability of third parties

10.285 Sums due towards the cost of residential care may be recovered by a local authority where a resident has disposed of assessable assets by way of gift or at an undervalue to a third party within 6 months before admission to residential accommodation, or whilst in the accommodation, knowingly and with the intention of avoiding charges for the accommodation.[179] The third party is liable to pay a contribution towards the assessed care fees, but only to the extent of the amount which they have received.

Deprivation of capital and notional capital

10.286 The resident may be treated as possessing an asset of which they have deprived[180] themselves at any time[181] for the purpose of avoiding or decreasing the amount they are financially assessed to pay.[182] This is known as 'notional capital'. Similar rules apply to income.[183] If capital has been converted to a disregarded asset, such as personal possessions or investment bonds, the local authority will look carefully, in case the conversion was a deliberate deprivation.[184] It does not apply to payments made in consequence of any personal injury for the first 52 weeks, or when the personal injury payment is placed on trust for the benefit of the resident.

10.287 Notional capital is deemed to reduce as it is treated as being spent on the fees, and notional income ceases to be taken into account when it would have ceased to be available anyway.

10.288 There is no time limit on the disposal, but clearly the longer it is since a gift was made the more difficult it will be to establish that the purpose was to avoid financial assessment. It would be unreasonable for the local authority to treat the transfer as a deliberate deprivation when the disposal took place at a time when the resident was fit and healthy and could not have foreseen the need for a move to residential accommodation.[185] The forseeability or immediacy of the need for care will therefore need to be established.

10.289 An asset given away before residential care was contemplated is unlikely to be caught by this rule, whereas any gift made immediately before (or after) admission to the

---

[179] HASSASSA 1983, s 21.
[180] Ie disposed of or given away.
[181] *Yule v South Lanarkshire Council* [1999] 1 CCL Rep 546.
[182] National Assistance (Assessment of Resources) Regulations 1992, SI 1992/2977, reg 25(1).
[183] Ibid, reg 17.
[184] CRAG, paras 6.061 and 6.065–6066.
[185] CRAG, para 6.064.

care home is vulnerable, even if a further purpose can be established.[186] It may be necessary to establish that the resident knew of the means-testing implications before making the gift, otherwise there could not be an intention to avoid them.[187] It is, however, the intention of the resident (subjective intent) which is important not what others think the resident intended (objective intent).[188]

Diminishing notional capital rule

10.290 Where a resident is deemed to possess notional capital and is thereby expected to pay contributions to care costs, there is a special rule that provides that this capital is deemed to diminish over a period of time so that ultimately the resident will re-qualify for care costs.[189]

Insolvency procedures

10.291 Some local authorities are prepared to resort to insolvency procedures[190] in order to recover the value of the assets given away. The resident is treated as unable to pay his debt[191] and made bankrupt, whereupon transactions at an undervalue or preferences between creditors may be set aside.

10.292 A gift is a transaction at an undervalue, but only those within 5 years prior to the petition are caught and if made more than 2 years previously it is necessary to establish insolvency at the time of the gift. It follows that the effective period is 2 years because the older person only becomes insolvent due to the effect of the subsequent means assessment. The local authority will have to be careful with timing and very persistent because three sets of proceedings will usually be required:

(1)   to obtain judgment against the resident for the unpaid contributions;

(2)   to make the resident bankrupt; and

(3)   to set aside the gift within the bankruptcy.[192]

Transactions at an undervalue

10.293 Other provisions in the Insolvency Act 1986[193] enable transactions at an undervalue to be set aside without time limit and without bankruptcy, if there was an intention to defraud creditors or potential creditors at the time of the transaction, even if the transferor was then solvent. These provisions are exceptionally broad in their terms and the court may make a range of orders to restore the position to what it would have been had the transaction not taken place. It is sufficient if the purpose was to put the asset beyond the reach of a person who might at some time make a claim or otherwise prejudice the interests of such a person.[194] This does not have to be the sole purpose and it may be sufficient for it to be a substantial rather than a dominant purpose, but the

---

[186]   There may be more than one purpose for disposing of a capital asset, only one of which is to avoid a charge for residential accommodation. Avoiding the charge need not be the main motive but it must be a significant one (CRAG, para 6.062).

[187]   *R (Beeson) v Dorset County Council* [2001] EWHC Admin 986.

[188]   Ibid.

[189]   National Assistance (Assessment of Resources) Regulations 1992, SI 1992/2977, reg 26.

[190]   Insolvency Act 1986, ss 339–340.

[191]   Ie the outstanding contribution to the fees assessed as payable to the local authority.

[192]   These proceedings are taken by the Official Receiver or trustee in bankruptcy who is likely to seek an indemnity as to costs from the local authority.

[193]   Insolvency Act 1986, ss 423–425.

[194]   See *Midland Bank plc v Wyatt* [1995] 1 FLR 696.

mere fact that the transaction was made without consideration does not of itself establish that it was made to defeat creditors: result cannot be equated with purpose.

10.294 As there is no binding appeal procedure for local authority funding the judge will first have to decide whether the local authority is a creditor in respect of care costs, but a finding of purpose sufficient for the resident's former home to be treated as notional capital would also appear to justify the subsequent setting aside procedure. As such a single hearing in the county court may result in the gift of a property being set aside or the donees being obliged to pay care home fees up to the value of the property.[195]

Discovery of the solicitor's file

10.295 Discovery of the file relating to the transfer may also reveal the true or dominant purpose of the gift or other transaction at an undervalue. The solicitor who dealt with the transfer will know the true purpose if they gave advice before it was made, and the file is likely to record such advice for the solicitor's own protection. Such file will normally be covered by legal professional privilege, but the court may order discovery if there is prima facie proof of fraud[196] and also for public policy considerations.

10.296 In a case where a bank sought to set aside a transaction at an undervalue which prejudiced its security the principles were considered and one of the issues was whether legal professional privilege applied to the solicitor's file relating to the transaction. The court identified the conflicting approaches of (a) knowing what happened and (b) allowing parties to speak frankly to their legal advisers. The authorities indicated that in the absence of iniquity the court should not order disclosure, and Schiemann LJ said:

> '... on a prima facie view, the client was seeking to enter into transactions at an undervalue the purpose of which was to prejudice the bank. I regard this purpose as being sufficiently iniquitous for public policy to require that communications between him and his solicitor in relation to the setting up of these transactions be discoverable.'[197]

It appears to follow that if the court considers that the purpose of the transaction may have been to avoid means-testing, then the court will order disclosure of the solicitor's file to ascertain whether this really was the case.

State benefits when in a care home

Background

10.297 It is clearly desirable for anyone funding the high cost of residential care to ensure that all available state benefits are being claimed. Local authorities who are paying the fees will wish to carry out a benefits check because they have an incentive to ensure that the resident is receiving the maximum state benefits from which to make a contribution, but this should only be with the informed consent of the resident. The policy is that the state should not be required to fund care costs once the local authority

---

[195]   *Derbyshire County Council v Akrill* [2005] EWCA Civ 308.

[196]   *Royscott Spa Leasing v Lovett* (16 November 1994) unreported, CA. A pleading of bad faith or impropriety may be sufficient in some situations – see *Nationwide Building Society v Various solicitors* (1998) *The Times*, 5 February, Blackburne J.

[197]   *Barclays Bank pic v Eustice* [1995] 4 All ER 511, [1995] 1 WLR 1238.

funds residential care so most disability benefits are then withdrawn. When an individual is in hospital or a similar institution most state benefits are withdrawn and the NHS must meet the cost.

Pension credit

10.298 Pension credit is subject to the normal rules of entitlement when a claimant is resident in a care home. Tariff income is applied at £10,000 whether or not the claimant is in a residential care home. Where the claimant is one of a couple, they will cease to be regarded as such on becoming permanently resident.

10.299 A person who is receiving attendance allowance (for people over 65 years) or the middle or higher care component of disability living allowance (for those under 65 years who have not yet been reassessed for personal independence payment[198]) or the daily living component of personal independence payment (for those over 65 years) is entitled to a severe disability addition.

10.300 When carrying out the means-test for paying for care, an additional disregard is available to those in receipt of savings credit. During 2013/14, for a single person, the disregard is £5.75 or £8.60 for couples.

Housing benefit for temporary residents

10.301 Where a claimant goes into residential care other than on a trial basis, housing benefit is payable for up to 52 weeks during the period of absence from the home. Housing benefit can only be paid in these circumstances where the claimant intends to return home within 52 weeks and the home is not occupied by another person or sub-let. Where a person goes into residential care on a trial basis, they can receive housing benefit for up to 13 weeks during the period of absence from the home.

Attendance allowance, disability living allowance or personal independence payments

10.302 Attendance allowance, the care component of disability living allowance, or daily living component of personal independence payment is not payable once the resident has lived for 28 days in a care home, which is either provided under Part III of the National Assistance Act 1948, or the cost of which is borne wholly or partly from public funds. This rule does not apply where the resident is self-funding. 'Self-funding' includes both the situation where the resident is responsible immediately for their own charges, and the situation where the resident will be responsible for their own charges once a house has been sold, but the local authority is making payments on the resident's behalf in the meantime.[199] This includes (but is not limited to) a deferred payment agreement.

10.303 Note that the value of the home is disregarded for the first 12 weeks during which the resident is permanently in residential care. If the local authority is funding care during this period, the 28-day rule will apply. However, once the 12-week period ends, the resident may become a self-funder, and so is entitled to reclaim attendance allowance, disability living allowance or personal independence payments.

---

[198] Disability living allowance (DLA) is being replaced by personal independence payments (PIP) and is being introduced in stages over a number of years. By 2015 most people who claimed DLA will be invited to reapply for PIP.

[199] In linked appeals CA/2937/97, CA/2604/98.

Effect on state benefits when going into hospital

10.304　The effect of being in hospital upon weekly state benefits depends upon the particular benefit and the length of the hospital stay, but benefits may be reinstated during temporary absences including the leaving and returning days. In most cases benefit is not reduced until the claimant has been an inpatient for 52 weeks. Attendance allowance, disability living allowance and personal independence payments cease after 28 days in an NHS hospital. This rule does not apply to a private hospital, nor to a hospice.

10.305　Carers allowance stops when attendance allowance, disability living allowance or personal independence payment stops, and a carer's premium or an addition paid with guarantee credit stops 8 weeks later. Where it is the carer who is in hospital, benefit continues for 12 weeks.

NHS funding

Preliminary

10.306　Support for an individual who is ill, infirm or otherwise in need of medical or nursing services is available through primary health care services, as well as an inpatient. Most health care provided under the NHS is free but there are charges for certain items.

Free and reduced rate health benefits

10.307　Prescriptions are free in Wales. In England, free prescriptions are available to those over 60 years of age, and people on low incomes or on means-tested state benefits get an exemption with the cost of prescriptions, or reduced charge for dental check-ups and treatment, sight tests and vouchers for glasses.[200] There are also certain medical grounds on which a person may qualify and these include a continuing physical disability which prevents the individual from leaving home except with the help of another person.

Travelling expenses to hospital

10.308　Assistance may be available for the cost of travel to hospital for treatment, and people in receipt of the same benefits as for free prescriptions are entitled to claim. Only the cost of travelling by the cheapest form of transport available is covered, but a companion's travelling expenses may also be paid where this is medically necessary. Claims are made to the hospital on form HC5T.

Other sources

Family

10.309　Financial support may also be given to a person by members of their family, normally on an informal basis without any legal commitment. Care should be taken to ensure that such support does not result in the reduction or loss of means-tested funding or increased charges for local authority services. It may be better to buy useful items and give these rather than to make gifts of money. Informal carers should not neglect to claim all financial benefits that are available as of right either for themselves or the person cared for.

---

[200]　See Forms HC11 – *Help with health costs* available from the NHS.

Concessions and subsidies

General

10.310 Various concessions and subsidies are available to older people in respect of significant items in the weekly budget such as travel, domestic fuel, telephone and television costs. These may be available in the private sector as well as the public sector but are sometimes marketing ploys. The following are some of the available concessions and subsidies available:

(1) Local authorities have power to set up travel concession schemes[201] and these also exist for public transport, such as senior railcards, the national bus pass.

(2) A free road tax disc is available in certain circumstances and there is no VAT on certain vehicles extensively modified to carry a person in a wheelchair.

(3) Suppliers of gas and electricity have codes of practice which should be referred to if problems arise and protection against disconnection is given to customers. Payments schemes include prepayment, monthly budget and flexible payments, and consumers receiving means-tested state benefits may arrange direct payments.

(4) BT operates rebate schemes and a protected service scheme which include elderly telephone subscribers. Help may be available with the cost of a telephone from the social services department.

(5) Television licences are available free of charge to anyone aged 75 or over, and concessions are available to retired people aged 60–75 who live in residential care homes and certain types of sheltered accommodation.[202]

Charities

General

10.311 Many charities, both local and national, exist for the purpose of giving support to disabled people, and older people may qualify for such assistance. The role of some other charities is specifically to support older people and this may be done by providing financial support, services or information.

Independent Living Fund

10.312 The Independent Living Fund was a charitable trust set up by the then Department of Social Security to give more help to very severely disabled people living in their own home. It was funded by the government but administered by a board of independent trustees. In April 1993 it was replaced by the Independent Living (Extension) Fund and the Independent Living (1993) Fund. From October 2007, the two funds were replaced by a single fund, the Independent Living Fund (2006). Financial help from this source is not taxable or taken into account when calculating means-tested benefits. The Independent Living Fund was closed to new applicants with effect from December 2010, and although the scheme was due to close by March 2016, following a successful legal challenge Ministers are now reviewing its future.

---

[201] Transport Act 1985, s 92.
[202] Wireless Telegraphy (Television Licence Fees) Regulations 1991, SI 1991/436.

CHAPTER 11

FINANCIAL AFFAIRS AND INCAPACITY

Gordon Ashton

'There is some magic in wealth, which can thus make persons pay their court to it, when it does not even benefit themselves. How strange it is, that a fool or knave, with riches, should be treated with more respect by the world, than a good man, or a wise man in poverty!'
Ann Radcliffe, The Mysteries of Udolpho, 1764

Those who cannot manage their own financial affairs need someone to do this for them. Legal procedures have for many years made this possible but have now been re-formulated within an all-embracing mental capacity jurisdiction. In this chapter we consider first some general procedures that are available, then the different forms of powers of attorney followed by involvement of the Court of Protection and the appointment of a financial deputy. Finally some guidance is offered on handling the affairs in practice.

INTRODUCTION

11.1   If an individual becomes unable to handle his own financial affairs a procedure is needed to enable another person or other persons to do so on his behalf, with safeguards to prevent the misuse of funds or assets. The management of other people's money is fraught with difficulties and widely varying practices are followed even by professionals. Confusion surrounds what can and cannot lawfully be done. Where there are only limited resources, relatives or carers find informal ways of dealing with financial matters as they arise. This is a practical response to the failure of the law to provide a simple and inexpensive procedure. The methods adopted may be of doubtful legal validity but are unlikely to be questioned and those involved are only concerned with whether they work. The Law Commission supported this informal approach by proposing that carers who receive money of the person cared for should be entitled to do what is reasonable with that money, having in mind the 'best interests' principle.[1] Where more than a small amount of money is involved or there is a dispute, it is necessary to use one of the legally recognised procedures that is available.

11.2   In this chapter we start by identifying circumstances in which specific financial powers may be delegated without the involvement of a court, and then we consider the manner in which an incapacitated person may delegate financial powers. Next an explanation is given of the powers that may be exercised or delegated by the Court of Protection, and we conclude with an overview of how the financial affairs of an

---

[1]   Mentally Incapacitated Adults and Decision-Making: A New Jurisdiction – No 128.

incapacitated person may be handled in practice. Although the law protects those who are incapable due to some mental aberration,[2] it does not interfere in the affairs of those who are merely incompetent or foolish.

11.3   In many instances the Court of Protection and the Office of the Public Guardian will be involved at some stage, and reference should be made to Chapter 2 for a further explanation of the status and function of these bodies and the general provisions of the Mental Capacity Act 2005 (MCA 2005).

GENERAL

Preliminary

11.4   There are a number of procedures available in specific or limited circumstances whereby financial affairs may be delegated, and these are now considered.

Wefare benefits

Agency

11.5   Welfare benefits, otherwise known as state benefits,[3] are administered by the Department for Work and Pensions (DWP)[4] which is divided into a number of operational organisations, notably the Pension Service, Jobcentre Plus and the Disability and Carers Service.[5] They are applied for by claimants through local DWP offices, or certain central offices or the local authority and this is generally paid by 'direct payment' to a nominated bank or building society account although 'simple payment' can be made through 'PayPoint' outlets set up in supermarkets or newsagents or a Post Office Card Account may be possible. Some benefits may be paid to someone on behalf of a claimant on the instructions of the claimant (for example, to a trusted relative who is assisting with financial affairs or the landlord in the case of housing benefit).

11.6   The 'agent' is merely entitled to receive the money for the claimant and is under an obligation to account for it but in practice may handle the money on behalf of the claimant with actual or tacit authority. This procedure should not be used for claimants who are incapable of handling their affairs because it relies upon an express delegation.

Appointee

11.7   If the claimant is unable for the time being to act because they are mentally incapable or severely disabled someone else can be appointed to act on behalf of the claimant in making a claim, and receiving and dealing with any sums payable.[6] If a financial deputy has been appointed by the Court of Protection, there will be someone with power to act for the claimant, so the appointee procedure is not appropriate. If there is a registered lasting or enduring power of attorney, the regulations are different and it is quite possible for a non attorney to collect benefits on behalf of the claimant.

---

[2]   This was previously a 'mental disorder' but under the Mental Capacity Act 2005 is now 'an impairment of, or a disturbance in the functioning of, the mind or brain'.
[3]   Previously 'Social Security Benefits'.
[4]   www.gov.uk/government/organisations/department-for-work-pensions.
[5]   See generally Ch 10.
[6]   Social Security (Claims and Payments) Regulations 1987, SI 1987/1968, reg 33.

11.8   The appointee assumes the rights and obligations of the claimant in regard to the claim including making declarations, reporting changes, receiving and dealing with any payments, and has a right of appeal.[7] All money collected by the appointee must be used for the benefit of the claimant, but the appointee's powers do not extend beyond handling the welfare benefit. A single appointment is made for all benefits from the DWP, but a separate application must be made to the local authority for housing benefit and similar procedures apply.

11.9   Application is in writing[8] and staff at the DWP must satisfy themselves as to the claimant's inability to manage his affairs and the suitability of the appointee. This usually involves seeing the claimant or receiving medical evidence and interviewing the appointee, but time pressures may result in only limited enquiries being made and the procedures are not adequate for dealing with disputes. If doubts arise as to the conduct of an appointee the matter should be referred to the DWP who may revoke the appointment if the appointee is not acting properly or in the best interests of the claimant.

11.10   The appointee will usually be an individual (typically a friend or relative) or a representative of an organisation (such as a solicitor or local authority). A close relative who lives with or someone else who cares for the claimant is regarded as the most suitable person. The proprietor of a residential care home should be appointed only as a last resort and not for administrative convenience, although in some cases this may be the only person available. Where there is no-one else available the director of social services may be appointed, as an office holder rather than an individual so that there will be continuity in the event of a change.

Direct payments

11.11   There are two additional powers of relevance to claimants who lack mental capacity although not specifically intended for them. First, the Secretary of State, acting through a senior local officer at the DWP, may direct that benefit shall be paid, wholly or in part, to another person acting on behalf of the claimant if this appears necessary for protecting the interests of the claimant or a dependant.[9] This power is used sparingly.

11.12   Second, deductions may be made from benefit with a view to direct payments being made to third parties on behalf of the claimant in accordance with detailed procedures.[10] This power is restricted to housing and accommodation costs and expenses for fuel and water services and there are limits on the amounts that can be deducted.

Miscellaneous

11.13   In addition to these procedures for welfare benefits, there are certain other specific circumstances in which an individual may acquire authority to receive money on behalf of someone who lacks capacity.

---

[7]   For further information refer to: www.gov.uk/become-appointee-for-someone-claiming-benefits.
[8]   Form BF56.
[9]   Social Security (Claims and Payments) Regulations 1987, SI 1987/1968, reg 34.
[10]   Social Security (Claims and Payments) Regulations 1987, SI 1987/1968, reg 35 and Sch 9.

11.14 The provision whereby any pay, pensions or other periodical payments due from the government to a person who was, by reason of mental disorder, unable to manage his affairs may be paid to the person having care of the individual for his benefit[11] has been repealed but payments already being made may continue.[12]

Hospitals

11.15 The administrative staff at a hospital may be controlling money belonging to a patient under their internal procedures, but such money belongs to the patient and not to the hospital which is merely providing a facility for it to be looked after. Usually this money will come from continuing state benefits and a welfare officer should be available to assist with claims[13] but an initial sum may be deposited by the patient. Where the patient is able to cope with small sums of cash, a form can be obtained and taken either by the patient or a member of staff to the hospital bank or cash office to effect withdrawals. The hospital must keep an account of all money held for a patient and produce this to the patient on request.

11.16 The hospital does not provide for all personal needs and some spending money in the hands of the patient is desirable. If relatives are attending to the financial affairs they may hand regular sums in cash to the patient when they visit, but if these visits are not regular or the patient cannot cope with cash it may be convenient to deposit regular sums in the hospital bank. Where there is no-one available to handle a patient's money, the hospital will deal with benefit claims and also administer the money under these procedures including making it available for the patient's benefit. Upon leaving hospital any balance must be accounted for to the patient or to the patient's representative or estate.

Tax returns and repayments

11.17 Tax returns must generally be signed by the taxpayer in person but may be signed by a deputy or an attorney under a registered lasting or enduring power of attorney in cases of mental incapacity, or by an ordinary attorney in cases of physical inability to sign.[14] A trustee will only have authority to sign tax returns relating to the particular trust. Someone who needs help from a relative or friend, or an adviser, to manage their tax affairs because of illness or disability may consent to that person dealing with HMRC on their behalf.

11.18 A spouse/civil partner or relative of someone who has difficulty making a claim or who has died, may be able to claim tax back for them by getting in touch with their usual HMRC Office or the HMRC Office that deals with repayment claims. In order to avoid the need for annual repayment claims there are further procedures whereby a parent, guardian, spouse, son or daughter of a person suffering from mental disorder may register on the person's behalf for interest to be paid without deduction of tax on bank and building society accounts.

---

11   Mental Health Act 1983, s 142. There were similar provisions for local government pensions.
12   MCA 2005, s 67 and Sch 6, para 29.
13   Refer to Ch 10 at **10.298** for entitlement to benefits whilst in hospital.
14   Taxes Management Act 1970, s 8.

Banking accounts

11.19 There was a time when a friendly local bank manager who knew the family circumstances could exercise discretion and overlook impaired capacity when satisfied that the money was being spent in the best interests of the customer, but with changes in management structures this type of approach can no longer be relied upon. Building societies also offer banking facilities that are similar to those traditionally provided by the banks, but these too have become more controlled by rules and the local manager or agent is unlikely to be left with discretion as to the manner in which an account may be conducted. Some banks will arrange limited facilities such as payment of maintenance charges for an account holder who is mentally incapable and some building societies allow withdrawals in certain circumstances.[15]

11.20 Some steps can be taken by an elderly person to anticipate the need for support in dealing with financial affairs. A *third party mandate* can be completed to allow another person to conduct an account and this may be convenient in cases of frequent absence or physical disability, but the mandate is revoked by the subsequent mental incapacity of the account-holder. As an alternative, money can be held in the joint names of an elderly individual and another person on the basis that either has power to sign, but such authority may also be revoked if either account-holder loses mental capacity.[16]

11.21 Money that belongs to an elderly individual can simply be held in the name of another person, but this creates vulnerability to misappropriation or misunderstandings so may not be suitable for larger sums, and it can result in tax, inheritance and state funding problems. It may be preferable for the money to be held by someone as express *nominee* for the elderly individual or for a trust to be formally acknowledged, although this is not possible if the elderly person is already mentally incapacitated.

Trusts

11.22 The use of trusts or settlements is one way of handling the financial affairs of another person, whether or not that person is incapable of dealing with his own affairs. Trustees hold and manage the trust property and may be given a discretion to expend both capital and income so as to support a particular beneficiary or beneficiaries. If they are given appropriate powers they may purchase assets and services for the use or benefit of the beneficiary rather than handing over the money.

11.23 The powers of the trustees will not, however, extend to property of the beneficiary that has not been vested in them as trustees, or to the personal life, residence or behaviour of the beneficiary, although their control over essential funding may give them considerable influence. There is no supervision over the conduct of trustees as long as they carry out the terms of the trust, and if they are given a wide discretion there can be no complaint if they do not exercise this in the manner that others might wish.

Informal arrangements

11.24 A simple form of trust arises where money is held in the name of another person who acknowledges, whether formally or informally, the true ownership. This is only suitable for relatively small sums because tax and other complications can arise. In some family situations a trust is not even created, but money or assets are given to children or

---

[15] MCA 2005, ss 7 and 8 may assist.
[16] This is not the view of some solicitors but it is the view of the clearing banks so problems can arise.

other relatives in the expectation that the resource will be made available in case of need. Whilst this may work in practice it can cause serious problems if the understanding is not honoured or unreasonable expectations are held.

Settlements

11.25 It is possible for an elderly person prior to but in expectation of becoming mentally incapable to transfer all money and assets to trustees upon the terms of a settlement whereby they continue to manage the trust fund for the support and benefit of that person. The trustees would not acquire any authority over assets that had not been or could not be transferred into the settlement, and the gift into the settlement might be set aside or disregarded in the event of subsequent insolvency or dependence upon means-tested benefits or services of the donor. The attractions of this course have been reduced by the availability of lasting powers of attorney (and previously enduring powers) which are more comprehensive in dealing with the financial powers of the individual.

11.26 Where it is desired to make financial provision for another person who may be or become incapable of dealing with his own affairs, this problem may be avoided by appointing trustees and leaving property to them on suitably worded trusts. The personal financial powers of the beneficiary will not be affected. The existence of the trust, if of a discretionary nature or interest only trusts, may also prevent the reduction or withdrawal of state benefits, or the charge for services, that would otherwise arise due to means-testing of the beneficiary's own assets and income, as explained in Chapter 12.

Income tax

11.27 Any income paid to or expended on behalf of a beneficiary will have had income tax deducted and in the case of a discretionary trust with income over £1,000 per annum this will be at a higher rate tax. Some or all of this tax can be reclaimed if the beneficiary has not otherwise utilised the annual personal allowance or is not liable to higher rates of tax. Care should be taken by the trustees to avoid any tax repayment being an unintended income in the hands of the beneficiary, and difficulties may arise in submitting tax repayment claims on behalf of a beneficiary who is mentally incapable.

Court awards

11.28 A party to civil proceedings who lacks the mental capacity to conduct those proceedings is called a 'protected party' and must be represented by a 'litigation friend'. No settlement or compromise of any money claim brought by or on behalf of a protected party is valid without the approval of the court, and there is provision for any settlement of a claim before proceedings are commenced to be approved on an application made to the court specifically for that purpose.[17]

11.29 Special procedures apply where a court awards damages to a person who is a 'protected beneficiary', namely:

> 'a protected party who lacks capacity to manage and control any money recovered by him or on his behalf or for his benefit in the proceedings.'

---

[17]　Civil Procedure Rules 1998, Part 21 and PD 21. This is dealt with in Ch 3 at **3.166** et seq.

That court must decide how those monies are to be handled and there are procedures which ensure that damages are transferred to the Court of Protection where this is desirable.[18] If a deputy has already been appointed or there is an attorney under an enduring or lasting power, the deputy or attorney will usually have brought the proceedings so will receive damages in that capacity and the procedures need not apply.

POWERS OF ATTORNEY

Preliminary

11.30 A power of attorney is a document whereby a person (the *donor*) gives another person (the *attorney*) power to act on his behalf in his name in regard to his financial affairs. It is a form of agency that has existed for centuries and the attorney contracts in the name of the donor and is not personally liable. A general power may be revoked by the donor at any time and is revoked by the death or subsequent mental incapacity of the donor. Statutory protection is provided for an attorney who acts in good faith without knowledge of revocation.[19]

11.31 The power must be executed as a deed by, or by the direction and in the presence of, the donor. Two witnesses are required where it is executed by the direction of the donor. Until 31 July 1990 it had to be 'signed sealed and delivered' but from that date need merely be 'signed as a deed'.[20] The power may be in general terms or limited to specific acts or circumstances, but a simple form of general power is available under which the attorney may do on behalf of the donor anything which he can lawfully do by an attorney.[21]

Production of powers

11.32 It may be necessary to register a power with many different financial bodies, but a statutory provision assists with these arrangements and makes it possible to retain the original in safekeeping. A photocopy which bears a certificate signed by the donor, or a solicitor or stockbroker, at the end of each page that it is a true and complete copy of the original must be accepted as proof of the contents of the original.[22] A certified copy of a certified copy must even be accepted if satisfying this requirement. The requirement that each page must be certified was not initially a problem because most powers consisted of one page, but the form of enduring and lasting power of attorney are many pages long but it is a necessary inconvenience to certify each page.

11.33 A lasting power of attorney can also be certified by the donor, solicitor or notary, provided it is certified as an 'accurate copy' of the original.[23]

---

[18] Refer to Ch 3 at **3.200** for the procedures that are available.
[19] Powers of Attorney Act 1971.
[20] Law of Property (Miscellaneous Provisions) Act 1989.
[21] Powers of Attorney Act 1971, Sch 1.
[22] Powers of Attorney Act 1971, s 3.
[23] Lasting Powers of Attorney, Enduring Powers of Attorney and Public Guardian Regulations 2007, SI 2007/1253, reg 11(3).

11.34 In the case of a registered enduring or lasting power an office copy issued by the Office of the Public Guardian is evidence of the contents. Office copies will only be produced in exceptional circumstances and at a cost of £35 each. It is not possible to certify an office copy as an original.[24]

Limitations of ordinary powers

11.35 Only a competent person can appoint an attorney, and an attorney under an ordinary power can only continue to act if the donor remains mentally capable. Thus although a power of attorney is potentially a very valuable document for an elderly person whose abilities are declining, it ceases to be of use at the very time that it is most needed. Some professionals will suggest creating general powers to operate whilst a lasting power is in the process of being registered with the Public Guardian to avoid any gap in decision-making when someone needs to act. This approach is only appropriate when the donor continues to have mental capacity as a general power should not be used when the donor is losing or has lost mental capacity.

Standard of care

11.36 A person who is appointed an attorney is not obliged to act, but if he does he owes a fiduciary duty to the donor and must act in good faith and keep accounts for production to the donor or the Office of the Public Guardian on request or order made by the Court of Protection. He must use such skill as he possesses and show such care as he would in conducting his own affairs. An attorney who is being remunerated must exercise the care, skill and diligence of a reasonable man, and if acting in the course of a profession must exercise proper professional competence. An attorney may not appoint a substitute or otherwise delegate his general authority, but may employ persons to do specific tasks.

Conflict of interest

11.37 An attorney must not allow a conflict of interest to arise between his duty to the donor and to someone else without disclosing this to the donor. If the donor is no longer mentally capable such disclosure will not be possible, but consultation with concerned members of the family or carers may resolve the problem as to what is really in the best interests of the donor. The enduring power should by then have been registered so directions can be sought from the Court of Protection where this is justified. This may be appropriate where self-interest arises, eg an attorney wishing to spend some of the donor's money on improvements to a home owned by the attorney in which the donor resides. Subject to any restrictions or conditions in the power, solicitors and other professional persons who are attorneys can charge for their services but ideally any express authority will have provided for some external supervision.

Enduring power of attorney

Preliminary

11.38 Legislation in 1985 created enduring powers of attorney ('EPAs') which remain valid notwithstanding the donor's subsequent incapacity to manage his own affairs.[25]

---

24 Public Guardian (Fees etc) Regulations 2007, SI 2007/2051, reg 10(d).
25 Enduring Powers of Attorney Act 1985.

These provided a practical, inexpensive way in which elderly or infirm people might anticipate incapacity. Ordinary powers were unaffected, but enduring powers were of general application so could be used instead if desired.

11.39 It has not been possible to create new EPAs since 1 October 2007 when the Mental Capacity Act 2005 came into force and replaced them with lasting powers of attorney, but the procedures are summarised here because many EPAs are still in use or available to be registered if the need arises.[26]

Requirements

Form

11.40 An EPA must have been executed in the manner and form prescribed in the regulations current at the date of execution, and there were three prescribed forms although some overlap was allowed at the time of each change.[27] The standard form is made up of pairs of alternatives with space for the inclusion of additional wording so that it might be adapted to the particular wishes of the donor by limiting the authority of the attorney or restricting the manner in which such authority may be exercised.

Execution

11.41 The explanatory information on the prescribed form told the donor the effect of executing the power and had to be read by or to the donor and understood by the donor. The form was signed by the donor first and then by each attorney to signify acceptance and acknowledgement of the duty to register in certain circumstances. The signatures of the donor and attorney(s) had to be witnessed by an independent person or persons and they could not witness each other's signatures nor should a spouse be a witness. A donor who was unable to sign could make a mark and the attestation clause would be amended to explain this and that the power and explanatory information had been read over to the donor who appeared fully to understand it. Deletions or additions need not be initialed as they are presumed to have been made before execution.

Restrictions

Voluntary

11.42 An EPA may be general in its terms or for specific purposes only. The donor could place restrictions or conditions on the power, for example that it may be used only for dealing with specific property. It may be expressed only to be effective if the donor ceases to have mental capacity or if it is registered, but in the absence of any such restriction it will be effective as a general power immediately.

Statutory

11.43 There are certain statutory restrictions on what an attorney under an EPA can do after it has been registered. He may not benefit himself or persons other than the donor except to the extent that the donor might have been expected to provide for his or their needs, and may not make gifts except for presents of reasonable value at Christmas, birthdays, weddings and such like to persons related to or connected with the donor or

---

[26] MCA 2005 repeals the former legislation but the provisions are repeated in Sch 4 so far as required.
[27] Enduring Powers of Attorney (Prescribed Form) Regulations 1986, 1987 and 1990.

charitable gifts which the donor might have been expected to make. The value of such gifts must not be unreasonable having regard to all the circumstances and in particular the size of the donor's estate.

The donor

11.44 An EPA is valid only if the donor had the necessary capacity at the time of its execution, and this means that he understood the nature and effect of the document. It does not mean that the donor must have been fully capable of managing his property and affairs. A valid power could be executed even though the person signing it did not have that level of capacity, although in such event the EPA would need to be registered immediately.

11.45 The decision of Mr Justice Hoffmann in *Re K, Re F* explains the reasons for this and also identifies what must be understood by the donor. It is repeated here because it has had a profound influence on the use of these powers and may also have some relevance to lasting powers of attorney:[28]

'The Act does not specify the mental capacity needed to execute an enduring power of attorney and the answer must therefore be found in the common law ... In principle ... an understanding of the nature and effect of the power was sufficient for its validity. At common law there is however the further rule that a power can no longer be validly exercised if the donor has lost the mental capacity to be a principal ... mental incapacity revokes the power. [It] would at common law have been revoked, at the latest, when [the donor] ceased to be able to manage and administer [his] property and affairs.

... There seems to me no logical reason why the validity of the power ... should be affected by considerations of whether it would have been exercisable. The court is not concerned with whether the power has been validly exercised but whether as a juristic act it should be registered with a view to its future exercise notwithstanding the donor's loss of mental capacity. The Act is intended to ensure that the power will continue to be exercisable notwithstanding mental incapacity. But ... I see no reason why the test for whether it was validly created should be the same as for whether it would have ceased to be exercisable. In principle they are clearly different ... In practice it is likely that many enduring powers will be executed when symptoms of mental incapacity have begun to manifest themselves. These symptoms may result in the donor being mentally incapable in the statutory sense that [he] is unable on a regular basis to manage [his] property and affairs. But [he] may execute the power with full understanding and with the intention of taking advantage of the Act to have [his] affairs managed by an attorney of [his] choice rather than having them put in the hands of the Court of Protection. The exercise of the power is ... hedged about on all sides with statutory protection for the donor. In these circumstances it does not seem to me necessary to impose too high a standard of capacity for its valid execution.

Finally I should say something about what is meant by understanding the nature and effect of the power. What degree of understanding is involved? Plainly one cannot expect that the donor should have been able to pass an examination on the provisions of the Act. At the other extreme, I do not think that it would be sufficient if he realised only that it gave [the attorney] power to look after his property. [Counsel] helpfully summarised the matters which the donor should have understood in order that he can be said to have understood the nature and effect of the power. First (if such be the terms of the power) that the attorney will be able to assume complete authority over the donor's affairs. Secondly, (if such be the terms of the power) that the attorney will in general be able to do anything with the donor's property which he himself could have done. Thirdly, that the authority will continue if the donor

---

28   [1988] 1 All ER 358.

should be or become mentally incapable. Fourthly, that if he should be or become mentally incapable, the power will be irrevocable without confirmation by the court ... I accept [counsel's] summary as a statement of the matters which should ordinarily be explained to the donor (whatever the precise language which may be used) and which the evidence should show he has understood.'

The attorney

11.46 Anyone who has attained their legal majority and is not bankrupt may act as an attorney, and although there is no statutory restriction upon an adult who is mentally incapable being appointed one would expect any objection on that ground to be readily upheld. Two or more people may be appointed to act jointly or jointly and severally but the regulations do not permit any two of several named attorneys to be appointed and the Court of Protection has severed such clauses on the basis the appointment is neither joint nor joint and several.[29]

11.47 Different attorneys may be appointed for different purposes and a trust corporation (such as a bank) may be appointed. Where there were fears that the attorney may not survive for long enough, a donor would simultaneously execute more than one power with only one coming into force initially and the other(s) worded so as to take effect at an appropriate later date (eg on the death of the previous attorney or on revocation of that power). Both powers are obliged to be registered when the donor has become or is becoming mentally incapable of managing his property and affairs, irrespective of whether the condition has been fulfilled.[30] It has since been held that a successor or replacement attorney may be appointed (this being expressly permitted for lasting powers of attorney).[31]

11.48 A person who is appointed an attorney under an EPA is not obliged to act but will be under a statutory duty to apply for registration when the time comes, unless he chooses to disclaim. He should keep accounts but only need produce these to the Office of the Public Guardian or court if so directed. Following registration of an EPA the court has jurisdiction to relieve the attorney of any liability incurred by reason of a breach of duty whether arising before or after the need for registration, and further statutory protection is available for attorneys in specific circumstances.

Supervision

11.49 The next stage with an outstanding EPA is registration. This provides safeguards because certain relatives must be given notice, and although the court has supervisory powers it is only where problems are brought to its attention that they may be used.[32]

Registration

11.50 An attorney is under a duty to apply to the Office of the Public Guardian for registration of the EPA as soon as practicable after he has reason to believe that the donor is or *is becoming* mentally incapable. Once this situation arises the EPA is suspended (save for essential action) until submission of an application for registration

---

[29] *Re Newman* (a judgment of the Senior Judge given on 30 July 2012).
[30] *Re J (Enduring Power of Attorney)* [2009] EWHC 436 (Ch), Lewison J.
[31] *Re J (Enduring Power of Attorney)* [2009] EWHC 436 (Ch), Lewison J.
[32] MCA 2005, Sch 4; Lasting Powers of Attorney, Enduring Powers of Attorney and Public Guardian Regulations 2007, SI 2007/1253 as amended.

when certain limited authority is automatically restored. Once the power has been registered the attorney can again exercise all his functions under it.

Notice

11.51 Notice must first be given to the donor and to the donor's closest relatives in the prescribed form (EP1PG), which states that the attorney proposes to apply for registration of the EPA and that the recipient may object to this within 4 weeks on any ground therein specified. Notice must be handed to the donor personally but relatives may be served by first class post and a covering letter may be helpful, but any explanation given must not prejudice the statutory requirements.

11.52 The specified relatives must be taken in order of priority from the statutory list, class by class, the classes being: spouse; children; parents; brothers and sisters (whole or half blood); widow or widower of a child; grandchildren; children of brothers and sisters of the whole blood; children of brothers and sisters of the half blood; uncles and aunts of the whole blood; children of uncles and aunts of the whole blood. At least three relatives must be served but if anyone from one class has to be served then all of that class must be served.

11.53 Notice need not be given to anyone who has not attained 18 years, is mentally incapable or cannot be traced. If there are less than three living relatives only they need be given notice, but this must be stated on the application to register. The attorney, if a relative entitled to notice, does not need to give notice to himself but may be included in the minimum of three and similarly any co-attorney who is joining in the application to register.[33]

Application

11.54 The attorney(s) must send the application in Form EP2PG together with the original EPA and registration fee to the Office of the Public Guardian. The fee (presently £110) is payable out of the estate of the donor but there is a generous exemption and remission policy for people with limited income or in receipt of means-tested state benefits.[34] If there are joint attorneys then they must jointly apply for registration, but if they are joint and several then one may apply alone but notice must be given to the other(s).

11.55 If the application is in order and no objections are received after 35 days from when the EP1PG was sent, the power is registered and the original is returned to the attorney(s) duly stamped as registered and bearing the Office of the Public Guardian validation stamp. No medical evidence is required as to the capacity of the donor either at the time of execution of the power or at the time of registration, but it would be advisable to obtain such evidence if a dispute is expected.

11.56 The persons to whom notice is given may object to registration on the grounds that the power was not validly created or no longer subsists, the application is premature, fraud or undue pressure was used to induce the donor to create the power or that having regard to all the circumstances and in particular the attorney's relationship

---

[33] An application to the Court of Protection can be made to dispense with giving notice to a person for special reasons. As this involves a court process and payment of the court fee, it would be exceptional for such an application to be made.

[34] Form LPA120 needs to be completed with evidence of income to be exempt from payment of the fee.

to or connection with the donor he or she is unsuitable to be the donor's attorney. The objector must notify the Office of the Public Guardian on form EP3PG, which has the effect of suspending registration and at the same time make an application to the Court of Protection on form COP8, with supporting evidence on form COP28. The matter should then proceed according to the court rules.

11.57 When an application is opposed, it is usually because someone in the donor's family does not know the attorney or does not trust him, and the underlying reason may be a struggle for influence over the donor.

Effect of registration

11.58 Once an EPA is registered the attorney(s) can again operate under its authority and the EPA cannot be revoked by the donor without the confirmation of the court. The court can cancel registration upon any ground upon which it could have refused the original registration and also on certain other grounds. An attorney can give notice of disclaimer to the donor while the donor is still mentally capable or to the OPG thereafter, and there is no prescribed form. In that event the power itself may be revoked and if so it must be delivered up to the court for cancellation.

11.59 The register is open to the public and free searches for information may be made on Form OPG100. Registration does not amount to certification that the EPA is valid so the power can still be challenged when attempts are made to use it and this is a major weakness of the procedure.

Lasting power of attorney

Preliminary

11.60 Enduring powers of attorney could no longer be created after 1 October 2007, although those then in existence can still be used. From that date a new but more complex version known as lasting powers of attorney (LPAs) came into existence. There are two types: (1) for property and affairs and (2) for personal welfare decisions, and they are explained in Chapter 2. In this Chapter we deal with the effective use of LPAs for property and affairs in financial management for an elderly person.

11.61 The essence of the LPA is that it is completed whilst the donor has capacity to appoint an attorney or attorneys of his choice. It may then be registered with the OPG, thereby pre-empting any future dispute as to validity or suitability. It cannot be used until it is registered, but unlike an EPA, registration does not signify the onset of a lack of mental capacity. Unless restricted, the property and affairs power may then be used prior to, or after, the onset of mental incapacity, and the donor is not precluded from entering into transactions for which he is capable.[35]

Creation and registration

11.62 Reference should be made to Chapter 2 at **2.62** et seq for the law and procedure relating to the creation of a valid LPA for property and affairs. Only additional practical guidance is provided here.

---

[35] In contrast, an LPA for personal welfare may only be used for decisions that the grantor is incapable of making.

Form

11.63 The first two pages contain information that the donor should read before completing Part A which sets out the core details of the appointment. The donor must specify the person(s) appointed, and if more than one, whether they are to act jointly, jointly and severally or joint in respect of some matters and jointly and severally in respect of other matters.[36] Further attorney(s) may be appointed to replace an attorney on the occurrence of a specified event which has the effect of terminating the attorney's appointment.[37]

11.64 The donor also identifies up to five persons (other than the named attorneys or any replacement attorney) to be notified of an application to register the power. If the donor dispenses with such notification two certificates of understanding must be obtained (see below).

11.65 Part B of the form comprises a certificate of understanding to be completed by a person of a prescribed description either at the time Part A is signed or as soon as reasonably practicable thereafter. This will be an independent person who has either known the donor for at least 2 years or is a suitable professional.[38]

11.66 Part C is for completion by the attorney(s) and includes a declaration that acknowledges the duties of the attorney. This should be read carefully. Supplementary pages allow for additional names, whether further or replacement attorneys or persons to be notified, and conditions, restrictions or guidance. A box is provided for inclusion of a charging clause in respect of a professional attorney.

11.67 Whilst restrictions and/or conditions may be imposed by the donor, these should be carefully considered to ensure they are appropriate, administratively possible and not forbidden by law, as they may cause unnecessary complications.[39] The donor should seek to appoint persons who can be trusted and then respect their judgment, as one can never anticipate all the situations that may arise. Helpful conditions include authority to inspect medical records or other confidential documents such as the donor's will, and authority to disclose information to relatives and others. It may be better to provide 'guidance' which the attorney(s) are obliged to take into account but not required to follow.

Registration

11.68 The LPA is ineffective until it is registered and it is unwise to wait until it is needed because there will then be a delay. This will be at least 6 weeks if the form is in order and there are no objections, but if it proves necessary for the Public Guardian to refer the form to the Court of Protection because of objections or ineffective provisions there will be considerable delay and it may then be too late for the donor to rectify matters. However, the cost of registration may be a disincentive, circumstances may change before the power is needed and the donor may not wish to confer authority on the attorney at this stage.

---

[36] This could be jointly in respect of some matters and jointly and severally (which means separately) in respect of others.

[37] Eg disclaimer, death, bankruptcy, dissolution of marriage, incapacity.

[38] Eg solicitor, registered health care professional or social worker, or independent mental capacity advocate.

[39] An invalid condition may be severed on an application to the Court of Protection. See Ch 2 at 2.81.

11.69 An application to register is made to the Public Guardian in form LPA002 with the original LPA and a cheque for the fee (presently £110) or remission application (form LPA120). Either the donor or an attorney may apply. The applicant gives notice in form LPA001 to persons named in the LPA for that purpose, but the Public Guardian gives notice in form LPA003 to the donor if an attorney applies, and to any other attorney if the donor or an attorney applies. Unless the Public Guardian receives a valid objection within 4 weeks of the last notice being given, or there is a defect in the document, the instrument must be registered as an LPA. It is stamped and returned to the applicant, and notice is given to the donor and attorney(s) on form LPA004.

11.70 The Public Guardian has only a limited right to determine the validity of the power and although registration may be refused (or cancelled) on technical or factual grounds, an objection on substantive grounds must be referred to the Court of Protection. Where an attorney or named person receives notice and objects on one of the prescribed grounds registration will be refused. The objection is made by notice being given to the Public Guardian on form LPA008 and an application to the court on form COP7 must then be made within 3 weeks.

11.71 If any other person wishes to object to registration on one of these grounds, or any person (including the donor or an attorney) wishes to apply for revocation of the LPA after it has been registered, a formal application must be made to the court on form COP1. The court has wide powers to determine the validity of and intervene in the operation of an LPA.[40]

Powers of the court and OPG

11.72 An attorney is expected to manage the donor's affairs in accordance with the terms of the EPA or LPA and without recourse to the court, taking advice from a solicitor where necessary, but the OPG and Court of Protection have some supervisory powers in relation to a registered power. The OPG has power to investigate the attorney, by requesting information and if need be can request a Court of Protection visitor the donor and the attorney for the purpose of preparing a report. If needed, the OPG can apply to the Court of Protection for suitable directions and as a last resort, the removal of the attorney.

11.73 The court may give directions as to the management or disposal by the attorney of the donor's property and affairs, direct the rendering of accounts by the attorney and the production of records, give directions regarding the attorney's remuneration and expenses, and require the attorney to furnish information or produce documents in his possession in the capacity of attorney. It may also give any consent or authority which the attorney would have had to obtain from a mentally capable donor and authorise the attorney to benefit himself, or other persons, in some way beyond the general statutory authority. The court may give such directions before registration of an EPA if it has reason to believe that the donor is becoming, or has become, mentally incapable.

11.74 These safeguards prevent the unscrupulous use of powers where the donor is not capable of understanding what is being done with his assets, but the court cannot exercise those powers itself nor can it enlarge those powers. It has been held that the statutory provision is only concerned with the administrative matters mentioned above and the court does not have unrestricted power in the disposal of the donor's property so

---

[40] MCA 2005, ss 22 and 23. See Ch 2 at **2.95**.

may not grant provision out of the donor's estate inconsistent with restrictions imposed in the EPA or LPA.[41] As a last resort the court could revoke the power and impose a deputyship if it thought fit or make orders under its own statutory jurisdiction.

COURT OF PROTECTION

Preliminary

11.75 Problems arise when an elderly person who has money or property becomes incapable of managing their financial affairs, does not have a valid enduring power of attorney that can be registered, and also does not have or is unable to execute a lasting power of attorney.[42] It is then necessary to apply to the Court of Protection which has power to direct how those affairs shall be managed.[43] The usual outcome is the appointment of a deputy, but the court does not always need to go that far and can make a one-off order if that will resolve the financial affairs.

11.76 The Court of Protection may only make decisions for a person, or appoint someone to do so, when it has determined that this person lacks capacity on the relevant matters. It will normally take this step following an application. However, pending determination of an application it does have power to make an interim order or give directions if there is reason to believe that the person lacks capacity in relation to the matter and it is in the person's interests to do so.[44]

11.77 The powers of the court extend to declaring whether the person lacks capacity to make a particular decision or range of decisions, declaring that an act done in relation to the person is lawful, making a decision on behalf of the person, or appointing a deputy to make decisions. The principles on which it acts are set out in the legislation.[45] Reference should be made to Chapter 2 at **2.98** et seq for a description of the Court of Protection and its powers. Only additional practical guidance is provided here.

Deputies

Overview

11.78 A deputy may be appointed for either (1) property and affairs or (2) personal welfare decisions, as explained in Chapter 2. Under this heading we only deal with the former.

11.79 Deputies are seldom appointed for personal welfare because a one-off decision will usually suffice when there is a dispute or uncertainty. But financial affairs are continuing and, despite the principle that the least restrictive intervention should be adopted, a practical approach requires that someone should be in continuous control of finances even if the appointment is to be reviewed at intervals. Such a review may be appropriate following the appointment of a deputy to manage the finances of a person

---

[41]   *Re R (Enduring Power of Attorney)* [1990] 2 All ER 893, Vinelott J. The court could not direct that the attorney dispose of the estate in the applicant's favour in recognition of a moral obligation.

[42]   The test of capacity to execute an LPA is less demanding than that to manage significant financial affairs. See **11.44** above for the capacity to execute an EPA. A similar approach is likely to be adopted.

[43]   For the powers of the Court of Protection see Ch 2.

[44]   MCA 2005, s 48.

[45]   MCA 2005. See generally Ch 2 at **2.11–2.18**.

who has just been awarded substantial damages following a brain injury, but not in the case of an elderly person whose life expectancy will inevitably be limited.

Appointment

Procedure

11.80 The application to the Court of Protection for the appointment of a deputy for property and affairs will be made by the person who wishes to be appointed or some other interested person. Permission to apply is not generally required.[46] Guidance on making an application and the relevant forms are available from the court website,[47] whereas guidance for deputies once appointed is available on the website of the Office of the Public Guardian (OPG).[48] An assessment of capacity (generally by a doctor) is required and a fee is payable but this may later be reimbursed from the estate of the elderly person. There is then a process whereby the person who is the subject of the application and other appropriate persons are notified of the application and given an opportunity to object.[49]

11.81 If the papers are in order and no objection is received by the court within the time limit, the application will be dealt with 'on paper' and a suitable Order issued to the applicant or deputy(ies). Otherwise a district judge will consider the file and give directions which may result in an attended hearing.

Choice and suitability

11.82 The person making the application will often be appointed but some other person may be appointed, although no-one may be appointed without their consent. Usually the deputy will be a relative or friend of the elderly individual, typically a spouse or adult child, but a solicitor, accountant or other professional person may be appointed, and if there is no-one suitable a local authority representative can be appointed in many (but not all) areas as the last resort.[50] The court decides who should be appointed in the event of a dispute and will accept the appointment of more than one deputy provided that there is no conflict between them. This may be appropriate to provide continuity where an elderly spouse is appointed with a child. Such an appointment will usually be made either jointly or joint and severally. It will not generally be appropriate for a person resident outside England and Wales, or a person with a conflict of interest, to be appointed.

Order

11.83 The following is a general form of Order suitable for most situations where the elderly person is male and a single deputy is appointed for property and affairs.

THIS DOCUMENT IS NOT VALID UNLESS IT BEARS THE IMPRESSED SEAL OF THE COURT OF PROTECTION ON ALL PAGES

COURT OF PROTECTION   No. [*Case number*]

---

[46] Court of Protection Rules 2007, rr 50–53.
[47] The Forms required are COP1 (Application), COP1A (Supporting information), COP3 (Assessment of capacity), COP4 (Deputy's declaration). An application pack may be downloaded at: www.justice.gov.uk/forms/hmcts/cop-packs.
[48] www.justice.gov.uk/forms/opg/deputies.
[49] Forms COP14, COP15, COP20A.
[50] This may be the holder of an office such as the Director of Social Services rather than a named person.

MENTAL CAPACITY ACT 2005

In the matter of
FULL NAME OF 'P'
ORDER APPOINTING A DEPUTY FOR
PROPERTY AND AFFAIRS

made by *Judge's name*
at *Court's London address*
on *date*

UPON the court being satisfied that [*P's name*] lacks capacity to make various decisions for himself in relation to a matter or matters concerning his property and affairs, and that the purpose for which this order is needed cannot be as effectively achieved in a way that is less restrictive of his rights and freedom of action.

IT IS ORDERED that:

1.　　　　Appointment of deputy

(a)　　　　[*Full name*] of [*address*] is appointed as deputy ("the deputy") to make decisions on behalf of [*P's name*] that he is unable to make for himself in relation to his property and affairs, subject to any conditions or restrictions set out in this order.

(b)　　　　The appointment will last until further order.

(c)　　　　The deputy must apply the principles set out in section 1 of the Mental Capacity Act 2005 ("the Act") and have regard to the guidance in the Code of Practice to the Act.

2.　　　　Authority of deputy

(a)　　　　The court confers general authority on the deputy to take possession or control of the property and affairs of [*P's name*] and to exercise the same powers of management and investment, including [selling and] letting property, as he has as beneficial owner, subject to the terms and conditions set out in this order.

(b)　　　　The deputy cannot purchase any freehold or leasehold property on [*P's name*]'s behalf without obtaining further authority from the court.

(c)　　　　[The deputy must not sell, lease or charge any freehold or leasehold property in which [*P's name*] has a beneficial interest without obtaining further authority from the court.]

(d)　　　　If the deputy considers it in [*P's name*]'s best interests to do so, the deputy may appoint an investment manager, who is regulated and authorised to undertake investment business, to manage his assets on a discretionary basis under the standard terms and conditions applicable to such service from time-to-time, and to permit the investments to be held in the name of the investment manager nominee company.

(e)　　　　The deputy may make provision for the needs of anyone who is related to or connected with [*P's name*] if he provided for, or might be expected to provide for, that person's needs by doing whatever he did, or might reasonably be expected to do, to meet those needs.

(f)　　　　The deputy may (without obtaining any further authority from the court) dispose of [*P's name*]'s money or property by way of gift to any charity to which he made, or might have been expected to make, such gifts, and, on customary occasions, to persons who are related to or connected with him, provided that the value of each such gift is not unreasonable having regard to all the circumstances and, in particular, the size of his estate.

(g)　　　　[*Optional paragraph*] On [*P's name*]'s behalf the deputy may take such steps as may be necessary to obtain (either alone or with a co-administrator) a grant of representation to the estate of [*name of P's deceased spouse*] and to use the share to which [*P's name*] is entitled for his benefit.

(h)　　　　For the purpose of giving effect to any decision the deputy may execute or sign any necessary deeds or documents.

3.　　　　Reports

(a)   The deputy is required to keep statements, vouchers, receipts and other financial records.

(b)   The deputy must submit a report to the Public Guardian as and when required.

4.   Costs and expenses

(a)   The deputy is entitled to be reimbursed for reasonable expenses incurred provided they are in proportion to the size of [*P's name*]'s estate and the functions performed by the deputy. [*This clause relates to Lay Deputies only*]

(b)   The deputy is authorised to pay [*name of P's solicitors*] fixed costs for this application, or, where the amount exceeds the fixed costs allowed, the deputy is authorised to agree the costs for making this application and to pay them from funds belonging to [*P's name*]. In default of agreement, or if the deputy or the solicitors would prefer the costs to be assessed, this order is to be treated as authority to the Senior Courts Costs Office to carry out a detailed assessment on the standard basis. [*This clause relates to Lay Deputies where a professional has submitted the application*]

(c)   The deputy is entitled to receive fixed costs in relation to this application, and to receive fixed costs for the general management of [*P's name*]'s affairs. If the deputy would prefer the costs to be assessed, this order is to be treated as authority to the Senior Courts Costs Office to carry out a detailed assessment on the standard basis. [*This clause relates to Professional Deputies only*]

5.   Security

(a)   The deputy is required forthwith to obtain and maintain security in the sum of £*amount* in accordance with the standard requirements as to the giving of security.

(b)   The deputy must ensure that the level of security ordered by the court is in place before discharging any of the functions conferred by this order.

6.   Right to apply for reconsideration of order

This order was made on the court's own initiative without hearing the parties, or giving them the opportunity to make representations. Any person who is affected by it may apply to the court within 21 days of the order being served for reconsideration of the order.

11.84 One of the variables is whether there should be authority for the deputy to sell the elderly person's own home (eg to enable care home fees to be paid). It is helpful to indicate the intention in the application form so as to avoid the expense of a further application for permission. If this authority is not given the value of the home will not be taken into account when calculating the amount of the security bond. Where the property is held in the joint names of the elderly person and another person, an additional application to authorise the sale is usually required. If a solicitor or other professional person is appointed the order makes provision for remuneration by way of costs.

Status and duties

11.85 The Deputy's Declaration on Form COP4 sets out 17 personal undertakings which must be given and these should be considered carefully. A deputy for property and affairs is responsible for administering the financial affairs in the best interests of the elderly person[51] in accordance with the principles in the Mental Capacity Act 2005.[52] Routine tasks will include collecting in the income, paying the bills, supervising the investments and safeguarding the assets. He must comply with all orders and directions

---

[51]   For amplification of 'best interests' see Ch 2 at **2.29** et seq.
[52]   See Ch 2 at **2.12** et seq.

issued by the court and act within the powers and authorities given to him, and must account to the court when required. He may not delegate his duties.

11.86 It should not be assumed that the deputy must do all these tasks personally. A solicitor may be employed to handle some of the work under the instructions of the deputy. Also, whilst the elderly person may be unable to handle his own affairs in an overall sense, there may be capacity to cope with small or day-to-day transactions, for example weekly social security benefit. The payment of a regular allowance for expenditure of choice may be beneficial to the elderly person's welfare and this should always be considered, because the purpose of the deputy appointment is not to deprive the person of all control over money. In suitable cases the elderly person may be supported in operating a personal bank or building society account.

Supervision, accounts and security bond

11.87 The OPG is responsible for ensuring that deputies act in the best interests of the person who lacks capacity and follow the directions of the court. The level of support and supervision the OPG allocates to a deputy is decided after carrying out an assessment of the individual circumstances of the case based on the complexity of the affairs, the types of decisions that need to be made, the care requirements of the person and the relationship between the deputy and the person who lacks capacity. There are four levels of supervision and fees are payable.

11.88 Type 1 is close supervision involving regular contact with the deputy. Type 2A is an intermediate level of supervision involving monitoring of new deputies or short term interventions. Type 2 is lighter touch supervision involving sample monitoring of cases and Type 3 applies to property and affairs deputies who manage limited assets and who the OPG will only contact periodically. The level of support and supervision will be regularly assessed to see if it is still relevant to the circumstances.

11.89 In most cases a security bond will be required.[53] The deputy should keep accounts, retaining receipts and handling all monies through a designated bank account. A basic account will be submitted to the OPG each year. The deputy may seek guidance from the OPG but if a significant doubt arises as to his powers he should make a formal application to the Court of Protection.

Powers

11.90 The powers of a deputy for property and affairs are limited to dealing with financial affairs and cannot extend to deciding where or with whom the elderly person shall live, consenting to medical treatment or other personal decisions, though in practice personal and financial decisions are often linked. A separate application would be required for personal welfare decisions, where there is a dispute.

11.91 Provided that he has the necessary authority the deputy may sign documents in his own name adding: 'as deputy of *name*'. He has a wide discretion and may be given general power to spend as much as is needed of the elderly person's income in maintaining this person and providing clothing and extra comforts, and income that is not needed may be accumulated (eg in a building society account). If it is clear that the

---

[53] A Public Guardian Practice Note is available at: www.justice.gov.uk/downloads/protecting-the-vulnerable/mca/pg-note-03-12-surety-bonds.pdf.

income will be insufficient to meet these expenses, perhaps because the elderly person is in a residential care home and the cost can be budgeted, authority may be given to resort to capital to the extent required to cover the shortfall. In the case of an elderly person, a deputy is generally now given the same wide powers as an attorney under a lasting power for property and affairs.

11.92 The deputy will also need to consider how he invests the money, in the best interests of the person for whom he acts. What is appropriate will depend on the person's age and life expectancy; the value and nature of his capital resources and financial needs; the impact of considered investments on state support; the views of the person concerned, including his attitude to risk, and where appropriate the views of others, as well as whether there are other people for whom he is responsible. In any event, he should obtain independent financial advice.[54]

Gifts, settlements and wills

11.93 The deputy has a general duty to maintain, so far as circumstances permit, any person whom the elderly person might have been expected to provide for. Whist this applies to an attorney acting under an EPA,[55] there is no specific provision for attorneys acting under an LPA to maintain, although the court has confirmed the attorney is able to maintain a spouse, civil partner or minor child, without necessitating an application to the Court of Protection for authority. In addition, in the course of managing the affairs of an elderly person the attorney or deputy may wish to make gifts, transfer funds to a settlement, or review testamentary provision.

Gifts

11.94 Although there is a limited discretion to make gifts, an application to the Court of Protection may be required to authorise these powers. The attorney under an LPA may make small gifts to charities and to people (including the attorney) who are related to or connected with the donor on special occasions, such as birthdays and weddings or civil partnerships, or on other customary occasions for the particular family.[56] The position is similar under an EPA except that other customary occasions are not included.[57] In all cases the gifts must be reasonable in the context of the value of the estate and the circumstances. The powers of a deputy depend upon the order under which appointed but the widely drafted order (see example above) generally adopts the same terms as for an LPA.

11.95 Larger gifts and any gift for tax planning would require the approval of the Court of Protection following a formal application and in some instances the appointment of the Official Solicitor to represent the interests of the elderly person, although a hearing might not be required in a straightforward case. In appropriate circumstances the court will consider tax planning where there are ample funds to provide for the remainder of the life of the elderly person.

---

[54] See *Re Buckley* [2013] EWHC 2965 (COP) for guidance for attorneys, 22 January 2013, SJ Lush.
[55] MCA 2005, Sch 4, para 3(2).
[56] MCA 2005, s 12. See Ch 2 at **2.74** for more detail.
[57] MCA 2005, Sch 4, para 3(2), (3).

Settlements

11.96 The Court of Protection may authorise the settlement of the elderly person's property either for his benefit or the benefit of another person.[58] There need to be special circumstances to justify this, because management by a deputy is generally considered to be more appropriate.

Statutory wills

11.97 The Court of Protection may authorise the execution of a will for a person who lacks testamentary capacity[59] and attorneys or deputies should always consider whether this is appropriate. This will usually be where there is a vacuum, either because there is no will or the last will has become seriously out of date, would be of little effect or made in dubious circumstances. It may also arise where an attorney or deputy has been obliged for the purpose of funding care needs to sell an asset that was specifically bequeathed under an existing will.[60]

11.98 Any application will be approached on the basis of the 'best interests' of the prospective testator and not (as under the previous law) on the assumption that the testator had a lucid interval. The court does not have power to resolve any dispute about the validity of any will, but has found it to be in the best interests of an incapacitated elderly person to authorise a new will where this would avoid an expensive probate dispute following death.[61]

HANDLING FINANCIAL AFFAIRS

Preliminary

11.99 Having identified the various legal procedures available for handling some or all of the financial affairs of an incapacitated person, we now consider what can be done to anticipate a decline in mental capacity and then what should be done when an elderly person actually becomes incapable of dealing with personal financial affairs. This situation may develop gradually, in which event there could be an opportunity to anticipate the problem and make arrangements, or it may arise quite suddenly perhaps due to illness or because the affairs have become more complicated and can no longer be coped with by less formal methods.[62] All too often the legal options have to be considered because an obstacle has arisen in dealing with the financial matters or there is a dispute relating to those affairs, rather than because there has been a specific assessment of incapacity.

---

[58] MCA 2005, s 18(1)(h). See Ch 2 at **2.105** for more detail.
[59] MCA 2005, s 18(1)(i). See Ch 2 at **2.105** for more detail.
[60] MCA 2005, Sch 2, paras 8 and 9 contain preserving provisions where the court has made an order for disposal, which may be used rather than an application for a statutory will.
[61] *VAC v JAD* [2010] EWHC 2159 (Ch).
[62] Eg an individual who has only had to cope with a small income from state benefits inherits capital or is awarded damages by a court.

Preparing for old age

Preliminary

11.100 What strategy should the older individual, family and advisers adopt to prepare for the potential impairment of mental capacity and a possible lack of capacity in the future? Obviously the provision of such support as is required for the time being is the primary step, but there may come a time when the supporter needs to take over conduct of the financial affairs.

Comparing the procedures

11.101 It is helpful to consider the relative advantages and disadvantages of the different methods of delegation that may be available. There are procedures of choice for the individual and also procedures that can be adopted on behalf of the individual if no advance planning has taken place. The difficulty is that much depends upon the point of view of the person judging the procedure and what may be seen as a disadvantage in one situation could be seen as an advantage in another.

Doing nothing

11.102 This is the default situation. It may be appropriate for an older person whose income is derived from state benefits and who has no property or investments. The existing financial resources can still be handled by family, a close friend or the local authority through its social services department following a loss of mental capacity. Any care provision or support that is required will be provided under community care policies and there may be little scope for means-testing to apply. Even if some asset exists that requires a more formal procedure, it may not be necessary to realise this asset prior to death although there remains the risk that this may prove a stumbling block.

11.103 There may however be a dispute as to who should manage the financial affairs. Most of us prefer to make our own decisions and manage our own affairs, often on a confidential basis, even if we rely upon a spouse, relative, friend or trusted adviser for guidance, assistance and reassurance. Leaving a vacuum is not helpful to those who must intervene following a loss of capacity, so adopting one of the options that appoints our personal choice of financial 'manager' is perhaps a duty that we owe to our loved ones. It may avoid conflict in the future.

Joint account

11.104 A simple option which can have advantages in the short term and help cope with a crisis is for the elderly person to place some money in a bank account in joint names with another person on the basis that either account holder may sign. A pension and other investment income could be mandated to this account. This facility, especially if a current account with a cheque book and debit card, may then be used by the elderly person for general living expenses thereby enabling continued personal management but with the option for the joint holder to assist, supervise and take over when necessary. The arrangement can work very well in practice provided a trustworthy and reliable joint holder is chosen, but it will only relate to the moneys in or passing through the account so is not a complete solution in many cases. Consideration needs to be given to ownership as the funds will generally pass to the surviving joint holder on the death of one joint holder. There may also be complications with regard to tax liabilities and ownership should the older person subsequently need community care services.

11.105   A problem is that once there is an impairment of capacity the underlining authority for the joint account may be revoked. The bank, once it becomes aware of this, may freeze the account until a proper legal procedure is put in place. It may be possible to rely upon the implied authority under ss 7 and 8 of the Mental Capacity Act 2005[63] but there can be no certainty about this.

Trusts

11.106   Another option is to place financial resources in the hands of someone else so that they can continue to manage these. This would be a 'bare trust'. It is not a fool-proof approach and there are many pitfalls even if this 'trustee' is entirely trustworthy and reliable (which they may not prove to be). There is no certainty that this other person, even if much younger, will survive or remain capable of fulfilling expectations. Ill-health or problems in their own life such as debt or divorce may create an unstable situation rendering the trust fund vulnerable. There can also be tax complications if the funds are held in the sole name of this person.

11.107   Some protection may be afforded by completing a 'declaration of trust' to identify the source and nature of the fund and its true ownership, and further by appointing two trustees (eg two adult children). The problem remains that only the funds put in this trust can be managed and whilst that could include the home and any investments, any pensions or other sources of income cannot be managed in this way. A trust is unlikely to be a total solution.

11.108   Advantages of the more formal trust (sometimes referred to as a 'settlement') are that the trustees are self-perpetuating and may be given wide discretionary powers. There is no need to obtain a security bond or pay fees and produce annual accounts to the Public Guardian and the financial authority of trustees cannot be questioned. Other people may credit money to the settlement for additional support and discretionary trusts may also be used to avoid means-testing for welfare benefits and contributions to the cost of local authority services.[64]

11.109   Disadvantages are that trusts cannot be set up by someone who is already incapacitated[65] and the trustees only have authority over money placed in the settlement. There is inadequate supervision with little control over administration costs or the charges of professional trustees, and trustees have no obligation to consult or visit an incapacitated beneficiary and no-one to turn to for approval of their actions. Problems may arise over unspent income and tax repayments in the hands of the beneficiary. If the trustees are given a discretion, and this may be desirable from many points of view, the exercise of this discretion cannot be questioned by or on behalf of the beneficiary. A formal settlement is likely to incur professional fees and result in tax complications.

Power of attorney

11.110   This is a procedure of choice made available initially in 1985 with enduring powers of attorney (EPL)[66] and since October 2007 with lasting powers of attorney (LPA).[67] An ordinary power of attorney is of limited benefit because continued use would be unlawful once the donor loses capacity. The enduring power was a simple

---

[63]   See Ch 2 at **2.49**.
[64]   This topic is dealt with in Ch 12.
[65]   Except by authority of the Court of Protection – s 18(1)(h). See Ch 2 at **2.104** for more detail.
[66]   See **11.60** et seq.
[67]   See **11.60** et seq.

document that anyone could complete and no expense need be involved until there was loss of capacity and it had to be registered. Unfortunately it was wide-open to abuse so its replacement is much more complex and potentially expensive to complete. Nevertheless, everyone whose personal finances would need to be managed should be encouraged to complete an LPA before it becomes too late!

11.111 Advantages of the LPA are that all financial affairs may be delegated, both before and after a loss of capacity, to a person or persons of choice thereby avoiding delay and a potential vacuum. It can be relatively cheap and easy to set up with little formality, is suitable for small as well as large estates, and is flexible with self-imposed restrictions upon financial powers. It is easy to operate, involves no annual fees and there is no need to produce annual accounts on a routine basis, though in case of challenge the attorney may be directed by the Court of Protection to render accounts and produce the records that should have been kept.[68] The attorney will use his discretion but there is a procedure whereby another person may challenge the conduct of the attorney.

11.112 Disadvantages include the fact that the power can only be created when there is sufficient capacity, and ceases to be available if the attorney dies or becomes incapable (unless another attorney is appointed jointly and severally or there is a replacement attorney). There is no effective supervision and no compulsion upon the attorney to consult or visit the donor although this would be assumed. The absence of a duty to produce annual accounts could also be seen as a disadvantage.

Deputy

11.113 The Court of Protection can appoint a deputy for property and affairs on the application of the proposed deputy or some other person.[69] The procedure is only available once the individual becomes mentally incapable. Advantages are that the procedure is available in all cases where there is a lack of capacity, relates to all money and property of the individual and involves some supervision by the Public Guardian. A change of deputy is possible and the authority of the deputy cannot be questioned provided that he acts within his powers. The deputy does not carry the responsibility alone and can turn to the Court of Protection for support and guidance which may be valuable when there is a dispute within the family.

11.114 Disadvantages are that deputyship is not suitable for small estates (though a simple order may be available which overcomes any obstacle) and is expensive to set up and operate (annual accounts must be produced and fees paid). The incapacitated individual has little choice as to who is appointed and the expectation that the deputy will consult or visit him or her may not be fulfilled.

Problem situations

11.115 Under this heading we identify some challenging situations that can arise and consider how they may be tackled.

---

[68] MCA 2005, Sch 4, para 16.
[69] For further consideration see Ch 2 at **2.102** et seq and also **11.78** et seq.

Dysfunctional families

11.116 All too often contested hearings in the Court of Protection arise where there is a struggle for control of the finances of an infirm elderly parent. A typical scenario is that the son applies for registration of an EPA and one of more of his siblings objects to this on the ground that mother did not know what she was signing or lacked capacity, and in any event the son is not a fit person to be an attorney. It generally transpires that the children have fallen out years before and this becomes the opportunity to ventilate their grievances! Nominated district judges are experienced in coping with these situations and will usually seek to diffuse them by pointing out that the role of the court is to address the best interests of the elderly parent, not to adjudicate upon past issues between the siblings. The court is bound to register the EPA unless it finds that one or more of the statutory grounds of objection are met.[70] To avoid the suspicion that may arise within the family the court may authorise and require the attorney to provide accounts to the siblings at intervals.

11.117 These cases are less frequent for LPAs because registration generally takes place when the donor still has capacity and can exercise some control of the children or at least confirm personal choices. Issues of this nature, which can prove extremely expensive and emotionally damaging, may be avoided where the elderly person keeps all the family informed of their wishes and intentions. The reality is that the frail elderly parent may seek to satisfy each child when with them, thereby giving mixed messages and contributing to the discord between the children when they later compare notes.

Lack of family

11.118 Some elderly people live alone and have no immediate family. They may by will leave their estate to charity because they have no dependants or friends whom they wish to benefit. It is all the more important that they complete an LPA because there will be no-one who will naturally take over control of their finances if they lose capacity. Their difficulty in identifying a prospective attorney may be resolved by appointing a local solicitor who is willing to adopt this role and experienced in doing so.[71]

Denial or retention of control

11.119 Most of us live in denial. We may frequently encounter people who have impaired mental capacity, but do not contemplate that this will happen to us even as we become elderly. When this is coupled with a natural reluctance to surrender control of our affairs to our children whose approach to life has appeared so different from our own, the prospect of signing a document having precisely that effect becomes unattractive. The legal advice may be to complete an LPA, but we do not wish to do that just yet so the opportunity is missed.

11.120 It can be counter-productive for children to persist in this situation, but a solicitor can give impartial advice as to the advantages and (few) disadvantages and, if so instructed, build safeguards into the document to ensure that it is not used prematurely or without adequate safeguards.

---

[70] See **11.56** for more detail.
[71] Members of *Solicitors for the Elderly* (SfE) are accustomed to this role: www.solicitorsfortheelderly.com. A member of the *Society of Trust and Estate Practitioners* (STEP) may also be suitable: www.step.org.

Large or complex estates

11.121 The choice of attorney or attorneys should be influenced by the task that will have to be undertaken. If an elderly parent with devoted children may need to be cared for in a retirement or nursing home in the future, one or more of the children could readily take over the finances under an LPA, sell the former family home, invest the proceeds and see that monthly accounts are paid and all personal requirements are met. That is the typical 'happy family' situation and the LPA (or failing this appointment of a deputy) is ideal for this.

11.122 The situation may be different where there is a dysfunctional family or the elderly person still has extensive business or property interests in which the family have never been involved. The independence or experience of a professional person may then be needed. A solicitor or accountant could be appointed as attorney or deputy, jointly where appropriate with a member of the family. The combination of professional experience and ability with the more emotional approach of an individual concerned about care provision may produce the best outcome for the elderly person. The duty of both is to act in that person's best interests, but this does not mean solely financial or medical best interests – a more holistic approach should be adopted.

Conclusion

11.123 Every adult, regardless of age, should have the potential advantages of the LPA drawn to their attention and be encouraged to complete one if they can identify an attorney(s) of choice. This may be viewed as a way of retaining autonomy in the event that some misfortune arises whereby there is a loss of mental capacity. The LPA for property and affairs is the most important because we all have financial lives. An LPA for personal welfare (which would include medical treatment) is a matter of choice because some people prefer to rely on fate or see the existing provisions as adequate where there are no disputes within a supportive family.[72] The advance decision in regard to medical treatment is also a matter of choice depending upon personal perspectives.[73]

11.124 Although different procedures are available for dealing with the financial affairs of an incapacitated person, in practice there may be no choice between them once incapacity has arisen. If there is an EPA it should now be registered. If an LPA has already been created by registration then there should be no problem provided that the attorney(s) are still able to perform their function. It is arguable that authority could be given by the court for the execution on behalf of the incapacitated individual of an LPA, but the court is unwilling to contemplate this on the basis that it is a procedure of choice and should only be used as such. There is little point in any event now that a deputy is generally given powers similar to those of the attorney and no longer needs to make constant requests to the court for authority (as was the case with receivers under the previous jurisdiction).

11.125 Where there are competing applications for registration of an EPA or LPA and for appointment of a deputy, the Court of Protection prefers the former as far as possible. However, notwithstanding the existence of a potentially valid EPA or LPA, where there is a seriously dysfunctional family there may be advantages in having the

---

[72] Mental Capacity Act 2005, ss 9–14. See Ch 2 at **2.62** et seq.
[73] Mental Capacity Act 2005, ss 24–26. See Ch 2 at **2.96** and Ch 8 generally.

potential attorney or some other person appointed as a deputy by the court so that the support of the court may be sought in the event of disputes, rather than facing frequent challenges as a more vulnerable attorney.

The work in practice

Initial steps

11.126   An initial over-reaction to a loss of capacity should be avoided, for this may be merely a temporary set-back in health followed by a degree of recovery. Unless it is clear that incapacity will be permanent, it is sufficient to deal with immediate issues and see how things develop. However, financial affairs do not improve with being left, so if a full application for the appointment of a deputy is going to have to be made then in general the sooner this is done the better.

11.127   It may be possible to get by without any formal steps if there is little capital and the only real income is from pensions. It may be time to claim additional state benefits,[74] but a suitable person (relative, carer or solicitor) can become an appointee for the purpose of claiming benefits and an occupational pension may already be paid into a current bank account on which the bank may allow drawing. If the only need is for a contribution to care home fees to be paid and sufficient money is available from these sources it may be possible to persuade the bank to accept a standing order or direct debit for the weekly fees even if capacity is in doubt. Longer-term decisions or serious and irreversible steps should never be taken without a clear medical report or at least the support of the GP.

11.128   Prevention is better than cure, and we should all prepare for old age and an inability to cope. Is it too late to get an LPA signed if one does not already exist? If such a document does exist, has it been registered? The test of capacity to execute this document is not as high as you may think and is not the same as the test of ability to handle one's own affairs. If the person can give instructions for an EPA at this stage a lot of later problems may be avoided, but a solicitor should be instructed and see the elderly person alone because that is the client, not the person who thinks that a power should be signed (in his or her favour!). The solicitor will take careful notes at this interview and see the client again if necessary to confirm consistency of instructions, and if in doubt will get a medical report. Some solicitors may see clients in their own home to make the whole experience less stressful for the client. When asked to see a new elderly client by a member of the family it is prudent for a solicitor to enquire if there is another solicitor who has usually acted for the client, and to be wary if there is, because he may have been brought in to avoid advice based upon knowledge of the background.

Practical steps

11.129   It helps to draw up a checklist of what needs to be done in taking over the affairs, both initially and thereafter on a regular basis. The first stage will be gathering information with a view to instructing a solicitor or making any necessary applications and preparing the action list. The second stage is actually drawing up and carrying out the action list. Each case is different, but the affairs of most elderly people follow a similar pattern and once these lists have been drawn up it is easier to consider the options that are available.

---

[74]   See generally Ch 10.

11.130 The actual arrangements depend upon the needs of the elderly person and should be made so as to be supportive yet provide as much freedom as circumstances permit. The primary objective is to make provision for maintenance and support, including food, clothing, accommodation, recreation, extra comforts, pocket money, holidays and medical attention. The attorney or deputy should be aware of the elderly person's wishes and use the available financial resources for their benefit during their lifetime. The GP and social services department for the area in which the elderly person resides should be consulted if guidance is needed as to accommodation, care and treatment.

Information

11.131 An attorney or deputy must start with personal information about the individual concerned, including full name and address with similar details for carers and next of kin, whether the present spouse is the parent of all children and whether there is a former spouse with a financial entitlement. Home status (whether owner-occupier, tenant or licensee) should be identified along with present arrangements for care. On the financial side it is necessary to ascertain income and capital (and any trust funds), clarify state benefits being claimed and ascertain bills to be paid both now and on a regular basis (these may include nursing home or other care fees). Insurance policies should be checked as well as arrangements, if any, for making tax returns.

11.132 The GP should be identified and contacted to see that all necessary medical arrangements have been made and whether any advance wishes as to treatment have been expressed or should be notified to the doctor if already known to exist. Finally it must be ascertained if a solicitor is already involved and if there is an appointee for state benefits or an EPA or LPA has been completed or an approach previously made to the Court of Protection. It helps to know if there is a will but difficulties may arise in inspecting any existing will at this stage.

11.133 The person making these enquiries will have no legal status at this stage and considerable tact may be required. It may not be possible to build up a complete picture but a start can be made, sufficient for an application to the Court of Protection if this is necessary, and outstanding information can be obtained when some legal authority over the affairs has been established. It is possible to apply to this court for an interim order authorising disclosure of information before a formal application is made for appointment of a deputy or to assist with such application.

Action

11.134 The action list follows from the information obtained but can conveniently be divided into topics. Many steps will have to await formal authority over the affairs or will be taken on a provisional basis pending such authority, but some action will be needed pending registration of an EPA/LPA or appointment of a deputy.

11.135 It will be appropriate to notify carers (including the staff at a residential care home) and next of kin of the arrangements, if only to ensure that they do not inadvertently seek to enter into transactions with or for the incapacitated individual or permit others to do so. It may also be prudent to consult certain of them in advance especially as some of the tasks may be delegated to them. As regards personal affairs, it may be necessary to arrange for physical security of home and possessions, care of pets, redirection of mail and cancellation of deliveries (milk, papers etc). A landlord should be notified and payment of future rent or mortgage subscriptions arranged along with any arrears that have arisen. Discussions may arise about personal care, involving the doctor and also a social worker who will consider whether a community care assessment is needed, and decisions may be needed about what can be afforded. It may be appropriate to arrange private medical treatment or care provision, in which event arrangements must be made to cover the fees, but contributions may also arise towards the cost of state provision.

11.136   Most of the financial arrangements will need to await the formal authority, but as soon as possible the representative should intercept state benefits and other income, ensure the security of documents (credit-cards, passbooks, share certificates, deeds, etc), confirm insurance arrangements, notify banks, building societies and any trustees and deal with tax affairs.

11.137   Where a local authority provides or sponsors residential care, the elderly person's financial circumstances must be disclosed so that an assessment may be made of ability to contribute towards the cost. The attorney or deputy should check these assessments and arrange reassessment at intervals as capital diminishes.

Options

11.138   Sooner or later a build-up of bills and other commitments may dictate that someone must take overall control of the financial affairs, and the available options then need to be considered. Two words of caution are appropriate whatever method of financial management is adopted. The first is that family members or friends may not only give a great deal of time and energy to looking after the elderly person, but it may also cost them money to do so even if only in extra heating and laundry bills. It is realistic for those handling the financial affairs to recognise this and ensure that such expenditure is adequately reimbursed where there is sufficient money available. The second is that conflicts of interest arise and should be recognised. The money belongs to the elderly person and should be spent for his or her benefit and not accumulated for the family (which may, and often will, include the person managing the affairs).

11.139   If there is an EPA, this should be registered when appropriate and can then be acted upon. If necessary arrangements can be made for the elderly person to be admitted to a suitable care home, any house can be sold, investments rearranged and a bank account opened to receive the income and to pay fees to the home. Less drastic measures of a caretaking nature may be sufficient if the elderly person is cared for by family.

11.140   If there is more than a little capital involved, there is no EPA or LPA and it is too late to get an LPA signed, the proper and only safe course is an application to the Court of Protection usually for the appointment of a deputy for property and affairs. Forms and guidance may be downloaded from the internet.[75] If these forms are fully and adequately completed and the necessary medical report is available, the appointment of the deputy may follow without undue further formality although certain people will have to be given notice of what is going on. The court fee will have to be paid and an insurance bond is required, but these expenses may later be reimbursed out of the elderly person's estate.

---

[75]   www.justice.gov.uk/forms/opg/deputies.

Involvement of professionals

Role of the solicitor

11.141 A solicitor will normally prepare any power of attorney but, though initial instructions may come from the intended attorney, the solicitor is acting for the donor and this will usually mean that he should see the donor personally. The solicitor should take instructions from the donor in the absence of the intended attorney so that independent advice may be given and in order to be satisfied of the true intentions and wishes of the donor. When acting on the instructions of the attorney a solicitor should remember that his client is the donor whose best interests should be safeguarded, even if this results in conflict with the attorney.

11.142 A solicitor will usually be employed to deal with the initial application for appointment of a deputy and, where necessary, also at later stages.[76]

11.143 The agency principle is truly established once an appointment has been made. Although the solicitor may receive instructions from the deputy (or attorney) it must be emphasised that his client is the incapacitated individual, and when the solicitor perceives a conflict between the actions of the deputy/attorney and the best interests of the individual he has a professional duty to refer the circumstances to the Public Guardian or the Court of Protection. This may create a conflict of interest for a solicitor employed by a local authority where an officer of the authority is appointed deputy, and it has been suggested that outside solicitors should be instructed in these cases. It is the solicitor's duty to advise the court on behalf of the incapacitated individual and in co-operation with a deputy to bring all relevant information to the notice of the court.

Involving a doctor

11.144 Whenever a doctor is approached for a medical report, the reason why this is required should be explained along with the relevant legal test of capacity. Appropriate information should also be given to the doctor because if he is expected to form a view as to whether his patient is incapable of dealing with financial affairs he will need to have a general idea what those affairs are. He will also need to confirm the existence of 'an impairment of, or a disturbance in the functioning of, the mind or brain'. It may be helpful to indicate to the doctor that he may issue a certificate dealing only with the particular situation involved and not expressing an opinion on capacity in other respects.[77] Where there are differences of opinion within a family, the family doctor may be reluctant to become involved and this can cause problems in obtaining a report for the Court of Protection or having an LPA witnessed by that doctor.

11.145 In relation to completion of an LPA at this late stage it is not enough simply to have a medical opinion confirming that the donor has the necessary capacity, but the solicitor will wish to satisfy himself that the donor has sufficient understanding when the power is actually signed. In cases of difficulty it may be helpful to see the donor on two separate occasions, at least once on his own, to see if the instructions given on each occasion are the same,[78] and if capacity fluctuates it is prudent to have the donor's signature witnessed by the doctor.

---

[76] *Solicitors for the Elderly* maintain a regional register of members who have particular experience in this field. This can be accessed from: www.solicitorsfortheelderly.com/public/search.

[77] For further consideration of the role of doctors, see Ch 1 at **1.107** et seq.

[78] If the solicitor knows the family and circumstances and is satisfied that the proposed power is in the donor's best interests, he may not wish to impose too rigid a test.

Wills

11.146 It is also desirable for the individual dealing with the financial affairs, or the solicitor acting in these arrangements, to be aware of the contents of the last will of the elderly person. This is so that the terms can be taken into account when deciding what property should be sold and when. Usually property which is specifically bequeathed should be sold after property which would fall into residue, though circumstances may dictate otherwise. Simply changing investments could also affect testamentary provision. If there is no will or the last will has become out of date, consideration can be given to applying to the Court of Protection for authority to make a statutory will.

Independent Financial Adviser

11.147 If significant investments or savings are involved an Independent Financial Adviser (IFA) should be consulted to implement a suitable investment policy. IFAs must be able to demonstrate to the Financial Conduct Authority and Prudential Regulation Authority that they review all the suitable products in a market and give fair, unbiased and unrestricted advice. They are no longer allowed to receive commissions from financial services companies on new sales of investments. Instead they have to set their own fees, based on the services they offer, and agree fees with their client before providing any services.

Management

11.148 A new bank account should be opened in the name of the attorney(s) or deputy as such,[79] for the purpose of receiving all income due to the elderly person, discharging liabilities and providing such funding as may be required. Surplus or accumulated income should be invested.

11.149 An official or certified copy of the relevant authority (EPA, LPA or court order) should be produced to all banks, building societies and other financial institutions that hold money or assets in the name of the elderly person so that control may be assumed over these. Arrangements should be made for dividends and other income to be credited to the new bank. The attorney or deputy should assume control of any investments and it should be considered whether these are the most suitable taking into account the needs of the elderly person.

11.150 Anyone dealing with the elderly person such as the staff at a residential care home and a social worker should be notified of the assumption of control by the attorney(s) or deputy so that they will not inadvertently seek to enter into transactions for the elderly person or allow others to do so. This is especially important where the elderly person has property of value and may be inclined to give it away to win favours.

11.151 It will be necessary to ensure that the elderly person is receiving all social security benefits to which he or she may be entitled, and contact may be needed with the local authority about services and contributions towards the cost. The attorney(s) or deputy also becomes responsible for dealing with the elderly person's tax affairs which will include completing the annual tax return or repayment claim.

---

[79]   Banks tend to have their own terminology, but the designation might be: 'GA & MA POAS for Mrs PA' or 'GA as deputy for Mrs PA'.

Care of property and possessions

11.152 The attorney(s) or deputy is under a duty to see that any house or flat belonging to the elderly person is kept in a reasonable state of repair, and will be empowered to carry out any repairs. Adequate insurance should be maintained. A list of possessions should be prepared so far as practicable, and appropriate insurance arranged. Where particular items are known to be left to specified persons by will it may be reasonable to permit those persons to have custody of the items on an appropriate undertaking.

CHAPTER 12

TESTAMENTARY PROVISION AND DEATH

Gordon Ashton

"The fear of death is more to be dreaded than death itself."
Publilius Syrus (~100 BC)

Preparation for death should not be overlooked as there is the ability to direct inheritance of wealth whilst minimising tax liabilities and to reduce the potential for subsequent uncertainty and disputes. Those who are left to face the reality of death must also know how to tackle the consequences. In this chapter we first consider provision of choice in the context of gifts, wills (including intestacy) and provision for dependants who are disabled or infirm. Then we identify how any testamentary provision may be changed by arrangement between beneficiaries or challenged as to adequacy or validity. Finally, we deal with matters arising immediately following death.

INTRODUCTION

12.1 An elderly person may give money or property away to people or charities of choice prior to death and there may be tax advantages in doing so. The individual may also by making a will stipulate who is to inherit any savings or assets owned at death and appoint executors to administer the estate, and if incapable of doing so the Court of Protection may direct that a suitable will be made. Special trust provision may be made by a will or settlement for a vulnerable dependant. In the absence of a will, the intestacy rules specify who is to receive the estate and the order of priority for administrators. Any beneficiary may disclaim an entitlement under a will or intestacy, and the beneficiaries may enter into a Deed of Family Arrangement and in effect rewrite a will or the effects of intestacy. Finally, the courts have power to provide for dependants and override the provisions of a will or the effect of intestacy, or they may be required to adjudicate upon the validity of a will.

12.2 All these matters are considered in this chapter and also, for the sake of completeness, an outline is given of the situation immediately following death. This extends to registration of the death, funeral arrangements, disposal of the body, organ donation and the role of the coroner.

PROVISION OF CHOICE

Preliminary

12.3 Under this heading we consider how an older person may choose to pass money and assets to other people or charities either during their lifetime or upon death, and also how the recipients may choose to redistribute the money or assets following that death. The law of intestacy is included because, in effect, there will have been a choice to leave the distribution of the estate to the law.

Gifts

12.4   There are several reasons why gifts may be contemplated, the most obvious being to assist the next generation of the family or pass wealth to them, but for larger estates a strategy to reduce the inheritance tax liability arising on death will be a factor. Other more negative reasons may be the desire to avoid benefiting particular relatives or dependants whom the donor wishes to disinherit, or assets falling into the hands of creditors on a bankruptcy. A relatively recent motivation is the desire to avoid means-testing for benefits or care services that the individual may subsequently become entitled to.

12.5   A lifetime gift should be considered only when the money or asset involved is surplus to the individual's present or anticipated requirements. Before making any substantial gift consideration should be given to the potential implications upon means-testing for state benefits or local authority services, including the need to be funded in a residential care or nursing home because there are anti-avoidance provisions.[1] Capital gains tax may also be a factor in the case of a gift of an asset that has increased in value during the donor's ownership, and a record should be kept of any large gifts for inheritance tax purposes. When making a gift the donor should consider whether any consequential changes are needed to any will.

12.6   The *rule against double portions* applies where a testator leaves a child a 'portion' (which may be a share of residue or a substantial legacy) and then makes a substantial lifetime gift to that child. The gift may be presumed to replace the provision in the will on the basis that the parent would not intend to benefit this child twice at the expense of the others. The lifetime gift is regarded as payment on account of the portion with the result that it adeems (is no longer payable) to the extent of such payment. It thus becomes necessary to establish the testator's intentions at the time of the gift.[2]

Validity

Capacity

12.7   A gift is only valid if the donor had capacity to make the gift at the time it was made.[3] This is based upon understanding and the ability to make a choice. That choice must be freely and voluntarily made and there must be no undue influence. If the individual does not have capacity to make the gift an attorney under an enduring or lasting power may be able to do so (subject to certain statutory restrictions), and failing this an approach may be made to the Court of Protection which has power to authorise gifts.[4]

12.8   The degree of understanding required is relative to the particular gift involved. If it is a trivial amount in relation to the donor's other assets a low degree of understanding

---

[1]   This is dealt with in Ch 10, but for gifts of the home see Ch 5 at **5.169**.
[2]   *Re Cameron (Deceased)* [1999] Ch 386. For cases involving the interpretation of 'portions' see *Kloosman v Aylen and Frost* [2013] EWHC 435 Ch; *Re Clapham* [2005] EWHC 3387 (Ch).
[3]   See generally Ch 1 at **1.2**.
[4]   See Ch 11 at **11.94** for gifts by attorneys or deputies.

will suffice, but if its effect is to dispose of the donor's only asset of value and thus, for practical purposes, to pre-empt the devolution of the donor's estate under a will or on intestacy, then the degree of understanding required might be compared with that for a will.[5] However, unlike in the case of a will, the donor must also take into account the effect upon the rest of his life of depriving himself of the asset involved so a greater level of understanding than that for testamentary capacity might be required.

12.9 Before making a substantial gift a donor must thus understand:

(1) that he is passing immediate ownership of property which will not be returned (as distinct from merely lending it or offering it as security);

(2) that this is voluntary and he is not getting anything in return (if that be the case) or that any promises given may not be legally enforceable;

(3) the identity of the recipient, reasons for making the gift and claims of others for whom the donor might be expected to have regard;

(4) whether any previous gifts have been made and whether the present gift is a 'one-off' or part of a series;

(5) the value of the gift and the effect on the donor's future standard of living taking into account likely needs and other financial resources.

Undue influence

12.10 Where there was a relationship of trust and confidence between donor and donee the making of a large gift which requires an explanation may give rise to a presumption of undue influence.[6] This would only be rebutted by a finding that the gift was made after full, free and informed thought and the absence of any pressure from the donee would not by itself be sufficient.[7] In a case where moneys were transferred to a joint account and would thereby pass by survivorship to the second wife, it was held that there was no undue influence.[8] Each case tends to turn on its own specific findings.[9]

Perfected gifts

12.11 A promise to make a gift is not enforceable. It is necessary for the title to any gifted property to be legally vested in the donee because 'there is no equity to perfect an imperfect gift'. How this is done will depend upon the nature of the property involved, but the donor must have done everything that he needs to do to effect the transfer although it may not matter that something remains to be done by a third party. Chattels and cash are transferable by delivery if there is an intention to give, but a letter is useful to confirm the intention and fix the date. A gift by cheque is not completed until the cheque is cleared so will not be effective if a donor who has signed the cheque dies before then. By contrast, in the case of securities such as stocks and shares it may be sufficient to hand over the certificates together with a signed transfer. Any transfer of land or of an interest in land must be by deed[10] and so must waiver of a debt (unless there is consideration).

---

5   *Re Beaney* [1978] 2 All ER 595.
6   *Royal Bank of Scotland Plc v Etridge (No 2)* [2001] 3 WLR 1021.
7   *Hammond v Osborne* [2002] EWCA Civ 885. Undue influence and unconscionable bargains are dealt with in Ch 4 at **4.160** and **4.173** respectively.
8   *Gorjat v Gorjat* [2010] EWHC 1537 (Ch).
9   The topic of undue influence is also considered in Ch 4 at **4.160** et seq.
10 Law of Property Act 1925, s 52.

Donatio mortis causa

12.12 An exception to the rule that a gift must be perfected, and also to the rule that a person may only dispose of property after death by will, arises in the case of *donationes mortis causa*. This applies where the donor makes a gift in contemplation (not necessarily expectation) of death, and delivers or causes delivery of the subject-matter of the gift to the donee[11] or transfers the means of getting at that subject matter, on the basis that the gift is conditional on the donor's death. Thus if a man on his death-bed tells his housekeeper that he wishes her to have some specific shares on his death and hands her the key to a safe containing the certificates, those shares belong to the donor until he dies and then the condition precedent is fulfilled and the gift takes effect.

12.13 Chattels, money, marketable securities and insurance policies can be given in this way, but not a personal cheque because it may not be met by the drawer's bank after death. Doubt as to whether land could be so given has been resolved in the affirmative in a case where the deceased handed over keys to a steel box containing the deeds to the house in which the donee lived with the words 'The house is yours …'.[12] Questions may still arise as to intention to make the conditional gift and capacity to do so.

Taxation

Capital gains tax (CGT)

12.14 A gift is a chargeable transfer for CGT, and *hold-over relief* (which means that the donee takes the gifted property at the donor's acquisition value and there is no charge to tax on the transfer) has been abolished except as between husband and wife, on disposal of a business asset and on transfers immediately chargeable to inheritance tax.[13] There is a right to pay tax by instalments over 10 years for certain types of gift. It is advantageous to make a gift of an asset with a fluctuating value when it has a relatively low value, but appreciating assets should be given sooner rather than later. The downside of making a gift may be the loss of the main residence exemption for a gift of the home and the loss of the CGT uplift on subsequent death.[14]

Inheritance tax (IHT)

12.15 The value of lifetime gifts is included in the estate of the donor, but a gift to a spouse or civil partner is exempt (as is any inheritance between such couples). There are several exemptions that can be taken advantage of by the older person, including small gifts,[15] an annual total sum that can be given by each donor,[16] gifts which are part of normal regular giving out of annual income, and payments for the maintenance of certain members of the family. Certain gifts of any size, with no benefit reserved will be *potentially exempt transfers* (PETs) which means that they become exempt if the donor survives the gift by 7 years, and there is tapering relief between 3 and 7 years. For this to apply they must be made to an individual or into a settlement for a disabled person.[17]

---

[11] The item may already be in the donee's possession as bailee – *Woodard v Woodard* [1991] Fam Law 470, CA.

[12] *Sen v Headley* [1991] Ch 425, CA.

[13] Relief is not available if the transferee is not resident or ordinarily resident in the UK.

[14] All assets are revalued for inheritance purposes but no CGT is chargeable.

[15] Presently £250 per donee or more on the marriage of the donee.

[16] Presently £3,000.

[17] A trust for a disabled person.

12.16 Any gift which is neither exempt nor a PET is a *chargeable transfer* liable to IHT if over the nil rate band in force (currently £325,000) immediately at half normal rates taking into account all chargeable transfers during the past 7 years. If the donor dies within 7 years the full rate is charged (subject to tapering relief). The primary liability for IHT on gifts falls on the donee, but there is a secondary liability on the estate of the deceased donor. It may therefore be worth arranging life assurance for the donee on the donor's life to cover the potential tax liability on a gift.

12.17 It follows that care should be taken with the timing of gifts, having in mind that the nil-rate band benefits earlier gifts first. It is also prudent to establish the value of gifted property at the time of the gift by getting a formal valuation. Complicated rules may result in an IHT liability in respect of any gift with a *reservation of benefit*.

Charities

12.18 Charities enjoy the benefit of considerable tax concessions, and giving to charities can be extremely tax-effective if the gift is made in certain ways. However, a distinction must be drawn between giving to charities and making arrangements with charities.

Tax incentives

12.19 As regards income tax, the traditional method of achieving tax benefits has been a *deed of covenant* because if this can exceed 3 years and there is no benefit in return the charity recovers basic rate tax on the gross amount to the extent that the donor pays such tax, and the donor gets higher rate tax relief on the gross amount. Deposit covenants could be arranged to cope with lump sum giving.

12.20 The statutory scheme known as *Gift Aid* has largely overtaken the use of covenants. A single gift by an individual is regarded as having been paid net of tax and the charity can recover the tax 'deducted' whilst the donor can obtain higher rate tax relief on the grossed-up amount. For this to apply it must be an outright gift in cash, free of any conditions or benefits accruing to the donor or his family, but there are schemes that allow a single gift to be divided among a number of charities.

12.21 There is no CGT on the transfer of an asset to a charity either by way of gift or at an under-value. The charity will not pay CGT on a subsequent disposal, so it may be better to transfer the asset to the charity and let it be sold by the charity than to sell it first and give the money after paying CGT. However, it is worth checking whether it is more tax-effective to sell the asset, pay the CGT and give the charity money as a Gift Aid donation.

12.22 A gift or legacy to a charity is exempt from IHT and the amount or value is not aggregated with the donor's estate. A beneficiary under a will may even be able to get the best of all worlds by entering into a Deed of Variation in favour of a charity thereby avoiding IHT on the amount transferred and also claiming income tax relief under Gift Aid on the same amount. Since April 2012, individuals with estates worth over the nil rate band and who leave 10% of their estate to charity in their will, benefit from a reduced rate of IHT at 36% instead of 40%.

Bargain-bounty rule

12.23 If a charity repeatedly or on a substantial scale contracts in return for gifts to provide that which it would normally provide as part of its charitable activities, it is in danger of losing its charitable status. Quite apart from this, tax relief on an individual gift may be withdrawn if such a bargain becomes established. A charity cannot legally bind itself to provide a service for a particular person in return for a gift, but of course having received a gift the charity may have regard to the wishes of the donor (especially if more gifts may be made) when it decides how its services are to be provided.

Succession

12.24 Under special rules property or money may pass to certain other persons following the death of the owner, and there are also circumstances where an individual may be denied benefit following the death of another.

Joint property

12.25 Any property or savings in joint names will normally pass direct to the surviving joint owner or owners upon the death of one of the owners. This may include bank or building society accounts, stock exchange investments etc. All that is required to complete the transfer is production of a death certificate. If the joint owners are trustees the survivors will still be obliged to carry out the terms of the trust.

12.26 In the case of freehold or leasehold property this outcome may be prevented by a declaration by deed, which may be in the deed vesting the property in joint names, to the effect that the property is held beneficially as tenants in common either in equal shares or such other shares as may be specified. The legal estate will then be held as joint tenants and the survivors will still become the legal owners following the death, but the property will be held by them on trust according to the terms of the declaration.[18] A similar result may be obtained in respect of personal property such as bank accounts by a declaration of trust under which the beneficial owners of the money are identified notwithstanding the names in which the money is invested.

12.27 Spouses will typically hold the matrimonial home as joint tenants because their intention is that it passes to the survivor. The joint tenancy may be 'severed' thereby creating a tenancy in common in equal shares by notice given by one joint owner to the other(s) and in certain other ways, such as conduct inconsistent with a joint tenancy.[19] This may be appropriate if the personal relationship breaks down. Property jointly owned in other circumstances will usually be held as tenants in common in specified shares whereby such shares may be part of the estate of a deceased co-owner.

Nominations

12.28 Certain assets may be disposed of on death by a written nomination, but this facility is less available than it used to be.[20] There are statutory nominations such as those for Industrial and Provident Society accounts, and non-statutory nominations under some pension schemes. A nomination will be of no effect if the nominee dies first.

---

[18] There are then restrictions upon the power of a sole legal owner to give title to the property and it may be necessary to appoint another trustee to effect a sale.

[19] Law of Property Act 1925, s 36(2). In *Re Woolnough, Perkins v Borden* [2002] WTLR 595, Ch D it was held that the making of wills by the parties had this effect.

[20] Nominations for National Savings Certificates and National Savings Bank accounts were discontinued in 1981 but any then in existence will still take effect.

Forfeiture

12.29 A person who causes the death of another is usually prevented from benefiting from the death of the victim, whether under a will, intestacy or gift, but there is now discretion in a case of manslaughter.[21] This could have implications in the case of a 'mercy killing' involving an elderly couple or suicide pacts which partly fail.

Wills

12.30 Everyone should make a will, but especially an elderly person. Among the advantages of doing so are the fact that the estate is disposed of according to the testator's wishes (and the beneficiaries know this), chosen executors may be appointed whose powers arise on death, special provision may be made to deal with particular situations and there is the opportunity for tax and welfare benefits planning. It is also desirable that any will is kept up-to-date. At the same time it is worth considering the signing of a lasting power of attorney and an advance decision.[22] It should never be assumed that the alternative to a will, the laws of intestacy, make the provision that one might wish for loved ones and dependants.

12.31 A clear record should also be kept and maintained of all savings, investments and other assets held, and of any significant gifts, so that this information may be available to the executors on death. This should include particulars of any life policies, pension funds, nominations, joint property and interests under trusts or settlements. Importantly any passwords should be recorded and stored safely in respect of on line accounts and digital assets, such as domain names and I-tunes and Facebook account.

Domicile

12.32 A person's domicile is the country (or jurisdiction) where the person resides with the intention of remaining there permanently or indefinitely. Everyone starts life with a domicile of origin based on that of their parent(s), and whilst this may be replaced by a domicile of dependency if the relevant parent moves, on attaining 16 years a different domicile of choice may be acquired. The domicile of origin may revive if a domicile of choice is abandoned and a new one is not acquired.

12.33 Domicile becomes relevant on death as to the validity of any will, liability for inheritance tax and the succession to the estate.[23] A person domiciled in England and Wales will be liable to inheritance tax on all assets in their estate including those which are located in and may be taxed in another jurisdiction, although there may be some double taxation relief. Although a will should be made in the place of domicile, it may also be desirable to make a will in any other jurisdiction where property is held. Care should be taken to ensure that there is no conflict between such provision.

Capacity

12.34 Subject to certain restrictions,[24] an individual is free to direct by will who shall inherit any savings or assets owned at death, and intestacy rules specify who is entitled

---

[21] This is provided under the Forfeiture Act 1982.

[22] See **11.60** and **8.103** et seq respectively.

[23] Some jurisdictions require immovable property to pass to designated relatives.

[24] Certain relatives or dependants may bring claims against the estate for financial provision under Inheritance (Provision for Family and Dependants) Act 1975. See **12.133** et seq.

in the absence of a will. In order to make a valid will a testator must have *testamentary capacity* at the time when it is made. There are two components of such capacity, the first being a status test (attainment of legal majority) and the second being a test based upon understanding and recollection. The testator must understand that he is giving his property to persons of his choice on his death, the extent of that property and the nature and extent of the obligations that he has to relatives and others.[25] This test is not the same as that for contractual capacity, because the testator must not only understand the effect of the document but must also possess an adequate memory and show a sufficient awareness of moral obligations.

12.35 No disorder of the mind must bring about a disposal which would not otherwise have been made, but the test does not depend upon the existence of a mental disorder. Capacity may be impaired by reason of mental illness or learning disabilities, or by physical illness or the effect of alcohol or drugs, but merely being frivolous or acting from bad motives is not by itself sufficient to upset a will. Mere eccentricity or foolishness does not invalidate a will but fraud or undue influence may do so. Where the testator has delusions the question is whether these directly affect the intentions as to disposal of the estate, and lack of capacity may also arise from the poisoning of affections.[26] In cases of doubt it is wise to obtain a medical opinion on capacity and even to arrange for the doctor to witness the will.[27]

12.36 Testamentary capacity is presumed unless it is contested. If a will is challenged the onus of proof is upon the person putting forward the will but there is a presumption in favour of a duly executed will if it appears rational. A previous finding overlapping the date of execution of the will that the testator was incapable of dealing with his property and affairs would potentially outweigh the presumption,[28] but this is not conclusive because there may still be testamentary capacity or it may be shown that the will was made during a lucid interval.

12.37 As capacity may vary from day to day, or even hour to hour, the evidence of persons present when instructions were given for the will and when it was signed may be of more significance than that of a doctor who has seen the testator on other occasions.[29] If the testator had testamentary capacity when giving instructions but then ceases to have that capacity, the will may still be valid if when it is signed the testator understands that he is signing a will which complies with those earlier instructions and it actually does so.[30] The 'golden rule' is that a will prepared for an elderly person, especially if infirm or a challenge was possible, should be witnessed by a medical practitioner who assesses capacity and records his findings.[31] Solicitors should consider any previous will and discuss reasons for change, and take instructions in the absence of anyone who stands to benefit or may have influence over the testator.

---

[25] The most often quoted test of testamentary capacity is found in the judgment of Cockburn CJ in *Banks v Goodfellow* (1870) LR 5, 549 QB.

[26] *Kostic v Chaplin* [2007] EWHC 2909 (Ch); *Ritchie, Ritchie and ors v National Osteoporosis Society* [2009] EWHC 709 (Ch).

[27] *Kenwood v Adams, The Times*, 29 November 1975. For a case where the medical evidence conflicted with that of other persons, see *Wood v Smith* [1992] 3 All ER 556, CA.

[28] This would be the case if a deputy had been appointed of the testator's affairs. In the absence of testamentary capacity a *statutory will* may be considered – see below.

[29] Hence the desirability for an older person in particular to have the will prepared by and signed in the presence of a solicitor who may then be expected to support the will.

[30] *Parker v Felgate* (1883) 8 PD 171; *Clancy v Clancy* (2003) *The Times*, 9 September, Rimer J.

[31] *Kenward v Adams* (1975) *The Times*, November 29. See also *Sharp v Adam* [2006] EWCA Civ 449.

Undue influence

12.38 An elderly person may have testamentary capacity yet be extremely vulnerable to persuasion, and a line has to be drawn between that which is acceptable and that which means that it is not the testator's own will. There is undue influence when the mind of the testator has been so dominated that the disposition in question is the result not of his own volition but of that of the person exerting the influence.[32] This is easier to state than to establish, but the conduct in question must amount to coercion, which may be physical or mental. Mere pressure is not sufficient, but the amount of pressure that is acceptable may depend upon the age or state of health of the testator and it is suggested that how close the testator is to the borderline of capacity will be relevant.[33]

Preparation

12.39 Before making a will the testator must obtain all appropriate information and work out a strategy for the outcome that it is intended to achieve. Married couples and civil partners generally have this discussion together so as to ensure that their respective provision does not conflict and the desired outcome will be achieved regardless of which of them dies first.

Matters taken into account

12.40 The testator must first identify the general nature and size of the estate (including any jointly-owned assets, business interests, life assurance, pensions, foreign property, and interests in trusts or settlements) and the extent of debts and liabilities. Then it is necessary to recall all personal and family obligations, any persons for whom the testator wishes to (or should) provide and any power of appointment that may be exercised. All this information influences the outcome and has to be carefully weighed in the mind of the testator along with influential matters such as the prospect of tax planning. Specific factors then to be taken into account are any need of a beneficiary to inherit particular assets, any problem situations (such as a prospective beneficiary going through a divorce or lacking mental capacity), and any substantial gifts made or to be made during lifetime. It is prudent to anticipate any changes that may occur before death in any of these respects.

Tax planning

12.41 The starting point is for the testator to identify his intentions and only then to consider how these may be carried into effect in the most tax effective way possible. The relevant importance of tax planning is to be determined by the particular testator, but all testators are entitled to know the tax implications of their estates. There are many strategies available, some of which are very complex or risky and these are beyond the scope of this book. Only some of the most basic tax planning approaches are mentioned here. The use of gifts has been mentioned earlier in this chapter.

12.42 It usually makes sense for older spouses to equalise their estates. If the entire estate is left to a surviving spouse there will be no inheritance tax on the death, but a greater charge to tax may arise on the death of the survivor because the combined estates then pass. The first slice of an estate is free of tax[34] so up to this sum was often left to children or others on the first death because this would escape any charge to tax.

---

[32] *Hall v Hall* (1868) LR 1 P & D 481.
[33] Undue influence is considered at **12.10** in respect of gifts and more generally in Ch 4 at **4.160** et seq.
[34] The 'nil rate band'. During 2009–2015 this amounts to £325,000.

If there was doubt as to whether there would be enough remaining to support the surviving spouse, the exempt slice was instead put in a nil-rate discretionary trust with that spouse as one of the potential beneficiaries. The surviving spouse may now benefit from that percentage of the nil-rate-band that was not utilised on the first death so this strategy has become less popular. It can actually work to the disadvantage of the family where many years elapse between the death of the spouses, because the nil-rate-band will have increased and the percentage reduction may far exceed the value previously passed to the children.

12.43 In addition, any property with beneficial tax treatment (eg business and agricultural property) may be left specifically to the other beneficiaries so that advantage is taken of such treatment (it is lost if the property is left to a surviving spouse).

Formalities

Execution

12.44 A will must be in writing and signed by the testator, or by some other person in his presence and by his direction, and it must appear that the testator intended by his signature to give effect to the will. That signature must be made or acknowledged by the testator in the presence of two or more witnesses present at the same time, and each witness must either attest and sign the will or acknowledge his signature in the presence of the testator (but not necessarily in the presence of each other).[35] The witnesses cannot benefit under the will.[36] A will is usually signed by the testator, but inability to produce a signature is not by itself an obstacle because a mark (generally a cross) will do.[37]

12.45 It is advisable for the testator's signature to be at the end of the will to avoid dispute, although this is no longer essential. Where a testator's name appeared in the attestation clause in her own handwriting and the evidence showed that she intended to give effect to the will, this was held to be sufficient.[38] An incomplete signature is only sufficient if it can be established that the testator was unable to finish it for physical reasons, and not because of a change of mind. If the testator could not read the will it is necessary to establish that he knew its contents before signing. A signature is sufficiently acknowledged if it appeared in a document produced to witnesses which all concerned knew was intended to be a will.[39]

12.46 An attestation clause setting out the manner in which the will has been executed is not a specific requirement but is desirable, and any variation from the normal method of executing a will should be explained in such a clause. This is also desirable where the testator's signature appears doubtful. Where the testator is blind or partially sighted the words 'with knowledge of the contents thereof' or 'the same having been read over to him' should be included.

Revocation

12.47 A will is not revoked by supervening incapacity and may only be revoked by the testator by destruction with intent to revoke or by a later will which declares that

---

[35] Wills Act 1837, s 9 substituted by Administration of Justice Act 1982, s 17.
[36] Wills Act 1837, s 15.
[37] A written name, even if not the normal signature, is capable of being a signature if that was the intention – *Wood v Smith* [1992] 3 All ER 556, CA.
[38] *Weatherhill v Pearce* (1994) *The Times*, 7 November.
[39] *Weatherhill v Pearce* (1994) *The Times*, 7 November.

intention. The capacity required for revocation is the same as that needed to make a will. A will is also revoked by a subsequent marriage unless expressed to be in contemplation of that marriage in which event, especially in the case of an elderly testator, it should make clear what happens if the marriage does not take place (for example, the testator dies prior thereto).

12.48 Termination of a marriage also affects the wills of the former spouses. Where, after the will is made, the marriage is dissolved or annulled any gift to the former spouse lapses (without prejudice to the right to make an inheritance claim), and the will takes effect as if any appointment of the former spouse as executor or trustee were omitted.[40] The same approach applies to civil partnerships.[41] Alternative provisions based upon prior death will not take effect unless the will so provides.[42]

Contents

12.49 There are many different styles of will, some using traditional language and others more modern. A will may be a long and complex document but for most people a simple will is preferred and may suffice. It generally commences with the name, address and description of the testator (or testatrix) followed by revocation of previous testamentary dispositions so as to ensure that it is the last will. This is followed by the appointment of executors (and guardians for any infant children), any specific or pecuniary legacies and then disposal of the residue of the estate. If the estate is not to be immediately distributed a trust fund will be set up with the executors, or other named persons, being the initial trustees. Various administrative clauses are then included to give them wider powers than those afforded by statute, but this can be briefly achieved by referring to standard published precedents.

12.50 The date of the will may be at the beginning or the end and will generally be written in to the printed document when the will is signed by the testator and witnesses.[43] A 'testimonium and attestation' clause at the end of the will confirms the manner in which it is signed and could be in the following form:

> IN WITNESS whereof I have set my hand this day of 2014
>
> SIGNED by the said [*name*] in our presence and by us in [his/hers]

The single person

12.51 The most simple will is that of a single person who leaves the entire estate to a younger adult. It could read as follows:

> I [*name*] of [*address and description*] REVOKE all former wills and testamentary dispositions made by me and DECLARE this to be my last will and testament
>
> I APPOINT [*name*] to be my [executor/executrix] and I GIVE to [him/her] absolutely all my real and personal property whatsoever and wheresoever
>
> IN WITNESS *etc*

---

[40] Wills Act 1837, s 18A (as amended by Family Law Act 1986, s 53).
[41] Civil Partnership Act 2004.
[42] *Re Sinclair* [1985] 1 All ER 1066, CA.
[43] A process known as 'execution of the will'.

The widow/widower with one adult child

12.52 A simple will may be possible in this situation also especially if the estate is modest, but it is always prudent to allow for the contingency of a principle beneficiary dying before the testator. In this instance there may be grandchildren and a short form of will could be as follows:

> I [*name*] of [*address and description*] REVOKE all former wills and testamentary dispositions made by me and DECLARE this to be my last will and testament

> I APPOINT [*name of child*] to be my [executor/executrix] and I GIVE to [him/her] absolutely all my real and personal property whatsoever and wheresoever ('my Estate') PROVIDED THAT if [he/she] predeceases me leaving a child or children living at my death then I appoint such of those children as have attained their legal majority to be my executors and I GIVE my Estate to such of those children as are living at my death and attain their legal majority and if more than one in equal shares absolutely

> IN WITNESS *etc*

The traditional family

12.53 In a 'happy family' situation where the children are adult and none have special needs, the residue after any legacies will be left to the surviving spouse conditional upon surviving by 28 days (or a calendar month) to allow for the uncertainty that would arise if both deaths were to arise in a common accident.[44] Alternative provisions then follow to deal with the situation where the spouse has died. Two or more of the children will typically be appointed as executors in that event, legacies may be left to the grandchildren living at the death of the testator[45] and then the residue is dealt allowing for the contingency of premature deaths.

12.54 The following is an example of such a will in traditional form where there are three children and there is a desire to support their spouses if a child dies before the testator. It is also prudent to allow for a grandchild being pregnant at the testator's death:[46]

> I [*name*] of [*address and description*] REVOKE all former wills and testamentary dispositions made by me and DECLARE this to be my last will and testament

1. Appointment of Executors

(a) IN THE EVENT of my wife [*name*] surviving me by one calendar month I APPOINT my said wife [*name of wife*] to be my sole executrix ('my Executrix')

(b) IN THE EVENT of my said wife not surviving me by one calendar month I APPOINT my children [*names*] to be my executors and trustees ('my Executors')

2. Legacies

---

[44] Where there is uncertainty the younger is deemed to have survived the elder under the 'commorientes' principle – Law of Property Act 1925, s 184.

[45] It is thoughtful for grandparents to leave legacies to daughters-in-law and sons-in-law in recognition of their role in the family and in cases of need a part of the share of residue of a deceased child may be diverted to the surviving spouse rather than the grandchildren.

[46] Allowing for any subsequent grandchildren would create a situation where it could be many years before the class of beneficiaries was finalised and the estate could be wound up.

I GIVE the following specific and pecuniary legacies free of any tax arising on my death

(a)   to [*name*] my [*specify item*]
(b)   to [*name*] the sum of [*amount*]

3. Residuary Estate

I GIVE all my estate not otherwise disposed of by this Will or any Codicil to it to my Executrix or my Executors as the case may be on trust

(a)   to pay my debts funeral and testamentary expenses and any inheritance tax on my estate
(b)   to hold the remainder ('my Residuary Estate') as set out below

4. Disposition of Residuary Estate

(a)   IN THE EVENT of my said wife [*name of wife*] surviving me by one calendar month my Executrix shall hold my Residuary Estate for herself my said wife absolutely
(b)   IN THE EVENT of my said wife not surviving me by one calendar month my Executors shall hold my Residuary Estate under the alternative provisions set out below

5. Alternative disposition of Residuary Estate

(a)   My Executors shall discharge the following specific and pecuniary legacies free of any tax arising on my death
        (i)   to [*name*] my [*specify item*]
        (ii)   to [*name*] the sum of [*amount*]
(b)   my Executors shall distribute the balance of my Residuary Estate after payment of such legacies as follows
        (i)   as to one-third to my said son [name]
        (ii)   as to one-third to my said son [name]
        (iii)   as to one-third to my said daughter [name]

PROVIDED ALWAYS that if any of my said children shall die in my lifetime the one-third share that such child would have taken had he or she survived shall be held as to twenty-five percent for any lawful widow or widower of such child living at my death and as to the remaining seventy-five per cent for such of the children of the whole blood of such deceased child as shall be living at (or born within 12 months of) my death and attain their legal majority and if more than one in equal shares absolutely

PROVIDED ALWAYS that if either of these provisions shall fail then my Executors shall hold the one-third share for the other twenty-five percent or seventy-five percent as the case may be

AND PROVIDED FURTHER that if both of these provisions shall fail then my Executors shall hold the one-third share for such of my grandchildren of the whole blood as shall be living at (or born within 12 months of) my death and attain their legal majority and if more than one in equal shares absolutely

6. Further Provisions

The Standard Provisions of the Society of Trust & Estate Practitioners (1st Edition) shall apply with the deletion of paragraph 5, Section 11 of the Trusts of Land & Appointment of Trustees Act 1996 (consultation with beneficiaries) shall not apply

7. IT IS MY WISH that my body may be cremated and my ashes scattered in the Garden of Remembrance – *or as appropriate*

IN WITNESS *etc*

The complex family

12.55 In less straightforward situations, especially where there are infant beneficiaries or continuing provision is intended, further clauses need to deal with the terms of any trust, any additional powers of the trustees and administrative provisions. If there are professional executors they are given power to charge because a trustee may not benefit from the trust unless authorised. Where one or both spouses have been married before, and especially where there are his children, her children and their children, the respective wills need to be carefully crafted so as to address future needs and intentions, thereby avoiding conflict between the wider family members after death.

12.56 Special provision may need to be made where there is a dependent relative who is disabled or lacks mental capacity and this is dealt with under a separate heading below.

Funeral wishes

12.57 It is often desired to include in a will any wishes as to burial or cremation or even the funeral arrangements themselves, but these should also be communicated to those close to the testator as the will may not be produced until after the funeral. Executors, especially if professional, and also family and friends are generally relieved if the testator has indicated arrangements of choice in this way, and the prospects of disagreement are reduced. Alternatively, these wishes may be set out in a separate letter retained with the will, but advantages of including them in the will itself are that they are more likely to be followed (if noticed in time) and the will can authorise the necessary expenditure which may go beyond that which is essential.

Mutual wills

12.58 Couples often make wills at the same time under which they leave their estates to each other and make common provisions to cover the death of the survivor. Usually the survivor is free to change those further provisions and it is often appropriate to do so due to a change of circumstances, but in some instances the parties undertake to each other that they will not do so. It is these cross-undertakings that create *mutual* wills, and the consequence is that the survivor, having inherited under the will of the former partner, may not revoke or alter the further provisions of his or her own will. It has been held that there do not need to be any reciprocal benefits between the parties to create mutuality, so where they each agreed to leave their estates direct to the children but left nothing to each other the survivor could not change this.[47]

12.59 The mere fact that a couple execute similar wills is not sufficient to make them mutual. They must have agreed to make their wills in agreed terms and not to amend them unilaterally, and the first to die must have continued to abide by that agreement.[48] Strong evidence is required of the existence and extent of that promise because it may not extend to all the provisions in the will, so where it is intended that mutual wills be

---

[47] *Re Dale* [1994] Ch 31.
[48] *Goodchild v Goodchild* [1997] 3 All ER 63.

created it is wise to record the existence of this agreement in the wills themselves.[49] Sometimes a declaration is included that wills are not mutual out of an abundance of caution. On the whole mutual wills are to be discouraged because they prevent testamentary wishes being adjusted to cope with a change of circumstances, but they may be appropriate where an elderly couple are making what are expected to be their final wills and especially when they wish to provide for each other but each have their own families from an earlier marriage. However, trust provision can achieve the same result and is generally to be preferred.

Statutory wills

12.60 A statutory will can be made on behalf of a person who lacks testamentary capacity and is subject to the jurisdiction of the Court of Protection.[50] It may replace an existing will which no longer represents what the wishes of the testator could reasonably be expected to be, or be made for a person who has never made a will and for whom intestacy would not be satisfactory. The costs of all parties are generally ordered to be paid out of the testator's funds and this should be taken into account when considering whether intestacy is to be avoided.

12.61 The test of capacity to marry is different so a person may be able to marry, which would have the effect of revoking an existing will, yet unable to make a new will; an application to the court for a statutory will might then be appropriate.

12.62 Before authorising the making of such a will the court needs all relevant information including medical evidence on the patient's mental condition, a comprehensive statement of the patient's assets and liabilities and full particulars of the patient's family and dependants. A Practice Direction specifies what is required.[51] When the court has all this information it is in a position to determine whether there is jurisdiction, to appreciate the extent of the property to be disposed of and to comprehend claims to which the patient should give effect. The need for a statutory will and its terms will be based on the court's assessment of the best interests of the testator, not what he might have considered appropriate although this will be a factor.[52]

12.63 The information, together with a draft of the proposed will, is usually contained in exhibits to the affidavit of the applicant filed in support of the application for the statutory will. The Official Solicitor may be, and usually is, asked to represent the patient and a hearing is normally arranged with certain persons being given notice.

Intestacy

12.64 The law makes provision as to who inherits what, where there is no will or the will does not provide for the disposal of all of the estate, and also as to who shall administer the estate.[53]

---

[49] For an appeal decision applying these principles see *Olins v Walters* [2008] EWCA Civ 782.
[50] MCA 2005, s 16. See **2.105**.
[51] Court of Protection Practice Direction PD9F: *Applications relating to Statutory Wills, Codicils, Settlements and Other Dealings with P's Property*.
[52] For the determination of 'best interests' see Ch 2 at **2.29** et seq.
[53] Administration of Estates Act 1925; Family Provision (Intestate Succession) Order 2009, SI 2009/135.

Administrators

12.65 Administrators may be appointed where there is no will, or where there is a will but there are no executors available to prove the will. The order of priority for appointment follows the order of entitlement to the estate in the absence of a will[54] and comprises as at the date of death the deceased's spouse, children and issue of a deceased child, parents, brothers and sisters of the whole blood and the issue of those who have died, (likewise) of the half blood, grandparents, uncles and aunts of the whole blood and the issue of those who have died, and (likewise) of the half blood. Where there is a will but no executor able and willing to act, priority follows entitlement to the estate according to complex rules.[55] Persons of higher priority must be cleared off before a grant can issue, and there cannot be more than four administrators but must be at least two (or a trust corporation) if there is a minority or life interest.

Entitlement

12.66 A surviving spouse[56] receives all personal chattels (as defined) and also the statutory legacy with interest.[57] In addition, when there is issue that spouse receives a life interest in half the residue and, when there is no issue but there is a specified relative surviving, half the residue absolutely.[58] When there is no issue and there are no specified relatives, the surviving spouse receives the entire estate absolutely. The spouse can make certain elections, including taking the matrimonial home at valuation as part of her share with the right to make up any shortfall.

12.67 In the event the Inheritance and Trustees' Powers Bill 2013 is passed, the intestacy rules will change. The result will be that a surviving spouse or civil partner, who leave no issue, will receive the entire estate, irrespective of whether there are parents or siblings alive. The rules for people with issue are amended so the position regarding the chattels and statutory legacy is retained but the life interest structure for the surviving spouse or civil partner is removed; instead they will receive their half of the residuary estate outright.

12.68 The issue (or the specified relatives if there is no issue) receive all that the surviving spouse does not receive, and this is on the *statutory trusts* which means equally between those who attain 18 years or marry before then, with children of a deceased child taking that child's share on the same basis. If there is no surviving spouse or issue the estate goes to a surviving parent or brothers and sisters of the whole blood on the statutory trusts, failing whom to remoter relatives (and ultimately to the Crown). Only a spouse, civil partner, blood relative or adopted person can benefit and a cohabitee has no rights on intestacy.

---

54   Non-Contentious Probate Rules 1987, SI 1987/2024, r 22(1).
55   Senior Courts Act 1981, s 119; Non-Contentious Probate Rules 1987, r 20.
56   A registered civil partner is treated in the same way as a spouse.
57   For deaths after 1 February 2009 this is £250,000 when there is issue and £450,000 when there is no issue but there is a specified relative surviving.
58   'Specified relatives' are parent, brother or sister of the whole blood or their issue.

Financial provision for a dependent relative

Introduction

12.69 As people get older they worry increasingly about how the responsibilities they have contemplated or accepted in their lifetime may be fulfilled after they have died. This may result in seeking to make testamentary provision for a relative, partner or friend who is dependent on them or others (including the state) for care and support by reason of mental or physical disability, infirmity, age or other cause. This situation typically occurs in respect of an infirm spouse or partner, but may also arise in the case of a parent of a mentally or physically disabled son or daughter, a son or daughter with an infirm parent, or elderly unmarried brothers or sisters for each other. In the case of a spouse there may be a legal obligation to provide continuing financial support.

12.70 Each case must be dealt with according to the circumstances and there is no simple solution, but an attempt is made here to explain the problems and indicate various options that are available. The solution may be to adopt a combination of these options tailor-made for the particular circumstances, but these must first be identified.[59]

Implications

12.71 The potential beneficiary is likely to be in need of expensive care provision and may also be improvident or incapable of dealing with financial affairs. If the beneficiary has, or will be provided with, adequate financial resources the first of these problems can be coped with and independent arrangements for care can be made and funded. Otherwise, support will be provided in the form of state benefits and provision by the local authority and/or NHS. Some form of trust provision may be desirable to avoid means-testing,[60] and this may be essential if improvidence or an application to the Court of Protection for the appointment of a deputy is to be avoided.[61] Although advantageous inheritance tax or capital gains tax treatment is available for certain kinds of trust provision, the adoption of such provision is likely to be counter-productive when it comes to means-testing.[62]

12.72 Under community care policies the local authority is obliged to assess and provide for any care needs but an assessment will also be made of the ability of the individual to contribute towards the cost.[63] It follows that any financial provision may be expended in meeting the cost of services that would otherwise have been provided without charge rather than being used as a long-term supplement. The testator does not necessarily wish to take on the full burden of funding care provision but rather to top up the resources already available or provide a 'lifeboat' in case things go wrong.

12.73 The intention may be to fund extras that have hitherto been provided as gifts without being means-tested and for this to continue for the beneficiary's life. Some

---

[59] For more detailed consideration see the author's material in *Butterworths Wills Probate and Administration Service* and *Encyclopaedia of Forms and Precedents*, vols 42(1) 'Wills and Administration' and 16(2) 'Family'.

[60] See generally Ch 10 at **10.208** et seq. The difficulty for the practitioner is that a working knowledge of state benefits and provision by social services and health authorities is required in addition to the ability to draft complex trusts — few practitioners are familiar with both fields of law and practice.

[61] See generally Ch 2.

[62] See **12.102** et seq. Those with sufficient funds to create capital tax liabilities may need to choose between tax efficient provision and welfare benefits planning.

[63] A similar financial assessment will be made in respect of any means-tested state benefits.

method must be found of making provision which supplements state and local authority benefits and provision rather than jeopardising them. This would be difficult enough to achieve if the circumstances could be known in advance and relied upon not to change throughout the beneficiary's life, but that is seldom the case.

The circumstances

12.74 In the case of a younger disabled person who has hitherto been cared for by the testator, there will be uncertainty as to future care needs, the cost of meeting those needs and the resources available. In the case of an older infirm person there may be uncertainty as to future needs and life expectancy. Not only may personal needs change but also care policies and public funding arrangements including rules for means-testing. Some flexibility is therefore desirable in the financial provision that is made and all likely changes should be anticipated.

Personal

12.75 The circumstances of the beneficiary will depend upon the nature and degree of the disability, the availability of personal carers or care provision and the funding that is available, whether private or from the state, local authority or health authority.[64] Any of these factors may change during the beneficiary's life, possibly even between the making of the will and the death of the testator when its provisions take effect.

Care provision

12.76 The first step is to ascertain by whom and on what basis the beneficiary will be cared for following the death of the testator. The beneficiary may be provided with a basic income and left to cope or may be actively cared for by another member of the family or friend. In these situations there may be no initial vulnerability to substantial means-testing so direct financial support from a trust fund can be beneficial. Others are able to cope in their own home with some supervision or day services or to live in a supervised home or hostel with other disabled or infirm people. But either of these situations may result in potential charges for services provided by the local authority.

12.77 The most expensive care is that provided in a residential care or nursing home, and this is the likely option for the elderly infirm individual whilst younger learning disabled people are cared for in small homes in the community.[65] Those in need of hospital treatment are still provided with this under the NHS without contributing to the cost and unless private medical treatment is contemplated additional financial resources may be of little benefit. However, the policy is to move people out of hospital when medical care is no longer required and means-testing then becomes relevant.

12.78 If the testator is a parent still looking after a learning disabled adult child no arrangements may have been made for the future and it may not be possible to anticipate what will happen to the child on the death of that parent.

---

[64]   These topics are dealt with in Ch 10.
[65]   This can be extremely expensive when full-time care is required. In the case of adults with learning disability there is an increasing tendency to arrange housing with care provision.

12.79 When the potential beneficiary is an elderly person who could not cope alone without the personal support of the testator and there is no-one else in the family available to replace that support, a move into a residential care home or nursing home is the likely outcome.

Financial arrangements

12.80 The beneficiary's own resources and all other sources of funding, actual and potential, should be taken into account. An elderly, infirm beneficiary whose income is insufficient to cover care needs will need some form of income supplement for life. A younger beneficiary with learning disabilities is unlikely to earn sufficient money to live independently without some supplement, and this will be provided in the form of state benefits and local authority provision perhaps topped up by informal funding from the family.

12.81 The problem lies in balancing the forms of supplement and trying to ensure that any private funding does not result in an equivalent reduction in state benefits or contribution towards the cost of local authority provision. At best a will can only provide a financial structure appropriate to the personal circumstances and if these are not correctly anticipated the results may be other than intended. There is the added complication that in some cases the testator may have an obligation to provide for the potential beneficiary, enforceable by an application to the court.[66]

Means-tests

12.82 Means-tests apply in respect of:

- state benefits paid to those whose income from other sources is insufficient to meet their deemed needs;
- assistance with the rent for housing whether provided by the local housing authority or the private sector; and
- residential, day and domiciliary services provided or funded by the social services department of the local authority.

These take into account the income and capital resources of the individual, but resources are calculated according to special rules which are frequently changed according to governmental policies.[67] Any trust provision should be designed to cope with means-testing rules throughout the lifetime of the beneficiary commencing with the testator's death.

12.83 Financial provision of an income nature may result in the loss of an equivalent amount of weekly state benefits or charges for local authority services, with the result that no additional benefit is enjoyed by the beneficiary. Financial provision of a capital nature may result in the withdrawal of weekly state benefits or a levy on the capital in excess of the income it produces, with the result that the capital is ultimately exhausted thereby frustrating the intention of providing a real long-term benefit.

---

[66] Inheritance provision is dealt with at **12.84** and **12.133** et seq.
[67] For a further explanation see Ch 10 at **10.213**.

Inheritance provision

12.84 The topic of inheritance provision is of general application and is considered under its own heading later in this chapter,[68] but some aspects are of special relevance here. Although the basic principle is that people can dispose of their estates on death as they wish, specified categories of person can apply for financial provision out of the estate and the court has wide powers to award such provision.[69] The application is made on the basis that the disposition of the deceased's estate effected by his will or on intestacy (or a combination of the two) is not such as to make reasonable financial provision for the applicant.

12.85 The court is required to take into account all the circumstances and to have regard to certain matters including the size of the estate, the financial resources and needs and any physical or mental disability of the applicant and any other beneficiaries, and past conduct. It will do so at the time of the hearing rather than the date of the will or death, but the testator's reasons for making only limited provision will be taken into account so a 'side letter' expressing reasons may be valuable.

12.86 It follows that a potential beneficiary who is disabled or infirm might be eligible to apply to the court for provision. This is likely to arise in the case of an infirm spouse or disabled child of the testator rather than a parent, brother or sister unless such relative was being maintained during the lifetime of the testator and that support has ceased on the death. A local authority may nominate a 'litigation friend' to apply in the name of a mentally incapacitated person for whom it has become financially responsible.[70] In the case of a physically disabled person the authority might under the means-testing rules treat a refusal to claim as failure to avail oneself of capital that would be available.[71]

Implications of means-tested provision

12.87 It has been held that there is no need to make provision for a daughter likely to remain for life in a mental hospital[72] and that it would not be unreasonable for a deceased to make no provision from a small estate when the only effect of doing so would be to relieve the national assistance fund to that extent.[73] In a later case, in response to the submission that there could not be said to be a failure to provide reasonable provision where the applicant was in receipt of support from the DSS, it was held that the fact of that support does not preclude consideration of whether the deceased has or has not made reasonable financial provision for the applicant.[74] No distinction was made between means-tested benefits and those available as of right, and the case may have been decided on its own facts.

12.88 When considering whether a father with limited means should be required to maintain his children following a divorce it was held that regard should be had to the

---

[68] See **12.133** et seq.
[69] Inheritance (Provision for Family and Dependants) Act 1975.
[70] For the procedure see Ch 3 at **3.172** et seq.
[71] This is a difficult argument to run, but if successful the amount that would have been recovered will be treated as *notional capital*.
[72] *Re Watkins, Hayward v Chatterton* [1949] 1 All ER 695, Roxburgh J. As this was under the National Health Service the question of means-testing did not apply.
[73] *Re E* [1966] 2 All ER 44, Stamp J. It was however held that receiving national assistance was 'a totally different consideration from the ability to rely on the national health service'.
[74] *Re Collins* [1990] 2 All ER 47, Hollins J. The headnote goes beyond the terms of the judgment in suggesting that the financial resources of the applicant do not include social security benefits.

availability of social security benefits for the mother.[75] However, awards have been made where the applicants would cease to be entitled to means-tested benefit but the provision ordered by the court would make them considerably better off.[76] There appear to be no reported cases involving community care and it may be that each case must be decided on its own merits having in mind that all the circumstances are to be taken into account.

Use of trust provision

12.89 In none of these cases was the court asked to consider provision by means of a trust targeted at the disabled applicant and structured so as to insulate the fund from means-testing. Nor were any of these cases brought for the benefit of the local authority as distinct from the disabled person. The legal test is 'has the testator made reasonable provision?' and this is quite different from asking whether the testator has acted reasonably, but a significant factor may be for how long a personal inheritance could have removed the applicant from dependence upon means-tested provision. Trust provision of the nature advocated in this chapter at least demonstrates an intention to make the best overall provision practicable for the lifetime of the disabled potential beneficiary.

12.90 In resolving an application the court has power to order a settlement for the benefit of the applicant and to include such supplementary provisions as it thinks fit and such powers for the trustees as it thinks expedient. If a testator makes no provision for a disabled person who is eligible to apply the court may be asked to create trust provision of a discretionary nature, but whether it would do so brings us back to the question to what extent can state benefits and community care provision be treated as a resource of the beneficiary. If they are to be ignored certain testators may have financial obligations arising on death which they did not have during their lifetimes.

Conclusions

12.91 The options available to the testator basically comprise:

- leaving the money to the disabled beneficiary with all the vulnerabilities that creates;
- leaving the money to other relatives in the hope that they will support the disabled beneficiary informally – and with the passage of time they may not; or
- creating a trust.

In many cases the potential beneficiary will be or may become unable to manage financial affairs, so for this reason alone it is desirable to create a trust fund under which the trustees have power to spend money on behalf of that beneficiary. Much then depends upon whether this beneficiary is or is likely to become dependent upon means-tested state or local authority funding or support. The testator has two potentially conflicting objectives, namely to give the trustees power to enhance or fill any gaps in care provision, and to ensure that moneys are not available if this will merely result in the loss of or a substantial reduction in other funding. If these objectives are to be achieved it is necessary to create a trust in suitable terms and enable the trustees to exercise their powers in an appropriate manner.

---

[75] *Delaney v Delaney* [1991] FCR 161, CA.
[76] *Re Debenham* [1986] 1 FLR 404, Ewbank J; *Millward v Shenton* [1972] 2 All ER 1025, CA.

Creating a trust

12.92 Because any of these fundamentals can change it is desirable to make the trust as flexible as circumstances will permit, but not to be so concerned with tax-effectiveness that welfare benefit planning is overlooked. Even when the beneficiary is likely to remain financially independent so that means-testing is not a problem, a discretionary trust may be desired so that more money is not transferred to the beneficiary than is actually needed for personal support. This would be the position where a testator desires to support an infirm elderly parent, brother or sister but for other residuary beneficiaries to receive any money that is not needed for this.

Information required

12.93 In addition to the usual information about the testator, the estate and other members of the family, the following information about the potential beneficiary should be ascertained:

- the nature and degree of the disability or infirmity;
- the prognosis and life expectancy;
- the present residence and arrangements for care, training and occupation, and any change that may arise in the foreseeable future or on the death of the testator;
- the present funding arrangements and any alteration that may arise;
- the present capital and income of the person and any other financial provision made or is likely to be made;
- whether a deputy has been appointed or there is an attorney under a registered enduring or lasting power of attorney.[77]

Choice of trustees

12.94 Unless different trustees are appointed, the executors will be the first trustees of a trust fund created by will and they should be asked in advance if they are willing to act in that capacity. There should be at least two, though this may be the optimum number, and there may not be more than four. The present trustees will have power to appoint their successors unless the testator gives someone else this power.[78]

12.95 Care should be taken over the choice of trustees, and they should be young enough to have the prospect of surviving the testator by a lengthy period. Between them they should have contact with the disabled beneficiary so as to be aware of any needs and also have the ability to administer the trust. It can be an onerous task, so a legacy should be considered for any trustee who is not also a beneficiary or authorised to charge professional fees. A solicitor or accountant may be a suitable trustee jointly with a concerned member of the family, but banks and other corporate trustees are less suitable because of the level of their annual fees and a lack of flexibility and personal touch that is so important in these situations.

Trust options

12.96 The terms of a trust can vary between the disabled beneficiary having a life interest or merely being included in a discretionary class of beneficiaries as regards

---

[77] See generally Ch 2.
[78] This is the statutory power under Trustee Act 1925, s 36.

income and/or capital. The choice will depend upon the extent to which the beneficiary is likely to remain self-reliant. If the beneficiary is likely to receive support from one of the many charitable organisations in the field of care provision, a trust for charitable purposes (limited to charities with specific objectives) may be the most satisfying course and there are also some special schemes set up by charities. If the beneficiary is younger than the testator and substantial funds are available, a combination of these options to fit the particular circumstances may be best.

The 'wait and see' option

12.97 A 2-year discretionary trust can be used to create an initial 'wait and see' period leaving the trustees to decide in what proportions to allocate the trust money between the available options in the light of experience after the death of the testator. A change in the distribution of an estate within 2 years of death under a family arrangement or by the exercise of powers given to the executors may, in certain circumstances, be treated as having been included in the original will for the purposes of capital taxation.[79]

Life interest

12.98 A life interest with capital passing to others is not appropriate for a beneficiary vulnerable to means-testing. A variation is a *protective trust* under which a discretionary trust is substituted for the life interest if any situation arises whereby the beneficiary may be deprived of the future right to receive the income.[80] This may be suitable for a beneficiary who is unlikely to be dependent on substantial means-tested funding but is vulnerable in other respects. There can be a discretion to accumulate income for up to 21 years, and also to give capital to the income beneficiary though this may cause problems as mentioned below. Power may be given to the trustees to terminate the trust by advancing the capital or resettling upon different trusts.

Discretionary trust

12.99 Where the disabled beneficiary is, or is likely to be, dependent upon means-tested funding or support, a discretionary trust lasting for at least the lifetime of this beneficiary is appropriate but there are tax disadvantages. The trustees will have a discretion to distribute income (and perhaps capital) amongst a wide class of beneficiaries including the disabled one, with power to accumulate for as long as the law allows. The class should be as wide as possible, perhaps including charities of a specified nature, and the trustees may be empowered to add people who support the disabled beneficiary. The exercise of the discretion could possibly be restricted so as to achieve one of the tax concessions mentioned below if this will not adversely affect means-testing or impair the flexibility of the trust. The intention will be to support the disabled beneficiary in the most effective way possible.

A (small) personal fund

12.100 It may be helpful to include a legacy to the disabled beneficiary of such amount as will not cause personal resources to exceed the relevant capital limit for means-tested benefits. If that beneficiary could not cope with money the sum may be left to trustees, who need not be the general trustees of the will, but unlike other provision this may be on the widest possible trusts for the benefit of the beneficiary. The trustees may then

---

[79] This is dealt with at **12.126** et seq.
[80] Trustee Act 1925, s 33.

hand over cash (either capital or income) in such amounts as the beneficiary can cope with, or expend the fund from time to time on items that are needed.

Charitable trusts

12.101 If substantial funds are available and the disabled beneficiary is likely to be supported by a charity (eg cared for in a home run by a charitable body), consideration should be given to creating a charitable trust.[81] Advantages of such a trust include freedom from capital and income taxation, no loss of state or local authority funding and the ability to benefit any charity for the time being supporting the disabled person. However, the money cannot be used for the direct benefit of that person.

Tax planning

12.102 Where a beneficiary under a trust is a disabled person (as strictly defined) there are certain tax concessions available. Relying on these could involve the trust in means-testing (where this applies) because that person must be given some minimum entitlement to capital compared with the other beneficiaries, so it may not be appropriate to draft a trust so as to take advantage of the concessions.

Inheritance tax

12.103 This concession applies to property held on trusts where the property can be applied for the benefit of the disabled person, and either the disabled person is entitled to all the income arising from the property or, if the disabled person is not entitled to all of it, none of the income can be applied for the benefit of anyone else. The trust must be capable of paying capital out, although there is no requirement that it must be actually be applied.

12.104 A lifetime transfer into such a trust will be a potentially exempt one and there are no 10-yearly charges, although there may be a charge on the death of the disabled person.[82]

Capital gains tax

12.105 The qualifying trust will enjoy in relation to capital gains tax the full annual exemption available to individuals instead of the reduced exemption normally available to trustees. This is without loss of the disabled person's own allowance, which is still available for any property which he may have.[83]

Drafting the trust

Terminology

12.106 Any trust should not be identified too closely with the disabled beneficiary. Under former means-testing regulations it was necessary to 'have regard to the real probabilities under the trust' and it would not be as easy to argue that other beneficiaries might receive all the money if it was described as 'Mary's Trust Fund'. For the same

---

[81] Whilst charities may be included in the class of beneficiaries under a discretionary trust, the usual tax advantages of charities will not then be available.

[82] Inheritance Tax Act 1984, s 89 as amended by Finance Act 2006.

[83] Taxation of Chargeable Gains Act 1992, Sch 1, para 1.

reason it is preferable to set aside on trust a specified share in the estate rather than 'the share to which Mary would have been entitled ...'.

Trustees' powers

12.107 Adequate discretionary trust powers should be included for the trustees, but not exercisable by a sole trustee. A family trustee may be personally affected by the manner in which the trustees exercise their discretionary powers, so it is reassuring though not strictly necessary to authorise such trustee to join in the exercise of powers notwithstanding any personal interest. To encourage an imaginative use of powers it is also appropriate to provide that no trustee shall be personally liable for any loss unless caused by personal fraud.

12.108 Power to invest in chattels and residential accommodation and permit use and occupation of trust assets is particularly valuable, as is the power to make loans on any terms that the trustees think fit as to interest and security. Being able to support a care provider may be more beneficial than directly benefiting the disabled beneficiary, especially in view of the prospect of means-testing, hence the advantage of having power to add to the discretionary class of beneficiaries any person who may have become a care provider.

12.109 A controversial question is whether trustees should be given power, perhaps with restrictions, to appoint capital to a disabled beneficiary. Other funding might be withheld because of the existence of such power, and the imprudent exercise of the power could have the same effect. It may be helpful to ask in what circumstances the power is needed, because if there are suitable powers of investment and appointing capital to other people the same objective can be achieved in other ways. Thus without risk of means-testing the trustees can purchase an item such as a television or wheelchair as a trust asset and let the beneficiary use it. Alternatively, the trustees could appoint capital to another beneficiary who has given items to the disabled beneficiary.

12.110 To ensure that there is a sufficient sum available to provide a proper funeral and memorial for the disabled beneficiary, especially as state benefits only cover basic costs, the trustees' powers should cover this expense and if necessary the trust period be extended for the purpose.

A 'side letter'

12.111 Instead of revealing in the will their wishes and intentions in regard to the administration of the trust, testators should prepare and sign a suitable letter addressed to the trustees setting these out. Not only will this reassure the testator but also the trustees when they consider the exercise of their powers in future years. The letter will be private and is not legally binding but may be relied upon by the trustees as guidance. The existence of such a letter may be of assistance if the will setting up the trust is challenged under the Inheritance (Provision for Family and Dependants) Act 1975.

Settlements

General

12.112 A lifetime settlement can create the desired trusts for the disabled beneficiary and then further moneys may be credited later, perhaps by a will which need merely leave money to the trustees on the terms of the settlement. This enables any will to be kept simple and has advantages where several people may wish to support the beneficiary, avoiding the need for each of them to create their own trust fund.[84]

12.113 Administration costs may make a small settlement uneconomical, although a nominal sum may be settled initially in anticipation of substantial sums being added under the will of the settlor or some other person. Potential disadvantages are the additional cost of creating the settlement, further administration costs on an annual basis, loss of flexibility and the difficulty of getting it right at that stage. If successive sums of capital are paid into a discretionary settlement without regard to the timing (as could happen in the case of moneys left by will) an unexpected liability to inheritance tax could arise by reason of the 10-yearly charge.

Charitable settlements

12.114 An exclusively charitable settlement benefits from tax exemptions (including inheritance tax on moneys introduced) and may also provide the benefits outlined above, but setting up a charitable trust can be costly. The Charities Aid Foundation offers a viable alternative.[85]

Administering a trust

12.115 Continuing trust provision will usually be required both for the avoidance of means-testing and to enable the moneys to be looked after and, to the extent required, expended for the benefit of the disabled or infirm beneficiary. The general law relating to the administration of trusts will apply in the normal way, but we now consider some specific aspects.

Beneficiary's needs

12.116 The trustees must first ascertain the circumstances and needs of the disabled or infirm beneficiary. Ideally the trustees will already know what care is being provided and the basis on which it is funded, but this may change as a result of the testator's death and what is then arranged may depend upon how the trustees exercise their powers. This is likely to be so where a parent has looked after a disabled child and died without making any arrangements, or where sisters have been living together and the survivor is infirm and in need of support.

12.117 The trustees should consider future plans and the extent to which the trust may be instrumental in carrying these into effect, and investment decisions will be made on the basis thereof. Any family trustee will probably have a role in planning future care, perhaps in co-operation with a social worker, whereas a professional co-trustee will concentrate upon the business side of the trust and advising as to the extent to which financial assistance may be forthcoming.

Policy

12.118 Usually the investment powers given to the trustees will be as wide as possible and equivalent to those of a beneficial owner. Where the disabled beneficiary is entitled to trust income but this is of no real benefit because of means-testing, the trustees may invest the capital to produce only a small income or none at all. If they acquire a house

---

[84] Such as grandparents of a child with learning disabilities, or several children in the case of an infirm parent.
[85] www.cafonline.org.

or flat for occupation by the beneficiary, this will be exempt from means-testing whilst preserving the capital. Where this is not appropriate they may still invest in assets that can be available for the beneficiary's use such as a television or wheelchair.

12.119   Once money leaves the trustees they will have no further legal control over it so they should take care to ensure that they do not create a situation where a deputy needs to be appointed for the beneficiary by the Court of Protection, when this would not otherwise be necessary. This could arise from tax repayments on income paid to or for the benefit of the beneficiary or capital advancements.

12.120   The trustees could be tempted to use capital as a supplement to the beneficiary's income, but if they do so on a regular basis, perhaps by making up the income to a fixed amount each year, the payment may be treated as income in the hands of the beneficiary and taxed as such even though partly derived from capital.[86] Of more significance may be the effect upon means-testing. Receipt of capital may cause those responsible for funding the beneficiary to enquire as to the source and attempt to assess the trust capital as if it belonged to the beneficiary or even withhold further support in the hope of forcing the trustees to exercise their discretionary powers.

12.121   The most effective way of improving the standard of living of a disabled beneficiary who has limited financial resources may be to provide extra funds for a personal carer or for a charity in whose accommodation the beneficiary resides. If this is done on a periodic basis the effectiveness of the strategy may be monitored.

12.122   THE CHARTS ON THE FOLLOWING PAGES ARE INTENDED TO ASSIST IN STEERING A COURSE BETWEEN THE OPTIONS AND CREATING A SUITABLE WILL FOR PARENTS OF A DISABLED CHILD

---

[86]   *Brodie's Will Trustees v IRC* (1933) 17 TC 432; but see also *Stevenson v Wishart* [1987] 2 All ER 428, CA.

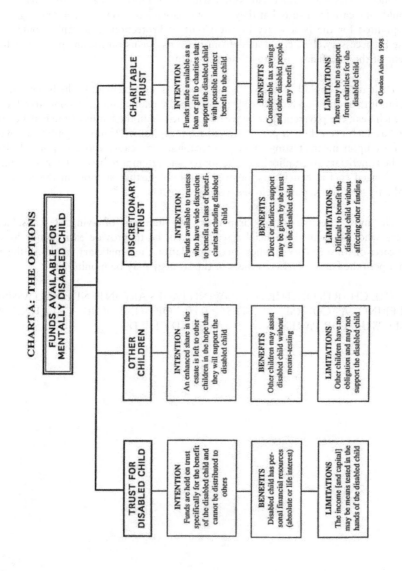

CHART A: THE OPTIONS

FUNDS AVAILABLE FOR MENTALLY DISABLED CHILD

TRUST FOR DISABLED CHILD

INTENTION
Funds are held on trust specifically for the benefit of the disabled child and cannot be distributed to others

BENEFITS
Disabled child has personal financial resources (absolute or life interest)

LIMITATIONS
The income [and capital] may be means tested in the hands of the disabled child

OTHER CHILDREN

INTENTION
An enhanced share in the estate is left to other children in the hope that they will support the disabled child

BENEFITS
Other children may assist disabled child without means-testing

LIMITATIONS
Other children have no obligation and may not support the disabled child

DISCRETIONARY TRUST

INTENTION
Funds available to trustees who have wide discretion to benefit a class of beneficiaries including disabled child

BENEFITS
Direct or indirect support may be given by the trust to the disabled child

LIMITATIONS
Difficult to benefit the disabled child without affecting other funding

CHARITABLE TRUST

INTENTION
Funds made available as a loan or gift to charities that support the disabled child with possible indirect benefit to the child

BENEFITS
Considerable tax savings and other disabled people may benefit

LIMITATIONS
There may be no support from charities for the disabled child

© Gordon Ashton 1998

CHART B: CHOOSING THE OPTIONS

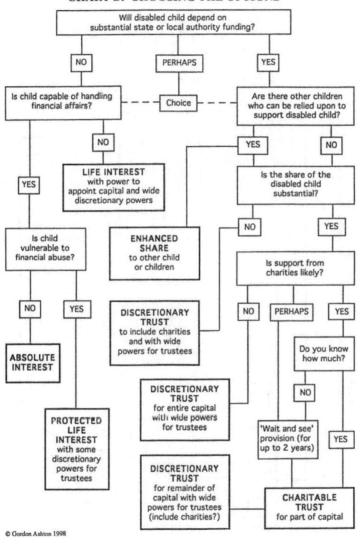

© Gordon Ashton 1998

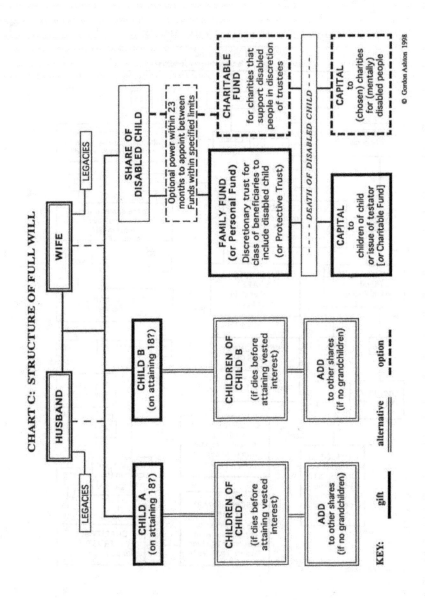

CHART C: STRUCTURE OF FULL WILL

© Gordon Ashton 1998

KEY: gift ▬▬ alternative ═══ option ▬ ▬ ▬

PROVISION AFTER DEATH

Preliminary

12.123 It is not too late following the death of an individual to change the provisions made by any will or the outcome of intestacy, and a testator can even provide for this to be done. Beneficial tax treatment may be available. An individual beneficiary may disclaim (decline to accept) any benefit under the will, or the relevant beneficiaries may collectively agree to vary the distribution of the estate. Certain people who consider that they should have had some (or more) provision made for them may apply to the court for reasonable provision to be made, and the court has power to override the provisions of the will. In this context it should not be assumed that the law of intestacy makes reasonable provision, and the court can also override the outcome. An alternative may be for disappointed people to dispute the purported will on the basis that it is not valid.

Voluntary provision

Powers of appointment

12.124 Where flexibility is required, possibly for tax reasons but also due to family circumstances, the testator may avoid the need for all beneficiaries to agree to a variation by giving the executors a power of appointment exercisable within 2 years.[87] There will usually be an initial discretionary trust of income with a default provision at the end of the period in case an appointment is not made. Inheritance tax will initially have to be paid, on applying for probate, on the basis that the powers of appointment are ignored, but will ultimately be paid as if the will had provided for the outcome effected under the appointment.[88] Thus if there is an initial discretionary trust, tax will be charged on the basis thereof on application for a grant. Any distributions made outside the 2-year period will be subject to the normal inheritance tax exit charge.

Precatory gifts

12.125 Where a testator expresses a wish that property bequeathed by the will be transferred by the legatee to other persons and the wish is complied with within 2 years of death, that disposition takes effect for inheritance tax as if the property had been originally bequeathed to the transferee.[89] No particular formality is required. This facility may be particularly valuable when dealing with furnishings and effects which may be left by will to the executors or to other persons with a view to being distributed informally.

Variations and disclaimers

12.126 It has always been possible for the beneficiaries under a will or intestacy to agree between themselves to distribute the estate in a different way. Any such variation is commonly referred to as a *family arrangement* and normally dealt with by deed. Alternatively, a beneficiary can simply state that he does not wish to take any benefit conferred upon him, and this is known as a *disclaimer*. It may be made as part of a family arrangement, or it may be made by the beneficiary without reference to anyone else.

---

[87] An example of this has been provided at **12.97** in regard to financial provision for a mentally disabled child.
[88] Inheritance Tax Act 1984, s 144 (there are no similar capital gains tax provisions).
[89] Inheritance Tax Act 1984, s 143.

12.127 There are other differences between a variation and a disclaimer. Receipt of a benefit may make it too late to disclaim, and part-disclaimer may not be allowed though one of two gifts could be disclaimed. As a variation depends upon agreement between all parties with a beneficial interest it can take place even if the property involved has been distributed and the estate administered. With a variation, either property or a share in the estate can be given to anyone whereas a disclaimer is merely a refusal to accept the entitlement under the will or intestacy and the subject matter passes to the next in line. A variation is not retrospective for income tax purposes, whereas in the case of a disclaimer the beneficiary is deemed never to have had an interest.

12.128 Where a necessary party to a deed of family arrangement lacks the necessary mental capacity an application may be made to the Court of Protection for approval to the proposed deed. This may be granted if it is in the best interests of the party but application should be made in good time so as to be sure of getting a decision within the 2-year time limit mentioned below.[90]

Inheritance tax

12.129 If, within 2 years of death, any dispositions are varied or benefits disclaimed, such variation or disclaimer may not be treated as a transfer of value and tax may be charged on the estate as if the variation had been made by the deceased or the disclaimed benefit had never been conferred.[91] This may result in a repayment of inheritance tax or additional tax having to be paid.

12.130 Certain requirements must be met if this tax treatment is to apply. The variation or disclaimer must be in writing, and must not have been made for any consideration in money or money's worth. A variation will only be read back to the date of death if a written election is made within 6 months of the variation being effective, but such election is not required in the case of a disclaimer.

Capital gains tax

12.131 Similar provisions exist whereby the variation or disclaimer need not be treated as a disposal for CGT.[92] An election to adopt this tax treatment is needed for a variation, but none is appropriate for a disclaimer. This is a separate election from that for inheritance tax and it is possible to make one without the other.

Tax planning

12.132 A variation or disclaimer may be used to achieve specific tax savings. If the deceased has not taken advantage of any of the available tax planning strategies, it may still be possible to implement these by a post-death variation. For example, if the entire estate passes to the surviving spouse, a variation may enable the nil-rate band to be used for the benefit of the children. If a beneficiary dies within 2 years of death the executors of that beneficiary may participate in a variation to achieve more advantageous overall tax treatment, and several possibilities exist. If a valuable property becomes worth very little within 2 years of death, the will may be varied so that it passes to charity (the value at death will then be exempt) perhaps instead of a cash gift.

---

90 See generally Ch 2 and Ch 11.
91 Inheritance Tax Act 1984, s 142.
92 Taxation of Chargeable Gains Act 1992, s 62(6)–(10).

Inheritance provision

Preliminary

12.133 Although the general principle is that a person can dispose of his estate by will as he wishes, most legal systems seek to protect close relatives from being disinherited unfairly and unreasonably. The methods employed fall into two categories. Some countries confer upon the courts a discretion to make suitable provision for the relative from the estate, and others give specified relatives a share in the estate calculated by fixed formulae, regardless of need. English law adopts the first method, though Scots law and that in many European countries employ the second. It follows that if property is owned in another country, enquiry should be made as to any restriction upon testamentary powers when considering the terms of a will. This is particularly relevant to older people who own homes abroad.

12.134 Under the Inheritance (Provision for Family and Dependants) Act 1975 (I(PFD)A 1975) various people or classes of people may apply to the court for financial provision out of the estate of a deceased person who was domiciled[93] in England and Wales and, if the court finds that reasonable provision has not been made for them, it has a discretionary power to redistribute the estate taking into account the obligations that the deceased had to the applicant and other persons affected.[94] The claim is personal to the applicant so cannot be pursued after his death, but any order that has been made may be enforced subsequently for the benefit of his estate.

Applications

Applicants

12.135 The people who may apply to the court for provision fall into five categories:

(1) the spouse or civil partner of the deceased;

(2) a former spouse (or civil partner) who has not remarried or been prevented by a court order made on the financial settlement following divorce;[95]

(3) a cohabitant, who must have lived in the same household with the deceased as husband or wife (or civil partner) for the whole of 2 years immediately before the death;[96]

(4) a child of the deceased, whether or not a dependant;

(5) any other person who was treated as a child of the family in relation to any marriage (or civil partnership)[97] to which the deceased was a party;

---

[93] For an explanation of domicile see **12.32**.

[94] Our Law Commission has recommended significant changes to this legislation (2009) and also further legislation dealing with cohabitants (2011). The papers are accessible at: lawcommission.justice.gov.uk.

[95] Such provision is routinely included as part of a court order imposing a clean-break financial settlement, but is not appropriate where there is a continuing liability to pay maintenance to the former spouse.

[96] This was added as I(PFD)A 1975, s 1(1)(ba) and s 1(1A) by the Law Reform (Succession) Act 1995 and as s 1(1B) by the Civil Partnership Act 2004.

[97] The Inheritance and Trustees' Powers Bill 2013, when passed and in force will amend this provision so that treatment of a child of the family will no longer be limited to situations where the deceased was married or in a civil partnership. The claimant will simply have to show that the nature of their treatment was akin to that between a parent and child.

(6)   any other person who immediately before the death was being maintained by the
        deceased, either wholly or partly, otherwise than for full valuable consideration.[98]

12.136   Different rules apply to these first two categories. As regards the final category,
the deceased must up to the time of death have been making a substantial contribution
in money or money's worth towards the reasonable needs of the applicant otherwise
than for full valuable consideration, and if this had ceased before death, even for a short
period, the claim will fail. In the case of cohabitees,[99] it was held that care provided by
the woman does not amount to full valuable consideration so as to offset the benefit of
free accommodation provided by the man,[100] but certain cohabitees may now claim as
such under category (3).

Procedure

12.137   Applications are made in the county court for the district in which the deceased
resided at the date of death and generally dealt with by district judges. There are criteria
for determining whether a case should be moved up to the High Court (Chancery
Division or Family Division) and this may be appropriate where it is exceptionally
complex or raises matters of importance to people who are not parties. Rules and
Practice Directions set out the detailed procedure to be followed.

Parties

12.138   The rules provide who shall or may be parties, and usually the personal
representatives and residuary beneficiaries under the will or intestacy are defendants.
The court has power to appoint someone to represent any person or class of persons
who may be interested in, or affected by, the proceedings when such person or class
cannot be ascertained or found or it appears to the court expedient for the purpose of
saving expense. When an application is first made the executors are under a duty to file
an affidavit giving particulars of the gross and net estate.

Time limit

12.139   An application must be made within 6 months from the date of the grant of
representation to the estate,[101] unless the court in its discretion gives leave to extend
time.[102] Permission to bring the claim out of time must be asked for in the originating
application and the grounds set out in an affidavit or statement in support. This will be
considered as a separate issue before the hearing of the substantive issue.

12.140   The Act does not lay down any principles, but the onus lies on the applicant to
make out a case for it being just and proper for the exercise of discretion and the court
will look at all the circumstances and consider whether 'it is reasonably clear that the
extension of time is required in the interests of justice'.[103] Relevant factors include the

---

[98]   The position adopted under the Inheritance and Trustees' Powers Bill 2013 makes it easier for applicants to
       pursue a claim based on maintenance as it will no longer be necessary for the applicant to show that the
       deceased contributed more to the relationship in financial terms or that the deceased assumed responsibility
       for their maintenance. Instead these will be factors to be taken into account by the court in determining
       whether an award should be made.
[99]   This would include the so-called 'common law spouse' who has no status as such in law.
[100] *Bishop v Plumley* [1991] 1 WLR 582, CA.
[101] A potential applicant may make a standing search in the Principal Registry for an office copy of any grant of
       representation to the estate.
[102] I(PFD)A 1975, s 4.
[103] *Re Ruttie* [1969] 3 All ER 1633.

interests of justice, the merits of the case, any prejudice caused to others, the reasons for delay, how promptly notice of the proposed application was given and whether the estate has been distributed.[104]

Basis of application

12.141 The application is made on the basis that the disposition of the deceased's estate effected by his will or the law relating to intestacy, or a combination of both, is not such as to make reasonable financial provision for the applicant. For a spouse this means 'such financial provision as it would be reasonable in all the circumstances of the case for a husband or wife to receive, whether or not that provision is required for his or her maintenance' but for any other applicant (including a former spouse) this same test applies but is restricted to that which it would be reasonable 'for the applicant to receive for his maintenance'.[105]

12.142 Maintenance includes payments which directly or indirectly enable the applicant in the future to discharge the cost of living, and has been stated to refer to 'no more and no less than the applicant's way of life and well-being, his health, financial security and allied matters'. What is proper maintenance depends upon all the facts and circumstances of the particular case; it does not mean just enough to enable a person to get by; on the other hand, it does not mean anything which may be regarded as reasonably desirable for his general benefit or welfare.[106]

Relevant matters

12.143 When determining whether reasonable financial provision has been made the court must have regard to certain matters set out in the statute, namely:[107]

- the financial resources and financial needs which the applicant has or is likely to have in the foreseeable future, any other applicant has or is likely to have and any beneficiary of the estate has or is likely to have;
- any obligation and responsibilities which the deceased had towards any applicant or beneficiary;
- the size and nature of the net estate;
- any physical or mental disability of any applicant or beneficiary;
- any other matter, including the conduct of the applicant or any other person, which in the circumstances of the case the court may consider relevant.

When the Inheritance and Trustees' Powers Bill 2013 is passed and in force, the court will also consider whether the deceased maintained the applicant and, if so, the length of time and extent of any contributions and the extent (if any) to which the deceased assumed responsibility for their maintenance.

---

[104] *Re Salmon* [1980] 3 All ER 532, Sir Robert Megarry VC.
[105] I(PFD)A 1975, s 1(2). In the case of a spouse, a comparison may be made with what would have been received on a divorce – s 3(2), but despite the Law Commission proposal in 1974 that the new Act should enable a surviving spouse to obtain a 'just share' in the family property the courts tend to provide only a life interest.
[106] *Re Coventry* [1979] 3 All ER 815, CA, per Goff LJ.
[107] I(PFD)A 1975, s 3.

12.144 In addition, on an application by a spouse or former spouse the court must have regard to the age of the applicant, the duration of the marriage and the contribution made by the applicant. On an application by a child or person treated as a child of the deceased it must have regard to the manner in which the applicant was being (or might be expected to be) educated or trained and, if treated as a child, also to the extent to which the deceased had assumed responsibility for maintenance and whether any other person was liable. Otherwise the court must have regard to the extent to which, and the basis upon which, the deceased assumed responsibility for the maintenance of the applicant, and the length of time for which the deceased discharged that responsibility. In any case the court may have regard to the standard of living enjoyed by the applicant during the lifetime of the deceased and the extent to which the deceased contributed to that standard.[108]

State benefits and support

12.145 In considering financial resources the court takes into account earning capacity, and in considering financial needs the court takes into account financial obligations and responsibilities.[109] It is not clear whether any means-tested state benefits that are being or could be received, or services provided by the local authority that are charged for on a means-tested basis, should be taken into account.[110]

Date for consideration

12.146 The facts as known to the court and the applicant's circumstances at the date of the hearing are relevant, rather than those at the date of the will or of the death, though any change between the date of death and the date of the hearing might be relevant. Where a child had been adopted between the date of the will and the date of a claim by that child, the court did not have jurisdiction to make an award out of the estate of the natural parent but would have been unlikely to do so in any event because at the date for consideration the child did not have any needs, being adequately supported by the adoptive parents.[111] The Inheritance and Trustees' Powers Bill 2013 includes changes which will ensure that children who are adopted after a parent's death do not lose their entitlement to share in that parent's estate as a result of the adoption.

12.147 When considering the deceased's obligations and responsibilities to the applicant it is those immediately before death that count, and the inheritance claim cannot be used to make good failures that have occurred at an earlier period (eg during the applicant's minority many years before). The relationship of father and son in the absence of special circumstances does not suffice to impose on the deceased a continuing obligation up to the time of death.[112]

Objective test

12.148 Courts originally asked the question whether, in all the circumstances, it was unreasonable on the part of the testator to make no provision for the applicant, or not to make a larger provision.[113] The deceased's moral obligation, if any, may be a relevant factor, though again this must be balanced against all the other factors and a blood

---

[108] I(PFD)A 1975, s 3(3) and (4). See *Harrington v Gill* (1983) 4 FLR 265, CA.
[109] I(PFD)A 1975, s 5(5) and (6).
[110] This has been further considered at **12.87** above.
[111] *Re Collins* [1990] 2 All ER 47.
[112] *Re Jennings* [1994] 1 FLR 536, CA.
[113] *Re Styler* [1942] Ch 387.

relationship by itself will not necessarily be sufficient.[114] More recent cases have made it clear that an objective test must be applied, namely does the disposition of the deceased's estate make reasonable financial provision for the applicant taking into account all relevant circumstances.[115] This is quite different from asking if the testator has acted reasonably, and may produce a different outcome.[116]

Deceased's reasons

12.149　The previous legislation[117] expressly required the court to consider the testator's reasons 'so far as ascertainable' for making no, or only limited, testamentary provision for the applicant. The court would take into account documentary and even oral evidence of the deceased's reasons but would not always follow them or comply with the deceased's wishes. The 1975 Act does not expressly provide that the deceased's reasons are to be considered by the court when dealing with an application, but such reasons may come within 'any other matter ... which in the circumstances of the case the court may consider relevant'.

12.150　Thus the previous decisions of the courts are still relevant[118] but the deceased's reasons and wishes comprise only part of the circumstances of the case and may be outweighed by other factors. A statement made by the deceased, whether or not in writing or signed, is admissible as evidence of any fact stated therein.[119] Any view expressed by a deceased that he wishes a particular person to benefit will generally be of little significance because the question is not subjective but objective, but any express reason for rejecting the applicant is a different matter and may be very relevant.[120]

Orders

12.151　Once the court is satisfied that the disposition of the estate does not make reasonable financial provision for the applicant it must decide whether, and if so in what manner, to exercise its powers. A wide variety of orders may be made,[121] and the court has a discretionary power to backdate the order[122] and may vary, discharge, suspend or revive orders that have been made.[123] Sometimes interim orders are made, but in all cases the order may only be made out of the net estate (as defined). An application may be adjourned if an immediate order is not required but provision may be required in the future.

12.152　The court may make an order in favour of the applicant for periodical payments, a lump sum, transfer of property or acquisition and transfer or settlement of property. An order for periodical payments will specify the period that the payments will be made, and such payments may be a specified amount, the income on part of the estate set aside for the purpose, a proportion of the income on the entire estate or as the court

---

[114]　*Re Coventry* [1979] 3 All ER 815, CA, Oliver J.

[115]　*Re Goodwin* [1968] 3 All ER 12, Megarry J.

[116]　*Millward v Shenton* [1972] 2 All ER 1025, CA, Denning MR.

[117]　Inheritance (Family Provision) Act 1938, s 1(7).

[118]　In *Re Collins*, it appears to have been held that the court may take into account any wish of the deceased expressed before death.

[119]　Civil Evidence Act 1995.

[120]　*Re Coventry* [1979] 3 All ER 815, CA, Goff LJ.

[121]　These are set out in I(PFD)A 1975, s 2. See **12.152**.

[122]　The court may not wish to do so when means-tested benefits have been paid. For a claim by a former wife, see *Lusternick v Lusternick* [1972] 1 All ER 592, CA.

[123]　I(PFD)A 1975, s 6.

thinks fit.[124] For the purpose of facilitating the making of financial provision the court may treat a joint tenancy in any property as severed and the deceased's beneficial share as part of the net estate to such extent as appears just in all the circumstances.[125]

12.153 There are also powers whereby the court may set aside dispositions made by the deceased within 6 years prior to the death with the intention of defeating an application for financial provision.[126]

Tax implications

12.154 Where an order is made in relation to any property forming part of the net estate, that property will be treated for inheritance tax purposes as if it had on the death devolved subject to the provisions of the order. There is no time limit and an election is not required, and this applies even to the provisions of a *Tomlin Order* to the extent that those provisions could have been included in an order made by the court.[127] However, a compromise recorded in such an order may extend to persons who could not have brought a claim, and if it does they will not be within this tax provision, though it may be possible to achieve the same result by treating the agreement as a deed of variation if it is within 2 years of the death.

Costs

12.155 The court has a discretion as to costs and may order costs to be paid out of the estate, by any party to the proceedings (or their solicitors), or out of the legal aid fund or may make no order. Most claims are settled due to the prospect of the substantial costs of all parties being awarded out of the estate thereby reducing the amount available for distribution between all the prospective beneficiaries.

Claims based on an estoppel

12.156 Under the principle of proprietory estoppel, where a person has relied upon a promise to his detriment, that person may be entitled to an interest in any property concerned. This situation may arise before or after the death of the promisor.

12.157 In a case where the deceased had made a promise to the claimant that a benefit in property would be received by him following the death, and he changed his position and acted to his detriment in reliance on this promise, the claimant received a share of the estate.[128] Where a widower persuaded his nephew and female partner with their children to move into his large house to support him, and there were discussions about the house being left to them, the court found on the facts that there was an estoppel and the house should be held on trust for the nephew.[129]

---

[124] The court must not set aside, in anticipation of future needs, more than is sufficient to meet, by the income thereof, the amount initially ordered to be paid – s 2(2) and (3).

[125] I(PFD)A 1975, s 9. Thus on an application by a widow, a one-half share in a home owned jointly by the deceased husband and his mistress was taken into account – *Jessop v Jessop* [1992] 1 FLR 591, CA. A life policy that reduces the mortgage in those circumstances may also be treated as part of the net estate – *Powell v Osbourne* [1993] 1 FLR 1001, CA.

[126] I(PFD)A 1975, s 10. It is necessary to establish such intention if the claim is to succeed.

[127] Inheritance Tax Act 1984, s 146. This is an order staying proceedings on agreed terms which are usually set out in a schedule.

[128] *Gillett v Holt* [2000] 2 All ER 289.

[129] *Bradbury v Taylor and Burkinshaw* [2012] EWCA Civ 1208.

Disputed wills

Powers of the court

12.158 There may be a dispute as to whether a particular document is a valid will and should be admitted to probate, and the courts have jurisdiction to deal with such matters.[130] A cohabitee who has not been provided for may wish to challenge the will in addition to making an inheritance claim. These 'contentious probate' claims are usually dealt with in the Chancery Division of the High Court although the county courts have jurisdiction where the estate does not exceed £30,000.[131] Even in the absence of a dispute the purported executors may apply to the court to resolve any uncertainty.

12.159 Most wills are proved routinely 'in common form' on production of the appropriate documents, but an application may be made for a decree pronouncing for or against the validity of a will 'in solemn form' or for the revocation of a grant that has already been made to the estate.[132]

Caveats and Citations

12.160 In order to prevent a grant being sealed a *caveat* may be lodged with the court and the person lodging this will then be notified of any application that is made and allowed a period within which to object.[133]

12.161 A citation is a document issued by the Principal Registry or a District Probate Registry on the application of a person interested in the estate calling upon the party cited to 'show cause' why a particular step should not be taken. There are three kinds: to take out a grant of probate in respect of a particular will (where the executor has inter-meddled in the estate), to accept or refuse a grant (thus potentially clearing off an executor who is not doing anything) and to propound a will (failing which an earlier will might be proved).

Validity

12.162 The validity of a will may be questioned for several reasons, the most obvious being that the document was not duly executed or has been revoked. The burden of proving due execution is upon the person putting forward the will, but this is presumed if the document on the face of it appears to be duly executed and the attesting witnesses are not available. Other reasons are lack of capacity to execute the will, undue influence, want of knowledge of the contents at the time of execution and forgery or fraud.[134]

Interpretation and rectification

12.163 Disputes relating to wills may also come before the courts in other ways. The court may be asked to interpret the provisions of the will where there is uncertainty, or a disappointed potential beneficiary may seek rectification of the will. The court has

---

[130] Non-Contentious Probate Rules 1987; available at: www.justice.gov.uk/courts/probate/rules.

[131] Proceedings should be issued in a county court where there is a Chancery District Registry and will be referred to a district judge who exercises that jurisdiction. The High Court may transfer a claim to the county court.

[132] This may be a grant of probate or of letters of administration. Revocation might be appropriate if a will, or a later will, is found.

[133] Non-Contentious Probate Rules 1987, r 44. The procedure is explained at: www.justice.gov.uk/courts/probate/caveats.

[134] For a recent case involving want of knowledge and approval see *Hawes v Burgess* [2013] EWCA Civ 94.

power to rectify a will where it fails to carry out the testator's intention by reason of a clerical error or a failure to understand the testator's instructions.[135]

MATTERS ARISING ON DEATH

Preliminary

12.164 There are various formalities to be observed immediately following a death and sometimes there is uncertainty as to what these are. By way of completeness the registration of death, role of the coroner and funeral arrangements are dealt with here. The Department for Work and Pensions has produced a helpful booklet entitled *What to do after a death*.[136]

Registration

Formalities

12.165 The death of every person dying in England or Wales must be registered by the Registrar of Births and Deaths for the sub-district in which the death occurred in a register kept for that sub-district.[137] Where a body is found and there is no information as to the place of death, registration is in the district where the body is found. The prescribed particulars to be registered are:

(1) date and place of death;

(2) name and surname (and maiden surname of a woman who has been married), sex, date and place of birth, occupation and usual address of the deceased;

(3) name, occupation and date of birth of any surviving spouse or civil partner;

(4) name and surname, qualification and usual address of the informant;

(5) cause of death; and

(6) signature of the informant and date of the registration.

Other non-obligatory information the Registrar may request includes the deceased birth and marriage (or civil partnership) certificates, National Insurance number and any state benefits in payment. The deceased's NHS medical card should be handed in if it is available.

Qualified informant

12.166 The person who must attend to the registration is known as a *qualified informant*, and where the death was in a house this means:

(1) the nearest relative[138] of the deceased person present at the death or in attendance during his last illness; or, if none

---

[135] Administration of Justice Act 1982, s 20. For the procedure see Non-Contentious Probate Rules 1987, r 55. The powers of the court were considered in *Wordingham v Royal Exchange Trust Co Ltd* [1992] 3 All ER 204 and *Re Segelman* [1995] 3 All ER 676.

[136] Available at: www.dwp.gov.uk/docs/dwp1027.pdf.

[137] Births and Deaths Registration Act 1953; Registration of Births and Deaths Regulations 1987, SI 1987/2088.

[138] This includes a relative by marriage and a civil partner.

(2) any other relative of the deceased residing or being in the sub-district where the death occurred; or, if none

(3) a person present at the death or the occupier of the house[139] if he knew of the happening of the death; or, if none

(4) each inmate of the house who knew of the happening of the death or the person causing the disposal the body.

12.167 Where death was in a hospital a qualified informant must still register the death. Where a person dies elsewhere or a dead body is found and no information as to the place of death is available, the qualified informant under a duty to register is:

(1) any relative of the deceased with knowledge of any of the particulars required to be registered concerning the death; or if none

(2) any person present at the death; or

(3) any person finding or taking charge of the body; or

(4) any person causing the disposal of the body.

Registered medical practitioner

12.168 A registered medical practitioner (RMP) who has attended a person during his last illness is required to send to the Registrar a medical certificate of cause of death (MCCD) stating to the best of his knowledge and belief the cause of death. A qualified informant who has received such a certificate from the RMP, generally in a sealed envelope, must deliver it to the Registrar. Where death was in a hospital the hospital may give the certificate to the Registrar direct. The RMP must also give to the qualified informant written notice in the prescribed form that a MCCD has been written and signed.

12.169 If there is no doctor who attended the deceased available to certify, or if the certifying doctor did attend the deceased but not within 14 days before death, or after death, then the doctor will seek advice of the coroner.

12.170 Guidance for doctors suggests that they should report a death to the coroner where it is due to accident, suicide, violence, neglect or industrial disease. Also where death is due to an unknown cause, before an operation or full recovery from an anaesthetic, or in (or shortly after release from) police or prison custody. The doctor should explain to the family why the death has been so referred.

Duty to register

12.171 The duty is to register within 5 days of the death or finding the body but if within that time written notice is given to the Registrar of the death accompanied by a written notice from the RMP that the MCCD has been signed, the registration need not be completed until 14 days after the death or finding. When one qualified informant gives information and signs the register the others are discharged from their duty to do so. It is an offence wilfully to give any false information upon registration. Once the time limit has expired the Registrar can require the attendance of, and information from, a qualified informant.

---

[139] 'House' includes public institutions such as prisons and hospitals, and prescribed charitable institutions.

12.172 The obligations placed upon qualified informants to register a death do not apply where an inquest is to be held. Upon conclusion the coroner completes a Coroner's Certificate in Form 99 and the death is registered without attendance by a qualified informant. Where the coroner instead completes Form 100A or 100B[140] the qualified informant remains under a duty to attend the Registrar and provide information.

Death certificate

12.173 If all is in order, the Registrar will issue:

(1) a certificate as to registration of death (the death certificate) and any duplicates that may be requested on payment of the stipulated fee;

(2) a certificate for claiming any social security benefits. This includes a claim form to be completed and returned to the relevant office in respect of any arrears of benefit to the date of death and may produce information on any benefits claimable by dependants of the deceased. Many registries are signed up to the government's 'Tell us Once' service which allows the bereaved person to inform central and local government services of the death via the registry, at one time rather than having to write, telephone or even attend each service individually;

(3) a certificate for burial or cremation, as required (the disposal certificate).

When a death has been referred to the coroner, the Registrar cannot proceed with registration of the death without the appropriate medical forms and coroner's certificate, but after an inquest has been opened the coroner can authorise burial or cremation, and also an interim death certificate.

12.174 If a person dies overseas the death must be registered in accordance with the procedures in that country. The bereaved may also register the death at the relevant British Consulate which enables a UK style death certificate to be issued.

Notification of disposal

12.175 The undertaker or other person causing the body to be disposed of must within 96 hours of the disposal deliver to the Registrar a notification in the prescribed form as to the date, place and means of disposal of the body. If this is not received the Registrar must make enquiry of the person to whom the certificate was issued.

Role of coroners

Preliminary

12.176 The law relating to coroners (coronial law) is a subject in itself and has a long history. The structure of the office and procedures adopted by coroners have lately been modernised and reformed,[141] to some extent, following the case of Harold Shipman, a general medical practitioner who murdered many of his patients.[142] From 25 July 2013

---

[140] 'Notification to the Registrar by the Coroner that he does not consider it necessary to hold an inquest'. One form is used where no postmortem is held and the other where there has been a postmortem.

[141] For the Government's press release see: www.gov.uk/government/news/major-overhaul-of-coroner-services-in-england-and-wales.

[142] The *Fundamental Review* and the *Shipman Enquiry* both reported in 2003.

the Coroners and Justice Act 2009, the Coroners (Inquests) Rules 2013 and the Coroners (Investigations) Regulations 2013 replace the previous provisions.[143]

12.177   Coroners are still appointed and funded by the local authority with jurisdiction in the area of that authority, but they must now be lawyers and cannot appoint their own deputies. Full-time coroners become 'senior coroners' and they are supported by area corners and assistant coroners. The mandatory retirement age is 70 years. A Chief Coroner has been appointed to oversee the system; coroners must meet a new national code of standards[144] and there is to be a *Charter for Bereaved People*.

12.178   The coroner is an independent judicial officer and thereby immune from legal proceedings in respect of acts done and words spoken in the exercise of his judicial duty.[145] A coroner's officer assists the coroner to carry out his duties and, although usually a serving police officer, reports to and receives instructions from the coroner. He deals with the public, searches for evidence, interviews witnesses, deals with lawyers and other representatives of interested parties, and generally makes all necessary arrangements for an inquest.

Duty to report

12.179   There is a general duty to give information which may lead to the coroner having notice of circumstances requiring the holding of an inquest. It is normal practice for an RMP to report a death to the coroner where there is doubt or suspicion, and he may seek advice from the coroner about his certificate. A registrar of births and deaths must report a death to the coroner when unable to obtain a duly complete certificate of cause of death and also if:[146]

- the deceased was not attended during his last illness by an RMP;
- the deceased was not seen by the certifying RMP either after death or within 14 days before death;
- the cause of death appears to be unknown;
- he has reason to believe the death to have been unnatural or caused by violence or neglect or to have been attended by suspicious circumstances;
- the death appears to have occurred during an operation or before recovery from the effect of anaesthetic; or
- the death appears from the contents of any medical certificate to have been due to industrial disease or industrial poisoning.

Investigation of death

12.180   The coroner for the area is under a duty to investigate a death where the dead body of a person is (or in some cases has been) lying within his jurisdiction and he is informed and there is reasonable cause to suspect that the person has died a violent or

---

[143] Coroners Act 1988 and the Coroners Rules 1984.
[144] *Guide to Coroners and Inquests and Charter for Coroner Services* (Ministry of Justice 2010). Available at: www.justice.gov.uk/downloads/burials-and-coroners/guide-charter-coroner.pdf.
[145] This does not extend to acts done and words spoken while acting in excess of or without jurisdiction – *Everett v Griffiths* [1921] 1 AC 631, HL.
[146] Registration of Births and Deaths Regulations 1987, reg 41.

an unnatural death, or a sudden death of which the cause is unknown, or in prison or in such place or in such circumstances as to require an inquest in pursuance of any Act.

12.181 The investigation will include the cause of death and the surrounding circumstances. It may be concluded without a post-mortem where a doctor has completed a certificate and the coroner concludes that there is no reason for him to intervene, and may be restricted to a post-mortem where the coroner is of the opinion that this is sufficient in cases of sudden death where the cause was unknown. In other circumstances the coroner may direct that there be an inquest. In certain circumstances the coroner may, after making a report to the Secretary of State, be directed to hold an inquest into the death even where there is no body.

12.182 The new Regulations make more extensive provision for disclosure. Where an interested person asks for disclosure of a document held by the coroner, it must be produced or a copy provided on payment of a fee unless the coroner considers that this is inappropriate for one of the specified reasons.[147]

Possession of the body

12.183 The coroner takes possession of the body until any inquest is concluded but may release it for earlier burial or cremation after he has received the results of the postmortem and any special examinations, and may issue an order for burial on Form 101 or certificate for cremation on Form CR6 without charge. He may need to retain it for a longer period where a second postmortem is requested or is required for criminal proceedings. Guidance states that bereaved people may 'ask the coroner, via the funeral director, for reasonable access to see the body before it is released for the funeral'.[148]

12.184 Any person intending to remove a body out of the country must first give notice to the coroner within whose jurisdiction the body is and certain formalities must then be complied with.[149]

Post-mortem examinations

12.185 A coroner may request a full or partial post-mortem examination (or merely a scan) either before or after deciding that an inquest is necessary, and may also after seeing the report decide that an inquest is unnecessary. Any post-mortem that is requested should be carried out as soon as reasonably practicable after the death, and notice is to be given to certain parties as to the time and place of the examination. Only a notified party who is a medical practitioner may attend but any such party may be represented at the examination by a medical practitioner. A person with a proper interest may view or request a copy of the results of the examination, and may request a further post-mortem examination at their cost.

Purpose of Inquest

12.186 The purpose of an inquest is to decide who the deceased was and how, when and where he came by his death. It must conclude with a determination (to be recorded on the record of the Inquest) under four heads, namely:

---

[147] Coroners (Investigations) Regulations 2013, regs 13–15.
[148] *Guide to Coroners and Inquests and Charter for Coroner Services,* para 29.2.
[149] Removal of Bodies Regulations 1954, SI 1954/448.

- who the deceased was;
- when the deceased came about his death;
- where the deceased came about his death;
- how the deceased came about his death.

The particulars required for registration as stated above will be ascertained and the coroner must report to the Registrar within 5 days of the conclusion of the inquest. A person with a proper interest may view or request a copy of the results of the examination.

12.187 It is not the function of an inquest to determine any question of criminal or civil liability or to attribute blame or responsibility, so a reference in the verdict to 'lack of care', or more correctly 'neglect', should not be made unless a clear and direct causal link was established between that conduct and the death.[150]

12.188 In the past, where the coroner considered that action should be taken to prevent similar fatalities in the future he might report the matter to the person or authority with power to take action and announce the fact at the inquest. This is now transformed into a duty and a report must be sent to the Chief Coroner and every interested person who in the coroner's opinion should receive it.[151] A copy of the report may be sent to any other person who the coroner believes may find it useful or of interest. The Chief Coroner may publish the report and a written response to it may be required.

Conduct of inquest

12.189 The coroner decides where and when an inquest is to be held, and it must normally be held in public and be formally opened and closed. A jury, which will comprise at least seven people, is only required in certain circumstances, but the coroner has a discretion to summon a jury. The procedure is inquisitorial and intended to investigate and formally record facts. Strict laws of evidence do not apply but the coroner may take a note and must record the proceedings.[152]

12.190 It is for the coroner to decide which witnesses to summon. Strict laws of evidence do not apply but witnesses give evidence on oath and enjoy privilege against self-incrimination. The coroner must examine anyone with knowledge of the facts whom he thinks it expedient to examine and anyone who wishes to give evidence. Medical witnesses may be called including for the purpose of expressing an opinion as to the cause of death. Witnesses are examined first by the coroner, then by any interested person who has asked to examine the witness and, if the witness is represented at the inquest, lastly by the witness's representative.[153]

12.191 The coroner has power to fine a person who will not attend or give evidence after being summoned, to issue a warrant for the arrest of a witness who fails to attend after being served with a summons and to commit a person for contempt in the face of the court (but not otherwise).

---

[150] *R v North Humberside and Scunthorpe Coroner, ex p Jamieson* [1994] 3 All ER 972, CA.
[151] Coroners and Justice Act 2009, Sch 5 para 7(1); Coroners (Investigations) Regulations 2013, reg 28.
[152] Coroners (Inquests) Rules 2013, r 26.
[153] Coroners (Inquests) Rules 2013, r 21.

12.192 The coroner may admit any relevant document made by the deceased, but documentary evidence from living people can only be admitted after interested persons have been given a chance to object and if they do, the coroner must be satisfied that the document maker could not give oral evidence within a reasonable period. Documentary evidence is usually read out aloud unless the coroner decides otherwise, as he might in the case of a suicide note.[154]

Conclusions of inquest

12.193 The coroner now reaches *conclusions* rather than delivering a verdict. A brief narrative conclusion may be made, but the listed conclusions are:

(1)   Accident or misadventure

(2)   Alcohol/drug related

(3)   Industrial disease

(4)   Lawful/unlawful killing

(5)   Natural causes

(6)   Open

(7)   Road traffic collision

(8)   Stillbirth

(9)   Suicide.

The standard of proof required for the short-form conclusions of 'unlawful killing' and 'suicide' is the criminal standard of proof. For all other short-form conclusions and a narrative statement the standard of proof is the civil standard of proof.

12.194 The proposal that there be an appeal process from the decision of a coroner has not been implemented, so judicial review proceedings have to be taken to quash a decision reached at an inquest and direct that a new inquest be held.

Funeral arrangements

Obligations

12.195 Although funeral wishes expressed by the deceased are not legally binding, even if included in a will, they are usually honoured as far as possible. The executors are primarily responsible for making funeral arrangements and discharging the cost from the assets of the deceased. It is not obligatory to use a funeral director and there is no necessity for a religious service. The court is reluctant to interfere at the suit of a relative with the executors' decision as to funeral arrangements, but there is nothing to stop other persons from arranging a separate memorial service.[155] In the case of an administrator the court may be prepared to make a decision.[156]

12.196 The same approach is likely to apply to those entitled to be administrators, but they will be the next of kin in any event because it is unlikely that a grant of letters of

---

[154] See generally Coroners (Inquests) Rules 2013, r 23.

[155] *Re Grandison* (1989) *The Times*, 10 July.

[156] *Hartshorne v Gardner* [2008] 2 FLR 1681.

administration to the estate will be obtained before the funeral. An unmarried partner will therefore have no status in this respect unless appointed as an executor by a valid will.

Financial liability

12.197 Usually the costs of the funeral, including refreshments and a memorial stone, will be paid out of the deceased's estate. Reasonable expenses are allowed as a deduction against the estate when calculating the inheritance tax liability.[157] There may be an insurance policy which was arranged to cover these expenses especially when the deceased had no savings. The person who actually instructs the funeral director may become personally responsible for the cost but will normally be entitled to an indemnity from the estate and the deceased's bank may release funds to an undertaker direct before probate, on production of the death certificate and funeral account. If the deceased leaves no money the funeral arrangements will be made by those prepared to pay the cost of the funeral.

State assistance

12.198 A funeral expenses payment may be claimed from the social fund by a person in receipt of certain means-tested benefits who takes responsibility for the cost of a funeral for a close family member where no other person could have taken primary responsibility for the cost of the funeral, but only essential expenses (as defined) will be covered and the payment is refundable out of the deceased's estate.[158]

12.199 The local authority (usually Environmental Health Department) must arrange and pay for a funeral where the deceased has no relatives or friends willing to do so and has not made advance arrangements.[159] The cost can be claimed from the estate, if there is one, or from any person liable to maintain the deceased. The NHS will make the arrangements if the death was in a hospital.

Advance payment

12.200 Previous generations tended to arrange life assurance policies to cover funeral expenses, but schemes are now available for pre-payment and these are becoming more popular especially as they provide some scope for planning. The individual selects a level of provision and pays for this either in a lump sum or by instalments. Although there are several trade associations,[160] funeral directors are not yet regulated so it would seem prudent to ensure that any moneys paid in advance are held in funds under independent control. If a scheme is entered into it is obviously important that the executors and next of kin know about it.

12.201 Advantages are that the individual may choose and cover the cost of the arrangements and relieve relatives of the responsibility or prospect of disagreement. Disadvantages depend upon the adequacy of the particular scheme but include inflexibility, reduction in choice (perhaps overcome by the ability to 'top-up'), the danger

---

[157] Inheritance Tax Act 1984, s 171.
[158] See Ch 10, at **10.154.**
[159] Public Health (Control of Disease) Act 1984, s 46.
[160] National Association of Funeral Directors (www.nafd.org.uk); Society of Allied and Independent Funeral Directors (www.saif.org.uk).

that the particular funeral directors may not be available or suitable when the time comes and the risk that the scheme may fail financially. There would not appear to be any inheritance tax implications because the value of the scheme will be offset by the allowance for funeral expenses. A payment should not be made to a scheme in the expectation of becoming entitled to means-tested benefits because if the payment was made for that purpose it may be disregarded and this is likely to be assumed from the consequence.

Disposal of the body

Authority

12.202   As we have seen, a disposal certificate ('green form') is issued by the Registrar, or by the coroner when he has investigated the death, and this will be required by the person effecting the disposal of the body. If after 14 days no notice as to the date, place and means of disposal of the body has reached the Registrar, he must make inquiry about this. The authority of the coroner is required for removal of a body from England and Wales.[161]

12.203   The decision about disposal of the body is strictly that of the executors or, in the absence of a will, the next of kin who will be the potential administrators, but directions may be in or with the will and it is prudent to check in all cases. Although these are not legally binding, they will invariably be followed where possible and will be compelling where there is disagreement between the executors. It may be that the deceased has already made arrangements for example by reserving a grave space. In the absence of clear wishes expressed by the deceased it is prudent for executors to consult the next of kin (and also tactful to consult any unmarried partner) and professional executors will usually follow their wishes but in cases of conflict will have to make a decision.

Organ donation

12.204   The executors can decide to donate the body for medical research and would usually follow any request of this nature in the will but are not obliged to do so. Organs can be removed soon after death if the deceased has indicated in writing a wish to be a donor (eg by carrying a donor card) or if no objections are raised by relatives when enquiries are made. If a death will be reportable to the coroner it will be necessary to obtain the coroner's consent before removing organs from a transplant donor.[162]

Burial

12.205   In theory everyone is entitled to be buried or have their ashes interred in the churchyard of the parish in which they died, lived at the time of death or were on the church electoral roll. This is qualified by two practical requirements: if there is one and if there is still room. The permission of the local clergy is required for burial in another churchyard, but grave space may have been bought in advance. The clergy may control the inscription on a gravestone.

---

[161]   Removal of Bodies Regulations 1954, SI 1954/448.
[162]   On this topic generally see Human Tissue Act 2004.

12.206   There are also cemeteries owned by local authorities or privately, but widely varying fees are charged.

Cremation

12.207   Before a cremation may take place three statutory forms must be completed. The first is by the next of kin or other suitable person authorising the cremation, the second by the doctor who attended the deceased in the last illness, and the third by another doctor who must also have seen the body. Both of these doctors will charge a fee. Where a coroner issues the certificate there is no fee and no need for the doctors' certificates, but the medical referee to the crematorium signs a document and a fee is charged for this.

APPENDIX

DIRECTORIES

ORGANISATIONS

Carers and nursing services

Name of organisation	Address
British Nursing Association	Group House 92–96 Lind Road Sutton SM1 4PL Tel: 0871 873 3324 Email: info@bna.org
Carers UK	20 Great Dover Street London SE1 4LX Tel: 020 7378 4999 Email: info@carersuk.org
Crossroads Care Association	10 Regent Place Rugby Warwickshire CV21 2PN Tel: 0845 450 0350
National Council for Palliative Care	The Fitzpatrick Building 188–194 York Way London N7 9AS Tel: 020 7697 1520 Email: enquiries@ncpc.org.uk
The Relatives and Residents Association	1 The Ivories 6–18 Northampton Street London N1 2HY Tel: 020 7359 8148 Email: info@relres.org
National Care Association	45–49 Leather Lane London EC1N 7TJ Tel: 020 7831 7090 Email: info@nationalcareassociation.org.uk

Name of organisation	Address
The Princess Royal Trust for Carers	142 Minories London EC3N 1LB Tel: 020 74807788 Email: info@carers.org

Elderly

Name of organisation	Address
Age UK	Tavis House 1–6 Tavistock Square London WC1H 9NA Tel: 0800 169 65 65 Email: contact@ageuk.org.uk
Age Cymru	Tŷ John Pathy 13/14 Neptune Court Vanguard Way Cardiff CF24 5PJ Tel: 029 2043 1555 Email: enquiries@agecymru.org.uk
Age NI	3 Lower Crescent Belfast BT7 1NR. Tel: 0808 808 75 75 Email: info@ageni.org
Age Scotland	Causewayside House 160 Causewayside Edinburgh EH9 1PR. Tel: 0845 125 97 32 Email: enquiries@ageconcernandscotland.org.uk
Action on Elder Abuse	PO Box 60001 Streatham SW16 9BY Tel: 020 8835 9280 Email: enquiries@elderabuse.org.uk
Aid for the Aged in Distress	Epworth House 25 City Road London EC1Y 1AA Tel: 0870 803 1950 Email: info@aftaid.org.uk
Alzheimer's Disease Society	Devon House 58 St Katharine's Way London E1W 1LB Tel: 020 7423 3500 Email: enquiries@alzheimers.org.uk

Name of organisation	Address
Charities Aid Foundation	25 Kings Hill Avenue West Malling Kent ME19 4TA Tel: 03000 123 000 Email: enquiries@caf.org
Charity Search	25 Portview Road Avonmouth Bristol BS11 9LD Tel: 0117 982 4060 Email: info@charitysearch.org.uk
Contact the Elderly	15 Henrietta Street London WC2E 8QG Tel: 020 7240 0630 Email: info@contact-the-elderly.org.uk
Counsel and Care for the Elderly	Twyman House 16 Bonny Street London NW1 9PG Tel: 020 7485 1550 Email: advice@counselandcare.org.uk
Dementia UK	6 Camden High Street London NW1 0JH Tel: 020 7874 7200 E-mail: info@dementiauk.org
National Benevolent Fund for the Aged, Elderly and Older People	1 Leslie Grove Place Croydon Surrey CR0 6TJ Tel: 020 8688 6655 Email: info@nbfa.org.uk

Financial

Name of organisation	Address
National Association of Pension Funds	Cheapside House 138 Cheapside London EC2V 6AE Tel: 020 7601 1700
Pensions Advisory Service	11 Belgrave Road London SW1V 1RB Tel: 0845 601 2923 Email: enquiries@opas.org.uk

Name of organisation	Address
Society of Pension Consultants	St Bartholomew House 92 Fleet Street London EC4Y 1DG Tel: 020 7353 1688 Email: info@spc.uk.com
Independent Age	6 Avonmore Road London W14 8RL Tel: 020 7605 4200 Email: charity@independentage.org.uk

General

Name of organisation	Address
Citizens Advice	Myddelton House 115–123 Pentonville Road London N1 9LZ Tel: 08444 111 444
National Council of Voluntary Organisations (NCVO)	Regent's Wharf 8 All Saints' Street London N1 9RL Tel: 020 7713 6161 Email: ncvo@ncvo-vol.org.uk
The Grandparents Association	Moot House The Stow Harlow Essex CM20 3AG Tel: 01279 428040 Email: info@grandparents-association.org.uk
The Samaritans	Freepost RSRB-KKBY-CYJK Chris PO Box 9090 Stirling FK8 2SA Tel: 08457 90 90 90 Email: jo@samaritans.org

Health and disability

Name of organisation	Address
Action against Victims of Medical Accidents (AVMA)	44 High Street Croydon Surrey CR0 1YB Tel: 0845 123 23 52

Name of organisation	Address
Arthritis Care	18 Stephenson Way London NW1 2HD Tel: 020 7380 6500 Email: info@arthritiscare.org.uk
Arthritis Research Campaign	Copeman House St Mary's Court, St Mary's Gate Chesterfield Derbyshire S41 7TD Tel: 0300 790 0400 Email: info@arc.org.uk
British Heart Foundation	Greater London House, 180 Hampstead Road London NW1 7AW Email: supporterservices@bhf.org.uk Tel: 020 7554 0000
British Red Cross	44 Moorfields London EC2Y 9AL Tel: 0844 871 11 11 Email: information@redcross.org.uk
Cancer Research UK	Angel Building 407 St John Street London EC1V 4AD Tel: 020 7242 0200 Email: info@cancerresearchuk.org
Diabetes Research and Wellness Foundation	Northney Marina Hayling Island Hampshire PO11 0NH Tel: 02392 637 808 Email: drwf@diabeteswellnessnet.org.uk
Diabetes UK	10 Parkway London NW1 7AA Tel: 020 7424 1000 Email: info@diabetes.org.uk
Disability Alliance	12 City Forum 250 City Road London EC1V 8AF Tel: 020 7247 8776 Email: office@disabilityalliance.org
Disabled Living Foundation	380–384 Harrow Road London W9 2HU Tel: 020 7289 6111 Email: info@dlf.org.uk

Name of organisation	Address
Disablement Information and Advice Lines (Dial UK)	Park Lodge St Catherine's Hospital Tickhill Road Doncaster DN4 8QN Tel: 01302 310 123 Email: informationenquiries@dialuk.org.uk
Macmillan Cancer Support	89 Albert Embankment London SE1 7UQ Tel: 020 7840 7840
Marie Curie Cancer Care	89 Albert Embankment London SE1 7TP Tel: 0800 716146 Email: info@mariecurie.org.uk
MIND	Granta House 15–19 Broadway Stratford London E15 4BQ Tel: 020 8519 2122 Email: contact@mind.org.uk
Motability	City Gate House 22 Southwark Bridge Road London SE1 9HB Tel: 0845 456 4566
Multiple Sclerosis Society	MS National Centre 372 Edgeware Road London NW2 6ND Tel: 020 8438 0700
MS Trust	Spirella Building Letchworth Herts SG6 4ET Tel: 01462 476700 Email: info@mstrust.org,uk
Parkinson's Disease Society	215 Vauxhall Bridge Road London SW1V 1EJ Tel: 020 7931 8080 Email: enquries@parkinsons.org.uk
Patients Association	PO Box 935 Harrow Middlesex HA1 3YJ Tel: 020 8423 9111 Email: helpline@patients-association.com

Name of organisation	Address
Royal Association for Disability and Rehabilitation (RADAR)	12 City Forum 250 City Road London EC1V 8AF Tel: 020 7250 3222 Email: radar@radar.org.uk
The Royal College of Surgeons	35–43 Lincoln's Inn Fields London WC2A 3PE Tel: 020 7405 3474
Royal National Institute of the Blind (RNIB)	105 Judd Street London W1H 9NE Tel: 020 7388 1266 Email: helpline@rnib.org.uk
Royal National Institute for Deaf People (RNID)	19–23 Featherstone Street London EC1Y 8SL Tel: 020 7296 8000 Email: helpline@rnid.org.uk
Stroke Association	Stroke House 240 City Road London EC1V 2PR Tel: 0845 3033100 Email: info@stroke.org.uk

Housing and care homes

Name of organisation	Address
Abbeyfield Society	Abbeyfield Society Abbeyfield House 53 Victoria Street St Albans Hertfordshire AL1 3UW Tel: 01727 857536 Email: enquiries@abbeyfield.com
Elderly Accommodation Counsel	3rd Floor 89 Albert Embankment London SE1 7TP Email: enquries@eac.org.uk
Help the Hospices	Hospice House 34–44 Britannia Street London WC1X 9JG Tel: 020 7520 8200 Email: info@helpthehospices.org.uk

Registered Nursing Home Association	Calthorpe House John Hewitt House Tunnel Lane Off Lifford Lane Kings Norton Birmingham B30 3JN Tel: 0121 451 1088 rankursell@rnha.co.uk
Shelter	88 Old Street London EC1V 9HU 0808 800 4444 Email: info@shelter.org.uk
Tenant Service Authority	Maple House 149 Tottenham Court Road London W1P OBN 0845 230 7000 Emailing enquiries@tsa.gsi.gov.uk

Human rights

Name of organisation	Address
Amnesty	99–119 Rosebery Avenue London EC1R 4RE Tel: 020 7814 6200 Email: info@amnesty.org.uk
JUSTICE	59 Carter Lane London EC4V 5AQ Tel: 020 7329 5100 Email@ admin@justice.org.uk
Liberty	21 Tabard Street London SE1 4LA Tel: 020 7403 3888 Email: info@liberty-human-rights.org.uk

Legal

Name of organisation	Address
Association of Personal Injury Lawyers	3 Alder Court Rennie Hogg Road Nottingham NG2 1RX Tel: 0115 9580585
Bar Council	289–293 High Holborn London WC1V 7HZ Tel: 020 7242 0082
The Law Society	113 Chancery Lane London WC2A 1PL Tel: 020 7242 1222
Legal Aid Practitioners' Group	242 Pentonville Road London N1 9UN Tel: 020 7833 7431
Society of Trust and Estate Practitioners	Artillery House (South) 11–19 Artillery Row London SW1P 1RT Tel: 020 7340 0500 Email: step@step.org
Solicitors for the Elderly	Suite 17, Conbar House Mead Lane Hertford Hertfordshire SG13 7AP Email: admin@solicitors for the elderly.com
Solicitors Regulation Authority	Ipsley Court Berrington Close Redditch B98 0TD Tel: 0870 606 2555

Official addresses

Name of organisation	Address
Care Quality Commission	Citygate Gallowgate Newcastle upon Tyne NE1 4PA Tel: 03000 616161
Charity Commission	PO Box 1227 Liverpool L69 3UG Tel: 0845 300 0218

Name of organisation	Address
HM Courts and Tribunals Service	Southside 105 Victoria Street London SW1E 6QT Tel: 020 7210 2266
Court Funds Office	Court Funds Office Glasgow G58 1AB Tel: 0845 223 8500 Email: enquiries@cfo.gsi.gov.uk
Court of Protection	PO Box 70185 First Avenue House 42–49 High Holborn London WC1A 9JA Tel: 0300 456 4600 Email: courtofprotectionenquiries@hmcts.gsi.goc.uk
Department of Health	Richmond House 79 Whitehall London SW1A 2NS Tel: 020 7210 4850
Department for Works and Pensions	Caxton House Tothill Street London SW1H 9DA
Equality & Human Rights Commission	3 More London Riverside Arndale House Arndale Centre Manchester M4 3EQ Tel: 0845 604 0300 Email: info@equalityhumanrights.com
Judicial Office for England and Wales	11th floor, Thomas More Building Royal Courts of Justice Strand London WC2A 2LL Email: general.enquiries@judiciary.gsi.gov.uk>
Law Commission	Steel House 11 Tothill Street London SW1H 9LJ Tel: 020 3334 0200 Email: enquries@lawcommission.gsi.gov.uk
Legal Services Commission	4 Abbey Orchard Street London SW1P 2BS Tel: 0207 783 7000

Name of organisation	Address
Ministry of Justice	102 Petty France London SW1H 9AJ Tel: 020 33343555 Email: general.queries@justice.gsi.gov.uk
Office of the Public Guardian	PO Box 16185 Birmingham B12 2WH Tel: 0300 456 0300 Email: customerservices@publicguardian.gsi.gov.uk
Official Solicitor and Public Trustee	Victory House 30–34 Kingsway London WC2B 6EX Tel: 020 3681 2750 (civil litigation) 020 3681 2752 (corporate services) 020 3681 2751 (Healthcare & Welfare) 020 3681 2758 (Property & Affairs) 020 3681 2754 (Private Law Family & Divorce) 020 3681 2755 (Public Law Family) 020 3681 2757 (REMO EU and Non EU Cases) 020 3681 2759 (Trust and Deputy Services) Email: enquiries@offsol.gsi.gov.uk
Royal Courts of Justice	Strand London WC2R 1PL Tel: 020 7936 6000
Treasury Solicitor's Department	One Kemble Street London WC2B 4TS Tel: 0207 2103000 Email: thetreasurysolicitor@tsol.gsi.gov.uk

Ombudsmen

Name of organisation	Address
Financial Ombudsman	South Quay Plaza 183 Marsh Wall Tel: 020 7964 1000 Email: complaint.info@financial-ombudsman.org.uk

Name of organisation	Address
Housing Ombudsman Service	81 Aldwych London WC2B 4HN Tel: 0300 111 3000 Email: info@housing-ombudsman.org.uk
Legal Ombudsman	PO Box 15870 Birmingham B30 9EB Tel: 0300 555 0333 Email: enquiries@legalombudsman.org.uk
Local Government Ombudsman	PO Box 4771 Coventry CV4 0EH Email: advice@lgo.org.uk
Parliamentary and Health Service Ombudsman	Millbank Tower Millbank London SW1P 4QP Tel: 0345 015 4033 Email: phso.enquiries@ombudsman.org.uk
Pensions Ombudsman	11 Belgrave Road London SW1V 1RB Tel: 020 7630 2200 Email: enquiries@pensions-ombudsman.org.uk

Publishers

Name of organisation	Address
Bloomsbury Professional	41–43 Boltro Road Haywards Heath West Sussex RH16 1BJ+44 01235 465500 Email: customerservices@bloomsburyprofessional.com
Child Poverty Action Group publications	94 White Lion Street London N1 9PF Email: bookorders@cpag.org.uk
Jessica Kingsley	116 Pentonville Road London N1 9JB Tel: +44 (020) 7833 2307 Email: post@jkp.com

Name of organisation	Address
Jordan Publishing	21 St Thomas Street Bristol BS1 6JS Tel: 0117 923 0600 Email: customerservice@jordanpublishing.co.uk
Lexis-Nexis	Halsbury House 35 Chancery Lane London WC2A 1EL Tel: 020 7400 2500 Email: customer.services@lexisnexis.co.uk
Oxford University Press	Great Clarendon Street Oxford OX2 6DP Tel: 01865 556767 Email: bookorders.UK@oup.com
Sweet & Maxwell	100 Avenue Road London NW3 3PF Tel: 020 7393 7000

WEBSITES

Financial

Website	Name
www.ft.com	Electronic Share Information
www.hmrc.gov.uk	Tax Rates and Allowances
www.landreg.gov.uk	Land Registry
www.napf.co.uk	National Association of Pension Funds
www.opra.co.uk	Occupational Pensions Regulatory Authority
www. pensionsadvisoryservice. org.uk	Pensions Advisory Service
www. thepensionsregulator. gov.uk	The Pensions Regulator
www.ship-ltd.org	Safe Home Income Plans (SHIP)
www.statistics.gov.uk	UK National Statistics

Government

Website	Name
www.appeals-service.gov.uk	The Appeals Service – Social Security
www.cabinetoffice.gov.uk	Cabinet Office
www.charity-commission.gov.uk	Charity Commission
www.communities.gov.uk	Department for Communities and Local Government
www.dft.gov.uk	Department for Transport
www.dh.gov.uk	Department of Health
www.direct.gov.uk	UK Government
www.dwp.gov.uk	Department for Work and Pensions
www.equalities.gov.uk	Government Equalities Office
www.hmrc.gov.uk	HM Revenue & Customs
www.hm-treasury.gov.uk	HM Treasury
www.homeoffice.gov.uk	Home Office
www.justice.gov.uk	Ministry of Justice
www.nationalarchives.gov.uk	The National Archives
www.number-10.gov.uk	No 10 Downing Street
www.parliament.uk	Houses of Parliament

Housing

Website	Name
www.housingcorp.gov.uk	Housing Corporation
www.nhbc.co.uk	National House Building Council

Human rights

Website	Name
www.amnesty.org.uk	Amnesty International
www.bihr.org.uk	British Institute of Human Rights
www.echr.coe.int	European Court of Human Rights
www.equalityhumanrights.com	Equalities and Human Rights Commission
www.hrw.org	Human Rights Watch
www.justice.org.uk	Justice
www.liberty-human-rights.org.uk	Liberty

Legal

Website	Name
www.civiljusticecouncil.gov.uk	Civil Justice Council
www.justice.gov.uk	Official Solicitor/Public Trustee/Court Funds Office
www.justice.gov.uk/about/hmcts/	HM Courts & Tribunals Service
www.judiciary.gov.uk	Judiciary of England & Wales
www.justice.gov.uk	The Law Commission
www.legalservices.gov.uk	Legal Services Commission
www.opsi.gov.uk	Office of Public Sector Information
www.justice.gov.uk/about/hmcts/	Office of the Public Guardian
www.justice.gov.uk/forms/opg	Office of the Public Guardian – forms

Legal information resources

Website	Name
www.bailii.org/	British and Irish Legal Information Institute

Website	Name
www.casetrack.com	Law Report Database
www.harassment-law.co.uk	Harassment law
www.infolaw.co.uk	Information for Lawyers Limited
www.justis.com	Full text legal database
www.lawdirect.co.uk	Solicitors Directory
www.lawgazette.co.uk	Legal Resource
www.lawontheweb.co.uk	General legal site
www.lawreports.co.uk	Incorporated Council of Law Reporting
www.lawtel.co.uk	Legal resource
www.legalhub.co.uk	Legal resource
www.makeawill.org.uk	Law Society's will site
www.online-law.co.uk	Online Law
www.monticello.org.uk	Law Resource
www.rightsnet.org.uk	Welfare Law Resource
www.venables.co.uk	Legal Resources

Legal professional

Website	Name
www.apil.org.uk	Association of Personal Injury Lawyers
www.apl.org.uk	Association of Pensions Lawyers
www.barcouncil.org.uk	Bar Council
www.lapg.co.uk	Legal Aid Practitioners Group
www.lawsociety.org.uk	The Law Society
www.lpld.org.uk	Lawyers for People with a Learning Disability
www.scl.org	Society for Computers & Law
www.solicitors-online.com	Law Society Directory of Solicitors

Website	Name
www.solicitorsforolderpeoplescotland.co.uk	Solicitors for Older People Scotland
www.solicitorsfortheelderly.com	Solicitors for the Elderly
www.spg.uk.com	Sole Practitioners Group
www.sra.org.uk	Solicitors Regulation Authority
www.step.org	Society of Trust and Estate Practitioners (STEP)
www.womensolicitors.org.uk	Association of Women Solicitors

Legal publishers

Website	Name
www.ark-group.com	Ark Group Publishing
www.bloomsburyprofessional.com	Bloomsbury Professional
www.cpag.org.uk	CPAG Publications
www.familylaw.co.uk	Family Law
www.FT.com	Financial Times
www.hammickslegal.co.uk	Hammicks Legal Bookshop
www.informa.com	Informa Group Publishers
www.jkp.com	Jessica Kingsley Publishers
www.jordanpublishing.co.uk	Jordan Publishing
www.lag.org.uk	Legal Action Group
www.legislation.gov.uk	UK Legislation
www.lexisnexis.co.uk	Lexis Nexis
www.opsi.gov.uk	Office of Public Sector Information
www.oup.co.uk	Oxford University Press
www.routledge.com	Routledge

Website	Name
www.sweetandmaxwell. co.uk	Sweet & Maxwell
www.the-lawyer.co.uk	The Lawyer
www.the-times.co.uk	The Times
www.tso.co.uk	The Stationery Office
www.wildy.com	Wildy's Legal Bookshop

Ombudsmen

Website	Name
www.fos.org.uk	The Financial Services Ombudsman
www.housing-ombudsman.org.uk	The Housing Ombudsman
www.lgo.org.uk	Local Government Ombudsman
www.legalombudsman. org.uk	The Legal Ombudsman
www.ombudsman.org. uk	Parliamentary and Health Service Ombudsman
www.pensions-ombudsman.org.uk	Pensions Ombudsman

Organisations – carers

Website	Name
www.aica.org.uk	Association of Independent Care Advisors
www.bettercaring.com	Better Caring resource
www.carers.org	The Princess Royal Trust for Carers
www.crossroads.org.uk	Crossroads Care
www.carersuk.org	Carers UK
www.cqc.org.uk	Care Quality Commission
www.nahf.org.uk/ hospice-directory.html	National Association of Hospices Directory
www.helpthehospices. org.uk	Help the Hospices Information Service

Website	Name
www.nursing-home-directory.co.uk	The Care Directory

Organisations – Elderly

Website	Name
www.abbeyfield.com	The Abbeyfield Society
www.aftaid.org.uk	Aid for the Aged in Distress
www.ageuk.org.uk	Age UK
www.alzheimers.org.uk	Alzheimer's Society
www.charitysearch.org.uk	Charity Search for Older People
www.communitycare.co.uk	Community Care resource
www.contact-the-elderly.org.uk	Contact the Elderly
www.dementiauk.org	Dementia UK
www.eac.org.uk	Elderly Accommodation Counsel
www.elderabuse.org.uk	Action on Elder Abuse
www.independentage.org.uk	Independent Age

Organisations – General

Website	Name
www.citizensadvice.org.uk	Citizen's Advice
www.avma.co.uk	Action against Medical Accidents (AvMA)
www.grandparents-association.org.uk	The Grandparents Association
www.salrc.org.uk	Society for the Assistance of Ladies in Reduced Circumstances
www.salvationarmy.org.uk	The Salvation Army

Website	Name
www.samaritans.org	The Samaritans
www.ncvo-vol.org.uk	National Council for Voluntary Organisations

Organisations – Health and disability

Website	Name
www.arthritisresearchuk.org	The Arthritis Research Campaign
www.arthritiscare.org.uk	Arthritis Care
www.bhf.org.uk	British Heart Foundation
www.cancerlinks.org	Cancer-Links
www.cancerresearchuk.org	Cancer Research UK
www.diabetes.org.uk	Diabetes UK
www.disabilityalliance.org.uk	Disability Alliance
www.dlf.org.uk	Disabled Living Foundation
www.dialuk.info	Disablement Information & Advice Lines
www.hpa.org	Health Protection Agency
www.hospicedirectory.org	Hospice Directory
www.lcm.org.uk	London City Mission
www.macmillan.org.uk	Macmillan Cancer Support
www.mariecurie.org.uk	Marie Curie Cancer
www.mencap.org.uk	MENCAP
www.mind.org.uk	MIND
www.motability.co.uk	Motability
www.mssociety.org.uk	MS Society
www.mstrust.org.uk	MS Trust
www.parkinsons.org.uk	Parkinson's UK
www.nhs.uk	The National Health Service

Website	Name
www.nhsdirect.nhs.uk	NHS Direct
www.nice.org.uk	National Institute for Health and Clinical Excellence
www.radar.org.uk	Royal Association for Disability and Rehabilitation
www.redcross.org.uk	British Red Cross Society
www.rnib.org.uk	Royal National Institute for the Blind
www.rnid.org.uk	Royal National Institute for Deaf People
www.shelter.org.uk	Shelter
www.stroke.org.uk	The Stroke Association

Organisations – Professionals

Website	Name
www.adass.org.uk	Association of Directors of Social Services
www.bma.org.uk	British Medical Association
www.bna.co.uk	British Nursing Association
www.saif.org.uk	National Society of Allied and Independent Funeral Directors
www.spc.uk.com	Society of Pension Consultants
www.tax.org.uk	Chartered Institute of Taxation

USEFUL PUBLICATIONS

Coroners

Blackstone's Guide to the Coroners and Justice Act 2009 (2010) Glassom & Knowles, OUP
Coroners: A Guide to the New Law (2010) Urpeth, Law Society
Coroners' Courts: A Guide to Law & Practice (2011) Dorries, OUP
Inquests: A Practitioner's Guide (2008) Thomas et al, LAG
Jervis on Coroners (2011) Matthews, Sweet & Maxwell

Courts and procedure

A Practitioner's Guide to the Court of Protection (2009) Terrell, Bloomsbury Professional

Civil Court Service 2014 Laws & Hickman, Jordan Publishing

Court of Protection Practice 2014 Ashton, Jordan Publishing

Court of Protection Law Reports, Jordan Publishing

Blackstone's Magistrates' Court Handbook 2013 (2012) Keogh, OUP

Family Lawyer and the Court of Protection (2010) Marin, Family Law

Heywood & Massey: Court of Protection (loose-leaf) Rees, Sweet & Maxwell

Legal Aid Handbook 2013–14 Ling, Pugh & Edwards, LAG

Solicitors' Duties and Liabilities (2009) Billins, Law Society

The Solicitor's Handbook (2013), Law Society

Todd's Relationship Agreements (2013) Todd, Sweet & Maxwell

Urgent Applications in the Court of Protection (2014) Pearce and Jackson, Jordan Publishing

Discrimination

Age Discrimination (2007) Davies, Bloomsbury Professional

Age Discrimination Handbook (2006) O'Dempsey et al, LAG

Age Discrimination – The New Law (2006) Cheetham, Jordan Publishing

Blackstone's Guide to the Equality Act 2010 Wadham, OUP

Discrimination in Employment: A Claims Handbook (2013) O'Dempsey, LAG

Disability Discrimination (2008) Doyle, Jordan Publishing

Disability Rights Handbook (2011) Disability Alliance

Discrimination Law Service (loose-leaf), Bloomsbury Professional

Equality and Discrimination (2010) Doyle, Jordan Publishing

Equality Act 2010: A Guide to the New Law (2010) Duggan, Law Society

Elderly clients

Elderly Client Handbook (2010) Bielanska, Terrell, Ashton, Law Society

Elderly Clients – A Precedent Manual (2013), Lush, Jordan Publishing

Elderly Client Adviser (journal) Ark Group Publishers

Elderly People and the Law (2014) Ashton and Bielanska, Jordan Publishing

Estate and financial management

A Practitioner's Guide to Executorship and Administration (2009) Thurston, Bloomsbury Professional

A Practitioner's Guide to Powers of Attorney (2010) Thurston, Bloomsbury Professional

Cretney & Lush on Lasting and Enduring Powers of Attorney (2013) Jordan Publishing

Drafting Trusts and Will Trusts (2012) Kessler and Sartin, Sweet & Maxwell

Finance and Law for the Older Client (loose-leaf), Lexis Nexis

Lasting Powers of Attorney: A Practical Guide (2011) Ward, Law Society

Law Relating to Trustees (2010) Underhill & Hayton, Lexis-Nexis

A Modern Approach to Lifetime Tax Planning for Private Clients (with Precedents) (2013) Whitehouse & King, Jordan Publishing

Pensions Law and Practice with Precedents (loose-leaf), Sweet & Maxwell

Pensions Law Handbook (2013), Nabarro, Bloomsbury Professional

Powers of Attorney (2007) Aldridge, Sweet & Maxwell

Practical Trust Precedents (loose-leaf), Sweet & Maxwell

The Law of Trusts (2012), Oxford University Press

Tolley's Pensions Administration and Trustees Service (loose-leaf), Lexis Nexis

Trust Drafting and Precedents (loose-leaf), Sweet & Maxwell

Trust Practitioner's Handbook (2012) Steel, Law Society

Health and medical care

Health Care Law (2011) Montgomery, OUP

Mason and McCall Smith's Law and Medical Ethics (2010), Mason and Laurie, OUP

Medical Law (2011) Herring, OUP

Medical Law and Ethics (2011) Herring, OUP

Medical Law and Ethics (2011) Shaun & Pattinson, Sweet & Maxwell

Medical Treatment Decisions and the Law (2010) Johnston, Bloomsbury Professional

Human rights

Blackstone's Guide to the Human Rights Act 1998 (2011), OUP

Human Rights Alerter, Sweet & Maxwell

Human Rights Law & Practice (2009) Lester and Pannick, Lexis Nexis

Human Rights Practice (looseleaf), Sweet & Maxwell

Human Rights Updater, Lexis Nexis

Mental health

Assessment of Mental Capacity: A Practical Guide for Doctors and Lawyers (2009) BMA, Letts, Law Society

Blackstone's Guide to the Mental Capacity Act 2006 (2008) Bartlett, OUP

Blackstone's Guide to the Mental Health Act 2007 (2008) Bowen, OUP

Dementia and the Law (2013) Harrop-Griffiths, Jordan Publishing

Mental Capacity Act Manual (2012) Jones, Sweet & Maxwell

Mental Capacity – A Guide to the New Law (2008) Gleaney, Law Society

Mental Health (2011) Fennell, Jordan Publishing

Mental Capacity – Law and Practice (2012) Ashton, Jordan Publishing
Mental Health Act Manual (2010) Jones, Sweet & Maxwell
Mental Health Law (2010) Hale, Sweet & Maxwell
Mental Health Law & Practice (2011) Fennell, Jordan Publishing
Mental Health Tribunals (2013) Butler, Jordan Publishing

Welfare

Care Standards: A Practical Guide (2010) Ridout, Jordan Publishing
Care Standards Legislation Handbook (2009) Pearl, Jordan Publishing

Community Care Law Reports, LAG
Community Care Law and Local Authority Handbook (2012) Butler, Jordan Publishing
Community Care Practice and the Law (2008) Mandelstam, Jessica Kingsley
Council Tax Handbook (2011) CPAG
Debt Advice Handbook (2012) CPAG
Fuel Rights Handbook (2013) CPAG

Coldrick on Care Home Fees (2012), Ark Group
Disability Rights Handbook (2013) Disability Rights UK
Guide to Housing Benefit and Council Tax Benefit (2013) Shelter
Safeguarding Adults and the Law (2013) Mandelstam, JKP

Welfare Benefits and Tax Credits Handbook (2013) CPAG
Welfare Law (loose-leaf), Bloomsbury Professional

Wills and probate

A Practitioner's Guide to Wills (2010) King et al, Wildy
Butterworths Wills, Probate and Administration Service (loose-leaf), Lexis Nexis

Inheritance Act Claims Law Practice and Procedures (loose-leaf) Francis and Lord Walker, Jordan Publishing
Inheritance Act Claims: Law Practice (2011) Ross, Sweet & Maxwell
Modern Approach to Wills, Administration and Estate Planning with Precedents (2013) King and Whitehouse, Jordan Publishing
Parker's Modern Wills Precedents (2011) Waterworth, Bloomsbury Professional
Practical Will Precedents (loose-leaf), Sweet & Maxwell
Probate Disputes and Remedies (2014) Withers, Jordan Publishing
Probate Practice Manual (loose-leaf), Sweet & Maxwell
Probate Practitioner's Handbook (2010) King, Law Society
Theobald on Wills (2010) Martin, Bridge and Oldham, Sweet & Maxwell
Tristram and Coote's Probate Practice (2011) D'Costa et al, Lexis Nexis

Will Draftsman's Handbook (2012) Riddett, Law Society

Williams, Mortimer & Sunnucks – Executors, Administrators and Probate (2013) Sunnucks, Sweet & Maxwell

Williams on Wills (2012) Lexis Nexis

INDEX

References are to paragraph numbers.